C++

P9-CKV-850

AN INTRODUCTION
TO COMPUTING

C++

AN INTRODUCTION
TO COMPUTING

Second Edition

Joel Adams

Sanford Leestma

Larry Nyhoff

Calvin College
Grand Rapids, Michigan

PRENTICE HALL
Upper Saddle River, New Jersey 07458

Library of Congress Cataloging-in-Publication Data

Adams, Joel
    C++: an introduction to computing/Joel Adams, Sanford Leestma,
Larry Nyhoff
    p. cm.
      includes index.
    ISBN 0-13-744392-7
    CIP data available

Publisher: *Alan Apt*
Editor: *Laura Steele*
Development Editor: *Sondra Chavez*
Production Editor: *Sharyn Vitrano*
Managing Editor: *Bayani DeLeon*
Editor-in-Chief: *Marcia Horton*
Director of Production and Manufacturing: *David W. Riccardi*
Creative Director: *Paula Maylahn*
Art Director: *Heather Scott*
Interior Designer: *Elm Street*
Cover Designer: *Davis Group*
Photo Researcher: *Rona Tucillo*
Manufacturing Buyer: *Donna Sullivan*
Editorial Assistant: *Toni Holm*

© 1998, 1995 by Prentice-Hall, Inc.
Simon & Schuster/A Viacom Company
Upper Saddle River, NJ 07458

All rights reserved. No part of this book may be
reproduced, in any form or by any means,
without permission in writing from the publisher

The author and publisher of this book have used their best efforts in preparing this book. The author
and publisher shall not be liable in any event for incidental or consequential damages in connection
with, or arising out of, the furnishing, performance, or use of these programs.

Printed in the United States of America

12 11 10   9   8   7   6   5   4   3   2

ISBN 0-13-744392-7

Prentice-Hall(UK) Limited, *London*
Prentice-Hall of Australia Pty. Limited, *Sydney*
Prentice-Hall Canada Inc., *Toronto*
Prentice-Hall Hispanoamericana, S.A., *Mexico*
Prentice-Hall of India Pribate Limited, *New Delhi*
Prentice-Hall of Japan, Inc., *Tokyo*
Simon & Schuster Asia Pte. Ltd., *Singapore*
Editora Prentice-Hall do Brasil, Ltda., *Rio de Janeiro*

Preface

When writing the first edition of this text, we felt strongly that to properly introduce students to computing, a first computing course should accomplish two goals:

1. Introduce students to the breadth of the discipline of computing, so that they come to understand the role of programming in the broader context of computing.

2. Introduce the methodologies and techniques of computer programming using C++, providing a (fairly) complete introduction to the language.

However, because C++ is such a large programming language, that edition went well past the 1000-pages mark at which point our editor issued the dictum "Enough is enough!" and we had to terminate the work with our goals only partially met.

Our goals for this new edition remain the same. To accomplish the first goal, we again include the PART OF THE PICTURE sections. They were well-received in the first edition and we have several new ones written by experts in various areas of computing.

We plan to use a divide-and-conquer strategy to accomplish the second goal. This book will be the first of a series of two, which together will provide a thorough presentation of the C++ language. This first volume will introduce the essential ideas of C++ programming and the breadth of the discipline of computing, making it ideal for a one-semester course in computer science. The second volume will cover the more advanced features of C++ programming (e.g., recursion, inheritance, and polynomophism) and will introduce topics that are traditionally taught in the second course including elementary data structures, algorithms, and complexity, and how these three topics converge in the C++ Standard Template Library. Together, these two texts will provide the beginning computer science student with a complete introduction to C++ and with a solid introduction to the discipline of computer science.

ORGANIZATION OF THE TEXT

A popular feature of our first edition was that each chapter began with an example problem that introduced the subject of that chapter (e.g., functions, if statements, loops, and so on). Once students had seen an example illustrating the topic, the concepts and details of that topic were explored. This approach has proven successful in providing students with a framework in which to place the concepts and details of the topic.

This new edition continues and expands upon this approach by incorporating a "use it, then build it" approach with respect to two of the most difficult topics for beginning C++ programmers: *functions* and *classes*. For example, to show students how functions are used, predefined functions are used already in Chapter 2 as components of expressions. Once students have experienced using (predefined) functions, Chapter 3 teaches them to build simple functions, and Chapters 5, 6 and 7 show how to build increasingly sophisticated functions. Similarly, students are introduced to the use of standard classes and function members in Chapter 4, with

v

more practice following in Chapters 5–8. Once students are firmly grounded in the use of (predefined, standard) classes, they learn to build classes in Chapter 10. As another example, students are first introduced to class templates in Chapter 7 and then use the Standard Template Library vector<T> template in Chapter 9, with additional practice in Chapters 12 and 13. Once students have extensive practice using templates, they learn to build class templates in an early chapter of Volume II. Through this "use it, then build it" approach, students receive extensive exposure to the concepts underlying each of these constructs, reducing the learning curve when the time comes to actually build those constructs.

SOME CHANGES

Thanks to constructive feedback from users of the first edition, this new edition incorporates a number of organizational changes, including the following:

- ▶ The background and introductory information has been consolidated into a Chapter 0 that instructors can cover in lecture, assign as reading, or omit as preferred. The presentation of computing history has been updated with more events and photos in a *time-line* of important people and events in the history of computing. Also, a superb new presentation of the major ethical issues in computing has been contributed by Anne Marchant of George Mason University.

- ▶ Chapter 1 introduces C++ programming through object-centered design, a four-phase graduated methodology that novice programmers can use as an aid in designing software solutions. This methodology is used consistently to solve the problems presented throughout the remainder of the text. As the reader learns new language constructs in subsequent chapters, (e.g., functions in Chapter 3, classes in Chapter 10, and so on), the methodology is expanded to incorporate these new constructs.

- ▶ Chapter 2 lays the foundation for the remainder of the book, introducing the basic ideas of types, operations, and expressions, including predefined functions.

- ▶ Chapter 3 introduces reusability, using functions as a way to write program statements that can be reused and then libraries as a way to store functions for later use. Object-centered design is expanded (phase II) to incorporate these new ideas.

- ▶ Chapter 4 builds on the ideas of Chapter 2, presenting the use of classes. The class is introduced as a means of creating a *new type,* and function members as a means of creating *operations* on such types. Standard classes (istream, ostream, and string) are used to illustrate these ideas.

- ▶ Chapters 5 and 6 expand on the introduction in Chapter 3 to control structures for selection and repetition. These control structures are used to build increasingly sophisticated functions. The use of standard classes (e.g., string) is reinforced in these chapters through examples. These chapters also include a concise but thorough summary of computer architecture contributed by William Stallings.

- ▶ Chapter 7 completes the study of "normal" functions, introducing reference parameters, scope, and recursion.

- ► Chapter 8 builds on Chapter 4, introducing the `ifstream` and `ofstream` classes for performing file I/O. Our colleague Keith Vander Linden kindly consented to add a new Part of the Picture section on databases.

- ► Chapter 9 begins by introducing C-style arrays and illustrates their use with several examples. After pointing out the inadequacies of such arrays, the second half of the chapter introduces the `vector<T>` class template from the Standard Template Library as an off-the-shelf component providing a more convenient way to process sequences of items. This two-part treatment provides maximum flexibility, by allowing both C-style arrays and vectors to be studied, C-style arrays to be examined and vectors skipped, or C-style arrays skipped and vectors studied.

- ► Chapter 10 builds on Chapters 4 and 8, showing how to create new types by building classes. Object-centered design is again expanded (phase III) to incorporate this new idea. An interesting new Part of the Picture by Keith Vander Linden describes how these ideas are applied in Artificial Intelligence.

- ► Chapter 11 extends the ideas of Chapter 2 by presenting enumerations as another way to create a new type. It also builds on Chapter 10 by showing how this can be done better by using enumeration classes.

- ► Chapter 12 introduces multidimensional arrays. It parallels the discussion of one-dimensional arrays in Chapter 9. Multidimensional arrays are first studied as C-style arrays and then a new class `Matrix` is constructed by deriving it from the `vector<double>` class. This makes this chapter the capstone of this first volume, reinforcing the idea of *reusability* through class *derivation* and *inheritance,* showing how one class can reuse the work of another. Object-centered design is expanded a final time (phase IV), resulting in object-oriented design.

- ► Chapter 13 begins with an introduction to pointers and run-time allocation. It then describes linked lists abstractly and how they can be processed using STL's `list<T>` class template. An application to TCP/IP addresses is followed by a new Part of the Picture section by William Stallings that describes the TCP/IP communications architecture more precisely.

STANDARD C++

At the time of this writing, the American National Standards Institute (ANSI) Committee X3J16 has completed a C++ draft standard, but it has not yet released a final standard. In the absence of a final standard, we have used the draft standard as our primary reference in preparing this text. Many of the changes in this new edition are revisions of the earlier edition to incorporate the changes proposed in the draft standard. For example, our presentation of types in Chapter 2 includes the `bool` type; in Chapter 4, we use the standard `string` class (instead of constructing a new `Strings` class as in the first edition); the previously supported `fstream` class (Chapter 8) has now been eliminated in favor of the `ifstream` and `ofstream` classes; we present `vector<T>` and `list<T>` from the Standard Template Library.

THE BREADTH OF COMPUTING

An important theme of recent curriculum recommendations published by the Association of Computing Machinery (ACM) is that an introductory course in computing should introduce the various knowledge areas of the discipline:

- ▶ Architecture
- ▶ Artificial Intelligence and Robotics
- ▶ Database and Information Retrieval
- ▶ Human–Computer Communication
- ▶ Numerical and Symbolic Computation
- ▶ Operating Systems
- ▶ Programming Languages
- ▶ Software Methodology and Engineering
- ▶ Social, Ethical, and Professional Context

In this text, we include a number of sections that introduce these areas, trying to capture the spirit of these curriculum guidelines in a natural, unobtrusive way. These sections have been carefully selected to provide an overview of the discipline of computer science and to provide a foundation for further study in theoretical and/or applied computer science. They have been highlighted in special PART OF THE PICTURE sections:

What Is Computer Science?
The History of Computing
Introduction to Computer Organization
Ethics and Computing (by Anne Marchant)
Data Representation
Computability Theory
Simulation
Boolean Logic and Digital Design
Computer Architecture (by William Stallings)
Introduction to Algorithm Analysis
Numerical Methods
Databases (by Keith Vander Linden)
Component Programming
Artificial Intelligence (by Keith Vander Linden)
The C++ Type Hierarchy
Computer Graphics
The TCP/IP Communications Architecture (by William Stallings)
Data Structures

A solid base is thus established for later courses in theoretical and/or applied computer science.

OTHER FEATURES

- ▶ Each chapter begins with an example problem, whose solution is used to introduce the ideas of that chapter. Following this example, the concepts and theory behind those ideas are explored, and other examples worked to reinforce the ideas. In this approach, students see the *practice* of a new topic before the *abstract* definitions and theory that underlie that topic, providing them with a framework in which those abstract aspects can be organized and understood.

▶ A wealth of examples illustrate each topic, allowing students to distinguish what is essential from what is optional. These examples are chosen from a wide range of applications, and have been written to model good structure and style. Those marked in the text with a spider web can be downloaded from the website http://cs.calvin.edu/c++/2e.

▶ Optional sections (marked with asterisks) delve into more advanced topics, without requiring that they be covered in a normal introductory course.

☞ ▶ Programming Pointers at chapter ends highlight important points, including:

    ✍ Proper techniques of design and style

    ⚡ Common programming pitfalls.

▶ Approximately 500 Quick Quiz questions provide a quick check of understanding of the material being studied. The answers to all of the Quick Quiz questions are given at the end of the text.

▶ Nearly 750 written exercises extend the Quick Quizzes and apply the material of the preceding section(s). No answers for these are provided in the text, and they can therefore be used for written assignments.

▶ The Programming Problems sections at the chapter ends contain more than 260 programming problems drawn from a wide range of application areas.

▶ A completely new design makes the text attractive and readable.

▶ Color is used to emphasize and highlight important features.

▶ Boxed displays make it easy to find descriptions of the basic C++ statements and constructs.

SUPPLEMENTARY MATERIALS

A solutions manual that contains answers to the written exercises in the text as well as solutions to many of the programming problems is available from the publisher to adopters of the text. A diskette containing the programming solutions is also available. A number of other instructional materials are available on the Internet at http://cs.calvin.edu/c++/2e including: source code for the programs, functions, libraries, and data files used in the text; transparency masters and other instructional materials; an errata list; and an on-line collection of closed laboratory exercises prepared by Professor Joel Adams.

In addition to our standard supplements package, we are offering a copy of the CodeWarrior Pro compiler and a free academic lab license to all professors who adopt the book for a class of twenty or more. Please let your local sales representative know that you will be adopting this second edition for your class and we will provide you with the CodeWarrior materials. CodeWarrior compatible source code for all examples to the text can be downloaded from the following site: http://cs.calvin.edu/c++/2e.

If you would like to incorporate the most current, real-world topics into your course, please contact your local sales representative so that you and your students can receive a free, biannual collection of articles excerpted from the *New York Times*.

SUGGESTIONS

The authors welcome feedback, both positive and negative. Comments on features of the text that work especially well, as well as those that could be improved, will aid us in the preparation of subsequent editions. We would also appreciate being notified of errors. Such comments can be directed to any of the authors at the following U.S. mail address:

Department of Computer Science
Calvin College
3201 Burton SE
Grand Rapids, MI 49546
USA

or to adams@calvin.edu, lees@calvin.edu, or nyhl@calvin.edu via the Internet.

ACKNOWLEDGMENTS

We express our sincere appreciation to all who helped in any way in the preparation of this text, especially our publisher Alan Apt, editor Laura Steele, development editor Sondra Chavez, and production editor Sharyn Vitrano. We also appreciate the valuable comments and suggestions made by the following reviewers: Ralph Ewton (Univ. of Texas - El Paso), Robert Holloway, (Univ. of Wisconsin), Lily Hou (Carnegie Mellon Univ.), Rex Jaeschke (chair, ANSI C committee), Steve Kolars (San Antonio College), Joel D. Kraft (Case Western Reserve University), Anne Marchant (George Mason Univ.), Bina Ramamurthy (SUNY at Buffalo), and Charles Welty (Univ. of Southern Maine). We also thank Anne Marchant, William Stallings, and Keith Vander Linden for writing Part of the Picture sections; Erin Fulp for the Internet address application in Chapter 13; Mike Nyhoff for the twine-ball photo in Chapter 2; and our students at Calvin College for serving as test subjects. And, of course, we must also thank our families—Barb and Roy; Marge, Sandy, Lori, Michelle, and Michael; Shar, Jeff, Dawn, Jim, Greg, Julie, Tom, Joni, Becca, Megan, and Joshua— for not complaining about the times that their needs and wants were slighted because of our busyness. Above all, we give thanks to God for giving us the opportunity, ability, and stamina to prepare this text.

JOEL ADAMS
SANFORD LEESTMA
LARRY NYHOFF

Contents

Chapter 0. BEGINNING SNAPSHOTS **1**

Part of the Picture: *What Is Computer Science?* 2

Part of the Picture: *The History of Computing* 4

Early Computing Devices 4
The Stored Program Concept 4
Mechanical Computers 5
Early Electronic Computers 6
Modern Computers 6
System Software 7
A Brief History of C++ and OOP 8

Part of the Picture: *Computing History* 10

Exercises 17

Part of the Picture: *Introduction to Computer Organization* 18

Computing Systems 18
Memory Organization 19
Exercises 21

Part of the Picture: *Ethics and Computing* (by Anne Marchant) 21

Exercises 26

Chapter 1. PROBLEM SOLVING AND SOFTWARE ENGINEERING **29**

1.1 Welcome to the World of C++ 32

1.2 Problem Solving through Software Engineering 34

Problem 34
Object-Centered Design 35
Coding in C++ 39
Testing, Execution, and Debugging 40
Maintenance 42

1.3   Example: Revenue Calculation   43

Problem   43
Object-Centered Design   43
Coding in C++   45
Testing, Execution, and Debugging   46
Program Maintenance   46
Quick Quiz 1.3   48
Exercises 1.3   48

Chapter 2. TYPES AND EXPRESSIONS   51

2.1   Introductory Example: Einstein's Equation   52

Problem   52
Object-Centered Design   52
Coding, Execution, and Testing   53

2.2   Declarations: Specifying an Object's Type   55

Fundamental Types   55
Constant Objects   62
Variable Objects   64
Variable Initialization   66
Quick Quiz 2.2   67
Exercises 2.2   68

 Part of the Picture: *Data Representation*   69

Integers   69
Reals   71
Characters and Strings   72
Booleans   73

2.3   Numeric Expressions   73

Operators   74
Numeric Functions   78
Quick Quiz 2.3   81
Exercises 2.3   81

2.4   Boolean Expressions   82

Simple Boolean Expressions   83
Compound Boolean Expressions   84

Operator Precedence   86
Short-Circuit Evaluation   87
Preconditions and the `assert()` Mechanism   88
Quick Quiz 2.4   89
Exercises 2.4   89

2.5   Character Expressions   90

Character-Processing Operations   91
Quick Quiz 2.5   91

2.6   Assignment Expressions   92

Assignment as an Operation   96
Chaining Assignment Operators   96
The Increment and Decrement Operations   97
Other Assignment Shortcuts   99
Transforming Expressions into Statements — Semicolons   101
A Final Word   102
Quick Quiz 2.6   102
Exercises 2.6   103

2.7   Input/Output Expressions   104

I/O Streams   104
Input Expressions   105
Output Expressions   108
Example: Calculating Wages   110
Output Formatting   111

2.8   Example: Truck Fleet Accounting   115

Problem   115
Object-Centered Design   115
Quick Quiz 2.8   118
Exercises 2.8   119

Programming Pointers   121

Program Style and Design   121
Potential Problems   122

Programming Problems   125

Chapter 3. FUNCTIONS 129

3.1   Computing with Expressions   130

Problem: Temperature Conversion   130
Object-Centered Design   130

3.2   Computing with Functions   132

Defining a Function   134
Function Prototypes   138
Calling a Function   140
Local Objects   140
Functions that Return Nothing   142
Summary   144
Quick Quiz 3.2   146
Exercises 3.2   147

3.3   Functions that Use Selection   148

Problem: Finding a Minimum of Two Values   148
Object-Centered Design   148
Sequential Execution   151
Selective Execution   152
Blocks   153
Style   154
Nested ifs   156
Quick Quiz 3.3   157
Exercises 3.3   158

3.4   Functions that Use Repetition   159

Problem: Computing Factorials   159
Object-Centered Design   160
Repeated Execution: The for Statement   163
Processing Several Input Values   166
Quick Quiz 3.4   171
Exercises 3.4   173

3.5   Example: An 8-Function Calculator   175

Problem   175
Object-Centered Design   175

3.6   An Introduction to Libraries   182

Constructing a Library   183
Using a Library in a Program   187
Translating a Library   188
Object-Centered Design: Incorporating Functions and Libraries   190
Summary   191
Quick Quiz 3.6   193

 Part of the Picture: *Computability Theory*   *193*

Programming Pointers   194

Program Style and Design   194
Potential Problems   196
Programming Problems   200

Chapter 4. CLASS TYPES AND EXPRESSIONS 205

4.1   Introductory Example: "The Farmer in the Dell"   206

Problem   206
Object-Centered Design   207

4.2   Introduction to Classes   212

Data Encapsulation   213
Function Members   215
Summary   216
Quick Quiz 4.2   216

4.3   The istream and ostream Classes   217

The istream Class   217
The ostream Class   222
Format Control   225
Quick Quiz 4.3   228
Exercises 4.3   229

4.4   Computing with string Objects   230

Declaring string Objects   231
String I/O   232
Other String Operations   233
Quick Quiz 4.4   245
Exercises 4.4   246

4.5   Example: Decoding Phone Numbers   247

Problem   247
Object-Centered Design   248

 Part of the Picture: *Simulation*   *252*

Random Number Generators—the `RandomInt` Class   253
Example: Modeling a Dice Roll   254
Normal Distributions   256

Programming Pointers   257

Program Style and Design   257
Potential Problems   257

Programming Problems   258

Chapter 5: SELECTION   **263**

5.1   Introductory Example: The School Mascot Problem   264

Problem   264
Object-Centered Design   264

5.2   Selection: The `if` Statement Revisited   268

Understanding the Multibranch `if`   269
Pitfall: The Dangling-else Problem   270
Pitfall: Confusing = and ==   271
Exercises 5.2   273

5.3   Selection: The `switch` Statement   274

Example: Temperature Conversions   274
Form of the `switch` Statement   278
The `break` Statement   279
Drop-Through Behavior   279
Example: Converting Numeric Codes to Names   280
Cases With No Action   283
Choosing the Proper Selection Statement   284

5.4   Example: Computing Letter Grades   286

Problem   286

Object-Centered Design   286
Quick Quiz 5.4   291
Exercises 5.4   292

*5.5   Selection: Conditional Expressions   293

Exercises 5.5   295

Part of the Picture: *Boolean Logic and Digital Design*   *296*

Early Work   296
Digital Circuits   297
Circuit Design: A Binary Half-Adder   297

Part of the Picture: *Computer Architecture*
(by William Stallings)   *300*

Processor Registers   301
Control and Status Registers   302
Instruction Execution   303
Instruction Fetch and Execute   303
I/O Function   304
The Memory Hierarchy   305
Input/Output Organization   307
I/O Module Function   307
To Probe Further   309

Programming Pointers   309

Program Style and Design   309
Potential Problems   313

Programming Problems   313

Chapter 6: REPETITION   **319**

6.1   Introductory Example: The Punishment of Gauss   320

The Summation Problem   320
Object-Centered Design   320

6.2   Repetition: The for Loop Revisited   323

Nested Loops: Displaying a Multiplication Table   327

Words of Warning   329
The Forever Loop   330

6.3   Repetition: The `while` Loop   333

Example: Follow the Bouncing Ball   333
Object-Centered Design   333
The `while` Statement   336
Loop Conditions vs. Termination Conditions   337
Words of Warning   338

6.4   Repetition: The `do` Loop   339

Example: How Many Digits?   339
Object-Centered Design   339
A Posttest Loop   343
Loop Conditions vs. Termination Conditions   344
Words of Warning   344
Quick Quiz 6.4   345
Exercises 6.4   347

6.5   Input Loops   350

Running Example: The Mean Time to Failure Problem   350
Object-Centered Design   350
Input Loops: The Sentinel Approach   351
Input Loops: The Counting Approach   358
Input Loops: The Query Approach   360

6.6   Choosing the Right Loop   364

Decision #1: Use a Counting Loop or a General Loop?   364
Decision #2: Which General Loop?   364
Quick Quiz 6.6   366

6.7   Example: Calculating Depreciation   366

Problem   366
Object-Centered Design   367

 Part of the Picture: *Introduction to Algorithm Analysis*   *373*

Programming Pointers   375

Program Style and Design   375
Potential Problems   376

Programming Problems   379

Chapter 7: FUNCTIONS IN DEPTH   **383**

7.1   Introductory Example: One-Step Integer Division   384

Problem   384
Object-Centered Design   384

7.2   Parameters in Depth   388

Value Parameters   388
Reference Parameters   389
const Reference Parameters   392
Using Parameters   395

7.3   Examples of Parameter Usage   395

Problem 1: Decomposing a Name   395
Problem 2: Designing a Coin Dispenser   398
Problem 3: Interchanging the Values of Two Variables   404
Quick Quiz 7.3   405
Exercises 7.3   406

7.4   Inline Functions   408

Inline Functions and Libraries   409
To inline or Not to inline: A Space-Time Tradeoff   410
Quick Quiz 7.4   410

7.5   Scope, Overloading, and Templates   411

Scope: Identifier Accessibility   412
Function Signatures and Overloading   419
Function Templates   421
Quick Quiz 7.5   425

*7.6   Introduction to Recursion   426

Example 1: The Factorial Problem Revisited   426
Example 2: Recursive Exponentiation   433
Example 3: Dry Bones!   435
Example 4: Towers of Hanoi   439
Recursion or Iteration?   442
Quick Quiz 7.6   443
Exercises 7.6   444

Part of the Picture: *Numerical Methods*   *446*

The Trapezoid Method of Approximating Areas   447
Problem: Road Construction   450
Object-Centered Design   450

Programming Pointers   453

Program Style and Design   453
Potential Problems   454

Programming Problems   456

Chapter 8:   FILES AND STREAMS   **461**

8.1   Introductory Example: Weather Data Analysis   462

Problem: Processing Meteorological Data   462
Object-Centered Design   463

8.2   ifstream and ofstream Objects   468

Declaring fstream Objects   468
The Basic fstream Operations   469
fstreams as Parameters   485
Summary   485
Quick Quiz 8.2   486
Exercises 8.2   487

8.3   Example: Scanning for a Virus   488

8.4   Additional fstream Operations   491

The seekg(), tellg(), seekp(), and tellp() Members   492
The peek() and putback() Members   498
The setstate() Member   500
The Formatting Manipulators   502
Quick Quiz 8.4   504

 Part of the Picture: *Database Systems* (by Keith Vander Linden)   *505*

Programming Pointers   511

Program Style and Design   511

Potential Problems   512

Programming Problems   514

Chapter 9: ARRAYS AND vector<T>s   519

9.1   Introductory Example: Quality Control   520

Problem: Mean Time to Failure   520
Object-Centered Design   521

9.2   C-Style Arrays   525

Array Initialization   528
The Subscript Operation   530
Processing Arrays with for Loops   531
Arrays as Parameters   532
The typedef Mechanism   532
Out-of-Range Errors   534
Predefined Array Operations   536
A Non-OOP Approach   537
An Object-Oriented Approach   540
Quick Quiz 9.2   541
Exercises 9.2   542

9.3   Example: Sorting Employee Information   544

Problem   544
Object-Centered Design   544

9.4   The vector<T> Class Template   547

A Quick Review of Function Templates   547
Class Templates   548
Defining vector<T> Objects   548
vector<T> Function Members   550
vector<T> Operators   553
The Standard Template Library   558
vector<T> Function Members Involving Iterators   564
Decision Making: Use a vector<T> or a C-Style Array?   565
Array and vector<T> Limitations   566

9.5   Example: Processing Test Scores   567

Problem   567
Object-Centered Design   567
Quick Quiz 9.5   574
Exercises 9.5   575

 Part of the Picture: *Component Programming*   *577*

Computer Hardware   578
Computer Software   578

Programming Pointers   579

Program Style and Design   579
Potential Problems   579

Programming Problems   581

Chapter 10:   BUILDING CLASSES   **585**

10.1   Introductory Example: Modeling Temperatures   586

Problem: Temperature Conversion   586
Preliminary Analysis   586
Extending Object-Centered Design   587
Object-Centered Design   588

10.2   Designing a Class   590

Class Design   591
The External and Internal Perspectives   591
Temperature Behavior   592
Temperature Attributes   592

10.3   Implementing Class Attributes   593

Encapsulation   593
Information Hiding   594
Class Invariants   595
Conditional Compilation and the Class "Wrapper"   595

10.4   Implementing Class Operations   597

Temperature Output   597
The Default-Value Constructor   600
Explicit-Value Constructors   602

Accessor Functions   605
Temperature Input   607
Conversion Functions   609
Overloading Operators   610
Summary: The Temperature Class   619

10.5   friend Functions   621

Quick Quiz 10.5   624
Exercises 10.5   625

10.6   Example: Retrieving Student Information   626

Problem: Information Retrieval   626
Object-Centered Design   627

Part of the Picture: *Artificial Intelligence*
(by Keith Vander Linden)   *636*

Programming Pointers   643

Program Style and Design   643
Potential Problems   644

Programming Problems   646

Chapter 11: ENUMERATIONS   **649**

11.1   Introductory Example: Wavelengths of Colors   651

Problem   651
Object-Centered Design   651

11.2   C-Style Enumerations   653

Enumeration Declarations   653
Defining Enumeration Objects   655
Using Enumerations   655
C-Style Enumeration Operations   656
Other Enumeration Operations   659
Libraries and Types   662
Quick Quiz 11.2   663
Exercises 11.2   663

11.3   Object-Oriented Enumerations   664

Declaring Enumeration Classes   664
Defining `Color` Operations   666
The `Color` Header File   677
Quick Quiz 11.3   679
Exercises 11.3   679

11.4   Example: Geological Classification   679

 Part of the Picture: *The C++ Type Hierarchy*   690

Programming Pointers   690

Program Style and Design   690
Potential Problems   691

Programming Problems   691

Chapter 12: MULTIDIMENSIONAL ARRAYS   **695**

12.1   Introductory Example: Mileage between Cities   696

Problem   696
Preliminary Analysis   696
Object-Centered Design   696

12.2   C-Style Multidimensional Arrays   698

Defining A Two-Dimensional Array   699
Predefined Two-Dimensional Array Operations   701
Defining Two-Dimensional Array Operations   702
Declaring Three-Dimensional Arrays   705
Operations on Three-Dimensional Arrays   706
Higher-Dimensional Arrays   707
Drawbacks of C-Style Arrays   710
Quick Quiz 12.2   711
Exercises 12.2   712

12.3   Multidimensional `vector<T>` Objects   714

Two-Dimensional `vector<T>` Objects   715
Two-Dimensional `vector<T>` Operations   718
Defining Two-Dimensional `vector<T>` Functions   720
Quick Quiz 12.3   723
Exercises 12.3   723

12.4   A `vector<T>`-Based Matrix Library   723

Matrix Multiplication   724
Building a `Matrix` Class: The External Approach   725
`Matrix` Operations   725
Building a `Matrix` Class: The Internal Approach   729
Object-Centered Design   737
Application: Solving Linear Systems   737
Quick Quiz 12.4   739
Exercises 12.4   739

 Part of the Picture: *Computer Graphics*   740

Examples: Function Graphing and Density Plots   741
GUI Windows Application Programming   747

Programming Pointers   749

Program Style and Design   749
Potential Problems   750

Programming Problems   751

Chapter 13: POINTERS AND RUN-TIME ALLOCATION   **761**

13.1   Introduction to Pointer Variables   762

Declaring and Initializing Pointers   763
Basic Pointer Operations   765

13.2   Run-Time Allocation Using `new` and `delete`   775

The `new` Operation   776
The `delete` Operation   783
Summary   790

13.3   The STL `list<T>` Class Template   792

A Limitation of `vector<T>`   792
Some `list<T>` Operations   795
Example: Internet Addresses   804

 Part of the Picture: *The TCP/IP Communications Architecture*
(by William Stallings)   *808*

*13.4   Pointers and Command-Line Arguments   815

Parameters of the Main Function   816
Example: A Square Root Calculator   818
Command-Line Arguments: Files and Switches   821

 Part of the Picture: *Data Structures*   *822*

Programming Pointers   823

Program Style and Design   823
Potential Problems   824

Programming Problems   825

Appendixes   829

A.   ASCII Character Set   829

B.   C++ Keywords   831

C.   C++ Operators   833

D.   Libraries and Classes   835

C Libraries   835
The `string` Class   838
The `list<T>` Class Template   844

Answers to Quick Quizzes   847

Index   857

Chapter 0

BEGINNING SNAPSHOTS

Is computer science a science? An engineering discipline? Or merely a technology, an inventor and purveyor of computing commodities? What is the intellectual substance of the discipline? Is it lasting, or will it fade within a generation?

FROM THE 1989 REPORT OF THE TASK FORCE ON THE CORE OF COMPUTER SCIENCE

I wish these calculations had been executed by steam.

CHARLES BABBAGE

Where a computer like the ENIAC is equipped with 18,000 vacuum tubes and weighs 30 tons, computers in the future may have only 1,000 vacuum tubes and weigh only $1\frac{1}{2}$ tons.

POPULAR MECHANICS, MARCH 1949

640K ought to be enough for anyone.

BILL GATES, 1981

For, contrary to the unreasoned opinion of the ignorant, the choice of a system of numeration is a mere matter of convention.

BLAISE PASCAL

One machine can do the work of fifty ordinary men. No machine can do the work of one extraordinary man.

ELBERT HUBBARD

Chapter Contents

PART OF THE PICTURE: What Is Computer Science?

PART OF THE PICTURE: The History of Computing

PART OF THE PICTURE: Computer Organization

PART OF THE PICTURE: Computer Ethics

1

A first course in computing should help students develop an accurate and balanced picture of computer science as a discipline. This is important to students majoring in computer science, for whom this introduction to the discipline will be fleshed out in later courses, as well as to students majoring in other disciplines, for whom the portrayal of computing should be a realistic one. Thus, although most of this text is devoted to developing problem-solving and programming skills, we attempt to give a more complete picture of computer science by including special "PART OF THE PICTURE" sections throughout the text that introduce topics from various areas of computer science. These opening sections give an overview of computer science, some historical background, basic principles of computer organization, and a perspective on social and ethical issues in the computer science community.

Part of the Picture: What Is Computer Science?

The term *computer science* has been a source of confusion. Although there are sciences called physics and biology, there are no disciplines called *telescope science* or *microscope science*. How can there be a *computer science* if a computer is simply another scientific tool or instrument?

Let us begin with what computer science is not. It is not simply writing computer programs. Although problem solving and programming are indeed the primary focus of this text, the discipline of computing consists of much more. The breadth of the discipline is evidenced by the following list of the main areas of computer science from *Computing Curricula 1991: Report of the ACM/IEEE-CS Joint Curriculum Task Force.*[1] In our attempt to portray computer science as a discipline, the PART OF THE PICTURE sections in this text will focus on many of these areas.

Area of Computer Science	What This Area Deals with
Algorithms and Data Structures	Specific classes of problems and their efficient solutions
	Performance characteristics of algorithms
	Organization of data relative to different access requirements
Architecture	Methods of organizing efficient, reliable computing systems
	Implementation of processors, memory, communications, and software interfaces
	Design and control of large, reliable computational systems
Artificial Intelligence and Robotics	Basic models of behavior
	Building (virtual or actual) machines to simulate animal and human behavior
	Inference, deduction, pattern recognition, and knowledge representation

---

[1] Allen B. Tucker, ed., *Computing Curricula 1991: Report of the ACM/IEEE-CS Joint Curriculum Task Force* (ACM Press and IEEE Computer Society Press, 1991).

Area of Computer Science	What This Area Deals With
Database and Information Retrieval	Organizing information and designing algorithms for the efficient access and update of stored information
	Modeling data relationships
	Security and protection of information in a shared environment
	Characteristics of external storage devices
Human–Computer Communication	Efficient transfer of information between humans and machines
	Graphics
	Human factors that affect efficient interaction
	Organization and display of information for effective utilization by humans
Numerical and Symbolic Computation	General methods for efficiently and accurately using computers to solve equations from mathematical models
	Effectiveness and efficiency of various approaches to the solution of equations
	Development of high-quality mathematical software packages
Operating Systems	Control mechanisms that allow multiple resources to be efficiently coordinated during execution of programs
	Appropriate service of user requests
	Effective strategies for resource control
	Effective organization to support distributed computation
Programming Languages	Notations for defining virtual machines that execute algorithms
	Efficient translation from high-level languages to machine codes
	Extension mechanisms that can be provided in programming languages
Software Methodology and Engineering	Specification, design, and production of large software systems
	Principles of programming and software development, verification, and validation of software
	Specification and production of software systems that are safe, secure, reliable, and dependable
Social and Professional Context	Cultural, social, legal, and ethical issues related to computing

Because to some people the term *computer science* seems inadequate to describe such a broad range of areas, the *Computing Curricula 1991 Report* suggests that *computing* is a more appropriate term than *computer science*. However, we will use the two terms interchangeably throughout this text.

Part of the Picture: The History of Computing

The modern electronic computer is one of the most important inventions of the twentieth century. It is an essential tool in many areas, including business, industry, government, science, and education; indeed, it has touched nearly every aspect of our lives. The impact of the twentieth-century information revolution brought about by the development of high-speed computing systems has been nearly as widespread as the impact of the nineteenth-century Industrial Revolution. As part of the picture of computing, it is necessary to be aware of some of the events that led to modern-day computing.

Two important concepts led to computers as we know them today: the **mechanization of arithmetic** and the **stored program** for the automatic control of computations. The timeline that follows this introduction shows some of the important events and devices that have implemented these concepts.

Early Computing Devices

A variety of computational devices were used by ancient, civilizations. Some of the earliest ones that might be considered forerunners of the modern computer are pictured in the timeline that appears later in this section and include the abacus, Stonehenge, Napier's bones, and the slide rule. The adding machine developed by Blaise Pascal in 1642 used a system of gears and wheels similar to that found in odometers and other counting devices to perform addition and subtraction. Pascal announced his calculating device as follows:

> Dear reader, this notice will serve to inform you that I submit to the public a small machine of my invention, by means of which you alone may, without any effort, perform all the operations of arithmetic, and may be relieved of the work which has often times fatigued your spirit, when you have worked with the counters or with the pen. As for simplicity of movement of the operations, I have so devised it that, although the operations of arithmetic are in a way opposed the one to the other—as addition to subtraction, and multiplication to division—nevertheless they are all performed on this machine by a single movement. The facility of this movement of operation is very evident since it is just as easy to move one thousand or ten thousand dials, all at one time, if one desires to make a single dial move, although all accomplish the movement perfectly. The most ignorant find as many advantages as the most experienced. The instrument makes up for ignorance and for lack of practice, and even without any effort of the operator, it makes possible shortcuts by itself, whenever the numbers are set down.

Although Pascal built more than 50 of his adding machines, his commercial venture failed because the devices could not be built with sufficient precision for practical use. A more reliable and accurate calculator that could perform multiplication as well as addition was developed by the German mathematician **Gottfried Wilhelm von Leibniz** in the 1670s. A number of other mechanical calculators followed that further refined Pascal's and Leibniz's designs, and by the end of the nineteenth century, these calculators had become important tools in science, business, and commerce.

The Stored Program Concept

The fundamental idea that distinguishes computers from calculators is the concept of a stored program that controls the computation. A **program** is a sequence of instructions that the computer follows to solve some problem. Programs made up of appropriate instructions perform a variety of tasks, from navigational control of the space shuttle to word processing to musical composition. Given different programs, the same machine can perform a variety of tasks. Because of this flexibility, the computer is sometimes called the **universal machine.**

An early example of an automatically controlled device is the weaving loom invented by the Frenchman **Joseph Marie Jacquard.** Holes punched in metal cards positioned the threads and directed the operation of the machine. Jacquard's loom is thus one of the first examples of a programmable machine. Within a decade, 11,000 of these machines were being used in French textile plants, resulting in what may have been the first incidence of unemployment caused by automation. Unemployed workers rioted and destroyed several of the new looms and cards. According to Jacquard, "The iron was sold for iron, the wood for wood, and I its inventor delivered up to public ignominy."

MECHANICAL COMPUTERS

The two fundamental concepts of mechanized calculation and stored program control were combined by the English mathematician **Charles Babbage** (1792–1871), who began work in 1822 on a machine that he called the **Difference Engine.** It was designed to compute polynomials for preparing mathematical tables. Babbage continued his work until 1833 when he abandoned this effort and went on to design a more sophisticated machine that he called his **Analytical Engine.** The operation of this machine was to be fully automatic, controlled by programs stored on punched cards, an idea based on Jacquard's earlier work. In fact, as Babbage himself observed: "The analogy of the Analytical Engine with this well-known process is nearly perfect." Its basic design corresponded remarkably to that of modern computers. A *mill* (like the central processing unit in modern machines) was designed to carry out the arithmetic computations; the *store* was the machine's memory for storing data and intermediate results; input was to be by means of punched cards; output was to be printed; and other components were designed for the transfer of information between components. A lifelong friend of Babbage, **Ada Augusta,** understood how the device was to operate and helped Babbage in its design. Considered by some to be the first programmer, she described the similarity of Jacquard's and Babbage's inventions: "The Analytical Engine weaves algebraic patterns just as the Jacquard loom weaves flowers and leaves." Although Babbage's machine was not built during his lifetime, it is nevertheless an important part of the history of computing because many of the concepts of its design are used in modern computers. For this reason, Babbage is sometimes called the "Father of Computing."

During the next hundred years, little progress was made in realizing Babbage's dream. About the only noteworthy event during this time was the invention by **Herman Hollerith** of a tabulating machine to assist the United States Census Bureau with compiling the 1890 census statistics. Hollerith's company eventually became the International Business Machines (IBM) Corporation.

Babbage's dream was finally realized in the Z-1, Z-2, Z-3, and Z-4 computers developed by the German engineer **Konrad Zuse.** One can only wonder how history might have been different if, in the middle of World War II, Adolf Hitler had agreed to fund Zuse's proposal to build the first fully electronic computer by replacing the electro-mechanical relays in his machines with vacuum tubes.

Meanwhile, World War II also spurred the development of computing devices in the United States and Britain. Repeating much of the work of Babbage, Howard Aiken designed a system consisting of several mechanical calculators working together. This work, which was supported by IBM, led to the invention in 1944 of the electromechanical **Mark I** computer, which is the best-known computer built before 1945. Other computing pioneers were John Atanasoff, J. Prespert Eckert, John Mauchly, Alan Turing, Grace Murray Hopper, and John von Neumann. Their contributions are described in the timeline that appears later.

EARLY ELECTRONIC COMPUTERS

The first fully electronic computer was developed by **John Atanasoff** at Iowa State University. With the help of his assistant, **Clifford Berry,** he built a prototype in 1939 and completed the first working model in 1942. The best known of the early electronic computers was the **ENIAC** (Electronic Numerical Integrator and Computer), constructed in 1946 by J. Prespert Eckert and John Mauchly at the Moore School of Electrical Engineering of the University of Pennsylvania. This extremely large machine could multiply numbers approximately 1000 times faster than the Mark I, but it was quite limited in its applications and was used primarily by the Army Ordnance Department to calculate firing tables and trajectories for various types of artillery shells. Eckert and Mauchly later left the University of Pennsylvania to form the Eckert-Mauchly Computer Corporation, which built the **UNIVAC** (Universal Automatic Computer), the first commercially available computer designed for both scientific and business applications. The first UNIVAC was sold to the Census Bureau in 1951.

The instructions that controlled the ENIAC's operation were entered into the machine by rewiring some of the computer's circuits. This complicated process was very time-consuming, sometimes taking a number of people several days; and during this time, the computer was idle. In other early computers, the instructions were stored outside the machine on punched cards or some other medium and were transferred into the machine one at a time for interpretation and execution.

A new scheme developed by Princeton mathematician **John von Neumann** and others used internally stored commands. The advantages of this stored program concept are that internally stored instructions can be processed more rapidly and, more important, that they can be modified by the computer itself while computations are taking place. The stored program concept made possible the general-purpose computers so commonplace today.

MODERN COMPUTERS

The actual physical components that make up a computer system are its **hardware.** Several generations of computers can be identified by the type of hardware used. The ENIAC and UNIVAC are examples of **first-generation** computers, which are characterized by their extensive use of *vacuum tubes.* Advances in electronics brought changes in computing systems, and in 1958, IBM introduced the first of the **second-generation** computers (the 7090 and other computers in their 7000 series) vaulting IBM from computer obscurity to first place. These computers were built between 1959 and 1965 and used *transistors* in place of vacuum tubes. Consequently, these computers were smaller, required less power, generated far less heat, and were more reliable than their predecessors. They were also less expensive. The first **minicomputer,** the PDP-8, which was introduced in 1963, sold for $18,000, in contrast with earlier computers whose six-digit price tags limited their sales to large companies. The **third-generation** computers that followed used *integrated circuits* and introduced new techniques for better system utilization, such as multiprogramming and time-sharing. The IBM System/360 introduced in 1964 is commonly accepted as the first of this generation of computers. Computers of the 1980s and 1990s, commonly called **fourth-generation** computers, use *very large-scale integrated* (VLSI) circuits on silicon chips and other microelectronic advances to shrink their size and cost still more while enlarging their capabilities. A typical chip is equivalent to millions of transistors, is smaller than a baby's fingernail, weighs a small fraction of an ounce, requires only a trickle of power, and costs but a few dollars. One of the pioneers in the development of transistors was Robert Noyce, one of the cofounders of the Intel Corporation, which introduced the 4004 microprocessor in 1971. Noyce contrasted microcomputers with the ENIAC as follows:

An individual integrated circuit on a chip perhaps a quarter of an inch square now can embrace more electronic elements than the most complex piece of electronic equipment that could be built in 1950. Today's microcomputer, at a cost of perhaps $300, has more computing capacity than the first electronic computer, ENIAC. It is twenty times faster, has a larger memory, consumes the power of a light bulb rather than that of a locomotive, occupies 1/30,000 the volume and costs 1/10,000 as much. It is available by mail order or at your local hobby shop.

Microprocessors like the Intel 4004 made possible the development of the personal computers (PCs) that are so common today. One of the most popular personal computers was the **Apple II,** introduced in 1977 by **Steven Jobs** and **Steve Wozniak,** then 21 and 26 years old, respectively. They founded the Apple Computer Company, one of the major manufacturers of microcomputers today. This was followed in 1981 by the first of **IBM's PCs,** which have become the microcomputer standard in business and industry.

Continued advances in technology have produced an array of computer systems, ranging from portable **laptop** and **notebook** computers to powerful desktop machines known as **workstations,** to **supercomputers** capable of performing billions of operations each second, and to **massively parallel computers,** which use a large number of microprocessors working together in parallel to solve large problems. Someone once noted that if progress in the automotive industry had been as rapid as in computer technology since 1960, today's automobile would have an engine that is less than 0.1 inch in length, would get 120,000 miles to a gallon of gas, have a top speed of 240,000 miles per hour, and would cost $4.

SYSTEM SOFTWARE

The stored program concept, introduced by John Von Neumann, was a significant improvement over manual programming methods, but early computers still were difficult to use because of the complex coding schemes used to represent programs and data. Consequently, in addition to improved hardware, computer manufacturers began to develop collections of programs known as **system software,** which make computers easier to use. One of the more important advances in this area was the development of **operating systems,** which allocate memory for programs and data and carry out many other supervisory functions. In particular, an operating system acts as an interface between the user and the machine. It interprets commands given by the user and then directs the appropriate system software and hardware to carry them out. One of the most popular operating systems is UNIX, begun in 1971 but still undergoing development today. It is the only operating system that has been implemented on computers ranging from microcomputers to supercomputers. For years, the most popular operating system for personal computers was MS-DOS, the first version of which was developed by the Microsoft Corporation in 1981. More recently, **graphical user interfaces (GUI),** such as MIT's X Window System for UNIX-based machines, Microsoft's Windows for PCs, and the Apple Macintosh interface have been devised to provide a simpler and more intuitive interface between humans and computers.

Another important advance in system software was the development of **high-level languages.** Early computers were very difficult to program. In fact, programming some of the earliest computers consisted of designing and building circuits to carry out the computations required to solve each new problem. Later, computer instructions could be coded in a language that the machine could understand. But these codes were very cryptic and programming was therefore very tedious and error-prone. High-level languages made it possible to enter instructions using an English-like syntax.

In addition to building electro-mechanical computers, Konrad Zuse in 1945 designed a high-level programming language that he named Plankalkül. Although Zuse wrote programs using this language, it was never actually implemented due to a lack of funding. As a result, it lay in obscurity until 1972 when Zuse's manuscripts were discovered. This language was amazingly sophisticated for its time—over 15 years passed before its features began to appear in other languages. Zuse designed programs to perform tasks as diverse as integer and floating point arithmetic, sorting lists of numbers, and playing chess.

One of the first high-level languages to gain widespread acceptance was **FORTRAN** (**FOR**mula **TRAN**slation), which was developed for the IBM 704 computer by **John Backus** and a team of 13 other programmers at IBM during a 3-year period (1954–1957). Since that time many other high-level languages have become popular, including ALGOL, BASIC, COBOL, Pascal, C, Ada, and Modula-2. In this text, we use the C++ programming language. Computers would not have gained widespread use if it had not been for the development of such high-level programming languages.

A program written in a high-level language is known as a **source program.** For most high-level languages, the instructions that make up a source program must be translated into **machine language,** that is, the language used directly by a particular computer for all its calculations and processing. This machine-language program is called an **object program.** The system programs that translate source programs into object programs are called **compilers.**

One of the primary advantages of high-level languages is portability. Programs written in machine language will run only on the type of computer for which they were written. This is the reason that an application written for a Macintosh computer will not run on an IBM PC. In contrast, a program written in a high-level language can be written and compiled on one computer and subsequently transferred to and compiled on an entirely different computer, so long as a compiler for the high-level language is available on the second computer. For this reason, programs written in high-level languages are **portable,** whereas programs written in low-level languages are not.

A Brief History of C++ and OOP

In 1969, a researcher named **Ken Thompson** was beginning the design and implementation of the **UNIX** operating system at AT&T's Bell Laboratories. His first implementation of UNIX was written in the assembly language of a spare Digital Equipment Corporation PDP-7.[2] It was not long before it became necessary to implement UNIX on a more powerful machine, a DEC PDP-11. However, because UNIX had been written in PDP-7 assembly language, it was not directly portable to the PDP-11. The prospect of rewriting the thousands of lines of UNIX in a different assembly language was distinctly unpleasant, particularly because it was obvious that this problem would recur each time Thompson wanted to implement UNIX on a new machine. To simplify the task of transferring UNIX to other computers, Thompson began to search for a high-level language in which to rewrite UNIX.

None of the high-level languages in existence at the time were appropriate; therefore, in 1970, Thompson began designing a new language called B that was based on an existing language BCPL. By 1972, it had become apparent that B was not adequate for implementing UNIX. At that time, **Dennis Ritchie,** also at Bell Labs, designed a successor language to B that he called **C,** and approximately 90 percent of UNIX was rewritten in C. This new language quickly became very popular in colleges and universities across the country and eventually spread to the business world as well. With the availability of inexpensive C compilers for microcomputers, C has become the language in which many microcomputer applications are written.

Although C is a very powerful language, it has two characteristics that make it inappropriate for a modern introduction to programming. First, C requires a level of sophistication in its users beyond that of the typical beginning programmer.Second, C was designed in the early 1970s, and the nature of programming has changed significantly since that time.

---

[2] See PART OF THE PICTURE: Computer Organization later in this chapter for a description of assembly language.

In 1967, the researchers Kristen Nygaard and Ole-Johan Dahl introduced a new language for creating real-world simulations named **Simula-67.** To facilitate the modeling of real-world objects, Simula provided a new language feature called the **class,** which could be extended through an *inheritance mechanism.* These capabilities laid the groundwork for **object-oriented programming (OOP),** a new approach to programming that emphasized the modeling of objects through classes and inheritance. By the late 1970s, it became apparent that this new approach held great promise for reducing the cost of upgrading and maintaining software. A research group at Xerox' Palo Alto Research Center (PARC) built upon these ideas and created the first truly object-oriented language, named **Smalltalk-80.**

Across the country at Bell Labs, another researcher named **Bjarne Stroustrup** undertook the project of extending C with object-oriented features. Stroustrup also added new features that eliminated many of the difficulties C posed for beginning programmers. The resulting language was first called *C with Classes,* but by 1983, more improvements had been added and the language was renamed **C++** (for reasons that will become clear in chapter 2). By blending the power of its parent C with the benefits of object-oriented programming, C++ has rapidly grown from obscurity to popularity.

PART OF THE PICTURE: COMPUTING HISTORY

3,000 B.C. - 1642

3000 B.C.: One of the earliest "personal calculators" was the **abacus**. It has movable beads strung on rods to count and to do calculations. Although its exact origin is unknown, the abacus was used by the Chinese perhaps 3000 to 4000 years ago and is still used today throughout Asia. Early merchants used the abacus in trading transactions.

STONEHENGE 1900 – 1600 B.C.: The ancient British stone monument **Stonehenge**, located near Salisbury, England, was built between 1900 and 1600 B.C. and, evidently, was used to predict the changes of the seasons.

TWELFTH CENTURY: A Persian teacher of mathematics in Baghdad, **Muhammad ibn-Musa al-Khowarizm**, developed some of the first step-by-step procedures for doing computations. The word *algorithm* used for such procedures is derived from his name.

NAPIER'S BONES 1612:

In Western Europe, the Scottish mathematician John Napier (1550-1617) designed a set of ivory rods (called **Napier's bones**) to assist with doing multiplications Napier also developed tables of **logarithms** and other multiplication machines.

SLIDE RULE 1630:
The English mathematician William Oughtred invented a circular **slide rule** in the early 1600s. Slide rules like that shown here were based on Napier's logarithms and were used by engineers and scientists through the nineteenth and first half of the twentieth centuries to do rapid approximate computations.

PASCALINE 1642: The young French mathematician **Blaise Pascal** (1623-1662) invented one of the first mechanical adding machines. The **Pascaline** could carry out additions and subtractions and was invented to help his father with calculating taxes. It used a series of eight ten-toothed wheels (one tooth for each decimal digit), which were connected so that numbers could be added or subtracted by moving the wheels.

1673 - 1842

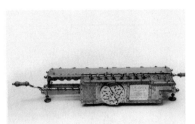

LEIBNIZ' CALCULATOR 1673: The German mathematician **Gottfried Wilhelm von Leibniz** invented an improved mechanical calculator that, like the Pascaline, used a system of gears and dials to do calculations. However, it was more reliable and accurate than the Pascaline and could perform all four of the basic arithmetic operations of addition, subtraction, multiplication, and division.

JACQUARD LOOM 1801: The weaving loom invented by the Frenchman **Joseph Marie Jacquard** (1752-1834) is an early example of an automatically controlled device. It used metal cards punched with holes to position threads in the weaving process. A collection of these cards made up a program that directed the loom. The **Jacquard loom** is still used today, although modern versions are controlled by programs stored on magnetic tape rather than punched cards.

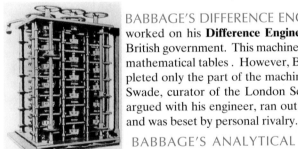

BABBAGE'S DIFFERENCE ENGINE 1822: **Charles Babbage** (1792-1871) worked on his **Difference Engine** from 1822 to 1933, with support from the British government. This machine was to be used in the preparation of accurate mathematical tables . However, Babbage abandoned this project, having completed only the part of the machine shown here, because, according to Doron Swade, curator of the London Science Museum, the cantankerous Babbage argued with his engineer, ran out of money, and was beset by personal rivalry.

BABBAGE'S ANALYTICAL ENGINE 1833: Babbage began the design of a much more advanced machine called the **Analytical Engine**. It was to have over 50,000 components, including a *store* for up to 1,000 50-digit numbers, a *mill* for calculating according to a sequence of instructions, input by means of punched metal cards, and printed output. When completed, it would have been as large as a locomotive, been powered by steam, been able to calculate to six decimal places of accuracy very rapidly and print out results, all controlled by a stored program.

ADA AUGUSTA 1842: **Ada Augusta** (1816-1852), Lord George Byron's daughter, the countess of Lovelace, was one of the few people other than Babbage who understood the Analytical Engine's design. This enabled her to develop "programs" for the machine, and for this reason she is sometimes called "the first programmer." In the 1980s, the programming language ADA was named in her honor.

1890 - 1944

HOLLERITH'S TABULATING MACHINE 1890:   There was a fear that, because of growing population, it would not be possible to complete processing of the 1890 census before the next one was to be taken. The tabulating machine invented by **Herman Hollerith** made it possible to complete the processing in two and a half years. The Hollerith Tabulating Company later merged with other companies to form IBM.

KONRAD ZUSE 1935-1938: The German engineer **Konrad Zuse** began work on his Z-1 computer, which was followed by the increasingly more sophisticated Z-2, Z-3, and Z-4. These machines, like modern computers, used binary arithmetic. Zuse's assistant Helmut Schreyer proposed using vacuum tubes in place of the relays to make a machine that would be hundreds of times faster. Zuse applied to the German government for funding, but in the middle of World War II, was turned down.

ATANASOFF'S ELECTRONIC DIGITAL COMPUTER (ABC) 1936-1939:

John Atanasoff and **Clifford Berry** developed the first fully electronic computer we now call the ABC (Atanasoff-Berry Computer) at Iowa State University to do long mathematical calculations in physics. Although the ENIAC bore the title of the first fully electronic computer for many years, a historic 1973 court decision ruled that Atanasoff was the legal inventor of the first electronic digital computer.

ALAN TURING 1937:   **Alan Turing** developed the universal machine concept, forming the basis of

computability theory. During World War II, he was a part of a team whose task was to decrypt intercepted messages of the German forces. Several machines resulted from this British war effort, one of which was the Collosus, finished in 1943.

GRACE HOPPER 1944:

MARK I 1944: The best-known computer built before 1945 was the **Harvard Mark I** (whose full name was the

Harvard-IBM Automatic Sequence Controlled Calculator). Repeating much of the work of Babbage, Howard Aiken and others at IBM constructed this large, automatic, general purpose, electromechanical calculator. It was sponsored by the U.S. Navy and (like Babbage's machines) was intended to compute mathematical and navigational tables.

Grace Murray Hopper (1907-1992) began work as a coder — what we today would call a programmer — for the Mark I. In the late 1950s, "Grandma COBOL," as she has affectionately been called, led the effort to develop the **COBOL** programming language for business applications.

1945 - 1957

COMPUTER BUG 1945: While working on the Mark II computer, Grace Hopper found the first **computer bug** — an actual bug stuck in one of the thousands of relays that has been preserved in the National Museum of American History of the Smithsonian Institution. She glued it into the logbook, and subsequent efforts to find the cause of machine stoppage were reported to Aiken as *debugging* the computer.

1945: John von Neumann wrote "First Draft of a Report on the EDVAC" computer which led to his being credited as the inventor of the stored-program concept. The architectural design he described is still known as the *von Neumann architecture*. (Others including Eckert and Mauchly, and Zuse claimed to have had similar ideas several years before this.)

VACUUM TUBES 1945-1956: **First-generation** computers used **vacuum tubes**. Although they could do calculations much more rapidly than mechanical and electromechanical computers, the heat generated by large numbers of vacuum tubes and their short lifetimes led to frequent failures.

ENIAC 1946: The ENIAC is arguably the best-known of the early electronic computers. It was designed at the University of Pennsylvania by **J. Prespert Eckert** and **John Mauchly** to calculate firing tables for the Army Ordnance Department. This 30-ton machine with its 18,000 vacuum tubes, 70,000 resistors, and 5 million soldered joints consumed 160 kilowatts of electrical power. Stories are told of how the lights in Philadelphia dimmed when the ENIAC was operating.

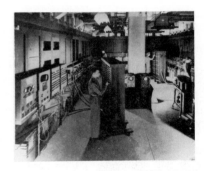

UNIVAC 1951: The **UNIVAC** (UNIVersal Automatic Computer), started in 1946 and completed in 1951, was the first general-purpose electronic digital computer designed for scientific and commercial use. It soon became the common name for computers, partly due to its correct (albeit unbelieved) prediction of the outcome of the 1952 U.S. presidential election.

1957: After 3 years of work, **John Backus** and his colleagues delivered the first **FORTRAN** program compiler for the IBM 704. Their first report commented that a programmer was able to write and debug in 4 to 5 hours a program that would have taken several days to do by hand. Fortran has undergone several revisions and remains a powerful language for scientific computing.

1956 - 1969

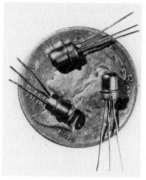

EARLY TRANSISTORS 1956-1963: **Second-generation** computers used **transistors** instead of the large, cumbersome vacuum tubes, marking the beginning of the great computer shrinking. Second-generation computers were smaller, faster, more reliable, and more energy-efficient than earlier machines.

1958: IBM produced the first of its 7000 series mainframes. These machines used transistors instead of vacuum tubes and were thus some of the first second-generation computers produced. The 7030 had 64-bit words and was designed to be a supercomputer for scientific work.

THIRD-GENERATION COMPUTER CHIPS–
INTEGRATED CIRCUITS 1964-1971: **Third-generation** computers used **integrated circuits (chips)**, which first became commercially available from the Fairchild Corporation. These ICs were based on the pioneering work of **Jack Kilby and Robert Noyce**. Another third-generation development was the use of operating systems to manage the computer's memory and allow them to run many different programs at once.

IBM 360 1964:
The **IBM System/360** is commonly accepted as the first of this generation of computers. Orders for this family of mutually compatible computers and peripherals climbed to 1000 per month within 2 years.

PDP-8 1965: Digital Equipment Corporation introduced the **PDP-8**, the first commercially successful **minicomputer**. Because of its speed, small size, and reasonable cost — $18,000, less than 20% of the price of a IBM 360 mainframe — it became a popular computer in many scientific establishments, small businesses, and manufacturing plants.

KEN THOMPSON 1969: Disillusioned by how work on the multiuser operating system Multics was proceeding, **Ken Thompson** of Bell Telephone Laboratories, using a spare PDP-7 computer, began work on a simpler OS aimed at the single user. In a pun on the name Multics, the new operating system was named **UNIX**.

1971 - 1981

4004 CHIP 1971: Intel's **Ted Hoff** designed the **4004 chip**, giving birth to the microprocessor, which marks the beginning of the **fourth-generation** of computers. This, along with the first use of an 8-inch floppy disk at IBM, ushered in the era of the personal computer.

1973:

■ **Dennis Ritchie** developed the **C programming language**, and in 1977 the UNIX operating system was rewritten in C.
■ **Ethernet** was developed at Xerox PARC.
■ A district court in Minneapolis ruled that John Atanasoff (and not Eckert and Mauchly) was the legal inventor of the first electronic digital computer.

1975:

■ The MITS **Altair 8800** hobby-kit computer was invented by Edward Roberts (who coined the term personal computer), William Yates, and Jim Bybee. It had 256 bytes of memory, but no keyboard, no display, and no external storage. It sold for $300 - $400.
■ **Bill Gates** and **Paul Allen** wrote a BASIC compiler for the Altair.
■ Working in a garage, **Steven Jobs** and **Steve Wozniak** developed the Apple I.

APPLE II 1976: Steven Jobs and Steve Wozniak produced the **Apple II**, assembled and complete with a keyboard and a monitor. Because of its affordabilty and the availability of basic software applications, it was an immediate success, especially in schools and colleges.

CRAY I

■ The first **supercomputer** and the fastest machine of its day, the **Cray I**, was introduced. It was built in the shape of a C so components would be close together, reducing the time for electronic signals to travel between them.
■ **Apple** and **Microsoft Corporations** are founded.

IBM PC 1981: IBM entered the personal computer market with the **IBM PC**, originally called the Acorn. It used the **DOS** operating system under an agreement that gave Microsoft all the profits in exchange for their having borne the development costs.

1983 - 1995

BJARNE STROUSTRUP 1983:   **Bjarne Stroustrup** introduced the redesigned and extended programming language *C With Classes* with the new name **C++**.

MAC-1984: Using a renowned George-Orwellian advertisement parodying the downtrodden masses, subservient to the IBM PC, Apple announced the **Macintosh** and its graphical user interface.

1985: Microsoft introduced **Windows 1.0**, its graphical user interface for IBM-PC compatibles. It was not until the release of Windows 3.0 in 1990, however, that it gained widespread acceptance.

INTEL 386 CHIP 1986: **Intel** released the **386 chip**, which became the best-selling microprocessor in history. It contained 275,000 transistors. The 486, released in 1989, had more than a million.

1993:
■ Intel introduced the **Pentium chip** containing more than 3 million transistors. The Pentium Pro released in 1995 has more than 5.5 million.
■ Motorola shipped the first **PowerPC chip**
1994:
■ **Netscape Navigator 1.0** was released
1995:
■ The new C++-based object-oriented programming language Oak, developed at Sun Microsystems, is renamed **Java** and bursts onto the computer scene. Applications created in Java can be deployed without modification to any computing platform, thus making versions for different platforms unnecessary.
■ Microsoft introduces **Windows 95**
■ Microsoft releases **Microsoft Internet Explorer** 1.0.

EXERCISES

1. What are two important concepts in the early history of computation?
2. Match each item in the first column with the associated item in the second column.

_____John von Neumann	A. early high-level language
_____Charles Babbage	B. first commercially available computer
_____Blaise Pascal	C. developed first fully electronic computer
_____Herman Hollerith	D. stored program concept
_____Grace Murray Hopper	E. Difference Engine
_____Konrad Zuse	F. designer of FORTRAN language
_____Alan Turing	G. Harvard Mark I
_____Howard Aiken	H. an early electronic computer
_____John Backus	I. integrated circuits (chips)
_____Joseph Jacquard	J. vacuum tubes
_____Ada Augusta	K. transistors
_____John Atanasoff and Clifford Berry	L. Apple Computer
	M. automatic loom
_____Bjarne Stroustrup	N. developed the UNIX operating system
_____Steven Jobs and Steve Wozniak	O. developed the C language
_____Ken Thompson	P. developed the C++ language
_____Dennis Ritchie	Q. the first computer bug
_____PDP-8	R. universal machine concept
_____UNIVAC	S. first programmer
_____FORTRAN	T. adding machine
_____ENIAC	U. punched card
_____first generation computers	V. minicomputer
_____second generation computers	W. developed pre-World-War-II computers
_____third generation computers	that used binary arithmetic

For Questions 3–21, describe the importance of the person to the history of computing:

3. al-Khowarizm
4. William Oughtred
5. Charles Babbage
6. Blaise Pascal
7. John von Neumann
8. Herman Hollerith
9. Joseph Jacquard
10. Gottfried Wilhelm von Leibniz
11. John Atanasoff
12. Steven Jobs and Steve Wozniak
13. Robert Noyce
14. J. Prespert Eckert
15. John Backus
16. Alan Turing
17. Konrad Zuse
18. Grace Murray Hopper
19. Ken Thompson
20. Dennis Ritchie
21. Bjarne Stroustrup

For Exercises 22–31, describe the importance of each item to the history of computing:

22.	ENIAC		**27.**	MITS Altair 8800
23.	Analytical Engine		**28.**	Apple II
24.	Jacquard loom		**29.**	Cray I
25.	UNIVAC		**30.**	DOS
26.	Mark I		**31.**	Java

32.   Distinguish the four different generations of computers.

Part of The Picture: Introduction to Computer Organization

Babbage's Analytical Engine (described in the preceding section) was a system of several separate components, each with its own particular function. This general scheme was incorporated in many later computers and is, in fact, a common feature of most modern computers. In this section we briefly describe the major components of a modern computing system and how program instructions and data are stored and processed. For a more complete description see PART OF THE PICTURE: Computer Architecture in Chapter 5.

COMPUTING SYSTEMS

The heart of any computing system is its **central processing unit (CPU).** The CPU controls the operation of the entire system, performs the arithmetic and logic operations, and stores and retrieves instructions and data. The instructions and data are stored in a high-speed **memory unit,** and the **control unit** fetches these instructions from memory, decodes them, and directs the system to execute the operations indicated by the instructions. Those operations that are arithmetical or logical in nature are carried out using the circuits of the **arithmetic-logic unit (ALU)** of the CPU.

The memory unit usually consists of several components. One of these components is used to store the instructions and data of the programs being executed and has many names, including **internal, main, primary,** and **random access memory (RAM).** A second component is a set of special high-speed memory locations within the CPU called **registers.** Values that are stored in registers can typically be accessed thousands of times faster than values that are stored in RAM.

One problem with both RAM and registers is that if the power to the computing system is shut off (either intentionally or accidently), values that are stored in these memory components are lost. To provide long-term storage of programs and data, most computing systems also have memory components that are called **external, auxiliary,** or **secondary memory.** Common forms of this type of memory include magnetic disks (such as hard disks and floppy disks) and magnetic tapes. These **peripheral devices** provide long-term storage for large collections of data, even if power is lost. However, the time required to access data that is stored on such devices can be thousands of times greater than the access time for data stored in RAM.

Other peripherals are used to transmit instructions, data, and computed results between the user and the CPU. These are the **input/output devices,** which have a variety of forms, such as terminals, scanners, voice input devices, printers, and plotters. Their function is to convert information from an external form understandable to the user to a form that can be processed by the computer system, and vice versa.

Figure 1 shows the relationship between these components in a computer system. The arrows indicate how information flows through the system.

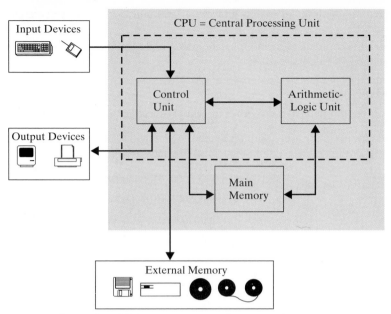

FIGURE 1.   Major components of a computing system.

MEMORY ORGANIZATION

The devices that make up the memory unit of a computer are two-state devices. If one of the states is interpreted as 0 and the other as 1, then it is natural to use a **binary scheme,** using only the two binary digits (**bits**) 0 and 1 to represent information in a computer. These two-state devices are organized into groups called **bytes.** Usually a byte consists of eight bits. Memory is commonly measured in bytes, and a block of $2^{10} = 1024$ bytes is called **1K** of memory. Thus, one **megabyte** (= 1024 K) of memory consists of $1024 \times 2^{10} = 2^{10} \times 2^{10} = 2^{20} = 1,048,576$ bytes, or, equivalently, $2^{20} \times 2^3 = 2^{23} = 8,388,608$ bits.

Bytes are typically grouped together into **words.** The number of bits in a word is equal to the number of bits in a CPU register. The word size thus varies on different computers, but common word sizes are 16 bits (= 2 bytes), 32 bits (= 4 bytes) and 64 bits (= 8 bytes). Associated with each word or byte is an **address** that can be used to directly access that word or byte. This makes it possible to store information in a specific memory location and then to retrieve it later. To understand how this is done, one must first understand the binary number system. The details of how various types of data are represented in a binary form and stored in a computer's memory are described in PART OF THE PICTURE: Data Representation in chapter 2.

Program instructions for processing data must also be stored in memory. They must be instructions that the machine can execute and they must be expressed in a form that the machine can understand, that is, they must be written in the **machine language** for that machine. These instructions consist of two parts: (1) a numeric **opcode,** which represents a basic machine operation such as load, multiply, add, and store; and (2) the address of the **operand.** Like all information stored in memory, these instructions must be represented in a binary form.

As an example, suppose that values have been stored in three memory locations with addresses 1024, 1025, and 1026 and that we want to multiply the first two values, add the third, and store the result in a fourth memory location 1027. To perform this computation, the following instructions must be executed:

1. Fetch the contents of memory location 1024 and load it into a register in the ALU.

2. Fetch the contents of memory location 1025 and compute the product of this value and the value in the register.

3. Fetch the contents of memory location 1026 and add this value to the value in the register.

4. Store the contents of the register in memory location 1027.

If the opcodes for load, store, add, and multiply are 16, 17, 35, and 36, respectively, these four instructions might be written in machine language as follows[3]:

1. 00010000000000000000010000000000

2. 00100100000000000000010000000001

3. 00100011000000000000010000000010

4. 00010001000000000000010000000011

$$\underbrace{}_{\text{opcode}} \qquad \underbrace{}_{\text{operand}}$$

These instructions can then be stored in four (consecutive) memory locations. When the program is executed, the control unit will fetch each of these instructions, decode it to determine the operation and the address of the operand, fetch the operand, and then perform the required operation, using the ALU if necessary.

As we noted in the preceding section, programs for early computers had to be written in machine language and only later did it become possible to write programs in **assembly language,** which uses mnemonics (names) in place of numeric opcodes and variable names in place of numeric addresses. For example, the preceding sequence of instructions might be written in assembly language as

1. MOV A, ACC

2. MUL B, ACC

3. ADD C, ACC

4. STO ACC, X

An **assembler,** which is part of the system software, translates such assembly language instructions into machine language.

Today, most programs are written in a high-level language such as C++, and a **compiler** translates each statement in the program into a sequence of basic machine- (or assembly-) language instructions. For example, for the preceding problem, the programmer could write the C++ statement

X = A * B + C;

which instructs the computer to multiply the values of A and B, add the value of C, and assign the value to X. The compiler translates this statement into the sequence of four machine (or assembly) language instructions considered earlier. For programs that use libraries, a **linker** will also be used to connect items that are defined outside of the object file with their definitions to produce an **executable program:**

---

[3] In binary notation, the opcodes 16, 17, 35, and 36 are 10000, 10001, 100011, and 100100, respectively, and the addresses 1024, 1025, 1026, 1027, are 10000000000, 10000000001, 10000000010, and 10000000011, respectively. (See the Web site described in the preface for algorithms to convert base-10 numbers to base-2.)

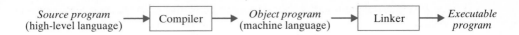

Source program (high-level language) → Compiler → Object program (machine language) → Linker → Executable program

EXERCISES

1. Match each item in the first column with the associated item in the second column.

_____compiler	A. random access memory
_____peripheral devices	B. language translator
_____bit	C. central processing unit
_____byte	D. 1024
_____megabyte	E. terminals, scanners, printers
_____object program	F. binary digit
_____source program	G. group of binary digits
_____CPU	H. 1024 K bytes
_____K	I. written in machine language
_____RAM	J. written in high-level language

Briefly define each of the terms in Exercises 2–15:

2. stored-program concept

3. FORTRAN

4. ALU

5. CPU

6. peripheral devices

7. bit

8. byte

9. word

10. K

11. megabyte

12. source program

13. object program

14. machine language

15. assembly language

16. What are the main functions of an assembler?

17. What are the main functions of a compiler?

18. What are the main functions of a linker?

Part of the Picture: Ethics and Computing

BY ANNE MARCHANT, PH. D.
GEORGE MASON UNIVERSITY

To be good is noble, but to show others how to be good is nobler, and no trouble.

MARK TWAIN

ETHICS AND SOCIETY

What will the future bring? Will we live a life of leisure with all our tedious chores performed by intelligent machines? Perhaps we will live instead in an "information prison" with all the details of our lives recorded and analyzed by government or by corporations that exist solely to buy and sell information. To a large extent, the future will be driven by the choices we make now.

Computers permeate every aspect of our lives. In addition to making businesses more productive, they also perform many life-critical tasks such as air-traffic control, medical diagnosis and treatment, and emergency communication. The field of computer science is unregulated. Programmers are not required to pass proficiency exams or obtain licenses to practice their art. In an effort to protect society from the obvious dangers, the field is regulating itself. It does this by encouraging the study of ethics and by demanding the highest level of integrity from its members. Professional organizations such as the Association for Computing Machinery (ACM) and the IEEE (Institute of Electrical and Electronics Engineers) have adopted and instituted Code of Ethics.[4] Students are encouraged to join these organizations and familiarize themselves with these codes. Most colleges and universities also have policies governing the responsible use of computers. Students are encouraged to read these carefully and to develop their own personal standards.

COMPUTER CRIME AND SECURITY

"Rogue software" is a class of software designed with some malicious intent. "Viruses" are programs that "infect" software in order to replicate. They usually do something harmful as well. A virus may corrupt or erase information on your disks. "Worms" are self-replicating programs that repeatedly propagate until they overwhelm the computer's resources. Viruses tend to be a problem on PCs. Worms create problems on networks. "Trojan horses" can occur anywhere. These are programs that appear to do something useful while secretly doing something malicious. An example might be a program that appears to be a space war game that secretly transmits the user's login, password, and user privileges to someone else. Trojan horses are of special concern on the Internet where Java Applets may harbor rogue code.

The term "hacker" has undergone a semantic shift in recent years. Originally the term meant someone who wrote poor programs (a "hack"). It then came to mean a computer enthusiast. Now it has come to mean a computer criminal (sometimes also called "crackers"). Hackers often justify their actions by claiming that they are just trying to learn about computers. Would-be hackers might consider that computer security is a rapidly expanding field. There is a tremendous need for "computer enthusiasts" with creative ideas. Creating a secure system is a much more challenging problem than breaking security. Students who put their energy into learning about computer security may well be on the way to a bright career!

How can we protect ourselves against hackers and rogue programs? The first line of defense is to use passwords that are not dictionary words and to change passwords frequently. It is very important to have at least two copies of every file at all times. It is also wise to keep backups at separate locations and in different media.

Users should keep antiviral software on their computers and be sure that they are familiar with how it works. Antiviral software needs to be updated periodically, at least every six months or so.

Firewalls are systems that monitor traffic between networks to ensure that all network traffic is legitimate. Every network connecting to the Internet should have a firewall in place. Institutions that allow modem access should consider installing a modem "call back" system to prevent unauthorized access.

Traditional security is especially important. Physically restricting access to computer systems can prevent many problems. The majority of computer crimes are not committed by hackers, but rather by employees or former employees of organizations. This means that employers need to screen applicants carefully, monitor employees' behavior, encourage a positive work ethic, and reward integrity. Grievance procedures should be in place to resolve work-related problems and diffuse hostilities when they arise. Secure audit systems should be in place to track fraud.

---

[4] See the Web site described in the preface.

HEALTH CONCERNS AND THE ENVIRONMENT

Today, our economy is based largely on information-related jobs. This means that many of us spend long hours behind the computer staring at monitors. The most obvious problem this creates is lack of exercise. We need to remember to make exercise a regular part of our lifestyle. A more insidious problem is a class of injuries known as repetitive stress injuries (RSIs) that result from performing the same actions repeatedly without taking breaks. Carpal tunnel syndrome is one such injury that may result from typing for many hours. These injuries can be incapacitating and may require surgery.

Questions have been raised as to whether computer use can cause problems such as miscarriages, birth defects, and cancer. These are still controversial. Some have suggested that stress and lack of exercise may be more harmful than electromagnetic radiation.

Staring at monitors for long periods of time may cause one to lose the ability to focus prematurely ("farsightedness"). One should reduce glare when possible and use the highest resolution screen possible. It is also advisable to look away from the screen and focus on distant objects periodically.

The ethical employer will insist on ergonomic work station design, encourage employees to take regular breaks and exercise, and watch for signs of excessive stress in fast-paced information-related jobs.

We think of the computer industry as being relatively friendly to the environment, but there are a number of serious concerns. The manufacture of computer chips can involve some chemicals that need to be carefully managed and disposed of. The ethical manager will see to it that paper and laser printer toner cartridges are recycled. Beyond that, each programmer and engineer needs to address the question: "Will my contributions make the world a better place or will my work cause harm?"

INFORMATION OWNERSHIP

Congress is granted the authority to "promote the Progress of Science and useful Art, by securing for limited Times to Authors and Inventors the exclusive Right to their respective Writings and Discoveries."

US CONSTITUTION, ART. 1, SECTION 8, CL. 8

Copyrights protect the original expression of ideas. You can't copyright a fact or the idea itself, but you can copyright the expression of an idea once it is fixed in a tangible medium. (This may be written text, recorded sound, or software stored on a disk.) A phone call can not be copyrighted (unless taped), but email or on-line chat may be copyrighted if it is saved to disk. (Note that some company contracts co-opt their employees email copyrights.) Under today's laws, a copyright notice © is not required to secure a copyright, nor need it be registered. However, these precautions will help to protect your work and support your case should you try to prove infringement. In 1989, the United States signed the Berne Convention, an international copyright agreement. With the growth of the Internet, international protection for intellectual property is a rising concern.

A copyright grants the copyright holder exclusive rights to the work's duplication, any derivative work, and the right of distribution or display. The integrity of the work must be maintained and the work must be properly attributed to the copyright holder. A copyright is valid for 75 years or 50 years after the death of the author for works created after 1977.

In a case of alleged copyright infringement, similarity and intent are evaluated. Damages up to $100,000 per infringement may be awarded. The law does allow for "fair use" of copyrighted material. In general, one may quote or copy a small amount of copyrighted material for educational purposes, or for use by the news media.

Students should be aware that it is an infringement to copy pictures or text from other web sites onto your own web page unless the copyright holder has granted permission. Creating a link to another page is legal (although this too may soon be challenged in court!). Similarly, it is illegal to scan in images to use on your web page without permission. You are essentially "publishing" someone else's work. Note that this is different from quoting something in a written paper that you submit as class work. As long as you include only a small portion of the work and properly attribute it to the author, this is considered "fair use."

Software is usually copyrighted. The holder of the copyright does not sell the software itself, but rather sells licenses to use the software. It is worth taking a minute to read the license that comes with software you purchase commercially. In general, it is illegal to make copies of commercial software except for the purposes of making a backup. As a rule, you must purchase a legal copy of the software for every machine you intend to install it on (although there are exceptions in some cases). Large companies and educational institutions will often purchase "site licenses" that allow them to install the software on a network file server. Duplicating software without paying for it is called "software piracy" or "bootlegging."

Sometimes software may be distributed as "shareware." Usually, shareware may be freely duplicated and distributed, but the author will require you to register the software and pay a fee if you decide to keep the software. Freeware is software that the author has placed in the public domain and may be duplicated freely.

Inventions, processes, and algorithms may be patented. An idea must pass a rigorous set of tests in order to be patented. The concept must be a new idea, it must be useful, and it must be "non-obvious" to other professionals working in the field. A patent may be held for 20 years and grants the patent holder the right to control sale of the invention and the right to royalties.

The legal system is struggling to manage the protection of electronic intellectual property. Does it make sense to grant an individual exclusive rights to an idea for 20 years in the rapidly changing field of computer science? As the use of computerized information continues to increase, society will need to adapt by making new laws and by changing existing laws. Exciting careers await those who combine the study of law and the study of computer science!

"NETIQUETTE" AND HOAXES

On-line "chat," newsgroups, and email provide a new realm of social interaction. In one sense, the lack of face-to-face interaction has a leveling effect on society. We make judgments based on a person's ideas instead of on their age, race, social standing, religion, ethnicity, or appearance. On the other hand, there is a disturbing lack of accountability that leads people to engage in inflammatory exchanges. These "flame wars" are usually viewed by more experienced users as a sign of immaturity and inexperience.

Chain mail is disallowed by many institutions and may be illegal in some instances. Be suspicious of mail that encourages you to forward the message to many other users. These messages may try to play on your emotions with such statements as: "Little Johnny is dying of cancer and would like your email messages before he dies. . . " or "Forward this mail to as many people as you can and it will bring you luck. If you don't, some serious harm will come to you." Such "chain mail" propagates quickly and overwhelms network resources. Don't be taken in!

Virus warnings are often hoaxes. Be especially leery of email viruses such as the "Good Times" virus. (This is a very old hoax!) Check with CERT (the Computer Emergency Response Team) to verify virus alerts (see CERT's web address provided at the end of this section).

Should anonymous email be permitted? Should we be accountable for the things that we say? On the one hand, we instinctively want to have the ability to "blow the whistle" anonymously—especially in cases where negative repercussions are likely. Anonymity may also protect such people as AIDs patients, abuse victims, etc. who need to get information or support. On the other hand, anonymous email makes it easy to harass other users or make libelous statements. Before sending anonymous email, ask yourself why you need to send it anonymously. Is it really because you may be unfairly punished or is it really just a way to say something you are not brave enough to take responsibility for?

PRIVACY

Database technology and the Internet make it very easy to store and transmit large quantities of information. Everything from our medical histories to our driving records are routinely bought and sold. As a society we need to come to terms with what information should be stored, how its accuracy can be verified, how it should be protected, and when it should be destroyed.

Ask yourself how you would feel if you were turned down for a loan because your credit history had been accidentally (or deliberately!) swapped with someone else's. When it is your word against the computer's, where is the burden of proof? Now imagine a worse scenario. Imagine that your name and social security number is very close to that of a convicted felon. Might this affect your ability to get a government job? On the other hand, law enforcement needs to maintain extensive data bases to assist them in preventing and solving crimes.

Recently, there has been discussion of implementing the routine "profiling" of airline passengers and subjecting those with suspicious profiles to extra searches. Profiles would be generated by matching information in a number of databases to try to identify "suspicious" persons. Is safety more important than civil liberty? Should you have the right to know what information about you is being stored?

With world populations continuing to rise, governments and economies become increasingly dependent on computerized systems to function. The danger is that if we do not make careful choices, we will be ever defined and controlled by data files. Worse, in the wrong hands, information systems can become the tools of oppressors.

As computer professionals, you can do your part to protect privacy by observing security precautions, restricting access to information, and by encouraging professional behavior among your colleagues. Remember that email should be treated as if it were a "post card," and not a sealed letter. Information that needs to be kept private should be encrypted and important documents should be digitally "signed." You should become familiar with the Electronic Communications Privacy Act (ECPA) of 1986 that protects private communications.

QUALITY CONTROL AND RISK REDUCTION

As you are beginning to learn, writing good software is extremely difficult. Software needs to be carefully designed, carefully developed, and tested as thoroughly as possible. Commercial software is routinely put through in-house testing ("alpha" testing) and then testing by select clients ("beta" testing). Some managers will even plant bugs in their products knowing that in the process of finding these bugs, their programmers will uncover other errors. Standards for software in life-critical applications need to be extremely high. Interfaces must be easy to learn and must be "bullet proof." They must anticipate user errors and safeguard against potentially serious mistakes. If serious flaws are detected, there should be some mechanism in place to report problems and correct them quickly.

Computers are powerful tools. This means that when we make mistakes with computers, they tend to be large scale! As students you should learn to do "back of the envelope" approximations to develop a sense when results are wrong. You should develop a style of coding that is readable. Remember that the person writing the code may well not be the one to maintain it! Even when code appears to work, make use of debuggers, the assert statement, or simply print out the values of variables to make sure that code is correct. Finally, document your code thoroughly with comments, "help" or "readme" files, manuals, or whatever system is required by the application.

THE FUTURE

Advances in technology are creating many admirable improvements in the quality of many lives. "Telecommuting" enables new parents to work, improves access for the disabled, and helps the environment by cutting down on traffic. "Distance learning" is making educational opportunities available throughout the world. All sorts of new economic possibilities are being created. Improvements in the speed of world-wide communication and the vast amount of information now readily available is bound to have profound implications we are only just beginning to imagine. Yet there are dangerous hazards to be negotiated. Choices we make now will determine how well we will meet these challenges.

EXERCISES

Briefly define each of the terms in Exercises 1–16.

1. ACM
2. chain mail
3. copyright
4. fair use
5. firewall
6. hacker
7. IEEE
8. patent
9. piracy
10. rogue software
11. RSI
12. site license
13. telecommuting
14. Trojan horse
15. virus
16. worm
17. Examine recent issues of the *New York Times, Time, Newsweek,* or other newspapers and news magazines to find articles that describe the following:
    (a) A new or novel application of computing
    (b) A problem caused by a computer error, either in hardware or software
    (c) Difficulties caused by a computer virus, worm, or other scheme that causes a computer system to shut down or to function abnormally, that destroys or damages data stored in the computer, or that generally is intended to interfere with the normal operation of, or use of, one or many computer systems
    (d) A break-in by a hacker or a group of hackers to databases containing sensitive information

    Write a report that summarizes the article and your reaction to it, especially to any ethical and moral issues that are involved.
18. Many of the publications of the professional computing societies contain articles that are of interest to and can be understood by students. Select one or several of the publications in the following list, locate an article dealing with some current ethical issue, and prepare a written summary of the article, the ethical or moral problem involved, suggestions for dealing with the problem, and your reaction.

Communications of the ACM

Computers and Society, a publication of the ACM Special Interest Group
on Computers & Society

COMPUTERWORLD

IEEE *Computer*

IEEE *Software*

IEEE *Spectrum*

New *Scientist*

SIGCAPH Newsletter, a publication of the ACM Special Interest Group
on Computers and the Physically Handicapped

SIGCHI Bulletin, a publication of the ACM Special Interest Group on
Computer & Human Interaction

Software Engineering Notes, an informal newsletter of the ACM Special
Interest Group on Software Engineering

19. Create your own "Code of Ethics"for an imaginary company. A good way to start
is to think about school or workplace behavior that you find objectionable. Try to
think of a code to address these problems.

20. Discuss freedom of speech and the Internet. Should any form of expression be permitted? Should individuals be free to post child pornography, hate, violence, or materials that might incite others to commit crimes? What happens when different
cultural standards collide? Are there technological solutions to these problems?

21. Create a web page on one of the topics below and include links to related pages:
CFAA (1986 Computer Fraud and Abuse Act)
ECPA (1986 Electronic Communications Privacy Act)
CDA (1996 Communications Decency Act)
FBI NCCS (National Computer Crime Squad. See http://www.fbi.gov)
encryption
software piracy
viruses

FOR FURTHER READING

Baase, S. *A Gift of Fire.* Prentice Hall, 1997.

Bowyer, K. *Ethics and Computing.* IEEE Computer Society Press, 1996.

Cavazos, E. & Morin, G. *Cyberspace and the Law.* MIT Press, 1995.

Cheswick, R. & Bellowin, S. *Firewalls and Internet Security.* Addison Wesley, 1994.

Hoffman, L. *Rogue Programs, Viruses, Worms, and Trojan Horses.* Van Nostrand Rein-
hold, 1990.

Icove, D.J. *Computer Crime: A Crime-fighter's Handbook.* O'Reilly Associates, 1995.

Johnson, D.G. & Nissenbaum, H. *Computer Ethics & Social Values.* Prentice Hall, 1995.

Neumann, P. *Computer Related Risks.* Addison Wesley, 1995.

Schneider, B. *Applied Cryptography.* J. Wiley and Sons, 1994.

Computer Emergency Response Team
http://www.cert.org

Computer Professionals for Social Responsibility
http://www.cpsr.org

Ethics References
http://www.cs.gmu.edu/~amarchan/ethics.html

Electronic Freedom Foundation
http://www.eff.org

MIT Ethics Web Page (many useful links)
http://www.mit.edu:8004/activities/ethics/home.html

Chapter 1

PROBLEM SOLVING AND SOFTWARE ENGINEERING

If we really understand the problem, the answer will come out of it, because the answer is not separate from the problem.

JIDDU KRISHNAMURTI

People always get what they ask for; the only trouble is that they never know, until they get it, what it actually is that they have asked for.

ALDOUS HUXLEY

If you don't know where you're going, you'll wind up somewhere else.

YOGI BERRA

It's the only job I can think of where I get to be both an engineer and an artist. There's an incredible, rigorous, technical element to it, which I like because you have to do very precise thinking. On the other hand, it has a wildly creative side where the boundaries of imagination are the only real limitation.

ANDY HERTZFELD

Chapter Contents

1.1   Welcome to the World of C++

1.2   Problem Solving through Software Engineering

1.3   Example: Revenue Calculation

We noted in the preceding chapter that the computer has become an indispensable tool in many areas. Its applications are far too many to enumerate, and those in the following list and those pictured in Figure 1.1 are intended only to show some of the diverse uses of computers. These and many other applications all require the

FIGURE 1.1.   (a) CAD design of an automobile.   (b) Automated insertion of components on electronic engine modules.   (c) Robot-controlled Chrysler automobile assembly plant.   (d) National Weather Service satellite imagery.   (e) Oil-drilling computerized tracking model.   (f) Northern Arizona University observatory.   (g) Flight deck of the space shuttle *Columbia*.

development of software, and the focus of this text is on how C++ can be used to write this software.

- ▶ Business and Finance
    - Mailing lists and billings
    - Payroll, accounts receivable, accounts payable
    - Inventory control
    - Reservations systems (airlines, car rentals, etc.)
    - Word processing
    - Data management
    - Spreadsheets
    - EFT (electronic funds transfer)
    - ATMs (automatic teller machines)
    - Electronic mail
    - Home banking
    - Financial planning
    - Processing of insurance claims

- ▶ Industry
    - Robots in assembly lines
    - CAD (computer-aided design)
    - CAM (computer-aided manufacturing)
    - CIM (computer-integrated manufacturing)
    - Market analysis
    - Project management and control
    - Production scheduling

- ▶ Government
    - Defense systems
    - Space programs
    - Compilation of census data
    - Weather forecasting by NOAA (National Oceanic and Atmospheric Administration)
    - Automated traffic-control systems
    - State and local lotteries
    - The FBI's NCIS (National Crime Information System)

- ▶ Medicine
    - CAT (computerized axial tomography) and MR (magnetic resonance) scans
    - On-line access to patients' medical records
    - Monitoring life-support systems
    - Expert diagnosis systems

- ▶ Entertainment
    - Animation, colorization, and creation of special effects in the film industry
    - Video games

- ▶ Science
    - Analysis of molecules
    - Study of crystal structures
    - Testing food quality
    - Simulation of large dynamical systems

Developing programs to solve problems is a complex process that is both an art and a science. It is an art in that it requires a good deal of imagination, creativity, and ingenuity. But it is also a science in that it uses certain techniques and methodologies. **Software engineering** applies these techniques to produce software solutions to problems. In this chapter we describe some of these methodologies and various phases of the software development process and illustrate them with an example.

1.1 WELCOME TO THE WORLD OF C++

A **program** is a collection of statements written in a programming language. Just as there are English *grammar rules* that specify how an English sentence is constructed, there are C++ grammar rules that determine how C++ statements are formed and how they are combined into more complex statements and into programs. Much of this text is devoted to learning how to write such statements and how to assemble them together into a program. In this section we take a first look at a simple C++ program.

Figure 1.2 shows a C++ program that greets its user. It asks the user to enter his or her first name and then displays a message personally welcoming the user to the world of C++. In the sample run of the program, the information entered by the user (`Sarah`) is underlined to distinguish it from the output produced by the program. We will use this program to illustrate the basic structure of C++ programs.

FIGURE 1.2   GREETING A USER.

```
/* greeting2.cpp greets its user.
 *
 * Input:  The name of the user
 * Output: A personalized greeting
 ************************************************************/

#include <iostream.h>              // cin, cout, <<, >>
#include <string>                  // string

int main()
{
   cout << "Please enter your first name: ";
   string firstName;
   cin >> firstName;

   cout << "\nWelcome to the world of C++, " << firstName << "!\n";

   return 0;
}
```

Sample run:

```
Please enter your first name: Sarah
Welcome to the world of C++, Sarah!
```
user input

The first line of the program begins with the pair of characters /* and the fourth line ends with the pair */. In a C++ program, anything contained between these character pairs is a **comment.** In Figure 1.2, the multiline comment in the first four lines of the program is **opening documentation** that describes what the program does, what is input to the program, and what output the program produces.

The two lines that follow begin with #include and are called **compiler directives.** They instruct the compiler to add to the program the items in the *library* iostream that are needed to perform input and output and the items in the library string that are needed to process character strings.

The rest of the program has the form

```
int main()
{
    A list of C++ statements
}
```

This is actually a function named main and is called the **main function** of the program. Here the word int preceding the word main is a C++ keyword that specifies the return type of the function and indicates that the main function will return an integer value to the operating system.

Execution of a C++ program begins with the first of the statements enclosed between the curly braces ({ and }) in this main function and proceeds through the statements that follow it. Note that each statement ends with a semicolon.

In the program in Figure 1.2, the first statement outputs (<<) a message to the screen (cout) prompting the user to enter her or his first name:

```
cout << "Please enter your first name: ";
```

The next statement

```
string firstName;
```

declares a *variable* firstName to store a character string and the statement

```
cin >> firstName;
```

actually reads (>>) the character string entered by the user from the keyboard (cin) and stores it in firstName. The next statement

```
cout << "\nWelcome to the world of C++, " << firstName << "!\n";
```

then displays on the screen a personalized greeting consisting of:

1. A special character (\n) that causes an advance to a new line followed by the string

   ```
   Welcome to the world of C++,
   ```

2. The character string that is stored in firstName
3. The character ! followed by the new-line character

The final statement in this program is a **return statement.** It causes execution of the program to terminate and returns the specified value. Because the return statement here is

```
    return 0;
```

execution will stop and the program will return the value 0 to the operating system. For most operating systems, a return value of 0 indicates normal termination and other return values indicate abnormal termination.

1.2 PROBLEM SOLVING THROUGH SOFTWARE ENGINEERING

As we noted in the introduction to this chapter, software engineering uses certain basic methodologies to obtain software solutions to problems. Although the problems themselves vary, several phases or steps are common in software development:

- ▸ **Design:**   The problem is analyzed and a solution is designed, resulting in an *algorithm* to solve the problem

- ▸ **Coding:**   The solution is written in the syntax of a high-level language (e.g., C++), resulting in a program

- ▸ **Testing, Execution, and Debugging:**   The program is rigorously tested and any errors (called *bugs*) are removed

- ▸ **Maintenance:**   The program is updated and modified, as necessary, to meet the changing needs of its users

In this section, we examine each of these stages in the **software life cycle** and illustrate them with an example. This is a rather simple example so that we can emphasize the main ideas in each stage without getting lost in a maze of details.

PROBLEM

The world's largest ball of twine is located in Cawker City, Kansas.[1] People in the area have been winding twine on the ball since 1953. At the time of this writing, the average radius of the ball was approximately $6\frac{1}{2}$ feet. Two common questions that tourists have are:

1.   How much does the ball weigh?

2.   How many miles would the twine reach if it were unrolled?

We will design a program to answer the first question. The second question is left as an exercise (see exercise 7 at the end of section 1.3).

[1] The hometown of one of the authors. For more information, see
http://skyways.lib.ks.us/kansas/towns/Cawker/cawker.html

The world's largest ball of twine. (Courtesy of Mike Nyhoff)

OBJECT-CENTERED DESIGN

Problems to be solved are usually expressed in a natural language, such as English, and often are stated imprecisely, making it necessary to analyze the problem and formulate it more precisely. For the preceding problem, this is quite easy:

Given the radius of a spherical ball of twine, compute the weight of the ball.

For many problems, however, this may be considerably more difficult, because the initial descriptions may be quite vague and imprecise. People who pose the problems often do not understand them well. Neither do they understand how to solve them nor what the computer's capabilities and limitations are.

We will call the approach we use in designing a software solution to a problem **object-centered design (OCD).** In its simplest form, it consists of the following steps:

1. *Behavior:* State how you want the program to behave, as precisely as possible

2. *Objects:* Identify the objects in your problem description, and categorize them

3. *Operations:* Identify the operations that are needed to solve the problem

4. *Algorithm:* Arrange the operations on the objects in an order that solves the problem

The arrangement of objects and operations that results from step 4 is called an **algorithm** for the problem, and this algorithm serves as a blueprint for writing the program.

The Desired Behavior. We begin by writing out exactly what we want our program to do (i.e., how we want it to behave). The remainder of our design depends on this step, so we must make it as precise as possible:

> *Behavior:*   A prompt for the radius of a spherical ball should appear on the screen. The user should enter this radius at the keyboard. The weight of the ball should be computed and appear on the screen.

Note that we have generalized the problem to calculating the weight of an arbitrary sphere. This **generalization** is an important aspect of analyzing a problem. The effort involved in later phases of solving a problem demands that the program eventually developed be sufficiently flexible to solve not only the given specific problem but also any related problem of the same kind with little, if any, modification required.

Objects.   Once we have decided exactly what should happen, we are ready for the next step, which is to identify the objects in the problem. One approach is to begin by identifying all of the *nouns* in our behavioral description, ignoring nouns like *user* and *program:*

> *Behavior:*   A <u>prompt for the radius of a spherical ball</u> should appear on the <u>screen</u>. The user should enter this <u>radius</u> at the <u>keyboard</u>. The <u>weight of the ball</u> should be computed and appear on the <u>screen</u>.

This gives us the following list of objects:

> **Objects:**   prompt for the radius of a spherical ball
> screen
> radius of a sphere
> keyboard
> weight of the ball

Next, it is useful to identify the *type* of each object, and whether the value of that object will *vary* or remain *constant* as the program executes. Objects whose values will vary are called **variables** and must be *named,* while objects whose values remain constant may or may not be named. In our example, we can classify our objects as follows:

Description	Type	Kind	Name
prompt for the radius of a sphere	`string`	constant	none
screen	`ostream`	variable	`cout`
radius of a sphere	`double`	variable	*radius*
keyboard	`istream`	variable	`cin`
weight of the ball	`double`	variable	*weight*

We will not name our first object, the prompt, because its value does not change during execution of the program and is unlikely to change in the future. Sequences of characters are called `string` values in C++, and within a program, string constants must be surrounded by double quotes.

Our second object, the screen (or window), has the predefined name `cout` in C++ and has the predefined type `ostream` (for *output stream*). Because the contents of the screen will change during program execution, the value of this object varies.

We have chosen the name *radius* for our third object, the radius of the sphere. Its value will vary, because the user enters that value from the keyboard. Numeric objects that can store real values (i.e., numbers with decimal points) are represented by the type `double` in C++.

The keyboard has the predefined name `cin` in C++ and its type is the predefined type `istream` (for *input stream*). Because values will be entered via the keyboard during program execution, the value of this object varies.

Finally, we have chosen the name *weight* for our last object, the weight of the ball. Because it will store a real value, its type is `double`. It is a variable, because its value will be computed by the program.

Operations.   Once we have identified and classified the objects in our program, we can proceed to the next step, which is to identify the operations needed to solve the problem. To identify the objects we identified the nouns in our behavioral description; to identify the operations we can begin by identifying the *verbs*:

> *Behavior:*   A prompt for the radius of a spherical ball should <u>appear</u> on the screen. The user should <u>enter</u> the radius at the keyboard. The weight of the ball should <u>be computed</u> and <u>appear</u> on the screen.

Using the objects we have identified, we can describe these operations as follows:

> **Operations:**   Output a prompt for the radius of a spherical ball to `cout`
> Input a real value from `cin` and store it in *radius*
> Compute *weight*
> Output *weight* to `cout`

C++ provides an output operator `<<` that can be used to insert string and numeric values into `cout`, which will display them on the screen. We can use this operator to display the prompt for the radius and to display the value of *weight*. Similarly, C++ provides an input operator `>>` that extracts values from `cin` (i.e., the keyboard) and stores them in variable objects. We can use this operator to input a real value from the keyboard and store it in *radius*.

Computing the weight of the ball requires some additional work. This is given by the formula

$$weight \;=\; density \,\times\, volume$$

The volume V of a sphere of radius r is given by

$$V \;=\; 4\pi r^3 / 3$$

Combining these two formulas gives the following formula for *weight*:

$$weight \;=\; density \times 4.0 \times \pi \times radius^3 / 3.0$$

This implies that we need to expand our list of operations:

> **Operations:**   Output a prompt for the radius of a spherical ball to `cout`
> Input a real value from `cin` and store it in *radius*
> Output a prompt for the density of a spherical ball to `cout`
> Input a real value from `cin` and store it in *density*

> Compute *weight*
>> Raise *radius* to the third power
>> Multiply real values (three times)
>> Divide real values
> Output *weight to* `cout`

As in most languages, real values can be multiplied in C++ using the `*` operator and can be divided using the `/` operator. Although there is no exponentiation operator, the standard math library contains a function named `pow()` that performs exponentiation. Thus, all of the operations needed to solve our problem are readily available.

However, our formula for computing the weight of the ball adds six new objects to our list:

Description	Type	Kind	Name
prompt for the radius of a spherical ball	`string`	constant	none
screen	`ostream`	variable	`cout`
radius of a sphere	`double`	variable	*radius*
keyboard	`istream`	variable	`cin`
prompt for the density of a spherical ball	`string`	constant	none
density of a spherical ball	`double`	variable	*density*
weight of the spherical ball (in pounds)	`double`	variable	*weight*
4.0	`double`	constant	none
π	`double`	constant	*PI*
3	`integer`	constant	none
3.0	`double`	constant	none

We have decided to use a name for π, because this increases readability and will also make it easier to modify the program if more or less precision is needed.

Algorithm. Once we have identified all of the objects and operations, we are ready to arrange those operations into an algorithm. If we have done the preceding steps correctly, this is usually straightforward:

Algorithm:

0. Declare constant *PI*.

1. Output a prompt for the radius of a spherical ball to `cout`.

2. Input a real value from `cin` and store it in *radius*.

3. Output a prompt for the density of a spherical ball to `cout`.

4. Input a real value from `cin` and store it in *density*.

5. Compute *weight* = *density* * 4.0 * *PI* * pow(*radius*, 3) / 3.0.

6. Output *weight* to `cout`.

This sequence of instructions is sometimes called a *pseudocode algorithm,* because it is not written in any particular programming language, and yet it bears some similarity to a program's code. This algorithm becomes our blueprint for the next stage of the process.

CODING IN C++

Once we have designed an algorithm for our problem, we are ready to translate that algorithm into a high level language like C++. The program that results is given in Figure 1.3:

FIGURE 1.3 WEIGHT OF A SPHERICAL BALL.

```cpp
/* sphere3.cpp computes the weight of a spherical ball.
 *
 * Input:   The radius (feet) and
 *          the density (pounds/cubic foot) of a spherical ball
 * Output: The weight of the sphere (pounds)
 *************************************************************/

#include <iostream.h>                    // cin, cout, <<, >>
#include <math.h>                        // pow()

int main()
{
   const double PI = 3.14159;

   cout << "Enter the radius of the spherical ball (feet): ";
   double radius;
   cin >> radius;
   cout << "Enter the density of the spherical ball (pounds/cubic feet): ";
   double density;
   cin >> density;

   double weight = density * 4.0 * PI * pow(radius, 3) / 3.0;

   cout << "\nThe weight of the spherical ball is approximately "
        << weight << " pounds.\n";

}
```

Sample run:

```
Enter the radius of the spherical ball of twine in feet: 6.5
Enter the density of the spherical ball (pounds/cubic feet): 14.6

The weight of the spherical ball is approximately 16795 pounds.
```

A software program called a *text editor* can be used to enter this program into a computer's memory.[2] The text editor is also used in the next stage of software development to correct any errors in the program.

TESTING, EXECUTION, AND DEBUGGING

There are a number of different points at which errors can be introduced into a program. Two of the most common are:

1. Violations of the grammar rules of the high-level language in which the program is written

2. Errors in the design of the algorithm on which the program is based

The process of finding such errors is called **debugging** the program.

The first kind of error is called a **syntax error,** because the program violates the syntax (i.e., the grammar rules) of the language. A **compiler** is a program that translates a program written in a high-level language into a functionally equivalent program in the machine language of a given computer.[3] As it performs this translation, the compiler checks whether the program it is translating conforms to the syntax rules of the language. If the program violates any of these rules, the compiler generates an *error* (or *diagnostic*) message that explains the (apparent) problem. For example, if we forgot to type the semicolon at the end of the line

```
double radius;
```

in the program in Figure 1.3, and entered

```
double radius
```

instead, the compiler would display a diagnostic message like the following:

```
sphere3.cpp:
    line 17: missing semicolon.
```

A different compiler might display a less precise diagnostic for the same error such as:

```
function main():
   18: parse error
```

---

[2] In the UNIX environment, common text editors include `vi` and `emacs`. Most microcomputer C++ implementations (e.g., Turbo C++, Visual C++, Symantec C++, and CodeWarrior) have a built in text editing window.

---

[3] Most microcomputer C++ implementations provide a `Compile` menu whose choices include `Compile` (to translate your program into machine language) and `Link` (to link calls to library functions like `pow()` to their definitions). Such menus also have a `Make` choice that performs both compilation and linking, although this usually requires the creation of a *project*. On UNIX systems, users of `g++` (the GNU C++ compiler) can compile a program from the command line by typing a line of the form

```
g++ progname.cpp -o progname
```

Users of the `emacs` text editor can compile from within the editor by using the `M-x compile` command. `emacs` will respond with `make -k` which can be replaced with a compile command like the preceding.

Here, the compiler displayed the number of the line it was processing when it detected that something was wrong, which is the line following the line containing the error. The diagnostic is also much less informative; it only indicates that the *parser* (a part of the compiler) encountered something unexpected. Learning to understand the messages that a particular compiler produces is an important skill. You can study these messages by intentionally introducing errors into a working program and see how the compiler responds.

The second kind of error is called a **logic error,** because such errors represent programmer mistakes in the design of the algorithm. For example, the program in Figure 1.3 contains the statement

```
double weight = density * 4.0 * PI * pow(radius, 3) / 3.0;
```

But suppose we misread the formula for the weight of the ball and typed a + in place of the first * operator:

```
double weight = density + 4.0 * PI * pow(radius, 3) / 3.0;
```

Because the resulting program violates none of the grammatical rules of C++, *the compiler* will not detect the error. It has no basis for identifying this statement as erroneous, because it is a valid C++ statement. Consequently, the program will compile and execute, but it will produce incorrect values because the formula used to compute the weight is not correct.

To determine whether a program contains a logic error, it must be run using sample data and the output produced checked for correctness. This **testing** of a program should be done several times using a variety of inputs, ideally prepared by people other than the programmer, who may be making non-obvious assumptions in the choice of test data. If *any* combination of inputs produces incorrect output, then the program contains a logic error.

Once it has been determined that a program contains a logic error, finding the error is one of the most difficult parts of programming. Execution must be traced step by step until the point at which a computed value differs from an expected value is located. To simplify this tracing, most implementations of C++ provide an integrated debugger[4] that allows a programmer to actually execute a program one line at a time, observing the effect(s) of each line's execution on the values of the program's objects. Once the error has been located, the text editor can be used to correct it.

Thorough testing of a program will increase one's confidence in its correctness, but it must be realized that it is almost never possible to test a program with every possible set of test data. There are cases in which apparently correct programs have been in use for more than ten years before a particular combination of inputs produced an incorrect output caused by a logic error. The particular data set that caused the program to execute the erroneous statement(s) had never been input in all that time!

---

[4] On popular microcomputer C++ implementations, the debugger is integrated with the compiler and editor and can be enabled via a `Debug` menu (or a `Debug` choice under the `Run` menu). In the GNU implementation of C++, the compiler `g++` and the debugger `gdb` can both be executed from within the text editor `emacs` (but the program must be compiled using the `-g` switch) providing the functional equivalent of an integrated environment.

As programs grow in size and complexity, the problem of testing them becomes increasingly more difficult. No matter how much testing is done, more could always be done. Testing is never finished; it is only stopped, and there is no guarantee that all the errors in a program have been found and corrected. Testing can only show the presence of errors, not their absence. It cannot prove that a program is correct; it can only show that it is incorrect.

MAINTENANCE

Student programs are often run once or twice and then discarded. By contrast, real-world programs often represent a significant investment of a company's resources and may be used for many years. During this time, it may be necessary to add new features or enhancements to the program. This process of upgrading a program is called **software maintenance.**

To illustrate, users of the program in Figure 1.3 might find it more informative to have the weight of the ball displayed in both pounds and tons. The program might be modified by making the changes (shown in color) in the program in Figure 1.4.

FIGURE 1.4   WEIGHT OF A SPHERICAL BALL — REVISED.

```
/* sphere4.cpp computes the weight of a spherical ball.
 *
 * Input:   The radius (feet) and
 *             the density (pounds/cubic foot) of a spherical ball
 * Output: The weight of the sphere (pounds and tons)
 ***************************************************************/

#include <iostream.h>                    // cin, cout, <<, >>
#include <math.h>                        // pow()

int main()
{
   const double PI = 3.14159;

   cout << "Enter the radius of the spherical ball (feet): ";
   double radius;
   cin >> radius;
   cout << "Enter the density of the spherical ball (pounds/cubic feet): ";
   double density;
   cin >> density;

   double weight = density * 4.0 * PI * pow(radius, 3) / 3.0;

   cout << "\nThe weight of the spherical ball is approximately "
        << weight << " pounds,\nwhich is the same as "
        << weight / 2000.0 << " tons.\n";
}
```

Sample run:

```
Enter the radius of the spherical ball (feet): 6.5
Enter the density of the spherical ball (pounds/cubic feet): 14.6

The weight of the spherical ball is approximately 16795 pounds,
which is the same as 8.39752 tons.
```

In other problems, it may be necessary to compute values for spheres whose radii are measured very precisely. When we execute the program, we find that it produces imprecise answers. This imprecision might be caused by the fact that the value for PI (3.14159) only uses five decimal places of precision, so we might increase the precision:

```
const PI = 3.14159265358979324;
```

1.3 EXAMPLE: REVENUE CALCULATION

PROBLEM

Sam Splicer installs coaxial cable for the Metro Cable Company. For each installation, there is a basic service charge of $25.00 and an additional charge of $2.00 for each foot of cable. The president of the cable company would like a program to compute the revenue generated by Sam in any given month. For example, if during the month of January, Sam installs a total of 263 yards of cable at 27 different locations, he generates $2253.00 in revenue.

OBJECT-CENTERED DESIGN

Following the principles of object-centered design, we describe the behavior of the program, identify the objects and operations, and then write an algorithm.

Behavior. The program should display on the screen a prompt for the number of installations performed and the total number of yards of cable installed. The user should enter those values from the keyboard. The program should compute and display on the screen the total amount of revenue resulting from these installations.

Objects. From our behavioral description, we can identify the following objects:

Description	Type	Kind	Name
screen	ostream	variable	cout
prompt	string	constant	none
number of installations	int	variable	*installations*
total number of yards of cable	double	variable	*yardsOfCable*
keyboard	istream	variable	cin
total amount of revenue	double	variable	*totalRevenue*

Operations.   From our behavioral description, we can identify the following operations:

> Display a prompt for installations and yards of cable to `cout`
>
> Read an integer from `cin` into *installations*
>
> Read a real from `cin` into *yardsOfCable*
>
> Compute *totalRevenue* from *installations* and *yardsOfCable*
>
> Display *totalRevenue* to `cout` (with some descriptive text)

Each of these operations is predefined in C++, except for computing *totalRevenue* from *installations* and *yardsOfCable*. Using information from the original problem description, we can break this step down into simpler operations:

> Compute *totalRevenue* from *installations* and *yardsOfCable*
>
>> Compute *installRevenue* = 25.00 * *installations*
>>
>> Compute *feetOfCable* = 3 * *yardsOfCable*
>>
>> Compute *cableRevenue* = 2.00 * *feetOfCable*
>>
>> Compute *totalRevenue* = *installRevenue* + *cableRevenue*

This refinement of the computation adds six new objects to our list:

Description	Type	Kind	Name
screen	`ostream`	varying	`cout`
prompt	`string`	constant	none
number of installations	`int`	varying	*installations*
total number of yards of cable	`double`	varying	*yardsOfCable*
keyboard	`istream`	varying	`cin`
total amount of revenue	`double`	varying	*totalRevenue*
installation revenue	`double`	varying	*installRevenue*
installation charge (25.00)	`double`	constant	*INSTALL_CHARGE*
feet of cable	`double`	varying	*feetOfCable*
number of feet in a yard (3)	`int`	constant	none
cable revenue	`double`	varying	*cableRevenue*
cable cost per foot (2.00)	`double`	constant	*CABLE_COST_PER_FOOT*

We give each of these new objects a name except for the number of feet in a yard, because it is a fixed quantity that will not change in the future, unlike the installation charge and the cable cost per foot, which may change.

Algorithm.   Given our objects and operations, we can order them into the following algorithm:

Algorithm:

1. Display a prompt for the number of installations and the total number of yards of cable to `cout`.

2. Read *installations* and *yardsOfCable* from `cin`.

3. Compute *installRevenue = INSTALL_CHARGE * installations.*
4. Compute *feetOfCable = 3 * yardsOfCable.*
5. Compute *cableRevenue = CABLE_COST_PER_FOOT * feetOfCable.*
6. Compute *totalRevenue = installRevenue + cableRevenue.*
7. Display *totalRevenue* to cout.

CODING IN C++

Once we have an algorithm to serve as our blueprint, we can encode it in C++ as shown in Figure 1.5. Constant objects like INSTALL_CHARGE and CABLE_COST_PER_FOOT, whose values are likely to change in the future, are defined at the beginning of the program, because this makes them easy to find when an update is necessary.

 FIGURE **1.5   REVENUE COMPUTATION.**

```
/* revenue5.cpp computes revenues for a cable installer.
 *
 * Input:  Number of installations, yards of cable installed
 * Output: The total revenue resulting from these installations
 ************************************************************/

#include <iostream.h>                    // cin, cout, <<, >>

int main()
{
  const double INSTALL_CHARGE = 25.00;
  const double CABLE_COST_PER_FOOT = 2.00;

  cout << "Enter the number of installations\n"
       << "followed by the total yards of cable installed: ";
  int installations;
  double yardsOfCable;
  cin >> installations >> yardsOfCable;

  double installRevenue = INSTALL_CHARGE * installations;
  double feetOfCable = 3.0 * yardsOfCable;
  double cableRevenue = CABLE_COST_PER_FOOT * feetOfCable;
  double totalRevenue = installRevenue + cableRevenue;

  cout << "\nThe total revenue for these installations is $"
       << totalRevenue << endl;

}
```

TESTING, EXECUTION, AND DEBUGGING

Once our program compiles without errors, we check that it is performing correctly by executing it using sample data:

```
Enter the number of installations,
followed by the total yards of cable installed: 1 1.0

The total revenue for these installations is $31
```

This data has been chosen because it is easy to verify the result. One installation results in an installation revenue of $25.00, and 1.0 yard of cable is 3.0 feet of cable, which at 2.00 per foot results in a cable revenue of $6.00. Because $25.00 + $6.00 = $31.00, our program performed correctly in this case.

We try another set of values for which it is easy to verify the result:

```
Enter the number of installations,
followed by the total yards of cable installed: 2 2.25

The total revenue for these installations is $63.5
```

The installation revenue is $25.00 * 2 = $50.00; 2.25 yards of cable is 6.75 feet of cable, which at 2.00 per foot gives a cable revenue of $13.50; and $50.00 + $13.50 = $63.50, which agrees with the output produced by our program. Testing with data sets like these increases our confidence in the correctness of our program, and we can run it with the input data given in the statement of the problem:

```
Enter the number of installations,
followed by the total yards of cable installed: 27 263.5

The total revenue for these installations is $2256
```

PROGRAM MAINTENANCE

Suppose that sometime after the program in Figure 1.5 was written, the Metro Cable Company raised the basic service charge for an installation from $25.00 to $30.00. Obviously, the program will no longer compute the correct revenue, so it must be modified to reflect the change. In the program in Figure 1.5, this is easily done by changing the line

```
const double INSTALL_CHARGE = 25.00;
```

to

```
const double INSTALL_CHARGE = 30.00;
```

and then recompiling the program. The program will then calculate installRevenue using the new value of INSTALL_CHARGE, so that its output will reflect the new service charge.

As a second example of program maintenance, suppose that the president of the Metro Cable Company requests that exactly two decimal digits be displayed for revenue, since this is customary for monetary values. Performing this upgrade involves formatting the value of totalRevenue before we display it. This in turn requires a better understanding of the C++ input/output system, which is discussed in chapters 2 and 4. Until then, Figure 1.6 shows how it can be done:[5]

FIGURE 1.6   REVENUE COMPUTATION — REVISED.

```
/* revenue6.cpp computes revenues for a cable installer.
 *
 * Input:  Number of installations, yards of cable installed
 * Output: The total revenue resulting from these installations
 ***************************************************************/

#include <iostream.h>          // cin, cout, <<, >>, fixed, showpoint
#include <iomanip.h>           // setprecision()

int main()
{
  const double INSTALL_CHARGE = 30.00;
  const double CABLE_COST_PER_FOOT = 2.00;

  cout << "Enter the number of installations\n"
       << "followed by the total yards of cable installed: ";
  int installations;
  double yardsOfCable;
  cin >> installations >> yardsOfCable;

  double installRevenue = INSTALL_CHARGE * installations;
  double feetOfCable = 3.0 * yardsOfCable;
  double cableRevenue = CABLE_COST_PER_FOOT * feetOfCable;
  double totalRevenue = installRevenue + cableRevenue;

  cout << "\nThe total revenue for these installations is $"
       << fixed << showpoint   // use fixed-point form, show decimal point,
       << setprecision(2)      // and 2 decimal places
       << totalRevenue << endl;

}
```

Sample run:
```
Enter the number of installations,
followed by the total yards of cable installed: 1 1.0
```

---

[5] If your compiler is not fully ANSI-C++ compliant, you may have to replace the line

```
<< fixed << showpoint
```

by

```
<< setiosflags(ios::fixed | ios::showpoint)
```

```
The total revenue for these installations is $36.00

...

Please enter the number of installations,
followed by the total yards of cable installed: 2 2.25

The total revenue for these installations is $73.50
```

✔ Quick Quiz 1.3

1. A _____ is a collection of statements written in a programming language.
2. In a C++ program, anything contained between /* and */ is a _____.
3. Execution of a C++ program begins with the first statement enclosed between _____ in the _____ function.
4. A _____ statement causes execution of a program to terminate and return a value to the operating system.
5. Name the four stages of the software life cycle.
6. List the four steps in object-centered design.
7. The _____ in a problem can be identified by finding the nouns in the behavioral description of the problem.
8. The _____ in a problem can be identified by finding the verbs in the behavioral description of the problem.
9. Objects whose values will change are called _____.
10. The screen has the predefined name _____ in C++ and its type is _____.
11. The keyboard has the predefined name _____ in C++ and its type is _____.
12. _____ is the output operator in C++ and _____ is the input operator.
13. Finding the errors in a program is called _____.
14. What are two types of errors that can occur in developing a program?

EXERCISES 1.3

For each of the problems described in exercises 1 and 2, give a precise description of how a program to solve that problem must behave. Then describe the data objects and operations needed to solve the problem and design an algorithm for it.

1. Calculate and display the perimeter and the area of a square with a given side.
2. Two common temperature scales are the Fahrenheit and Celsius scales. The boiling point of water is 212° on the Fahrenheit scale and 100° on the Celsius scale. The freezing point of water is 32° on the Fahrenheit scale and 0° on the Celsius scale. Assuming that the relationship between these two temperature scales is $F = \frac{9}{5}C + 32$, convert a temperature on the Celsius scale to the corresponding Fahrenheit temperature.
3. Enter and execute the following C++ program on your computer system:

```
/* This program adds the values of variables x and y.
 *
 * Output (screen):  The value x + y
 **************************************************************/
```

```
#include <iostream.h>

int main()
{
   int x = 214,         // the first value
       y = 2057,        // the second value
       sum = x + y;

   // output the resulting value
   cout << "\nThe sum of " << x << " and " << y
        << " is " << sum << endl;

   return 0;
}
```

4. Make the following changes in the program in exercise 3 and execute the modified program:

   (a) Change 214 to 1723 in the statement that gives x a value.

   (b) Change the variable names x and y to alpha and beta throughout.

   (c) Add the comment

   ```
   // find their sum
   ```

   following the declaration of sum.

   (d) Change the variable declaration to

   ```
   int alpha = 214,                  // the first value
       beta = 2057,                  // the second value
       difference = alpha - beta,    // find their difference
       sum = alpha + beta;           // find their sum
   ```

   and add the following statement after the output statement:

   ```
   cout << "\nThe difference of " << alpha << " and "
        << beta <<   " is  " << difference <<  endl;
   ```

5. Using the programs in this chapter as a guide, write a C++ program to solve the problem in exercise 1.

6. Using the programs in this chapter as a guide, write a C++ program to solve the problem in exercise 2.

7. Consider the program developed in section 1.2 to solve part of the ball-of-twine problem. There we also stated a second part of the problem:

   How many miles would the twine reach if it were unrolled?

   (a) Extend the behavior of the program to solve this problem also.

   (b) Extend the list of objects as necessary for this problem.

   (c) Extend the list of operations to include those needed to solve this problem. Assume that approximately 350 feet of the twine must be wound to form a ball that weighs 1 pound and there are 5280 feet in a mile, so the total length of the twine in the ball is 350 *weight* / 5280 miles.

   (d) Modify the algorithm so that it will also solve this problem.

   (e) Modify the program in Figure 1.3 so that it will also solve this problem.

8. Extend the program in exercise 7 to calculate the length of the twine in both feet and miles.

Chapter 2

TYPES AND EXPRESSIONS

In language, clarity is everything.

CONFUCIUS

Kindly enter them in your notebook.
And, in order to refer to them conveniently,
let's call them A, B, and Z.

THE TORTOISE IN LEWIS CARROLL'S
WHAT THE TORTOISE SAID TO ACHILLES

Arithmetic is being able to count up to twenty without taking off your shoes.

MICKEY MOUSE

A little inaccuracy sometimes saves tons of explanation.

SAKI (H.H. MUNROE)

Chapter Contents

2.1   Introductory Example: Einstein's Equation

2.2   Declarations: Specifying an Object's Type

PART OF THE PICTURE: Data Representation

2.3   Numeric Expressions

2.4   Boolean Expressions

2.5   Character Expressions

2.6   Assignment Expressions

2.7   Input/Output Expressions

2.8   Example: Truck Fleet Accounting

An important part of using a computer to solve a problem is encoding the algorithm for solving that problem as a program. Whereas algorithms can be described somewhat informally in a pseudoprogramming language, the corresponding program must be written in strict compliance with the rules of some programming language. In this chapter, we begin a detailed study of the language C++.

In 1989, the American National Standards Institute (ANSI) convened committee X3J16 to establish a standard for the C++ language. This committee is the major contributor to an international effort to standardize C++, under the auspices of the International Standards Organization (ISO) working group WG21. In 1995, a "frozen"*ANSI/ISO C++ Standard Draft Working Paper* was released for public comment and review. At the time of this writing, the initial review period has ended, and work continues on a finalized standard for the language. It is the working draft that is the principal reference used in preparing this text.

2.1 INTRODUCTORY EXAMPLE: EINSTEIN'S EQUATION

PROBLEM

Suppose we are given the task of writing a program to find the amount of energy released by a quantity of matter, given its mass. In developing this program, we will apply the steps of object-centered design.

OBJECT-CENTERED DESIGN

Behavior.   The program should display on the screen a prompt for the quantity of matter (i.e., its mass). The user will enter a nonnegative real value at the keyboard. The program should read this number and use Einstein's equation to compute the energy that can be produced by that quantity of matter. It should display this amount of energy along with a descriptive label.

Objects.   From our behavioral description, we can identify the following objects:

Description	Type	Kind	Name
screen	ostream	varying	cout
prompt	string	constant	none
quantity of matter	double	varying	*mass*
keyboard	istream	varying	cin
quantity of energy	double	varying	*energy*
descriptive label	string	constant	none

Operations.   Again, from our behavioral description, we have the following operations:

i. Display a string (the prompt)

ii. Read a nonnegative number (*mass*)

iii. Compute *energy* from *mass*

iv. Display a number (*energy*) and a string

Each of these operations is provided for us by C++, with the exception of computing energy from mass. It requires the use of Einstein's equation:

$$e = m \times c^2$$

where *m* is the mass, *c* is the speed-of-light constant, and *e* is the energy produced. Performing this operation thus requires the following operations:

Exponentiation (c^2)

Multiplication of reals ($m \times c^2$)

Storage of a real ($e = m \times c^2$)

This refinement to step 3 adds two additional objects to our object list:

Description	Type	Kind	Name
screen	ostream	varying	cout
prompt	string	constant	none
quantity of matter	double	varying	*mass*
keyboard	istream	varying	cin
quantity of energy	double	varying	*energy*
descriptive label	string	constant	none
speed of light	double	constant	*SPEED_OF_LIGHT*
2	int	constant	none

Algorithm. Organizing these objects and operations into an algorithm gives:

1. Display to cout a prompt for the mass to be converted into energy.
2. Read a nonnegative number from cin into *mass*.
3. Compute *energy* = *mass* × *SPEED_OF_LIGHT*^{2}.
4. Display to cout a descriptive label and *energy*.

Coding, Execution, and Testing. Figure 2.1 shows one way to implement the preceding algorithm as a program.[1] Also shown are two sample runs with test data for which the output can be easily verified and a third execution with "real" data.

---
[1] Recent changes in the C++ standard provide alternative ways to include libraries. One that may become widely accepted will use the names iostream, cassert, and cmath, in place of iostream.h, assert.h, and math.h, respectively, and add the statement using namespace std; after the #includes.

FIGURE 2.1   MASS-TO-ENERGY CONVERSION.

```
/* energy1.cpp computes energy from a given mass using
 * Einstein's mass-to-energy conversion equation.
 *
 * Input:       The mass (in kilograms) being converted to energy
 * Precondition: mass >= 0
 * Output:      The amount of energy (in kilojoules) corresponding
 *                 to mass
 ************************************************************************/

#include <iostream.h>                    // cin, cout, <<, >>
#include <assert.h>                      // assert()
#include <math.h>                        // pow()

int main()
{
    const double SPEED_OF_LIGHT = 2.997925e8;   // meters/sec

    cout << "To find the amount of energy obtained from a given mass,\n"
            "enter a mass (in kilograms): ";
    double mass;
    cin >> mass;                         // get mass
    assert(mass >= 0);                   // make sure it's nonnegative
                                         // compute energy
    double energy = mass * pow(SPEED_OF_LIGHT, 2);
                                         // display energy
    cout << mass << " kilograms of matter will release "
         << energy << " kilojoules of energy.\n";
}
```

Sample runs:

```
To find the amount of energy obtained from a given mass,
enter a mass (in kilograms): 1
1 kilogram of matter will release 8.98755e+16 kilojoules of energy.


To find the amount of energy obtained from a given mass,
enter a mass (in kilograms): 2
2 kilograms of matter will release 1.79751e+17 kilojoules of energy.


To find the amount of energy obtained from a given mass,
enter a mass (in kilograms): 125.5
125.5 kilograms of matter will release 1.12794e+19 kilojoules of energy.
```

This program uses several different kinds of expressions. In the remainder of this chapter, we will explore the rich variety of expressions available in C++.

2.2   DECLARATIONS: SPECIFYING AN OBJECT'S TYPE

As we discussed in chapter 1, object-centered programming involves identifying the data objects used by a program, identifying what operations on those data objects are needed, and then constructing and encoding an algorithm that manipulates those data objects. To allow the C++ compiler to check that the objects within a program are being used properly, C++ requires that the types of the objects be specified, or **declared,** before those objects are used. In this section, we examine the fundamental types C++ provides for object declarations. The PART OF THE PICTURE section that follows shows how data values of these types are commonly stored in memory.

FUNDAMENTAL TYPES

The most important fundamental data types provided in C++ are as follows:[2]

- ▸ **integers:**   whole numbers and their negatives: of type `int`
- ▸ **integer variations:**   types `short`, `long`, and `unsigned`
- ▸ **reals:**   fractional numbers: of type `float`, `double`, or `long double`
- ▸ **characters:**   letters, digits, symbols, and punctuation: of type `char`
- ▸ **booleans:**   logical values `true` and `false`:   of type `bool`

A constant of one of these types is called a **literal.** For example, `123` is an integer literal, `-45.678` is a real literal, and `true` is a boolean literal.

C++ provides this diversity so that different types of data can be processed and memory can be used most efficiently. Table 2.1 shows the storage typically allocated for each of these fundamental types.

Type	Typical Number of Bits
`char`[3]	8
`bool`	the word size of the machine
`short int`	16
`int`	the word size of the machine
`long int`	32
`float`	32
`double`	64
`long double`	implementation dependent

TABLE 2.1   STORAGE FOR FUNDAMENTAL TYPES

---

[2] Other fundamental types are the `signed char` and `unsigned char` integer types, the wide character type `wchar_t`, and the `void` type for an empty set of values (see section 3.2).

---

[3] The ASCII and EBCDIC character sets store characters in 8 bits. The ISO character set stores characters in 16 bits.

We now discuss these types in detail.

Integers. As indicated in Table 2.1, the number of bits used to store an int value depends on the word size of the machine. Usually, a 16-bit machine will store int values using 16 bits, a 32-bit machine will use 32 bits, and a 64-bit machine will store int values using 64 bits. This can cause portability problems, because a program that uses int values may execute differently on different machines.

To deal with this problem, C++ allows int declarations to be modified with one of the key words short or long. These modifiers have the following effects:

- ▶ A short int (or just short) is usually a 16-bit value, ranging from -32768 $(= -2^{15})$ through 32767 $(= 2^{15} - 1)$

- ▶ A long int (or just long) is usually a 32-bit value,[4] ranging from -2147483648 $(= -2^{31})$ through 2147483647 $(= 2^{31} - 1)$

Programmers who are concerned with efficiency and portability can use short for integer data objects with relatively small values and long for those that may have larger values. In this text we will use int in most of our examples.

The internal representation of an integer typically uses one bit as a **sign bit,** so that the largest positive value of a 16-bit integer is $2^{15} - 1$ and not $2^{16} - 1$ (see the PART OF THE PICTURE that follows this section). However, some data objects never have negative values. For example, in a program for processing student test scores, a score would (hopefully) never be negative. To avoid wasting the sign bit for integer objects whose values are never negative, C++ provides the modifier unsigned:

- ▶ An unsigned int (or just unsigned) is a nonnegative integer whose size usually is the word size of the particular machine being used

- ▶ An unsigned short is usually a 16-bit value, ranging from 0 through 65535 $(= 2^{16} - 1)$

- ▶ An unsigned long is usually a 32-bit value, ranging from 0 through 4294967295 $(= 2^{32} - 1)$

By default, whole numbers (e.g., -30, 0, 1, 12, 365) are treated as type int by the C++ compiler. Appending the letter L or l to a literal (e.g., -30L, 0L, 1L, 12L, 365L) instructs the compiler to treat a literal value as a long instead of as an int.[5] Similarly, to instruct the compiler to treat a literal value as an unsigned instead of as an int, the letter U or u can be appended to the literal (e.g., 0U, 1U, 12U, 365U). Appending both of the suffixes L (or l) and U (or u) in either order causes a literal to be treated as unsigned long.

Integer literals are taken to be decimal integers unless they begin with 0. In this case,

- ▶ A sequence of digits that begins with 0 is interpreted as an **octal** integer (provided that the digits are octal digits 0, 1, . . . , 7)

---

[4] On machines whose word size is 64 bits, a long value may be stored in 64 bits instead of 32.

[5] We prefer the uppercase L, because the lowercase l is easily confused with 1.

▸ A sequence of digits preceded by 0x is interpreted as a **hexadecimal** integer; the hexadecimal digits for ten, eleven, . . . , fifteen are A, B, . . . , F, respectively, or their lowercase equivalents a, b, . . . , f

▸ Any other digit sequence is a decimal (base-ten) integer

For example, the literal

    12

has the decimal value $12_{10} = 1 \times 10^1 + 2 \times 10^0$, but the literal

    012

has the octal value $12_8 = 1 \times 8^1 + 2 \times 8^0 = 10_{10}$, and

    0x12

has the hexadecimal value $12_{16} = 1 \times 16^1 + 2 \times 16^0 = 18_{10}$. Table 2.2 is a quick guide to the C++ representation of integer values in the three bases. (See the Web site described in the preface for additional details about binary, octal, and hexadecimal number systems.)

Decimal	Octal	Hexadecimal
0	0	0x0
1	01	0x1
2	02	0x2
3	03	0x3
4	04	0x4
5	05	0x5
6	06	0x6
7	07	0x7
8	010	0x8
9	011	0x9
10	012	0xA
11	013	0xB
12	014	0xC
13	015	0xD
14	016	0xE
15	017	0xF
16	020	0x10
17	021	0x11
18	022	0x12
19	023	0x13
20	024	0x14

TABLE 2.2   C++ INTEGER CONSTANTS

Reals. C++ provides three types of real values:

- ▶ `float`, usually a 32-bit real value
- ▶ `double`, usually a 64-bit real value
- ▶ `long double`, typically a 96-bit or a 128-bit real value[6]

The type chosen for an object should be determined by the degree of precision required for that data object. The range of values and the precision of each of these types is implementation-dependent. These are defined in one of the standard libraries `float` or `limits` (described later in this section) that C++ implementations provide.

Like most programming languages, C++ provides two ways to represent real values, fixed-point notation and floating-point notation. A **fixed-point** real literal has the form

```
m.n
```

where either the integer part `m` or the decimal part `n` (but not both) can be omitted. For example,

```
5.0
0.5
5.
 .5
```

are all valid fixed-point real literals in C++.

Scientists often write very large or very small real numbers using a special notation called *exponential, scientific,* or *floating-point* notation. For example, a scientist might write the number 12 billion (12,000,000,000) as:

$$0.12 \times 10^{11}$$

In C++, a **floating-point** real literal has one of the forms

```
xEn
```
or
```
xen
```

where x is an integer or fixed-point real literal and n is an integer exponent (that can be positive or negative). For example, 12 billion = 0.12×10^{11} can be written in any of the following forms:

```
0.12e11
1.2E10
12.0E9
12.e9
12E9
```

C++ compilers treat all real literals (whether fixed- or floating-point) as being of type `double`. This means that if a value is computed using real literals and

---

[6] Some C++ environments implement `long double` as 80-bit values.

assigned to a `float` variable, then the value stored in the variable does not have the precision of the computed value. For this reason, *many programmers never use the type* `float`, *and instead always use the type* `double` *for real objects.*

To instruct the compiler to process a real literal as a `float`, an F or f can be appended to it (e.g., `1.0F`, `3.1316F`, `2.998e8F`). Similarly, appending an L or l to a real literal instructs the compiler to treat it as a long double (e.g., `1.0L`, `0.1E1L`).

Characters. The `char` type is used to represent *individual characters* in the machine's character set (commonly the ASCII character set shown in appendix A). This includes the uppercase letters A through Z; lowercase letters a through z; common punctuation symbols such as the semicolon (;), comma (,), and period (.); and special symbols such as +, =, and >.

Characters are represented in memory by numeric codes, and in C++, values of type `char` are stored using these integer codes. (See the next section for a description. Also, see Potential Problem 2 at the end of this chapter to see how this can lead to confusion.) *Character literals* are usually written in C++ as single character symbols enclosed in apostrophes (or single quotes).[7] For example,

```
'A', '@', '3', '+'
```

are all examples of C++ character literals. The C++ compiler stores these values using their numeric codes, which in ASCII are

65, 43, 51, and 124

respectively.

Using an apostrophe as a delimiter raises the question, What is the character literal for an apostrophe? A similar question arises for characters such as the newline character, for which there is no corresponding symbol. For such characters that have a special purpose and cannot be described using the normal approach, C++ provides **escape sequences.** For example, the character literal for an apostrophe can be written as

```
'\''
```

and the newline character by

```
'\n'
```

Table 2.3 lists the escape sequences provided in C++.

---

[7] Character literals of the form L`'x'` where *x* consists of one or more characters are *wide-character literals* and are used to represent alternate character sets. They are of type `wchar_t` and have implementation-dependent values.

Character	C++ Escape Sequence
Newline (NL or LF)	\n
Horizontal tab (HT)	\t
Vertical tab (VT)	\v
Backspace (BS)	\b
Carriage return (CR)	\r
Form feed (FF)	\f
Alert (BEL)	\a
Backslash (\)	\\
Question mark (?)	\?
Apostrophe (single quote, ')	\'
Double quote (")	\"
With numeric octal code ooo	\ooo
With numeric hexadecimal code hhh	\x$hhh$

TABLE 2.3   C++ CHARACTER ESCAPE SEQUENCES

Strings. A different, but related, type of literal is the *string literal,* which consists of a sequence of characters enclosed in double quotes.[8] For example,

```
"Hello, there"
"Enter id number on one line\n\tand your name on the next.\n "
"\nThe revenue = $"
"Hamlet said, \"To be or not to be ... \""
```

are all string literals. Note that escape sequences can be used within string literals. The double newline character string literal

```
"\n\n"
```

can be used to separate lines of output with blank lines, making the output more readable. For example, consider the output of a string literal of the form

```
"One line\n\nAnother line"
```

The first newline (shown as ⏎ in the following output) ends the line on which One line appears and the second newline makes the next line a blank line, after which Another line appears:

```
One line⏎
⏎
Another line
```

Inserting blank lines into output is a simple way to increase its readability.

---

[8] String literals of the form L" . . . " are wide string literals; they may contain wide characters.

Two string literals that are consecutive or are separated only by **white space** (spaces, tabs, and end-of-lines) are automatically concatenated to form a single literal. For example, for

```
"John " "Doe"
```

or

```
"John"
"Doe"
```

the two string literals will be combined to form the single literal

```
"John Doe"
```

IDENTIFIERS

We have given *names* to most of the objects used in the programs considered thus far. These names are called **identifiers.** In C++, an identifier should begin with a letter, which may be followed by any number of letters, digits or underscores.[9] This allows the user to give an object a meaningful name that describes what that object represents. For example, the identifier

```
mass
```

is more meaningful than the identifier

```
m
```

which could represent *mass, mean, meters, megabytes,* and so on. *Identifiers should be as descriptive as possible, because this makes programs much easier to read.* They may not be C++ **keywords** (e.g., `int`, `const`, `double`, etc.), which are words that have predefined meanings. A complete list of the C++ keywords is given in appendix B.

Also, *C++ is case sensitive—that is, it distinguishes between uppercase and lowercase.* For example,

```
MASS
mass
Mass
MaSs
```

are four different identifiers in C++. One must be careful to use the same name consistently.

The primary goal in choosing identifiers is to enhance the program's readability. Although different programmers may use different naming conventions, one of the most common is the following:

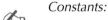

Constants: Names are given in uppercase. If a name consists of several words, these words are separated by underscore (_) characters. Some examples are `PI`, `AVOGADROS_NUMBER`, and `SPEED_OF_LIGHT`

---

[9] Identifiers that begin with an underscore (_) followed by an uppercase letter or that contain two *consecutive* underscores (_ _) are reserved for special use and should be avoided.

Variables: Names are given in lowercase, except that if a name consists of several words, the first letter of the second and each following word is capitalized. Some examples are `mass`, `energy`, `firstName`, and `myLastName`

This naming convention makes it easy to distinguish an object whose value is constant from one whose value can vary.

To use an identifier in a program, we must provide the compiler with the meaning of that identifier before its first use. This is accomplished by using a **declaration statement.** Thus far we have seen two kinds of identifiers, those for constant objects and those for variable objects, and we now describe their declarations in greater detail.

CONSTANT OBJECTS

We have seen that C++ permits the declaration of objects whose values remain constant. For example, the program in Figure 2.1 contains the constant declaration

```
const double SPEED_OF_LIGHT = 2.997925e8;    // meters/sec
```

The ability to define constant objects is especially useful when a program uses universal constants, such as the speed of light c or the geometric constant π, but it is also useful for describing any object whose value remains fixed during execution of a program:

```
const int YEAR = 2001;          // A Space Odyssey

const char
    MY_MIDDLE_INITIAL = 'C', // using a normal character
    FORM_FEED = '\f',         // using an escape sequence
    SPACEBAR = '\040';        // using an octal (ASCII) code
```

In general, a **constant declaration** has the following form:

Constant Declaration

Form:

const type CONSTANT_NAME = expression;

where:

`const` is a C++ keyword;

type may be any type that is known to the compiler;

CONSTANT_NAME is a valid C++ identifier; and

expression is any valid expression (as described in later sections) whose value is of type *type*.

Purpose:

Declares and provides a value for a named constant. Any attempt to change this value within a program is an error.

There are two important reasons for using constants instead of the literals they represent. One reason is *improved readability*. To illustrate, consider which of the following statements is more readable:

```
PopulationChange = (0.1758 - 0.1257) * Population;
```

or

```
PopulationChange = (BIRTH_RATE - DEATH_RATE) * Population;
```

If we define the constants `BIRTH_RATE` and `DEATH_RATE` by

```
const double
   BIRTH_RATE = 0.1758, // rate at which people are born
   DEATH_RATE = 0.1257; // rate at which people die
```

we can use the second statement, and that part of our program becomes much easier to understand.

A second benefit of using constants is that they *facilitate program modification*. To illustrate, suppose that you are solving a population-related problem, and that you use the birth rate and death rate literals `0.1758` and `0.1257` throughout your program. Suppose further that new values are published for the birth and death rates of the population you are studying. To modify your program to use these new values, you must find each occurrence of the old values and replace them with the new values.

If you had instead declared constants `BIRTH_RATE` and `DEATH_RATE` and used them throughout the program, you could simply change their declarations:

```
const double
   BIRTH_RATE = 0.1761, // rate at which people are born
   DEATH_RATE = 0.1252; // rate at which people die
```

Changing the values of `BIRTH_RATE` and `DEATH_RATE` in these declarations will change their values throughout the program without any further effort on your part.

It is considered good programming practice to *place all declarations of constants at the beginning of the function in which they are used.* This makes it easy to locate these declarations when it is necessary to modify the value of a constant.

In addition to programmer-defined constants, C++ provides many predefined constants in its various libraries. One very useful predefined constant is the character constant

`endl`	new-line character `'\n'`

defined in `iostream.h`. The library `limits` contains

`INT_MIN`	minimum `int` value
`INT_MAX`	maximum `int` value
`UINT_MIN`	minimum `unsigned int` value
`UINT_MAX`	maximum `unsigned int` value
`LONG_MIN`	minimum `long int` value
`LONG_MAX`	maximum `long int` value

and the library float contains

FLT_MIN	minimum float value
FLT_MAX	maximum float value
DBL_MIN	minimum double value
DBL_MAX	maximum double value
LDBL_MIN	minimum long double value
LDBL_MAX	maximum long double value

These lists are by no means exhaustive; for example, in addition to the minimum and maximum of each of the real types, float contains constants for the precision of each real type, the minimum and maximum exponent permitted in scientific notation, and so on.

VARIABLE OBJECTS

As scientists study the world, they discover relationships that exist between the objects they are studying. Such relationships can often be expressed by a *formula*. For example, the program in Figure 2.1 makes use of the formula

$$e = m \times c^2$$

which describes the relationship between a given mass and the amount of energy to which it can be converted. These symbolic names, e and m, are called variable objects, or just **variables.** If a specific value is substituted for m, then this formula can be used to calculate e, the energy.

When a variable object is declared in a C++ program, the compiler associates its name with a particular memory location. The value of a variable at any time is the value stored in its associated memory location at that time. One might think of a variable and its memory location as a mailbox—that can hold only one item at a time—with the name of the variable on the outside and the value of the variable placed inside:

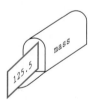

Variable names are identifiers and thus must follow the rules for valid identifiers.

As discussed previously, a **variable declaration** indicates to the compiler the kind of data that a variable object is to contain by associating a type with that variable. It has the following form:

Variable Declaration

Form:

```
type variable_name;
```

> where:
>
> *type* may be any type that is known to the compiler; and
>
> *variable_name* is a valid C++ identifier.
>
> **Purpose:**
>
> Instructs the C++ compiler to reserve sufficient memory to store a value of type *type,* and associates that memory with the name *variable_name.*

For example, the following are all valid declarations of variables that might be used to store information about a student:

```
long idNumber;

double cumulativeHours,
       hoursThisTerm,
       gradePointAverage;

short currentYear;
```

The type specified for a variable enables the compiler to associate the proper amount of memory with the variable. For example, it would be wasteful to use 4 bytes to store a character when a single byte is sufficient or 8 bytes to store a small integer when 2 are sufficient. Consequently, the type of a C++ variable must be one of the data types described previously (or one of the other data types to be discussed later).

C++ allows variable declarations to be placed (almost) anywhere before their first use in a function body. For example, in the program segment

```
        .
        .
        .
int main()
{
    const double SPEED_OF_LIGHT = 2.997925e8;   // meters/sec

    cout << "To find the amount of energy obtained from a "
            "given mass,\nenter a mass (in kilograms): ";
    double mass;
    cin >> mass;                      // get mass
    assert(mass >= 0);                // make sure it's nonnegative
                                      // compute energy
    double energy = mass * pow(SPEED_OF_LIGHT, 2);
        .
        .
        .
}
```

program statements and the declarations of SPEED_OF_LIGHT, mass, and energy are intermixed.

Of course, C++ does not prohibit declaring all variables at the beginning of the function, and some programmers prefer this style, to keep all the declarations together. To illustrate, we could have written the preceding program segment as follows:

```
      .
      .
      .
int main()
{
    const double SPEED_OF_LIGHT = 2.997925e8;   // meters/sec.
    double mass,                    // the amount of matter
           energy;                  // the amount of energy

    cout << "To find the amount of energy obtained from a"
            "given mass,\nenter a mass (in kilograms): ";
    cin >> mass;                    // get mass
    assert(mass >= 0);              // make sure it's nonnegative
                                    // compute energy
    energy = mass * pow(SPEED_OF_LIGHT, 2);
      .
      .
      .
}
```

 Where variable declarations are placed is largely a matter of programming style. In this text, we usually declare variables just prior to their first use rather than at the beginning of a function, because declaring a variable near its first use makes it easier to ensure that the variable is used in a manner consistent with its type.

 It is good programming practice to use meaningful variable names that suggest what they represent, since this makes the program more readable and easier to understand. Complete words are preferable to abbreviations, because such names help make a program **self-documenting.**

For additional documentation, many programmers also like to include a **data dictionary,** *consisting of brief comments that indicate what the variables represent, how they are to be used, and so on.* The following declarations illustrate this style:

Data dictionary
↓

```
long idNumber;              // Student Id Number

double cumulativeHours,     // Total credits earned to date
       hoursThisTerm,       // Credits this semester
       gradePointAverage;   // Cumulative GPA

short year;                 // 1 - freshman, 2 - sophomore
                            // 3 - junior, 4 - senior,
                            // 5 - continuing
```

VARIABLE INITIALIZATION

In the programs we have seen thus far, we have often provided a value, called an **initial value,** for a variable when it is declared. The general form of an initialization declaration is as follows:

Initialization Declaration

Form:

```
type variable_name = expression;
```

where

expression is any valid expression whose value is the same type as *type*.

Purpose:

This statement declares and provides an initial value for a variable.

The following are thus valid variable initializations:

```
int     count = 1,
        sum = 0;
double  gradePointAverage = 4.0;
char    letterGrade = 'A';
```

Variable initialization takes place when execution passes through the declarations. Thus, if the preceding declarations are in the main function of a progam, count and sum will be initialized with the integer values 1 and 0 respectively, gradePointAverage with the real value 4.0, and letterGrade with the character A when execution passes through these declarations.

✔ Quick Quiz 2.2

1. List the fundamental data types provided in C++.
2. List the three integer type variations.
3. List the three real types.
4. A constant of a particular type is called a(n) _____.
5. (True or false)   0123 and 123 represent the same integer value.
6. (True or false)   0xA and 10 represent the same integer value.
7. (True or false)   All real literals are treated as being of type double.
8. Character literals must be enclosed in _____.
9. (True or false)   '1/n' is a valid character literal.
10. (True or false)   '\n' is a valid character literal.
11. '\n' is an example of a(n) _____ sequence.
12. String constants must be enclosed in _____.
13. endl is a named constant whose value is _____

For questions 14–17, tell whether each is a legal identifier. If is it not legal, indicate the reason.

14. 55MPH   15. W_D_4_0   16. N/4   17. First Name

For questions 18–25, tell whether each is an integer literal, a real literal, or neither.

18. `1234`   **19.** `1,234`   **20.** `1.234`   **21.** `123e4`
22. `123-4`   **23.** `0.123E-4`   **24.** `0x123E4`   **25.** `0199`

For questions 26–33, tell whether each is a character literal, a string literal, or neither.

26. `'A'`   **27.** `'AB'`   **28.** `"ABC"`   **29.** `"@#'%&"`
30. `'/'`   **31.** `'\\'`   **32.** `'\123'`   **33.** `"John Doe'`

34. Write a constant declaration to associate `GRAVITY` with the integer 32.

35. Write constant declarations to associate `EARTH` with 1.5E10 and `MARS` with 1.2E12.

36. Write a declaration for a variable `distanceTraveled` of type `int`.

37. Write declarations for variables `idNumber` of type `unsigned`, `salary` of type `float`, and `employeeCode` of type `char`.

38. Repeat question 36, but initialize `distanceTraveled` to zero.

39. Repeat question 37, but initialize `idNumber` to 9999, `salary` to zero, `employeeCode` to a blank.

EXERCISES 2.2

For exercises 1–16, determine if each is a valid C++ identifier. If it is not, give a reason.

1. `XRay`   **2.** `X-Ray`   **3.** `Jeremiah`   **4.** `R2_D2`
5. `3M`   **6.** `PDQ123`   **7.** `PS.175`   **8.** `x`
9. `4`   **10.** `N/4`   **11.** `$M`   **12.** `Z_Z_Z_Z_Z_Z`
13. `night`   **14.** `ngiht`   **15.** `nite`   **16.** `to day`

For exercises 17–36, classify each as an integer literal, a real literal, or neither. If it is neither, give a reason.

17. `12`   **18.** `12.`   **19.** `12.0`   **20.** `"12"`
21. `8 + 4`   **22.** `-3.7`   **23.** `3.7-`   **24.** `1,024`
25. `+1`   **26.** `$3.98`   **27.** `0.357E4`   **28.** `24E0`
29. `E3`   **30.** `five`   **31.** `3E.5`   **32.** `.000001`
33. `1.2 × 10`   **34.** `-(-1)`   **35.** `0E0`   **36.** `1/2`

For exercises 37–48, determine if each is a valid string literal. If it is not, give a reason.

37. `"X"`   **38.** `"123"`   **39.** `IS"`   **40.** `"too yet"`
41. `"DO\"ESNT"`   **42.** `"isn't"`   **43.** `"constant"`   **44.** `"$1.98"`
45. `"DON\'T"`   **46.** `"12 + 34"`   **47.** `"\'twas"`   **48.** `"\"A\"\"B\"\"C\""`

For exercises 49–52, write constant declarations to associate each name with the specified literal:

49. `1.25` with the name `RATE`

50. `40.0` with the name `REGULAR_HOURS` and `1.5` with the name `OVERTIME_FACTOR`

51. `1776` with the name `YEAR`, the letter `F` with `FEMALE`, and a blank character with `BLANK`

52. `0` with `ZERO`, `*` with `ASTERISK`, and an apostrophe with `APOSTROPHE`

For exercises 53–56, write declarations for each variable.

53. `item`, `number`, and `job` of type `double`

54. `shoeSize` of type `int`

55. `mileage` of type `double`, `cost` and `distance` of type `unsigned`

56. `alpha` and `beta` of type `long`, `code` of type `char`, and `root` of type `double`

For exercises 57–58, write declarations to declare each variable to have the specified type and initial value.

57. `numberOfDeposits` and `numberOfChecks` to be of type `int`, each with an initial value of `0`; `totalDeposits` and `totalChecks` to be of type `double`, each with an initial value of `0.0`; and `serviceCharge` to be of type `double` with an initial value of `0.25`

58. `symbol_1` and `symbol_2` to be of type `char` and with a blank character and a semicolon for initial value, respectively; and `debug` to be of type `char` with an initial value of `T`

59. Write constant declarations that associate the current year with the name `YEAR` and 99999.99 with `MAXIMUM_SALARY` and variable declarations that declare `number` and `prime` to be of type `int` and `initial` to be of type `char`.

Part of the Picture: Data Representation

The third PART OF THE PICTURE section in chapter 1—Introduction to Computer Organization—noted that a binary scheme having only the two binary digits 0 and 1 is used to represent information in a computer. It also described how instructions can be represented in base-two and stored in memory. We now look at how literals of the various data types can be represented and stored in binary.

INTEGERS

When an integer value must be stored in the computer's memory, the binary representation of that value is typically stored in one word of memory. To illustrate, consider a computer whose word size is 32 and suppose that the integer value 58 is to be stored. The base-two representation of 58 is[10]

$$58 = 111010_2$$

If 58 is being used as an `unsigned` literal, all 32 bits are used for the binary digits of the value. The six bits in the binary representation of 58 can be stored in the rightmost bits of the memory word and the remaining bits filled with zeros:

| 0 | 0 | 0 | 0 | 0 | 0 | 0 | 0 | 0 | 0 | 0 | 0 | 0 | 0 | 0 | 0 | 0 | 0 | 0 | 0 | 0 | 0 | 0 | 0 | 0 | 0 | 1 | 1 | 1 | 0 | 1 | 0 |

Unlike `unsigned` values, which are always nonnegative, `int` values may be negative and so they must be stored in a binary form in which the sign of the integer is part of the

---

[10] See the website described in the preface for additional information about nondecimal number systems (binary, octal, and hexadecimal).

representation. There are several ways to do this, but one of the most common methods is the **two's complement** representation. In this scheme, positive integers are represented in binary form, as just described, with the leftmost bit set to 0 to indicate that the value is positive. Thus, if 58 is being used as an int literal, 31 bits are used for the binary digits of the value and one bit for the sign:

The two's complement representation of a negative integer $-n$ is obtained by first finding the binary representation of n, complementing it—that is, changing each 0 to 1 and each 1 to 0—and then adding 1 to the result. For example, the two's complement representation of -58 using a string of 32 bits is obtained as follows:

1. Represent 58 by a 32-bit binary numeral:

    00000000000000000000000000111010

2. Complement this bit string:

    11111111111111111111111111000101

3. Add 1:

    11111111111111111111111111000110

This string of bits is then stored:

Note that the sign bit in this two's complement representation of a negative integer is always 1, indicating that the number is negative.

The number of bits used to store an integer value determines the range of the integers that can be stored internally. For example, the largest `unsigned` value that can be stored in 32 bits is

$$11111111111111111111111111111111_2 = 2^{32} = 4294967296$$

The range of integers that can be represented using 32 bits is

$$10000000000000000000000000000000_2 = -2^{31} = -2147483648$$

through

$$01111111111111111111111111111111_2 = 2^{31} - 1 = 2147483647$$

Representation of an integer outside the allowed range would require more bits than can be stored, a phenomenon known as **overflow.** Using more bits to store an integer will enlarge the range of integers that can be stored, but it does not solve the problem of overflow; the range of representable integers is still finite.

REALS

Digits to the left of the binary point in the binary representation of a real number are coefficients of nonnegative powers of two, and those to the right are coefficients of negative powers of two. For example, the expanded form of 10110.101_2 is

$$(1 \times 2^4) + (0 \times 2^3) + (1 \times 2^2) + (1 \times 2^1) + (0 \times 2^0)$$
$$+ (1 \times 2^{-1}) + (0 \times 2^{-2}) + (1 \times 2^{-3})$$

which has the decimal value

$$16 + 0 + 4 + 2 + 0 + \frac{1}{2} + 0 + \frac{1}{8} = 22.625$$

There is some variation in the schemes used for storing real numbers in computer memory, but one floating-point representation was standardized in 1985 by the Institute for Electrical and Electronic Engineers (IEEE) and has become almost universal. This **IEEE Floating Point Format** specifies how reals can be represented in two formats: *single precision,* which uses 32 bits, and *double precision,* which uses 64 bits. The double precision format is simply a wider version of the single precision format, so we will consider only single precision.

We begin by writing the binary representation of the number in **floating-point form,** which is like scientific notation except that the base is two rather than ten:

$$b_1.b_2b_3 \cdots \times 2^k$$

where each b_i is 0 or 1, and $b_1 = 1$ (unless the number is 0). $b_1.b_2b_3 \ldots$ is called the **mantissa (or fractional part or significand)** and k is the **exponent (or characteristic).** To illustrate it, consider the real number 22.625, which we have seen can be written in binary as

$$10110.101_2$$

Rewriting this in floating-point form,

$$1.0110101_2 \times 2^4$$

is easy since multiplying (dividing) a base-two number by 2 is the same as moving the binary point to the right (left). 1.0110101_2 is the mantissa and 4 is the exponent.

In the IEEE format for single precision real values,

▶ the leftmost bit stores the sign of the mantissa, 0 for positive, 1 for negative

▶ the next 8 bits store the binary representation of the exponent + 127; 127 is called a **bias**

▶ the rightmost 23 bits store the bits to the right of the binary point in the mantissa (the bit to the left need not be stored since it is always 1)

For 22.625, the stored exponent would be $4 + 127 = 10000011_2$ and the stored mantissa would be $01101010000000000000000_2$:

sign

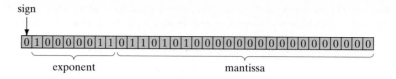

exponent   mantissa

The IEEE representation for double precision uses an 11-bit exponent with a bias of 1023 and 53 bits for the signed mantissa.

Because the binary representation of the exponent may require more than the available number of bits, we see that the **overflow** problem discussed in connection with integers also occurs in storing a real number whose exponent is too large. An 8-bit exponent restricts the range of real values to approximately -10^{38} to 10^{38}, and overflow occurs for values outside this range. A negative exponent that is too small to be stored causes an **underflow.** Real values represented using an 8-bit exponent must be greater than approximately 10^{-38} or less than -10^{-38}, and underflow occurs between these values:

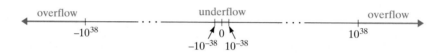

Also, there obviously are some real numbers whose mantissas have more than the allotted number of bits; consequently, some of these bits will be lost when such numbers are stored. In fact, most real numbers do not have finite binary representations and thus cannot be stored exactly in any computer. For example, the binary representation of the real number 0.7 is

$$(0.10110011001100110011001100110 \ldots)_2$$

where the block 0110 is repeated indefinitely. Because only a finite number of these bits can be stored, the stored representation of 0.7 will not be exact (e.g., 0.6999999284744263). This error in the stored representation of a real value, called **round-off error,** can be reduced, but not eliminated, by storing a larger number of bits. A 24-bit mantissa gives approximately 7 significant decimal digits for real values and a 48-bit mantissa gives approximately 14 significant digits.

CHARACTERS AND STRINGS

The schemes used for the internal representation of character data are based on the assignment of a numeric code to each of the characters in the character set. Several standard coding schemes have been developed, such as ASCII (American Standard Code for Information Interchange) and EBCDIC (Extended Binary Coded Decimal Interchange Code) and Unicode.[11]

---

[11] See appendix A for a table of ASCII codes for all characters.

Characters are represented internally using these binary codes. For example, the ASCII code of c is $99 = 01100011_2$ which can be stored in one 8-bit byte,

and the character string code can be stored in a 32-bit word with the code for c in the first byte, the code for o in the second byte, and so on:

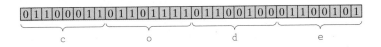

Character strings whose length exceeds the number of bytes in a word are usually stored in adjacent memory words.

Unicode is designed for use with most of the written languages of the world and must therefore provide codes for many characters. Whereas ASCII can encode only 128 characters, Unicode provides codes for more than 65,000 characters. To accomplish this it uses 16-bit codes. For example, the code for c (99—same as in ASCII) would be stored in two bytes:

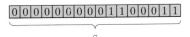

The code for the non-ASCII character π (Greek pi) is $960 = 0000001111000000_2$ and can also be stored in two bytes:

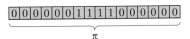

BOOLEANS

There are only two boolean values: `false` and `true`. If `false` is encoded as 0 and `true` as 1, then a single bit is all that is needed to store a `boolean` value. Usually, however, an entire word or byte is used with all bits set to 0 for `false` and any other bit string representing `true`.

2.3 NUMERIC EXPRESSIONS

A C++ **expression** is a sequence of one or more objects called *operands*, and zero or more *operators* that combine to produce a value. For example, is an expression that consists of one object (12) and no operators, producing the integer value twelve. Similarly,

$$2.2 + 3.3$$

is an expression that consists of two operands, 2.2 and 3.3, one operator (+), and produces the real value 5.5.

In this section, we examine the arithmetic operators and functions that are used in writing numeric expressions in C++ programs.

OPERATORS

In C++, addition and subtraction are denoted by the usual plus (+) and minus (−) signs. Multiplication is denoted by an asterisk (*). This symbol must be used to denote every multiplication. That is, to multiply n by 2, we can write 2*n or n*2 but not 2n. Division is denoted by a slash (/), which is used for both real and integer division. Another operation closely related to integer division is the **modulus** or **remainder** operation, denoted by percent (%), which gives the remainder in an integer division. The following table summarizes these operators.

Operator	Operation
+	addition, unary plus
−	subtraction, unary minus
*	multiplication
/	real and integer division
%	modulus (remainder in integer division)

For the operators +, −, *, and /, the operands may be of either integer or real type. If both are integer, the result is integer, but if either is real, the result is real. For example,

$$2 + 3 = 5$$
$$2 + 3.0 = 5.0$$
$$2.0 + 3 = 5.0$$
$$2.0 + 3.0 = 5.0$$
$$7.0 / 2.0 = 3.5$$
$$7 / 2 = 3$$

It is important to understand the difference between integer and real division. Consider the two expressions

$$3 / 4$$

and

$$3.0 / 4$$

Since both operands in the first expression, 3 and 4, are integers, integer division is performed, producing the integer quotient 0. By contrast, the second expression has a real operand, 3.0, and so real division is performed, producing the real result 0.75.

Integer division produces both a quotient and a remainder and C++ provides one operator (/) that gives the integer quotient and another operator (%) that gives the remainder from an integer division.[12] The following are some examples:

$$9 \; / \; 3 \rightarrow 3 \qquad\qquad 9 \; \% \; 3 \rightarrow 0$$
$$86 \; / \; 10 \rightarrow 8 \qquad\qquad 86 \; \% \; 10 \rightarrow 6$$
$$197 \; / \; 10 \rightarrow 19 \qquad\qquad 197 \; \% \; 10 \rightarrow 7$$

Type Conversions. We just saw that the division operation in the expression

$$3.0 \; / \; 4$$

performs real division and produces a real value as its result, even though only one of the operands is a real value. Some languages do not allow integer and real values to be intermixed within an expression in this manner. Although the extent to which mixed-type expressions are allowed is implementation-dependent in C++, most implementations will automatically *widen* the values in such an expression that are stored in the smaller number of bits. For example, suppose that in the expression

$$3.0 \; / \; 4$$

the double value 3.0 is stored in 64 bits and the int value 4 is stored in 32 bits. C++ will typically *widen* the narrower value (4) to a 64-bit value, so that the division can be performed on two 64-bit values, producing a 64-bit value as the result. No information or precision is lost, as would happen if the wider value were narrowed to the size of the narrower value.

This automatic widening of a narrower value to the size of a wider value in an expression is often described as **promotion** of the narrower value. Promotion is what permits short, unsigned, int, and long integer values to be freely intermixed in C++ expressions; and most implementations of C++ will promote integer values to real values when necessary. Two values are said to be **compatible** if one of the following is true:

▶ They are both of the same type
▶ The type of one value can be promoted to the type of the other value
▶ The types of both can be promoted to the same type

For example, char and int are compatible, since char can be promoted to int.

Operator Precedence. The arithmetic operators can be grouped into two groups: the **additive** operators (+ and -) and the **multiplicative** operators (*, /, and %). These groupings are important because they determine the order in which operators in an expression are applied. The order of evaluation in an expression is determined by **operator precedence** (or **priority**):

In an expression involving several operators the multiplicative operators have higher precedence than (i.e., are applied before) the additive operators.

----

[12] Neither i / j nor i % j is defined if j is zero.

Thus, in the expression

$$2 + 3 * 5$$

* has higher precedence than +, so the multiplication is performed before the addition; therefore, the value of the expression is 17.

Operator Associativity. In C++ the operators +, -, *, /, and % are all **left-associative** operators, which means that in an expression having two operators that have the same priority, the left operator is applied first. Thus,

$$9 - 5 - 1$$

is evaluated as

$$(9 - 5) - 1 \rightarrow 4 - 1 \rightarrow 3$$

In a later section, we will see that some C++ operators are *right-associative*.

Associativity is also used in more complex expressions containing different operators of the same priority. For example, consider

$$7 * 10 - 5 \% 3 * 4 + 9$$

There are three high-priority operations, *, %, and *, and so the leftmost multiplication is performed first, giving the intermediate result

$$70 - 5 \% 3 * 4 + 9$$

Because of left associativity, % is performed next, giving

$$70 - 2 * 4 + 9$$

and the second multiplication is performed last, yielding

$$70 - 8 + 9$$

The two remaining operations, - and +, are equal in priority, and so left associativity causes the subtraction to be performed first, giving

$$62 + 9$$

and then the addition is carried out, giving the final result

$$71$$

Using Parentheses. Parentheses can be used to change the usual order of evaluation of an expression as determined by precedence and associativity. Parenthesized subexpressions are first evaluated in the standard manner, and the results are then combined to evaluate the complete expression. If the parentheses are "nested"— that is, if one set of parentheses is contained within another—the computations in the innermost parentheses are performed first.

For example, consider the expression

$$(7 * (10 - 5) \% 3) * 4 + 9$$

The subexpression $(10 - 5)$ is evaluated first, producing

$$(7 * 5 \% 3) * 4 + 9$$

Next, the subexpression (7 * 5 % 3) is evaluated left to right, giving

$$(35 \ \% \ 3) \ * \ 4 \ + \ 9$$

followed by

$$2 \ * \ 4 \ + \ 9$$

Now the multiplication is performed, giving

$$8 \ + \ 9$$

and the addition produces the final result

$$17$$

Care must be taken in writing expressions containing two or more operations to ensure that they are evaluated in the order intended. Even though parentheses may not be required, they should be used freely to clarify the intended order of evaluation and to write complicated expressions in terms of simpler expressions. It is important, however, that the parentheses balance—each left parenthesis has a matching right parenthesis that appears later in the expression—since an unpaired parenthesis will result in a compilation error.

Unary Operators. The operators + and – can also be used as **unary operators** (i.e., they can be applied to a single operand); for example, $-x$ and $+34$ are allowed. Similarly, the expression $3 \ * \ -4$ is a valid C++ expression, producing the value -12. Unary operations have higher priority than the binary operations $+, -, *, /,$ and $\%$.

Summary. In summary, the following rules govern the evaluation of arithmetic expressions.

Precedence Rules

Higher: unary +, unary –

          *, /, and %

Lower: binary +, binary –

1. Higher-priority operations are performed before lower-priority operations.
2. Operators having the same priority are applied according to their associativity.
3. If an expression contains subexpressions enclosed within parentheses, these are evaluated first, using the standard order specified in rules 1 and 2. If there are nested parentheses, the innermost subexpressions are evaluated first.

C++ also provides other numeric operators, for example, bitwise operations that can be applied to integer data: ~ (negation), & (bitwise and), | (bitwise or), ^

(bitwise exclusive or), << (bitshift left) and >> (bitshift right). See appendix C for a complete list of the C++ operators.

NUMERIC FUNCTIONS

In the program in Figure 2.1, we computed the value of `energy` using the following statement:

```
energy = mass * pow(SPEED_OF_LIGHT, 2);
```

Here we see that in addition to simple objects like literals, constants, and variables, an operand may also be a value returned by a function. In this case, we used the standard math library function `pow()`, which provides the exponentiation operation in C++.

Many languages provide standard functions, such as square root, logarithm, and absolute value, as part of the language. This is convenient because a program can simply call such functions when they are needed. The problem is that these functions may add to the size of the compiled program, regardless of whether the program uses them or not. This is a significant price (in terms of space) to pay for the convenience of built-in functions.

C++ provides so many predefined functions that even a simple program (such as that in Figure 2.1) would be huge if all of the predefined functions were added to the program. Instead, C++ stores its predefined functions in various **libraries.**

As the name implies, a library is a place where objects and functions can be stored, so that a program can "borrow" them when necessary. For example, the **iostream library** is where the stream objects `cin` and `cout` are stored along with input (>>) and output (<<) functions. Similarly, the **math library** stores `pow()`, `sqrt()`, and other math-related functions. The **standard library** contains many other commonly used functions such as the absolute value function `abs()` for integers and `exit()`, which can be used to terminate program execution if an error occurs. Becoming familiar with the functions available in these libraries is an important part of learning to program in C++, because they provide many commonly needed operations.

To use objects and functions stored in a library, a program must use the `#include` directive to insert that library's **header file**—a special file containing the declarations of the library's objects and functions. Thus, since the program in Figure 2.1 uses the `pow()` function, which is stored in the math library, the program must contain the directive

```
#include <math.h>                // pow()
```

to make the contents of the math library available to the program. It is good programming practice to follow a `#include` directive with a comment like that shown, that lists the items from the library that are being used.[13]

---

[13] As noted earlier, recent changes to the C++ standard make it possible to use other names for libraries—e.g., `iostream`, `cmath`, `cassert`, and `cstlib`, instead of `iostream.h`, `math.h`, `assert.h`, and `stdlib.h`, respectively.

Since the program in Figure 2.1 reads numeric values from the keyboard via `cin`,

```
cin >> mass;
```

and writes values to the screen via `cout`,

```
cout << mass << " kilograms of matter will release "
     << energy << " kilojoules of energy.\n";
```

and since the objects `cin`, `cout` and their operations are stored in the `iostream` library, whose header file is `iostream.h`, the program must contain the directive:

```
#include <iostream.h>        // cin, cout, <<, >>
```

The `iostream` library is discussed in greater detail in section 4.3.

Finally, because the program uses `assert()`, which is declared in the `assert` library, the program contains the directive:

```
#include <assert.h>          // assert()
```

When the C++ compiler processes a `#include` directive, the contents of that file are *inserted* into the program. The angle brackets (< and >) around the name of the header file tell the compiler to look for that file in a special system *include directory* that contains the header files of most of the standard C++ libraries.[14]

To *call* any of the functions from a library whose header file has been included, we simply give the function name, followed by any **arguments** it requires—constants, variables, or expressions to which the function is to be applied—enclosed within parentheses. For example, the program in Figure 2.1 uses the call

```
pow(SPEED_OF_LIGHT, 2)
```

Computing x^n requires two operands, x and n, so the `pow()` function requires two arguments. By contrast, if we wanted to find the absolute value of an integer value, we could use the standard library function `abs()`, which takes a single argument:

```
positiveValue = abs(intValue);
```

but to do so, we must first have included the header file of the standard library `stdlib`:

```
#include <stdlib.h>
```

Table 2.4 lists several of the functions provided by the math library. Each of these functions takes one or more arguments of type `double` and returns a value of type `double`. Thus, to calculate the square root of 5, we can write

```
sqrt(5.0)
```

Most implementations will also allow

```
sqrt(5)
```

since the `int` value 5 can be promoted to the `double` value `5.0`.

---

[14] Different platforms store the include directory in different places. See your instructor or system manuals for the location of the include directory for your particular system.

Function	Description
abs(x)	Absolute value of real value x
pow(x, y)	x raised to power y
sqrt(x)	Square root of x
ceil(x)	Least integer greater than or equal to x
floor(x)	Greatest integer less than or equal to x
exp(x)	Exponential function e^x
log(x)	Natural logarithm of x
log10(x)	Base-10 logarithm of x
sin(x)	Sine of x (in radians)
cos(x)	Cosine of x (in radians)
tan(x)	Tangent of x (in radians)
asin(x)	Inverse sine of x
acos(x)	Inverse cosine of x
atan(x)	Inverse tangent of x
sinh(x)	Hyperbolic sine of x
cosh(x)	Hyperbolic cosine of x
tanh(x)	Hyperbolic tangent of x

TABLE 2.4   MATH LIBRARY FUNCTIONS

As a more complicated example, if we wish to calculate $\sqrt{b^2 - 4ac}$, we could write

```
sqrt(pow(b, 2) - 4.0 * a * c)
```

Note that if the value of the expression

```
pow(b, 2) - 4.0 * a * c
```

is negative, then an error results because the square root of a negative number is not defined.

Type Conversions. If `intVal` is an integer variable and `doubleVal` is a `double` variable, then the expression

```
double(intVal)
```

produces the `double` value equivalent to `intVal`. Similarly, the expression

```
int(doubleVal)
```

will truncate the fractional part and produce the integer part of `doubleVal` as its value. More generally, the type of an expression can be explicitly converted to a different type as follows:[15]

---

[15] The C++ standard recently added new type-conversion operators: `const_cast`, `dynamic_cast`, `reinterpret_cast`, and `static_cast`. For example, the preceding expression could be written `static_cast<int>(doubleVal)`.

> ## Explicit Type Conversion
>
> **Forms:**
>
> *type (expression)*
>
> or
>
> *(type) expression*
>
> where:
>
> *type* is a valid C++ type; and
>
> *expression* is any C++ expression.
>
> **Purpose:**
>
> The type of the value produced by *expression* is converted to *type* (if possible). The first form is sometimes referred to as *functional notation* and the second form as *cast notation*.

Explicitly converting the type of an expression is sometimes called **casting** the expression.

✔ ## Quick Quiz 2.3

Find the value of each of the expressions in questions 1–12, or explain why it is not a valid expression.

1. `3 - 2 - 1`   **2.** `2.0 + 3.0 / 5.0`

3. `2 + 3 / 5`   **4.** `5 / 2 + 3`

5. `7 + 6 % 5`   **6.** `(7 + 6) % 5`

7. `(2 + 3 * 4) / (8 - 2 + 1)`   **8.** `12.0 / 1.0 * 3.0`

9. `sqrt(6.0 + 3.0)`   **10.** `pow(2.0, 3)`

11. `floor(2.34)`   **12.** `ceil(2.34)`

Questions 13–20 assume that `two`, `three`, and `four` are reals with values 2.0, 3.0, and 4.0, respectively, and `intEight` and `intFive` are integers with values 8 and 5, respectively. Find the value of each expression.

13. `two + three * three`   **14.** `intFive / 3`

15. `(three + two / four) * 2`   **16.** `intEight / intFive * 5.1`

17. `four * 2 / two * 2`   **18.** `intFive * 2 / two * 2`

19. `sqrt(two + three + four)`   **20.** `pow(two, intFive)`

21. Write a C++ expression equivalent to $10 + 5B - 4AC$.

22. Write a C++ expression equivalent to the square root of $A + 3B^2$.

EXERCISES 2.3

Find the value of each of the expressions in questions 1–24, or explain why it is not a valid expression.

1.	`9 - 5 - 3`	**2.**	`2 / 3 + 3 / 5`
3.	`9.0 / 2 / 5`	**4.**	`9 / 2 / 5`
5.	`2.0 / 4`	**6.**	`(2 + 3) % 2`
7.	`7 % 5  % 3`	**8.**	`(7 % 5)  % 3`
9.	`7 % (5  % 3)`	**10.**	`(7 % 5  % 3)`
11.	`25 * 1 / 2`	**12.**	`25 * 1.0 / 2`
13.	`25 * (1 / 2)`	**14.**	`-3.0 * 5.0`
15.	`5.0 * -3.0`	**16.**	`12 / 2 * 3`
17.	`((12 + 3)/2)/(8 - (5 + 1))`	**18.**	`((12 + 3) / 2) / (8 - 5 + 1)`
19.	`(12 + 3 / 2) / (8 - 5 + 1)`	**20.**	`sqrt(pow(4.0,2))`
21.	`sqrt(pow(-4.0,2))`	**22.**	`pow(sqrt(-4.0),2)`
23.	`ceil(8.0 / 5.0)`	**24.**	`floor(8.0 / 5.0)`

Questions 25–32 assume that `r1` and `r2` are reals with values 2.0 and 3.0, respectively, and `i1`, `i2`, and `i3` are integers with values 4, 5, and 8, respectively. Find the value of each expression.

25.	`r1 + r2 + r2`	**26.**	`i3 / 3`
27.	`i3 / 3.0`	**28.**	`(r2 + r1) * i1`
29.	`i3 / i2 * 5.1`	**30.**	`pow(i1,2) / pow(r1,2)`
31.	`pow(i2,2) / pow(r1,2)`	**32.**	`sqrt(r1 + r2 + i1)`

Write C++ expressions to compute each of the quantities in exercises 33–39.

33. $10 + 5B - 4AC$

34. Three times the difference $4 - n$ divided by twice the quantity $m^2 + n^2$

35. The square root of $a + 3b^2$

36. The square root of the average of m and n

37. $|A / (m + n)|$ (where $|x|$ denotes the absolute value of x)

38. a^x, computed as $e^{x \ln a}$ (where ln is the natural logarithm function)

39. The real quantity *Amount* rounded to the nearest hundredth

40. Using the given values of `cost`, verify that the statement

```
cost = double(int(cost*100.0 + 0.5))/100.0;
```

can be used to convert a real value `cost` to dollars, rounded to the nearest cent.
(a) 12.342   **(b)** 12.348   **(c)** 12.345   **(d)** 12.340   **(e)** 13.0

41. Write an expression similar to that in exercise 40 that rounds a real amount `x` to the nearest tenth.

42. Write an expression similar to that in exercise 40 that rounds a real amount `x` to the nearest thousandth.

2.4 BOOLEAN EXPRESSIONS

In the mid-1800s, a self-taught British mathematician George Boole (1815–1864) developed an algebra of logic in which expressions could be formed to process logical values. Such logical expressions, which produce either the value *true* or the value *false,* have thus come to be known as **boolean expressions.** They are also often called **conditions,** and we will use the two terms interchangeably.

Every modern programming language provides some means for constructing boolean expressions, and in this section we consider how they are constructed in C++. We look first at simple boolean expressions and then at how logical operators can be used to combine boolean expressions to form compound expressions.

SIMPLE BOOLEAN EXPRESSIONS

In C++, the type `bool` has two literals: `false` and `true`.[16] A boolean expression is thus a sequence of operands and operators that combine to produce one of the boolean values, `true` or `false`.

The operators that are used in the simplest boolean expressions test some *relationship* between their operands. For example, the program in Figure 2.1 contains the boolean expression

```
mass >= 0
```

which compares the operands `mass` and `0` using the *greater-than-or-equal-to* relationship, and produces the value `true` if the value of `mass` is nonnegative, and produces the value `false` if the value of `mass` is negative. Similarly, the C++ boolean expression

```
count == 5
```

tests the *equality* relationship between the (variable) operand `count` and the (literal) operand 5, producing the value `true` if the value of `count` is 5 and the value `false` otherwise. Operators like `>=` and `==` that test a relationship between two operands are called **relational operators** and they are used in boolean expressions of the form

expression₁   relational_operator   expression₂

where *expression₁* and *expression₂* are two C++ compatible expressions and the *relational_operator* may be any of the following:

Relational Operator	Relation Tested
<	Is less than
>	Is greater than
==	Is equal to
!=	Is not equal to
<=	Is less than or equal to
>=	Is greater than or equal to

These relational operators may be applied to operands of any of the standard data types: `char`, `int`, `float`, `double`, and so on. For example, if x, a, b, and c are of

---

[16] For historical reasons, C++ also allows integers to be used as boolean values: 0 in place of `false`, and any nonzero value can be used for `true`, with 1 being the most commonly used nonzero value.

type `double`, `number` is `int`, and `initial` is of type `char`, then the following are valid boolean expressions formed using these relational operators:

```
x < 5.2
b * b >= 4.0 * a * c
number == 500
initial != 'Q'
```

For numeric data, the relational operators are commonly used to compare numbers. Thus, if `x` has the value 4.5, then the expression

```
x < 5.2
```

produces the value `true`. Similarly, if `number` has the value 17, then the expression

```
number == 500
```

produces the value `false`.

Characters are compared using their numeric codes (see appendix A). Thus, if ASCII is used,

```
'A' < 'B'
```

is a true boolean expression because the ASCII code of `A` (65) is less than the ASCII code of `B` (66). This expression thus produces the value `true`. Similarly, the expression

```
'a' < 'b'
```

produces the value `true`, because the ASCII code of `a` (97) is less than the ASCII code of `b` (98). The boolean expression

```
'a' < 'A'
```

is `false`, because the ASCII code of `a` (97) is not less than the ASCII code of `A` (65).[17]

COMPOUND BOOLEAN EXPRESSIONS

Many relationships are too complicated to be expressed using only the relational operators. For example, a typical test score is governed by the mathematical relationship

$$0 \leq \text{test score} \leq 100$$

which is true if the test score is between 0 and 100 (inclusive), and is false otherwise. However, this relationship *cannot* be correctly represented in C++ by the expression

```
0 <= testScore <= 100
```

---

[17] The boolean expressions `'A' < 'B'` and `'a' < 'b'` will both be true on a system using the EBCDIC character codes, but the expression `'a' < 'A'` will also evaluate to `true`, because the EBCDIC code for a (129) is less than the EBCDIC code for A (193).

To see why, suppose that `testScore` has the value 101, which would mean that the expression should be false. Because these relational operators are left-associative, the preceding expression is processed as

$$(0 <= 101) <= 100$$

The subexpression

$$(0 <= 101)$$

is evaluated first, producing the value `true`, which is treated in C++ as the `int` value 1. This 1 is then used as an operand for the second `<=` operator, so that the expression

$$(1 <= 100)$$

is evaluated. It, of course, is `true`, which is not the value of the original mathematical expression.

To avoid this difficulty, we must rewrite the mathematical expression

$$0 \le \text{test score} \le 100$$

in the form

$$(0 \le \text{test score}) \text{ and } (\text{test score} \le 100)$$

This expression can be correctly coded in C++, because C++ provides **logical operators** that combine boolean expressions to form **compound boolean expressions.** These operators are defined as follows:

Logical Operator	Logical Expression	Name of Operation	Description
!	!p	*Not* (*Negation*)	!p is false if p is true; !p is true if p is false.
&&	p && q	*And* (*Conjunction*)	p && q is true if both p and q are true; it is false otherwise.
||	p || q	*Or* (*Disjunction*)	p || q is true if either p or q or both are true; it is false otherwise.

These definitions are summarized by the following **truth tables,** which display all possible values for two conditions p and q and the corresponding values of the logical expression:

p	!p
true	false
false	true

p	q	p && q	p || q
true	true	true	true
true	false	false	true
false	true	false	true
false	false	false	false

We can thus use the `&&` operator to represent the mathematical expression

$(0 \le \text{test score})$ and $(\text{test score} \le 100)$

by the compound boolean expression

```
(0 <= testScore) && (testScore <= 100)
```

In this case, if `testScore` has the value 101, the expression will be evaluated as follows:

1. The relational expression `0 <= 101` is evaluated giving `true`
2. The relational expression `101 <= 100` is evaluated giving `false`
3. The `&&` operator is applied to these two values, `true && false`, producing the value `false`

OPERATOR PRECEDENCE

A boolean expression that contains an assortment of arithmetic operators, boolean operators, and relational operators is evaluated using the following precedence (or priority) and associativity rules:

Operator	Priority	Associativity
`!`	highest	Right
`/, *, %`		Left
`+, -`		Left
`<, >, <=, >=`		Left
`==, !=`		Left
`&&`		Left
`||`		Left
`=, +=, *=, . . .`	lowest	Right

An operator with a higher priority is applied before an operator with a lower priority.

To illustrate, consider the boolean expression

```
n != 0 && x < 1.0/n
```

The `/` operator has highest priority, and so this operator is applied first, producing an intermediate real value `r` and the expression

```
n != 0 && x < r
```

Of the remaining operators, `<` has the highest priority, so that operator is applied next, producing an intermediate boolean value `b1` and the expression

```
n != 0 && b1
```

Of the remaining two operators, != has the higher priority, so that operator is applied next, producing an intermediate (boolean) value b2 and the expression

```
b2 && b1
```

Finally, the && operator is applied to the two (boolean) intermediate values to produce the value of the expression.

Because it is difficult to remember so many precedence levels, it is helpful to remember the following:

- ▶ ! is the highest-precedence operator (that we have seen so far)
- ▶ *, /, and % have higher precedence than + and –
- ▶ Every numeric operator has higher precedence than every relational and/or logical operator (except !)
- ▶ Every relational operator has higher precedence than the logical operators && and ||
- ▶ Use parentheses for all the other operators to clarify the order in which they are applied

SHORT-CIRCUIT EVALUATION

An important feature of the && and || operators is that they do not always evaluate their second operand. For example, if p is false, then the condition

```
p && q
```

is false, regardless of the value of q, and so C++ does not evaluate q. Similarly, if p is true, then the condition

```
p || q
```

is true, regardless of the value of q, and so C++ does not evaluate q. This approach is called **short-circuit evaluation,** and has two important benefits:

1. One boolean expression can be used to *guard* a potentially unsafe operation in a second boolean expression

2. A considerable amount of time can be saved in the evaluation of complex conditions

As an illustration of the first benefit, consider the boolean expression

```
(n != 0) && (x < 1.0 / n)
```

No division-by-zero error can occur in evaluating this expression, because if n is 0, then the first expression

```
(n != 0)
```

is false and the second expression

```
(x < 1.0 / n)
```

is not evaluated. Similarly, no division-by-zero error will occur in evaluating the condition

```
(n == 0) || (x >= 1.0 / n)
```

because if n is 0, the first expression

```
(n == 0)
```

is true and the second expression is not evaluated.

PRECONDITIONS AND THE assert() MECHANISM

In many problems, the set of possible input values is much larger than the set of input values for which the program is designed. This creates a potential problem: if the user inputs an invalid value, the program will not compute the correct result. For example, in the mass-to-energy conversion problem we considered in section 2.1, the problem is only defined for nonnegative masses. If the user should enter a negative value for mass, the result produced by the program will not be correct.

In problems like this, a restriction imposed on the set of valid input values is called a **precondition**—a condition that must be true before the computation can proceed correctly. For example, the mass-to-energy problem has the following precondition:

mass must be nonnegative.

Boolean expressions can be used to construct expressions to represent such preconditions. For example, the preceding precondition can be represented by the boolean expression

```
mass >= 0
```

C++ also provides the assert() mechanism (defined in the assert library) as a convenient way to check that a precondition is true. For example, the program in Figure 2.1 contains the statement

```
assert(mass >= 0);
```

When this statement is executed, the boolean expression mass >= 0 is evaluated. If it is true, then execution proceeds normally. However, if the expression is false, execution of the program will be terminated and a diagnostic message such as

```
failed assertion: mass >= 0
```

will be displayed to inform the user that the value entered for mass did not satisfy the program's precondition. The program is thus prevented from processing invalid inputs.

In general, the assert() mechanism can be described as follows:

The assert( ) Mechanism

Form:

```
assert(boolean_expression);
```

where

boolean_expression is any valid expression evaluating to true or false.

> **Purpose:**
> Checks a condition that must be true at a given point in a program.
> If *boolean_expression* is true, then execution proceeds normally. If it is false, the program is terminated and a diagnostic message is displayed.

✔ Quick Quiz 2.4

1. The two `bool` literals are _____ and _____.
2. List the six relational operators.
3. List the three logical operators.

For questions 4–8, assume that `p`, `q`, and `r` are boolean expressions with the values `true`, `true`, and `false`, respectively. Find the value of each boolean expression.

4. `p && !q`   **5.** `p && q || !r`
6. `p && !(q || r)` **7.** `!p && q`
8. `p || q && r`

For questions 9–13, assume that `number`, `count`, and `sum` are integer variables with values 3, 4, and 5, respectively. Find the value of each boolean expression, or indicate why it is not valid.

9. `sum - number <= 4`
10. `number*number + count*count == sum*sum`
11. `number < count || count < sum`
12. `0 <= count <= 5`
13. `(number + 1 < sum) && !(count + 1 < sum)`
14. Write a boolean expression to express that `x` is nonzero.
15. Write a boolean expression to express that `x` is strictly between −10 and 10.
16. Write a boolean expression to express that both `x` and `y` are positive or both `x` and `y` are negative.

EXERCISES 2.4

For exercises 1–10, assume that `m` and `n` are integer variables with the values −5 and 8, respectively, and that `x`, `y`, and `z` are real variables with the values −3.56, 0.0, and 44.7, respectively. Find the value of the boolean expression.

1.	`m <= n`	**2.**	`2 * abs(m) <= 8`
3.	`x * x < sqrt(z)`	**4.**	`int(z) == (6 * n - 4)`
5.	`(x <= y) && (y <= z)`	**6.**	`!(x < y)`
7.	`!((m <= n) && (x + z > y))`	**8.**	`!(m <= n) || !(x + z > y)`
9.	`!((m <= n) || (x + z > y))`	**10.**	`!((m > n) && !(x < z))`

For exercises 11–16, use truth tables to display the values of the boolean expression for all possible (boolean) values of `a`, `b`, and `c`:

11.   a || !b   **12.**   !(a && b)

13.   !a || !b   **14.**   (a && b) || c

15.   a && (b || c)   **16.**   (a && b) || (a && c)

For exercises 17–25, write C++ boolean expressions to express the following conditions:

17.   x is greater than 3.

18.   y is strictly between 2 and 5.

19.   r is negative and z is positive.

20.   Both alpha and beta are positive.

21.   alpha and beta have the same sign (both are negative or both are positive).

22. $-5 < x < 5$.

23.   a is less than 6 or is greater than 10.

24.   p is equal to q, which is equal to r.

25.   x is less than 3, or y is less than 3, but not both.

Exercises 26–28 assume that a, b, and c are boolean values.

26.   Write a C++ boolean expression that is true if and only if a and b are true and c is false.

27.   Write a C++ boolean expression that is true if and only if a is true and at least one of b or c is true.

28.   Write a C++ boolean expression that is true if and only if exactly one of a and b is true.

2.5 CHARACTER EXPRESSIONS

As mentioned in section 2.2, C++ provides the char type for representing values from the machine's character set. As discussed there, a char literal consists of a character surrounded by single quotes; and objects of type char can be defined and initialized in a manner similar to int and double objects; for example,

```
const char myMiddleInitial = 'C';
char direction = 'N';                    // N, S, E or W
```

Character values can be assigned in the usual manner,

```
myMiddleInitial = 'C';
```

can be read from the keyboard via cin,

```
cin >> myMiddleInitial;
```

and can be written to the screen via cout:

```
cout << myMiddleInitial;
```

We also saw in section 2.4 that C++ allows char values to be compared using the relational operators. For example, suppose we are solving a problem that has the precondition that a character variable *letter* must have an uppercase value. This precondition can be expressed in C++ using a compound boolean expression:

```
('A' <= letter) && (letter <= 'Z')
```

We can thus use the `assert()` mechanism as follows to test this precondition:

```
assert('A' <= letter && letter <= 'Z');
```

CHARACTER-PROCESSING OPERATIONS

In addition to the operations just mentioned, the library `ctype` provides a number of functions for performing commonly needed operations on character values. The most useful of these character-processing functions are shown in Table 2.5. These functions provide the programmer with a variety of "off-the-shelf" solutions to common problems that involve character values. For example, an alternative way to write the earlier assertion that `letter` is an uppercase letter is

```
assert(isupper(letter));
```

Operation	Description
isalnum(*ch*)	true if *ch* is a letter or a digit, `false` otherwise
isalpha(*ch*)	true if *ch* is a letter, `false` otherwise
iscntrl(*x*)	true if *ch* is a control character, `false` otherwise
isdigit(*ch*)	true if *ch* is a decimal digit, `false` otherwise
isgraph(*ch*)	true if *ch* is a printing character except space, `false` otherwise
islower(*ch*)	true if *ch* is lower case, `false` otherwise
isprint(*ch*)	true if *ch* is a printing character, including space, `false` otherwise
ispunct(*ch*)	true if *ch* is a punctuation character (not a space, an alphabetic character, or a digit), `false` otherwise
isspace(*ch*)	true if *ch* is a white space character (space, `'\f'`, `'\n'`, `'\r'`, `'\t'`, or `'\v'`), `false` otherwise
isupper(*ch*)	true if *ch* is upper case, `false` otherwise
isxdigit(*ch*)	true if *ch* is a hexadecimal digit, `false` otherwise
toupper(*ch*)	returns the uppercase equivalent of *ch* (if *ch* is lower case)
tolower(*ch*)	returns the lowercase equivalent of *ch* (if *ch* is upper case)

TABLE 2.5   CHARACTER OPERATIONS IN `ctype`

✔ **Quick Quiz 2.5**

1. A character literal must be enclosed in _____.
2. (True or false) `char x = '1/2';` is a valid initialization declaration.
3. (True or false) `char x = '\12';` is a valid initialization declaration.
4. Using relational operators, write an `assert` statement to test the condition that the value of the `char` variable c is one of the digits `'0'`, `'1'`, `'2'`, . . ., `'9'`.
5. Repeat question 4 but use a function from `ctype`.
6. Write a statement that checks if the value of the `char` variable c is an uppercase or lowercase vowel.

2.6 ASSIGNMENT EXPRESSIONS

An **assignment expression** uses the assignment operator (=) to assign a value to a variable.

Assignment Expression

Form:

```
variable = expression
```

where:

variable is a valid C++ identifier, declared as a variable;

expression may be a constant, another variable to which a value has previously been assigned, or a formula to be evaluated, whose type is the same as that of *variable*.

Behavior:

1. *expression* is evaluated, producing a value v;

2. The value of *variable* is changed to v; and

3. The = operator produces the value v.

For example, suppose that xCoord and yCoord are real variables, number and position are integer variables, and code is a character variable, declared as follows:

```
double xCoord, yCoord;
int number, position;
char code;
boolean isOkay;
```

These declarations associate memory locations with the six variables. This might be pictured as follows, with the question marks indicating that these variables are initially **undefined:**

xCoord	?
yCoord	?
number	?
position	?
code	?
isOkay	?

Now consider the following assignment statements:

```
xCoord = 5.23;
yCoord = sqrt(25.0);
```

```
number = 17;
code = 'M';
isOkay = false;
```

Note that the value of a variable of type char is a single character and not a string of characters.

The first assignment statement assigns the real constant 5.23 to the real variable xCoord, and the second assigns the real constant 5.0 to the real variable yCoord. The next assignment statements assign the integer constant 17 to the integer variable number, the character M to the character variable code, and the boolean constant false to the boolean variable isOkay. Thinking of variables as mailboxes, as described in section 2.2, we might picture the results as follows:

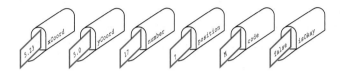

More precisely, when these assignment statements are executed, the values 5.23, 5.0, and 17, the numeric code for M, and the integer 0 (representing false) are stored in the memory locations associated with the variables xCoord, yCoord, number, code, and isOkay, respectively. The variable position is still undefined, and the content of the memory location associated with it is uncertain.

xCoord	5.23
yCoord	5.0
number	17
position	?
code	M (65)
isOkay	false (0)

These values are substituted for the variables in any subsequent expression containing these variables. Thus, in the assignment statement

```
position = number / 3 + 2;
```

the expression number / 3 + 2 is evaluated (with the value 17 substituted for the variable number) yielding 7. This value is then assigned to the integer variable position; the value of number remains unchanged.

xCoord	5.23
yCoord	5.0
number	17
position	7
code	M (65)
isOkay	false (0)

Compare this with the assignment statement

```
xCoord = 2.0 * xCoord;
```

in which the variable xCoord appears on both sides of the assignment operator (=). In this case, the current value 5.23 for xCoord is used in evaluating the expression 2.0 * xCoord, yielding the value 10.46; this value is then assigned to xCoord. The old value 5.23 is lost because it has been replaced with the new value 10.46.

xCoord	10.46
yCoord	5.0
number	17
position	7
code	M (65)
isOkay	false (0)

In every assignment statement, the variable whose value is to be changed must appear on the left of the assignment operator (=), a valid expression must appear on the right, and both the variable and the expression should be of the same type. Although mixing of numeric types is permitted in C++, the practice should be avoided, since assigning a real value to an integer variable truncates the real value (i.e., discards its fractional part). For example,

```
number = 4 / yCoord;
```

will evaluate the expression 4 / yCoord, and since yCoord is of type double, this expression produces the real result 0.8. Assigning this real value to the integer variable number truncates the fractional part (.8), and assigns the integer portion (0) to number. Significant information can be lost through careless mixing of real and integer values.

An unusual feature of C++ is that it treats characters as integers. This means that unusual assignments like

```
code = 65 + 1;
```

or

```
number = 'A' + 'B';
```

are allowed in C++. If ASCII is used, the first statement assigns the value 66 (the numeric code for 'B') to code and the second assigns the value 131 (65 + 66) to number. Such statements are poor programming style and should be avoided. *Assign character values to character variables, integer values to integer variables, and real values to real variables.*

The following are examples of *invalid* C++ assignment statements. A reason is given for each to explain why it is not valid. The variables in these statements are assumed to have the types specified earlier.

Statement	Error
5 = number	A variable must appear on the left of the assignment operator.
xCoord + 3.5 = 2.7	Arithmetic expressions may not appear on the left of the assignment operator.
code = "ABC"	The value of a char variable is a single character.
number = "12" + "34"	"12" + "34" is not a valid expression.

 It is important to remember that *the assignment statement is a replacement statement*. Some beginning programmers forget this and write an assignment statement like

    a = b;

when the statement

    b = a;

is intended. These two statements produce very different results: The first assigns the value of b to a, leaving b unchanged, and the second assigns the value of a to b, leaving a unchanged.

```
a   8.5       a = b;      a   9.37
b   9.37    ──────────►   b   9.37

a   8.5       b = a;      a   8.5
b   9.37    ──────────►   b   8.5
```

To illustrate further the replacement property of an assignment, suppose that the integer variables alpha and beta have values 357 and 59, respectively, and that we wish to interchange these values. For this, we use an auxiliary integer variable temp to store the value of alpha while we assign beta's value to alpha; then we can assign this stored value to beta.

```
temp = alpha;
alpha = beta;
beta = temp;
```

```
alpha  357   temp =    alpha  357   alpha =   alpha   59   beta =    alpha   59
beta    59   alpha;    beta    59   beta;     beta    59   temp;     beta   357
temp     ?  ─────────► temp   357  ─────────► temp   357  ─────────► temp   357
```

Assignment as an Operation

We have seen that an assignment

```
variable = expression
```

produces three actions:

1. *expression* is evaluated, producing a value v
2. The value of `variable` is changed to v
3. The = operator produces the value v

Thus far in our discussion, we have concentrated on actions (1) and (2), but we now turn our attention to action (3) in this description.

Just as the expression

```
2 + 2
```

produces the value 4, the assignment

```
number = 4
```

is an expression that produces the value 4. The assignment operator = *is a binary infix operator whose result is the value assigned to the left operand.* For example, if the value of `number` is 4, then in the expression

```
number = number * 2
```

the * is applied first (the precedence of the = operator is lower than almost all other C++ operators),

```
number = (number * 2)
```

producing the result 8. That value is then assigned to `number`,

```
number = 8
```

which changes the value of `number` to 8, after which the = operator produces the result 8. *It is important to remember that = is a value-producing operator.*

Chaining Assignment Operators

Because = is a value-producing operator, several assignment operators may be chained together in a single statement such as

```
xCoord = yCoord = 2.5;
```

which is equivalent to the two separate statements

```
yCoord = 2.5;
xCoord = yCoord;
```

Unlike the arithmetic operators we have seen thus far, the assignment operator = is **right-associative,** hence in the statement

```
xCoord = yCoord = 2.5;
```

the rightmost = is applied first,

```
xCoord = (yCoord = 2.5);
```

which changes the value of yCoord to 2.5; and because this = operator produces the value assigned to yCoord (i.e., 2.5), the leftmost = is then applied using this value:

```
xCoord = 2.5
```

This changes the value of xCoord to 2.5, after which this = produces the assigned value 2.5 as its result.

Chained assignment operators can be used to assign a group of variables the same value; for example,

```
a = b = c = d = 1;
```

will set d to 1, c to 1, b to 1, and finally, a to 1. Similarly, in the statement

```
area = (length = 2.0) * (width = 2.5);
```

length is set to 2.0, width is set to 2.5, and area is set to the product (5.0) of the values produced by these assignments.

THE INCREMENT AND DECREMENT OPERATIONS

Algorithms often contain instructions of the form

"Increment *counter* by 1."

One way to encode this instruction in C++ is

```
counter = counter + 1;
```

Such a statement, in which the same variable appears on both sides of the assignment operator often confuses beginning programmers. Although we read English sentences from left to right, execution of this statement *begins to the right of the assignment operator,* so that:

1.   The expression counter + 1 is evaluated; and
2.   The resulting value is assigned to counter (overwriting its previous value).

For example, if counter has the value 16, then

1.   The value of counter + 1, 16 + 1 = 17, is computed; and
2.   This value is assigned as the new value for counter:

As we have seen, the old value of the variable is lost because it was replaced with a new value.

This kind of assignment (i.e., incrementing a variable) occurs so often that C++ provides a special unary **increment operator ++** for this operation.[18] It can be used as a postfix operator,

```
variableName++
```

or as a prefix operator,

```
++variableName
```

where *variableName* is an integer variable whose value is to be incremented by 1. Thus, the assignment statement

```
counter = counter + 1;
```

can also be written

```
counter++;
```

or

```
++counter;
```

The difference between the postfix and prefix use of the operator is subtle. To explain it, consider the following program segments where counter, number1, and number2 are int variables:

```
//POSTFIX:  Use first, then increment                    Output
counter = 10;
cout << "counter = " << counter << endl;                 counter = 10

number1 = counter++;
cout << "number1 = " << number1 << endl;                 number1 = 10
cout << "counter = " << counter << endl;                 counter = 11
```

and

```
//PREFIX:  Increment first, then use                     Output
counter = 10;
cout << "counter = " << counter << endl;                 counter = 10

number2 = ++counter;
cout << " number2 = " << number2 << endl;                number2 = 11
cout << "counter = " << counter << endl;                 counter = 11
```

Note that after execution of both sets of statements, the value of counter is 11. However, in the first set of assignments, the value assigned to number1 is 10, whereas in the second set of assignments, the value assigned to number2 is 11.

To understand this difference, we must remember that these increment expressions are assignment expressions and thus produce values. If counter has the value 10, then in the *prefix* expression

```
++counter
```

---

[18] The name C++ stems from this increment operator—C++ is C that has been incrementally improved.

counter is incremented (to 11), and *the value produced by the expression is the incremented value* (11). By contrast, if counter again has the value 10, then in the *postfix* expression

```
counter++
```

counter is still incremented (to 11), but *the value produced by the expression is the original value* (10). That is, the assignment

```
number2 = ++counter;
```

is equivalent to

```
counter = counter + 1;
number2 = counter;
```

By contrast, the assignment

```
number1 = counter++;
```

is equivalent to

```
number1 = counter;
counter = counter + 1;
```

It does not matter whether the prefix or postfix form is used if the increment operator is being used simply to increment a variable as a stand-alone statement:

```
counter++;
```

or

```
++counter;
```

Both of these statements produce exactly the same result; namely, the value of counter is incremented by 1.

Just as you can increment a variable's value with the ++ operator, you can decrement the value of a variable (i.e., subtract 1 from it) using the **decrement operator** (--), For example, the assignment statement

```
counter = counter - 1;
```

can be written more compactly as

```
counter--;
```

or

```
--counter;
```

The prefix and postfix versions of the decrement operator behave in a manner similar to the prefix and postfix versions of the increment operator.

OTHER ASSIGNMENT SHORTCUTS

The increment and decrement operations are special cases of a more general assignment that changes the value of a variable using some expression that involves its original value. For example, the pseudocode statement

"Add *counter* to *sum*"

implicitly changes the value of *sum* to the value of *sum + counter*. This can be encoded in C++ as

```
sum = sum + counter;
```

The following diagram illustrates this for the case in which the integer variables sum and counter have the values 120 and 16, respectively.

This operation occurs so frequently that C++ provides special operators for it. Instead of writing

```
sum = sum + counter;
```

we can write

```
sum += counter;
```

to accomplish the same thing.

Each of the arithmetic operators can be used in this way. For example, the statement

```
number = number / 2;
```

can be written

```
number /= 2;
```

In general, a statement of the form

```
alpha = alpha Δ beta;
```

can be written :

```
alpha Δ= beta;
```

where Δ is any of the operators +, -, *, /, or %. Each of the following is, therefore, an acceptable variation of the assignment operator:[19]

```
+=,      -=,      *=,      /=,      %=
```

Like the regular assignment operator, each of these is right-associative and produces the value assigned as its result. Thus, if xCoord has the value 4.0 and yCoord the value 2.5, then the statement

```
xCoord *= yCoord += 0.5;
```

---

[19] In addition to those listed here, the bitwise operators can be applied in this manner: <<=, >>=, &=, |=, ^=.

has the effect of:

1. Assigning yCoord the value 2.5 + 0.5 = 3.0, and then
2. Assigning xCoord the value 4.0 * 3.0 = 12.0.

    Chaining such operators together should normally be avoided so that the readability of the program does not suffer. Programs that are cleverly written but are difficult to read are of little use because they are too costly to maintain.

TRANSFORMING EXPRESSIONS INTO STATEMENTS — SEMICOLONS

We are finally ready to understand the meaning of the semicolon in C++. *An expression followed by a semicolon becomes an* **expression statement.** For example, in the statement

```
number = 2 + 2;
```

the following actions occur:

1. The expression 2 + 2 is evaluated, producing the value 4
2. The expression number = 4 is evaluated, which
    (a) Changes the value of number to 4
    (b) Produces the value 4
3. The semicolon terminates the statement, causing the value 4 (produced by the assignment operator) to be discarded

The semicolon can thus be thought of as an operator that causes the expression to its left to be evaluated and then discards the result of that expression.

Any C++ expression can become a statement simply by appending a semicolon. Thus,

```
'A';
```

and

```
sqrt(1.234);
```

and even

```
;
```

(where the expression is empty) are valid C++ statements; they just don't accomplish any useful work the way an assignment expression does.

Thinking of the semicolon this way gives a different insight into the behavior of an assignment statement:

```
variable = expression;
```

Such an assignment is really an expression that returns the value of *expression* and has the **side effect** of changing the value of *variable*.

A FINAL WORD

In a C++ program, *variables are undefined until their values have been explicitly specified* by a declaration initialization, an input statement, an assignment statement, or by one of the other statements discussed later.[20] The results of attempting to use undefined variables are unpredictable.

✔   **Quick Quiz 2.6**

Questions 1–15 assume that the following declarations have been made:

```
int m, n;
double pi;
char c;
```

Tell whether each is a valid C++ statement. If it is not valid, explain why it is not.

1. pi = 3.0;	**2.** 0 = n;	**3.** n = n + n;
4. n+n = n;	**5.** m = 1;	**6.** m = "1";
7. m = n = 1;	**8.** c = '65';	**9.** c = 65;
10. m = m;	**11.** pi = m;	**12.** m = pi;
13. m++;	**14.** m + n;	**15.** ++pi;

For questions 16–25, assume that the following declarations have been made:

```
int intEight = 8, intFive1 = 5, intFive2 = 5, jobId;
double two = 2.0, three = 3.0, four = 4.0, xValue;
char code = 'A', letter;
bool check;
```

Find the value assigned to the given variable or indicate why the statement is not valid.

16. xValue = three + two / four;

17. xValue = intEight / intFive1 + 5.1;

18. jobId = intEight / intFive1 + 5.1;

19. xValue = sqrt(three * three + four * four);

20. jobId = abs(three − 4.5);

21. jobId = intFive1++;

22. jobId = ++intFive2;

23. intEight *= 8;

24. letter = tolower(code);

25. check = isupper(code);

For each of questions 26-28, write a C++ assignment statement that calculates the given expression and assigns the result to the specified variable.

---

[20] Variables of storage class `auto` (see section 3.2) are undefined until explicitly given a value. However, variables of storage class `static` are automatically initialized to zero when the program is loaded into memory.

26. *rate* times *time* to *distance*   **27.** $\sqrt{a^2 + b^2}$ to *c*

28. Assuming that *x* is an integer variable, write four different statements that increment *x* by 1.

Exercises 2.6

Exercises 1–16 assume that `number` is an integer variable, `xValue` and `yValue` are real variables, and `grade` is a character variable. Tell whether each is a valid C++ statement. If it is not valid, explain why it is not.

1. `xValue = 2.71828;`   **2.** `3 = number;`

3. `grade = 'B+';`   **4.** `number = number + number;`

5. `xValue = 1;`   **6.** `grade = A;`

7. `number + 1 = number;`   **8.** `xValue = '1';`

9. `xValue = yValue = 3.2;`   **10.** `yValue = yValue;`

11. `xValue = 'A';`   **12.** `grade = grade + 10;`

13. `xValue /= yValue;`   **14.** `xValue = number;`

15. `number = yValue;`   **16.** `xValue = yValue++;`

For exercises 17–36, assume that the following declarations have been made:

```
int int1 = 16, int2 = 10, int3;
double real1 = 4.0, real2 = 6.0, real3 = 8.0, xCoord;
char numeral = '2', symbol;
bool check;
```

Find the value assigned to the given variable or indicate why the statement is not valid.

17. `xCoord = (real1 + real2) * real2;`

18. `xCoord = (real2 + real1 / real3) * 2;`

19. `xCoord = int1 / int2 + 5;`

20. `int3 = int1 / int2 + 5;`

21. `xCoord = pow(int2,2) / pow(int1,2);`

22. `int3 = pow(int2,2) / pow(int1,2);`

23. `symbol = 4;`

24. `symbol = numeral;`

25. `symbol = '4';`

26. `symbol = real3;`

27. `real1 = 2;`

28. `real1 = '2';`

29. `real1 = numeral;`

30. `int1 = int1 + 2;`

31. `int3 = 1 + numeral;`

32. `int3 = ceil(pow(int1 % int2, 2) / real3);`

33. `check = isdigit(numeral);`

34. `check = (int1 == 16);`

35. `check = (1 < int1 < 20);`

36. `check = (real1 > 5) || (real2 > 5);`

For each of exercises 37–41, write an assignment statement that changes the value of the integer variable `number` by the specified amount.

37. Increment `number` by 77.

38. Decrement `number` by 3.

39. Increment `number` by twice its value.

40. Add the rightmost digit of `number` to `number`.

41. Decrement `number` by the integer part of the real value `xCoord`.

For each of exercises 42–47, write a C++ assignment statement that calculates the given expression and assigns the result to the specified variable. Assume that all variables are of type `double`, except where otherwise noted.

42. `rate` times `time` to `distance`

43. `xCoord` incremented by an amount `deltaX` to `xCoord`

44.
$$\frac{1}{\dfrac{1}{res1} + \dfrac{1}{res2} + \dfrac{1}{res3}} \text{ to } \texttt{resistance}$$

45. Area of a triangle with a given `base` and `height` (one-half base times height) to `area`

46. The last three digits of the integer `stockNumber` with a decimal point before the last two digits to `price` (e.g., if `stockNumber` is 1758316, `price` is assigned the value 3.16)

47. `tax` rounded to the nearest dollar to `tax`.

For each of exercises 48–50, give values for the integer variables `a`, `b`, and `c` for which the two given expressions have different values:

48. `a * (b / c)` and `a * b / c`

49. `a / b` and `a * (1 / b)`

50. `(a + b) / c` and `a / c + b / c`

2.7 INPUT/OUTPUT EXPRESSIONS

In many high-level languages, values are input to a program by using an input statement, often some kind of *Read* statement; and values are output by using some kind of *Print or Write* statement or some other output statement. In C++, however, input and output are carried out using special input and output operators. Thus, to perform input, we write an input expression; to perform output, we write an output expression. In this section we will take a first look at input/output; a more complete discussion is given in chapters 4 and 8.

I/O STREAMS

C++ avoids the nitty-gritty details about how I/O is actually carried out on any particular machine by dealing with **streams,** which connect an executing program with an input/output device. When characters are entered from the keyboard, they enter an input stream called an `istream` that transmits the characters from the keyboard to the program. Similarly, when output is to be displayed by a program on the screen, the output characters are placed in an output stream called an `ostream` that transmits the characters to the monitor.[21]

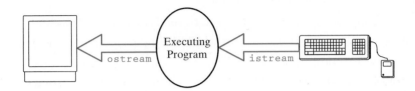

C++ has no input or output facilities built into the language. Instead, `istreams` and `ostreams` are provided by a special library `iostream`. This library defines three important data objects:

▸ An `istream` object named `cin`, which is associated with the *keyboard*

▸ An `ostream` object named `cout`, which is associated with the *monitor*

▸ An `ostream` object named `cerr`, which is associated with the *monitor,* and is used to display error messages

Input and output are operations on these data objects.

INPUT EXPRESSIONS

The program in Figure 2.1 contains the input statement

```
cin >> mass;
```

where `mass` is a real variable. We have seen that `cin` is the name of the `istream` data object defined in `iostream`, but what is the purpose of the `>>`? The answer is that it is the operator that performs the input operation. Just as the expression

```
x + 2
```

consists of the *addition* operator (+) and two operands (x and 2), and

```
y = 1
```

consists of the *assignment* operator (=) and two operands (y and 1),

```
cin >> mass
```

is an input expression in which the **input** (or **extraction**) **operator >>** is applied to the two operands `cin` and `mass`. That is, the `>>` symbol is a binary operator that acts as follows:

---

[21] The names `istream` and `ostream` are not a part of the C++ language but are the names of two *classes* (see section 4.3). The ability to develop an entire I/O system using classes provides some indication of their powerful capabilities.

Input Expression

Form:

input_stream >> *variable*

where:

input_stream is the name of any declared C++ input stream; and

variable is any C++ variable for which the input operator >> is defined.

Behavior:

1. A value *v* is read from *input_stream*. (If there is none, program execution is suspended until one is entered.)
2. The value *v* is shifted from *input_stream* into *variable*.
3. The >> operator produces the value *input_stream*.

The >> operator is *left-associative*, which, along with part 3 of its behavior, allows input expressions to be chained together. For example,

```
cin >> x >> y;
```

is evaluated as

```
(cin >> x) >> y;
```

in the following manner:

1.   The next value is read from `cin` (if none is present, program execution is suspended until a value is entered), and the >> operator produces the value `cin`, giving

     ```
     cin >> y;
     ```

2.   The next value is read from `cin` (if none is present, program execution is suspended until a value is entered), and the >> operator produces the value `cin`, giving

     ```
     cin;
     ```

3.   The expression `cin` is evaluated and discarded by the semicolon

Note that just as a semicolon serves to make an assignment expression into an assignment statement, a semicolon serves to make an input expression into an input statement. We can thus describe a typical C++ (interactive) input statement as follows:

> ## C++ Interactive Input Statement
>
> **Form:**
>
> cin >> *variable*₁ >> *variable*₂ >> ⋯ >> *variable*ₙ;
>
> where:
>
> cin is the istream declared in iostream;
>
> >> is the input operator; and
>
> each *variable*ᵢ is a variable for which >> is defined.
>
> **Purpose:**
>
> Execution of an input statement reads a sequence of n values from the input device with which cin is associated, storing them in *variable*₁, *variable*₂, ..., *variable*ₙ.

Note that the user must enter a value (of the appropriate type) for each variable in the statement before execution of the program will resume. Thus, if side1, side2, and side3 are real variables, the statement

```
cin >> side1 >> side2 >> side3;
```

is executed, and the user enters the values

```
2.0 3.0
```

then execution will not resume until the user enters a third value:

```
4.0
```

The first value is then stored in the first variable, the second value in the second variable, and so on. In our example, the value of side1 will be 2.0, the value of side2 will be 3.0, and the value of side3 will be 4.0. Program execution then resumes. Any **white space** (spaces, tabs, or newlines) can be used to separate input values. For example, the user could separate the values with newlines by entering each data item on a separate line,

```
2.0
3.0
4.0
```

and produce the same result.

Because execution is suspended and because the correct number and types of values must be entered before execution can resume, *it is good practice to provide an informative message to prompt the user whenever it is necessary to enter data values.* This is accomplished by preceding input statements with output statements that display appropriate prompts; for example,

```
cout << "Enter the three sides of the triangle: ";
```

We turn now to a study of such output statements.

There is a natural correspondence between C++ input and output statements. To illustrate, consider the input statement

```
cin >> mass;
```

and the output statement

```
cout << "Enter a mass (in kilograms): ";
```

Just as `cin` is the name of an `istream` data object, `cout` is the name of an `ostream` data object defined in `iostream`. Just as `>>` is the `istream` input (or extraction) operator, `<<` is the `ostream` **output** (or **insertion**) **operator.** And, just as the expression

```
cin >> mass
```

performs the *input* operation (`>>`) using two operands (`cin` and `mass`), the expression

```
cout << "Enter a mass (in kilograms): "
```

performs the *output* operation (`<<`) using two operands (`cout` and `"Enter a mass (in kilograms): "`. The `<<` symbol is a binary operator that behaves as follows:

Output Expression

Form:

output_stream `<<` *expression*

where:

output_stream is the name of any declared C++ output stream, and *expression* is any C++ expression for which `<<` is defined.

Behavior:

1.   *expression* is evaluated, producing a value *v*.
2.   The value of *v* is shifted into *output_stream*.
3.   The `<<` operator produces the value *output_stream*.

Like `>>`, the `<<` operator is *left-associative,* which, along with part 3 of its behavior, allows output expressions to be chained together. Thus,

```
cout << "Perimeter = " << side1 + side2 + side3 << endl;
```

is evaluated as

```
((cout << "Perimeter = ") << side1 + side2 + side3) << endl;
```

and its behavior is thus as follows:

1. The expression `"Perimeter = "` is evaluated and inserted into `cout`, and the `<<` operator produces the value `cout`, giving

   ```
   cout << side1 + side2 + side3 << endl;
   ```

2. The expression `side1 + side2 + side3` is evaluated and shifted onto `cout`, and the `<<` operator produces the value `cout`, giving

   ```
   cout << endl;
   ```

3. The expression `endl` is evaluated and shifted onto `cout`, and the `<<` operator produces the value `cout`, giving

   ```
   cout;
   ```

4. The expression `cout` is evaluated and discarded by the semicolon

We can thus describe a typical C++ (interactive) output statement as follows:

C++ Interactive Output Statement

Form:

   ```
   cout << expr₁ << expr₂ << ··· << exprₙ;
   ```

where:

   `cout` is the `ostream` declared in `ostream`;

   `<<` is the output operator; and

   each $expr_i$ is a C++ expression for which `<<` is defined.

Purpose:

Execution of an output statement displays the values of $expr_1, expr_2, \ldots,$ $expr_n$ on the output device with which `cout` is associated.

For example, the statement

```
cout << side1 << ' ' << side2 << '\n' << side3 << '\n';
```

displays the values of `side1` and `side2` on one line and the value of `side3` on the next line. Subsequent output would begin on yet another line.

Note that if white space is to appear in the output, it must be specified explicitly. For example, if the values of the integer variables a and b are 2 and 3, respectively, then the output statement

```
cout << "The sum of" << a << "and" << b
     << "is" << a + b << endl;
```

will display the output

```
The sum of2and3is5
```

whereas the output statement

```
cout << "The sum of " << a << " and " << b
     << " is " << a + b;
```

will display

```
The sum of 2 and 3 is 5
```

Newline escape sequences must be used to cause values being displayed to appear on separate lines. For example, the output statement

```
cout << "Rats\nSnails\n\nPuppy Dog Tails\n";
```

will display the output

```
Rats
Snails

Puppy Dog Tails
```

EXAMPLE: CALCULATING WAGES

The program in Figure 2.2 calculates wages for an employee. It uses output statements to prompt the user and display results, as well as input statements to enter values from the keyboard.

 FIGURE 2.2   CALCULATING WAGES—VERSION 1.

```
/* wages2.cpp computes the wages of an employee.
 *
 * Input:    The employee's number, the hours worked, and hourly rate
 * Output:   The employee's number, hours worked, hourly rate, and
 *           total wages
 ***********************************************************************/

#include <iostream.h>                 // cin, cout, <<, >>

int main()
{
   cout << "Enter the employee number: ";

   int empNumber;                     // employee number

   cin >> empNumber;

   cout << "Enter the hours worked and the pay rate: ";

   double hours,                      // hours worked by employee
          rate;                       // employee's hourly rate

   cin >> hours >> rate;

   double wages = hours * rate;       // gross wages earned by employee
```

```
cout << "\nEmployee #" << empNumber
     << "\nHours Worked: " << hours
     << "\nHourly Rate: $" << rate
     << "\nTotal Wages: $" << wages << endl;

    return 0;
}
```

Sample run:

```
Enter the employee number: 31564

Enter the hours worked, and the pay rate: 38.5 8.75

Employee #31564
Hours Worked: 38.5
Hourly Rate: $8.75
Total Wages: $336.875
```

OUTPUT FORMATTING

The output produced by the preceding program is not really satisfactory because the real values are displayed with a precision that is not suitable for monetary values. This can be remedied by inserting **format manipulators** into the output list, which specify the appearance of the output. A few manipulators are given here; a more complete description of the capabilities provided by the `iostream` and `iomanip` libraries can be found in section 4.3 and in chapter 8.[22]

Format Manipulators

Manipulators:	Description:
From `iostream`:	
`showpoint`	Display decimal point and trailing zeros for all real numbers

---

[22] Compilers that are not fully ANSI-C++ compliant may not support the use of format manipulators from `iostream` as described here. The `boolalpha` manipulator may not be provided, and it may be necessary to include `<iomanip.h>` and use `setiosflags(flag1 | flag2 | ...)` in the output statement where each `flagi` is one of `ios::fixed`, `ios::showpoint`, `ios::right`, and so on. For example,

```
cout << setiosflags(ios::showpoint | ios::fixed | ios::right) << ...
```

You may also have to use `resetiosflags(flagi)` to reset the `ostream` to a default value. See chapter 8 for more details.

`noshowpoint`	Hide decimal point and trailing zeros for whole real numbers (default)
`fixed`	Use fixed-point notation for real values
`scientific`	Use scientific notation for real values
`boolalpha`	Display boolean values as strings "true" and "false"
`left`	Display values left justified within a field
`right`	Display values right justified within a field (default)

From `iomanip`:

`setw(w)`	Display the next value in a field of size w (default 1)
`setprecision(p)`	Display p fractional digits for all subsequent output of real values (common default is 6)

Purpose:

When inserted into an output list, these format manipulators specify the appearance of the output (i.e., its format) of subsequent items in the list.

Note: `setw()` applies to only the next output item; the other format manipulators apply to all subsequent items in output statements.

To illustrate the use of format manipulators, consider the statements

```
double alpha = 8.0 / 3.0,
       beta = 9.0 / 3.0;

cout << '(' << alpha << ")\n" << '(' << beta << ")\n";
```

While the default format depends on the particular C++ implementation, the output displayed by these statements might appear as

```
(2.666667)
(3)
```

Using the `showpoint` manipulator will cause the decimal point and trailing zeros of `beta` to be displayed, and using the `fixed` manipulator will ensure that values are displayed in fixed-point (rather than scientific) form,

```
cout << showpoint << fixed
     << '(' << alpha << ") \n" << '(' << beta << ")\n";
```

which will cause the output to appear as

```
(2.66667)
(3.00000)
```

If we wish to alter the precision to display only three decimal places, we can insert the `setprecision()` manipulator from the `iomanip` library

```
cout << showpoint << fixed
     << setprecision(3)
     << '(' << alpha << ")\n" << '(' << beta << ")\n";
```

which will alter the output as follows:

```
(2.667)
(3.000)
```

Similarly, we can use the `setw()` manipulator from `iomanip` to change the width of the field in which an output value appears:

```
cout << showpoint << fixed
     << setprecision(3)
     << '(' << setw(10) << alpha << ")\n"
     << '(' << alpha << ")\n" << '(' << beta << ")\n";
```

Here, the number of positions (5) required to display the value of `alpha` is now smaller than the width of the field (10) being used to display it. If values are left justified in their fields, the output will appear as

```
(2.667     )
(3.000)
```

and if they are right justified, it will be

```
(     2.667)
(3.000)
```

To specify the justification, we can use the `left` and `right` manipulators. For example,

```
cout << showpoint << fixed << right
     << setprecision(3)
     << '(' << setw(10) << alpha << ")\n"
     << '(' << alpha << ")\n" << '(' << beta << ")\n";
```

will produce the latter output.

The `setw()` and `right` manipulators can be used to align right-justified values in a column. For example, inserting another `setw()` before outputting `beta`

```
cout << showpoint << fixed << right
     << setprecision(3)
     << '(' << setw(10) << alpha << ")\n"
     << '(' << setw(10) << beta << ")\n";
```

changes the output to

```
(     2.667)
(     3.000)
```

It is important that you note the difference between `setw()` and the other manipulators. `setw()` *affects the format of only the next value to be displayed, whereas the other manipulators affect the appearances of all values that follow.*
We noted earlier that the output produced by the program in Figure 2.2 is not really satisfactory. Figure 2.3 shows how format manipulators can be used to display the results in a more acceptable format.

 FIGURE 2.3   CALCULATING WAGES — VERSION 2.

```
/* wages3.cpp computes the wages of an employee.
       .
       .
       .

#include <iostream.h>          // cin, cout, <<, >>, fixed, showpoint
#include <iomanip.h>           // setprecision(), setw()

int main()
{
          .
          .
          .

   cout << "\nEmployee #" << empNumber
        << setprecision(2)        // precision for money values
        << showpoint << fixed     // force fixed point and .00 to display
        << right                  // and right justify
        << "\nHours Worked: " << setw(7) << hours
        << "\nHourly Rate: $" << setw(7) << rate
        << "\nTotal Wages: $" << setw(7) << wages
        << "\n\n";

   return 0;
}
```

Sample run:

```
Enter the employee number: 31564

Enter the hours worked, and the pay rate: 38.5 8.75

Employee #31564
Hours Worked:   38.50
Hourly Rate: $   8.75
Total Wages: $ 336.88
```

2.8 EXAMPLE: TRUCK FLEET ACCOUNTING

PROBLEM

Suppose that a manufacturing company maintains a fleet of trucks to deliver its products. On each trip, the driver records the distance traveled in miles, the number of gallons of fuel used, the cost of the fuel, and other costs of operating the truck. As part of the accounting process, the controller needs to calculate and record for each truck and for each trip the miles per gallon, the total cost of that trip, and the cost per mile. A simple program is to be designed to assist the controller in performing these calculations for a given trip.

 OBJECT-CENTERED DESIGN

Behavior.   The program should display on the screen a prompt for the distance traveled in miles, the number of gallons of fuel used, the cost per gallon of the fuel, and the per-mile cost of operating the truck. The program should read these values from the keyboard. The program should then calculate and display the truck's mileage (in miles per gallon), the total cost of the trip, and the cost per mile.

Objects.   From the behavioral description, we can identify the following objects:

Description	Type	Kind	Name
screen	`ostream`	variable	`cout`
total miles traveled	`double`	variable	*miles*
total gallons of fuel used	`double`	variable	*gallonsOfFuel*
cost per gallon of fuel	`double`	variable	*unitFuelCost*
operating cost per mile	`double`	variable	*unitOperatingCost*
keyboard	`istream`	variable	`cin`
miles per gallon	`double`	variable	*milesPerGallon*
total cost of the trip	`double`	variable	*totalTripCost*
cost per mile	`double`	variable	*costPerMile*

Operations.   From the behavioral description, we can identify the following operations:

  i.   Display a prompt for input on the screen
  ii.   Read a sequence of four real values from the keyboard
  iii.   Compute the number of miles driven per gallon
       — Divide the number of miles traveled by the number of gallons of fuel used
  iv.   Compute the total cost of the trip
       — Compute the cost of fuel: multiply gallons used by price per gallon
       — Compute the operating costs: multiply miles driven by cost per mile and then add these two products

    v. Compute the cost of the trip per mile
       — Divide the total cost of the trip by the number of miles traveled

    vi. Output three real values

Solving this problem thus requires only the standard C++ arithmetic and I/O operations. Note that the problem assumes that all of the input values are positive, making this a *precondition* for the problem.

Algorithm.   Organizing these operations into an algorithm gives the following. Note that we have used two new objects, *fuelCost* and *operatingCost* in calculating *totalTripCost.*

Algorithm for Truck Cost Problem

1. Display a prompt via `cout` for *miles, gallonsOfFuel, unitFuelCost,* and *unitOperatingCost.*

2. Read values from `cin` into *miles, gallonsOfFuel, unitFuelCost,* and *unitOperatingCost.*

3. Check that each of these values is positive.

4. Compute *milesPerGallon = miles / gallonsOfFuel.*

5. Compute *fuelCost = gallonsOfFuel * unitFuelCost.*

6. Compute *operatingCost = unitOperatingCost * miles.*

7. Compute *totalTripCost = fuelCost + operatingCost.*

8. Compute *costPerMile = totalTripCost / miles.*

9. Via `cout`, display *milesPerGallon, totalTripCost* and *costPerMile,* with descriptive labels.

Coding and Testing.   A C++ implemention of this algorithm and two sample runs are shown in Figure 2.4:

 FIGURE 2.4   TRUCKING COSTS.

```
/* truck4.cpp calculates the total cost and miles per gallon
 * of a vehicle, based on the miles traveled, fuel consumed,
 * cost per gallon of fuel, and operating cost per mile.
 *
 * Input: The total miles traveled, total fuel consumed,
 *        unit cost of the fuel, and operating cost per mile.
 * Precondition: miles, gallonsOfFuel, unitFuelCost and
 *        unitOperatingCost are all positive.
 * Output: The miles per gallon, total cost of the trip
 *        and the cost per mile.
 ******************************************************************/

#include <iostream.h>        // cin, cout, <<, >>, fixed, showpoint
#include <iomanip.h>         // setw(), setprecision()
#include <assert.h>
```

```
int main()
{
   const int WIDTH = 7;                          // width of output field

   cout << "Enter:\n\ttotal miles traveled,"
        << "\n\tgallons of fuel used,"
        << "\n\ttotal cost per gallon of the fuel, and"
        << "\n\toperating cost per mile."
        << "\n\t---> ";

   double miles,                                 // total miles traveled
          gallonsOfFuel,                         // total gallons used
          unitFuelCost,                          // fuel cost per gallon
          unitOperatingCost;                     // operating cost per mile

   cin >> miles >> gallonsOfFuel
       >> unitFuelCost >> unitOperatingCost;

   assert(miles > 0 && gallonsOfFuel > 0 &&
          unitFuelCost > 0 && unitOperatingCost > 0);

   double milesPerGallon = miles / gallonsOfFuel,
          fuelCost = unitFuelCost * gallonsOfFuel,
          operatingCost = unitOperatingCost * miles,
          totalTripCost = fuelCost + operatingCost,
          costPerMile = totalTripCost / miles;

   cout << showpoint << fixed << setprecision(2)
        << "\n\tMiles per gallon: " << setw(WIDTH) << milesPerGallon
        << "\n\tTotal cost:       $" << setw(WIDTH) << totalTripCost
        << "\n\tCost per mile:    $" << setw(WIDTH) << costPerMile
        << endl << endl;
}
```

Sample runs:

```
Enter:
   total miles traveled,
   gallons of fuel used,
   total cost per gallon of the fuel, and
   operating cost per mile.
   ---> 10 1 1.50 3.50

Miles per gallon:   10.00
Total cost:       $ 36.50
Cost per mile:    $  3.50
```

```
Enter:
    the total miles traveled,
    the gallons of fuel used,
    the total cost per gallon of the fuel, and
    the operating cost per mile.
    ---> 100 10 15 10

Miles per gallon:    10.00
Total cost:        $1150.00
Cost per mile:     $  11.50
```

✔ Quick Quiz 2.8

1. In C++, input and output are carried out using _____, which connect an executing program with an input/output device.

2. (True or false) C++ has no input or output facilities built into the language.

3. _____ is the stream object associated with the keyboard; its type is _____.

4. _____ and _____ are stream objects associated with the monitor; their type is _____.

5. The input operator is _____.

6. The output operator is _____.

7. The value produced by the input expression `cin >> x` is _____.

8 The value produced by the output expression `cout << x` is _____.

9. The input and output operators are (left or right) _____ associative.

10. _____ can be inserted into an output list to format the output of items.

Questions 11–13 assume the declarations

```
int number = 123;
double rate = 23.45678;
```

For each, show precisely the output that the set of statements produces, indicating blanks with ⊔, or explain why an error occurs.

11. `cout << number << rate << endl;`

12. `cout << '\n' << setw(5) << number << number + 1`
       `<< setw(5) << number + 2`
       `<< setw(1) << number + 4 << endl;`

13. `cout << showpoint << fixed`
       `<< setw(8) << setprecision(0) << rate << endl`
       `<< setw(8) << setprecision(1) << rate << endl`
       `<< setw(8) << setprecision(2) << rate << endl`
       `<< setw(8) << rate << endl`
       `<< setprecision(1) << rate << endl;`

Questions 14–17 assume the declarations

```
int number1, number2, number3;
double real1, real2, real3;
```

For each, tell what value, if any, will be assigned to each variable, or explain
why an error occurs, when the statement is executed with the given input data:

14. `cin >> number1 >> number2 >> number3;`   **Input**   11 22
                                                              33 44

15. `cin >> real1 >> real2 >> real3;`   **Input**   1.1 2 3.3 4

16. `cin >> number1 >> number2 >> number3;`   **Input**   1.1 2 3.3 4

17. `cin >> number1 >> real1 >> number2`   **Input**   1.1 2
`>> real2 >> number3 >> real3;`   3.3 4
                                                           5.5 6

EXERCISES 2.8

Exercises 1–8 assume the declarations

```
double alpha = -567.392, beta = 0.0004;
int rho = 436;
```

For each, show precisely the output that each of the statements produces, indicating blanks
with ⊔, or explain why an error occurs.

1. `cout << rho << rho + 1 << rho + 2;`

2. `cout << "alpha ="`
`<< setw(9) << setprecision(3) << alpha << endl`
`<< setw(10) << setprecision(5) << beta << endl`
`<< setw(7) << setprecision(4) << beta << endl;`

3. `cout << setprecision(1) << setw(8) << alpha << endl`
`<< setw(5) << rho << endl`
`<< "Tolerance:"`
`<< setw(8) << setprecision(5) << beta << endl;`

4. `cout << "alpha =" << setw(12) << setprecision(5)`
`<< alpha << endl`
`<< "beta =" << setw(6) << setprecision(2)`
`<< beta << endl`
`<< "rho =" << setw(6) << rho << endl`
`<< setw(15) << setprecision(3)`
`<< alpha + 4.0 + rho << endl;`

5. `cout << "Tolerance =" << setw(5)`
`<< setprecision(3) << beta;`
`cout << setw(2) << rho << setw(4) << alpha;`

6. `cout << setw(8) << setprecision(1) << 10 * alpha`
`<< setw(8) << ceil(10 * alpha);`
`cout << setprecision(3) << setw(5) << pow(rho / 100, 2.0)`
`<< setw(5) << sqrt(rho / 100);`

7. `cout << "rho =" << setw(8) << setprecision(2) << rho`
`<< "*****";`

8. `cout << setw(10) << alpha << setw(10) << beta;`

For Exercises 9 and 10, assume the declarations

```
int i = 15, j = 8;
char c = 'c', d = '-';
double x = 2559.50, y = 8.015;
```

Show precisely the output that each of the statements produces; indicate blanks with ⊔.

9.   cout << setw(j) << setprecision(2) <<   "new balance ="
         << x << ' ' <<   setw(i % 10) << c
         << setw(j) << setprecision(j-6) << y;

10. cout << "i =" << setw(i) << i
         << "j =" << setw(j) << setprecision(j) << j << endl
         << setw(j) << i << ' '
         << setw(i) << j;

For Exercises 11–14, assume the declarations

```
int n1 = 39, n2 = -5117;
char c = 'F';
double r1 = 56.7173, r2 = -0.00247;
```

For each exercise, write output statements that use these variables to produce the given output:

11.   __56.7173___F___39
          -5117PDQ-0.00247__

12.   __56.717_____-0.0025***39__F
          ____56.72__39-5117_____

13.   Roots_are__56.717_and_-0.00247

14.   Approximate_angles:__56.7_and_-0.0
          Magnitudes_are_____39_and__5117___

For exercises 15–21, assume that a, b, and c are integer variables and x, y, and z are real variables. Tell what value, if any, will be assigned to each of these variables, or explain why an error occurs, when the input statements are executed with the given input data:

15. cin >> a >> b >> c   Input: 1   2   3
              >> x >> y >> z;   4 5.5 6.6

16. cin >> a >> b >> c;   Input: 1
         cin >> x >> y >> z;   2
                                             3
                                             4
                                             5
                                             6

17. cin >> a >> x;   Input: 1 2.2
         cin >> b >> y;   3 4.4
         cin >> c >> z;   5 6.6

18. cin >> a >> b >> c;   Input: 1 2.2
         cin >> x >> y >> z;   3 4.4
                                              5 6.6

19. cin >> a;   Input: 1   2   3
         cin >> b >> c;   4 5.5 6.6
         cin >> x >> y;
         cin >> z;

20. `cin >> a`   Input: 1   2   3
        `>> b >> c`   4   5.5   6.6
        `>> x >> y`
        `>> z;`

21. `cin >> a >> b;`   Input: 1   2   3
        `cin >> c >> x >> y >> z;`   4   5.5   6.6
                                                7   8.8   9.9
                                               10   11.11   12.12
                                               13   14.14   15.15

☞ PROGRAMMING POINTERS

In this section we consider some aspects of program design and suggest guidelines for good programming style. We also point out some errors that may occur in writing C++ programs.

✍ PROGRAM STYLE AND DESIGN

1. In the examples in this text, we adopt certain stylistic guidelines for C++ programs, and you should write your program in a similar style. In this text we use the following standards; others are described in the Programming Pointers of subsequent chapters.

▶ *Put each statement of the program on a separate line.*

▶ *Use uppercase and lowercase letters in a way that contributes to program readability;* for example, put identifiers in lowercase, capitalizing the first letter of each word after the first.

▶ *Put each* { *and* } *on a separate line.*

▶ *Align each* { *and its corresponding* }. *Indent the statements enclosed by* { *and* }.

▶ *When a statement is continued from one line to another, indent the continued line(s).*

▶ *Align the identifiers in each constant and variable declaration, placing each on a separate line;*

for example,

```
const double taxRate = 0.1963,
             interestRate = 0.185;

int empNumber;

double hours,
       rate,
       wages;
```

▶ *Insert blank lines between declarations and statements and between blocks of statements to make clear the structure of the program.*

▶ *Separate the operators and operands in an expression with spaces to make the expression easy to read.*

▶ *Declare constants at the beginning of a function, and declare variables near their first use.* This makes it easy to find constants when they must be modified. It also reduces the tendency to declare unused variables, since declarations are deferred until they are needed.

2. *Programs cannot be considered to be correct if they have not been tested.* Test all programs with data for which the results are known or can be checked by hand calculations.

3. *Programs should be readable and understandable.*

▶ *Use meaningful identifiers.* For example,

```
wages = hours * rate;
```

is more meaningful than

```
w = h * r;
```

or

```
z7 = alpha * x;
```

Also, avoid "cute" identifiers, as in

```
baconBroughtHome = hoursWasted * pittance;
```

▶ *Use comments to describe the purpose of a program or other key program segments.* However, do not clutter the program with needless comments; for example, the comment in the statement

```
counter++;     // add 1 to counter
```

is not helpful and should not be used.

▶ *Label all output produced by a program.* For example,

```
cout << "Employee # " << empNumber
     << "  Wages = $" << wages;
```

produces more informative output than

```
cout << empNumber << wages;
```

4. *Programs should be general and flexible.* They should solve a class of problems rather than one specific problem. It should be relatively easy to modify a program to solve a related problem without changing much of the program. Using named constants instead of "magic numbers," as described in section 2.2, is helpful in this regard.

5. *Identify any preconditions a program has, and check them using the* assert() *mechanism.* Preconditions are assumptions made in a program, often one or more restrictions on what comprises a valid input value. The assert() mechanism evaluates a boolean expression and terminates the program if it is false. Identify the preconditions in a problem and use assert() to check them.

⚡ POTENTIAL PROBLEMS

1. *Character constants must be enclosed in single quotes.* In particular,

▶ *Character string constants cannot be assigned to variables of type* `char`. **For example, the declaration**

```
char ch = "x";
```

is not valid.

2. *Values of type* `char` *are stored as their (integer) numeric codes.* This can be confusing, since strange things like the following are allowed in C++:

```
char letterGrade = 65;
```

On machines using the ASCII character set, this causes `LetterGrade` to have exactly the same value as if it had been initialized to `'A'` (since 65 is the decimal ASCII code for `'A'`). Such mixing of integer and character values within an expression should normally be avoided.

3. *Character string constants must be enclosed within double quotes.* If either the beginning or the ending double quote is missing, an error will result. Escape sequences, such as `\"`, are used to represent double quotes, single quotes, tabs, newlines, etc.

4. *The type of value stored in a variable should be the same as or promotable to the type of that variable.*

5. *If an integer value is to be stored in a real variable, most implementations will automatically promote the integer to a real type. By contrast, if a real value is to be stored in an integer variable, then the real value is truncated, possibly resulting in the loss of information.*

6. *Parentheses in expressions must be paired.* That is, for each left parenthesis, there must be exactly one matching right parenthesis that occurs later in the expression.

7. *Both real and integer division are denoted by /; which operation is performed is determined by the type of the operands. Thus,* `8 / 5 = 1`, but `8.0 / 5.0 = 1.6`.

8. *All multiplications must be indicated by* `*`. For example, `2*n` is valid, but `2n` is not.

9. *A semicolon must appear at the end of each expression (assignments, input, output, etc.) that is meant to be a programming statement.*

10. *Comments are enclosed within* `/*` *and* `*/` *or between* `//` *and the end of the line.* Be sure that:

▶ *Each beginning delimiter* `/*` *has a matching end delimiter* `*/`. Failure to use these in pairs can produce strange results. For example, in the program segment

```
/* Read employee data
cin >> empNumber >> hours >> rate;
/* Calculate wages */
wages = hours * rate;
```

everything from "Read employee data . . ." through "Calculate wages," including the input statement, is a single comment. No values are read for `empNumber`, `hours`, and `rate`, and so `hours` and `rate` are undefined when the statement `wages = hours * rate;` is executed.

▶ *There is no space between the / and the * or between the two slashes.* Otherwise these pairs will not be considered to be comment delimiters.

11. *Every* `{` *must be matched by a* `}`. Failure to include either one produces a compilation error.

12. *All identifiers must be declared.* Attempting to use an identifier that has not been declared will produce a compilation error. In this connection, remember that:

▸ *C++ distinguishes between uppercase and lowercase letters.* For example, declaring

```
double sumOfXValues;
```

and then later in the program writing

```
sumOfXvalues += X;
```

causes a compile-time error since the identifier `sumOfXvalues` has not been declared.

13. *Variables should be initialized at their declarations, unless they are going to be immediately changed by an input or assignment statement;* in this case there is little point in giving it an initial value, since that value will be overwritten by the input value. Other variables should be initialized appropriately, since the value of an uninitialized variable is *undefined.* This means that it is not possible to predict the contents of the memory location associated with a variable until a value has been explicitly assigned to that variable. For example, the statements

```
int x, y;
    . . .
y = x + 1;
```

will produce a "garbage" value for y, since x has not previously been initialized or assigned a value, as in

```
int x = 0, y;
    . . .
y = x + 1;
```

14. *Keywords, identifiers, and constants may not be broken at the end of a line, nor may they contain blanks (except, of course, a string constant may contain blanks).* Thus, the statements

```
empNumber = 12345;
cout << "The number of the current employee is "
     << empNumber;
```

are valid, whereas the statements

```
empNumber = 12 345;
cout << "The number of the current employee
        is " << empNumber;
```

are not valid. If it is necessary to split a string over two lines, as in the second statement, the string should be split into two separate strings, each enclosed in double quotes, and placed as consecutive items in the output list,

```
cout << "The number of the current employee "
        "is " << empNumber;
```

or separated by the output operator,

```
cout << "The number of the current employee "
     << "is " << empNumber;
```

or placed in separate output statements:

```
cout << "The number of the current employee ";
cout << "is " << empNumber;
```

15. *Use parentheses in complex expressions to indicate those subexpressions that are to be evaluated first.* The precedence of the operators used thus far is as follows:

`!`	Highest (performed first)
`/, *, %`	
`+, -`	
`<<, >>`	
`<, >, <=, >=`	
`==, !=`	
`&&`	
`||`	
`=, +=, *=,` etc.	Lowest (performed last)

However, there are so many operators in C++ (these are fewer than half of those available), that remembering their precedence levels is difficult. For this reason, we recommend using parentheses in complex expressions to specify clearly the order in which the operators are to be applied.

16. *When real quantities that are algebraically equal are compared with* `==`, *the result may be a false boolean expression, because most real numbers are not stored exactly.* For example, even though the two real expressions `x * (1/x)` and `1.0` are algebraically equal, the boolean expression `x * (1/x) == 1.0` may be false for some real numbers `x`.

17. *One of the most common errors in writing boolean expressions is to use an assignment operator* (`=`) *when an equality operator* (`==`) *is intended.* For example, if `x` is an integer variable, the statements

```
cin >> x;
bool isOne = (x = 1);          // should be (x == 1)
```

will assign `true` to `isOne` regardless of what value is input for `x`, because `x = 1` assigns 1 to `x` and produces the value 1, which is interpreted as true.

Programming Problems

1. Write a program that reads two three-digit integers, and then calculates and displays their product and the quotient and the remainder that result when the first is divided by the second. The output should be formatted to appear as follows:

```
   739              61 R    7
                  -----
x   12        12 ) 739
-----
 8868
```

2. Write a program to read the lengths of the two legs of a right triangle, and to calculate and display the area of the triangle (one-half the product of the legs) and the length of the hypotenuse (square root of the sum of the squares of the legs).

3. Write a program to read values for the coefficients a, b, and c of the quadratic equation $ax^2 + bx + c = 0$, and then find the two roots of this equation by using the quadratic formula

$$\frac{-b \pm \sqrt{b^2 - 4ac}}{2a}$$

Execute the program with several values of a, b, and c for which the quantity $b^2 - 4ac$ is nonnegative, including $a = 4$, $b = 0$, $c = -36$; $a = 1$, $b = 5$, $c = -36$; and $a = 2, b = 7.5, c = 6.25$.

4. Write a program to convert a measurement given in feet to the equivalent number of **(a)** yards, **(b)** inches, **(c)** centimeters, and **(d)** meters (1 ft = 12 in, 1 yd = 3 ft, 1 in = 2.54 cm, 1 m = 100 cm). Read the number of feet, number of inches, number of centimeters, and number of meters.

5. Write a program to read a student's number, his or her old grade point average, and the old number of course credits (e.g., 31479, 3.25, 66), and to then print these with appropriate labels. Next, read the course credit and grade for each of four courses— for example, `course1Credits = 5.0`, `course1Grade = 3.7`, `course2Cred-its = 3.0`, `course2Grade = 4.0`, and so on. Calculate:

old # of honor points = (old # of course credits) * (old GPA)

new # of honor points = `course1Credits * course1Grade +`
`course2Credits * course2Grade + ···`

total # of new course credits = `course1Credits + course2Credits + ···`

$$\text{current GPA} = \frac{\text{# of new honor points}}{\text{# of new course credits}}$$

Print the current GPA with an appropriate label. Finally, calculate

$$\text{cumulative GPA} = \frac{(\text{# of old honor points}) + (\text{# of new honor points})}{(\text{# of old course credits}) + (\text{# of new course credits})}$$

and display this with a label.

6. The shipping clerk at the Rinky Dooflingy Company is faced with the following problem: Dooflingies are very delicate and must be shipped in special containers. These containers are available in four sizes: huge, large, medium, and small, which can hold 50, 20, 5, and 1 dooflingy, respectively. Write a program that reads the number of dooflingies to be shipped and displays the number of huge, large, medium, and small containers needed to send the shipment in the minimum number of containers, and with the minimum amount of wasted space. Use constant definitions for the number of dooflingies each type of container can hold. The output should be similar to the following:

```
Container  Number
=========  ======
   Huge      21
   Large      2
   Medium     1
   Small      3
```

Execute the program for 3, 18, 48, 78, and 10598 dooflingies.

7. Write a program that reads the amount of a purchase, the amount received in payment (both amounts in cents), and then computes and displays the change in dollars, half-dollars, quarters, dimes, nickels, and pennies.

8. Angles are often measured in degrees (°), minutes (')', and seconds ("). There are 360 degrees in a circle, 60 minutes in one degree, and 60 seconds in one minute. Write a program that reads two angular measurements given in degrees, minutes, and seconds, and then calculates and displays their sum. Use the program to verify each of the following:

$$74°29'13'' + 105°8'16'' = 179°37'29''$$

$$7°14'55'' + 5°24'55'' = 12°39'50''$$

$$20°31'19'' + 0°31'30'' = 21°2'49''$$

$$122°17'48'' + 237°42'12'' = 0°0'0''$$

9. Write a program that reads two three-digit integers and then displays their product in the following format:

```
      749
x     381
------
      749
   5992
  2247
-------
  285369
```

Execute the program with the following values: 749 and 381; −749 and 381; 749 and −381; −749 and −381; 999 and 999.

10. In a certain region, pesticide can be sprayed from an airplane only if the temperature is at least 70°, the relative humidity is between 15 and 35%, and the wind speed is at most 10 miles per hour. Write a program that accepts three numbers representing temperature, relative humidity, and wind speed; assigns the value true or false to the boolean variable okToSpray according to these criteria; and displays this value.

11. A certain credit company will approve a loan application if the applicant's income is at least $25,000 or the value of his or her assets is at least $100,000; in addition, the applicant's total liabilities must be less than $50,000. Write a program that accepts three numbers representing income, assets, and liabilities; assigns the value true or false to the boolean variable creditOK according to these criteria; and displays this value.

12. Write a program that reads three real numbers, assigns the appropriate boolean value to the following boolean variables, and displays these values.

triangle: true if the real numbers can represent lengths of the sides of a triangle (the sum of any two of the numbers must be greater than the third); false otherwise.

equilateral: true if triangle is true and the triangle is equilateral (the three sides are equal); false otherwise.

isosceles: true if triangle is true and the triangle is isosceles (at least two sides are equal); false otherwise.

scalene: true if triangle is true and the triangle is scalene (no two sides are equal); false otherwise.

Chapter 3

FUNCTIONS

Great things can be reduced to small things, and small things can be reduced to nothing.

CHINESE PROVERB

If you can keep your head, when all around are losing theirs.

RUDYARD KIPLING

Those who do not learn from history are doomed to repeat its mistakes.

UNKNOWN

I never met a library I didn't like.

V. OREHCK III (fictitious)

Chapter Contents

3.1   Computing with Expressions

3.2   Computing with Functions

3.3   Functions That Use Selection

3.4   Functions That Use Repetition

3.5   Example: An 8-Function Calculator

3.6   An Introduction to Libraries

PART OF THE PICTURE: Computability Theory

Most people dislike unnecessary work, and the theme of this chapter is to show how to avoid it in programming by writing *reusable code*. We will first describe reusability on a "local" level in which segments of code are *encapsulated in a function* that is separate from the program. Such a function can then be used anywhere in the program, and because it is separate from the program, it is easy to copy and paste it for use with other programs.

A better way to facilitate such reusability on a larger scale, however, is to store such functions in a *library*. Any program can then retrieve functions from the library and use them, just as the program in Figure 2.1 used the function `pow()` from the math library.

In this chapter we will first look at functions in some detail and give several examples, because understanding how to construct and use functions is fundamental to writing reusable code. In the last section we will show how libraries are constructed. It must be realized, however, that this first look at functions and libraries is only an introduction. Many more features and uses will be given in the chapters that follow.

3.1 COMPUTING WITH EXPRESSIONS

There are many problems whose solutions involve the use of one or more formulas, such as the problem in section 2.1 of computing the amount of energy released by a quantity of matter, that was solved using Einstein's equation $e = m \times c^2$. Writing programs to solve such problems is usually straightforward if we know how to write C++ expressions for the formulas. Another example, which we will use throughout this chapter, is the following temperature-conversion problem.

PROBLEM: TEMPERATURE CONVERSION

Two scales used to measure temperature are the Fahrenheit and Celsius scales. A program is needed to convert temperatures in Fahrenheit to the equivalent Celsius temperatures.

OBJECT-CENTERED DESIGN

Behavior.   The program will display on the screen a prompt for a Fahrenheit temperature. The user will enter a numeric value from the keyboard, which the program will read. The program will compute the Celsius temperature equivalent to that Fahrenheit temperature and display this Celsius temperature on the screen along with descriptive text.

Objects.   From the statement of the desired behavior, we can identify the following objects:

Description	Type	Kind	Name
screen	`ostream`	varying	`cout`
prompt	`string`	constant	none
Fahrenheit temperature	`double`	varying	*tempFahrenheit*
keyboard	`istream`	varying	`cin`
Celsius temperature	`double`	varying	*tempCelsius*
descriptive text	`string`	constant	none

Operations. The formula for converting temperature measured in Fahrenheit to Celsius is

$$C = (F - 32)/1.8$$

where F is the Fahrenheit temperature and C is the corresponding Celsius temperature. This gives two additional data objects—the numeric values 32 and 1.8. We will not include in our data-object list constant values such as these that are unlikely to change in the foreseeable future.

From this formula and our statement of the desired behavior, we can identify these operations:

   i.   Display a string on the screen
   ii.   Read a number from the keyboard
   iii.   Compute the Celsius equivalent of a Fahrenheit temperature
      a. Perform real subtraction
      b. Perform real division
   iv.   Display a number on the screen

Algorithm.   As in all of our programs thus far, each of these operations is provided in C++, so we can organize them into an algorithm, as follows:

   1. Output a prompt for a Fahrenheit temperature to `cout`.
   2. Input *tempFahrenheit* from `cin`.
   3. Calculate *tempCelsius* = (*tempFahrenheit* − 32)/1.8.
   4. Output *tempCelsius* (and descriptive text) to `cout`.

Coding and Testing. A C++ program that solves this problem is given in Figure 3.1.[1]

---

[1] As we noted in chapter 1, recent changes in the C++ standard provide other ways to include libraries such as `iostream` in programs.

FIGURE 3.1 **CONVERTING A TEMPERATURE—VERSION 1.**

```
/* temperature1.cpp converts a temperature from Fahrenheit to Celsius,
 * using the standard Fahrenheit-to-Celsius conversion formula.
 *
 * Input:   tempFahrenheit
 * Output:  tempCelsius
 ***********************************************************************/

#include <iostream.h>                    // cin, cout, <<, >>

int main()
{
    cout << "This program converts a temperature\n"
            "from Fahrenheit to Celsius.\n";

    cout <<"\nEnter a Fahrenheit temperature: ";
    double tempFahrenheit;
    cin >> tempFahrenheit;

    double tempCelsius = (tempFahrenheit - 32.0) / 1.8;

    cout << tempFahrenheit << " degrees Fahrenheit is equivalent to "
         << tempCelsius << " degrees Celsius\n";
}
```

Sample runs:

```
This program converts a temperature
from Fahrenheit to Celsius.

Enter a Fahrenheit temperature: 212
212 degrees Fahrenheit is equivalent to 100 degrees Celsius


This program converts a temperature
from Fahrenheit to Celsius.

Please enter a Fahrenheit temperature: 32
32 degrees Fahrenheit is equivalent to 0 degrees Celsius
```

3.2 COMPUTING WITH FUNCTIONS

Before writing a program like that in Figure 3.1, we should ask whether we (or someone else) might someday need to expand this program or perhaps write new programs that will use the same conversions. If so, we should construct a function that *encapsulates* the code used to carry out the conversion as illustrated in the program in Figure 3.2, rather than build the conversion into our program, like we did in Figure 3.1.

FIGURE 3.2 CONVERTING A TEMPERATURE—VERSION 2.

```cpp
/* temperature2.cpp converts a temperature from Fahrenheit to Celsius,
 * using a conversion function named FahrToCelsius().
 *
 *   Input:  tempFahrenheit
 *   Output: tempCelsius
 ***********************************************************************/

#include <iostream.h>                    // cin, cout, <<, >>


double FahrToCelsius(double tempFahr);           // function prototype

int main()
{
    cout << "This program converts a temperature\n"
            "from Fahrenheit to Celsius.\n";

    cout << "\nEnter a Fahrenheit temperature: ";
    double tempFahrenheit;
    cin >> tempFahrenheit;

    double tempCelsius = FahrToCelsius(tempFahrenheit);

    cout << tempFahrenheit << " degrees Fahrenheit is equivalent to "
         << tempCelsius << " degrees Celsius\n";
}

/* FahrToCelsius converts a temperature from Fahrenheit to Celsius.
 *
 * Receive: tempFahr, a Fahrenheit temperature
 * Return:  the equivalent Celsius temperature
 ***********************************************************************/

double FahrToCelsius(double tempFahr)           // function definition
{
    return (tempFahr - 32.0) / 1.8;
}
```

The program in Figure 3.2 produces exactly the same output as that in Figure 3.1, but the flow of execution is very different. Here the Fahrenheit-to-Celsius conversion is performed using a function that is defined following the main function. The following diagram illustrates the flow of control in this new program.

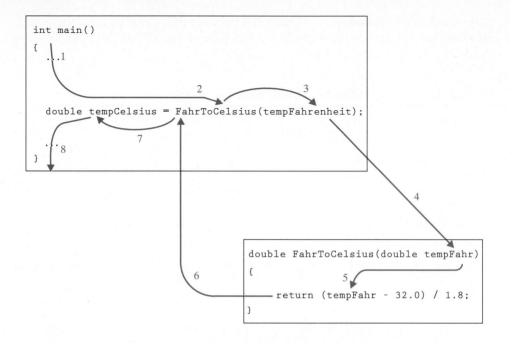

When the program is run, execution proceeds from the beginning of the program in the usual manner (1), until the assignment statement containing the **call** to function FahrToCelsius() is reached (2).[2] At that time, the function's **argument** tempFahrenheit is evaluated (3) and copied into the **parameter** tempFahr in the function FahrToCelsius() (4). Control is transferred from the main function to the function FahrToCelsius(), which begins execution (5). The expression

```
(tempFahr - 32.0) / 1.8
```

is evaluated, and since tempFahr contains a copy of the value of tempFahrenheit, the resulting value is the Celsius equivalent of the value of tempFahrenheit. The return statement makes this value the **return value** of FahrToCelsius(), and transfers execution back to the main function (6). There, the return value of FahrToCelsius() is assigned to tempCelsius (7), and execution proceeds normally through the rest of the main function (8).

We now describe how such C++ functions are constructed, using the program in Figure 3.2 to illustrate the discussion.

Defining a Function

A C++ function definition can be described as follows:

---

[2] We will use notation of the form *FunctionName*() for functions, with the parentheses used to distinguish them from identifiers that do not represent functions.

C++ Function Definition

Form:

```
return_type function_name(parameter_declaration_list)
{
    statement_list
}
```

where:

    return_type is the type of value returned by the function or the keyword void if the function does not return a value;

    function_name is an identifier that names the function;

    parameter_declaration_list is a list of declarations of the function's parameters, separated by commas; it is omitted if there are no parameters;

    statement_list is a sequence of statements that describe the behavior of the function.

Purpose:

Defines a function. A call to the function causes execution of the statements in the statement list and a return to the calling program unit after execution of the function is terminated, usually by encountering a return statement.

Thus, in the program in Figure 3.2, the lines

```
double FahrToCelsius(double tempFahr)
{
    return (tempFahr - 32.0) / 1.8;
}
```

constitute the definition of the function `FahrToCelsius()`. The first occurrence of `double` specifies the return type of the function; `FahrToCelsius` is the identifier naming the function; and the parentheses identify `FahrToCelsius` as a function (and not a variable). Inside the parentheses, the parameter declaration list declares a single parameter whose type is `double` and whose name is `tempFahr`. The **body** of the function consists of a pair of curly braces surrounding a return statement, whose syntax is

```
return expression;
```

where the type of *expression* matches the return type of the function.

Functions are often called **subprograms,** because defining a function is similar to defining a program. The same steps used to design a program can be used to design a function:

1. Behavior

2. Objects

3. Operations
4. Algorithm
5. Coding
6. Testing, execution, and debugging
7. Maintenance

Behavior. In addition to any objects that must be input from the keyboard or output to the screen, the behavior of a function typically describes:

- Any data objects that the function must **receive** from the calling function; and
- Any data objects that the function must **return** to the calling function.

For example, we might describe the behavior of `FahrToCelsius()` as follows: The function should receive from its caller a Fahrenheit temperature to be converted to Celsius. The function should return to its caller the Celsius temperature equivalent to this Fahrenheit temperature.

Objects. It is especially important for a function's behavior to specify each value that the function must receive and/or return to solve its problem. This receive and/or return information is often described as the function's **specification,** because it specifies the behavior of the function. Since received values can be thought of as flowing from the caller *into* the function, and returned values as flowing from the function *out* to the caller, we call this characteristic the **movement** of the objects with respect to the function, and note it in the object list for the function:

Description	Type	Kind	Movement	Name
a Fahrenheit temperature	double	varying	received (in)	*tempFahr*
the equivalent Celsius temperature	double	varying	returned (out)	none

Function Design. The **heading** in a function definition must include the following:

1. **Parameters**—variables declared within the function heading's parentheses—to hold the data objects that are *received*. If no objects are received, the parameter list is empty;
2. The *return type* of the function is the type of the object being returned. If the function does not return an object, then its return type is indicated by the keyword **void**—the absence of any type.

The specification of the function provides this information. For example, the specification for `FahrToCelsius()` tells us that

1. `FahrToCelsius()` requires one parameter of type `double`
2. The return type of `FahrToCelsius()` is `double`

Once we have this information, we can begin defining the function. If we choose the name `tempFahr` for the parameter, we can construct the following **function stub** for `FahrToCelsius()`:

```
double FahrToCelsius(double tempFahr)
{
}
```

A function stub is a complete function definition consisting of a function heading and a function body (enclosed in curly braces) that contains no statements. Once we have written such a stub, all that remains is to design an algorithm that solves the problem, and then encode that algorithm within the body of the function stub.

Designing the algorithm for a function is almost the same as designing the algorithm for a program. The only differences are as follows:

Algorithm for a Program	Algorithm for a Function
Usually includes a step to *input* the data values required in the solution of the problem	Usually *the parameters already contain the data values* because values of the arguments are copied into the function's parameters when the function is called
Usually includes a step to *output* data values	Usually contains a step to *return* a data value to the function that calls it

Thus, when the function `FahrToCelsius()` begins execution, we can assume that parameter `tempFahr` already contains the Fahrenheit temperature to be converted. This leaves the following operations to be performed:

Operations:
  Real subtraction (`tempFahr - 32.0`)
  Real division (`(tempFahr - 32.0) / 1.8`)
  Return a real value

These operations can be organized into the following simple algorithm for function `FahrToCelsius()`:

Algorithm for Fahrenheit-to-Celsius Conversion Function

1. Return (*tempFahr* − 32.0)/1.8.

Coding a Function. Given a C++ function stub and a pseudocode algorithm, this algorithm is encoded in C++ by inserting appropriate C++ statements into the stub. In our example, the `return` statement and predefined C++ operations can be used to code the single instruction in the algorithm:

```
double FahrToCelsius(double tempFahr)
{
    return (tempFahr - 32.0) / 1.8;
}
```

As this example illustrates, the specification of a function determines the form of a function's heading, and its algorithm determines the content of the function's body:

Design Component	Determines
Specification	The form of the function heading
Algorithm	The content of the function body

For a simple function like `FahrToCelsius()`, the specification and design steps may seem like extra work, but they are absolutely essential for more complicated problems. A well-defined specification makes the process of constructing the function heading almost mechanical, and a well-defined algorithm can make the process of coding the body of the function similarly straightforward.

Testing, Execution, and Debugging. Just as a program must be tested to verify its correctness, a function should also be rigorously tested to ensure that it is correct. Functions written for real-world software projects are often large and complex, and they must be thoroughly checked for logical errors before they are incorporated into the project.

To test a function, we can write a program that calls the function with specific values and displays the values returned by the function. Such a program is called a **driver program** because it "test drives" the function. Figure 3.3 shows a simple driver program for `FahrToCelsius()`. The sample run indicates that `FahrToCelsius()` is performing correctly for the test values we have chosen.

FIGURE 3.3   A SAMPLE DRIVER PROGRAM.

```
#include <iostream.h>                    // cin, cout, <<, >>

double FahrToCelsius(double tempFahr);        // function prototype

int main()
{
   cout << "212F => " << FahrToCelsius(212)
        << "C\n 32F => " << FahrToCelsius(32)
        << "C\n";
}

double FahrToCelsius(double tempFahr)       // function definition
{
   return (tempFahr - 32.0) / 1.8;
}
```

Sample run:

```
212F => 100C
 32F => 0C
```

FUNCTION PROTOTYPES

The programs in Figures 3.2 and 3.3 each contain the line

```
double FahrToCelsius(double tempFahr);
```

before the main function. This is called the **prototype,** or **declaration,** of the function `FahrToCelsius()`.[3] Recall from chapter 2 that C++ requires that an object must be declared before it is used, so that the compiler can check if it is being used in a manner consistent with its type. For the objects we have seen thus far (i.e., data objects), their declarations and definitions have been synonymous. For a function, however, its definition can be separated from its prototype (declaration). A function definition must *fully describe* the function, but a function prototype need only *specify its characteristics:*

- The *return type* of the function
- The function's *name*
- The *number of parameters* for the function
- The *type* of each parameter

The (simplified) syntax of a function prototype is as follows:

C++ Function Prototype

Form:

```
return_type function_name(parameter_declaration_list);
```

where:

`return_type` is the type of value returned by the function or the keyword `void` if the function does not return a value;

`function_name` is the name of the function;

`parameter_declaration_list` is a list of declarations of the function's parameters, separated by commas. (Parameter names are optional, but it is good practice to include them to indicate what the parameters represent.)

Purpose:

Declares a function. Provides sufficient information for the compiler to check that the function is being called correctly, with respect to the number and types of the parameters and the return type of the function.

Note that as with other declarations, a semicolon is placed at the end of a function prototype to make it a statement.

A function prototype can thus be the same as the heading in a function definition followed by a semicolon. For example, to prototype `FahrToCelsius()` in Figures 3.2 and 3.3, we wrote

```
double FahrToCelsius(double tempFahr);
```

---

[3] We will use the term *prototype* because beginning programmers often confuse the words "declaration" and "definition."

This is sufficient to inform the compiler that the return type of the function is `double`, that its name is `FahrToCelsius`, that it has one parameter, and that the type of that parameter is `double`. Thus, if we should call the function incorrectly, such as passing it two arguments as in

```
double tempCelsius = FahrToCelsius(32.0, 'F');
```

the compiler can generate an error message to inform us of the mistake.

   Although C++ allows functions to be declared inside a calling function, in this text we will declare them outside, because this is consistent with the use of libraries (see section 3.6). It also improves readability, because placing function prototypes inside calling functions tends to clutter and obscure the structure of these functions.

CALLING A FUNCTION

Since a function call returns a value, it is a kind of expression, which means that a function can be called at any point where an expression whose type matches the function's return type is permitted. Thus, because the return type of `FahrToCelsius()` is `double`, a call to `FahrToCelsius()` can be used to initialize a variable of type `double` such as `tempCelsius` in the program in Figure 3.2:

```
double tempCelsius = FahrToCelsius(tempFahrenheit);
```

Similarly, the output statement in the driver program in Figure 3.3,

```
cout << "212F => " << FahrToCelsius(212)
     << "C\n 32F => " << FahrToCelsius(32)
     << "C\n";
```

which contains two calls to `FahrToCelsius()`, is a valid statement, since the `<<` operator can be used to output a `double` expression to `cout`.

LOCAL OBJECTS

The only variable used by the function `FahrToCelsius()` is the parameter `tempFahr`. Many functions, however, use other variables or constants in computing their return values. For example, one of the formulas for computing the wind chill index is given by the rather complicated formula

$$\text{wind chill} = 91.4 - (0.474677 - 0.020425 \times v + 0.303107 \times \sqrt{v}) \times (91.4 - t)$$

where v is the wind speed in miles per hour and t is the temperature in degrees Fahrenheit.[4] The function `WindChill()` in Figure 3.4 uses this formula to compute the wind chill index, but it breaks it up into two steps to simplify the computation:

1.   Compute $v\_part = 0.474677 - 0.020425 \times v + 0.303107 \times \sqrt{v}$.
2.   Compute wind chill $= 91.4 - v\_part \times (91.4 - t)$.

The variable `v_part` is used to store the result computed in step 1. Figure 3.4 also shows a simple driver program to test `WindChill()`.

---

[4] The formula is not valid for wind speeds less than 4 mph or for temperatures greater than 50° F.

FIGURE 3.4   COMPUTING WIND CHILL.

```
/* This is a driver program to test the WindChill() function.
 ************************************************************/

#include <iostream.h>                          // cin, cout, <<, >>


double WindChill(double tempFahr, double windSpeed); // function prototype

int main()
{
   double temp,    // Fahrenheit temperature
          wind;    // wind speed (mph)

   cout << "Enter Fahrenheit temperature and wind speed (mph): ";
   cin >> temp >> wind;
   cout << "Wind chill index is " << WindChill(temp, wind) << endl;
}


/* WindChill computes wind chill.
 *
 * Receive: tempFahr, a Fahrenheit temperature
 *          windSpeed, in miles per hour
 *
 * Return:  the wind chill
 ******************************************************************************/

# include <math.h>              // sqrt

double WindChill(double tempFahr, double windSpeed)  // function definition
{
   double v_part =
           0.474677 - 0.020425 * windSpeed + 0.303107 * sqrt(windSpeed);
   return 91.4 - v_part * (91.4 - tempFahr);
}
```

Sample runs:

```
Enter Fahrenheit temperature and wind speed (mph): 10 5
Wind chill index is 5.90396

Enter Fahrenheit temperature and wind speed (mph): 0 20
Wind chill index is -38.5445

Enter Fahrenheit temperature and wind speed (mph): -10 45
Wind chill index is -69.71
```

Variables such as `v_part`, constants, and parameters that are declared in a function are called **local** objects, because they are *defined only while the function is executing;* they are undefined both before and after its execution.[5] (See Potential Problem 2 in the Programming Pointers at the end of the chapter.) This means that they can be accessed only within the function; any attempt to use them outside the function is an error. It also means that the name of a local object may be used outside the function for some other purpose without conflict.

FUNCTIONS THAT RETURN NOTHING

In applying object-centered design, one sometimes encounters an operation that returns nothing to its caller. For example, in a problem that involves monetary calculations, we might need to display a dollar amount via `cout`, formatted as a monetary value. Because there is no one predefined C++ operation that performs this operation, we would probably use the output operator and several format manipulators[6]

```
int main()
{
   // ...
   cout << fixed << showpoint
        << right << setprecision(2)
        << '$' << dollarAmount;
}
```

to display a dollar amount in a nice format like

```
$4.95
```

Putting such details in a main function, however, can make a program messy and cluttered, especially when they must be used at several different places. It would be much better if we could simply write a single statement such as

```
int main()
{
   // ...
   PrintAsMoney(dollarAmount);
}
```

In C++ this can be accomplished by writing a function named `PrintAsMoney()`. A specification for this function is:

Receive: `dollars`, a `double`

Output: `dollars`, appropriately formatted as a monetary value

---

[5] These are also called **automatic** objects because they automatically begin to exist when the function begins executing and automatically cease to exist when it is finished. Prepending the keyword `static` to a local object's declaration makes it a **static** object, which will retain its value from one function call to the next.

---

[6] As noted in chapter 2 (see footnote 22), if your compiler is not fully ANSI-C++ compliant, you may have to use the `setiosflags` manipulator from `<iomanip.h>` to do some of the formatting. See chapter 8 for more details.

Note how this specification clarifies the problem. It does not require the function to return anything to its caller, but instead it performs output for its caller.

From this specification, we see that the function `PrintAsMoney()` will have a `double` parameter named `dollars`, but what do we use as the return type of a function that returns nothing to its caller? For such situations, C++ provides the keyword `void` to denote the absence of any type. Because function `PrintAsMoney()` returns nothing to its caller, its return type should be given as `void`:

```
void  PrintAsMoney(double dollars);
```

Since `void` functions do not return values, they cannot be called in the same way as the functions we have considered up to now. They are not used in expressions but rather are called in statements of the form

```
Function_Name(argument_list);
```

For example, the statement

```
PrintAsMoney(dollarAmount);
```

can be used to display the value of `dollarAmount`. Attempting to use such function calls in expressions such as

```
cout << "Amount due: "
     << PrintAsMoney(dollarAmount)   // ERROR!
     << endl;
```

is an error, because `PrintAsMoney(dollarAmount)` returns no value.

Figure 3.5 gives the complete definition of `PrintAsMoney()`. It also shows a program that inputs the amount of a purchase and the amount received, and uses `PrintAsMoney()` to display the amount returned to the customer.

FIGURE 3.5   MONETARY TRANSACTIONS.

```
/* money5.cpp computes the amount to be returned for a purchase.
 *
 * Input:  purchase, payment
 * Output: amount returned to customer (via PrintAsMoney())
 ****************************************************************/

#include <iostream.h>                 // cin, cout, <<, >>,
                                      // fixed, showpoint, right
#include <iomanip.h>                  // setprecision

void PrintAsMoney(double dollars);    // function prototype
int main()
{
   double purchase,                   // amount of purchase
          payment;                    // amount paid
```

```
    cout << "Enter amount of purchase: ";
    cin >> purchase;
    cout << "Enter amount paid (>= purchase): ";
    cin >> payment;
    cout << "Amount to return is: ";
    PrintAsMoney(payment - purchase);
    cout << endl;
}
```

```
/* PrintAsMoney displays an amount in monetary format.
 *
 * Receive: dollars, the double value to be displayed
 * Output:  dollars in monetary format
 *****************************************************************/

void PrintAsMoney(double dollars)
{
    cout << fixed << showpoint
         << right << setprecision(2)
         << '$' << dollars;
}
```

Sample runs:

```
Enter amount of purchase: 4.01
Enter amount paid (>= purchase): 5.00
Amount to return is: $0.99

Enter amount of purchase: 9.00
Enter amount paid (>= purchase): 20.00
Amount to return is: $11.00
```

The effect of shifting details from `main()` to `PrintAsMoney()` is to "clean up" the main function by hiding the money-format details in a function, which makes the main function easier to read. In computer science, such detail hiding is called an **abstraction.** An abstraction is a view of something that simplifies it by hiding some of its details. Our `PrintAsMoney()` function is therefore an abstraction of the display-a-monetary-value operation, because it "hides" the details of how the operation is accomplished (at least as far as readers of the main function are concerned).

SUMMARY

Functions are an essential part of C++, because they are used to write program components that are reusable. Because they are so fundamental to C++ programming, we review some of the important ideas about functions that have emerged thus far:

▶ For each value that a function must receive from its caller, a *variable* to hold that value must be declared within the parentheses of the function heading. Such variables are called the *parameters* of the function. For example, in the definition of the function `FahrToCelsius()`,

```
double FahrToCelsius(double tempFahr)     // function definition
{
    return (tempFahr - 32.0) / 1.8;
}
```

the variable `tempFahr` is a parameter of `FahrToCelsius()`.

▶ A *value* that is supplied to a function when it is called is an *argument* to that function call. For example, in the function call

```
    double tempCelsius = FahrToCelsius(tempFahrenheit);
```

`tempFahrenheit` is an argument to the function `FahrToCelsius()`. When execution reaches this call, the value of the argument `tempFahrenheit` is *passed* (i.e., copied) from the main function to the parameter `tempFahr` in function `FahrToCelsius()`.

▶ When one function `F()` calls another function `G()`, the flow of execution is from `F()` to `G()` and then back to `F()`. To illustrate, consider again the main function's call of function `FahrToCelsius()` in Figure 3.2:

```
    .
    .
    .
int main()
{
    .
    .
    .
    double tempCelsius = FahrToCelsius(tempFahrenheit);
    .
    .
    .
}
```

When the call to `FahrToCelsius()` is encountered, execution proceeds as follows:

1. The value of the argument `tempFahrenheit` is determined.

2. This value is passed from the main function to `FahrToCelsius()`, and copied into the parameter `tempFahr`.

3. Control is then transferred from the line containing the function call (in `main()`) to the first statement of `FahrToCelsius()`, which begins execution using the value of its parameter.

4. When a `return` statement (or the final statement of the function) is executed, control is transferred back to the caller (i.e., the main function), and execution of the caller resumes.

▶ *Local objects are defined only while the function containing them is executing.* They can be accessed only within the function, and any attempt to use them outside the function is an error.

▶ void is used to specify the return type of a function that returns no values. Such functions are called with statements of the form *Function_Name(argument_list)*;

The ability to define functions is a powerful tool in object-oriented programming. If the solution of some problem requires that an operation not provided in C++ (as an operator or as a predefined function) be applied to some data object, we can simply

1. Define a function to perform that operation, and
2. Apply that function to the data object

as we did with the temperature-conversion operation FahrToCelsius(). As we shall see in section 3.6, such functions can then be stored in a library, from which they can be retrieved when needed.

✔ Quick Quiz 3.2

1. In addition to input and output objects, what two other kinds of objects are usually included in the description of a function's behavior?

2. In the function heading double Sum(int a, char b), a and b are called _____.

3. For a function whose heading is double Sum(int a, char b), the type of the value returned by the function is _____.

4. The keyword _____ is used to indicate the return type of a function that returns no value.

5. A function stub is a function definition in which the function's body contains _____.

Questions 6–10 deal with the following function definition:

```
int What(int n)
{
    return (n * (n + 1)) / 2;
}
```

6. If the statement number1 = What(number2); appears in the main function, number2 is called a(n)_____ in this function call.

7. If the statement int number = What(3); appears in the main function, the value assigned to number will be _____.

8. (True or false) The value assigned to number by the statement int number = What(2+3); in the main function will be 15.

9. (True or false) The value assigned to number by the statement int number = What(1, 5); in the main function will be 3.

10. Write a prototype for function What().

11. Write a function definition that calculates values of $x^2 + \sqrt{x}$.

12. Write a function definition that calculates the integer average of two integers.

13. Write a function definition that displays three integers on three lines separated by two blank lines.

EXERCISES 3.2

The following exercises ask you to write functions to compute various quantities. To test these functions, you should write driver programs as instructed in Programming Problems 1–12 at the end of this chapter.

1. Write a function `CelsiusToFahr()` that returns the Fahrenheit equivalent of a Celsius temperature.

2. U.S. dollars are typically converted to another country's currency by multiplying the U.S. dollars by an *exchange rate,* which varies over time. For example, if on a given day, the U.S.-to-Canada exchange rate is 1.22, then $10.00 in U.S. currency can be exchanged for $12.20 in Canadian currency. Write a function `US_to_Canadian()` that, given a dollar amount in U.S. currency and the exchange rate, returns the equivalent number of dollars in Canadian currency.

3. Proceed as in exercise 2, but write a function `Canadian_to_US()` that, given a dollar amount in Canadian currency and the exchange rate, returns the equivalent number of dollars in U.S. currency.

4. Write a function `Range()` that, given two integers, returns the range between them—that is, the absolute value of their difference.

5. Write a function `Wages()` that, given the number of hours worked and an hourly pay rate, returns the wages earned.

6. Write a function that, given the radius of a circle, returns its circumference. ($C = 2\pi r$)

7. Write a function that, given the radius of a circle, returns its area. ($A = \pi r^2$)

8. Write a function that, given the lengths of the sides of a rectangle, returns its perimeter. ($P = 2l + 2w$)

9. Write a function that, given the lengths of the sides of a square, returns its area. ($A = s^2$)

10. Write a function that, given the lengths of the three sides of a triangle, returns its perimeter. ($P = s_1 + s_2 + s_3$)

11. Write a function that, given the lengths of the three sides of a triangle, returns its area. (The area of a triangle can be found by using *Hero's formula:*

$$\sqrt{s(s - a)(s - b)(s - c)}$$

    where $a, b,$ and c are the lengths of the sides and s is one half of the perimeter.)

12. The number of bacteria in a culture can be estimated by $N \cdot e^{kt}$, where N is the initial population, k is a rate constant, and t is time. Write a function to calculate the number of bacteria present for given values of $N, k,$ and t.

13. Write a function that, given a number of seconds, returns the equivalent number of minutes.

14. Write a function that, given a number of minutes, returns the equivalent number of hours.

15. Write a function that, given a number of hours, returns the equivalent number of days.

16. Using the functions from exercises 13–15, write a function that, given a number of seconds, returns the equivalent number of days.

17. Write a function that accepts a 7-digit integer representing a phone number and displays it in the format *abc-defg.*

18. The wind chill index, described in the text, was developed in 1941. It is a measure of discomfort due to the combined cold and wind, and is based on the rate of heat loss due to various combinations of temperature and wind. The *heat index,* developed in 1979, is a measure of discomfort due to the combination of heat and high humidity, and is based on studies of evaporative skin cooling for combinations of temperature and humidity. It is computed using the following formula:

$$
\begin{aligned}
\text{heat index} = (&-42.379 + 2.04901523 \times t + 10.14333127 \times r \\
&- 0.22475541 \times t \times r - (6.83783\text{E}{-}3) \times t^2 \\
&- (5.481717\text{E}{-}2) \times r^2 + (1.22874\text{E}{-}3) \times t^2 \times r \\
&+ (8.5282\text{E}{-}4) \times t \times r^2 - (1.99\text{E}{-}6) \times t^2 \times r^2)
\end{aligned}
$$

where t is the temperature in degrees Fahrenheit and r is the relative humidity. Write a function to compute the heat index.

19. Write four functions `PrintZero()`, `PrintOne()`, `PrintTwo()`, and `Print-Three()` to produce "stick numbers" like those on a calculator display, for the digits 0, 1, 2, and 3, respectively:

3.3 FUNCTIONS THAT USE SELECTION[7]

Although the C++ language features we have studied thus far are sufficient to write functions that encode a variety of formulas, there are many problems whose solutions require more. To see this, consider the following problem:

PROBLEM: FINDING A MINIMUM OF TWO VALUES

Write a function that, given two real values, returns the minimum of the two values.

OBJECT-CENTERED DESIGN

Behavior. Our function should receive two real values from its caller. If the first is less than the second, the function should return the first value; otherwise, it should return the second value.

Objects. From the behavioral description, we can identify the following objects:

---

[7] This section provides only an introduction to the `if` statement. A complete treatment of selection structures appears in chapter 5, and those who prefer to study them first can jump ahead to that chapter and return to this section later.

Data Object	Kind	Type	Movement	Name of Object
The first value	variable	double	received	*first*
The second value	variable	double	received	*second*
The minimum value	variable	double	returned	none

We can thus specify this problem as follows:

Receive: *first* and *second*, two real values

Return: the minimum of *first* and *second*.

From this information, we can write the following stub for our function:

```
double Minimum(double first, double second)
{
}
```

To fill in the body of the stub, we must look at what operations are needed to solve the problem.

Operations.   Again, from our behavioral description, we can identify the following operations:

i.   Receive two real values from the function's caller

ii.   Compare two real values to see if one is less than the other

iii.   Return the first value

iv.   Return the second value

v.   Select either iii or iv (but not both), based on the result of ii

The first operation will occur automatically through the normal function-call mechanism, because we are providing two parameters to hold the values received:

```
double Minimum( double first, double second )
```

The second operation can be performed using the relational operator < described in section 2.4:

```
first < second
```

We have also seen that `return` statements can be used to perform the third and fourth operations:

```
return first;
return second;
```

Our difficulty is with the last operation. How can we select one and only one of these two `return` statements? The answer is to use a new statement called the **if statement,** which allows the selection of either of a pair of statements.

Algorithm.   We can use a pseudocode version of an `if` statement to express the logic of our solution as follows:

Algorithm for Minimum of Two Numbers

If *first* < *second*

return *first;*

otherwise

return *second.*

Coding.   In the syntax of C++, this algorithm can be expressed as shown in Figure 3.6:

FIGURE 3.6.   FUNCTION `Minimum()`.

```
/* Minimum finds the minimum of two doubles.
 *
 * Receive:  first and second
 * Return:   the smaller of first and second
 *************************************************/

double Minimum(double first, double second)
{
   if (first < second)
      return first;
   else
      return second;
}
```

Testing.   To verify that our function is correct, we can test it with a simple driver program like that in Figure 3.7 that calls the function, using a variety of input combinations to "exercise" it. Once we have verified that `Minimum()` behaves correctly, it could be moved to a library as described in section 3.6 for convenient reuse by any program needing its functionality.

FIGURE 3.7.   DRIVER FOR `Minimum()`.

```
/* minimum7.cpp is a driver program to test the Minimum function.
 *******************************************************************/

#include <iostream.h>                  // cin, cout, <<, >>

double Minimum(double first, double second);

int main()
{
   double num1, num2;
   cout << "Enter two numbers: ";
   cin >> num1 >> num2;
   cout << "Minimum is " << Minimum(num1, num2) << endl;
}
```

```
/*** Insert the definition of function Minimum()
     from Figure 3.6 here. ***/
```

Sample runs:

```
Enter two numbers: -2 -5
Minimum is -5

Enter two numbers: -2 3
Minimum is -2

Enter two numbers: 3 3
Minimum is 3

Enter two numbers: 3 5
Minimum is 3
```

Sequential Execution

Sequential execution, as illustrated in the following diagram, refers to the execution of a sequence of statements in the order in which they appear, so that each statement is executed exactly once. The arrows in this diagram, called **flow lines,** indicate the order in which the statements are executed. In the case of a sequential structure, they clearly show the *straight line* pattern of execution. All the sample programs in earlier chapters were straight-line programs in which only sequential control is used.

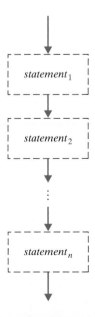

For situations where statements must be executed **selectively,** C++ provides the **if statement** (and other selection statements described in chapter 5). If we think of the flow of execution through a program as traveling along a roadway, we might visualize an if statement as a *fork* in the road:

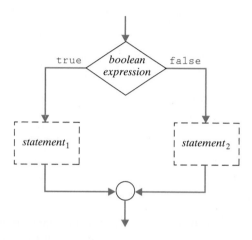

Based on the value of a boolean expression, execution will pass through *statement₁* or through *statement₂*, *but not both,* before proceeding to the next statement.

When execution reaches an if statement, the boolean expression is evaluated.

```
if (first < second)
    return first;
else
    return second;
```

If the expression is true, then the first statement is executed, and the trailing else and its statement are skipped:

```
if (true)
    return first;
else
    return second;
```

However, if the boolean expression evaluates to false, then the first statement is skipped, and the statement in the else part is executed:

```
if (false)
    return first;
else
    return second;
```

In general, the form of the if statement can be summarized as follows:

if Statement (General Form)

Form:

```
if (boolean_expression)
    statement
```

or

```
if (boolean_expression)
    statement₁
else
    statement₂
```

or

```
if (boolean_expression₁)
    statement₁
else if (boolean_expression₂)
    statement₂
          .
          .
          .
else if (boolean_expressionₙ)
    statementₙ
else
    statementₙ₊₁
```

where:

if and else are keywords;
each $statement$, $statement_1$, $statement_2$, . . . is a C++ statement
(and may be compound).

Purpose:

In the first form, if the $boolean\_expression$ is true, then $statement$ is executed; otherwise $statement$ is bypassed.

In the second form, if the $boolean\_expression$ is true, $statement_1$ is executed and $statement_2$ is bypassed; otherwise $statement_1$ is bypassed and $statement_2$ is executed.

In the last form, if $boolean\_expression_1$ is true, $statement_1$ is executed and the remainder of the statement is bypassed; otherwise if $boolean\_expression_2$ is true, $statement_2$ is executed and the remainder of the statement is bypassed; and so on. If none of the $boolean\_expression_i$ is true, $statement_{n+1}$ (if present) is executed.

BLOCKS

When a group of statements must be selected for execution, we enclose them between curly braces { and } to form a single statement. This is called a **block,** or a **compound statement:**

Block (Compound Statement)

Form:

```
{
    statement₁
    statement₂
        .
        .
        .
    statementₙ
}
```

where:

each $statement_i$ is a C++ statement.

Purpose:

The sequence of statements is treated as a single statement, in which $statement_1$, $statement_2$, ..., $statement_n$ are executed in order, with each statement being executed exactly once.

Note that the block does not require a semicolon after the final curly brace; a block is a complete statement by itself.

We have already seen examples of blocks—the body of a function is a block. Thus, the general form of a function definition can be described by

```
return_type function_name(parameter_declaration_list)
block
```

A block can also be used to *wrap* several statements into a single statement when more than one statement must be selected in an `if` statement; for example,

```
if (hours > 40.0)
{
    overtime = hours - 40.0;
    overtimePay = 1.5 * overtime * rate;
    regularPay = 40.0 * rate;
}
else
{
    regularPay = hours * rate;
    overtimePay = 0.0;
}

totalPay = regularPay + overtimePay;
```

If the value of `hours` is more than 40.0, the three statements in the first block are executed and the second block is bypassed. If the value of `hours` is 40.0 or less, the first block is bypassed and the second block is executed.

 STYLE

There are a variety of styles used by programmers to write `if` statements. They differ in the placement of the statements with respect to the `if` and `else` keywords, and where the curly braces are placed when the statements are blocks.

Some styles are more popular than others, but each follows some basic principle, such as:

Minimize the number of lines of code occupied by an `if` statement.

Follow one simple rule consistently.

Use consistent indentation to emphasize the structure of the code.

Always use blocks, even when a single statement is being selected.

In our opinion, the key issue is *readability:*

Use a form that is easy to read.

Accordingly, we will

1. Align the `if` and the `else`, and
2. Use white space and indentation to clearly mark the statements that are being selected by the `if` and `else`.

When a single statement is being selected, we will usually indent that statement on the line below the `if` or the `else`; for example,

```
if (first < second)
    return first;
else
    return second;
```

When a block of statements is involved, we will place the curly braces on separate lines, aligned with the `if` and `else`, and indent the statements they enclose; for example,

```
if (hours > 40.0)
{
    overtime = hours - 40.0;
    overtimePay = 1.5 * overtime * rate;
    regularPay = 40.0 * rate;
}
else
{
    regularPay = hours * rate;
    overtimePay = 0.0;
}
```

In our opinion, consistent alignment of curly braces produces more readable code, and it reduces the chance of omitting the closing curly brace, a common problem for beginning programmers.

When writing `if-else-if` statements (the third form), we will place the `else` and the following `if` on the same line, and indent the statements in each part; for example,

```
if (percentage >= 90)
    grade = 'A';
```

```
else if (percentage >= 80)
   grade = 'B';
else if (percentage >= 70)
   grade = 'C';
else if (percentage >= 60)
   grade = 'D';
else
   grade = 'F';
```

Occasionally, when an `if` selects a single statement and has no associated `else`, we will place the statement on the same line as the `if`; for example,

```
if (x == 0) break;
```

To improve readability, we will usually put blank lines above and below such statements.

NESTED IFS

The statements selected by `if` and `else` may be any C++ statements; in particular, they may be other `if` statements. In this case, an inner `if` statement is said to be **nested** within the outer `if` statement.

When one `if` statement is nested within another, it may not be clear with which `if` an `else` is associated. (See Potential Problem 7 in the Programming Pointers at the end of this chapter.) This ambiguity is resolved in C++ by the following important rule:

> *In a nested* `if` *statement, an* `else` *is matched with the nearest preceding unmatched* `if`.

Aligning each `else` with its corresponding `if` helps make this clear.

It should be noted that the `if-else if` form we considered earlier is really a nested `if` statement—we are simply writing

```
if (boolean_expression₁)
   statement₁
else statement
```

where `statement` happens to be an `if` statement that begins on the same line:

```
if (boolean_expression₁)
   statement₁
else if (boolean_expression₂)
   statement₂
else statement
```

and so on. Each `if` in an `else if` clause is actually a new `if` statement that is only executed if the conditions in all of the preceding `if` statements are false. Similarly, each `else` in an `else if` clause is actually associated with the `if` of the preceding `else if` clause (or the first `if`), as shown by the arrows in the following diagram:

```
if ( boolean_expression₁)
            statement₁
else if ( boolean_expression₂)
            statement₂
else if ( boolean_expression₃)
            statement₃
         .
         .
         .
else if ( boolean_expressionₙ)
            statementₙ
    else
         statementₙ₊₁
```

✔   Quick Quiz 3.3

Questions 1–3 refer to the following `if` statement:

```
if (x >= y)
    cout << x;
else
    cout << y;
```

1. Describe the output produced if $x = 6$ and $y = 5$.

2. Describe the output produced if $x = 5$ and $y = 5$.

3. Describe the output produced if $x = 5$ and $y = 6$.

Questions 4–6 refer to the following `if` statement:

```
if (x >= 0)
  if (y >= 0)
        cout << x + y;
  else
        cout << x - y;
else
  cout << y - x;
```

4. Describe the output produced if $x = 5$ and $y = 5$.

5. Describe the output produced if $x = 5$ and $y = -5$.

6. Describe the output produced if $x = -5$ and $y = 5$.

Questions 7–11 refer to the following `if` statement:

```
if (n >= 90)
    cout << "excellent\n";
else if (n >= 80)
    cout << "good\n";
```

```
   else if (n >= 70)
      cout << "fair\n";
   else
      cout << "bad\n";
```

7. Describe the output produced if n = 100

8. Describe the output produced if n = 90.

9. Describe the output produced if n = 89.

10. Describe the output produced if n = 70.

11. Describe the output produced if n = 0.

12. Write a statement that displays "Out of range" if number is negative or is greater than 100.

13. Write an efficient if statement to assign n the value 1 if $x \leqslant 1.5$, 2 if $1.5 < x < 2.5$, and 3 otherwise.

EXERCISES 3.3

Exercises 1–4 refer to the following if statement:

```
if (x * y >= 0)
   cout << "yes\n";
else
   cout << "no\n";
```

1. Describe the output produced if $x = 5$ and $y = 6$.

2. Describe the output produced if $x = 5$ and $y = -6$.

3. Describe the output produced if $x = -5$ and $y = 6$.

4. Describe the output produced if $x = -5$ and $y = -6$.

Exercises 5–7 refer to the following if statement:

```
if (abs(n) <= 4)
   if (n > 0)
      cout << 2*n + 1;
   else
      cout << 2*n;
else
   cout << n << " out of range";
```

5. Describe the output produced if $n = 2$.

6. Describe the output produced if $n = -7$.

7. Describe the output produced if $n = 0$.

For exercises 8–10, write if statements that will do what is required.

8. If taxCode is 'T', increase price by adding taxRate percentage of price to it.

9. If code is 1, input values for x and y and calculate and display the sum of x and y.

10. If a is strictly between 0 and 5, set b equal to $1/a^2$; otherwise set b equal to a^2.

For exercises 11–14, write functions that will do what is required. To test these functions, you should write driver programs as instructed in Programming Problems 14–18 at the end of this chapter.

11.   Given a distance, return a cost, according to the following table:

Distance	Cost
0 through 100	5.00
More than 100 but not more than 500	8.00
More than 500 but less than 1000	10.00
1000 or more	12.00

12.   A quadratic equation of the form $Ax^2 + Bx + C = 0$ has real roots if the discriminant $B^2 - 4AC$ is nonnegative. Write a function that receives the coefficients A, B, and C of a quadratic equation, and returns true if the equation has real roots and false otherwise.

13.   A certain city classifies a pollution index less than 35 as "pleasant," 35 through 60 as "unpleasant," and above 60 as "hazardous." Write a function that displays the appropriate classification for a pollution index.

14.   A wind chill of 10° F or above is not considered dangerous or unpleasant; a wind chill of $-10°$ F or higher but less than 10° F is considered unpleasant; if it is $-30°$ F or above but less than $-10°$ F, frostbite is possible; if it is $-70°$ F or higher but below $-30°$ F, frostbite is likely and outdoor activity becomes dangerous; if the wind chill is less than $-70°$ F, exposed flesh will usually freeze within half a minute. Write a function that displays the appropriate weather condition for a wind chill index.

3.4 FUNCTIONS THAT USE REPETITION[8]

The problems we considered in the preceding chapters and those at the beginning of this chapter required only *sequential* processing of instructions for their solution. In the last section, we saw that there are problems whose solutions require *selection.* In this section we consider *repetition,* a form of control that is needed to solve many problems.

PROBLEM: COMPUTING FACTORIALS

The **factorial** of a nonnegative integer n, denoted by $n!$, is defined by:

$$n! = \begin{cases} 1 & \text{if } n = 0 \\ 1 \times 2 \times \cdots \times n & \text{if } n > 0 \end{cases}$$

Write a function that, given an integer $n \geq 0$, computes n factorial.

---

[8] This section provides only an introduction to the `for` statement. A complete treatment of repetition structures appears in chapter 6, and those who prefer to study them first can jump ahead to that chapter and return to this section later.

OBJECT-CENTERED DESIGN

Behavior. To describe how the function should behave, we might begin by looking at how to solve the problem by hand. We would probably begin with 1, multiply it by 2, multiply that product by 3, and so on, until we multiply it by n. For example, to find 5!, we might do the following computation:

$$
\begin{array}{r}
1 \\
\times\ 2 \\
\hline
2 \\
\times\ 3 \\
\hline
6 \\
\times\ 4 \\
\hline
24 \\
\times\ 5 \\
\hline
120
\end{array}
$$

If we want our function to imitate this approach, we need to identify the various objects in the solution and the roles they play. It should be clear that we are keeping a running product and incrementing a counter:

$$
\begin{array}{r}
1 \quad \leftarrow \text{initial running product} \\
\times\ 2 \quad \leftarrow \text{initial count} \\
\hline
2 \quad \leftarrow \text{new running product} \\
\times\ 3 \quad \leftarrow \text{new count} \\
\hline
6 \quad \leftarrow \text{new running product} \\
\times\ 4 \quad \leftarrow \text{new count} \\
\hline
24 \quad \leftarrow \text{new running product} \\
\times\ 5 \quad \leftarrow \text{new count} \\
\hline
120 \quad \leftarrow \text{new running product}
\end{array}
$$

Our list of objects can thus be summarized as follows:

Data Object	Kind	Type	Movement	Name of Object
nonnegative integer	variable	`int`	received	*n*
the running product	variable	`int`	returned	*product*
the counter	variable	`int`	none (local)	*count*

We can specify the problem as follows:

Receive: *n*, an integer

Precondition: $n \geq 0$

Return: *product* = *n*!, an integer

From this information, we can write a stub for the function:

```
int Factorial(int n)
{
}
```

To fill in the body of this stub, we must consider the operations required in the computation.

Operations. Analysis of the operations performed in the preceding approach gives the following list:

i. Check the precondition ($n \geq 0$)

ii. Define and initialize two integer variables (*product* and *count*)

iii. Multiply two integers (*product* and *count*) and assign the result to an integer (*product*)

iv. Increment an integer variable (*count*)

v. Repeat operations iii and iv so long as *count* is less than or equal to *n*

In chapter 2 we saw how the `assert` mechanism can be used for the first operation:

```
assert(n >= 0);
```

The second operation is also familiar:

```
int product = 1;
int count = 2;
```

We have also seen how to perform operation iii,

```
product *= count;
```

and operation iv:

```
count++;
```

The difficulty lies with the last operation. How can statements be executed more than once? Here we will use a C++ **for loop** to repeatedly execute a statement once for each number in a given range.

Algorithm. The idea of the `for` loop can be captured in pseudocode as shown in the following algorithm for our problem:

Algorithm for Factorial Computation

1. Initialize *product* to 1.

2. Repeat the following for each value of *count* in the range 2 to *n*:

> Multiply *product* by *count*.

3. Return *product*.

Coding. The C++ function in Figure 3.8 implements this algorithm:

FIGURE 3.8.   FUNCTION `Factorial()`.

```
/* Factorial computes the factorial of a nonnegative integer.
 *
 * Receive:      n, an integer
 * Precondition: n is nonnegative
 * Return:       n!
 ***************************************************************/

#include <assert.h>                  // assert()

int Factorial(int n)
{
    assert(n >= 0);

    int product = 1;

    for (int count = 2; count <= n; count++)
        product *= count;

    return product;
}
```

Testing. To test this function, we can write a simple driver program like that in Figure 3.9 to display the values returned by the function for some easy-to-check inputs. Note in the sample runs that both valid and invalid input values are used. The results indicate that `Factorial()` computes correct values for valid inputs (at least those we tried), and the `assert()` mechanism prevents output of values for negative inputs. Once it has been fully tested, `Factorial()` could be moved to a library as described in section 3.6 for convenient reuse by programs that need this mathematical function.

FIGURE 3.9.   DRIVER FOR `Factorial()`.

```
/* factorial9.cpp is a driver program to test the Factorial function
 *
 ***************************************************************/

#include <iostream.h>                // cin, cout, <<, >>

int Factorial(int n);

int main()
{
    cout << "To compute n!, enter n: ";
    int theNumber;
    cin >> theNumber;
```

```
      cout << theNumber << "! = "
           << Factorial(theNumber) << endl;
}

/*** Insert the #include directive and the definition of
     Factorial() from Figure 3.8 here. ***/
```

Sample runs:

```
To compute n!, enter n: 1
1! = 1

To compute n!, enter n: 2
2! = 2

To compute n!, enter n: 5
5! = 120

To compute n!, enter n: -1
factorial9.cpp:22: failed assertion 'n >= 0'
-1! = Abort
```

REPEATED EXECUTION: THE for STATEMENT

For algorithms like that for factorials in which a statement must be executed more than once, C++ provides the **for** **statement** (and other repetition statements described in chapter 6). It executes a statement *repeatedly,* as long as a boolean expression is true.

To illustrate, consider the for statement from Figures 3.11 and 3.12:

```
for (int count = 2; count <= n; count++)
   product *= count;
```

When it is executed, this statement behaves as shown in the flow-graph on the next page. Such statements are called **loops** because the flow of execution moves in a circular path.

When execution reaches the loop for the first time, the variable count is created and initialized to 2. The value of count is then tested against n. If count exceeds n, control passes immediately to the next statement. However, if count is less than or equal to n, then the statement controlled by the loop is executed, so product is multiplied by count. The value of count is then incremented, after which control returns to the top of the loop where the boolean expression count <= n is re-evaluated and the cycle starts again. This cyclic behavior continues so long as the boolean expression evaluates to true.

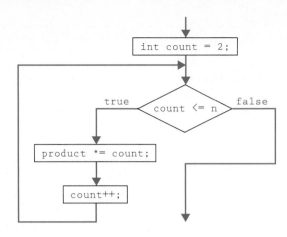

Another way to understand the execution of such a loop is with a **trace table,** which traces the execution of the loop's statements, one at a time. The following is a trace table for the execution of `Factorial(5)`:

Time	Statement Executed	product	count	Comment
0	int count = 2;	1	2	loop initialization
1	count <= n	1	2	true, loop executes
2	product *= count;	2	2	product updated
3	count++;	2	3	count incremented
4	count <= n	2	3	true, loop executes
5	product *= count;	6	3	product updated
6	count++;	6	4	count incremented
7	count <= n	6	4	true, loop executes
8	product *= count;	24	4	product updated
9	count++;	24	5	count incremented
10	count <= n	24	5	true, loop executes
11	product *= count;	120	5	product updated
12	count++;	120	6	count incremented
13	count <= n	120	6	false, repetition ceases

A `for` statement has the following general form:

for Statement

Form

```
for (init_expression; boolean_expression; step_expression)
    statement
```

where:

for is a keyword;

init_expression, *boolean_expression*, and *step_expression* are C++ expressions; and *statement* is a C++ statement (simple or compound).

Purpose:

When execution reaches a for statement, the following actions occur:

1. *init_expression* is evaluated
2. *boolean_expression* is evaluated
3. If *boolean_expression* is true, then
   a. *statement* is executed
   b. *step_expression* is evaluated
   c. Control returns to step (2)
   Otherwise
       Control passes to the statement following the for statement

Note that like the if statement, a for loop controls access to a *statement*, called the **body** of the loop, which can be either a single statement, as in

```
for (int count = 2; count <= n; count++)
    product *= count;
```

or a block of statements:

```
cout << "How many values? ";
int numValues;
cin >> numValues;
for (int count = 1; count <= numValues; count++)
{
    cin >> newValue;
    sum += newValue;
    sum_of_Squares += newValue * newValue;
}
```

Note also that allowing the *step_expression* to be an arbitrary expression makes the C++ for loop quite flexible. For example, to count downwards from 10 to 1, we could write:

```
for (int value = 10; value >= 1; value--)
    cout << value << ' ';
```

which will display

```
10 9 8 7 6 5 4 3 2 1
```

Similarly, to count from 0 to 2 by 0.5, we could write:

```
for (double counter = 0.0; counter <= 2.0; counter += 0.5)
    cout << counter << ' ';
```

which will display on many systems as follows:

```
0 0.5 1 1.5 2
```

Finally, note that when the `for` statement is being used to count by 1s, the prefix and the postfix forms of the increment (or decrement) operator can be used interchangeably. That is, to count from 1 to 10, we can write either

```
for (int count = 1; count <= 10; count++)
    statement
```

or

```
for (int count = 1; count <= 10; ++count)
    statement
```

The two are interchangeable, because both expressions add 1 to the value of `count`, which is the value being used to control the loop.

PROCESSING SEVERAL INPUT VALUES

The driver program in 3.8 for computing factorials suffers from one major drawback: It processes only one value of n. To compute factorials for other values, the program must be re-executed, which involves retyping its name, reclicking on its icon, or whatever is necessary for a particular system.

A more user-friendly program would permit the user to process any number of values before it terminated. One way to do this is to have the user specify in advance how many values are to be processed and then *wrap* the body of the program in a `for` loop that counts from 1 to that number:

```
        .
        .
        .

int main()
{
    cout << "This program computes n! for n >= 0.\n"
            "How many factorials do you wish to compute? ";
    int numValues;
    cin >> numValues;
```

```
        for (int count = 1; count <= numValues; count++)
        {
           cout << "\nEnter n: ";
           int n;
           cin >> n;
           cout << n << "! = " << Factorial(n) << endl;
        }
   }
            .
            .
            .
```

A sample run might appear as follows:

```
This program computes n! for n >= 0.
How many factorials do you wish to compute? 3

Enter n: 5
5! = 120

Enter n: 2
2! = 2

Enter n: 1
1! = 1
```

By enclosing the critical portion of a driver program within a loop, we can process several input data values without having to re-execute the program.

The difficulty with this approach is that it requires knowing the number of input values in advance and counting a long list of values is inconvenient. Morever, when testing a program, we usually do not know in advance how many data values will be used.

Fortunately, the `for` loop can be used in a better way to process sets of values. Figure 3.10 illustrates.

 FIGURE 3.10   COMPUTING SEVERAL FACTORIALS.

```
/* factorial10.cpp is a driver program to test the Factorial
 * function.  It computes any number of factorials.
 *
 ****************************************************************/

#include <iostream.h>                 // cin, cout, <<, >>

int Factorial(int n);

int main()
{
```

```
for (;;)
{
    cout << "To compute n!, enter n (a negative number to quit): ";
    int theNumber;
    cin >> theNumber;
    if (theNumber < 0) break;

    cout << theNumber << "! = "
         << Factorial(theNumber) << "\n\n";
}
```

```
}
/*** Insert the #include directive and the definition of
     Factorial() from Figure 3.8 here. ***/
```

Sample run:

```
To compute n!, enter n (a negative number to quit): 1
1! = 1

To compute n!, enter n (a negative number to quit): 2
2! = 2

To compute n!, enter n (a negative number to quit): 5
5! = 120

To compute n!, enter n (a negative number to quit): 6
6! = 720

To compute n!, enter n (a negative number to quit): -1
```

We call the special kind of loop used in this program a **forever loop** because it repeats its body an arbitrary number of times. More precisely, if the *init_expression*, *boolean_expression*, and *step_expression* are omitted from a for loop as in the preceding main function, the statements in the loop body will be repeated an *indefinite* number of times. For this reason, such loops are sometimes referred to as **indefinite loops.**[9]

Since the boolean expression that normally controls repetition is omitted in a forever loop, some other means of terminating repetition must be provided. This is typically accomplished with an **if-break combination:** an if statement that selects a **break statement** when its boolean expression is true:

---

[9] Almost all modern programming languages provide indefinite loops. For example, *Ada* and *Turing* provide the loop statement, *Modula-2* and *Modula-3* the LOOP statement, and *Fortran 90* the DO loop. Many *Fortran 90* programmers use only indefinite input loops and *Turing* provides *only* an indefinite loop.

```
for (;;)
{
    cout << "To compute n!, enter n (a negative number to quit): ";
    int theNumber;
    cin >> theNumber;

    if (theNumber < 0) break;

    cout << theNumber << "! = "
         << Factorial(theNumber) << "\n\n";
}
```

When it is executed, the break statement immediately transfers control to the first statement that follows the loop (in this case, the end of the main function). Since it is selected only when the boolean expression theNumber <= 0 evaluates to true, repetition will stop when a negative value is entered for theNumber. Such a boolean expression is called a **termination condition** or an **exit condition.**

In this example, the user is instructed to enter an invalid value called a **sentinel** when there are no more values to process. (Here, any negative value can serve as a sentinel, because factorials are defined only for nonnegative integers.) This general pattern

```
for (;;)
{
    // prompt for a value
    // input a value

    if (the value is the sentinel) break;

    // if execution gets here, then the value is not the sentinel,
    // so process it as a normal value.
}
```

is called **sentinel-based input processing,** and can be used for a wide variety of problems that involve processing lists of data.[10]

---

[10] Some programmers whose experience is with earlier programming languages prefer using a while loop for sentinel-based processing:

```
// prompt for a value
// input a value
while (the value is not the sentinel)
{
    // process the value

    // prompt for a value
    // input a value
}
```

However, this approach requires prompting for and inputting values before the loop is entered, and again at the bottom of the loop body. Such duplication of code is eliminated in an indeterminate loop approach. This form of input loop also seems to be less intuitive for a beginning programmer.

A general form for the forever loop is as follows:[11]

The Forever Loop

Form

```
for ( ; ; )
{
    statement_list₁

    if (boolean_expression) break;
    // or if (boolean_expression) return;

    statement_list₂
}
```

where:

for, if, and break are C++ keywords; and

$statement\_list_1$ and $statement\_list_2$ are sequences of zero or more C++ statements.

Purpose

$statement\_list_1$ is executed and the $boolean\_expression$ is then evaluated. If it is true, repetition terminates; otherwise $statement\_list_2$ is executed, $statement\_list_1$ is executed, and the $boolean\_expression$ is evaluated again. This continues until the $boolean\_expression$ eventually becomes true.

In the case of an if-break combination, execution of the loop will terminate, and execution will continue with the next statement after the loop.

In the case of an if-return combination, the loop and the function containing it are terminated, and control returns to the calling function.

Note that $statement\_list_1$ and $statement\_list_2$ are optional. If $statement\_list_2$ is omitted,

---

[11] Some C++ programmers prefer to write forever loops using a while loop of the form

```
while(true)
   body of loop
```

The two forms are completely equivalent. We use the for-loop version in this text because this has been the "standard" way to write such loops in C, the parent language of C++. If desired, for(;;) may be replaced everywhere with while(true) and the programs will work.

```
for (;;)
{
  statement_list₁
  if (boolean_expression) break;
}
```

the loop is called a **posttest** or **test-at-the-bottom loop.** Posttest loops have special uses, because testing the exit condition at the bottom guarantees that *the loop body is executed at least once.*

By contrast, if `statement_list₁` is omitted,

```
for (;;)
  {
      if (boolean_expression) break;
      statement_list₂
  }
```

then the loop is called a **pretest** or **test-at-the-top loop.** Pretest loops also have special uses, because testing the exit condition at the top means that *if the exit condition is initially true,* `statement_list₂` *will not be executed.* As we will see in chapter 6, C++ provides other statements for pretest and posttest loops that provide a more convenient way to write such loops.

✔ **Quick Quiz 3.4**

For questions 1–8, describe the output produced.

1. `for (int i = 1; i <= 5; i++)`
       `cout << "Hello\n";`

2. `for (int i = 1; i < 4; i++)`
       `cout << "Hello";`

3. `for (int i = 1; i <= 5; i += 2)`
       `cout << "Hello\n";`

4. `for (int i = 1; i < 7; i++)`
       `cout << i << ' ' << i + 1 << endl;`

5. `for (int i = 6; i > 0; i--)`
       `cout << endl << i*i << endl;`

6. `for (int i = 6; i <= 6; i++)`
       `cout << "Hello\n";`

7. `for (int i = 6; i <= 5; i++)`
       `cout << "Hello\n";`

8. `for (int i = 1; i <= 10; i++)`
   `{`
       `cout << i << endl;`
       `i++;`

   `}`

9. How many lines of output are produced by the following?

```
for (int i = 1; i < 6; i++)
{
   cout << i << endl;
   for (int j = 0; j <= 3; j++)
      cout << i + j << endl;
}
```

10. What is the difference between a pretest and a posttest loop?

11. (True or false) A pretest loop is always executed at least once.

12. (True or false) A posttest loop is always executed at least once.

13. Assuming that `number` is an integer variable initialized to 1, describe the output produced by the following loop:

```
for (;;)
{
   if (number > 100) break;
   cout << number << endl;
   number *= 2;
}
```

14. Assume that `number` and `limit` are integer variables in the following program segment:

```
cin >> limit;
number = 0;
for (;;)
{
   if (number > limit) break;
   cout << number << endl;
   number++;
}
```

Describe the output produced for the following inputs:

(a) 4   (b) −2

15. Assume that `number` and `limit` are integer variables in the following program segment:

```
cin >> limit;
number = 0;
for (;;)
{
   cout << number << endl;
   number++;
   if (number > limit) break;
}
```

Describe the output produced for the following inputs:

(a) 4   (b) −2

EXERCISES 3.4

For questions 1–5, describe the output produced.

1.
```
for (int i = -2; i <= 3; i++)
    cout << i << " squared = " << i*i << endl;
```
2.
```
for (int i = 1; i <= 5; i++)
{
    cout << i << endl;
    for (int j = i; j >= 1; j--)
        cout << j << endl;
}
```
3.
```
int k = 5;
for (int i = -2; i <= 3; i++)
{
    cout << i + k << endl;
    k = 1;
}
```
4.
```
for (int i = 1; i <= 3; i++)
    for (int j = 1; j <= 3; j++)
        for (int k = 1; k <= j; k++)
            cout << i << j << k << endl;
```
5.
```
for (int i = 1; i <= 3; i++)
    for (int j = 1; j <= 3; j++)
    {
        for (int k = i; k <= j; k++)
            cout << i << j << k << endl;
        cout << endl;
    }
```

For exercises 6–8, assume that i, j, and k are integer variables. Describe the output produced.

6.
```
i = 0;
j = 0;
for (;;)
{
    k = 2 * i * j;
    if (k > 10)  break;
    cout << i << j << k << endl;
    i++;
    j++;
}
cout << k << endl;
```
7.
```
i = 0;
j = 0;
for (;;)
{
    k = 2 * i * j;
    if (k > 10) break;
    cout << i << j << k << endl;
    if (i + j > 5) break;
    i++;
    j++;
}
cout << k << endl;
```

8.
```
i = 5;
for (;;)
{
    cout << i;
    i -= 2;
    if (i < 1) break;
    j = 0;
    for (;;)
    {
        j++;
        cout << j;
        if (j >= i) break;
    }
    cout << "###\n";
}
cout << "***\n";
```

Each of the program segments in exercises 9–11 is intended to find the smallest integer number for which the sum $1 + 2 + \cdots + \text{number}$ is greater than limit. For each exercise, make three trace tables that display the values of number and sum, one table for each of the following values of limit:

(a) 10   (b) 1   (c) 0

9.
```
/* Using a pretest loop */
number = 0;
sum = 0;
for (;;)
{
    if (sum > limit) break;
    number++;
    sum += number;
}
```

10.
```
/* Using a posttest loop */
number = 0;
sum = 0;
for (;;)
{
    number++;
    sum += number;
    if (sum > limit) break;
}
```

11.
```
/* Using a test-in-the middle loop */
number = 0;
sum = 0;
for (;;)
{
    number++;
    if (sum > limit) break;
    sum += number;
}
```

For exercises 12 and 13, write functions that will do what is required. To test these functions, you should write driver programs as instructed in Programming Problems 21 and 22 at the end of this chapter.

12.   For a positive integer n, use a for loop to find the sum $1 + 2 + \cdots + n$ and return this sum.

13.   For two integers m and n with $m \leq n$, use a for loop to find the sum $m + (m + 1) + \cdots + n$ and return this sum.

For exercises 14–20, write a loop to do what is asked for.

14. Display the squares of the first 100 positive integers in increasing order.

15. Display the cubes of the first 50 positive integers in decreasing order.

16. Display the square roots of the first 25 odd positive integers.

17. Display a list of points (x, y) on the graph of $y = x^3 - 3x + 1$ for x ranging from -2 to 2 in steps of 0.1.

18. Display the value of x and decrease x by 0.5 as long as x is positive.

19. Read values for a, b, and c and print their sum, repeating this as long as none of a, b, or c is negative.

20. Calculate and display the squares of consecutive positive integers until the difference between a square and the preceding one is greater than 50.

3.5 EXAMPLE: AN 8-FUNCTION CALCULATOR

PROBLEM

Write an 8-function calculator program that allows the user to perform addition, subtraction, multiplication, division, exponentiation, base-ten logarithm, factorial, and quit operations.

OBJECT-CENTERED DESIGN

Behavior. The program will display on the screen a menu of the eight operations, telling the user to enter +, −, *, /, ^, l, !, or q to specify the operation to be performed. The program will read the operation from the keyboard. If the user enters q, execution will terminate. Otherwise, the program will display on the screen a prompt for the first operand, which it will then read from the keyboard. If the operation requires two operands, the program will display on the screen a prompt for the second operand, which it will then read from the keyboard. The program will then compute the result of performing the specified operation using the operand(s) provided and output this result. The program should repeat this behavior until the user specifies the q operation.

Objects. We can immediately identify the following objects from our behavioral description:

Data Object	Kind of Value	Type of Object	Name of Object
screen	variable	ostream	cout
prompt for the first operand	constant	string	none
first operand	variable	double	*operand1*
keyboard	variable	istream	cin
menu of operations	constant	string	*MENU*
the operation	variable	char	*theOperation*
second operand	variable	double	*operand2*
the result	variable	double	*result*

(We will be studying `string` objects in detail in the next chapter. Here we will introduce them by building a `string` object to represent the menu.)

This object list enables us to specify the problem more precisely:

Output: Prompts for input

Input: *operand1,* a real;
                     theOperation, a character;
                     and (possibly) *operand2,* a real

Precondition: *theOperation* is one of +, −, *, /, ^, 1, !, or q

Output: the *result* of applying *theOperation* to *operand1* and *operand2*

Operations. From our behavioral description, we can identify the following operations:

Operation Needed	C++ Operation/Statement
i. Output a character string to the screen (prompts, the menu)	<<
ii. Input a character from the keyboard (the operator)	>>
iii. Input a real value from the keyboard (*operand1, operand2*)	>>
iv. Compute the result	none
v. Output a real value to the screen (result)	<<
vi. Repeat the preceding steps, unless the user entered q in step ii	forever loop

With the exception of operation iv, each of these operations is provided by a C++ operation or statement as noted at the right of the operations. We will construct a function to perform operation iv. Given such a function, we can organize our operations into the following algorithm:

Algorithm for 8-Function Calculator Problem

Loop:

   1. Display *MENU* via `cout`.

   2. Read *theOperator* from `cin`.

   3. If *theOperator* is q, terminate the repetition. Otherwise continue with the following.

   4. Display a prompt for the first operand via `cout`.

   5. Read *operand1* from `cin`.

   6. If *theOperator* is a binary operator:

       a. Display a prompt for the second operand via `cout`.

       b. Read *operand2* from `cin`.

7. Compute *result* using *theOperator, operand1,* and *operand2.*

8. Output *result.*

Refinement. Step 7 of this algorithm involves a nontrivial operation. We will develop a function to perform it using the same design steps we are using to solve the "big" problem.

Function's Behavior. The function should receive *theOperator, operand1,* and *operand2* from its caller, and then do the following:

If *theOperator* is:	The function should:
+	Return the sum of *operand1* and *operand2*
–	Return the difference of *operand1* and *operand2*
*	Return the product of *operand1* and *operand2*
/	Return the quotient of *operand1* and *operand2*
^	Return $operand1^{operand2}$
l	Return the logarithm of *operand1*
!	Compute the factorial of the integer part of *operand1* and return the real number equivalent
invalid	Display an error message and return 0

Function's Objects. From this behavioral description, we can identify the following objects:

Data Object	Kind	Type	Movement	Name of Object
operator	variable	`char`	received	*theOperator*
first operand	variable	`double`	received	*operand1*
second operand	variable	`double`	received	*operand2*
return value	variable	`double`	returned	none

Using this list of object names, we can specify the subproblem this function must solve as follows:

Receive: *theOperator,* a character
operand1, a real value
operand2, a real value

Return: the result of applying *theOperator* to *operand1* and *operand2*

This suggests that we can define the following stub for this function:

```
double OperationResult(char theOperator,
                       double operand1, double operand2)
{
}
```

(Note that we name our operator `theOperator` instead of `operator`, because `operator` is a keyword in C++.)

Function's Operations. From the function's behavioral description, we can identify the following operations:

Operation needed	C++ Operation/statement
i. Sum two reals	`+`
ii. Subtract two reals	`-`
iii. Multiply two reals	`*`
iv. Divide two reals	`/`
v. Raise a real to an integer power	`pow()`
vi. Find the base-ten logarithm of a real	`log10()`
vii. Convert a real to an integer and an integer to a real	type casts
viii. Compute the factorial of an integer	`Factorial()`
ix. Display a character string (the error message)	`<<`
x. Select from among i–ix, based on the value of *theOperator*.	`if`

For step x, where we must select one of i–ix, based on *theOperator,* we need selective execution; that is, an `if` statement.

Function's Algorithm. We can organize these operations into the following algorithm:

Algorithm for Result Calculation Function

1. If *theOperator* is '+':
    Return *operand1* + *operand2*.

2. Otherwise, if *theOperator* is '−'
    Return *operand1* − *operand2*.

3. Otherwise, if *theOperator* is '*'
    Return *operand1* * *operand2*.

4. Otherwise, if *theOperator* is '/'
    Return *operand1* / *operand2*.

5. Otherwise, if *theOperator* is '^'
    Return `pow`(*operand1, operand2*).

6. Otherwise, if *theOperator* is 'l'
    Return `log10`(*operand1*).

7. Otherwise, if *theOperator* is '!'
    Return `Factorial`(*integer-part-of-operand1*) converted to a real.

8. Otherwise,
>   **a.** Display an error message.
>   **b.** Return 0.

Function's Coding. The algorithm for our function can be expressed in C++ as shown in Figure 3.11:

FIGURE 3.11   RESULT CALCULATION FUNCTION.

```
/* OperationResult applies theOperator to operand1 and operand2.
 *
 * Receive:      theOperator, a character
 *               operand1 and operand2, two doubles
 * Precondition: theOperator is one of +, -, *, /, ^, l, !
 * Return:       the result of applying theOperator to operand1
 *               and operand2
 ***********************************************************************/

#include <math.h>              // pow(), log10()

double OperationResult(char theOperator, double operand1, double operand2)
{
   if (theOperator == '+')
      return operand1 + operand2;
   else if (theOperator == '-')
      return operand1 - operand2;
   else if (theOperator == '*')
      return operand1 * operand2;
   else if (theOperator == '/')
      if (operand2 != 0)
         return operand1 / operand2;
      else
         cerr << "Operation Result: division by 0 -- result undefined!\n";
   else if (theOperator == '^')
      return pow(operand1, operand2);
   else if (theOperator == 'l')
      return log10(operand1);
   else if (theOperator == '!')
      return (double)Factorial((int)operand1);
   else                ( int Factorial (int operand1 ));
   {
      cerr << "OperationResult: invalid operator "
           << theOperator << " received!\n";
      return 0.0;
   }
}
```

Coding the Program. Once the operations are available for each step of the algorithm, we can write a program like the following in Figure 3.12 that encodes the algorithm for the original problem.

FIGURE 3.12.   PROGRAM TO SOLVE THE CALCULATOR PROBLEM.

```cpp
/* calculator12.cpp implements a simple 8-function calculator.
 *
 * Input:  operand1, theOperator, operand2
 * Output: the result of applying theOperator to operand1 and operand2.
 ********************************************************************/

#include <iostream.h>                 // cin, cout, <<, >>
#include <string>                     // string

double OperationResult(char theOperator, double operand1, double operand2);
int Factorial(int n);

int main()
{
    const string MENU = "Enter:\n"
                        "  + for the addition operation\n"
                        "  - for the subtraction operation\n"
                        "  * for the multiplication operation\n"
                        "  / for the division operation\n"
                        "  ^ for the exponentiation operation\n"
                        "  l for the base-10 logarithm operation\n"
                        "  ! for the factorial operation and\n"
                        "  q to quit.\n"
                        "--> ";

    cout << "Welcome to the 8-function calculator!\n\n";

    double operand1,
           operand2,
           result;
    char theOperator;

    for (;;)
    {
        cout << MENU;
        cin >> theOperator;

        if (theOperator == 'q') break;

        cout << "Enter the first operand: ";
        cin >> operand1;

        if (theOperator == '+' || theOperator == '-' ||
            theOperator == '*' || theOperator == '/' ||
            theOperator == '^')
        {
            cout << "Enter the second operand: ";
            cin >> operand2;
        }
```

```
        result = OperationResult(theOperator, operand1, operand2);

        cout << "The result is " << result << endl << endl;
    }
}
```

```
/*** Insert the #include directives and the definitions of functions
     Factorial() from Figures 3.8 and OperationResult() from
     Figure 3.11 here.  ***/
```

Sample run:

```
Welcome to the 8-function calculator!

Enter:
  + for the addition operation
  - for the subtraction operation
  * for the multiplication operation
  / for the division operation
  ^ for the exponentiation operation
  l for the base-10 logarithm operation
  ! for the factorial operation and
  q to quit
--> /
Enter the first operand: 2
Enter the second operand: 3
The result is 0.666667

Enter:
  + for the addition operation
  - for the subtraction operation
  * for the multiplication operation
  / for the division operation
  ^ for the exponentiation operation
  l for the base-10 logarithm operation
  ! for the factorial operation and
  q to quit
--> ^
Enter the first operand: 2
Enter the second operand: 3
The result is 8

Enter:
  + for the addition operation
  - for the subtraction operation
  * for the multiplication operation
  / for the division operation
  ^ for the exponentiation operation
  l for the base-10 logarithm operation
  ! for the factorial operation and
  q to quit
```

```
--> !
Enter the first operand: 4
The result is 24


Enter:
   + for the addition operation
   - for the subtraction operation
   * for the multiplication operation
   / for the division operation
   ^ for the exponentiation operation
   l for the base-10 logarithm operation
   ! for the factorial operation and
   q to quit
--> q
```

Testing. The sample runs show only a small group of the tests that must be performed to verify the correctness of the program. In particular, since we are using selective execution, it is possible for one path through the program to contain an error that goes undetected if execution does not follow that path. Thus, each possible execution path through the program (i.e., each operation) must be tested to ensure that it is behaving correctly.

3.6 AN INTRODUCTION TO LIBRARIES

In the preceding sections, we have seen how functions enable us to extend the collection of operations provided in C++. If a problem requires some new operation, we can define and call a function to perform that operation, just as if C++ did provide it.

Although this is a significant improvement over using only expressions, it does not by itself make it easy for us to reuse our work. For example, to use the function `Factorial()` in the calculator program of the preceding section, we have to copy its prototype and its definition from the program in Figure 3.9 and insert them at the appropriate places in the program in Figure 3.12. We might use the *copy-and-paste* capabilities of a word processor to do this. If we needed the function `FahrToCelsius()` from Figure 3.2 in a new program, we might use this same copy-and-paste method or we might simply make a copy of the program in Figure 3.2, delete everything between the prototype and definition of `FahrToCelsius()`, and then write the new program between this prototype and definition.

Although these approaches may be acceptable in languages not designed for reusability, C++ provides a better approach by supporting **libraries,** which are collections of files containing declarations and definitions of items that can be used in programs and in other libraries. C++ inherited the idea of libraries from its parent language C, which defined a number of standard libraries, some of which we have described in earlier chapters.

Libraries are one feature that make C a powerful language, because they make it possible to share commonly-used functions between different programs. For example, we noted in chapter 2 that the standard C library provides the function `exit()` that can be used to terminate execution of a program at any point in the program. When executed, the function call

```
exit(1);
```

will terminate a program and make its return value 1. (Recall from chapter 1 that a C++ program is a function named `main()` whose return value is normally 0.) To use the `exit()` function, we need only include the library's header file `stdlib.h` in the program:

```
#include <stdlib.h>
```

The C++ libraries provide a variety of different functions, several of which are described in appendix D.[12] In this section we give a brief description of how such libraries are constructed.

CONSTRUCTING A LIBRARY

If we examine the libraries of functions provided in the various C++ implementations, we see that the functions in each library are *related* in some way. For example, the `iostream` library provides functions for performing input and output and the `math` library provides functions that are commonly needed in mathematical computations. It would be silly (and confusing) to put the `sin()` function in the `iostream` library or to put one of the input functions in the `math` library.

The first step in constructing a library, therefore, is to identify its *organizing principle;* that is, what kind of functions it should contain. For example, if we intend to store the temperature-conversion function `FahrToCelsius()` in a library and temperature measures heat, we might call the library `Heat`. It will contain items that are in some way related to heat and temperature, just as the `iostream` library contains functions that are related to input and output streams.

Once we have decided what kind of items will be in the library, we must identify the particular items that we want it to provide. By careful planning and trying to anticipate what items related to heat might be reused, we hope to save time in the future—long-term rather than short-term planning.

One way to select the functions to store in a library is to view them as the operations on a type of data object. For example, if the library is to contain functions that are related to temperature, and we view temperature as a type, then the library should provide the operations commonly performed on that type. Thus, in addition to a Fahrenheit-to-Celsius conversion, we should perhaps also include the inverse operation of Celsius-to-Fahrenheit conversion. Functions to convert a temperature in each scale to Kelvin and back are other possible additions.

It is important to note that we are not limited to storing functions in a library. For example, we might also store important heat-related constants in our library, such as the heat of fusion of water (79.71 calories/gram) and the heat of vaporization of water (539.55 calories/gram). The important thing is to identify useful items that are related to heat or temperature and put them into the library, so that a user can retrieve and use these items (and thus avoid "reinventing the wheel").

Once the items that the library is to contain have been selected, we are ready to begin construction of the library. A library is a collection of files:

---

[12] The header files of these inherited libraries have alternative names in standard C++. For example, the C header files `stdlib.h`, `math.h`, and `ctype.h` are also named `cstdlib`, `cmath`, and `cctype`, respectively. In general, the new name of a header file that C++ inherits from C is modified by prepending a `c` to its name and dropping its `.h` extension.

▶ A **header file** that contains the *declarations* and *prototypes* of the items in the library. It is inserted into a program (or another library) using a #include directive. It serves as an *interface* between the library and a program that uses the library and is thus sometimes called the library's **interface file.**

▶ An **implementation file** that contains the *definitions* of items not defined in the header file. It must be separately compiled and then linked to a program needing to access its contents.

▶ A **documentation file** that contains *documentation* for the items in the library.[13]

Building the Header File. A header file contains declarations of all items stored in the library. For functions stored in the library, it contains the *prototypes* of the functions but usually *not their definitions.* Thus, just as iostream (or iostream.h in older versions of C++) is a file containing declarations of items needed to perform stream input and output, Heat will be a header file containing declarations of items needed for processing heat and temperature objects. It might begin as shown in Figure 3.13:

FIGURE 3.13   HEADER FILE FOR LIBRARY Heat.

```
/* Heat.h provides an interface for a library of
 * heat-related constants and functions.
 *
 * Created by: Jane Roe, January, 1997, at Yoyodyne Industries.
 * Modification History: Kelvin functions added April, 1997 -- JR.
 ************************************************************************/

const double HEATOFFUSION = 79.71;          // calories per gram

const double HEATOFVAPORIZATION = 539.55;   // calories per gram

double FahrToCelsius(double tempFahr);      // degrees Celsius

double CelsiusToFahr(double tempCels);      // degrees Fahrenheit

double FahrToKelvin(double tempFahr);       // degrees Kelvin

double KelvinToFahr(double tempKelv);       // degrees Fahrenheit

double CelsiusToKelvin(double tempCels);    // degrees Kelvin

double KelvinToCelsius(double tempKelv);    // degrees Celsius
```

If a program includes this header file (using a #include directive) before its main function, the compiler will insert these statements into the program at that point. Since these statements are declarations of the library's constants and proto-

---

[13] An alternative approach is to document each object and/or function in the header file. However, this tends to clutter the header file and reduce its overall readability. For this reason, we will put this documentation in a separate file.

types of the library's functions, these items can be used at any point thereafter in the program.

It is not necessary to compile the header file separately. It gets compiled when it is *inserted* into a program; that is, when the program that names it in a #include directive is compiled, the contents of the header file also get compiled.

Building the Implementation File. As noted earlier, the *definitions* of a library's functions are stored in the implementation file of the library.[14] The implementation file is so named because it implements (i.e., defines) the functions that are declared in the header file. Part of the implementation file for our library Heat is given in Figure 3.14:

FIGURE 3.14   IMPLEMENTATION FILE FOR LIBRARY Heat.

```
/* Heat.cpp provides the function implementations for Heat,
 * a library of heat-related constants and functions.
 *
 * Created by: Jane Roe, January, 1997, at Yoyodyne Industries.
 * Modification History: Kelvin functions added April, 1997 — JR.
 ****************************************************************/

#include "Heat.h"

//---------------------------------------------

double FahrToCelsius(double tempFahr)
{
   return (tempFahr - 32.0) / 1.8;
}

//---------------------------------------------

double CelsiusToFahr(double tempCels)
{
   return tempCels * 1.8 + 32.0;
}

// . . . Definitions of other functions omitted to save space . . .
```

It is important to note that, unlike the header file, a library's implementation file must be compiled. This is the reason that this implementation file contains the line

```
#include "Heat.h"
```

in addition to the definitions of the various temperature-related functions. When the library's implementation file is compiled, the compiler will insert and pro-

---

[14] Although the name of a library's header file usually has a .h extension, the extension for an implementation file is the same as that of a source file (e.g., .cpp).

cess the function prototypes from the header file and then process their definitions in the library's implementation file. Because the compiler processes both the prototypes and the definitions of the functions, it can check that they are *consistent*; if it detects any inconsistencies, the compiler will display an error message.

It is also important to note that:

▶ Items defined in the implementation file that are declared in the header file can be accessed in any program that uses the `#include` directive to insert the header file

▶ Items defined in the implementation file that are *not* declared in the header file *cannot* be accessed outside of the implementation file, even by a program that inserts the header file

Stated differently, items in the header file can be thought of as **public** information, whereas information in the implementation file is **private** within the library.

Building The Documentation File. The documentation file is a copy of the header file, but it is annotated with documentation that describes each object and provides the specification for each function prototype. Figure 3.15 shows part of `Heat.doc`, the documentation file for library `Heat`.

FIGURE 3.15   DOCUMENTATION FILE FOR LIBRARY Heat.

```
/* Heat.doc provides the documentation for Heat,
 * a library of heat-related constants and functions.
 *
 * Created by: Jane Roe, January, 1997, at Yoyodyne Industries.
 * Modification History: Kelvin functions added March, 1997 -- JR.
 *************************************************************/

// the amount of heat needed to change water from liquid to solid
const double HEATOFFUSION = 79.71;          // calories per gram

// the amount of heat needed to change water from liquid to gas
const double HEATOFVAPORIZATION = 539.55;   // calories per gram

/* FahrToCelsius converts a temperature from Fahrenheit to Celsius.
 *
 * Receive:  A Fahrenheit temperature
 * Return:   The equivalent Celsius temperature
 */
double FahrToCelsius(double tempFahr);      // degrees Celsius

/* CelsiusToFahr converts a temperature from Celsius to Fahrenheit.
 *
 * Receive:  A Celsius temperature
 * Return:   The equivalent Fahrenheit temperature
 */
double CelsiusToFahr(double tempCels);      // degrees Fahrenheit

// ... Documentation of other functions omitted to save space ...
```

Such a documentation file serves a secondary purpose: as an annotated copy of the header file, it serves as a *backup* for the header file.

USING A LIBRARY IN A PROGRAM

Once the library Heat has been constructed, it can be used in a program like that in Figure 3.16 for solving the temperature-conversion problem.

FIGURE 3.16   CONVERTING A TEMPERATURE—VERSION 3.

```
/* temperature16.cpp converts a temperature from Fahrenheit to Celsius,
 * using function FahrToCelsius() that is stored in library Heat.
 *
 * Input:    tempFahrenheit
 * Output:   tempCelsius
 ***********************************************************************/

#include <iostream.h>                        // cin, cout, <<, >>

#include "Heat.h"                            // the library's header file


int main()
{
    cout << "This program converts a temperature\n"
            "from Fahrenheit to Celsius.\n";

    cout << "\nEnter a Fahrenheit temperature: ";
    double tempFahrenheit;
    cin >> tempFahrenheit;

    double tempCelsius = FahrToCelsius(tempFahrenheit);

    cout << tempFahrenheit << " degrees Fahrenheit is equivalent to "
         << tempCelsius << " degrees Celsius\n";
}
```

Execution of this program is identical to that in Figure 3.2. In this program, how-ever, the prototype of FahrToCelsius() before the main function has been re-placed by the line

```
#include "Heat.h"
```

and the definition of FahrToCelsius() is no longer present. The prototype and the definition of FahrToCelsius() are not given in this file, because the proto-type is in the header file of library Heat and the definition is in the library's imple-mentation file.

It is important to understand the difference between the notation

```
#include "Heat.h"
```

used to include the `Heat` library's header file, and the different notation

```
#include <iostream.h>
```

used to include the `iostream` library's header file. If the name of a library's header file is surrounded by *angle brackets* (`<` and `>`), the C++ compiler will search for that file in the special system `include` directory described in chapter 2. By contrast, if the name of a library's header file is enclosed in *double quotes,* the C++ compiler will search for that file in the directory that contains the source file being compiled.

C++ also permits the programmer to store a library in a different directory (e.g., a library directory) and then instruct the compiler to search that directory when looking for files named by `#include` directives. The details of how to do this vary from one environment to another.[15]

TRANSLATING A LIBRARY

Translation of a program consists of two separate steps:

1. **Compilation,** in which a source program is translated to an equivalent machine-language program, called an *object program,* which is stored in an *object file*[16]

2. **Linking,** in which any calls to functions that are defined within a library are linked to their definitions, creating an *executable program,* which is stored in an *executable file*

Since a programmer-defined library must also be compiled (if it isn't already), translation of a program that uses a library may require three separate actions:[17]

1. Separate compilation of the program's source file, creating an object file

2. Separate compilation of the library's implementation file, creating a different object file (unless the library's implementation file has already been compiled)

3. Linking the function calls in the program's object file to the function definitions in the library's object file, creating an executable program

---

[15] In Turbo C++, this is done by adding the directory to the appropriate list in the *Compile Options* dialogue box. In GNU C++, this is done using the `-I   Path` switch, where `Path` is the path to the new directory.

[16] DOS object files end in the extension .`OBJ`, UNIX object files end in the extension .`o`, and Macintosh object files are stored within the Project, and thus have no separate extension.

[17] In GNU C++, the -c switch can be used to compile the source file separately (e.g., `g++  -c  temperature16.cpp`), and to compile the library's implemenation file separately (e.g., `g++  -c  Heat.cpp`). The two object files can then be linked (e.g., `g++  temperature16.o  Heat.o  -o  temp16`). In *Turbo C++, Visual C++, Symantec C++,* and *CodeWarrior C++,* separate compilation can be coordinated by creating a `Project`, to which the names of the source file and library implementation files are added. Given a `Project`, the `Make` operation can be used to perform all necessary compilation and linking steps in one convenient step.

It makes no difference whether the source program or the library's implementation file is compiled first, but *both source and library implementation files must be compiled before linking can be performed.* The following diagram illustrates this process:

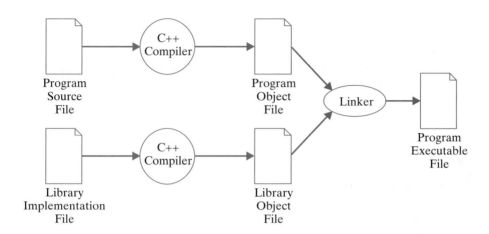

While the mechanics of translation differ from one system to another, there are two basic approaches: translation from the *command-line,* and translation using a *project file.* In a command-line environment such as UNIX, Linux, or MS-DOS, the user interacts with the computer by typing commands. Compiling and linking the source code in the files `temperature16.cpp` and `Heat.cpp` thus requires several commands. For example, if we are using the GNU C++ compiler (`g++`) on a UNIX system, we begin by entering the command to separately compile the source file `temperature16.cpp`,

```
g++ -c temperature16.cpp
```

which creates the object file `temperature16.o`. Next, we do the same for the library's implementation file,

```
g++ -c Heat.cpp
```

which creates a second object file `Heat.o`. Finally, we link these two object files together,

```
g++ temperature16.o Heat.o -o temp16
```

which produces a binary executable file named `temp16` that can be executed simply by typing its name:

```
temp16
```

In a GUI C++ development environment such as *CodeWarrior* for Macintosh, *Symantec C++* for Macintosh and Windows, *Visual C++* for Windows, or *Turbo C++* for Windows, a multi-file translation is coordinated by creating a special file called a *project*.[18] By selecting a menu choice (such as `Project` → `Add Files`), a dialogue box appears through which one can add source files such as `tempera-ture16.cpp` and `Heat.cpp` (but *not* `Heat`) to the project. Once this has been done, translation is accomplished using the `Make` menu choice (usually `Pro-ject` → `Make`, or `Compile` → `Make`), which automatically compiles each file in the project and then links the resulting object files into a binary executable. This binary executable can then be executed from within the environment by choosing the `Run` menu choice (usually `Project` → `Run`, or `Compile` → `Run`), or from the operating system by double-clicking its icon.

Although the extra step of compiling a library separately from the source program may seem like an inconvenience, it has two significant benefits:

1.   The compilation time for the source program is significantly reduced;

2.   Any errors that occur are (most likely) confined to the source program.

These long-term advantages far outweigh the short-term inconvenience.

To illustrate this, suppose that we have written a library containing a large number of functions that a friend wishes to use in a program she is writing. Because C++ allows us to link together separately-compiled files, translation of her program requires

1.   Compilation of her source program; and

2.   Linking the resulting object file to our library's object file.

By contrast, if it were necessary to recompile the library's implementation file each time she translated her program, the translation would probably take much longer. Moreover, since our library is compiled separately (and, we hope, is error-free), any errors generated during compilation must lie in her source file. *Separate compilation and linking eliminate needless recompilation of a library and allow errors to be isolated in a file.*

OBJECT-CENTERED DESIGN: INCORPORATING FUNCTIONS AND LIBRARIES

Up to now, we have designed software solutions to problems using object-centered design (OCD), which we described as follows:

Behavior: State how you want the program to behave as precisely as possible;

Objects: Identify the objects in the problem description and categorize them;

Operations: Identify the operations that are needed to solve the problem;

---

[18] Many command-line environments provide a `make` utility that uses a special file called a `Makefile` to coordinate the multi-file translation. Discussion of the `make` utility is beyond the scope of this text—for an introduction, see the lab manual *Hands On C++ (GNU version)* by Adams (Prentice Hall, 1995); or for a complete discussion, see *Mastering Make* by Tondo, Nathanson and Yount (Prentice Hall, 1994).

Algorithm: Arrange the operations on the objects in an order that solves that problem.

Now that we have seen how to build functions and store them in libraries, we need to integrate these new capabilities into OCD. Since a function can be thought of as a way to extend C++ by adding an operation not predefined in the language, we will expand OCD as follows:

Behavior: State how you want the program to behave as precisely as possible;

Objects: Identify the objects in the problem description and categorize them;

Operations: Identify the operations that are needed to solve the problem;

             If an operation is not predefined, then

              a. Write a function to implement that operation;

              b. If that function seems likely to be reused in the future, store it in a library;

Algorithm: Arrange the operations on the objects in an order that solves that problem.

Thus, any time a problem requires an operation that is not provided in C++, we will write a function to implement that operation. Functions that are likely to be reused in the future should be stored in a library instead of in the file containing the main function.

SUMMARY

Libraries are fundamental to the object-oriented approach to programming, because they provide the following benefits:

Functions in a Library Are Reusable.   A library *extends the language* by making additional items—functions, constants, and so on—available to any program (or other library). There is no need for a programmer to "reinvent the wheel" each time these items are needed.

Libraries Hide Implementation Details.   To use the items in a library, the programmer needs to know only the information in the header file; the details in the implementation file are of no concern. The header and documentation files must be provided to users, but the source code in the implementation file need not be made available—only its compiled object file, so that it can be linked to their programs. The details in the implementation file can thus remain "hidden" in the machine code of the object file provided to the user. This **information hiding** makes it possible to use the library without being concerned about these details. For example, one can use the square root function `sqrt()` from the math library without worrying about the details of how the operation is performed.

Libraries Make Programs Easier to Maintain.   Information hiding is one of the most important benefits of using libraries, because it makes programs using the libraries *easier to maintain.* When programmers are permitted to access the contents of the implementation file, they may be tempted to use the implementation details in their programs. However, if the implementation file is subsequently changed (e.g., perhaps a faster square root function is devised and substituted for the old one), then such programs may no longer work correctly. Maintaining such programs requires that they be modified to remove the references to the obsolete details, be recompiled, and then be relinked with the new implementation object file.

By contrast, if the implementation details are hidden in the implementation file, a programmer is unable to access those details and is thus forced to use the interface provided in the header file. The benefit is that if a library's implementation file changes (but its interface does not), then maintaining the program that uses the library requires only that it be relinked to the new implementation object file. By forcing programs to use the library's interface instead of the implementation details, no modification or recompilation of the program is necessary when those implementation details change.

Libraries Permit Separate Compilation. Another benefit that results from this separation of programs and libraries is that they can be compiled separately. **Separate compilation** makes it possible to change the implementation file of a library and recompile only the implementation file; programs or other libraries that use the library need not be changed or recompiled. For example, if function `FahrToCelsius()` in the implementation file of the library `Heat` is changed, then only the implementation file needs to be recompiled. A program using `FahrToCelsius()` need not be recompiled, because the prototype of `FahrToCelsius()` has not changed, only its definition. All that would be needed is to relink the program to the new object file of library `Heat`. However, if the interface in the header file is altered, then both the library's implementation file and all programs and other libraries that name that header file in a `#include` directive must be recompiled and relinked.

Libraries Support Independent Coding. Libraries introduce a higher level of *modularity* into software design by allowing related functions to be grouped together into independent units. This is especially useful in large programming projects that involve several programmers. A team of programmers might jointly identify the objects and operations required to complete a large software project. By categorizing the operations according to the kind of object on which they operate, a library can be designed to house the operations on each particular kind of object. Once the needed libraries have been identified (as well as the operations they are to contain), the header files of these libraries can be easily constructed.

When the header files have been created, the work of the project can be divided among the programming team, with one group of programmers working on the program(s) that will use the functions in the libraries, and different groups of programmers assigned to construct the implementation files of the various libraries. Because the work is partitioned into manageable "chunks", the entire project can be completed much more rapidly. Moreover, since the work in one portion of the project proceeds independently of the work in another portion of the project, the likelihood of errors is greatly diminished.

Libraries Simplify Testing. Separate libraries can be developed and tested independently (using driver programs) by completely different programmers or teams of programmers. Again, because the project has been divided into smaller libraries, each library can be tested much more thoroughly (and rapidly) than can a project stored in a single, monolithic file.

✔ Quick Quiz 3.6

1. (True or false) Libraries were first provided in the language C++.

2. What are the three types of files included in a library?

3. What are the main benefits of using libraries?

4. A library's _____ file contains the declarations and prototypes of the items in the library.

5. A library's _____ file contains the definitions of the functions in the library.

6. A library's _____ file is sometimes called its interface file.

7. The items in a library's header file contain _____ information, whereas the items in its implementation file contain _____ information (public or private).

8. If a program contains #include_____, the compiler will search for the file lib in a special system include directory.

9. If a program contains #include_____, the compiler will search for the file lib in the directory that contains the program being compiled.

10. What two steps are required to translate a program that uses libraries?

11. (True or false) A library's header file is usually compiled separately from a program that uses the library.

12. (True or false) If a library's header file is modified then all programs that use the library must be recompiled.

13. _____ makes it possible to use a library without knowing all the details of how it is implemented.

Part of the Picture: Computability Theory

At the beginning of this chapter, we were limited to designing functions that applied operations to objects in a sequential fashion. The statements presented in sections 3.3 and 3.4 now allow us to design functions that apply operations *selectively* or *repetitively*.

Selection and repetition enable us to build functions that are more powerful than those limited to sequential execution. There are functions that use sequence and selection for which there is no equivalent function that uses only sequential execution. Similarly, there are functions that use sequence, selection, and repetition for which there is no equivalent function that uses only sequence and selective execution.

Stated differently, *the set of all operations that can be performed using only sequential execution is a proper subset of the set of all operations that can be performed using sequence and selection. And the set of all operations that can be performed using only sequential and selective execution is a proper subset of the set of all operations that can be performed using sequence, selection, and repetition.* The **Venn Diagram** on the next page pictures the relationship between these three categories of functions. Selection statements allow us to design and implement operations that are more powerful than those we can build using only sequence; and adding repetition statements allows us to design and implement operations that are more powerful than those that can be built using only sequence and selection.

This is a result from *Computability Theory,* a branch of computer science that investigates (from a theoretical viewpoint) interesting questions such as the following:

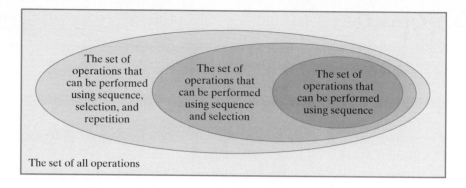

- ▶ What can (or cannot) be computed?
- ▶ How can functions be classified, and what relationships exist among those classes?
- ▶ What is the most efficient algorithm for solving a particular problem?

Rather than ask questions about programs written in an existing language or that run on a particular hardware platform, both of which become obsolete all too soon, theoreticians represent programs *abstractly*, using mathematical models (e.g., *the set of all functions that use only sequence*). The advantage of this is that when a theoretician discovers something that is true about the model, then that result is true for all programs represented by that model, regardless of the language in which those programs are written and regardless of the hardware on which those programs execute! This **language and hardware independence** gives theoretical work a sense of *timelessness:* although programming languages and hardware platforms come and go, theoretical results endure.

☞ *PROGRAMMING POINTERS*

✎ PROGRAM STYLE AND DESIGN

1. *Functions should be documented in the same way as programs.* The documentation should include specifications and descriptions of

   - ▶ The *purpose* of the function
   - ▶ Any items *input to* the function
   - ▶ Any items *output by* the function
   - ▶ What the function *receives*
   - ▶ What the function *returns*

   In this text, to avoid cluttering the header and implementation files, we place the documentation for functions stored in a library, in a separate documentation file.

2. *Functions are separate program components, and the white space in a program should reflect this.* In this text, we

   - ▶ Insert appropriate documentation before each function defined in the main function's file, to separate it from other program components
   - ▶ Indent the declarations and statements within each function

3. *All guidelines for programming style apply to libraries.* The stylistic standards de-

scribed in earlier chapters for programs and functions should be applied to libraries as well.

4. *Once a problem has been analyzed to identify the data objects and the operations needed to solve it, an algorithm should be constructed that specifies the order in which the operations are applied to the data objects.*

5. *Operations that are not predefined (or are nontrivial) in C++ should be encoded as functions, separate from the main function.*

6. *A function that encodes an operation should be designed in the same manner as the main function.*

7. *A function that returns no values should have its return type declared as* void.

8. *A function that receives no values should have no parameters.*

9. *If a problem requires the selection of one or more operations, use a selection statement like the* if *statement.*

10. *If a problem requires the repetition of one or more operations, and the number of repetitions can be computed in advance, use a repetition statement like the* for *statement.*

11. *If a problem requires the repetition of one or more operations an indeterminant number of times, use a repetition statement like the forever loop.*

12. *If a function is sufficiently general that it might someday prove useful in solving a different problem, a library should be constructed to store that function, rather than declaring and defining it in the program's source file.*

13. *A library's files should be documented in much the same way as programs.* For each library we provide a special documentation file that describes clearly, precisely, and completely the contents of the library and how to use items in it, any special algorithms it implements, and other useful information such as the author, a modification history, and so on. This documentation file should be kept in the same place as the other files of a library, so that users can refer to that file in order to understand and use the objects and functions stored in the library.

14. *When the header file of a less commonly used library is inserted in a program (using* #include*), a comment should be used to explain its purpose.* For example, simply writing

```
#include <stdlib.h>
```

tells the reader nothing about why the library is needed in this program. A simple comment

```
#include <stdlib.h>  // exit()
```

tells the reader what role the library is playing in solving the particular problem.

15. *Libraries provide the following benefits:*

   ▶ *A library extends the language, since its objects can be made available to any program or to another library.*

   ▶ *The items in a library's interface can be used without being concerned about the details of their implementation.*

   ▶ *Programs and libraries can be compiled separately. Changing the implementation file of a library requires recompilation of only that implementation file.*

   ▶ *Libraries provide another level of modularity in software design; related functions and other objects can be grouped together in independent libraries.*

POTENTIAL PROBLEMS

1. *When a function is called, the list of arguments is matched against the list of parameters from left to right, with the leftmost argument associated with the leftmost parameter, the next argument associated with the next parameter, and so on. The number of arguments must be the same as the number of parameters (for exceptions see the website described in the preface) and the type of each argument must be compatible with the type of the corresponding parameter.* For example, consider the function with the heading

   ```
   int F(int number1, int number2)
   ```

   The statements

   ```
   y = F(x);
   ```

   and

   ```
   y = F(2, 3.75);
   ```

   are incorrect. In the first case, the number of arguments (1) does not agree with the number of parameters (2). In the second case, the real value `3.75` should not be passed to the integer parameter `number2`.

2. *Identifiers defined within a function (e.g., parameters, local variables, and local constants) are defined only during the execution of that function; they are undefined both before and after its execution.* Any attempt to use such identifiers outside the function (without redeclaring them) is an error. For example, in the function

   ```
   void F(int x, float y)
   {
      int a, b;

         .
         .
         .

   }
   ```

   neither the local variables `a` and `b` nor the parameters `x` and `y` can be accessed outside of function `F()`.

3. *If a function changes the value of its parameter, the value of the corresponding argument is not altered.* A parameter is a completely separate variable into which the argument value is copied. Any change to the parameter changes the copy, not the corresponding argument. For example, if a function `F()` is defined as

   ```
   int F(int x)
   {
      x = x * 5;
   }
   ```

   and then called by

   ```
         .
         .
         .
   int y = 1,
       z;
   ```

```
z = F(y);
        .
        .
        .
```

the value of y is still 1 following the call to function F(). Even if the calling function uses an argument with the same name as the corresponding parameter,

```
int x = 1;
z = F(x);
```

the value of x will still be 1 after the function call.

4. *A function must be declared before it is called. For example, if the function* F() *is to call the function* G(), *then a prototype of* G() *must precede its call in* F():

```
int G(...);   // prototype of function G
        .
        .
        .

int F(...)    // definition of function F
{
        .
        .
        .

    int x = G(...); // call to function G
        .
        .
        .

}
```

5. *Each { must have a matching }.* To make it easier to find matching braces, we align each { with its corresponding }.

6. *One of the most common C++ errors is using an assignment operator (=) when an equality operator (==) is intended. Each equality comparison in a boolean expression should be double-checked to make certain that the equality operator is being used and not the assignment operator. It is easy to forget that in C++, = is the assignment opera-*tor, and to incorrectly encode an instruction of the form

> If *variable* is equal to *value,* then
>> *statement*

as

```
if (variable = value)
   statement
```

perhaps because = is used in many programming languages to check equality. However, instead of testing whether *variable* is equal to *value*, the condition in this if statement assigns *value* to *variable*. If *value* happens to be zero, then the result of the assignment is zero, which C++ interprets as false, and so the *statement* will not be executed, regardless of the value of *variable*. If *value* is nonzero, then the result of the assignment is nonzero, which C++ interprets as true, and so *statement* will be executed, regardless of the value of *variable*. For example, execution of the following incorrect function for finding the reciprocal of a real number,

```
double Recip(double x)
{
    if (x = 0)
    {
        cout << "\n***Error:  Cannot divide by zero!\n";
        return 0.0;
    }
    else
        return 1.0 / x;
}
```

will always produce a division-by-zero error, regardless of the value of parameter x, because

1. x is not compared to zero, but is assigned the value zero, which changes the value of x to 0 and produces the value 0 as its result;
2. The value 0 (produced by the assignment operator) is treated as false by the if statement, and so the statement

```
return 1.0 / x;
```

is selected; and
3. The expression 1.0 / x is evaluated, and since x was set to 0, a division-by-zero error occurs.

7. *In a nested if statement, each* else *clause is matched with the nearest preceding un-matched* if. For example, consider the following statements, which are given without indentation:

```
if (x > 0)
if (y > 0)
z = x + y;
else
z = x + abs(y);
w = x * y * z;
```

With which if is the else associated? According to the rule just stated, these statements are executed as

```
if (x > 0)
    if (y > 0)
        z = x + y;
    else
        z = x + abs(y);
w = x * y * z;
```

where the else clause matches the if statement containing the condition y > 0. Use indentation and alignment to show such associations.

8. *When using repetition, care must be taken to avoid infinite looping.*

   ▶ In a for statement, be sure that the boolean expression controlling repetition eventually becomes true. For example, executing the following code fragment,

   ```
   for (double num = 0.0; num != 1.0; num += 0.3)
       cout << num << endl;
   ```

   results in an infinite loop:

   ```
   0.0
   0.3
   0.6
   ```

```
0.9
1.2
 .
 .
 .
```

because the boolean expression controlling the loop is always false. Rewriting the loop as

```
for (double num = 0.0; num <= 1.0; num += 0.3)
    cout << num << endl;
```

corrects the problem.

▶ The body of a forever loop should always contain an `if-break` (or `if-return`) combination and statements that cause the exit condition of the loop to eventually become true.

9. *In a* for *loop, neither the control variable nor any variable involved in the loop condition should be modified within the body of the* for *loop, since it is intended to run through a specified range of consecutive values.* Strange or undesirable results may be produced otherwise. To illustrate, the statement

```
for (int i = 1; i <= 4; i++)
{
    cout << i << endl;
    i++;
}
```

produces the output

```
1
3
```

The statement

```
for (int i = 1; i <= 4; i++)
{
    cout << i << endl;
    i--;
}
```

results in an infinite loop, displaying the output

```
1
1
1
1
```

```
 .
 .
 .
```

10. *If a function needs data objects or functions from a library, the header file of that library must be inserted (using* #include*) before the definition of that function.* For example, if a function attempts to perform input using the `istream` data object `cin` and

```
#include <iostream.h>
```

does not precede the function's definition, then an error message such as the following is produced:

```
cin:  Unknown identifier
```

11. *The implementation file of a library should always insert the header file of that library (using* `#include`) *so that the compiler can verify that each function's prototype is consistent with its definition.* Failure to follow this rule is a common source of **linking errors.**

12. *A function that is defined in the implementation file of a library but not declared in that library's header file cannot be called outside the library (but it can be called inside the library).* For example, if a library's implementation file contains the two function definitions

```
int F(...)
{
     .
     .
     .
}

int G(...)
{
     .
     .
     .
}
```

and the library's header file declares `G()` but does not declare `F()`, then

`G()` can be called by a program in which `#include` is used to insert the library's header file, but `F()` cannot be called.

`F()` can call `G()` because there is a declaration of `G()` before the definition of `F()` in the header file, and `G()` can call `F()` because the definition of `F()` precedes that of `G()`.

Programming Problems

Section 3.2

1. Write a driver program to test the temperature-conversion function `CelsiusToFahr()` of exercise 1.

2. Write a driver program to test the monetary-conversion functions `US_to_Canadian()` and `Canadian_to_US()` of exercises 2 and 3.

3. Write a driver program to test the function `Range()` of exercise 4.

4. Write a driver program to test the function `Wages()` of exercise 5.

5. Write a driver program to test the circle-processing functions of exercises 6 and 7.

6. Write a driver program to test the rectangle-processing functions of exercises 8 and 9.

7. Write a driver program to test the triangle-processing functions of exercises 10 and 11.

8. Write a driver program to test the culture-of-bacteria function of exercise 12.

9. Write a driver program to test the time-conversion functions of exercises 13–16.

10. Write a driver program to test the phone-number function of exercise 17.

11. Write a driver program to test the heat-index function of exercise 18.

12. Write a driver program to test the stick-number functions of exercise 19.

13. Complete problem 12 by writing and testing the additional functions needed to display all digits.

Section 3.3

14. Write a driver program to test the distance-calculation function of exercise 11.

15. Write a driver program to test the quadratic-equation function of exercise 12. Execute the program with the following values for A, B, and C: $1, -5, 6$; $1, -2, 1$; $1, 0, 4$; $1, 1, 1$; $2, 1, -3$.

16. Modify the quadratic-equation function of exercise 12 so that it returns 0 if the quadratic equation has no real roots (discriminant is negative), 1 if it has a repeated real root (discriminant is 0), and 2 if it has two distinct real roots (discriminant is positive). Test the function with a driver program using the values in problem 15 for A, B, and C.

17. Construct a driver program to test the pollution-index function in exercise 13 and execute it with the following data: $20, 45, 75, 35, 60$.

18. Construct a driver program to test the wind-chill function in exercise 14 and execute it with the following data: $-80, 10, 0, -70, -10, -5, 10, -20, -40$.

19. Write a program that reads an employee's number, hours worked, and hourly rate, calls a function to calculate his or her wages, and then displays the employee information, including wages. All hours over 40 are paid at 1.5 times the regular hourly rate. Execute the program with the following values for employee number, hours worked, and hourly rate: $123, 38, 7.50; 175, 39.5, 7.85; 223, 40, 9.25; 375, 44.5, 8.35$.

20. Write a wage-calculation program like the one in problem 19, but with the following modification: if an employee's number is greater than or equal to 1000, the program should read an annual salary and calculate the employee's weekly pay as this salary divided by 52. If the employee's number is less than 1000, wages are calculated on an hourly basis, as described in problem 19. Execute the program with the data in Problem 19 and the following data: $1217, 25500; 1343, 31775$.

SECTION 3.5

21. Write a driver program to test the summation function of exercise 12.

22. Write a driver program to test the summation function of exercise 13.

23. The sequence of *Fibonacci numbers* begins with the integers 1, 1, 2, 3, 5, 8, 13, 21, . . . where each number after the first two is the sum of the two preceding numbers. Write a program that reads a positive integer n and uses a for loop to generate and display the first n Fibonacci numbers.

24. Ratios of consecutive Fibonacci numbers 1/1, 1/2, 2/3, 3/5, . . . approach the *golden ratio* $(\sqrt{5} - 1)/2$. Modify the program in problem 23 so that it also displays the decimal values of the ratios of consecutive Fibonacci numbers.

25. A certain product is to sell for unitPrice dollars. Write a program that reads values for unitPrice and totalNumber and then produces a table showing the total price of from 1 through totalNumber units. The table should have a format like the following:

```
Number of Units    Total Price
===============    ===========
          1          $ 1.50
          2          $ 3.00
          3          $ 4.50
          4          $ 6.00
          5          $ 7.50
```

26. Suppose that at a given time, genotypes AA, AB, and BB appear in the proportions x, y, and z, respectively, where $x = 0.25$, $y = 0.5$, and $z = 0.25$. If individuals of type AA cannot reproduce, the probability that one parent will donate gene A to an offspring is

$$p = \frac{1}{2}\left(\frac{y}{y + z}\right)$$

since $y/(y + z)$ is the probability that the parent is of type AB and $\frac{1}{2}$ is the probability that such a parent will donate gene A. Then the proportions x', y', and z' of AA, AB, and BB, respectively, in each succeeding generation are given by

$$x' = p^2, \quad y' = 2p(1 - p), \quad z' = (1 - p)^2$$

and the new probability is given by

$$p' = \frac{1}{2}\left(\frac{y'}{y' + z'}\right)$$

Write a program to calculate and display the generation number and the proportions of AA, AB, and BB under appropriate headings for 30 generations. (Note that the proportions of AA and AB should approach 0, since gene A will gradually disappear.)

27. Write a program that uses a sentinel-based input loop to read data values as shown in the following table, calculates the miles per gallon in each case, and displays the values with appropriate labels:

Miles Traveled	Gallons of Gasoline Used
231	14.8
248	15.1
302	12.8
147	9.25
88	7
265	13.3

28. Write a program that uses a sentinel-based input loop to read several values representing miles, converts miles to kilometers (1 mile = 1.60935 kilometers), and displays all values with appropriate labels.

29. Write a program to read a set of numbers, count them, and calculate and display the mean, variance, and standard deviation of the set of numbers. The *mean* and *variance* of numbers $x_1, x_2, \ldots, x_n$ can be calculated using the formulas

$$\text{mean} = \frac{1}{n}\sum_{i=1}^{n} x_i \quad \text{variance} = \frac{1}{n}\sum_{i=1}^{n} x_i^2 - \frac{1}{n^2}\left(\sum_{i=1}^{n} x_i\right)^2$$

The *standard deviation* is the square root of the variance.

SECTION 3.6

30. Construct a library `Exchange` that contains the monetary-conversion functions from exercises 2 and 3 in section 3.2. Write a driver program to test your library.

31. Construct a library `Geometry` that contains the functions from exercises 6–11 in section 3.2. Write a driver program to test your library.

32. Write a program to read one of the codes `C` for circle, `R` for rectangle, or `T` for triangle, and the radius of the circle, the sides of the rectangle, or the sides of the triangle, respectively. Using the functions in the library `Geometry` of problem 31, the program should then calculate and display with appropriate labels the perimeter and the area of that geometric figure.

33. Construct a library `Time` that contains the time-conversion functions from exercises 13–16 in section 3.2. Write a driver program to test your library.

34. Write a library containing functions to compute the surface area and volume of a sphere. For a sphere of radius r, these values can be calculated using

$$\text{Surface Area} = 4\pi r^2$$
$$\text{Volume} = \frac{4\pi r^3}{3}$$

Write a driver program to test your library.

35. Write a library `Cylinder` containing functions to compute the total surface area, lateral surface area, and volume of a right-circular cylinder. For a cylinder of radius r and height h, these can be calculated using:

$$\text{Total Surface Area} = 2\pi r(r + h)$$
$$\text{Lateral Surface Area} = 2\pi rh$$
$$\text{Volume} = \pi r^2 h$$

Write a driver program to test your library.

36. Construct a library `Measures` containing functions that will allow a user to freely convert within the following categories of measurement:

Length: inches, feet, yards, miles

Weight: ounces, pounds, tons

Volume: teaspoons, tablespoons, cups, quarts, gallons

Chapter 4

CLASS TYPES AND EXPRESSIONS

The old order changeth, yielding place to the new.

ALFRED, LORD TENNYSON

Buying a new tire costs less than reinventing the wheel.

V. OREHCK III (fictitious)

The moving finger writes; and having writ
Moves on: not all your piety nor wit
Shall lure it back to cancel half a line,
Nor all your tears wash out a word of it.

THE RUBAIYAT

Chapter Contents

4.1   Introductory Example: "The Farmer in the Dell"

4.2   Introduction to Classes

4.3   The `istream` and `ostream` Classes

4.4   Computing with `string` Objects

4.5   Example: Decoding Phone Numbers

       PART OF THE PICTURE: Simulation

The word *class* is often used to describe a group or category of objects that have a set of attributes in common. For example, the high school football teams in one state are described as

- *class A*, if they have fewer than 100 students in 3 grades
- *class AA*, if they have between 101 and 500 students in 3 grades
- *class AAA*, if they have between 501 and 1000 students in 3 grades
- *class AAAA*, if they have 1000 or more students in 3 grades

The U.S. Navy describes ships as belonging to certain *classes;* for example, *Skipjack class, Thresher class,* and *Sturgeon class* have been used to characterize different kinds of submarines.[1] Economists describe families as *lower class, middle class,* or *upper class,* based on their annual income. Karl Marx described history as a *class struggle* between the workers and the bourgeoisie. Used in this way, the word *class* is a synonym for the word *type,* since it provides a name for a group of related objects.

In chapter 2, we studied some of the types provided in C++, including `int`, `long`, `unsigned`, `double`, `char`, and `bool`. These are called **fundamental types,** because they can be used to model basic objects like numbers and characters. However, consider modeling the name of a person. Since a name consists of several characters and the fundamental type `char` can only store single characters, the `char` type is inadequate to model a name.

For situations like this where the fundamental types are inadequate to model an object, C++ allows a programmer to create a new type for representing the object by building a **class.** A class can thus be thought of as an *extension* to C++; by building a class and storing it in a library, a programmer can add new types to C++ that other programmers can reuse.

In this chapter, we examine three types that have been added to C++ using the class mechanism: the `istream` class for modeling a computer's keyboard, the `ostream` class for modeling a computer's screen, and the `string` class for modeling arbitrary sequences of characters. None of these types existed in the original C++ language; all of them have been added to the language using the class mechanism.

4.1 INTRODUCTORY EXAMPLE: "THE FARMER IN THE DELL"

PROBLEM

"The Farmer in the Dell" is a children's song that most people have sung at one time or another:

    The farmer in the dell
    The farmer in the dell
    Hi-ho, the derry-o
    The farmer in the dell

---

[1] To carry on this theme, the Enterprise on the popular television show *Star Trek* was described as a *Constitution Class* starship. On the succeeding show *Star Trek: The Next Generation,* the new and improved Enterprise is a *Galaxy class* starship.

The farmer takes a wife
The farmer takes a wife
Hi-ho, the derry-o
The farmer takes a wife

The wife takes a child
The wife takes a child
Hi-ho, the derry-o
The wife takes a child

The child takes a nurse
. . .

The nurse takes a cow
. . .

The cow takes a dog
. . .

The dog takes a cat
. . .

The cat takes a rat
. . .

The rat takes the cheese
. . .

The cheese stands alone
The cheese stands alone
Hi-ho, the derry-o
The cheese stands alone

We want to write a program that prints the lyrics of this song.

 ## OBJECT-CENTERED DESIGN

Preliminary Analysis.   One obvious solution is a "brute force" solution, in which the program consists of a large main function containing a single output statement that displays the lyrics on the screen:

```
int main()
{
    cout << "The farmer in the dell\nThe farmer in the dell\n"
            "Hi-ho, the derry-o\nThe farmer in the dell\n\n"
            "The farmer takes a wife\nThe farmer takes a wife\n"
            "Hi-ho, the derry-o\nThe farmer takes a wife\n\n"
            "The wife takes a child\nThe wife takes a child\n"
            "Hi-ho, the derry-o\nThe wife takes a child\n\n"

         // etc., etc., etc.
}
```

However, writing such a program is tiresome and boring, because we are typing almost exactly the same thing over and over again. *Anytime a plan requires repeating the same work over and over, there is something wrong with the plan!*

If we examine the structure of the song, and identify what is common to the verses, we see that each verse has the following form:

> The *restOfLine*
> The *restOfLine*
> Hi-ho, the derry-o
> The *restOfLine*

In the first verse, *restOfLine* is "farmer in the dell"; in the second verse, it is "farmer takes a wife"; and so on, until in the tenth verse, *restOfLine* is "cheese stands alone". This suggests that the song can be viewed as a sequence of verses, rather than as a single monolithic song. More precisely, what we should do is write a function to display on the screen a single verse of the song, with a `string` parameter to store *restOfLine,* and then call that function 10 times, passing it different lines.

Behavior.   Our program should display on the screen the lyrics of a verse of "The Farmer in the Dell" using "farmer in the dell", followed by a verse using "farmer takes a wife", followed by a verse using "wife takes a child", and so on.

Objects.   In this approach, our objects are as follows:

Description	Kind	Type	Name
screen	Variable	ostream	cout
lyrics of a Farmer-in-the-Dell verse	Constant	string	none
"farmer in the dell"	Constant	string	none
"farmer takes a wife"	Constant	string	none
"wife takes a child"	Constant	string	none
"child takes a nurse"	Constant	string	none
"nurse takes a cow"	Constant	string	none
"cow takes a dog"	Constant	string	none
"dog takes a cat"	Constant	string	none
"cat takes a rat"	Constant	string	none
"rat takes the cheese"	Constant	string	none
"cheese stands alone"	Constant	string	none

Operations.   There are 10 operations to perform:

Display on the screen a verse of the song using:
  i.   "farmer in the dell"
  ii.   "farmer takes a wife"
  iii.   "wife takes a child"

iv.	"child takes a nurse"
v.	"nurse takes a cow"
vi.	"cow takes a dog"
vii.	"dog takes a cat"
viii.	"cat takes a rat"
ix.	"rat takes the cheese"
x.	"cheese stands alone"

Since the operation "Display on the screen a verse of the song using _____" is not predefined in C++, we will construct a function to perform this operation.

Algorithm.   Once we have such a function `PrintVerse()`, we simply call it 10 times, once with each of the phrases listed above. Thus we can solve our problem with the following algorithm, which eliminates the redundant coding that afflicts the brute force approach:

Algorithm for Displaying the Lyrics of *The Farmer in the Dell*

Call `PrintVerse()` with each of the 10 arguments listed above.

Function's Behavior.   Our function must receive from its caller a phrase to complete the first, second, and last lines. It should construct a verse of "The Farmer in the Dell" using that phrase, and then display that verse on the screen.

Function's Objects.   Our behavioral description contains these objects:

Description	Type	Kind	Movement	Name
screen	ostream	varying	none	cout
a verse of "The Farmer in the Dell"	string	constant	none	*verse*
a phrase	string	varying	received (in)	*restOfLine*

From these objects, we can specify the problem our function solves as follows:

Receive: *restOfLine,* a `string` object.

Output: a verse of "The Farmer in the Dell" using *restOfLine.*

Function's Operations.   To construct a function having the specified behavior, we need the following operations:

i.   Build *verse,* a `string` consisting of the lyrics to a verse of "The Farmer in the Dell," containing *restOfLine* in the first, second, and last lines.

ii.   Display *verse* on the screen.

Algorithm for Function.   After our analysis of the structure of a verse, we arrive at the following sequence of steps to solve the problem:

Algorithm for Function `PrintVerse()`

1.   Build *verse* = "The" + *restOfLine* + "\n"
                           "The" + *restOfLine* + "\n"
                           "Hi-ho, the derry-o\n"
                           "The" + *restOfLine* + "\n\n"

2.   Display *verse* via `cout`.

The listed values are all strings, and the C++ `string` class provides the + operator to perform the necessary operation of *concatenating* (i.e., joining) strings into a single string. Each operation in this algorithm is thus predefined, and we can continue to the coding phase.

Coding. Now that we have an algorithm for the program and for the function, we can proceed to code the program. Figure 4.1 presents the solution. Compared with the brute force approach, it is surely more *space efficient* (i.e., it is shorter), and exhibits good design style, because its structure reflects the structure of the song.

 FIGURE 4.1.   "THE FARMER IN THE DELL".

```
/* song1.cpp displays the lyrics for "The Farmer in the Dell".
 * using a function PrintVerse().
 *
 * Input:   none
 * Output:  lyrics for the "The Farmer in the Dell"
 ******************************************************************/

#include <iostream.h>              // cin, cout, >>, <<
#include <string>                  // string

void PrintVerse(string restOfLine);

int main()
{
   PrintVerse("farmer in the dell");
   PrintVerse("farmer takes a wife");
   PrintVerse("wife takes a child");
   PrintVerse("child takes a nurse");
   PrintVerse("nurse takes a cow");
   PrintVerse("cow takes a dog");
   PrintVerse("dog takes a cat");
   PrintVerse("cat takes a rat");
   PrintVerse("rat takes the cheese");
   PrintVerse("cheese stands alone");
}


/* PrintVerse() prints one verse of "The Farmer in the Dell".
 *
 * Receive: restOfLine, a string.
 * Output:  a verse with restOfLine inserted appropriately.
 ******************************************************************/
```

```
void PrintVerse(string restOfLine)
{
    const string verse =
                        "The " + restOfLine + "\n" +
                        "The " + restOfLine +  "\n" +
                        "Hi-ho, the derry-o\n" +
                        "The " + restOfLine + "\n\n";

    cout << verse;
}
```

Sample run:

```
The farmer in the dell
The farmer in the dell
Hi-ho, the derry-o
The farmer in the dell

The farmer takes a wife
The farmer takes a wife
Hi-ho, the derry-o
The farmer takes a wife

The wife takes a child
The wife takes a child
Hi-ho, the derry-o
The wife takes a child

The child takes a nurse
The child takes a nurse
Hi-ho, the derry-o
The child takes a nurse

The nurse takes a cow
The nurse takes a cow
Hi-ho, the derry-o
The nurse takes a cow

The cow takes a dog
The cow takes a dog
Hi-ho, the derry-o
The cow takes a dog

The dog takes a cat
The dog takes a cat
Hi-ho, the derry-o
The dog takes a cat
```

```
The cat takes a rat
The cat takes a rat
Hi-ho, the derry-o
The cat takes a rat

The rat takes the cheese
The rat takes the cheese
Hi-ho, the derry-o
The rat takes the cheese

The cheese stands alone
The cheese stands alone
Hi-ho, the derry-o
The cheese stands alone
```

4.2 INTRODUCTION TO CLASSES

In chapter 2, we saw that a programmer can model items in a computation by declaring objects. For example, we used

```
double hours,
       rate;
```

to declare objects `hours` and `rate` to model hours worked by employees and their hourly rates. In chapter 3, we saw that a programmer can effectively create new operations for a computation by declaring and defining functions, such as the temperature-conversion function whose prototype was

```
double FahrToCelsius(double tempFahr);
```

These C++ features are adequate for many programming tasks in which the objects being modeled are sufficiently simple.

The problem, however, is that most objects in the real world are not simple. For example, suppose we want to represent cars. If we begin by thinking of the different characteristics of a car, we can quickly compile a sizeable list:

1. name (Acura Integra, Ford Mustang, Pontiac GrandAm, Volkswagen Beetle, . . .)

2. number of doors

3. number of cylinders

4. engine size

        .
        .
        .

Suppose, for simplicity, that we use only these four characteristics. One way to proceed would be to declare a separate variable for each of these characteristics:

```
string carName;
int carDoors;
int carCylinders;
int carEngineSize;
```

This approach is on the right track, but it has some serious deficiencies. To see why, consider a function to display the information about a car via cout:

```
void ShowCarInfo(string itsName, int itsDoors,
                int itsCylinders, int itsEngineSize)
{
    cout << itsName << endl
         << "Doors: " << itsDoors << endl
         << "Cylinders: " << itsCylinders << endl
         << "Engine Size: " << itsEngineSize << endl;
}
```

Given such a function and the variables defined earlier, we can call it as follows:

```
ShowCarInfo(carName, carDoors, carCylinders, carEngineSize);
```

A function to input information about a car would be similar (with one major difference that we will see in chapter 7) and would be called in virtually the same way:

```
GetCarInfo(carName, carDoors, carCylinders, carEngineSize);
```

The problems with this approach should be clear: every function we define for a "car operation" must have a separate parameter for each attribute needed by that operation. Similarly, each function call must pass the correct argument to each of those parameters. Obviously, the more complex the object, the more information must be passed and the more cumbersome this approach becomes. Just imagine how inelegant a program would be if it had 50 function calls, each having 100 or more arguments.

The basic difficulty with this approach is that there is *one* kind of object (a car) that we want to model, and yet we must pass *more than one* piece of information to the operations. To solve this problem, C++ provides the **class.** When programmers create a class, they create a *new type,* with space for the characteristics of objects of that type. For example, the type string used in Figure 4.1 is actually a class that was created by some programmer.

In the discussion that follows, we will describe the major features of classes, leaving most of the details for a later chapter. By the end of this section, you should know what a class is, and how to use one (but not how to create your own classes, which will be described in chapter 10).

Data Encapsulation

Classes provide a way to encapsulate the characteristics of an object within a single "wrapper." For example, to create a class named Car with the four characteristics described previously, we could use

```
class Car
{
 public:
    string itsName;
    int itsDoors;
    int itsCylinders;
    int itsEngineSize;
};
```

The identifiers itsName, itsDoors, itsCylinders, and itsEngineSize are called the **data members** of the class.

The name of the class, Car, is treated by C++ as *the name of a new type*, and can therefore be used to declare objects:

```
Car dadsCar,
    momsCar;
```

Such declarations create distinct Car objects, each of which can store its own characteristics:

dadsCar

Yugo	itsName
2	itsDoors
4	itsCylinders
120	itsEngineSize

momsCar

Porsche 911	itsName
2	itsDoors
8	itsCylinders
454	itsEngineSize

(We will see how to initialize the data members of a class object in chapter 10.)

This encapsulation is important, because a single object like dadsCar now contains all of its own information. This solves our earlier problem, because it allows us to pass a complicated object to a function by using just one argument (and just one parameter); for example,

```
void DisplayCarInfo(Car theCar)
{
   cout << theCar.itsName << endl
        << "Doors: " << theCar.itsDoors << endl
        << "Cylinders: " << theCar.itsCylinders << endl
        << "Engine Size: " << theCar.itsEngineSize << endl;
}
```

Note that the public members of a class object are accessed using **dot notation.** The expression

```
theCar.itsDoors
```

will access the itsDoors member of the Car object associated with parameter theCar.

If we call this function with

```
DisplayCarInfo(dadsCar);
```

the values of the data members of dadsCar will be displayed:

```
Yugo
Doors: 2
Cylinders: 4
Engine Size: 120
```

If we call the same function with a different argument,

```
DisplayCarInfo(momsCar);
```

the values of momsCar's data members will be displayed:

```
Porsche 911
Doors: 2
Cylinders: 8
Engine Size: 454
```

For complicated objects, classes thus provide a convenient way to package the data items needed to describe that object in one container. This is what is meant by **data encapsulation.**

FUNCTION MEMBERS

There is more to classes than data encapsulation. Besides making it possible to package the data characteristics of an object, classes can also store function proto-types that make up the *operations* on such objects. For example, to provide an input function Read() and an output function Print() for our Car class, we could use

```
class Car
{
 public:
    void Read();
    void Print();
 private:
    string itsName;
    int itsDoors;
    int itsCylinders;
    int itsEngineSize;
};
```

Members Read() and Print() are called **function members.** Each function member performs its particular operation using the data members of the class. For example, the Print() function could be defined by

```
void Car::Print()
{
    cout << itsName << endl
         << "Doors: " << itsDoors << endl
         << "Cylinders: " << itsCylinders << endl
         << "Engine Size: " << itsEngineSize << endl;
}
```

(The unusual Car:: notation will be explained in chapter 10. We show it here to give you an idea of how a function member does its job.)

Usually, we would provide a rich set of function members to perform operations on Car objects. When this is done, the data members are designated private as shown in class Car to prevent users of the class from performing unauthorized op-erations. However, since this is just an introduction to classes, we will keep this ex-ample simple and use only the two function members Read() and Print().

When class objects are declared, as in

```
Car dadsCar,
    momsCar;
```

each has its own members—data members and function members. As we saw earlier, any public member can be called using dot notation; thus to display the information stored in `dadsCar`, we would call its `Print()` function,

```
dadsCar.Print();
```

and to display the information stored in `momsCar`, we would call its `Print()` function:

```
momsCar.Print();
```

Similarly, we can call

```
momsCar.Read();
```

to read data into `momsCar` and

```
dadsCar.Read();
```

to read data into `dadsCar`.

Classes also make it possible to redefine C++ operators. For example, the `string` class redefines the + function so that when it is given two strings, it *concatenates* (joins) those strings. For example, the declaration

```
string name = "Popeye" + " the " + "Sailor";
```

initializes the object `name` with the `string` value `"Popeye the Sailor"`. Redefining a function with a new definition is called **overloading** that function, a topic discussed in chapter 7.

Once a class has been built, it is usually stored in a library, with its declaration stored in the library's header file and the definitions of its function members in an implementation file. For example, to use the `string` class we must include the header file `string`, and to use the `istream` or `ostream` classes we must include the header file `iostream.h`.

This brief introduction to classes should indicate their importance in C++. Classes are the single biggest difference between C++ and its parent language C. (In fact, prior to 1983, the C++ language was called "C with Classes.") An important part of learning to program in C++ is learning how to use the standard classes that are part of the language, to avoid reinventing the wheel. In the rest of this chapter, we will examine three of these classes: `ostream`, `istream`, and `string`.

SUMMARY

C++ provides the class mechanism for building types to represent complicated objects. This mechanism allows us to create a single structure that encapsulates (i) *data members* defining the characteristics of the object, and (ii) *function members* defining the operations on the object. Class members that are designated `public` within the class can be accessed using *dot notation*.

✔ **Quick Quiz 4.2**

1. Packaging data items needed to describe an object in one container is known as data _____ .

2. Classes have two kinds of members: _____ members and _____ members.

3. Redefining a function with a new definition is called _____ that function.

4. Public members of a class can be accessed using _____ notation.

Questions 5–7 assume the following declarations:

```
class Date
{
 public:
    void Display();
 private:
    string month;
    int day;
    int year;
};

Date birth;
```

5. List the data members of Date.

6. List the function members of Date.

7. Write a statement to call the Display function in birth.

4.3 THE istream AND ostream CLASSES

When C++ was first developed in 1980, it did not have its own I/O system, but instead relied upon the I/O system of its parent language C.[2] Jerry Schwarz, one of the early users of C++, decided to see just how powerful these new things called classes really were, and used them to develop a better I/O system. After much work, feedback from users, and revision, the resulting set of classes is today's iostream library. Two of these classes are the istream class and the ostream class, which we examine in this section.

THE istream CLASS

One problem in designing a general purpose model for input is that where the input comes from depends on how the user is interacting with the program. Regardless of whether the user is using a computer terminal on a mainframe, a workstation, or a microcomputer, the input to the program must come from that terminal's keyboard. What complicates the problem is that the program to which the input is being sent may reside on the same computer, or it may be running on an entirely different computer across a network.

The challenge in creating a modern I/O system is to provide a single system that hides this complexity from the programmer—to create an *abstraction* for input that programmers can use without having to concern themselves with the messy details of how data actually gets from the keyboard to the program. What model can capture the basic idea of *every* input system, regardless of the low-level details?

---

[2] The C standard I/O system provided in stdio is fully useable in C++, but its use is discouraged because its design and use reflect the procedural approach of C and not the object-oriented approach of C++.

Streams. Building on an idea from C and UNIX, Bjarne Stroustrup, the designer of C++, developed such an abstraction, which he called a **stream.** Stroustrup envisioned a stream of characters flowing from the keyboard to a program, like a stream of water flowing from one place to another. Schwarz used this idea to create the `istream` class—a class representing a flow of characters from an arbitrary input device to an executing program:

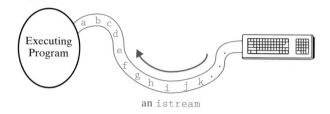

an `istream`

He then defined an `istream` object in the `iostream` library, so that any C++ program that included the library's header file would automatically have an input stream flowing from the keyboard to the program. This object is named `cin`:

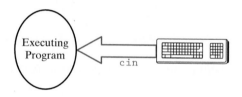

The >> Operator. Schwarz also defined the input operator `>>` so that when it is applied to an `istream` object and a variable object,

```
istream_object >> variable_object
```

the operator tries to extract a sequence of characters corresponding to a value of the type of `variable_object` from `istream_object`. If there are no characters, it *blocks execution* from proceeding until characters are entered.

To illustrate, suppose that `cin` is initially empty and the following statements are executed:

```
int age;
cin >> age;
```

When the `>>` function attempts to read an integer value for `age`, it finds that `cin` is empty and so blocks execution. If the user enters 18, the characters 1 and 8 are entered into the `istream` named `cin`,

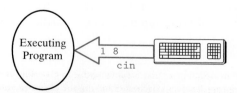

and since cin is now no longer empty, the >> function resumes its execution. It reads the characters 1 and 8 from the istream, converts them to the integer value 18, and stores this value into its right operand age.

Because the behavior of the >> operator is to extract values from an istream, it is often called the *extraction operator*.

The Status Functions. In our discussion of the >> operator, we assumed that the user entered appropriate values. Suppose, however, in the preceding example that 18 was mistyped as q8. The stream cin will then contain the characters q and 8:

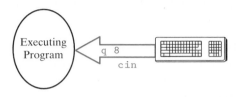

What happens when the >> operator tries to extract an integer and encounters the character q?

One of the attributes of an istream is its **state** or condition. If all is well with the stream, its state is said to be *good*. If something has gone wrong with the stream, its state is *bad*. If the last operation on the stream did not succeed, its state is *fail*. The istream class essentially maintains a boolean variable called a **flag** for each of these states,[3] with the *good* flag initialized to true and the *bad* and *fail* flags initialized to false.

In our scenario, encountering the letter q while trying to read an integer will set the stream's *good* flag to false, its *bad* flag to true, and its *fail* flag to true. In general, if either the *bad* or *fail* flag is true, then the *good* flag is false. In most circumstances, if the *bad* flag is true, then the *fail* flag is also true, and vice versa.

For each of these flags, the istream class provides a boolean function member having the same name as its flag, that reports on the value of that flag.

Function Call	Returns True if and only if
cin.good()	all is well in the istream
cin.bad()	something is wrong with the istream
cin.fail()	the last operation could not be completed

We can use the function member good() to check that an input step has succeeded:

```
assert(cin.good());
```

Alternatively, we could call one of the other functions; for example,

```
assert(!cin.fail());
```

---

[3] There is a fourth *end-of-file* state that occurs when the last input operation encountered an end-of-file mark before finding any data, and an eof() function member that reports this state.

Combined with the `assert()` mechanism, these status functions provide a simple way to guard against data-entry errors.

The `clear()` Member. Once the *good* flag of an `istream` has been set to false, no subsequent input operations can be performed on that stream until its state is cleared. This is accomplished by calling the function member `clear()`,

```
cin.clear();
```

which resets the `good()` flag to true and the other flags to false. As we shall see in chapter 6, this `clear()` function is useful in writing fool-proof loops for reading data values.

The `ignore()` Member. The function member `clear()` resets the status flags, but it does not actually clear the offending input from the `istream`. For this, the `istream` class provides the function member `ignore()`. As its name implies, it can be used to ignore one or more characters in the stream. The function call

```
cin.ignore();
```

will skip the next character in `cin`.

More generally, `ignore()` can be called with a statement of the form

```
cin.ignore(num_chars_to_skip, stop_char);
```

where *num_chars_to_skip* is an integer expression and *stop_char* is a character. It will skip *num_chars_to_skip* characters in `cin`, unless *stop_char* is encountered. The default value of *num_chars_to_skip* is 1 and the default value of *stop_char* is the end-of-file mark.[4] For example, the call

```
cin.ignore(1024, ' ');
```

might be used to skip all characters up to the next blank, and

```
cin.ignore(1024, '\n');
```

to skip all characters remaining on a given line of input. Like `clear()`, `ignore()` is useful for writing fool-proof input loops.

White space. One of the nice features of the `>>` operator is that, by default, it *skips leading* **white space** — blanks, tabs, and returns. To illustrate, consider the statements

```
double height, weight;
cout << "Enter your height (inches) and weight (pounds): ";
cin >> height >> weight;
```

and suppose the user enters 70.5 and 180. Then `cin` contains the following characters where ␣ represents a blank and ↵ represents the return character:

---

[4] Different operating systems use different control characters as an end-of-file mark. On UNIX systems and the Macintosh, `Control-d` can be entered as this mark, while DOS-based systems use `Control-z` followed by `Enter`.

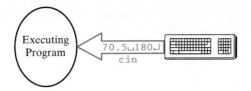

When the input statement

```
cin >> height >> weight;
```

is executed, the first (leftmost) >> reads 70.5 and stores it in `height`, leaving the blank (⊔) unread:

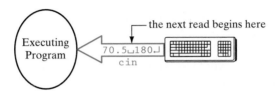

The second >> begins reading where the previous one left off, but since the first character is a blank, it skips this character:

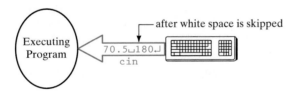

It then reads 180 and stores it in `weight`:

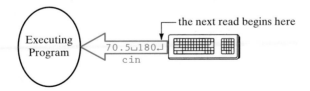

The return character is left unread in the stream. Since a return character is a white-space character, it will be skipped by any subsequent calls to the >> operator.

Note that white space is skipped even when reading a single character, as in

```
char ch;
cin >> ch;
```

`>>` will read the first non-white-space character from `cin` into `ch`. Any leading white-space characters in `cin` will be skipped.

Suppose, however, that we want to read all characters, including white-space characters; for example, a word-processing program may need to count the lines of input by reading each input character and incrementing a counter each time that character is a return character. One way to read white-space characters is to use an **input manipulator**—an identifier that changes some property of the `istream` when it is used in an input statement. If we use the **noskipws manipulator** in an input statement,

```
cin >> ...  >> noskipws  ...
```

then in all subsequent input, white-space characters will not be skipped. The **skipws manipulator** can be used to reactivate white-space skipping.[5]

Alternatively, the `istream` class provides a function member named **get()** that reads a single character without skipping white space. More precisely,

```
cin.get(ch);
```

where `ch` is of type `char`, will read the next character from `cin` into `ch`, regardless of whether or not it is a white-space character.

THE ostream CLASS

Just as the idea of a stream of characters abstractly describes the nature of input, it also describes the nature of output. This level of abstraction is needed because of the different destinations to which the output might be sent. If a text-only computer terminal is being used, then the output from the program must be sent to that terminal's screen. By contrast, if a computer running a windowing system (e.g., X-windows, Macintosh, or Windows 95) is being used, then the output must be sent to the appropriate window on that machine. Complicating things even more is the fact that a program may be running *locally* (i.e., on the local computer) or *remotely* (i.e., on a different machine, across a network).

The abstract notion of a stream can be used to hide these low-level details from the programmer, and so the `iostream` library provides the `ostream` class to represent the "flow" of characters from an executing program to an arbitrary output device:

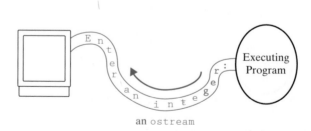

an ostream

---

[5] As noted before, some older C++ compilers may not support the use of manipulators in this way. It may be necessary to include the `iomanip.h` header file and use `resetiosflags(ios::skipws)` in the input statement to turn off white-space skipping and `setiosflags(ios::skipws)` to turn it back on.

After creating an `ostream` class, Schrwarz defined two `ostream` objects in the `iostream` library so that any C++ program that includes the library's header file will automatically have two output streams from the program to whatever device the user is using for output—a window, a terminal, etc.:

1.   `cout`, an `ostream` for displaying *normal* output; and
2.   `cerr`, an `ostream` for displaying *error* or diagnostic messages.

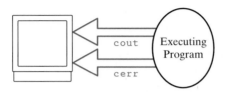

The `assert()` mechanism typically writes its diagnostic messages to `cerr`, not to `cout`.

The << Operator. Schwarz also defined the << operator so that when it is applied to an `ostream` object and an expression:

```
ostream_object << expression
```

it will evaluate the expression and insert the sequence of characters corresponding to that value into the `ostream` object. Thus, if the constant `PI` is defined by

```
const double PI = 3.1416;
```

then, in the output statement

```
cout << PI;
```

the << function converts the `double` value 3.1416 into the corresponding characters 3, ., 1, 4, 1, and 6, and inserts each character into `cout`:

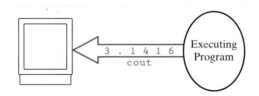

These characters actually remain in the `ostream`, without appearing on the screen, until the `ostream` is *flushed,* which, as its name suggests, empties the stream onto the screen. This can sometimes cause confusion. For example, suppose we insert output statements in a function to trace calls to the function:

```
double f(double x, double y)
{
   cout << "Entering f";
      .
      .
      .
   cout << "Exiting f";
   return z;
}
```

The output `"Entering f"` may not appear on our screen when we expect it to, because the `ostream` is not being flushed.

One common way to flush an `ostream` is to use an **output manipulator**—an identifier that affects the `ostream` itself when it is used in an output statement, rather than simply generating a value to appear on the screen. The manipulator most often used to flush an output stream is the **endl manipulator:**

```
double f(double x, double y)
{
   cout << "Entering f" << endl;
      .
      .
      .
   cout << "Exiting f" << endl;
   return z;
}
```

It inserts a newline character (`'\n'`) into the `ostream` and then flushes it, thus ending a line of output.

A less commonly used alternative is the **flush manipulator,** which simply flushes the `ostream` without inserting anything:

```
double f(double x, double y)
{
   cout << "Entering f" << flush;
      .
      .
      .
   cout << "Exiting f" << flush;
   return z;
}
```

Of course, without insertion of a newline character, the output will appear on the same line,

```
Entering fExiting f
```

which is the reason `endl` is usually used instead.

The `ostream` `cout` *is also flushed automatically whenever the* `istream` `cin` *is used.* Thus, when the statements

```
cout << "Enter radius: ";
double radius;
cin >> radius;
```

are executed, the call to the << operator inserts the prompt "Enter radius: "
into the ostream,

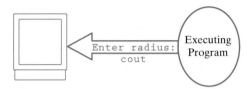

but it is actually the later call to the >> operator that moves the prompt "Enter
radius: " out of the ostream and onto your screen or window:

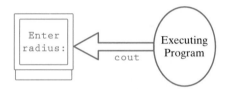

FORMAT CONTROL

The form in which a value is displayed or is entered is called its *format,* and **format
manipulators** can be used to specify various format features. For example, in the
program in Figure 1.6, we used the statement

```
cout << "\nThe total revenue for these installations is $"
     << fixed << showpoint
     . . .
```

Here, fixed is a format manipulator that ensures that subsequent real values
will be displayed in fixed-point notation instead of in scientific notation, and
showpoint is a format manipulator that ensures that the decimal point will be
displayed. The following is a complete list of the format manipulators provided by
the iostream class. They and other manipulators are described in more detail in
chapter 8.[6]

---

[6] As we noted before, some older C++ compilers may not support the use of format manipulators in
this way. For example, it may be necessary to include the iomanip.h header file, use
setiosflags(ios::fixed | ios::showpoint) in the output statement, and use resetios-
flags(ios::*flagname*) to reset the ostream to its default value. See chapter 8 for more details.

Format Manipulator	Description
fixed	Use fixed-point notation for real values
scientific	Use scientific notation for real values
showpoint	Show decimal point and trailing zeros for whole real numbers
noshowpoint	Hide decimal point and trailing zeros for whole real numbers
dec	Use base-10 notation for integer input or output
hex	Use base-16 (hexadecimal) notation for integer input or output
oct	Use base-8 (octal) notation for integer input or output
showbase	Display integer values indicating their base (e.g., 0x for hex)
noshowbase	Display integer values without indicating their base
showpos	Display + sign for positive values
noshowpos	Do not display + sign for positive values
boolalpha	Read or display bool values as true or false
noboolalpha	Do not read or display bool values as true or false
uppercase	In scientific, use E; in hexadecimal, use symbols A−F
nouppercase	In scientific, use e; in hexadecimal, use symbols a−f
flush	Write contents of stream to screen (or file)
endl	Insert newline character into output stream and flush the stream
left	Left-justify displayed values, pad with fill character on right
right	Right-justify displayed values, pad with fill character on left
internal	Pad with fill character between sign or base and value
skipws	Skip white space on input
noskipws	Do not skip white space on input

As we have seen, manipulators are inserted directly into the stream, but they affect the stream itself. For example, if we were to write

```
int i = 17;

cout << showbase
     << oct << i << endl
     << dec << i << endl
     << hex << i << endl;
```

then the result would be

```
021
17
0x11
```

because $21_8 = 17_{10} = 11_{16}$.

Some format manipulators require arguments, and to use them, the file ioma-nip.h must be included. There are many programs in which we want to specify the number of decimal places, or **precision**, to use in displaying real values. For this, iomanip provides the **setprecision(n)** manipulator, which sets the number of decimal places of precision in subsequent reals to n. We used this manipulator in the program in Figure 1.6 to display monetary values with two decimal places:

```
cout << "\nThe total revenue for these installations is $"
     << fixed << showpoint
     << setprecision(2)
     << totalRevenue << endl;
```

Another kind of format has to do with the space or *field* in which a data value is displayed. The width of an output field is 0 by default, and automatically grows to accomodate the value being displayed. This is convenient, because it is what the programmer usually wants. However, there are some situations where we would like to have a field wider than the data value. The **setw(n)** manipulator can be used to set the width of the *next* field to n. However, every insertion automatically resets the field width to zero, and so setw() *must be used immediately prior to the insertion of each value whose field width is to be altered.*

To illustrate the use of setw(), suppose we are creating a budget report, and want the decimal points in our monetary values to be aligned. If we use

```
cout << showpoint << fixed
     << setprecision(2)
     << "Expenditures:  $" << expenditures << endl
     << "Receipts:      $" << receipts << endl
     << "----------------------" << endl
     << "Profit:        $" << profit << endl;
```

then the output appears as follows:

```
Expenditures:   $1013.51
Receipts:       $998.49
----------------------
Profit:         $15.02
```

This would look better if the decimal points were aligned, and one way to do this is to use the setw() manipulator to increase the size of the field for the monetary values, and the right manipulator to right justify the values in these fields:

```
cout << showpoint << fixed
     << setprecision(2) << right
     << "Expenditures:  $" << setw(7) << expenditures << endl
     << "Receipts:      $" << setw(7) << receipts << endl
     << "----------------------" << endl
     << "Profit:        $" << setw(7) << profit << endl;
```

which generates the output

```
Expenditures:   $1013.51
Receipts:       $ 998.49
----------------------
Profit:         $  15.02
```

When a value is smaller in width than its field, the character used to fill the empty part of a field is called the **fill character.** It is a *space* by default, but it can be changed to another character ch by using the **setfill(ch)** manipulator. For example, if we changed the preceding output statement to

```
cout << showpoint << fixed
     << setprecision(2) << right
     << setfill('*')
     << "Expenditures:  $" << setw(7) << expenditures << endl
     << "Receipts:      $" << setw(7) << receipts << endl
     << "----------------------" << endl
     << "Profit:        $" << setw(7) << profit << endl;
```

the resulting output will be

```
Expenditures:    $1013.51
Receipts:        $*998.49
----------------------
Profit:          $**15.02
```

✔   Quick Quiz 4.3

1. Who designed the C++ language?

2. Who developed the classes that constitute the `iostream` library?

3. What are two of the main classes in the `iostream` library?

4. A _____ is an abstraction that models how input gets from the keyboard to a program, or from a program to the screen.

5. _____ is a class for inputting characters from an arbitrary input device to an executing program.

6. _____ is an `istream` object defined in the `iostream` library, which is a stream from the keyboard to a program.

7. Three states of an `istream` are _____, _____, and _____.

8. The statement `assert(cin.____)`; will stop program execution if there is a data-entry error.

9. The function member _____ of the `istream` class is used to reset the states of an input stream.

10. The function member _____ of the `istream` class is used to skip characters in an input stream.

11. (True or false) By default, `>>` skips white space in an input stream.

12. (True or false) The function member `get()` skips white space in an input stream.

13. _____ is a class for outputting characters from an executing program to an arbitrary output device.

14. _____ and _____ are `ostream` objects defined in the iostream library, which are streams from a program to an output device.

15. Two manipulators that can be used to flush an output stream are _____ and _____.

16. (True or false) When the statement, `cout << setw(10) << 1.234 << 5.678 << endl`; is executed, the real numbers 1.234 and 5.678 will be displayed in 10-space fields.

17. (True or false) When the statement, `cout << setprecision(1) << 1.234 << 5.678 << endl`; is executed, the real numbers 1.2 and 5.7 will be displayed.

EXERCISES 4.3

For exercises 1–11, assume that i1, i2, and i3 are int variables, r1, r2, and r3 are double variables, and c1, c2, and c3 are char variables. Tell what value, if any, will be assigned to each of these variables, or explain why an error occurs, when the input statements are executed with the given input data.

1. cin >> i1 >> i2 >> i3   Input: 1   2   3
        >> r1 >> r2 >> r3;   4 5.5 6.6

2. cin >> i1 >> i2 >> i3;   Input: 1
        cin >> r1 >> r2 >> r3;   2
                                                3
                                                4
                                                5
                                                6

3. cin >> i1 >> r1;   Input: 1 2.2
        cin >> i2 >> r2;   3 4.4
        cin >> i3 >> r3 ;   5 6.6

4. cin >> i1 >> i2 >> i3   Input: 1 2.2
        >> r1 >> r2 >> r3;   3 4.4
                                                5 6.6

5. cin >> i1 >> c1 >> r1   Input: 1 2.2
        >> i2 >> c2 >> r2   3 4.4
        >> i3 >> c3 >> r3;   5 6.6

6. cin >> noskipws   Input: 1 2.2
        >> i1 >> c1 >> r1   3 4.4
        >> i2 >> c2 >> r2   5 6.6
        >> i3 >> c3 >> r3;

7. cin >> i1 >> c1 >> i2   Input: 1A 2B 3C
        >> c2 >> i3 >> c3;

8. cin >> i1 >> i2 >> i3;   Input: 012 345 678

9. cin >> dec >> i1 >> i2 >> i3;   Input: 012 345 678

10. cin >> oct >> i1 >> i2 >> i3;   Input: 012 345 678

11. cin >> hex >> i1 >> i2 >> i3;   Input: 12 3A BC

For exercises 12–20, assume that alpha and beta are real variables with values -567.392 and 0.0004, respectively, and that num1 and num2 are integer variables with values 12 and 436, respectively. Show precisely the output that each of the sets of statements produces, or explain why an error occurs.

12. cout << num2 << num2 + 1 << num2 + 2;

13. cout << num2 << setw(4) << num2 + 1 << num2 + 2;

14. cout << num1 << num1 + 1 << num1 + 2;

15. cout << oct << num1 << num1 + 1 << num1 + 2;

16. cout << showbase << oct << num1 << num1 + 1 << num1 + 2;

17. cout << hex << num1 << num1 + 1 << num1 + 2;

18. cout << showbase << hex << num1 << num1 + 1 << num1 + 2;

19.
```
cout << fixed << showpoint << right
     << setw(9) << setprecision(3) << alpha << endl
     << setw(10) << setprecision(5) << beta << endl
     << setw(7) << setprecision(4) << beta << endl;
```

20.
```
cout << scientific << showpoint << left
     << setprecision(1) << setw(10) << alpha << endl
     << setw(5) << beta << endl
     << "Tolerance:"
     << setw(12) << setprecision(3) << beta << endl;
```

For exercises 21 and 22, assume that i and j are integer variables with i = 15 and j = 8, that ch is a character variable with ch = 'c', and that x and y are real variables with x = 2559.50 and y = 8.015. Show precisely the output produced, or explain why an error occurs.

21.
```
cout << setw(j) << setprecision(2)
     << fixed << showpoint << right
     << "New balance =" << x << ' ' << setw(i % 10) << ch
     << setw(j) << setprecision(j-6) << y << endl;
```

22.
```
cout << i =" << setw(i) << i
     << fixed << showpoint << right
     << "j = << setw(j) << setprecision(j) << j << endl
     << setw(j) << i << ' '
     << setw(i) << j << endl;
```

For exercises 23–26, assume that n1 and n2 are integer variables with values 39 and −5117, respectively; that r1 and r2 are real variables with values 56.7173 and −0.00247, respectively; and that ch is a character variable with the value 'F'. Write output statements that use these variables to produce the given output.

23. 56.7173___F___39__
         -5117PDQ-0.00247__

24. 56.717_____-0.0025***39__F__
         56.72__39-5117_____

25. Roots_are__56.717_and_-0.00247

26. Approximate_angles:__56.7_and_-0.0
         Magnitudes_are_____39_and__5117___

4.4 COMPUTING WITH string OBJECTS

The word *compute* usually suggests arithmetic computations performed on numeric data; thus computers are sometimes thought to be mere "number crunchers"— devices whose only purpose is to process numeric information—and in the early days of computing, this was largely true.

However, to facilitate communication between a human and a running program, computer scientists soon devised a code by which alphabetic characters could be represented and manipulated. Since words consist of sequences or **strings** of characters, the problem of storing and processing strings of characters followed naturally. In this section, we examine C++'s solution to the problem, the standard string class. It is declared in the header file string (*not* string.h, which is a C library), which must be included to use the class.

DECLARING string OBJECTS

Since string is the name of a class and the name of a class is a type, string objects can be declared and initialized in the same manner as other objects we have studied. For example, the declaration

```
string name;
```

creates a string object named name and initializes it to an **empty string,** which contains no characters. A literal for the empty string can be written as two consecutive double quotes (" ").

A declaration of a string object can also initialize that object by providing a string expression for its initial value. For example, the declarations

```
string play = "Hamlet",
       author = "W. Shakespeare",
       mainCharacter = play;
```

create three string objects play, author, and mainCharacter, and initialize play to contain 6 characters,

author to contain 14 characters,

and mainCharacter to contain a copy of the string in play:

These string objects are *variables,* and they can be assigned new values as in

```
play = "The Tempest";
mainCharacter = "Prospero";
```

and these two objects will be modified:

```
play   T h e   T e m p e s t
```

```
mainCharacter   P r o s p e r o
```

Constant string objects are defined by preceding a normal string declaration with the keyword const; for example,

```
const string PASSWORD = "Romeo-Romeo";
```

As with other constants, the string value of such objects cannot subsequently be changed.

STRING I/O

String input and output are quite similar to input and output for other types of objects. More precisely, the `string` class has overloaded the `<<` operator to perform `string` output and the `>>` operator to perform `string` input.

Output. The output operator `<<` can be used to display `string` literals and expressions. For example, the statements

```
string name = "John Doe";
cout << "My name is " << name << ".\n";
```

will display

```
My name is John Doe.
```

Input Using >>. The input operator `>>` can be used to input values for `string` variables. For example, consider the following statements:

```
cout << "Enter your name: ";
string name;
cin >> name;
cout << "Welcome, " << name << "!\n";
```

If these statements are executed and the user enters `Al`,

```
Enter your name: Al
Welcome, Al!
```

we see that the string `Al` is assigned to `name`. If, however, the user enters `Al  E. Cat` instead, execution will proceed as follows:

```
Enter your name: Al E. Cat
Welcome, Al!
```

The string `Al` is assigned to `name` as before, but what happened to the `E. Cat`?

When the input operator `>>` is applied to a string object, it gets the next word from the input stream. More precisely, `>>` *extracts characters from an* `istream` *and transfers them into a* `string` *object until a white-space character (space, tab or newline) is encountered.* In the preceding example, the unread characters `E. Cat` remain in the `istream` and will be read by subsequent input statements, which is probably not what was intended. For this reason, it is a good idea to *always prompt the user as precisely as possible when reading* `string` *values using* `>>`; for example,

```
cout << "Enter your first name (e.g., Jane): ";
string firstName;
cin >> firstName;
```

or

```
cout << "\nEnter your full name (e.g., John Quincy Doe): ";
string firstName,
       middleName,
       lastName;
cin >> firstName >> middleName >> lastName;
```

Input Using `getline()`. Sometimes we want to read an entire line of text into a `string` variable. This can be done using the function `getline()` provided in the `string` library. For example, if we rewrite the earlier code segment as

```
cout << "Enter your name: ";
string name;
getline(cin, name);
cout << "Welcome, " << name << "!\n";
```

and the user enters Al, execution will proceed as before:

```
Enter your name: Al
Welcome, Al!
```

However, if the user instead enters Al E. Cat, execution will produce

```
Enter your name: Al E. Cat
Welcome, Al E. Cat!
```

because the `getline()` function reads the entire line. More precisely, *the* `getline()` *function extracts characters from an* `istream` *and transfers them into a* `string` *variable until a newline character is encountered.*

Thus, to read an *entire line* of input, the `getline()` function should be used. To read a *word* of input, the input operator `>>` should be used.

OTHER STRING OPERATIONS

The `string` class provides several other operations. We will discuss the more commonly used operations here; the others are described in appendix D.

The Subscript Operation. The variables of previous chapters are called **scalar** variables to indicate that they can only store single values. In contrast, a `string` object can be viewed as a *container* for storing a sequence of values. Each *element* of a `string` object is like a scalar character variable in that it can store a single character, and anything that can be done with a single character can be done to an element of a `string` object.

When a `string` object is created, the compiler automatically associates an integer called an **index** with each character in the string. For example, suppose that name is declared by

```
string name = "John Doe";
```

When this declaration is encountered, a container is automatically built for the object name, with each element of name being numbered, starting from zero, and the characters J, o, h, n, a blank, D, o, and e, are stored in these elements:

name	J	o	h	n		D	o	e
	0	1	2	3	4	5	6	7

The **subscript operator** `[]` uses the index of an element to access the character stored in that element. An expression of the form

```
string_object[index]
```

is a char object whose value is the character stored at the specified *index* of *string_object*. To illustrate, consider the following assignment statements:

```
name[1] = 'a';
name[2] = name[3];
name[3] = 'e';
name[5] = 'R';
```

The first assignment changes the character at index 1 of name to 'a'. The second assignment copies the character 'n' at index 3 to index 2. The third assignment changes the character at index 3 to 'e'. The final assignment changes the character at index 5 to 'R'. The result is that name is changed as follows:

A for loop is often used in conjunction with the subscript operator to process string objects. Since the index values of a string are consecutive integers, a for loop can run through those numbers. For example, the for loop

```
for (int i = 7; i >= 0; i--)
    cout << name[i];
```

displays the characters of name in reverse order:

```
eoR enaJ
```

Here, the notation

```
name[i]
```

is being used to access the character at index i in name. On the first pass through the loop, i is 7, and so the last character is displayed; on the next pass, i is 6, and so the next-to-last character is displayed; and so on.

The preceding for loop assumes that the index of the last character is 7. If a larger or smaller string value is assigned to name, this loop will no longer work correctly. To avoid this difficulty, we need to be able to determine the *size* of a string.

The size() Operation. The string class provides a function member size() that returns the **size** of a given string object; that is, the number of characters in it. For example, the function call

```
name.size()
```

will return the value 8.

Note that because indices start at zero, *the index of the last character in a string is always* size() - 1. We can use this property to design a for loop that runs through all the characters of a string, regardless of its size. For example, the for loop for displaying the reverse of name could be better written

```
for (int i = name.size() - 1; i >= 0; i--)
    cout << name[i];
```

If name is "Jane Roe", then name.size() is 8, and so 7 is the index of the final character. If name is "William Shakespeare", then name.size() is 19, and so 18 is the index of the final character. By using *name*.size() - 1 as the index of the final character, this loop will always correctly begin with the last character in name, regardless of the string stored in it.

The empty() Operation.   As we noted earlier, a string containing no characters is called the empty string. The string class provides the function member empty() to test whether a string is empty. It returns the boolean value true if its string object is empty and false otherwise. For example, if we declare

```
string oneString,
       anotherString = "Hi There";
```

then the expression

```
oneString.empty()
```

returns true, while the expression

```
anotherString.empty()
```

returns false.

Assignment.   The assignment operator can be used to assign values to variable string objects. The size of the string object will be the number of characters in the string value being assigned. For example,

```
string quote = "To be is to do - Aristotle.";
```

will initialize quote with the indicated string so that quote.size() will be 27. If we later assign

```
quote = "To do is to be - Sartre.";
```

then this new string replaces the string in quote, and quote.size() changes to 24. Similarly, a later assignment

```
quote = "Doobee-Doobee-Doo - Sinatra.";
```

will change quote's value as indicated and quote.size() to 28.

   In each of these examples, the value assigned has been a string literal, but a string object can also be assigned to another string object. For example, the declarations

```
string today = "Monday",
       yesterday;
```

initialize today to contain the string "Monday" and yesterday to an empty string:

today	M	o	n	d	a	y
	0	1	2	3	4	5

yesterday

If we subsequently write

```
yesterday = today;
today = "Tuesday";
```

then `yesterday` is assigned the value `"Monday"` and the value of `today` is changed to `"Tuesday"`:

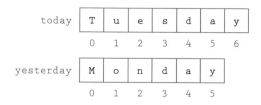

The Relational Operators. The relational operators have all been overloaded in class `string` and can be used to compare `string` objects and/or character string literals. For each operation, the elements of the string operands are compared element by element until a mismatch occurs or the end of one (or both) of the strings is reached.

To illustrate, consider the declarations

```
string hisName = "James",
       herName = "Jan";
```

The objects produced are

hisName	J	a	m	e	s
	0	1	2	3	4

herName	J	a	n
	0	1	2

If these two objects are compared with the boolean expression

```
hisName < herName
```

the < function begins by comparing the characters at index 0:

hisName	J	a	m	e	s
	0	1	2	3	4

herName	J	a	n
	0	1	2

Since these characters are the same, the function compares the next two characters,

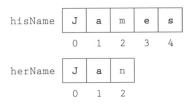

and, because they are also the same, it proceeds to the next two characters:

Here, the first mismatch occurs. Since the character code for 'm' is less than the character code for 'n' (see appendix A), the < function returns true, indicating that "James" is less than "Jan". If the end of one of the strings is reached without a mismatch, then the shorter string is considered to be less than the longer one. For example,

```
herName < "Jane"
```

returns true.

Expressions involving the other relational operators such as

```
hisName == herName
```

```
hisName != herName
```

```
hisName > herName
```

```
hisName <= herName
```

```
hisName >= herName
```

use this same character-by-character comparison. For the given values of hisName and herName, they will return false, true, false, true, and false, respectively.

Concatenation.   Another useful string operation is **concatenation**—combining two strings into a single string. For example, the concatenation of the string "list" and the string "en" produces the string "listen". Ordering is important in concatenation—if we concatenate the string "en" and the string "list", the string "enlist" is produced. The concatenation operation can be thought of as forming a string whose value is the second string appended to the first string.

The plus symbol (+) has been overloaded in class string so that when its two operands are `string` objects or character string literals, concatenation is performed. For example, given the declarations:

```
string state = "Michigan",
       greatLake;
```

the expression

```
greatLake = "Lake " + state;
```

concatenates the `string` literal `"Lake "` and the `string` stored in `state`, and assigns the resulting `string` to `greatLake`:

Concatenation thus builds a larger `string` out of two smaller `string` values. The concatenation operator returns the `string` object it produces, so that multiple concatenations can be chained together, as in:

```
string firstName = "Popeye",
       middleName = "the",
       lastName = "Sailor",
       fullName = firstName + " " + middleName + " " + lastName;
```

which initializes `fullName` to be a `string` object containing

```
Popeye the Sailor
```

To append `man` to this string, we could write:

```
fullName = fullName + "man";
```

but the += shortcut

```
fullName += "man";
```

is preferable. In either case, `"man"` is appended to the `string` in name so that the value in `fullName` is `"Popeye the Sailorman"`.

Substring. The subscript operation provides access to a particular character in a string, but it is sometimes useful to access a substring of characters. To illustrate, suppose that the following string objects have been declared:

```
string fullName = "John Quincy Doe",
       firstName,
       middleName,
       lastName;
```

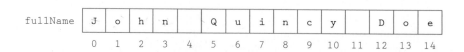

Also, suppose we want to access the first, middle, or last name within `fullName`.

The string class provides a function member substr() that makes this easy. The assignments

```
firstName = fullName.substr(0, 4);
middleName = fullName.substr(5, 6);
lastName = fullName.substr(12, 3);
```

set the value of firstName to "John", the value of middleName to "Quincy", and the value of lastName to "Doe", leaving fullName unchanged.

The general form of a call to the string function member substr() is as follows:

```
string_object.substr(first, num_chars)
```

where first is the index in string_object of the first character to be selected and num_chars is the size of the substring to be selected. It returns a string value consisting of the num_chars characters beginning at position first in string_object.

Note the differences between this *substring* operation and the *subscript* operation:

Subscript Operation	Substring Operation
Uses square brackets: []	Uses parentheses: ()
Uses one index	Uses an index and a size
Returns a char value	Returns a string value

Another difference is that the subscript operation does not check that the index it receives is within the bounds of the string; hence, logic errors can occur and go undetected if one tries to access a position past the end of the string, as in

```
string name = "Sam"
char initial = name[4];        // ERROR, no notification
```

When these statements are executed, initial will be assigned whatever "garbage" character happens to be 2 characters past the end of "Sam".

By contrast, the substring() member function checks the validity of its index. If one tries to access a substring that begins past the end of the string,

```
string name1 = "Sam",
       name2 = name1.substr(4, 2);  // ERROR: fatal
                                    // with notification
```

an **out-of-bounds exception** will occur and execution of the program is terminated. If the size passed to substr() is larger than the number of characters remaining in the string,

```
string name1 = "Sam",
       name2 = name1.substr(1, 5);  // ERROR: no notification
```

the size argument (5) will be ignored and all of the characters from the specified starting position (1) to the end of the string will be selected.

Substring Replacement. We have seen that the substring operation does not modify the string object to which it is applied. However, it is sometimes necessary to modify some portion of a `string`, leaving the rest of it unaltered. The `string` class provides the member function `replace()` to perform this operation. To illustrate, consider again the declaration:

```
string fullName = "John Quincy Doe";
```

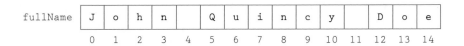

The function call

```
fullName.replace(0, 4, "Jane");
```

replaces the first 4 characters in `fullName` with `"Jane"`:

Individual characters can also be replaced with the `replace()` function. For example, the call

```
fullName.replace(12, 1, 'R');
```

replaces the single character at index 12 with `'R'`, changing the last name to `"Roe"`:

In the preceding examples, the length of `fullName` did not change, because the replacement string and the substring being replaced had the same length. In general, however, they may have different lengths. For example, execution of the statement

```
fullName.replace(5, 6, "Eyre");
```

replaces the 6-character substring "Quincy" with the 4-character string "Eyre". As a result, the size of `fullName` decreases from 15 to 13:

The general form of a call to the function member `replace()` is

```
string_object.replace(first, num_chars, replacement)
```

where *first* is the index of the first character to be replaced, *num_chars* is the number of characters to be replaced, and *replacement* is a `string` object, string literal, or character. It modifies *string_object* by replacing the substring *string_object*.substr(*first, num_chars*) with *replacement*; the size of *string_object* increases or decreases as necessary. Bounds checking is performed to ensure that *first* is a valid index of *string_object*.

Substring Removal. Another useful string operation is removal of a substring. The string class provides a function member remove() to perform this operation. For example, consider the declaration

```
string commonName = "John Quincy Doe";
```

which initializes the string object commonName as

commonName	J	o	h	n		Q	u	i	n	c	y		D	o	e
	0	1	2	3	4	5	6	7	8	9	10	11	12	13	14

The statement

```
commonName.remove(5, 6);
```

removes the 6 characters starting at position 5 from commonName,

commonName	J	o	h	n		D	o	e
	0	1	2	3	4	5	6	7

and the size of commonName decreases to 8.

The general form of a call to the string function member remove() is

```
string_object.remove()
```

or

```
string_object.remove(first, num_chars)
```

where *first* is the index of the first character to be removed and *num_chars* is the number of characters to be removed. The first version makes *string_object* the empty string, removing all its characters. The second version modifies *string_object* by removing the substring *string_object*.substr(*first, num_chars*). The length of *string_object* decreases by *num_chars*. Bounds checking is performed to ensure that *first* is a valid index of *string_object*.

Substring Insertion. The inverse of the deletion operation for a string object is the insertion of a substring into a string. The string class provides the function member insert() to perform this operation. For example, consider the declaration

```
string signature = "Jane Doe";
```

which initializes signature to "Jane Doe":

signature	J	a	n	e		D	o	e
	0	1	2	3	4	5	6	7

The function call

```
signature.insert(5, "E. ");
```

will insert the string `"E. "` into `signature` beginning at position 5, giving

signature	J	a	n	e		E	.		D	o	e
	0	1	2	3	4	5	6	7	8	9	10

The size of `signature` increases to 11.

The general form of a call to the `string` function member `insert()` is

> `string_object.insert(position, new_string)`

where *position* is the index at which insertion is to begin, and *new_string* is a string object, `string` literal, or a character. It modifies *string_object* by inserting the *new_string* with its first character at *position*. The size of *string_object* increases by *new_string*.`size()`. Bounds checking is performed to ensure that *position* is a valid index of *string_object*.

Substring Pattern Matching.   Another common string operation is finding the location of a given substring within a string, an operation known as **pattern matching.** The `string` function members `find()` and `rfind()` provide this capability. For example, given the declaration

```
string quote = "If it walks like a duck, "
               "and quacks like a duck,\n"
               "then it just may be a duck - Reuther";
```

the call

```
int position = quote.find("duck", 0);
```

searches `quote` for the substring `"duck"`, beginning the search at index 0. In this case, the call returns the value 19, since 19 is the index of the first occurrence of the substring `"duck"` within object `quote`. The positions of later occurrences of the same substring `"duck"` can be found by searching from one past the last position. For example, if `position` is 19, then the call

```
position = quote.find("duck", position + 1)
```

will search for `"duck"` again, but starting from the character at index 20. In this case, the call returns the value 43, which is assigned to `position`. A subsequent call

```
position = quote.find("duck". position + 1);
```

will begin the search at position 44, and return the value 71. If we try again,

```
position = quote.find("duck", position + 1);
```

the search fails, and the function returns **npos**, a special constant (-1 on many systems) defined in the `string` library.

The find() and replace functions can be called in a loop to find and replace all occurrences of a substring in a string object. For example, the statements

```
int position = -1;
for (;;)
{
    position = quote.find("a duck", position + 1);
    if (position == string::npos) break;
    quote.replace(position, 6, "an aardvark");
}
```

will replace all occurrences of "a duck" in quote with "an aardvark". Note that position is initialized to − 1 so that on the first pass through the loop, the search will begin correctly at index 0.

The general form of a call to the string pattern-matching operation is

```
string_object.find(pattern, position)
```

where *pattern* is a string object or string literal, and *position* is the index at which the search is to commence. It returns the index at which the substring *pattern* begins within *string_object*. If *pattern* is not found (i.e., if the search *fails*), npos is returned. Bounds checking is performed to ensure that *position* is a valid index of *string_object*.

In general, it is good programming practice to check the return value of operations that can easily fail (like pattern matching) to ensure that they were successful before continuing. For example, instead of simply writing

```
int location = quote.find(some_string, 0);
```

and then proceeding to use location, the value of location should be checked before continuing:

```
int location = quote.find(some_string, 0);

if (location == string::npos)
    cerr << some_string << "does not occur within \'quote\'";
else
{
    // ... process using valid location value
}
```

Otherwise, if *some_string* is a value that does not occur within quote, find() will return the value npos, so that a subsequent access to quote using location may generate a fatal out-of-bounds exception.

The function member find() searches in a forward direction, by incrementing the index being examined. To search in a backward direction, the string class provides the function member rfind(). It is used in a manner similar to the find() function, except that the search should begin at the index of the last character instead of the first character. Here is the rfind() version of the earlier loop that replaces all occurrences of "a duck" in quote with "an aardvark":

```
    int position = quote.size();

    for (;;)
    {
        position = quote.rfind("a duck", position - 1);

        if (position == string::npos) break;

        quote.replace(position, 6, "an aardvark");
    }
```

Note that in this version `position` is initialized to one greater than the index of the final character in `quote`, and we then subtract 1 from `position` on each pass through the loop.

The `find()` and `rfind()` functions are used to search for strings. To search a `string` object for the first occurrence of any of a set of characters, the `string` class provides the `find_first_of()` function member, which searches a string in a forward direction for the first occurrence of any of a given list of characters. To illustrate, consider the declaration:

```
    string quote = "I wouldn't want to belong to any club\n"
                   "that would accept me as a member "
                   "- Groucho Marx.";
```

We can use the following statements to find the indices of the vowels in `quote`:

```
    int position = -1;

    for (;;)
    {
        position = quote.find_first_of("aeiouAEIOU", position + 1);

        if (position == string::npos) break;

        cout << position << ' ';
    }
```

Execution of these statements produces

0 3 4 12 17 20 22 27 29 35 40 44 45 49 52 57 59 62 65 68 75 76 79 82

The general form of a call to `find_first_of()` is

```
    string_object.find_first_of(pattern, position)
```

where *pattern* is a `string` object, `string` literal, or character, and *position* is the index at which the search is to begin. It returns the index $\geq$ *position* of the first occurrence of any character in *pattern* within *string_object*. If no character in *pattern* is found, the predefined constant `npos` is returned. Bounds checking is carried out to ensure that *position* is a valid index of *string_object*.

The `string` class also provides other character-searching functions, including:

▶ *string_object*.`find_last_of`(*pattern, position*) returns the index $\leq$ *position* of the *last* occurence of any of the characters in *pattern*

▶ *string_object*.find_first_not_of(*pattern, position*) returns the index ≥ *position* of the *first* occurrence of a character *not* in *pattern*

▶ *string_object*.find_last_not_of(*pattern, position*) returns the index ≤ *position* of the *last* occurrence of a character *not* in *pattern*

These complementary operations simplify some kinds of searches. For example, to find the consonants in quote with the find_first_of() function, *pattern* would have to list all 21 consonants in both upper and lower case:

```
"bcdfghjklmnpqrstvwxyzBCDFGHJKLMNPQRSTVWXYZ"
```

It is much simpler to use the find_first_not_of() function and the string of vowel characters for *pattern*:

```
firstConsonantIndex = quote.find_first_not_of("AEIOUaeiou", 0);
```

✔ **Quick Quiz 4.4**

1. A string that contains no characters is called a(n) _____ string.
2. Write a declaration that initializes a string variable label to an empty string.
3. Write a declaration that initializes a string constant UNITS to "meters".
4. If the input for the statement cin >> s1 >> s2;, where s1 and s2 are string variables, is

   ```
   ABC
       DEF GHI
   ```

   then s1 will be assigned the value _____ and s2 the value _____.

Questions 5–21 assume the following declarations:

```
string s1 = "shell",
       s2 = "seashore",
       s3 = "She sells seashells by the seashore.",
       s4;
```

For questions 5–18 find the value of the expression, and for 20–22 give the new value of the variable (s1, s2, or s3).

5. s1[2]
6. s2.size()
7. s4.size()
8. s3.empty()
9. s4.empty()
10. s1 > s2
11. s1 < s3
12. s2 + s1
13. s1.substr(0,3)
14. s3.find("sea", 0)
15. s3.rfind("sea", 35)
16. s3.find_first_of("abc",0)
17. s3.find_last_of("abc",35)
18. s3.find_first_not_of("abc",0)
19. s3.find_last_not_of("abc",35)
20. s1.replace(0, 2, 'b');
21. s2.insert(3, "1 on the ");
22. s3.remove(9, 13);

EXERCISES 4.4

Exercises 1–26 assume the following declarations:

```
string s1,
       s2 = "row, row, row your boat",
       s3 = "row",
       s4 = "boat.";
```

For exercises 1–21 find the value of the expression or explain why an error occurs.

1. `s2[3]`

2. `s1.size() + s4.size()`

3. `s3 < s4`

4. `s3 <= s2`

5. `s3 + s4`

6. `"fl" + s4.substr(1,3) + " a " + s4`

7. `s1.substr(1,3)`

8. `s2.substr(1,3)`

9. `s2.find("ow", 1)`

10. `s2.find("ow", 2)`

11. `s2.find("ow", 12)`

12. `s2.rfind("ow", 12)`

13. `s2.rfind("ow", 11)`

14. `s2.rfind("ow", 1)`

15. `s2.find_first_of(s4, 0)`

16. `s2.find_first_of(s4, 2)`

17. `s2.find_first_not_of(s4, 0)`

18. `s2.find_first_not_of(s4, 1)`

19. `s2.find_last_of(s3, 22)`

20. `s2.find_last_of(s3, 19)`

21. `s2.find_last_not_of(s3, s2.size() - 1)`

For exercises 22–26, give the output produced, or explain why an error occurs.

22.
```
int i = s2.find_last_of(s3, s2.size() - 1);
cout << s2.substr(i, s2.size() - i) << endl;
```

23.
```
s1 = s3 + s4;
s1[0] = 'g';
s1.replace(2, 2, " fl");
cout << s1 << endl;
```

24.
```
s1 = s2;
s1.remove(3, 10);
s1.insert(0, "Bor");
cout << s1 + "?\n";
```

25.
```
s1 = s2;
s1[s1.find("b", 0)] = 'g';
for (int i = 0; i <= 10; i += 5)
   s1[i] = 'm';
cout << s1 << endl;
```

26.
```
s1 = s2;
int i = -1;
for (;;)
{
   int i = s1.find_first_of("aeiou", i + 1);
   if (i == string::npos) break;
   s1.replace(i, 1, "xx");
}
cout << s1 << endl;
```

27. Given that `string` variable `last_first` has the value `"Smith, Bill"`, write statements to extract the first and last names from `last_first` and then combine them, so that the value `"Bill   Smith"` is assigned to the `string` variable `first_last`.

Exercises 28–34 ask you to write functions to compute various quantities. To test these functions, you should write driver programs as instructed in Programming Problems 7–13 at the end of this chapter.

28.   Write a function that accepts a month number and returns the name of the month.

29.   Write a function that accepts the name of a month and returns the number of the month.

30.   Write a function that, given a string of lowercase and uppercase letters, returns a copy of the string in all lowercase letters; and another function that, given a string of lowercase and uppercase letters, returns a copy of the string in all uppercase letters. (Hint: Use a `for` loop and the functions provided in `ctype`).

31.   Write a function `replace_all()`, such that a call

        newString = replace_all(str, substring, newSubstring);

will return a copy of string *str* with each occurrence of *substring* replaced by *newSubstring*.

32.   Write a function that, given the three components of a name (first name, middle name or initial, and last name), returns a single `string` object consisting of the last name, followed by a comma, and then the first name and middle initial, followed by a period. For example, given `"John"`, `"Quincy"`, and `"Doe"`, the function should return the string `"Doe, John Q."`.

33.   Proceed as in exercise 32, but design the function to accept a single `string` object consisting of a first name, a middle name or initial, and a last name. As before, the function should return a single `string` object consisting of the last name, followed by a comma, and then the first name and the middle initial. For example, given `"John Quincy Doe"`, the function should return the string `"Doe, John Q."`.

34.   A `string` is said to be a palindrome if it does not change when the order of its characters is reversed. For example:

        madam
        463364
        ABLE WAS I ERE I SAW ELBA

are palindromes. Write a function that, given a string, returns true if that string is a palindrome and returns false otherwise.

4.5 EXAMPLE: DECODING PHONE NUMBERS

PROBLEM

To dial a telephone number, we use the telephone's keypad to enter a sequence of digits. For a long-distance call, the telephone system must divide this number into its area code, exchange, and local number; but if the number is a local call, it splits the number into its exchange and local number. For example, if a person enters 12345556789 in the United States, the system extracts the area code (234), the exchange (555), and the local number (6789); but if the person enters 5556789, the system extracts the exchange (555) and the local number (6789).

We want to develop a program that, given a phone number (a sequence of seven digits or a sequence of 11 digits beginning with 1), extracts and displays the area code (if a long distance number), the exchange, and the local number. For example, for the input 12345556789, the program should display (234)-555-6789; and for the input 5556789, it should display 555-6789.

OBJECT-CENTERED DESIGN

Behavior.   The program should display a prompt for a phone number on the screen, and then read a phone number from the keyboard. It should check that the number is a valid telephone number. If the number begins with 1, the program should extract and display the area code, exchange, and local number. Otherwise, the program should extract and display the exchange and local number.

Objects.   From our behavioral description, we can identify the following objects:

Description	Type	Kind	Name
prompt	string	constant	*PROMPT*
phone number	string	varying	*phoneNumber*
screen	ostream	varying	cout
keyboard	istream	varying	cin
area code	string	varying	none
exchange	string	varying	none
local number	string	varying	none

Note that the phone number cannot be represented by an integer, because the maximum (unsigned long) integer value on 32-bit systems is 429496725, which is considerably less than a long distance number such as 12345556789. Thus, we will treat phone numbers as sequences of characters and use the type string to store them.

Operations.   From the statement of the problem, we can identify these operations:

  i.   Display a string on the screen (the input prompt)
 ii.   Read a string from the keyboard (*phoneNumber*)
iii.   Check that a string constitutes a valid phone number
 iv.   If the number begins with '1':

  a. Extract and display the second, third, and fourth characters from a string (the area code)
  b. Extract and display the fifth, sixth, and seventh characters from a string (the exchange)
  c. Extract and display the eighth through the eleventh characters from a string (the local number)

  v.   Otherwise

  a. Extract and display the first, second, and third characters from a string (the exchange)

b. Extract and display the fourth through seventh characters from a string (the local number)

Algorithm. Assuming the availability of a function for each of the operations, we can arrange them into an algorithm for the problem.

Algorithm for Phone Number Decoder

1. Display *PROMPT*.
2. From `cin`, read *phoneNumber*.
3. Check that *phoneNumber* is a valid phone number.
4. If *phoneNumber* begins with 1:
   a. Display the area code = characters 1–3 of *phoneNumber*.
   b. Display the exchange = characters 4–6 of *phoneNumber*.
   c. Display the local number = characters 7–10 of *phoneNumber*.
5. Otherwise
   a. Display the exchange = characters 0–2 of *phoneNumber*.
   b. Display the local number = characters 3–6 of *phoneNumber*.

Refinement. All of the operations except the third are provided in C++ or by the `string` class. We need to define a function to perform this operation.

Function's Problem. Write a function to check that the value stored in a string is a valid phone number.

Function's Behavior. The function should receive a string from its caller and check that it contains either 7 or 11 characters. For a string with 11 characters, it should check that the first digit is 1. For a string with 7 characters, it should check that the first digit is not 1 or 0. It should also check that each of the characters in the string is a digit. For a string that fails any of these tests, the function should display an appropriate diagnostic message and terminate execution.

Function's Objects. From our behavioral description, we can identify the following objects for this function:

Description	Type	Kind	Movement	Name
a string	string	varying	received	*aString*
first digit of a string	char	constant	none	none

We will not name the first digit of a string, since it can be accessed directly using the subscript operator.

Function's Operations. From our behavioral description, we can identify the following operations:

   i.   Check that the string contains either 7 characters or 11 characters
   ii. If the string contains 11 characters, check that the first digit is a 1
  iii. If the string contains 7 characters, check that the first digit is not 1 or 0
  iv. Check that each of the characters in the string is a digit

v.   If any of tests i–iv fail, display a diagnostic message and terminate the program

As we shall see, each of these operations is readily available, so we can go on to organize them into an algorithm.

Function's Algorithm. With a bit of thought, we can arrange the preceding operations into the following algorithm:

Algorithm for Function that Checks a Phone Number

1. Receive *aString*.

2. If the size of *aString* is neither 7 nor 11
>   Display a diagnostic message and terminate.

> Otherwise

>> If *aString* has size 7 and begins with 0 or 1
>>>   Display a diagnostic message and terminate.

>> Otherwise if *aString* has size 11 and does not begin with 1
>>>   Display a diagnostic message and terminate.

>> Otherwise if there are any non-digit characters in *aString*
>>>   Display a diagnostic message and terminate.

Function's Coding. The following function `CheckValidity()` in Figure 4.2 implements this algorithm:

FIGURE 4.2   VERIFYING PHONE NUMBERS.

```
/* CheckValidity ensures that a string is a valid phone number.
 *
 * Receive: aString, a string
 * Return:  nothing if aString is valid
 *          (terminate the program otherwise)
 ***************************************************************/

void PhoneError(string message);

void CheckValidity(string aString)
{
   if (aString.size() != 7 && aString.size() != 11)
     PhoneError("A phone number has 7 or 11 characters");
   else
   {
     if (aString.size() == 7 && (aString[0] == '0' || aString[0] == '1'))
        PhoneError("A local call cannot begin with 0 or 1");
     else if (aString.size() == 11 && aString[0] != '1')
        PhoneError("A long distance call must begin with 1");
     if (aString.find_first_not_of("0123456789", 0) != string::npos)
        PhoneError("A phone number must consist of all digits");
   }
}
```

```
/* PhoneError displays an error msg and terminates the program
 *
 * Receive: message, a string.
 * Output:  message, with phone-specific text
 * Postcondition: Program has been terminated.
 ************************************************************/

#include <stdlib.h>                       // exit()

void PhoneError(string message)
{
   cerr << "Your call cannot be completed because:\n"
        << message <<   ".\nPlease try again." << endl;
   exit(1);
}
```

Note the use of the various string operations. We use the `size()` function to check that the number of characters is correct,

```
if (aString.size() != 7 && aString.size() != 11)
```

the subscript operator to check that the first character of `aString` is correct,

```
if (aString.size() == 7 && (aString[0] == '0' || aString[0] == '1'))
```

and the `find_first_not_of()` function to search `aString` for non-digits:

```
if (aString.find_first_not_of("0123456789", 0) != string::npos)
```

Also note that to "clean up" the function, we wrote a simple `PhoneError()` function which, given a diagnostic message, displays that message, and terminates the program using the `exit()` function provided in `stdlib`. This provides a convenient way to customize the diagnostic messages without cluttering the function with redundant code.

Coding and Testing. A C++ program that solves the original problem is given in Figure 4.3.

 FIGURE 4.3   **PROCESSING PHONE NUMBERS.**

```
/* phone3.cpp simulates the processing of a phone number
 * by the telephone company.
 *
 * Input:   phoneNumber.
 * Output:  areaCode, exchange and localNumber.
 ************************************************************/

#include <iostream.h>                  // cin, cout, >>, <<
#include <string>                      // string

void CheckValidity(string aString);
```

```
int main()
{
  const string PROMPT = "\nEnter a phone number: ";
  cout << PROMPT;

  string phoneNumber;
  cin >> phoneNumber;

  CheckValidity(phoneNumber);

  if (phoneNumber[0] == '1')
     cout << '(' << phoneNumber.substr(1, 3) << ")-"
          << phoneNumber.substr(4, 3) << '-'
          << phoneNumber.substr(7, 4) << endl;
  else
     cout << phoneNumber.substr(0, 3) << '-'
          << phoneNumber.substr(3, 4) << endl;
}

/*** Insert the contents of Figure 4.2 here:
       the prototype for PhoneError
       the definition of CheckValidity
       #include <stdlib.h>
       the definition of PhoneError    ***/
```

Sample runs:

```
Enter a phone number: 12345556789
(234)-555-6789

Enter a phone number: 5556789
555-6789

Enter a phone number: 1234

Your call cannot be completed because:
A phone number has 7 or 11 characters.
Please try again.
```

Part of the Picture: Simulation

The term **simulation** refers to modeling a dynamic process and using this model to study the behavior of the process. The behavior of some **deterministic** processes can be modeled with an equation or a set of equations. For example, processes that involve exponential growth or decay are commonly modeled with an equation of the form

$$A(t) = A_0 e^{kt}$$

where $A(t)$ is the amount of some substance A present at time t, A_0 is the initial amount of the substance, and k is a rate constant.

In many problems, however, the process being studied can be modeled using **randomness;** for example, Brownian motion, the arrival of airplanes at an airport, the number of defective parts manufactured by a machine, and so on. Computer programs that simulate such processes use random number generators to introduce randomness into the values produced during execution.

RANDOM NUMBER GENERATORS—THE `RandomInt` CLASS

A **random number generator** is a subprogram that produces a number selected *at random* from some fixed range in such a way that a sequence of these numbers tends to be uniformly distributed over the given range. Although it is not possible to develop an algorithm that produces truly random numbers, there are some methods that produce sequences of **pseudorandom numbers** that are adequate for most purposes. Most of these algorithms have two properties:

1. Some initial value called a *seed* is required to begin the process of generating random numbers. Different seeds will produce different sequences of random numbers.

2. Each random number produced is used in the computation of the next random number.

Although C++ does not provide a random number generator, its parent language C does. We have used this random number generator to construct a class `RandomInt` that can be used to define integer data objects whose values are pseudorandom numbers. (See the website described in the preface for more information about this class.)

Two basic operations on a `RandomInt` object are provided that correspond directly to the properties of a (pseudo-)random number generator given above:

i. *Construction* (i.e., declaration), which initializes the object to a random number

ii. *Generation,* which provides the object with a new random number

Additional operations, such as assignment (=) and output (<<) are also provided. The class is also designed so that any of the operations (numeric, relational, etc.) that can be applied to integers can be applied to class objects, although the result is an `int`, as opposed to a `RandomInt`.

Construction. A `RandomInt` object can be constructed by writing a declaration of the form:

```
RandomInt
    object_name(lower_bound, upper_bound);
```

Such a declaration constructs a `RandomInt` object named *object_name* whose value is a random number in the range *lower_bound* to *upper_bound*. If *lower_bound* and *upper_bound* are omitted, a random number is generated in the range 0 to some (large) upper limit defined in the `RandomInt` class.

Generation. The second operation is to generate a new random number. Given a `RandomInt` object constructed as just described, this can be done using the function member `Generate()`:

```
object_name.Generate();
```

The effect of such a call is that the value of *object_name* is changed to another random integer, from the range specified when *object_name* was constructed.[7] In addition to changing the value of *object_name*, `Generate()` returns that value to the function that called it.

---

[7] Optional arguments *lower_bound* and *upper_bound* can be used with the `Generate()` function to alter the range in the random number to be generated.

Example: Modeling a Dice Roll

Suppose we wish to model the random process of tossing a pair of dice. Using the RandomInt class, we might define the objects

```
RandomInt
    die1(1, 6),
    die2(1, 6);
```

to initialize the random number generator and construct the objects die1 and die2 as random integers in the range 1 through 6. We might then use statements like the following

```
die1.Generate();
die2.Generate();

int pair = die1 + die2;
```

to simulate one roll of two dice; the value of pair is the total number of dots showing. The program in Figure 4.4 uses statements similar to these in its simulation.

If the random number generator is suitably constructed, the relative frequency of each value from 2 through 12 for pair should correspond to the probability of that number occurring on one throw of a pair of dice. These probabilities, rounded to three decimal places, are given in the following table:

Outcome	Probability
2	0.028
3	0.056
4	0.083
5	0.111
6	0.139
7	0.167
8	0.139
9	0.111
10	0.083
11	0.056
12	0.028

The program in Figure 4.4 reads an integer numRolls indicating the number of times that two dice are to be tossed, then repeatedly asks the user to enter a possible outcome of a roll of the dice, and displays the relative frequency of this outcome. Comparing the relative frequencies produced against the entries in the preceding probability table, we see that the RandomInt class provides a reasonable simulation of a dice roll.

 FIGURE 4.4   DICE-ROLL SIMULATION.

```
/* dice4.cpp simulates a given number of pairs of dice rolls,
 * and counts the number of times a specified number occurs.
 *
 * Input:    number of dice rolls, the number to be counted,
 *           and user's response to "More rolls?" query
 * Output:   user prompts, and the relative frequency of
 *           the number of spots
 *************************************************************/
```

```cpp
#include <iostream.h>                      // cout, cin, <<, >>
#include "RandomInt.h"                     // the type RandomInt

int main()
{
   cout
      << "This program simulates a given number of dice-pair rolls,\n"
      << "counting the number of times a given roll occurs.\n";

   int numRolls;                           // number of rolls of dice

   cout << "\nHow many times are the dice to be rolled? ";
   cin >> numberOfRolls;

   RandomInt die1(1, 6),                   // the first die
            die2(1, 6);                    // the second die
   int pair,                               // the sum of the dice
       numberOfSpots,                      // number of spots to count
       occurrences;                        // the counter variable

   for(;;)                                 // input loop:
   {                                       //    get outcome to count
      cout << "Enter number of spots to count (2-12, 0 to stop): ";
      cin >> numberOfSpots;

      if (numberOfSpots <= 0) break;       //    terminate input loop

      occurrences = 0;                     //    set counter to zero
                                           //    for loop to repeat
      for (int rollCount = 1;              //      the following
           rollCount <= numRolls;          //      numRolls times:
           rollCount++)
      {                                    //       roll the dice
         pair = die1.Generate() + die2.Generate();

         if (pair == numberOfSpots)        //       if the number came up
            occurrences++;                 //         increment the counter
      }                                    //    end for loop

                                           //    display the result
      cout << "The relative frequency of " << numberOfSpots
           << " was " << double(occurrences) / double(numRolls)
           << "\n\n";
   }                                       // end input loop

   return 0;
}
```

Sample run:

```
This program simulates a given number of dice rolls,
counting the number of times a given roll occurs.

How many times are the dice to be rolled ? 10000

Enter number of spots to count (2-12, 0 to stop): 2
The relative frequency of 2 was 0.0281

Enter number of spots to count (2-12, 0 to stop): 6
The relative frequency of 6 was 0.1365

Enter number of spots to count (2-12, 0 to stop): 7
The relative frequency of 7 was 0.1691

Enter number of spots to count (2-12, 0 to stop):  8
The relative frequency of 8 was 0.141

Enter number of spots to count (2-12, 0 to stop): 11
The relative frequency of 11 was 0.0543

Enter number of spots to count (2-12, 0 to stop): 0
```

NORMAL DISTRIBUTIONS

Most random number generators generate random numbers having a **uniform distribution,** but they can also be used to generate random numbers having other distributions. The **normal distribution** is especially important because it models many physical processes. For example, the heights and weights of people, the lifetime of light bulbs, the tensile strength of steel produced by a machine, and, in general, the variations in parts produced in almost any manufacturing process, have normal distributions. The normal distribution has the familiar bell-shaped curve,

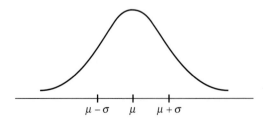

$$\mu - \sigma \quad \mu \quad \mu + \sigma$$

where μ is the mean of the distribution, σ is the standard deviation, and approximately two thirds of the area under the curve lies between $\mu - \sigma$ and $\mu + \sigma$.

A normal distribution having $\mu = 0$ and $\sigma = 1$ is called a **standard normal distribution,** and random numbers having approximately this distribution can be generated quite easily from a uniform distribution with the following algorithm:

Algorithm for the Standard Normal Distribution

1. Set *Sum* equal to 0.

2. Do the following 12 times:

    a. Generate a random number X from a uniform distribution.

    b. Add X to *Sum*.

3. Calculate $Z = Sum - 6$.

The numbers Z generated by this algorithm have an approximate standard normal distribution. To generate random numbers Y having a normal distribution with mean μ and standard deviation σ, we simply add the following step to the algorithm:

4. Calculate $Y = \mu + \sigma * Z$.

Implementing this algorithm as a program is left as an exercise.

☞ *Programming Pointers*

✍ PROGRAM STYLE AND DESIGN

1. *If any of the objects needed to solve a problem have been identified but cannot be defined using the fundamental types, examine the predefined classes of C++ to see if any of them is appropriate for representing such objects.* Don't be afraid to discuss your problem with experienced programmers who may know of classes that will make the problem easier to solve.

2. *If any of the operations needed to solve a problem involve a class object, study the available documentation for that class to see if any of its function members perform that operation.* In the worst case, this may involve looking at the header file for that class, and experimenting with the function members.

3. *If you find yourself doing the same work repeatedly, look for what you are doing wrong. A primary tenet of object-centered programming is, "Don't reinvent the wheel!".* If you find yourself writing redundant code, isolate the code in a function and call the function wherever it is needed.

⚡ POTENTIAL PROBLEMS

1. *The index of the first character in a* `string` *object is 0.* This zero-based indexing is a legacy from C, the parent language of C++, that simplifies the mapping of a subscript access `string_object[index]` to an actual memory address.

2. *The* `string` *subscript operation uses square brackets containing an index,*

   `stringVariable[index]`

   whereas the `string` *substring operation uses parentheses containing an index and a size:*

   `string_object.substr(index, num_chars)`

3. *Run-time bounds checking is performed on most string functions that use an index.* This bounds checking causes an out-of-bounds exception if the index is negative or greater than the size of the `string`, which terminates the program and displays a diagnostic.

4. *Run-time bounds checking is* not *performed on the subscript operation.* Special care must be taken when accessing the characters of a `string` with the subscript operator, to ensure that all accesses fall within the boundaries of the `string`.

5. *To fill a* `string` *object with a* word *from an* `istream`, *use the input operator* `>>`:

    ```
    cin >> someString;
    ```

    to fill a `string` *object with a* line *from an* `istream`, *use the* `getline()` *function:*

    ```
    getline(cin, someString);
    ```

Programming Problems

SECTION 4.1

1. Write a program to display the lyrics of "Happy Birthday to You".
2. Write a program to display the lyrics of "Old MacDonald had a Farm".
3. Write a program to display the lyrics of "This Old Man".
4. Write a program to display the lyrics of "She'll be Comin' 'Round the Mountain".
5. Write a program to display the lyrics of "When the Saints Go Marchin' In".
6. Write a program to display the lyrics of "The Hokey Pokey".

SECTIONS 4.2–4.5

7. Write a driver program to test the name-of-a-month function of exercise 28.
8. Write a driver program to test the number-of-a-month function of exercise 29.
9. Write a driver program to test the case-conversion functions of exercise 30.
10. Write a driver program to test the function `replace_all()` of exercise 31.
11. Write a driver program to test the name-conversion function of exercise 32.
12. Write a driver program to test the name-conversion function of exercise 33.
13. Write a driver program to test the palindrome-checker function of exercise 34.
14. Write a function to count occurrences of a string in another string. Then write a driver program to input a string and then input several lines of text, using the function to count occurrences of the string in the lines of text.
15. Write a program to input a string and then input several lines of text, determine whether the first string occurs in each line, and if so, print asterisks (*) under each occurrence.
16. Write a program to print personalized contest letters like those frequently received in the mail. They might have a format like that of the following sample. The user should enter the three strings in the first three lines, and the program then prints the letter with the underlined locations filled in.

    ```
    Mr. John Q. Doe
    123 SomeStreet
    AnyTown, AnyState 12345

    Dear Mr. Doe:

       How would you like to see a brand new Cadillac parked in
    front of 123 SomeStreet in AnyTown, AnyState?  Impossible, you
    say?  No, it isn't, Mr. Doe.  Simply keep the enclosed raffle
    ticket and validate it by sending a $100.00 tax-deductible
    political contribution and 10 labels from Shyster & Sons chewing
    tobacco.  Not only will you become eligible for the drawing to
    be conducted on February 29 by the independent firm of G. Y. P.
    Shyster, but you will also be helping to reelect Sam Shyster.
    That's all there is to it, John.  You may be a winner!!!
    ```

17. There are 3 teaspoons in a tablespoon, 4 tablespoons in a quarter of a cup, 2 cups in a pint, and 2 pints in a quart. Write a program to convert units in cooking. The program should call for the input of the amount, the units, and the new units desired.

18. Write a function that accepts two character strings and determines whether one is an anagram of the other; that is, whether one character string is a permutation of the characters in the other string. For example, "dear" is an anagram of "read," as is "dare." Write a driver program to test your function.

19. The game of Hangman is played by two persons. One person selects a word and the other tries to guess the word by guessing individual letters. Design and implement a program to play Hangman.

20. Reverend Zeller developed a formula for computing the day of the week on which a given date fell or will fall. Suppose that we let a, b, c, and d be integers defined as follows:

a = The number of a month of the year, with March = 1, April = 2, and so on, with January and February being counted as months 11 and 12 of the preceding year

b = The day of the month

c = The year of the century

d = The century

For example, July 31, 1929 gives $a = 5, b = 31, c = 29, d = 19$; January 3, 1988 gives $a = 11, b = 3, c = 87, d = 19$. Now calculate the following integer quantities:

w = The integer quotient $(13a - 1)/5$

x = The integer quotient $c/4$

y = The integer quotient $d/4$

$z = w + x + y + b + c - 2d$

$r = z$ reduced modulo 7; that is, r is the remainder of z divided by 7: $r = 0$ represents Sunday; $r = 1$ represents Monday, and so on

Write a function `Day_of_the_Week()` that receives the name of a month, the day of the month, and a year, and returns the name of the day of the week on which that date fell or will fall. Write a program that inputs several strings representing dates, calls the function `Day_of_the_Week()`, and displays the day returned by the function.

(a) Verify that December 12, 1960 fell on a Monday, and that January 1, 1991 fell on a Tuesday.

(b) On what day of the week did January 25, 1963 fall?

(c) On what day of the week did June 2, 1964 fall?

(d) On what day of the week did July 4, 1776 fall?

(e) On what day of the week were you born?

Part of the Picture: Simulation

21. A coin is tossed repeatedly, and a payoff of 2^n dollars is made, where n is the number of the toss on which the first head appears. For example, TTH pays $8, TH pays $4, and H pays $2. Write a program to simulate playing the game several times and to print the average payoff for these games.

22.   Suppose that a gambler places a wager of $5 on the following game: a pair of dice is tossed, and if the result is odd, the gambler loses his wager. If the result is even, a card is drawn from a standard deck of fifty-two playing cards. If the card drawn is an ace, 3, 5, 7, or 9, the gambler wins the value of the card (with aces counting as 1, Jacks as 11, Queens as 12, and Kings as 13); otherwise, he loses. What will be the average winnings for this game? Write a program to simulate the game.

23.   Johann VanDerDoe, centerfielder for the Klavin Klodhoppers, has the following life-time hitting percentages:

Out	63.4%
Walk	10.3%
Single	19.0%
Double	4.9%
Triple	1.1%
Home run	1.3%

Write a program to simulate a large number of times at bat, for example, 1000, for Johann, counting the number of outs, walks, singles, and so on, and calculating his

$$\text{batting average} = \frac{\text{number of hits}}{\text{number of times at bat} - \text{number of walks}}$$

24.   The classic **drunkard's walk problem** is as follows: Over an 8-block line, the home of an intoxicated chap is at block 8, and a pub is at block 1. Our poor friend starts at block n, $1 < n < 8$, and wanders at random, one block at a time, either toward or away from home. At any intersection, he moves toward the pub with a certain proba-bility, say 2/3, and toward home with a certain probability, say 1/3. Having gotten ei-ther home or to the pub, he remains there. Write a program to simulate 500 trips in which he starts at block 2, another 500 in which he starts at block 3, and so forth up to block 7. For each starting point, calculate and print the percentage of time he ends up at home and the average number of blocks he walked on each trip.

25.   A slab of material is used to shield a nuclear reactor, and a particle entering the shield follows a random path by moving forward, backward, left, or right with equal likeli-hood, in jumps of one unit. A change of direction is interpreted as a collision with an atom in this shield. Suppose that after 10 such collisions, the particle's energy is dissi-pated and that it dies within the shield, provided that it has not already passed back inside the reactor or outside through the shield. Write a program to simulate particles entering this shield and to determine what percentage of them reaches the outside.

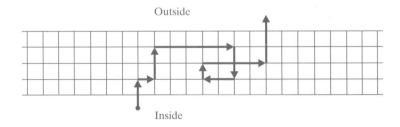

26.   Consider a quarter circle inscribed in a square whose sides have length 1:

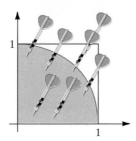

Imagine throwing q darts at this square and counting the total number p that hit within the quarter circle. For a large number of throws, we would expect

$$\frac{p}{q} \sim \frac{area\ of\ quarter\ circle}{area\ of\ square} = \frac{\pi}{4}$$

Write a program to approximate π using this method. To simulate throwing the darts, generate two random numbers X and Y and consider point (X,Y) as being where the dart hits.

27. The famous **Buffon Needle problem** is as follows: A board is ruled with equidistant parallel lines, and a needle of length equal to the distance between these lines is dropped at random on the board. Write a program to simulate this experiment and estimate the probability p that the needle crosses one of these lines. Display the values of p and $2/p$. (The value of $2/p$ should be approximately equal to a well-known constant. What constant is it?)

28. The tensile strength of a certain metal component has an approximate normal distribution with a mean of 10,000 pounds per square inch and a standard deviation of 100 pounds per square inch. Specifications require that all components have a tensile strength greater than 9800; all others must be scrapped. Write a program that uses the algorithm described in this section to generate 1000 normally distributed random numbers representing the tensile strength of these components, and determine how many must be rejected.

Chapter 5

SELECTION

When you get to the fork in the road, take it.

YOGI BERRA

We are all special cases.

ALBERT CAMUS

"Would you tell me, please, which way I ought to go from here?"
"That depends a great deal on where you want to get to," said the Cat.

LEWIS CARROLL

'Less is more' does not appear to be the philosophy behind C++.

V. OREHCK III (fictitious)

Chapter Contents

5.1   Introductory Example: The School Mascot Problem

5.2   Selection : The `if` Statement Revisited

5.3   Selection: The `switch` Statement

5.4   Example: Computing Letter Grades

*5.5   Selection: Conditional Expressions

       PART OF THE PICTURE: Boolean Logic and Digital Design

       PART OF THE PICTURE: Computer Architecture

In chapter 3, we saw that functions play an important role in programming in C++. We also saw that the logical flow of execution through a function is governed by three basic control mechanisms: **sequence, selection,** and **repetition.** The functions that we examined used the `if` statement to perform selective execution and the `for` statement to perform repetitive execution. In this chapter, we take a closer look at the selection mechanism by examining the `if` statement in more detail, and by introducing the `switch` statement that sometimes provides a more efficient way to perform selection.

5.1 INTRODUCTORY EXAMPLE: THE SCHOOL MASCOT PROBLEM

PROBLEM

The Big 10 Conference of the NCAA consists of the following universities, whose mascots are as shown:

University	Mascot
University of Illinois	Fighting Illini
University of Indiana	Hoosiers
University of Iowa	Hawkeyes
University of Michigan	Wolverines
Michigan State University	Spartans
University of Minnesota	Golden Gophers
Northwestern University	Wildcats
Ohio State University	Buckeyes
Pennsylvania State University	Nittany Lions
Purdue University	Boilermakers
University of Wisconsin	Badgers

We want to develop a function `Mascot()` that, given the name of a Big 10 university, returns its mascot.[1]

OBJECT-CENTERED DESIGN

Behavior.   Our function should receive from its caller the name of a Big 10 university. It should return the university's mascot.

Objects.   Examining this problem, we identify two objects:

Description	Type	Kind	Movement	Name
the name of a Big 10 university	string	varying	received	*university*
its mascot	string	varying	returned	none

---

[1] We have restricted our universities to the Big 10 conference to keep the problem manageable in size. Extending the function to include additional universities is straightforward and is left as an exercise.

The problem can be specified in terms of these objects as follows:

Receive: *university,* a string

Return: the mascot of that university, a string

Given this specification, we can build the following stub for our function:

```
string Mascot(string university)
{
}
```

Operations. From the problem description, we can identify 11 operations:

  i. Compare *university* to "Michigan State University"; if true, return "Spartans"

 ii. Compare *university* to "Northwestern University"; if true, return "Wildcats"

iii. Compare *university* to "Ohio State University"; if true, return "Buckeyes"

  .
  .
  .

 xi. Compare *university* to "University of Wisconsin"; if true, return "Badgers"

Because the `string` class defines the equality operator (`==`) to compare two `string` values, a series of `if` statements can be used to perform these operations.

Algorithm. These operations can be organized into the following algorithm. To save the user from having to enter "University" or "University of", we will use the common name for each school.

Algorithm for Big 10 University Mascot Computation

 1. If *university* is "Illinois"
       return "Fighting Illini".

 2. Otherwise, if *university* is "Indiana"
       return "Hoosiers".

 3. Otherwise, if *university* is "Iowa"
       return "Hawkeyes".

 4. Otherwise, if *university* is "Michigan State"
       return "Spartans".

 5. Otherwise, if *university* is "Minnesota"
       return "Golden Gophers".

 6. Otherwise, if *university* is "Northwestern"
       return "Wildcats".

 7. Otherwise, if *university* is "Ohio State"
       return "Buckeyes".

 8. Otherwise, if *university* is "Penn State"
       return "Nittany Lions".

 9. Otherwise, if *university* is "Purdue"
       return "Boilermakers".

10. Otherwise, if *university* is "Michigan"
       return "Wolverines".

11. Otherwise, if *university* is "Wisconsin"
   return "Badgers".

12. Otherwise
   a. Display an error message.
   b. Return on empty string as a default value.

Coding. Given this algorithm, completing our function is straightforward, as shown in Figure 5.1.

FIGURE 5.1   THE Mascot() Function.

```
/* Mascot returns the mascot for a Big 10 university.
 *
 * Receive:      university, a string
 * Precondition: university is a Big 10 university
 * Return:       the (string) mascot of university
 ********************************************************/

string Mascot(string university)
{
   if (university == "Illinois")
      return "Fighting Illini";
   else if (university == "Indiana")
      return "Hoosiers";
   else if (university == "Iowa")
      return "Hawkeyes";
   else if (university == "Michigan")
      return "Wolverines";
   else if (university == "Michigan State")
      return "Spartans";
   else if (university == "Minnesota")
      return "Golden Gophers";
   else if (university == "Northwestern")
      return "Wildcats";
   else if (university == "Ohio State")
      return "Buckeyes";
   else if (university == "Penn State")
      return "Nittany Lions";
   else if (university == "Purdue")
      return "Boilermakers";
   else if (university == "Wisconsin")
      return "Badgers";
   else
   {
      cerr << "Mascot: " << university
           << " is not known by this program!";
      return "";
   }
}
```

Testing. To test this function, we write a simple driver program like that in Figure 5.2. Note that it uses getline() to read the name of a university, because some names consist of more than one word (e.g., Michigan State, Penn State). If we used the input operator >>, only the first word of such names would be read, as described in section 4.4.

FIGURE 5.2   DRIVER FOR THE Mascot() FUNCTION.

```
/* mascot2.cpp is a driver program to test the Mascot() function.
 *
 * Input:   names of Big 10 schools
 * Output:  prompts, mascots of schools
 *****************************************************************/

#include <iostream.h>              // cin, cout, <<, >>
#include <string>                  // string, ==, getline()

string Mascot(string university);

int main()
{
  string school;

  for (;;)
  {
    cout << "\nEnter a Big 10 school (Q to quit): ";
    getline(cin, school);

    if (school == "Q" || school == "q") break;

    cout << Mascot(school) << endl;
  }
}

/*** Insert definition of Mascot() from Figure 5.1 here ***/
```

Sample run:

```
Enter a Big 10 school (Q to quit): Michigan
Wolverines

Enter a Big 10 school (Q to quit): Ohio State
Buckeyes

Enter a Big 10 school (Q to quit): Missouri
Mascot: Missouri is not known by this program!

Enter a Big 10 school (Q to quit): Minnesota
Golden Gophers

Enter a Big 10 school (Q to quit): Q
```

The sample run indicates that the function is working correctly.

5.2 SELECTION: THE `if` STATEMENT REVISITED

In chapter 3, we saw three different forms of the `if` statement:

the **single-branch** or **simple `if`** form:

```
if (boolean_expression)
    statement
```

the **dual-branch** or **`if-else`** form:

```
if (boolean_expression)
    statement₁
else
    statement₂
```

the **multi-branch** or **`if-else-if`** form:

```
if (boolean_expression₁)
    statement₁
else if (boolean_expression₂)
    statement₂
...
else if (boolean_expressionₙ)
    statementₙ
else
    statementₙ₊₁
```

The boolean expressions in these `if` statements are sometimes called **conditions.**
   While these may look like three distinct statements, C++ really has only one `if` statement with two different forms:

The `if` Statement (General Form)

Forms

```
if (boolean_expression) statement₁
```
or
```
if (boolean_expression) statement₁ else statement₂
```
where:

   `if` and `else` are keywords; and

   $statement_1$ and $statement_2$ are C++ statements (either simple or compound).

Purpose

If the `boolean_expression` is true, then $statement_1$ is executed and $statement_2$ is bypassed, if present. If the `boolean_expression` is false, then $statement_1$ is bypassed and $statement_2$ is executed, if present. In either case, execution continues with the next statement in the program.

UNDERSTANDING THE MULTIBRANCH if

While it may look like a different statement, the multibranch or if-else-if form is really an if statement of the second form

```
if (boolean_expression) statement₁ else statement₂
```

where *statement₂* is another if statement.

It is important to understand that this multibranch form is simply a series of nested if statements written as one. That is, if we were to write a 5-branch if-else-if and we were to start each new if statement on a new line with each else aligned with its corresponding if, our code would appear as follows:

```
if (boolean_expression₁)
    statement₁
else
    if (boolean_expression₂)
        statement₂
    else
        if (boolean_expression₃)
            statement₃
        else
            if (boolean_expression₄)
                statement₄
            else
                statement₅
```

However, the free-form nature of C++ allows us to write each nested if on the same line as the preceding else and align the else-if combinations:

```
if (boolean_expression₁)
    statement₁
else if (boolean_expression₂)
    statement₂
else if (boolean_expression₃)
    statement₃
else if (boolean_expression₄)
    statement₄
else
    statement₅
```

This latter style reflects more clearly the multibranch nature and is therefore more readable. It is important, however, to understand that each else is really a continuation of the preceding if:

```
            if (boolean_expression₁)
        ↑       statement₁
            else if (boolean_expression₂)
              ↗ statement₂
            else if (boolean_expression₃)
              ↗ statement₃
            else if (boolean_expression₄)
              ↗ statement₄
            else
                statement₅
```

PITFALL: THE DANGLING-else PROBLEM

We have just seen that the multibranch form of the if statement is actually an if-else form

    if (*boolean_expression*) *statement₁* else *statement₂*

in which *statement₂* is another if statement. However, suppose that *statement₁* is another if statement; for example,

```
if (x > 0)
    if (y > 0)
        z = sqrt(x) + sqrt(y);
```

When such nested if statements are followed by an else, it is not evident with which if the else corresponds. Does the else match the outer if?

```
if (x > 0)
    if (y > 0)
        z = sqrt(x) + sqrt(y);
else
    cerr << "\n*** Unable to compute z!" << endl;
```

Or does it match the inner if?

```
if (x > 0)
    if (y > 0)
        z = sqrt(x) + sqrt(y);
    else
        cerr << "\n*** Unable to compute z!" << endl;
```

This ambiguity is known as the **dangling else problem,** and C++ resolves it by stipulating that

> *In a nested* if *statement, an* else *is matched with the nearest preceding unmatched* if.

Thus, for the preceding if statement, the second matching is used; that is, the else is associated with the inner if (whose condition is y > 0). Consequently, the output statement is executed only in the case that x is positive and y is nonpositive. If we wish to associate this else with the outer if, we can force the association by surrounding the inner if with curly braces, as follows:

```
if (x > 0)
{
    if (y > 0)
        z = sqrt(x) + sqrt(y);
}
else
    cerr < "*** Unable to compute z!" << endl;
```

Putting the inner if inside a block makes it a complete statement, so that the else must associate with the outer if. Thus, the output statement is executed whenever x is nonpositive.

PITFALL: CONFUSING = AND ==.

We describe now what is probably *the most common error in constructing boolean expressions,* and, as a consequence, in if statements. We begin by examining two features of C++ that are relevant to this problem.

1. *True and false in C++.* To maintain compatibility with its parent language C, C++ interprets the value 0 as equivalent to the boolean value false and any nonzero value as equivalent to the boolean value true.[2] Thus, the statement

   ```
   if (0)
       cout << "T\n";
   else
       cout << "F\n";
   ```

   will always display F, because the condition controlling the selection is zero, which C++ treats as false. Similarly, the statement

   ```
   if (23)
       cout << "T\n";
   else
       cout << "F\n";
   ```

   will always display the value T, because the condition controlling the selection is nonzero, which is interpreted as true in C++.

2. *Assignments are expressions.* We saw in chapter 2 that in C++, assignment (=) is an operator that returns the value being assigned as its result. For example, the assignment expression

   ```
   x = 32
   ```

   does two things: It assigns x the value 32 and it produces the value 32 as its result. Similarly, the assignment

   ```
   x = 0
   ```

   both assigns x the value 0 and produces the value 0 as its result.

By themselves, neither of these C++ features is particularly troublesome, but when coupled with the similarity of the assignment and equality operators, they make it easy to write if statements that contain logical errors. To illustrate, suppose that a programmer encodes the instruction

    If x is equal to zero, then

        Display the character string "Zero"

    Otherwise

        Display the character string "Nonzero"

as

```
if (x = 0)
    cout << "Zero\n";
```

---

[2] C has no bool type. In its place, C uses the zero/nonzero mechanism described here.

```
else
    cout << "Nonzero\n";
```

Because the assignment operator

```
x = 0
```

is used instead of an equality comparison

```
x == 0
```

and the value returned by the assignment operator is the value that was assigned, this statement is equivalent to

```
if (0)
    cout << "Zero\n";
else
    cout << "Nonzero\n";
```

Because 0 is treated as false, the statement to output Nonzero will always be selected, regardless of the value of x.

Similarly, if a programmer writes

```
cout << MENU;              // display menu of choices: A, B, C
cin >> choice;

if (choice = 'A')
    statement₁            // do something when choice is A
else if (choice = 'B')
    statement₂            // do something else when choice is B
else if (choice = 'C')
    statement₃            // do something else when choice is C
else
    cout << choice << " must be A, B, or C.\n";
```

then the statement associated with choice A will always be selected, regardless of the value entered by the user. The reason is that instead of the first condition testing whether choice is equal to A,

```
choice == 'A'
```

it assigns choice the numeric code of A (65 in ASCII):

```
choice = 'A'
```

The result produced by the assignment operator is the value assigned (65), and so this if-else-if form is equivalent to

```
cout << MENU;             // display menu of choices: A, B, C
cin >> choice;

if (65)
    statement₁            // do something when choice is A
else if (66)
    statement₂            // do something else when choice is B
```

```
else if (67)
   statement₃          // do something else when choice is C
else
   cout << Choice << " must be A, B, or C.\n";
```

Because nonzero values are treated as true, the value 65 is treated as true, so *statement₁* will be executed, and *statement₂*, *statement₃*, and the output statement will be bypassed, regardless of the value of `choice`.

This kind of error is one of the most frequent errors in constructing boolean expressions. Unfortunately, these errors can be fiendishly difficult to find, because the equality operator (==) and the assignment operator (=) are similar in appearance. *Any time an algorithm calls for an equality comparison, the code that implements the algorithm should be carefully checked to ensure that an assignment operator has not been inadvertently used instead of the equality operator.*

EXERCISES 5.2

1.   Describe the output produced by the following poorly-indented program segment:

```
int number = 4;
double alpha = -1.0;
if (number > 0)
   if (alpha > 0)
       cout << "first\n";
else
   cout << "second\n";
   cout << "third\n";
```

Exercises 2 and 3 refer to the following `if` statement, where `honors`, `awards`, and `good-Student` are of type `bool`:

```
if (honors)
   if (awards)
       goodStudent = true;
   else
       goodStudent = false;
else if (!honors)
   goodStudent = false;
```

2.   Write a simpler `if` statement that is equivalent to this one.

3.   Write a single assignment statement that is equivalent to this `if` statement.

For exercises 4–8, you are asked to write functions. To test these functions, you should write driver programs as instructed in Programming Problems 1–5 at the end of this chapter.

4.   In a certain region, pesticide can be sprayed from an airplane only if the temperature is at least 70°, the relative humidity is between 15 and 35 percent, and the wind speed is at most 10 miles per hour. Write a boolean-valued function `OkToSpray()` that receives three numbers representing temperature, relative humidity, and wind speed, and returns true if the conditions allow spraying and false otherwise.

5.   A certain credit company will approve a loan application if the applicant's income is at least $25,000 or the applicant's assets are at least $100,000; in addition, the applicant's total liabilities must be less than $50,000. Write a boolean-valued function `CreditApproved()` that receives three numbers representing income, assets, and liabilities, and returns true if the criteria for loan approval are satisfied and false otherwise.

6. Write a function that returns true if the value of an `int` parameter `year` is the number of a leap year and return false otherwise. (A leap year is a multiple of 4; and if it is a multiple of 100, it must also be a multiple of 400.)

7. Write a function that returns the number of days in a given `int` parameter `month` (1, 2, ..., 12) of a given parameter `year`. Use exercise 6 to determine the number of days if the value of `month` is 2.

8. Proceed as in exercise 7, but assume that `month` is a `string` variable whose value is the name of a month.

5.3   SELECTION: THE `switch` STATEMENT

An `if` statement can be used to implement a multialternative selection statement in which exactly one of several alternative actions is selected and performed. In the `if-else-if` form described in the preceding section, a selection is made by evaluating one or more boolean expressions. Because selection conditions can usually be formulated as boolean expressions, an `if-else-if` form can be used to implement virtually any multialternative selection.

In this section we describe another multialternative selection statement called the `switch` statement. Although it is not as general as the `if` statement, it is more efficient for implementing certain forms of selection. As usual, we begin with an example that illustrates the use of the statement.

EXAMPLE: TEMPERATURE CONVERSIONS

In the early sections of chapter 3, we considered the problem of converting temperatures from the Fahrenheit scale to the Celsius scale. In section 3.1, we constructed a function to do this conversion, and in section 3.6 we showed how a library `Heat` could be created to store various functions for converting temperatures between the Fahrenheit, Celsius, and Kelvin scales.

Now that we know about selective execution, we can consider a more general version of the problem—writing a program that allows the user to choose which conversion to be performed: Fahrenheit to Celsius (or vice versa), Fahrenheit to Kelvin (or vice versa), or Celsius to Kelvin (or vice versa).

Problem. Write a program that allows the user to perform arbitrary temperature conversions.

Behavior. Our program should display on the screen a menu of the six possible conversion options and then read the desired conversion from the keyboard. Next, it should display on the screen a prompt for a temperature, which it should read from the keyboard. The program should then display the result of converting the input temperature, as determined by the specified conversion.

Objects. From our behavioral description, we have the following objects: [3]
We can thus specify the problem as follows:

---

[3] Since almost every problem will use the screen, keyboard, and prompt objects, we will omit them from our lists of objects and simply assume they are needed. This will save space and will also allow us to focus our attention on user-defined objects.

Description	Type	Kind	Name
menu	string	constant	*MENU*
conversion	char	varying	*conversion*
temperature	double	varying	*temperature*
result	double	varying	*result*

Input: *temperature*, a double; and *conversion*, a char

Precondition: *conversion* is in the range A–F (or a–f)

Output: *MENU*, prompts for input, and the *result* of converting the temperature

Operations. Our behavioral description leads to the following list of operations:

i. Display prompts and *MENU* (strings) on the screen

ii. Read *temperature* (a double) from the keyboard

iii. Read *conversion* (a char) from the keyboard

iv. Select the conversion function corresponding to *conversion* and apply it to *temperature*

All of these are provided in C++. For operation iv, we must compare *conversion* to each of the valid menu choices, and based upon that comparison, select an appropriate conversion function.

Algorithm. The following algorithm applies this strategy.

Algorithm to Convert Arbitrary Temperatures

1. Display *MENU* via cout.

2. Read *conversion* from cin.

3. Display a prompt for a temperature via cout.

4. Read *temperature* from cin.

5. If *conversion* is 'A' or 'a'
    Convert *temperature* from Fahrenheit to Celsius and store in *result*.
Otherwise, if *conversion* is 'B' or 'b'
    Convert *temperature* from Celsius to Fahrenheit and store in *result*.
Otherwise, if *conversion* is 'C' or 'c'
    Convert *temperature* from Celsius to Kelvin and store in *result*.
Otherwise, if *conversion* is 'D' or 'd''
    Convert *temperature* from Kelvin to Celsius and store in *result*.
Otherwise, if *conversion* is 'E' or 'e'
    Convert *temperature* from Fahrenheit to Kelvin and store in *result*.
Otherwise, if *conversion* is 'F' or 'f'
    Convert *temperature* from Kelvin to Fahrenheit and store in *result*.
Otherwise
    Display an error message.

Coding and Testing. We could implement the algorithm using an `if-else-if` construct:

```
if (conversion == 'A' || conversion == 'a')
    result = FahrToCelsius(temperature);
else if (conversion == 'B' || conversion == 'b')
    result = CelsiusToFahr(temperature);
             .
             .
             .
else
{
    cerr << "\n*** Invalid conversion: " << conversion << endl;
    result = 0.0;
}
```

The C++ `switch` statement, however, provides a more convenient way to do this, as shown in the program in Figure 5.3.[4]

FIGURE 5.3   ARBITRARY TEMPERATURE CONVERSIONS.

```
/* temperature3.cpp converts temperatures from one scale to another scale.
 *
 * Input:  menu choices, temperatures
 * Output: menu, temperatures on other scale
 ***************************************************************************/

#include <iostream.h>              // cin, cout, <<, >>
#include <string>                  // string

#include "Heat.h"

int main()
{
    const string MENU = "To convert arbitrary temperatures, enter:\n"
                        "    A - to convert Fahrenheit to Celsius;\n"
                        "    B - to convert Celsius to Fahrenheit;\n"
                        "    C - to convert Celsius to Kelvin;\n"
                        "    D - to convert Kelvin to Celsius;\n"
                        "    E - to convert Fahrenheit to Kelvin; or\n"
                        "    F - to convert Kelvin to Fahreneht.\n"
                        "--> ";
    cout << MENU;
    char conversion;
    cin >> conversion;
```

---
[4] This program uses the conversion functions from the library `Heat` from section 3.6. If this section was omitted, simply replace the directive `#include "Heat.h"` with the prototypes of the conversion functions, and append the definitions of these functions after the main program

```
      cout << "\nEnter the temperature to be converted: ";
      double temperature;
      cin >> temperature;

      double result;
      switch (conversion)
      {
         case 'A': case 'a':
                            result = FahrToCelsius(temperature);
                            break;
         case 'B': case 'b':
                            result = CelsiusToFahr(temperature);
                            break;
         case 'C': case 'c':
                            result = CelsiusToKelvin(temperature);
                            break;
         case 'D': case 'd':
                            result = KelvinToCelsius(temperature);
                            break;
         case 'E': case 'e':
                            result = FahrToKelvin(temperature);
                            break;
         case 'F': case 'f':
                            result = KelvinToFahr(temperature);
                            break;
         default:
                            cerr << "\n*** Invalid conversion: "
                                 << conversion << endl;
                            result = 0.0;
      }
      cout << "The converted temperature is " << result << endl;
}
```

Sample run:

```
To convert arbitrary temperatures, enter:
   A - to convert Fahrenheit to Celsius;
   B - to convert Celsius to Fahrenheit;
   C - to convert Celsius to Kelvin;
   D - to convert Kelvin to Celsius;
   E - to convert Fahrenheit to Kelvin; or
   F - to convert Kelvin to Fahreneht.
--> B
Enter the temperature to be converted: 100
The converted temperature is 212
```

Note the convenience of the switch statement: by allowing us to specify the *cases* for a given alternative, we can test the value of conversion quite conveniently, regardless of whether it is uppercase or lowercase:

```
switch (conversion)
{

   case 'A': case 'a':
      result = FahrToCelsius(temperature);
      break;
         .
         .
         .

}
```

The equivalent `if-else-if` version seems clumsy by comparison and many people find it to be more work and less readable. In addition, using a `switch` statement to select from among several alternatives is typically *more time-efficient* than using an `if` statement, as discussed at the end of this section.

FORM OF THE switch STATEMENT

A (simplified) general form for the C++ `switch` statement is as follows:

The switch Statement

Form
```
switch (expression)
{
   case_list₁ :
               statement_list₁;
   case_list₂ :
               statement_list₂;
               .
               .
               .
   case_listₙ :
               statement_listₙ
   default :
               statement_listₙ₊₁
}
```
where:

 switch and default are keywords;

 expression is an integer (or integer-compatible) expression;

 each *case_listᵢ* is a sequence of cases of the form

    case *constant_value* :

 the default clause is optional; and

 each *statement_listᵢ* is a sequence of statements.

Purpose

 When the `switch` statement is executed, *expression* is evaluated. If the value of *expression* is in *case_listᵢ*, then execution begins in *statement_listᵢ* and continues until one of the following is reached:

A break statement

A return statement

The end of the switch statement

If the value of *expression* is not in any *case_list$_i$*, then *statement_list$_{n+1}$* in the default clause is executed. If the default clause is omitted and the value of *expression* is not in any *case_list$_i$*, then execution "falls through" the switch statement.

Note that *expression* must be an integer-compatible expression (i.e., it may not evaluate to a real or a string value).

THE break STATEMENT

As illustrated in the program in Figure 5.3, each of the statement lists in a switch statement usually ends with a **break statement** of the form

```
break;
```

When it is executed, this statement transfers control to the first statement following the switch statement. As we saw in chapter 3, the break statement is also used to terminate repetition of a forever loop. The behavior of the break is the same in both statements: execution jumps to the first statement following the statement in which it appears.

DROP-THROUGH BEHAVIOR

An important feature to remember when using the switch statement is its *drop-through behavior*. To illustrate it, suppose we had written the switch statement in Figure 5.3 without the break statements

```
switch (conversion)
{
   case 'A': case 'a':
                     result = FahrToCelsius(temperature);
   case 'B': case 'b':
                     result = CelsiusToFahr(temperature);
   case 'C': case 'c':
                     result = CelsiusToKelvin(temperature);
   case 'D': case 'd':
                     result = KelvinToCelsius(temperature);
   case 'E': case 'e':
                     result = FahrToKelvin(temperature);
   case 'F': case 'f':
                     result = KelvinToFahr(temperature);
   default:
                     cerr << "\n*** Invalid conversion: "
                        << conversion << endl;
                     result = 0.0;
}

cout << "The converted temperature is " << result << endl;
```

The output produced when this modified version is run may be rather unexpected. Here is one example:

```
To convert arbitrary temperatures, enter:
   A - to convert Fahrenheit to Celsius;
   B - to convert Celsius to Fahrenheit;
   C - to convert Celsius to Kelvin;
   D - to convert Kelvin to Celsius;
   E - to convert Fahrenheit to Kelvin; or
   F - to convert Kelvin to Fahreneht.
--> B
Enter the temperature to be converted: 100

*** Invalid conversion: B
The converted temperature is 0
```

As before, in the sample run in Figure 5.3, the value of `conversion` is B, so control is transferred to the statement:

```
result = CelsiusToFahr(temperature);
```

However, there is no break following this statement to transfer control past the other statements, and so execution drops through to the statement in the next case, which resets `result`:

```
result = CelsiusToKelvin(temperature);
```

Again, there is no break statement, so execution drops through to the statement in the next case, which resets `result` again:

```
result = KelvinToCelsius(temperature);
```

This drop-through behavior continues until a `break`, a `return`, or the end of the `switch` statement is reached. Because there are no `break` or `return` statements here, execution proceeds through the next two cases and reaches the `default` case, which displays

```
*** Invalid conversion: B
```

and sets result to zero. The output statement following the `switch` then displays

```
The converted temperature is 0
```

 To avoid this behavior, we must remember to end each statement list in a `switch` statement with a `break` or `return` statement (except for the final statement list, where it is not necessary).

The program in Figure 5.3 uses the `switch` statement in a `main` function, but it is perhaps more commonly used to control selection in functions other than `main`. In this case, the function is probably using the `switch` to select its return value, and so a `return` statement can be used instead of a `break` statement. The following example illustrates this.

 Example: Converting Numeric Codes to Names

Problem. Suppose that a university uses numeric codes to store certain information about a student: 1 for freshman, 2 for sophomore, 3 for junior, 4 for senior, and

5 for graduate. When information about a freshman named Jane Doe is displayed, output of the form

```
Doe, Jane D. (Freshman)
```

is more descriptive than

```
Doe, Jane D.    (1)
```

Write a function that, given the numeric code for a year, returns the name of the year corresponding to that code (e.g., 1 → Freshman, 2 → Sophomore, and so on).

Objects. From our behavioral description, we have two objects:

Description	Type	Kind	Movement	Name
a year code	int	varying	received	*yearCode*
the name of the year	string	varying	returned	none

We can thus specify our problem as:

Receive: *yearCode*, an integer

Precondition: *yearCode* is in the range 1–5

Return: The character string corresponding to that year code ("Freshman", "Sophomore", . . .)

From this specification, we can build the following stub for our function:

```
string YearName(int yearCode)
{
}
```

Operations. From the behavioral description, we have only one operation:

Return the name of the year corresponding to *yearCode*.

Here, the key word is *corresponding*. Because we must return the name of the year corresponding to *yearCode*, we must compare *yearCode* to each of the possible year codes, and then select an appropriate return statement.

Algorithm. The following algorithm applies this strategy.

Algorithm to Convert a Year Code

If *yearCode* is 1
    Return "Freshman".
Otherwise, if *yearCode* is 2
    Return "Sophomore".
Otherwise, if *yearCode* is 3
    Return "Junior".
Otherwise, if *yearCode* is 4
    Return "Senior".

Otherwise, if *yearCode* is 5
Return "Graduate".

Otherwise
Display an error message.
Return the empty string.

Although we clearly could implement this algorithm using an `if` statement, the function in Figure 5.4 solves this problem using a `switch` statement. Note that no `break` statements are required in the cases of this `switch`. The function uses the `switch` to select a `return` statement, and a `return` statement causes execution of the function to terminate.

 FIGURE 5.4   YEAR-CODE CONVERSION.

```
/* YearName returns the name of a year, given a year code.
 *
 * Receive: an int year code (1-5)
 * Return:  the appropriate (string) year name
 *          (Freshman, Sophomore, Junior, Senior, Graduate)
 ************************************************************/

string YearName(int yearCode)
{
   switch (yearCode)
   {
      case 1:
              return "Freshman";
      case 2:
              return "Sophomore";
      case 3:
              return "Junior";
      case 4:
              return "Senior";
      case 5:
              return "Graduate";
      default:
              cerr << "YearName: code error: " << yearCode << endl;
              return "";
   }
}
```

Testing. To test our function, we can write a simple driver program like that in Figure 5.5. Note the use of the `for` statement in testing our function. By varying `i` over the range 1–6 and passing each value of `i` to the function, we can easily check that the function is behaving correctly for each valid value and one invalid value.

FIGURE 5.5   DRIVER TO TEST YearName().

```
/* year5.cpp is a driver program to test function YearName().
 *
 * Input:   none
 * Output: names of years (Freshman, Sophomore, ... )
 ************************************************************/

#include <iostream.h>                    // cout, <<
#include <string>                        // string

string YearName(int yearCode);

int main()
{
   for (int i = 1; i <= 6; i++)
     cout << YearName(i) << endl;
}

/*** Insert the definition of YearName() from Figure 5.4 here ***/
```

Sample run:

```
Freshman
Sophomore
Junior
Senior
Graduate
YearName: code error: 6
```

CASES WITH NO ACTION

Occasionally, no action is required for certain values of the expression in a switch statement. In such situations, the statement lists associated with these values should consist of a single break or return statement, so that no action is taken. For example, a program to count aces and face cards might use a switch statement like the following:

```
char card;
int aces = faceCards = 0;
   .
   .
   .
switch (card)
{
   case 'A':                          aces++;
                                      break;

   case 'J': case 'Q': case 'K': faceCards++;
                                      break;
```

```
case '2': case '3': case '4': // these 'cards' are
case '5': case '6': case '7': //  not being counted
case '8': case '9': case '0':
                              break;

default:
        cout << "*** Error: Illegal card: "
             << card << endl;
}
```

 Note that white space is ignored in the case lists and statement lists. Where these items are positioned is largely a matter of personal style, but the goal should be to write readable `switch` statements in which there is a clear association between each case list and its corresponding statement list.

 It is important to remember that *the expression and the constants in the case lists must be integer-compatible* (e.g., `int`, `char`, *and so on*). In particular, they may not be real or string expressions. For example, we cannot write the preceding `switch` statement as

```
string card;
int aces = faceCards = 0;
     .
     .
     .
switch (card)
{
    case "ACE":                 aces++;       // STRINGS
                                break;        // ARE
    case "JACK": case "QUEEN":                // NOT
    case "KING":                faceCards++;  // ALLOWED
                                break;
        .
        .
        .
}
```

because the expression controlling a `switch` statement must be integer-compatible, which precludes `string` and real expressions.

 ## CHOOSING THE PROPER SELECTION STATEMENT

Now that we have two different ways to perform multialternative selection, it is important to understand when an `if-else-if` should be used and when a `switch` statement is appropriate. If a selection step in an algorithm is written in the form

If *expression* is equal to *constant*$_1$
    statement_list$_1$

Otherwise, if *expression* is equal to *constant*$_2$
    statement_list$_2$
      .
      .

Otherwise, if *expression* is equal to *constant*$_n$
    statement_list$_n$

Otherwise
> statement_list$_{n+1}$

and if *expression* is integer-compatible, then this selection step is most effectively coded as a switch statement:

```
switch (expression)
{
    case constant₁:
                    statement_list₁
                    break;
    case constant₂:
                    statement_list₂
                    break;

        .
        .
        .

    case constantₙ:
                    statement_listₙ
                    break;
    default:
                    statement_listₙ₊₁
}
```

The reason is that in the if-else-if form, execution of statement_list$_1$ requires the evaluation of one boolean expression, execution of statement_list$_2$ requires the evaluation of two boolean expressions, . . . , and execution of statement_list$_n$ (or statement_list$_{n+1}$) requires the evaluation of n boolean expressions. Because it takes time to evaluate each expression, there is a performance penalty associated with statements that occur later in an if-else-if construct.

For example, we already saw that it would be *correct* to code the temperature-conversion algorithm at the beginning of this section using an if-else-if as follows:

```
if (conversion == 'A' || conversion == 'a')
    result = FahrToCelsius(temperature);
else if (conversion == 'B' || conversion == 'b')
    result = CelsiusToFahr(temperature);
else if (conversion == 'C' || conversion == 'c')
    result = CelsiusToKelvin(temperature);
else if (conversion == 'D' || conversion == 'd')
    result = KelvinToCelsius(temperature);
else if (conversion == 'E' || conversion == 'e')
    result = FahrToKelvin(temperature);
else if (conversion == 'F' || conversion == 'f')
    result = KelvinToFahr(temperature);
else
{
    cerr << "\n*** Invalid conversion: " << conversion << endl;
    result = 0.0;
}
```

But this requires that 12 boolean expressions be evaluated for a Kelvin-to-Fahrenheit conversion, whereas only one is evaluated for a Fahrenheit-to-Celsius conversion.

By contrast, a `switch` statement is usually implemented so that each statement list requires approximately one comparison,[5] regardless of whether it is first or last. A `switch` statement is thus to be preferred over the `if-else-if` when

1. The equality (==) comparison is being performed;
2. The same expression (e.g., `conversion`) is being compared in each condition; and
3. The value to which this expression is being compared is `int`-compatible.

5.4 EXAMPLE: COMPUTING LETTER GRADES

PROBLEM

In many courses, students submit homework, take tests, and take a final exam. In computing a final grade, the average scores for these components are calculated, multiplied by a weighting factor, and then added to give a final weighted average. A program is needed that, given averages for homework, tests, and a final exam score, will compute a student's letter grade, assuming that homework constitutes 20 percent, tests 50 percent, and the final exam 30 percent of the final grade.

OBJECT-CENTERED DESIGN

Behavior. Our program should display on the screen a prompt for the homework average, test average, and the final exam score. It should then read these quantities from the keyboard and compute the final weighted average. From the weighted average, it should compute the corresponding letter grade and display this grade.

Objects. From the statement of the problem and our behavioral description, we can identify the following objects:

Description	Type	Kind	Name
homework average	`double`	varying	*homeworkAverage*
test average	`double`	varying	*testAverage*
final exam score	`double`	varying	*examScore*
final weighted average	`double`	varying	*finalAverage*
homework weight	`double`	constant	*HOMEWORK_WEIGHT*
test weight	`double`	constant	*TEST_WEIGHT*
final exam weight	`double`	constant	*EXAM_WEIGHT*
letter grade	`char`	constant	*grade*

---

[5] The mechanism by which this is accomplished is beyond the scope of this text. The interested reader should see *Compiler: Principles, Techniques and Tools* by Aho, Sethi, and Ullman (Reading, Mass.: Addison-Wesley, 1986).

The problem can thus be specified in terms of these objects as follows:

Input: *homeworkAverage, testAverage,* and *examScore,* three real values
Output: The letter grade earned

Operations.   From our behavioral description, we can identify the following operations:

i.   Display a prompt (a character string) on the screen
ii.   Read three (real) quantities from the keyboard
iii.   Compute a weighted average using the three inputs and three weights
iv.   Compute the letter grade corresponding to a weighted average
v.   Display that (char) letter grade

Operations i, ii, and v are predefined, and iii is a simple formula:

$$finalAverage = HOMEWORK\_WEIGHT * homeworkAverage +$$
$$TEST\_WEIGHT * testAverage +$$
$$EXAM\_WEIGHT * examScore$$

Operation iv is more complicated, so we will write a function to perform it.

Algorithm.   Once we have a function to perform operation iv, we can solve our problem using the following algorithm:

Grade-Computation Algorithm

1. Prompt for the homework average, test average, and exam score.
2. Enter *homeworkAverage, testAverage,* and *examScore.*
3. Calculate *finalAverage* = *HOMEWORK_WEIGHT* * *homeworkAverage* +
            TEST_WEIGHT * *testAverage* +
            EXAM_WEIGHT * *examScore.*
4. Calculate and display the letter grade corresponding to *finalAverage.*

Function's Problem. Calculate the letter grade corresponding to a weighted average.

Function's Behavior. The function should receive from its caller a weighted average, which is a real value. It should return the letter grade corresponding to that weighted average.

Function's Objects. From our behavioral description, we can identify the following objects:

Description	Type	Kind	Movement	Name
the weighted average	double	varying	received (in)	*weightedAverage*
the corresponding letter grade	char	constant	returned (out)	none

We can thus specify the behavior of our function as

Receive: *weightedAverage,* a double
Return: the (char) letter grade corresponding to *weightedAverage*

and from this specification, we can build a stub for the function:

```
char LetterGrade(double weightedAverage)
{
}
```

Function's Operations. The key to our problem is recognizing that it requires selective execution. The function must return a letter grade for a given value of *weightedAverage,* as given by the following table:

weightedAverage	Return
weightedAverage $\geq$ 90	A
80 $\leq$ *weightedAverage* $<$ 90	B
70 $\leq$ *weightedAverage* $<$ 80	C
60 $\leq$ *weightedAverage* $<$ 70	D
weightedAverage $<$ 60	F

Function's Coding. We could perform this operation using an `if` statement, as described in section 5.2, but a `switch` statement is more efficient. There are, however, two problems to be resolved. First, the parameter `weightedAverage` will be of type `double` (i.e., a real) and the expression in a `switch` statement cannot be a real. This problem can be solved by converting `weightedAverage` to an `int` value,

```
int(weightedAverage)
```

which truncates the decimal portion of `weightedAverage`.

The second problem is that when `weightedAverage` has been converted from a real to an integer, there are still 10 or more values in each case list. For example, the values for a 'B' are

$$80, 81, 82, 83, 84, 85, 86, 87, 88, 89$$

This means that a case list like

```
case 80: case 81: case 82: case 83: case 84:
case 85: case 86: case 87: case 88: case 89:
```

would be required for each grade to be displayed. However, if we divide each of these values by 10, the same quotient (8) results. Thus, assuming that the weighted average does not exceed 100, we can use the expression

```
int(weightedAverage) / 10
```

in a `switch` statement that will have manageable case lists. The function in Figure 5.6 uses this approach.

FIGURE 5.6   GRADE COMPUTATION.

```
/* LetterGrade computes the appropriate Grade for a given weightedAverage.
 *
 * Receive:     a (double) weighted average.
 * Precondition: 0 <= weightedAverage<= 100.
 * Return:      the appropriate (char) letter grade (A, B, C, D, or F)
 ***********************************************************************/

char LetterGrade(double weightedAverage)
{
   switch ( int(weightedAverage) / 10 )
   {
      case 10:                    // int(100)/10 -> 10
      case 9:                     // int(90-99)/10 -> 9
             return 'A';
      case 8:                     // int(80-89)/10 -> 8
             return 'B';
      case 7:                     // int(70-79)/10 -> 7
             return 'C';
      case 6:                     // int(60-69)/10 -> 6
             return 'D';
      default:                    // not so good!
             return 'F';
   }
}
```

Coding and Testing. We can now code the algorithm for the original problem, as shown in Figure 5.7.

FIGURE 5.7   THE LETTER GRADE PROGRAM.

```
/* grader7.cpp computes a final course average using the homework
 * average, the average on tests, and a final exam score, and
 * assigns a letter grade.
 *
 * Input:  three real values representing a student's homework
 *            average, average on tests, and a final exam score
 * Output: the final average and the letter grade
 ***********************************************************************/

#include <iostream.h>                 // cin, cout, >>, <<

char LetterGrade(double weightedAverage);

int main()
{
   const double HOMEWORK_WEIGHT = 0.2, // weights for homework,
                TEST_WEIGHT = 0.5,     //    tests,
                EXAM_WEIGHT = 0.3;     //    and the exam.
```

```
      cout << "This program computes a final course grade using the\n"
              "homework average, test average, and a final exam "
              "score.\n";

      cout << "\nEnter the homework average, test average, "
              "and exam score:\n";

      double homeworkAverage,      // the average of the homework scores
             testAverage,          // the average of the test scores
             examScore;            // the final exam score

      cin >> homeworkAverage >> testAverage >> examScore;

      double finalAverage = HOMEWORK_WEIGHT * homeworkAverage +
                            TEST_WEIGHT * testAverage +
                            EXAM_WEIGHT * examScore;

      char grade = LetterGrade(finalAverage);     // the letter grade received

      cout << "Final Average = " << finalAverage
           << ", Grade = " << grade << "\n\n";
}

/*** Insert definition of LetterGrade() from Figure 5.6 here ***/
```

Sample runs:

```
This program computes a final course grade using the
homework average, test average, and a final exam score.

Enter the homework average, test average, and exam score:
100 100 100
Final Average = 100, Grade = A


. . .
Enter the homework average, test average, and exam score:
30 40 50
Final Average = 41, Grade = F


. . .
Enter the homework average, test average, and exam score:
56.2 62.7 66.5
Final Average = 62.54, Grade = D


. . .
Enter the homework average, test average, and exam score:
87.5 91.3 80
Final Average = 87.15, Grade = B
```

✔ Quick Quiz 5.4

For the following questions, assume that `number` is an `int` variable, `code` is a `char` variable, and `x` is a `double` variable.

1. If `number` has the value 99, tell what output is produced by the following `switch` statement, or indicate why an error occurs:

```
switch(number)
{
    case 99:
                cout << number + 99 << endl;
                break;
    case -1:
                cout << number - 1 << endl;
                break;
    default:
                cout << "default\n";
}
```

2. Proceed as in question 1, but suppose the `break` statements are omitted.
3. Proceed as in question 1, but suppose `number` has the value 50.
4. Proceed as in question 2, but suppose `number` has the value 50.
5. Proceed as in question 1, but suppose `number` has the value − 1.
6. Proceed as in question 2, but suppose `number` has the value − 1.
7. If the value of `code` is the letter B, tell what output is produced by the following `switch` statement, or indicate why an error occurs:

```
switch (code)
{
    case 'A':
    case 'B':
                cout << 123 << endl;
                break;
    case 'P':
    case 'R':
    case 'X':
                cout << 456 << endl;
                break;
}
```

8. Proceed as in question 7, but suppose the value of `code` is the letter X.
9. Proceed as in question 7, but suppose the value of `code` is the letter M.
10. If the value of `x` is 2.0, tell what output is produced by the following `switch` statement, or indicate why an error occurs:

```
switch (x)
{
    case 1.0:
                cout << x + 1.0 << endl;
                break;
```

```
        case 2.0:
                cout << x + 2.0 << endl;
                break;
    }
```

EXERCISES 5.4

1. Write a `switch` statement that increases `balance` by adding `amount` to it if the value of the character variable `transCode` is `'D'`; decrease `balance` by subtracting `amount` from it if `transCode` is `'W'`; display the value of `balance` if `transCode` is `'P'`; and display an illegal-transaction message otherwise.

2. Write a `switch` statement that, for two given integers a and b, and a given character op, computes and displays a + b, a - b, a * b, or a / b according to whether op is `'+'`, `'-'`, `'*'`, or `'/'`, and displays an illegal-operator message if it is not one of these.

For exercises 3–6, write functions that use `switch` statements to compute what is required. To test these functions, you should write driver programs as instructed in Programming Problems 9–12 at the end of this chapter.

3. Given a number representing a TV channel, return the call letters of the station that corresponds to that number, or some message indicating that the channel is not used. Use the following channel numbers and call letters (or use those that are available in your locale):

   2: WCBS
   4: WNBC
   5: WNEW
   7: WABC
   9: WOR
   11: WPIX
   13: WNET

4. Given a distance less than 1000, return a shipping cost as determined by the following table:

Distance	Cost
0 through 99	5.00
At least 100 but less than 300	8.00
At least 500 but less than 600	10.00
At least 600 but less than 1000	12.00

5. Given the number of a month, return the name of a month (or an error message indicating an illegal month number).

6. Proceed as in 5, but return the number of days in a month. (See exercise 9 of section 5.2 regarding the determination of leap years.)

*5.5 SELECTION: CONDITIONAL EXPRESSIONS

The selection statements (`if` and `switch`) we have considered thus far are similar to statements provided by other languages. However, C++ has inherited a third selection mechanism from its parent language C, an expression that produces either of two values, based on the value of a boolean expression (also called a *condition*).

To illustrate it, consider a simplified form of the letter grade computation problem from the preceding section, in which we wish to determine whether a student is passing or failing, based on an average of homework average, test average, and final exam score. If `average` is this average, the output statement

```
cout << "You are "
     << ( (average > PASS_FAIL_LINE) ? "passing." : "failing." );
```

will display

```
You are passing.
```

if the condition `average > PASS_FAIL_LINE` is true, but it will display

```
You are failing.
```

if the condition `average > PASS_FAIL_LINE` is false.

Because the value produced by such expressions depends on the value of their condition, they are called **conditional expressions,**[6] and have the following general form:

The Conditional Expression

Form

   condition ? *expression*$_1$: *expression*$_2$

where:

  condition is a boolean expression; and

  expression$_1$ and *expression*$_2$ are type-compatible expressions.

Behavior

condition is evaluated.

If the value of *condition* is true (i.e., nonzero),
   then the value of *expression*$_1$ is returned as the result.

If the value of *condition* is false (i.e., zero),
   then the value of *expression*$_2$ is returned as the result.

---

[6] A conditional expression has the form `C ? A : B` and is actually a *ternary* (three-operand) operation, in which `C`, `A`, and `B` are the three operands and `? :` is the operator.

Note that in a conditional expression, only one of *expression*$_1$ and *expression*$_2$ is evaluated. Thus, an assignment such as

```
reciprocal = ( (x == 0) ? 0 : 1 / x);
```

is safe because if the value of x is zero, the expression 1 / x will not be evaluated, and so no divide-by-zero error results. A conditional expression can thus sometimes be used in place of an if statement to guard a potentially unsafe operation. When it is used as a subexpression in another expression, the conditional expression should be enclosed in parentheses, because its precedence is lower than most of the other operators (see appendix C).

This mechanism has many different uses, because it can be used anywhere that an expression can appear. In fact, the conditional expression can be used in place of most if-else statements. To illustrate, suppose that we wanted to write a function LargerOf() to find the maximum of two int values. Although we could do this with an if statement,

```
int LargerOf(int value1, int value2)
{
   if (value1 > value2)
      return value1;
   else
      return value2;
}
```

a conditional expression provides a simpler alternative:

```
int LargerOf(int value1, int value2)
{
   return ( (value1 > value2) ? value1 : value2);
}
```

Using such a function, we can write

```
max = LargerOf(x, y);
```

and max will be assigned the larger of the two values x and y.

As a final example, suppose that numCourses is an int variable containing the number of courses a student is taking in the current semester. Then the output statement

```
cout << "\nYou are taking " << numCourses << " course"
     << ( (numCourses == 1) ? "" : "s" )
     << " this semester.\n";
```

will display the *singular* message

```
You are taking 1 course this semester.
```

if numCourses is equal to 1, and will display a *plural* message if numCourses has a value other than 1:

```
You are taking 3 courses this semester.
```

EXERCISES 5.5

1. Describe the operation that the following function performs:

```
int DoSomething1(int value)
{
    return ( (value >= 0) ? value : -value );
}
```

2. Describe the operation that the following function performs:

```
char DoSomething2(char ch)
{
    return ( ( ('A' <= ch) && (ch <= 'Z') ) ? ch+32 : ch );
}
```

3. Write conditional expressions that can replace the blanks in the output statement

```
cout << _____ << month << '/'
     << _____ << day << '/'
     << _____ << year % 100<< endl;
```

so that the output produced will be as follows:

month	day	year	Output
12	25	1997	12/25/97
10	1	1980	10/01/80
7	4	1915	07/04/15
1	1	1901	01/01/01

4. Write a conditional expression that can replace the blank in the output statement

```
cout << _____ << number<< endl;
```

so that the output produced will be as follows:

number	Output
123	123
23	023
3	003

5. Write a function `SmallerOf()` that returns the smaller of two given integer values.

6. Using nested conditional expressions, write a function:
   (a) `LargestOf()` that, given three int values, returns the largest of the three.
   (b) `SmallestOf()` that, given three int values, returns the smallest of the three.

7. The mathematician Carl Friedrich Gauss discovered that the sum of the integers from 1 through n is given by the formula

$$\frac{n(n + 1)}{2}$$

Using a conditional expression, construct a function `Sum()` that returns the value according to Gauss's formula if the value of its parameter is positive and zero otherwise.

Part of the Picture: Boolean Logic and Digital Design

The PART OF THE PICTURE: Introduction to Computer Organization section in chapter 0 and the PART OF THE PICTURE: Computer Architecture that follows this section describe one of a computer's components, the CPU (central processing unit). The arithmetic operations performed by the CPU must be carried out using special electrical circuits called **logic circuits** that are used to implement boolean (or digital) logic in hardware. In this section we investigate the design of such circuits, which is one small part of the broader area of computer architecture.

EARLY WORK

The foundations of circuit design were laid in the early 1900s by the English mathematician George Boole, after whom the C++ bool type is named. Boole formalized several axioms of logic, resulting in an algebra for writing logical expressions, which have since come to be known as boolean expressions.

In C++ syntax, some of the basic axioms of boolean logic are as follows:[7]

The Relational Laws

1a. !(X == Y) ≡ (X != Y)   1b. !(X != Y) ≡ (X == Y)
2a. !(X < Y) ≡ (X >= Y)   2b. !(X >= Y) ≡ (X < Y)
3a. !(X > Y) ≡ (X <= Y)   3b. !(X <= Y) ≡ (X > Y)

The Boolean Laws

4a. X || false ≡ X   4b. X && false ≡ false
5a. X || true ≡ true   5b. X && true ≡ X

Idempotent Laws

6a. X || X ≡ X   6b. X || X ≡ X

Involution Law

7a. !(!X) ≡ X

Laws of Complementarity

8a. X || (!X) ≡ true   8b. X && (!X) ≡ false

Commutative Laws

9a. X || Y ≡ Y || X   9b. X && Y ≡ Y && X

Associative Laws

10a. (X || Y) || Z ≡ X || (Y || Z)   10b. (X && Y) && Z ≡ X && (Y && Z)

Distributive Laws

11a. X && (Y || Z) ≡   11b. X || (Y && Z) ≡
     (X && Y) || (X && Z)   (X || Y) && (X || Z)

Simplification Theorems

12a. (X && Y) || (X && !Y) ≡ X   12b. (X || Y) && (X || !Y) ≡ X
13a. X || (X && Y) ≡ X   13b. X && (X || Y) ≡ X
14a. (X || !Y) && Y ≡ X && Y   14b. (X && !Y) || Y ≡ X || Y

DeMorgan's Laws

15a. !(X && Y) ≡ !X || !Y   15b. !(X || Y) ≡ !X && !Y

It is especially useful for programmers to know DeMorgan's Laws because they can simplify complicated boolean expressions. As a simple illustration, suppose that done and error are bool objects, and consider the following if statement:

---

[7] In the statements of these laws, the symbol ≡ denotes is equivalent to. A statement of the form $p \equiv q$ means that p and q always have the same truth values (true or false).

```
if (!done && !error)
    // ... do something...
```

DeMorgan's law tells us that the boolean expression involving two negated values,

```
!done && !error
```

can be simplified to

```
!(done || error)
```

The original expression contained 2 NOT operations and 1 AND operation, but the simplified expression contains only 1 NOT operation and 1 OR operation—1 less operation. Applying DeMorgan's law repeatedly to a boolean expression of the form

```
!b₁ && !b₂ && ... && !bₙ
```

containing n NOTs and $n - 1$ ANDs, gives the simpler expression

```
!(b₁ || b₂ || ... || bₙ)
```

containing only 1 NOT and $n - 1$ ORs. The complexity of the expression is thus reduced by $n - 1$ NOT operations, which can result in a significant increase in performance.

DIGITAL CIRCUITS

With the invention of the digital computer in the late 1930s, the work of Boole moved from obscurity to prominence. The axioms and theorems of his boolean algebra became extremely important as mathematicians, engineers, and physicists sought to build the arithmetic and logic circuitry of the early computers. These circuits utilize three basic electronic components: the **AND gate,** the **OR gate,** and the **NOT gate** or **inverter,** whose symbols are as follows:

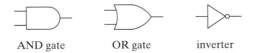

AND gate   OR gate   inverter

The inputs to these gates are electrical voltages, where a voltage that exceeds a certain threshold value is interpreted as 1 (i.e., true), and a voltage below that threshold is interpreted as 0 (i.e., false). In the case of an AND gate, a 1 is produced only when there are 1s on both input lines. An OR gate produces a 1 only when there is a 1 on at least one of the input lines. The output of a NOT gate is the opposite of its input. Because these three components behave in the same fashion as the AND, OR, and NOT operators from boolean algebra, a circuit can be constructed to represent any boolean expression, and boolean expressions can be used to design circuits!

CIRCUIT DESIGN: A BINARY HALF-ADDER

To illustrate, consider the problem of adding two binary digits `digit1` and `digit2`. The truth table below summarizes the behavior of the addition operation, which produces two results—a `sum` bit and a `carry` bit:

digit1	digit2	carry	sum
0	0	0	0
0	1	0	1
1	0	0	1
1	1	1	0

There are two important things to note:

1. The `carry` output is 1 (true) only when `digit1` and `digit 2` are both 1 (true)
2. The `sum` output is 1 (true) only when `digit1` is 0 (false) and `digit2` is 1 (true), or when `digit1` is 1 (true) and `digit2` is 0 (false)

It is easy to see that we can represent these outputs by the following pair of boolean expressions:

```
bool carry = digit1 && digit2,
     sum = (!digit1 && digit2) || (digit1 && !digit2);
```

The expression for `sum` has the form `(!A && B) || (A && !B)` and can be simplified by applying the axioms from boolean logic as follows:

```
(!A && B) || (A && !B)
          ⇓                      (Apply 9a to switch two operands of ||)
(A && !B) || (!A && B)
          ⇓                      (Apply 11b with  X = (A && !B),  Y = !A,  Z = B)
((A && !B) || !A) && ((A && !B) || B))
          ⇓                      (Apply 14b to second expression with  X = A and Y = B)
((A && !B) || !A) && (A || B)
          ⇓                      (Apply 9a to switch two operands of first &&)
((!B && A) || !A) && (A || B)
          ⇓                      (Apply 14b to first expression with  X = !B and Y = !A)
(!B || !A) && (A || B)
          ⇓                      (Apply 15a to first || expression with X = B and Y = A)
!(B && A) && (A || B)
          ⇓                      (Apply 9a to switch two operands of first &&)
!(A && B) && (A || B)
          ⇓                      (Apply 9a to switch two operands of second &&)
(A || B) && !(A && B)
```

This means that the boolean expression for `sum` can be rewritten as

```
sum = (digit1 || digit2) && !(digit1 && digit2);
```

which has one less NOT operation than the original expression.

This may seem like a lot of work for not much improvement. On the contrary, this simplification means that a circuit for this expression will require one less inverter than a circuit for the original expression and will therefore be less expensive to manufacture. If half-adders are mass-produced, then this circuit may be manufactured millions of times with a savings that is millions of times the cost of an inverter!

Using the boolean expressions

```
bool carry = digit1 && digit2,
     sum = (digit1 || digit2) && !(digit1 && digit2);
```

for `sum` and `carry`, we can design the following circuit, called a **binary half-adder,** that adds two binary digits:

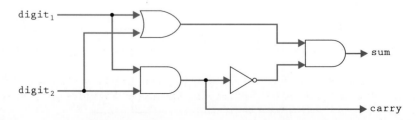

It accepts two inputs, `digit1` and `digit2`, and produces two outputs, `sum` and `carry`.
   Once a boolean expression is found to represent a circuit, it is easy to write a simple program to check its behavior. For example, the program in Figure 5.8 simulates the action of a binary half-adder. It reads binary digits (0 or 1) for `digit1` and `digit2`. The values of the two boolean expressions representing the sum and carry outputs are then assigned to the variables `sum` and `carry`, respectively, and are displayed.

FIGURE 5.8   A BINARY HALF-ADDER.

```
/* halfadder8.cpp calculates the outputs from boolean expressions
 * that represent the logical circuit for a binary half-adder.
 *
 *   Input (keyboard): two binary digits
 *   Output (screen):  two binary values representing the sum and carry
 *                     that result when the input values are added
 ********************************************************************/

#include <iostream.h>                          // cout, cin, <<, >>

int main()
{
   cout << "Enter two binary inputs: ";
   short digit1, digit2;                        // the two binary inputs
   cin >> digit1 >> digit2;
                                                 // the two circuit outputs
   bool sum = (digit1 || digit2) && !(digit1 && digit2),
        carry = (digit1 && digit2);
   cout << "Carry = " << carry << " Sum = " << sum << "\n\n";
}
```

Sample runs:

```
Enter two binary inputs: 0 0
Carry = 0 Sum = 0


Enter two binary inputs: 0 1
Carry = 0 Sum = 1


Enter two binary inputs: 1 0
Carry = 0 Sum = 1

Enter two binary inputs: 1 1
Carry = 1 Sum = 0
```

A binary *full-adder* for adding two binary digits and a carry bit, and an *adder* for numbers having more than one binary digit, are described in the Programming Problems at the end of the chapter.

Part of the Picture: Computer Architecture

BY WILLIAM STALLINGS

At a top level, a computer consists of processor, memory, and I/O components, with one or more modules of each type. These components are interconnected in some fashion to achieve the main function of the computer, which is to execute programs. Thus, there are four main structural elements:

- ▶ **Processor:** Controls the operation of the computer and performs its data processing functions. When there is only one processor, it is often referred to as the *central processing unit* (*CPU*).

- ▶ **Main Memory:** Stores data and programs. This memory is typically volatile; it is also referred to as *real memory* or *primary memory*.

- ▶ **I/O Modules:** Move data between the computer and its external environment. The external environment consists of a variety of external devices, including secondary memory devices, communications equipment, and printers.

- ▶ **System Interconnection:** Some structure and mechanisms that provide for communication among processors, main memory, and I/O modules.

Figure 5.9 depicts these top-level components. The processor controls operations. One of its functions is to exchange data with memory. For this purpose, it typically makes use of two internal (to the processor) registers: a **memory address register (MAR),** which specifies the address in memory for the next read or write; and a **memory buffer register (MBR),** which contains the data to be written into memory or which receives the data read from memory. Similarly, an **I/O address register (I/OAR)** specifies a particular I/O device. An **I/O buffer register (I/OBR)** is used for the exchange of data between an I/O module and the processor.

FIGURE 5.9   COMPUTER COMPONENTS: TOP-LEVEL VIEW

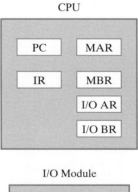
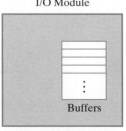
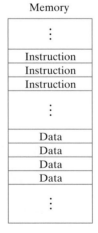

PC   = Program counter
IR   = Instruction register
MAR   = Memory address register
MBR   = Memory buffer register
I/O AR = I/O address register
I/O BR = I/O buffer register

A **memory module** consists of a set of locations, defined by sequentially numbered addresses. Each location contains a binary number that can be interpreted as either an instruction or data. An I/O module transfers data from external devices to processor and memory, and vice versa. It contains internal buffers for temporarily holding this data until it can be sent on.

Processor Registers

Within the processor, there is a set of registers that provide a level of memory that is faster and smaller than main memory. The registers in the processor serve two functions:

▶ **User-visible registers:** These enable the assembly-language programmer to minimize main memory references by optimizing the use of registers. For high-level languages, an optimizing compiler will attempt to make intelligent choices of which variables to assign to registers and which to main memory locations. Some high-level languages, such as C and C++, allow the programmer to suggest to the compiler which variables should be held in registers.

▶ **Control and status registers:** These are used by the processor to control the operation of the processor and by privileged, operating-system routines to control the execution of programs.

There is not a clean separation of registers into these two categories. For example, on some machines the program counter is user visible, but on many it is not. For purposes of the following discussion, however, it is convenient to use these categories.

User-Visible Registers. A user-visible register is one that may be referenced by means of the machine language that the processor executes and that is generally available to all programs, including application programs as well as system programs. The following types of registers are typically available: data, address, and condition codes.

Data registers can be assigned to a variety of functions by the programmer. In some cases, they are general purpose in nature and can be used with any machine instruction that performs operations on data. Often, however, there are restrictions. For example, there may be dedicated registers for floating-point operations.

Address registers contain main memory addresses of data and instructions, or they contain a portion of the address that is used in the calculation of the complete address. These registers may themselves be somewhat general purpose, or they may be devoted to a particular addressing mode. Examples include:

▶ **Index register:** Indexed addressing is a common mode of addressing that involves adding an index to a base value to get the effective address.

▶ **Segment pointer:** With segmented addressing, memory is divided into variable-length blocks of words called *segments.* A memory reference consists of a reference to a particular segment and an offset within the segment; this mode of addressing is important in memory management. In this mode of addressing, a register is used to hold the address of the base (starting location) of the segment. There may be multiple registers; for example, one for the operating system (i.e., when operating-system code is executing on the processor) and one for the currently executing application.

▶ **Stack pointer:** If there is user-visible stack addressing, then typically the stack is in main memory and there is a dedicated register that points to the top of the stack. This allows the use of instructions that contain no address field, such as push and pop.

A final category of registers, which is at least partially visible to the user, holds **condition codes** (also referred to as *flags*). Condition codes are bits set by the processor hardware as the result of operations. For example, an arithmetic operation may produce a positive, negative, zero, or overflow result. In addition to the result itself being stored in a register or memory, a condition code is also set. The code may subsequently be tested as part of a conditional branch operation.

Condition code bits are collected into one or more registers. Usually, they form part of a control register. Generally, machine instructions allow these bits to be read by implicit reference, but they cannot be altered by the programmer.

Control and Status Registers. There are a variety of processor registers that are employed to control the operation of the processor. Most of these, on most machines, are not visible to the user. Some of them may be accessible by machine instructions executed in a control or operating-system mode.

Of course, different machines will have different register organizations and use different terminology. We will list common register types, with a brief description.

In addition to the MAR, MBR, IOAR, and IOBR registers mentioned earlier, the following are essential to instruction execution:

- ▶ **Program counter (PC):** Contains the address of an instruction to be fetched.
- ▶ **Instruction register (IR):** Contains the instruction most recently fetched.

All processor designs also include a register or set of registers, often known as the **program status word (PSW),** which contains status information. The PSW typically contains condition codes plus other status information. Common fields and flags include the following:

- ▶ **Sign:** Contains the sign bit of the last arithmetic operation.
- ▶ **Zero:** Set when the result of an arithmetic operation is zero.
- ▶ **Carry:** Set if an operation resulted in a carry (addition) into or borrow (subtraction) out of a high-order bit. Used for multi-word arithmetic operations.
- ▶ **Equal:** Set if a logical compare result is equality.
- ▶ **Overflow:** Used to indicate arithmetic overflow.
- ▶ **Interrupt Enable/Disable:** Used to disable or enable interrupts. When interrupts are disabled, the processor ignores them. This is often desirable when the operating system is in the midst of dealing with another interrupt.
- ▶ **Supervisor:** Indicates whether the processor is executing in supervisor or user mode. Certain privileged instructions can be executed only in supervisor mode, and certain areas of memory can be accessed only in supervisor mode.

There are a number of other registers related to status and control that might be found in a particular processor design. In addition to the PSW, there may be a pointer to a block of memory containing additional status information. In machines using multiple types of interrupts, a set of registers may be provided, with one pointer to each interrupt-handling routine. If a stack is used to implement certain functions (e.g., procedure call), then a system stack pointer is needed. Memory management hardware requires dedicated registers. Finally, registers may be used in the control of I/O operations.

A number of factors go into the design of the control and status register organization. One key issue is operating system support. Certain types of control information are of specific utility to the operating system. If the processor designer has a functional understanding of the operating system to be used, then the register organization can to some extent be tailored to the operating system.

Another key design decision is the allocation of control information between registers and memory. It is common to dedicate the first (lowest) few hundred or thousand words of memory for control purposes. The designer must decide how much control information should be in more expensive, faster registers and how much in less expensive, slower main memory.

INSTRUCTION EXECUTION

The basic function performed by a computer is program execution. The program to be executed consists of a set of instructions stored in memory. The processor does the actual work by executing instructions specified in the program.

The simplest point of view is to consider instruction processing as consisting of two steps: The processor reads (*fetches*) instructions from memory one at a time, and executes each instruction. Program execution consists of repeating the process of instruction fetch and instruction execution. The instruction execution may involve several operations and depends on the nature of the instruction.

The processing required for a single instruction is called an *instruction cycle*. In simple terms, the instruction cycle consists of a *fetch cycle,* in which the processor reads an instruction from memory, and the *execute cycle,* in which the processor executes the instruction. This instruction cycle is performed repeatedly.

INSTRUCTION FETCH AND EXECUTE

At the beginning of each instruction cycle, the processor fetches an instruction from memory. In a typical processor, a register called the **program counter (PC)** is used to keep track of which instruction is to be fetched next. Unless told otherwise, the processor always increments the PC after each instruction fetch so that it will fetch the next instruction in sequence (i.e., the instruction located at the next higher memory address). So, for example, consider a computer in which each instruction occupies one 16-bit word of memory. Assume that the program counter is set to word location 300. The processor will next fetch the instruction at location 300. On succeeding instruction cycles, it will fetch instructions from locations 301, 302, 303, and so on. This sequence may be altered, as explained presently.

The fetched instruction is loaded into a register in the processor known as the **instruction register (IR).** The instruction is in the form of a binary code that specifies what action the processor is to take. The processor interprets the instruction and performs the required action. In general, these actions fall into four categories:

▸ **Processor-memory:** Data may be transferred from processor to memory or from memory to processor.

▸ **Processor-I/O:** Data may be transferred to or from a peripheral device by transferring between the processor and an I/O module.

▸ **Data processing:** The processor may perform some arithmetic or logic operation on data.

▸ **Control:** An instruction may specify that the sequence of execution be altered. For example, the processor may fetch an instruction from location 149, which specifies that the next instruction be from location 182. The processor will remember this fact by setting the program counter to 182. Thus, on the next fetch cycle, the instruction will be fetched from location 182 rather than 150.

Of course, an instruction's execution may involve a combination of these actions.

Let us consider a simple example using a hypothetical machine that includes the characteristics listed in Figure 5.10. The processor contains a single data register, called an **accumulator (AC).** Both instructions and data are 16 bits long. Thus it is convenient to organize memory using 16-bit locations, or words. The instruction format provides four bits for the opcode; thus there can be as many as $2^4 = 16$ different opcodes, and up to $2^{12} = 4,096$ (4K) words of memory can be directly addressed.

FIGURE 5.10 CHARACTERISTICS OF A HYPOTHETICAL MACHINE

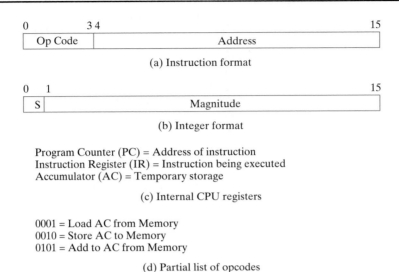

Figure 5.11 illustrates a partial program execution, showing the relevant portions of memory and processor registers. The program fragment shown adds the contents of the memory word at address 940 to the contents of the memory word at address 941 and stores the result in the latter location. Three instructions, which can be described as three fetch and three execute cycles, are required:

1. The program counter (PC) contains 300, the address of the first instruction. This address is loaded into the instruction register (IR). Note that this process would involve the use of a memory address register (MAR) and a memory buffer register (MBR). For simplicity, these intermediate registers are ignored.

2. The first 4 bits in the IR indicate that the accumulator (AC) is to be loaded. The remaining 12 bits specify the address, which is 940.

3. After the load is complete, the PC is incremented and the next instruction is fetched.

4. The old contents of the AC and the contents of location 941 are added and the result is stored in the AC.

5. The PC is incremented and the next instruction is fetched.

6. The contents of the AC are stored in location 941.

In this example, three instruction cycles, each consisting of a fetch cycle and an execute cycle, are needed to add the contents of location 940 to the contents of 941. With a more complex set of instructions, fewer cycles would be needed. Most modern processors include instructions that contain more than one address. Thus the execution cycle for a particular instruction may involve more than one reference to memory. Also, instead of memory references, an instruction may specify an I/O operation.

I/O FUNCTION

An I/O module (e.g., a disk controller) can exchange data directly with the processor. Just as the processor can initiate a read or write with memory, designating the address of a specific location, the processor can also read data from or write data to an I/O module. In this

FIGURE 5.11   EXAMPLE OF PROGRAM EXECUTION

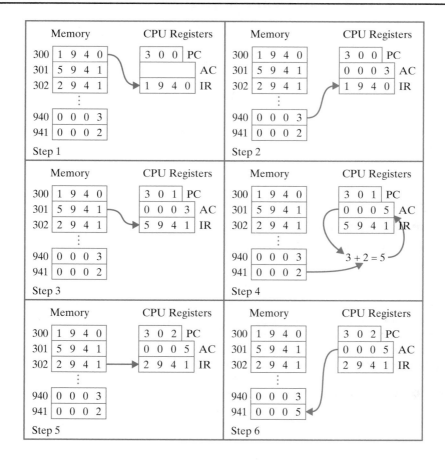

latter case, the processor identifies a specific device that is controlled by a particular I/O module. Thus, an instruction sequence similar in form to that of Figure 5.11 could occur, with I/O instructions rather than memory-referencing instructions.

In some cases, it is desirable to allow I/O exchanges to occur directly with memory. In such a case, the processor grants to an I/O module the authority to read from or write to memory, so that the I/O-memory transfer can occur without tying up the processor. During such a transfer, the I/O module issues read or write commands to memory, relieving the processor of responsibility for the exchange. This operation is known as **direct memory access (DMA).**

THE MEMORY HIERARCHY

The design constraints on a computer's memory can be summed up by three questions: How much? How fast? How expensive?

The question of how much is somewhat open-ended. If the capacity is there, applications will likely be developed to use it. The question of how fast is, in a sense, easier to answer. To achieve greatest performance, the memory must be able to keep up with the processor. That is, as the processor is executing instructions, we would not want it to have to pause waiting for instructions or operands. The final question must also be considered. For a practical system, the cost of memory must be reasonable in relationship to other components.

As might be expected, there is a tradeoff among the three key characteristics of memory: namely cost, capacity, and access time. At any given time, a variety of technologies are used to implement memory systems. Across this spectrum of technologies, the following relationships hold:

▶ Smaller access time, greater cost per bit
▶ Greater capacity, smaller cost per bit
▶ Greater capacity, greater access time

The dilemma facing the designer is clear. The designer would like to use memory technologies that provide for large-capacity memory, both because the capacity is needed and because the cost per bit is low. However, to meet performance requirements, the designer needs to use expensive, relatively lower-capacity memories with fast access times.

The way out of this dilemma is not to rely on a single memory component or technology, but to employ a **memory hierarchy.** A traditional hierarchy is illustrated in Figure 5.12. As one goes down the hierarchy, the following occur:

(a) Decreasing cost/bit
(b) Increasing capacity
(c) Increasing access time
(d) Decreasing frequency of access of the memory by the processor

Thus, smaller, more expensive, faster memories are supplemented by larger, cheaper, slower memories. By employing a variety of technologies, a spectrum of memory systems exist that satisfy conditions (a) through (c). Fortunately, condition (d) is also generally valid.

The basis for the validity of condition (d) is a principle known as *locality of reference.* During the course of execution of a program, memory references by the processor, for both instructions and data, tend to cluster. Programs typically contain a number of iterative loops and subroutines. Once a loop or subroutine is entered, there are repeated references to a small set of instructions. Similarly, operations on tables and arrays involve access to a clustered set of data words. Over a long period of time, the clusters in use change, but over a short period of time, the processor is primarily working with fixed clusters of memory references.

FIGURE 5.12   THE MEMORY HIERARCHY

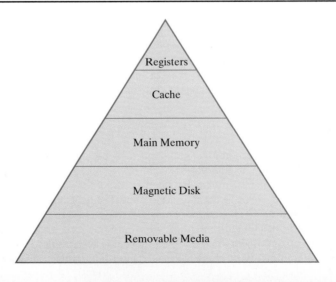

Accordingly, it is possible to organize data across the hierarchy such that the percentage of accesses to each successively lower level is substantially less than that of the level above. Consider a simple two-level memory. Let Level 2 memory contain all program instructions and data. The current clusters can be temporarily placed in Level 1. From time to time, one of the clusters in Level 1 will have to be swapped back to Level 2 to make room for a new cluster coming in to Level 1. On average, however, most references will be to instructions and data contained in Level 1.

This principle can be applied across more than two levels of memory. Consider the hierarchy shown in Figure 5.12. The fastest, smallest, and most expensive type of memory consists of the registers internal to the processor. Typically, a processor will contain a few dozen such registers, although some machines contain hundreds of registers. Skipping down two levels, main memory, also referred to as real memory, is the principal internal memory system of the computer. Each location in main memory has a unique address, and most machine instructions refer to one or more main memory addresses. Main memory is usually extended with a higher-speed, smaller *cache*. The cache is not usually visible to the programmer or, indeed, to the processor. It is a device for staging the movement of data between main memory and processor registers to improve performance.

The three forms of memory just described are, typically, volatile and employ semiconductor technology. The use of three levels exploits the fact that semiconductor memory comes in a variety of types, which differ in speed and cost. Data are stored more permanently on external mass storage devices, of which the most common are hard disk and removable media, such as removable disk, tape, and optical storage. External, nonvolatile memory is also referred to as *secondary* or *auxiliary memory*. These are used to store program and data files and are usually visible to the programmer only in terms of files and records, as opposed to individual bytes or words. Disk is also used to provide an extension to main memory known as *virtual storage* or *virtual memory*.

INPUT/OUTPUT ORGANIZATION

In addition to one or more processors and a set of memory modules, the third key element of a computer system is a set of I/O modules. Each module interfaces to the system bus or other interconnection structure and controls one or more external devices. An I/O module is not simply mechanical connectors that wire a device into the system bus. Rather, the I/O module contains some "intelligence," that is, it contains logic for controlling the flow of data between the external device and the bus.

An I/O module has two major functions:

- ► Interface to the processor and memory via the system bus or other interconnection structure.
- ► Interface to one or more external devices by tailored data links.

I/O MODULE FUNCTION

The major functions or requirements for an I/O module fall into the following categories:

- ► Control and timing
- ► Communication with processor
- ► Communication with external device
- ► Data buffering
- ► Error detection

During any period of time, the processor may communicate with one or more external devices in unpredictable patterns, depending on the program's need for I/O. The internal resources, such as main memory and the system bus, must be shared among a number of activities, including I/O. Thus, the I/O function includes a **control and timing** requirement, to coordinate the flow of traffic between internal resources and external devices. For example, the control of the transfer of data from an external device to the processor might involve the following sequence of steps:

1.   The processor interrogates the I/O module to check the status of the attached device.
2.   The I/O module returns the device status.
3.   If the device is operational and ready to transmit, the processor requests the transfer of data, by means of a command to the I/O module.
4.   The I/O module obtains a unit of data (e.g., 8 or 16 bits) from the external device.
5.   The data are transferred from the I/O module to the processor.

If the system employs a bus, then each of the interactions between the processor and the I/O module involves one or more bus events.

The preceding simplified scenario also illustrates that the I/O module must have the capability to engage in **communication with the processor** and with the external device. Communication with the processor involves:

▶ **Command decoding:** The I/O module accepts commands from the processor. These commands are generally sent as signals on the *control bus*. For example, an I/O module for a disk drive might accept the following commands: READ SECTOR, WRITE SECTOR, SEEK track number, and SCAN record ID. The latter two commands each include a parameter that is sent on the *data bus.*

▶ **Data:** Data are exchanged between the processor and the I/O module over the data bus.

▶ **Status reporting:** Because peripherals are so slow, it is important to know the status of the I/O module. For example, if an I/O module is asked to send data to the processor (read), it may not be ready to do so because it is still working on the previous command. This fact can be reported with a status signal. Common status signals are BUSY and READY. There may also be signals to report various error conditions.

▶ **Address recognition:** Just as each word of memory has an address, so does each I/O device. Thus, an I/O module must recognize one unique address for each peripheral it controls.

On the other side, the I/O module must be able to **communicate with external devices.** This communication also involves commands, status information, and data.

An essential task of an I/O module is **data buffering.** Whereas the transfer rate into and out of main memory or the processor is quite high, the rate is orders of magnitude lower for most peripheral devices. Data coming from main memory are sent to an I/O module in a rapid burst. The data are buffered in the I/O module and then sent to the external device at its data rate. In the opposite direction, data are buffered so as not to tie up the memory in a slow transfer operation. Thus, the I/O module must be able to operate at both device and memory speeds.

Finally, an I/O module is often responsible for **error detection** and for subsequently reporting errors to the processor. One class of errors includes mechanical and electrical malfunctions reported by the device (e.g., paper jam, bad disk track). Another class consists of unintentional changes to the bit pattern as it is transmitted from device to I/O module. Some form of error-detecting code is often used to detect transmission errors. A common example is the use of a *parity bit* on each character of data. For example, the ASCII character occupies 7 bits of a byte. The eighth bit is set so that the total number of 1s in the byte is even (even parity) or odd (odd parity). When a byte is received, the I/O module checks the parity to determine whether an error has occurred.

To Probe Further

The topics in this section are covered in detail in *Computer Organization and Architecture: Designing for Performance, Fourth Edition,* by William Stallings (Prentice Hall, 1996). Links to web sites with further information can be found at http://www.shore.net/~ws/COA4e.

☞ *Programming Pointers*

✍ Program Style and Design

In this text, we use the following conventions for formatting the selection statements considered in this chapter.

1. *For an* if *statement,* if (boolean_expression) *is on one line, with its statement indented on the next line. If there is an* else *clause,* else *is on a separate line, aligned with* if*, and its statement is indented on the next line. If the statements are compound, the curly braces are aligned with the* if *and* else *and the statements inside the block are indented.*

```
if (boolean_expression)
    statement₁
else
    statement₂

if (boolean_expression)
{
    statement₁
        .
        .
        .
    statementₖ
}
else
{
    statementₖ₊₁
        .
        .
        .
    statementₙ
}
```

An exception is made when the if-else-if *form is used to implement a multialternative selection structure. In this case the format used is*

```
if (boolean_expression₁)
    statement₁
else if (boolean_expression₂)
    statement₂
        .
        .
        .
else if (boolean_expressionₙ)
    statementₙ
else
    statementₙ₊₁
```

2. *For a* switch *statement,* switch (expression) *is on one line, with its curly braces aligned and on separate lines; each case list is indented within the curly braces, and*

each statement list and break *or* return *statement is indented past its particular case list.*

```
switch (expression)
{
    case_list₁:
                    statement_list₁
                    break;                  // or return
    case_list₂:
                    statement_list₂
                    break;                  // or return



                .
                .
                .


    case_listₙ:
                    statement_listₙ
                    break;                  // or return



    default:
                    statement_list_{n+1}
}
```

Alternatively, each $statement\_list_i$ may be positioned on the line following $case\_list_i$.

3. *Program defensively by using the* if *statement to test for illegal values.* This provides an alternative to the assert() mechanism that does not terminate the program on a failed precondition. For an example, see the first if statement in the function ScoreToGrade() in the next programming pointer.

4. *Multialternative selection constructs can be implemented more efficiently with an* if-else-if *construct than with a sequence of separate* if *statements.* For example, consider the function

```
char ScoreToGrade(int score)
{
    if (score < 0 || score > 100)
    {
        cout << score << " is not a valid score.\n";
        return '?';
    }
    if (score >= 90) && (score <= 100))
        return 'A';
    if ((score >= 80) && (score < 90))
        return 'B';
    if ((score >= 70) && (score < 80))
        return 'C';
    if ((score >= 60) && (score < 70))
        return 'D';
    if (score < 60)
        return 'F';
}
```

Here, all the if statements are executed for each score processed and 5 of the boolean expressions are compound expressions, so that a total of 16 operations are performed, regardless of the score being processed. By contrast, for the function

```
char ScoreToGrade(int score)
{
   if (score < 0 || score > 100)
   {
      cout << score << " is not a valid score.\n";
      return '?';
   }
   else if (score >= 90)
      return 'A';
   else if (score >= 80)
      return 'B';
   else if (score >= 70)
      return 'C';
   else if (score >= 60)
      return 'D';
   else
      return 'F';
}
```

most of the boolean expressions are simple, and not all of them are evaluated for each score, so that only 3 to 7 operations are performed, depending on the score being processed.

5. *Multialternative selection statements of the form*

```
if (variable == constant₁)
   statement₁
else if (variable == constant₂)
   statement₂

   .
   .
   .

else if (variable == constantₙ)
   statementₙ
else
   statementₙ₊₁
```

where `variable` *and each* `variableᵢ` *are* int*-compatible, are usually implemented more efficiently using a* switch *statement* like that in the preceding Programming Pointer 2, with *expression* replaced by *variable* and *case_listᵢ* by case *constantᵢ*. For example, we might implement `ScoreToGrade()` even more efficiently as follows:

```
char ScoreToGrade(int score)
{
   switch (score / 10)
   {
      case 10: case 9:
                        return 'A';
      case 8:
                        return 'B';
      case 7:
                        return 'C';
      case 6:
                        return 'D';
      case 5: case 4:
      case 3: case 2:
```

```
             case 1: case 0:
                             return 'F';
             default:

                             cout << score
                                  << " is not a valid score.\n";
                             return '?';

      }
  }
```

This version of ScoreToGrade() will perform the same number of operations regardless of the value of score.

A second advantage of the switch statement is that a problem solution implemented with a switch is often more readable than an equivalent solution implemented using an if statement. For example, consider the problem of classifying the
value of a char variable ch as an arithmetic operator (+, -, *, /, %), a relational operator (<, >), an assignment operator (=), or a punctuation symbol (semicolon or
comma). Using a switch statement, we might write

```
switch (ch)
{
   case '+': case '-':
   case '*': case '/':
   case '%':
                       cout << "Arithmetic operator\n";
                       break;
   case '<': case '>':
                       cout << "Relational operator\n";
                       break;
   case '=':
                       cout << "Assignment operator\n";
                       break;
   case ';': case ',':
                       cout << "Punctuation\n";
                       break;
   default:
                       cout << "identification of "
                            << ch << " is not supported.\n";
}
```

which is more readable than an equivalent implementation using an if statement:

```
if ((ch == '+') || (ch == '-')  || (ch == '*')
|| (ch == '/') || (ch == '%'))
   cout << "Arithmetic operator\n";
else if ((ch == '<') || (ch == '>'))
   cout << "Relational operator\n";
else if (ch == '=')
   cout << "Assignment operator\n";
else if ((ch == ';') || (ch == ','))
   cout << "Punctuation\n";
else
   cout << "identification of " << ch
        << " is not supported.\n";
```

The potential error of inadvertently substituting the assignment operator (=) for one
of the several equality operators (==) in this if statement is also avoided by the
switch statement.

⚡ POTENTIAL PROBLEMS

1. *One of the most common errors in an* if *statement is using an assignment operator (=) when an equality operator (==) is intended.* See Potential Problem 6 at the end of chapter 3.

2. *When real quantities that are algebraically equal are compared with ==, the result may be a false boolean expression, because most real numbers are not stored exactly.* For example, even though the two real expressions x * (1/x) and 1.0 are algebraically equal, the boolean expression x * (1/x) == 1.0 may be false for some real numbers x.

3. *In a nested* if *statement, each* else *clause is matched with the nearest preceding unmatched* if. For example, consider the following statements, which are given without indentation:

```
if (x > 0)
if y > 0)
z = x + y;
else
z = x + abs(y);
w = x * y * z;
```

With which if is the else associated? According to the rule just stated, these statements are executed as

```
if (x > 0)
   if (y > 0)
      z = x + y;
   else
      z = x + abs(y);
w = x * y * z;
```

where the else clause matches the if statement containing the condition y > 0. Use indentation and alignment to show such associations.

4. *Each* switch *statement and block must contain matching curly braces.* A missing } can be very difficult to locate. In certain situations, the compiler may not find that a { is unmatched until it reaches the end of the file. In such cases, an error message such as

```
Error...: Compound statement missing } in function ...
```

will be generated.

5. *The selector in a* switch *statement must be integer-compatible.* In particular, the values of the selector in case lists

   ▶ May *not* be real constants, such as 1.5, − 2.3, 3.414159 or 2.998E8; and

   ▶ May *not* be string constants such as "JACK", "QUEEN", or "KING".

Programming Problems

SECTION 5.2

1. Write a driver program to test the function OKToSpray() of exercise 4.
2. Write a driver program to test the function CreditApproved() of exercise 5.
3. Write a driver program to test the leap-year function of exercise 6.

4. Write a driver program to test the days-in-a-month function of exercise 7.

5. Write a driver program to test the days-in-a-month function of exercise 8.

6. Suppose that charges by a gas company are based on consumption according to the following table:

Gas Used	Rate
First 70 cubic meters	$5.00 minimum cost
Next 100 cubic meters	5.0¢ per cubic meter
Next 230 cubic meters	2.5¢ per cubic meter
Above 400 cubic meters	1.5¢ per cubic meter

Write a function that computes the charges for a given amount of gas usage. Use this function in a program in which the meter reading for the previous month and the current meter reading are entered, each a four-digit number and each representing cubic meters, and that then calculates and displays the amount of the bill. *Note:* The current reading may be less than the previous one; for example, the previous reading may be 9897, and the current one may be 0103. Execute the program with the following meter readings: 3450, 3495; 8810, 8900; 9950, 0190; 1275, 1982; 9872, 0444.

7. Write a program that reads values for the coefficients A, B, C, D, E, and F of the equations

$$Ax + By = C$$
$$Dx + Ey = F$$

of two straight lines, and then determine whether the lines are parallel (their slopes are equal) or the lines intersect. If they intersect, determine whether the lines are perpendicular (the product of their slopes is equal to -1).

8. Write a program that reads the coordinates of three points and then determines whether they are collinear.

SECTIONS 5.3 & 5.4

9. Write a driver program to test the TV-channel function of exercise 3.

10. Write a driver program to test the distance-cost function of exercise 4.

11. Write a driver program to test the month-name function of exercise 5.

12. Write a driver program to test the days-in-month function of exercise 6.

13. Locating avenues' addresses in mid-Manhattan is not easy; for example, the nearest cross street to 866 Third Avenue is 53rd Street, whereas the nearest cross street to 866 Second Avenue is 46th Street. To locate approximately the nearest numbered cross street for a given avenue address, the following algorithm can be used:
    Cancel the last digit of the address, divide by 2, and add or subtract the number given in the following abbreviated table:

1st Ave.	Add 3
2nd Ave.	Add 3
3rd Ave.	Add 10
4th Ave.	Add 8
5th Ave. up to 200	Add 13
5th Ave. up to 400	Add 16
6th Ave. (Ave. of the Americas)	Subtract 12
7th Ave.	Add 12
8th Ave.	Add 10
10th Ave.	Add 14

Write a function that uses a `switch` statement to determine the number of the nearest cross street for a given address and avenue number according to the preceding algorithm. Then write a program to test your function.

14. A wholesale office supply company discounts the price of each of its products depending on the number of units bought and the price per unit. The discount increases as the numbers of units bought and/or the unit price increases. These discounts are given in the following table:

Number Bought	Unit Price (dollars)		
	0–10.00	10.01–100.00	100.01–
1–9	0%	2%	5%
10–19	5%	7%	9%
20–49	9%	15%	21%
50–99	14%	23%	32%
100–	21%	32%	43%

Write a function that calculates the percentage discount for a specified number of units and unit price. Use this function in a program that reads the number of units bought and the unit price, and then calculates and prints the total full cost, the total amount of the discount, and the total discounted cost.

15. An airline vice president in charge of operations needs to determine whether the current estimates of flight times are accurate. Because there is a larger possibility of variations due to weather and air traffic in the longer flights, he allows a larger error in the time estimates for them. He compares an actual flight time with the estimated flight time and considers the estimate to be too large, acceptable, or too small, depending on the following table of acceptable error margins:

Estimated Flight Time in Minutes	Acceptable Error Margin in Minutes
0–29	1
30–59	2
60–89	3
90–119	4
120–179	6
180–239	8
240–359	13
360 or more	17

For example, if an estimated flight time is 106 minutes, the acceptable error margin is 4 minutes. Thus, the estimated flight time is too large if the actual flight time is less than 102 minutes, or the estimated flight time is too small if the actual flight time is greater than 110 minutes; otherwise, the estimate is acceptable. Write a function that uses a `switch` statement to determine the acceptable error for a given estimated flight time, according to this table. Use your function in a program that reads an estimated flight time and an actual flight time, and then determines whether the estimated time is too large, acceptable, or too small. If the estimated flight time is too large or too small, the program should also print the amount of the overestimate or underestimate.

16. Write a function `ConvertLength()` that receives a real value and two strings

inUnits and outUnits, then converts the value given in inUnits to the equivalent metric value in outUnits and displays this value. The function should carry out the following conversions:

inUnits	outUnits	
I	c	(inches to centimeters; 1 in = 2.54001 cm)
F	c	(feet to centimeters; 1 ft = 30.4801 cm)
F	m	(feet to meters; 1 ft = 0.304801 m)
Y	m	(yards to meters; 1 yd = 0.914402 m)
M	k	(miles to kilometers; 1 mi = 1.60935 km)

Also, write a driver program to test your function. What happens if you enter units other than those listed?

17. Proceed as in problem 16, but write a function ConvertWeight() that carries out the following conversions:

inUnits	outUnits	
O	g	(ounces to grams; 1 oz = 28.349527 g)
P	k	(pounds to kilograms; 1 lb = 0.453592 kg)

18. Proceed as in problem 16, but write a function ConvertVolume() that carries out the following conversions:

inUnits	outUnits	
P	l	(pints to liters; 1 pt = 0.473167 L)
Q	l	(quarts to liters; 1 qt = 0.94633 L)
G	l	(gallons to liters; 1 gal = 3.78541 L)

19. Write a menu-driven program to test the three functions ConvertLength(), ConvertWeight(), and ConvertVolume() of problems 16–18. It should allow the user to select one of three options according to whether lengths, weights, or volumes are to be converted, read the value to be converted and the units, and then call the appropriate function to carry out the conversion.

PART OF THE PICTURE: Boolean Logic and Digital Design

20. A *binary full-adder* has three inputs: the two bits a and b being added, and a "carry-in" bit cIn (representing the carry bit that results from adding the bits to the right of a and b in two binary numbers). It can be constructed from two binary half-adders and an OR gate:

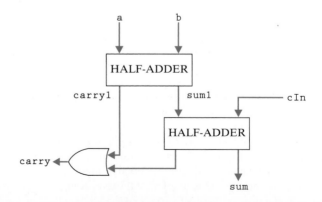

(a) Write boolean expressions for

    (i) `sum1` and `carry1` in terms of `a` and `b`

    (ii) `sum` and `carry` in terms of `cIn`, `sum1`, and `carry1`

(b) Write a program to implement this binary full-adder, and use it to verify the results shown in the following table:

a	b	cIn	sum	carry
0	0	0	0	0
0	0	1	1	0
0	1	0	1	0
0	1	1	0	1
1	0	0	1	0
1	0	1	0	1
1	1	0	0	1
1	1	1	1	1

21.   An *adder* to calculate binary sums of two-bit numbers

```
      a2  a1
  +   b2  b1
cOut  s2  s1
```

where `s1` and `s2` are the sum bits and `cOut` is the carry-out bit, can be constructed from a binary half-adder and a binary full-adder:

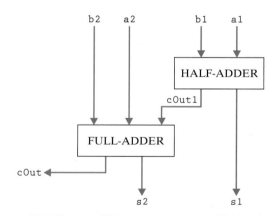

(a) Write logical expressions for

    (i) `s1` and `cOut1` in terms of `a1` and `b1`

    (ii) `s2` and `cOut` in terms of `a2`, `b2`, and `cOut1`

(b) Write a program to implement this adder and use it to demonstrate that $00 + 00 = 000$, $01 + 00 = 001$, $01 + 01 = 010$, $10 + 01 = 011$, $10 + 10 = 100$, $11 + 10 = 101$, and $11 + 11 = 110$.

Chapter 6

REPETITION

Progress might be a circle, rather than a straight line.

EBERHARD ZEIDLER

But what has been said once can always be repeated.

ZENO OF ELEA

It's deja vu all over again.

YOGI BERRA

A rose is a rose is a rose.

GERTRUDE STEIN

My new computer game runs circles around me and makes my head spin. But once my head gets spinning fast enough, I start doing better.

V. OREHCK III (fictitious)

Chapter Contents

6.1   Introductory Example: The Punishment of Gauss

6.2   Repetition: The `for` Loop Revisited

6.3   Repetition: The `while` Loop

6.4   Repetition: The `do` Loop

6.5   Input Loops

6.6   Choosing the Right Loop

6.7   Example: Computing Depreciation

       PART OF THE PICTURE: Introduction to Algorithm Analysis

As we saw in chapter 3, the three control behaviors used in writing functions are **sequence, selection,** and **repetition.** In chapter 5 we examined selection in detail, and in this chapter we take a closer look at the third control structure, repetition.

6.1 INTRODUCTORY EXAMPLE: THE PUNISHMENT OF GAUSS

Although sequence and selection are powerful control mechanisms, they are by themselves not powerful enough to solve all computing problems. In this section, we consider a problem that can be solved using repetition and review the most familiar C++ repetition statement: the `for` loop.

THE SUMMATION PROBLEM

Our problem begins with an incident in the life of Carl Friedrich Gauss, one of the greatest mathematicians of all time. When Gauss was young, he attended a school in Brunswick, Germany, and one day when the students were being particularly mischievous, the teacher asked them to sum the integers from 1 to 100, expecting that this would keep them busy for awhile. However, Gauss produced the correct answer (5050) almost immediately, using a particularly clever approach described at the end of this chapter.

Although calculating the sum of the integers from 1 to 100 is not a particularly important computation, a generalization of this problem has many applications. The problem is to construct a function that, given a positive integer n, calculates and returns the sum of the integers from 1 to n:

$$1 + 2 + \cdots + n$$

OBJECT-CENTERED DESIGN

Behavior. The function should receive the value n from its caller. It should compute the sum $1 + \cdots + n$ and return this value to its caller.

Objects. From the statement of the problem and the function's behavior, we see two data objects that are needed:

Description	Kind	Type	Movement	Name
The limit value, n	varying	integer	received	n
$1 + 2 + \cdots + n$	varying	integer	returned	none

This gives the following specification

    Receive: a real value n
    Return: $1 + 2 + \cdots + n$

from which we can build the following stub for the function:

```
integer Sum(integer n)
{
}
```

Operations.   Because most of us do not have Gauss' ability, we will solve this problem using the approach probably used by his classmates (and intended by his teacher). We simply begin adding consecutive integers, keeping a running total as we proceed:

$$
\begin{array}{rl}
0 & \leftarrow \text{running total} \\
\underline{+1} & \leftarrow \text{count} \\
1 & \leftarrow \text{running total} \\
\underline{+2} & \leftarrow \text{count} \\
3 & \leftarrow \text{running total} \\
\underline{+3} & \leftarrow \text{count} \\
6 & \leftarrow \text{running total} \\
\underline{+4} & \leftarrow \text{count} \\
10 & \leftarrow \text{running total} \\
\underline{+5} & \leftarrow \text{count} \\
15 & \leftarrow \text{running total} \\
\vdots &
\end{array}
$$

This procedure consists of the following steps:

1.   Initialize a *running total* to 0.

2.   Initialize *count* to 1.

3.   Loop through the following steps:

    a.   Add *count* to the *running total;*
    b.   Add 1 to *count.*

The steps in the loop must be repeated as long as the value of *count* is less than or equal to *n*. Thus, if *n* has the value 100, the loop must be repeated so long as the value of *count* is less than or equal to 100:

$$
\begin{array}{rl}
\vdots & \\
4950 & \leftarrow \text{running total} \\
\underline{+\ \ 100} & \leftarrow \text{count} \\
5050 & \leftarrow \text{running total}
\end{array}
$$

We see that this procedure uses two new data objects: the *running total* and the *counter,* and that when it is finished, the running total is the value to be returned by the function. We can thus amend our list of data objects as follows:

Description	Kind	Type	Movement	Name
The limit value, *n*	varying	integer	received	*n*
$1 + 2 + \cdots + n$	varying	integer	returned	*runningTotal*
A counter	varying	integer	none	*count*

The preceding description of how the problem can be solved suggests that the following operations are needed:

  i.   Receive an integer (*n*)

  ii.   Initialize an integer (*runningTotal* to 0, *count* to 1)

  iii. Add two integers (*count* and *runningTotal*) and store the result

  iv.   Repeat the preceding step for each value of *count* in the range 1 through *n*

  v.   Return an integer (*runningTotal*)

All of these can be implemented using predefined C++ operations and functions.

Algorithm.   We organize these operations in the following algorithm:

Algorithm for the Summation Problem

  1. Initialize *runningTotal* to 0.

  2. For each value of *count* in the range 1 through *n*:
           Add *count* to *runningTotal.*

  3. Return *runningTotal* .

Coding and Testing.   Note that the two data objects *runningTotal* and *count* are not received by the function, but they are required to solve the problem. It is important to remember that such objects should be declared as *local variables within the definition of the function.* By contrast, *n* must be *received* from the caller, and so it is declared as a *parameter* of the function. Figure 6.1 gives a definition of Sum(). In the next section, we will review the for statement used to implement the loop in Sum() .

FIGURE 6.1   FUNCTION Sum() — for LOOP VERSION.

```
/* Sum(n) computes the sum of the integers from 1 to n.
 *
 * Receive:      n, an integer
 * Precondition: n > 0
 * Return:       the sum 1 + 2 + ... + n
 ************************************************************/

int Sum (int n)
{
   assert (n > 0);

   int runningTotal = 0;

   for (int count = 1; count <= n; count++)
      runningTotal += count;

   return runningTotal;
}
```

The program in Figure 6.2 uses this function to solve specific summation problems. The prototype of Sum() is placed before main() and its definition follows main(). Alternatively, Sum() could be stored in a library (e.g., MyMath) so that other programs needing to compute sums can use it. In this case we would store the definition of Sum() in the implementation file and the prototype of Sum() in

the header file, and use a directive such as #include "MyMath.h" (instead of
including the prototype of Sum() and its definition in the source program.)

FIGURE 6.2   DRIVER PROGRAM FOR FUNCTION **Sum()**.

```
/* summation2.cpp is a driver program to test function Sum().
 *
 *    Input:    an integer n
 *    Output:   the sum of the integers from 1 through n
 ******************************************************************/

#include <iostream.h>          // cout, cin, <<, >>
#include <assert.h>            // assert

int Sum(int n);               // prototype for Sum()

int main()
{
  cout << "This program computes the sum of the integers from "
          "1 through n.\n";

  cout << "Enter a value for n: ";
  int n;
  cin >> n;

  cout << "--> 1 + ... + " << n << " = " << Sum(n) << endl;

}

/*** Insert the definition of function Sum()
     from Figure 6.1 here. ***/
```

Sample runs:

```
This program computes the sum of the integers from 1 through n.
Enter a value for n: 5
--> 1 + ... + 5 = 15
```

```
This program computes the sum of the integers from 1 through n.
Enter a value for n: 100
--> 1 + ... + 100 = 5050
```

6.2 REPETITION: THE for LOOP REVISITED

Counting loops, or **counter-controlled loops,** are loops in which a set of statements
is executed once for each value in a specified range:

> for each value of a *counter _variable* in a specified range:
>   *statement*

For example, our solution to the summation problem uses a counting loop to execute the statement

```
runningTotal += count;
```

once for each value of `count` in the range 1 through `n`.

Because counting loops are used so often, nearly all programming languages provide a special statement to implement them. In C++ this is the **for statement** or **for loop.** We saw the four components of a counting `for` loop in Section 3.4:

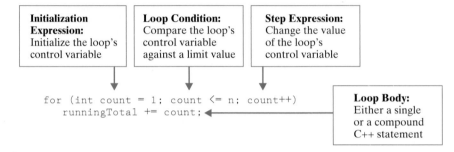

We have also seen that a trace table is a good tool to trace the action of a loop (especially in debugging). For example, in the first sample run of Figure 6.1 where the value 5 is entered for `n`, the loop counts through the values 1 through 5, so that the body of the `for` loop is executed five times. The following table shows the value of the various data objects as the function `Sum()` executes:

count	n	count <= n	Action	runningTotal
1	5	true	Execute loop body	1
2	5	true	Execute loop body	3
3	5	true	Execute loop body	6
4	5	true	Execute loop body	10
5	5	true	Execute loop body	15
6	5	false	Terminate repetition	15

A similar trace table for the second sample run where `n` has the value 100 would show that the loop counts through the values 1 through 100, so that the loop body is executed 100 times.

There are two forms of the `for` statement that are commonly used to implement counting loops: an ascending form, in which the loop control variable is incremented,

```
for (int control_variable = initial_value;
         control_variable <= limit_value;
         increment_expression)
    statement
```

and a descending form, in which the loop control variable is decremented:

```
for (int control_variable = initial_value;
         control_variable >= limit_value;
         decrement_expression)
    statement
```

The first form counts through an *ascending range,* and the second counts through a *descending range.*

The Ascending Form. To illustrate the first form, consider the following for statement:

```
for (int number = 1; number <= 10; number++)
    cout << number << '\t' << number * number << endl;
```

Here, number is the control variable, the initial value is 1, the limit value is 10, and the increment expression is number++. This for loop will execute the statement

```
cout << number << '\t' << number * number << endl;
```

once for each value of number in the ascending range 1 through 10. On the first pass through the loop, number will have the value 1; on the second pass it will have the value 2; and so on until the final pass when number will have the value 10. Thus, the output produced will be

```
1    1
2    4
3    9
4    16
5    25
6    36
7    49
8    64
9    81
10   100
```

The ascending form executes as shown in the following diagram:

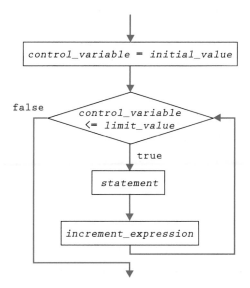

By using an appropriate increment expression, a for statement can be used to step through a range of values in increments of size other than 1. For example, the for statement

```
for (int number = 0; number <= 100; number += 20)
    cout << number << '\t' << number * number << endl;
```

uses the expression

```
number += 20
```

to count upwards in increments of 20, producing the output

```
0       0
20      400
40      1600
60      3600
80      6400
100     10000
```

The Descending Form. The second form of a `for` loop performs a decrement operation following each execution of the loop body. For example, the following loop

```
for (int number = 10; number > 5; number--)
    cout << number << '\t' << number * number << endl;
```

will count downward from 10 to 6, producing the output:

```
10      100
9       81
8       64
7       49
6       36
```

The descending form executes as shown in the following diagram:

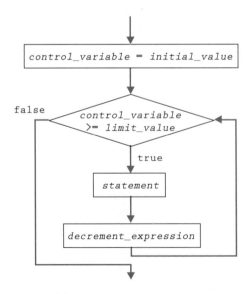

Note that whereas the ascending form continues the repetition as long as the control variable is less than or equal to the limit value, the descending form is counting downwards, and so must continue the repetition as long as the control variable is *greater than or equal to* the limit value.

NESTED LOOPS: DISPLAYING A MULTIPLICATION TABLE

The statement that appears within a for statement may itself be a for statement; that is, one for loop may be *nested within* another for loop. As an example, Figure 6.3 presents a program that displays a multiplication table by calculating and displaying products of the form x * y for each x in the range 1 through lastX and each y in the range 1 through lastY (where lastX and lastY are arbitrary integers). The multiplication table is generated by using nested for statements:

```
for (int x = 1; x <= lastX; x++)
   for (int y = 1; y <= lastY; y++)
   {
      product = x * y;
      cout << setw(2) << x << " * "
           << setw(2) << y << " = "
           << setw(3) << product << endl;
   }
```

The loop that has x as its control variable is called the **outer loop,** and the loop that has y as its control variable is called the **inner loop.**

FIGURE 6.3   PRINTING A MULTIPLICATION TABLE.

```
/* multiply3.cpp calculates and displays a multiplication table.
 *
 * Input:    lastX and lastY, the largest numbers to be multiplied
 * Output:   a list of products: 1*1 ... lastX * lastY
 *************************************************************/

#include <iostream.h>              // cout, cin, <<, >>, right
#include <iomanip.h>               // setw()

int main()
{
   cout << "This program constructs a multiplication table\n"
           "for the values 1*1 through lastX*lastY.\n";

   int lastX,          // the largest numbers being multiplied
       lastY,
       product;        // the product of the two numbers

   cout << "\nEnter two integer limit values (lastX and lastY): ";
   cin >> lastX >> lastY;
```

```
for (int x = 1; x <= lastX; x++)
   for (int y = 1; y <= lastY; y++)
   {
       product = x * y;
       cout << right
               << setw(2) << x << " * "
               << setw(2) << y << " = "
               << setw(3) << product << endl;
   }
}
```

Sample run:

```
This program constructs a multiplication table
for the values 1*1 through lastX*lastY.

Enter two integer limit values (lastX and lastY): 3 4
  1 *  1 =    1
  1 *  2 =    2
  1 *  3 =    3
  1 *  4 =    4
  2 *  1 =    2
  2 *  2 =    4
  2 *  3 =    6
  2 *  4 =    8
  3 *  1 =    3
  3 *  2 =    6
  3 *  3 =    9
  3 *  4 =   12
```

In the sample run, `lastX` is given the value 3 and `lastY` the value 4. When control reaches the outer loop, its control variable `x` is assigned its initial value 1. The statement it controls (the inner loop) is then executed, which counts through the values 1 through 4 for `y` and thus calculates and displays the first four products: 1 * 1, 1 * 2, 1 * 3, and 1 * 4. Control then passes from the inner loop to the increment expression of the outer loop, where the value of `x` is incremented to 2. The statement it controls (the inner loop) is then executed again. It again counts through the values 1 through 4 for `y`, but since the value of `x` is now 2, this pass calculates and displays the next four products: 2 * 1, 2 * 2, 2 * 3, and 2 * 4. The control variable `x` is then incremented to 3, so that when the inner loop is executed again, the last four products, 3 * 1, 3 * 2, 3 * 3, and 3 * 4, are produced. `x` is then incremented again (to 4), making the loop condition `x <= lastX` false, so that repetition stops. The compound statement

```
{
    product = x * y;
    cout << setw(2) << x << " * "
            << setw(2) << y << " = "
            << setw(3) << product << endl;
}
```

is executed a total of 12 times, because the inner loop is executed 4 times for each of the 3 executions of the outer loop.

WORDS OF WARNING

A for loop must be constructed carefully to ensure that its initialization expression, loop condition, and increment expression will eventually cause the loop condition to become false. In particular:

> *If the body of a counting loop alters the values of any variables involved in the loop condition, then the number of repetitions may be changed.*

It is generally considered poor programming practice to alter the value of any variables in the loop condition within the body of a counting loop, because this can produce unexpected results. For example, execution of

```
int limit = 1;

for (int i = 0; i <= limit ; i++)
{
   cout << i << endl;
   limit++;
}
```

produces an infinite sequence of integers[1]

```
0
1
2
3
.
.
.
```

because on each pass through the loop, the expression limit++ increments limit by 1 before i++ increments i. As a result, the loop condition i <= limit is always true.

Similarly, the loop

```
for (int i = 0; i <= limit; i++)
{
   cout << i << '\n';
   i--;
}
```

will output infinitely many zeros,

```
0
0
0
.
.
.
```

---

[1] In some environments, execution will terminate when i is MAXINT and limit is MAXINT + 1 = MININT.

because the expression `i--` in the body of the loop decrements `i` by 1 before the step expression `i++` increments it by 1. As a result, `i` is always 0 when the loop condition is tested.

THE FOREVER LOOP

The primary use of `for` loops is to implement counting loops where the number of repetitions is known (or can be computed) in advance. For example, in computing the sum of the integers from 1 to n, we know that the loop's body must be executed exactly n times. However, there are many problems in which the number of repetitions cannot be determined in advance. For these situations, most modern programming languages provide a general loop statement that provides for *indefinite repetition*. This loop is often implemented by a statement that is different from the statements used for other loops.[2]

C++, however, does not provide a separate statement for indefinite loops, but instead allows the programmer to construct such a loop from other loops. One way this can be done is by removing the initialization expression, the loop condition, and the step expression from a for loop, as illustrated in the following general form:[3]

The Forever Loop

Form

```
for ( ; ; )          // forever loop
    statement
```

where:

`for` is a C++ keyword; and

statement is a simple or a compound statement (but is usually compound).

Behavior

The specified *statement* is executed infinitely many times, unless it contains a `break` or `return` statement (usually an `if-break` or `if-return` combination).

If a `break` statement is encountered, execution of the loop will terminate and will continue with the statement following the loop.

If a `return` statement is encountered, the loop and the function containing it are terminated and control returns to the calling function.

---

[2] *Ada* and *Turing* have the `loop` statement, *Modula-2* and *Modula-3* the `LOOP` statement, and *Fortran 90* the `DO` loop.

[3] Alternatively, we can achieve the same effect with either of these forms:

```
while (true) statement   or   do statement while (true);
```

Because such a loop contains no loop condition specifying the condition under which repetition terminates, it is an **indefinite loop** that executes the statements in its body without stopping. We will call such a loop a **forever loop.**

To illustrate, consider the following forever loop:

```
for ( ; ; )                        // forever loop
   cout << "Help ! I'm caught in a loop!\n";
```

This statement will produce the output

```
Help ! I'm caught in a loop!
Help ! I'm caught in a loop!
Help ! I'm caught in a loop!
Help ! I'm caught in a loop!

        .
        .
        .
```

an unlimited number of times, unless the user *interrupts* execution (usually by pressing the Control and C keys).

To avoid this infinite looping behavior, the body of a forever loop is usually a compound statement, containing

1.   Those statements that must be repeatedly executed in order to solve the problem; and

2.   A statement that will *terminate* execution of the loop when some condition is satisfied.

The terminating statement is usually an **if-break combination**—an if statement containing a break statement,

```
if (condition) break;
```

where *condition* is a boolean expression. Execution of a break statement within a loop terminates execution of the loop and transfers control to the statement following the loop.

Note that unlike other loops (counting loops and the loops considered in the next sections), repetition continues as long as the condition in the if-break combination is *false*—it terminates when the condition becomes true. To distinguish this condition from the loop conditions of the other loops we will call it a **termination condition** instead of a *loop condition*.

Most forever loops, therefore, have the following form:

```
for (;;)                                   // loop:
{
   statement_list₁
   if (termination_condition) break;
   statement_list₂
}                                          // end loop
```

where either *statement_list₁* or *statement_list₂* can be empty.

To illustrate forever loops, consider the following utility function GetMenu-Choice() that receives a menu and the characters that denote the first and last choices on the menu. (A precondition of this function is that the menu choices are denoted by consecutive characters such as A, B, C, D.) It repeatedly displays the menu and reads the user's choice until that choice is in the range of valid choices:

```
char GetMenuChoice(string MENU, char firstChoice, char lastChoice)
{
   char choice;                              // what the user enters

   for (;;)                                  // loop:
   {
      cout << MENU;                          //    statement_list₁
      cin >> choice;

                                             //    if-break combination
      if ((choice >= firstChoice) && (choice <= lastChoice))
         break;
                                             //    statement_list₂
      cerr << "\nI'm sorry, but " << choice
           << " is not a valid menu choice.\n";
   }                                         // end loop

   return choice;
}
```

The effect here is to "trap" the user inside the forever loop until a valid menu choice is entered. For each invalid menu choice, the termination condition is false, so the break statement is bypassed and the output statement displays an error message. Control then returns to the beginning of the loop for the next repetition and gives the user another chance. When a valid choice is entered, the termination condition becomes true, so the break statement is executed and transfers control to the return statement following the loop.

Returning From A Loop. In functions like GetMenuChoice() where the statement following a forever loop is a return statement, it is slightly more efficient to replace the break statement with a return statement:

```
char GetMenuChoice(string MENU, char firstChoice, char lastChoice)
{
   char choice;                              // what the user enters

   for (;;)                                  // loop:
   {
      cout << MENU;                          //    statement_list₁
      cin >> choice;

                                             //    if-return combination
      if ((choice >= firstChoice) && (choice <= lastChoice))
         return choice;
                                             //    statement_list₂
      cerr << "\nI'm sorry, but " << choice
           << " is not a valid menu choice.\n";
   }                                         // end loop
}
```

As before, if the user enters an invalid choice, an error message is displayed and the body of the loop is repeated. However, when the user enters a valid choice, the termination condition is true, and so the `return` statement is selected. Since execution of a `return` statement causes the function to terminate, it also terminates the loop in the function.

6.3 REPETITION: THE while LOOP

A loop of the form

> loop
>   if (*termination_condition*) exit the loop.
>   other statements
> end loop

in which the termination test occurs before the loop's statements are executed is called a **pretest** or **test-at-the-top** loop. Such loops can be implemented in C++ using a forever loop:

```
for (;;)                          // loop:
{
   if (termination_condition) break;
   statement_list₂
}                                 // end loop
```

However, C++ provides another statement with a simpler syntax for these pretest loops—the **while statement** or **while loop.** We will use a `while` loop to solve the following problem.

EXAMPLE: FOLLOW THE BOUNCING BALL

Suppose that when a ball is dropped, it bounces from the pavement to a height one-half of its previous height. We want to write a program that will simulate the behavior of the ball when it is dropped from a given height. It should display the number of each bounce and the height of that bounce, repeating this until the height of the ball is very small (e.g., less than 1 millimeter).

OBJECT-CENTERED DESIGN

Behavior.   The program should first obtain the initial height. It should then display 1 and the height of the first rebound, display 2 and the height of the second rebound, and so on, until the height of the rebound is less than some very small number.

Objects.   Given this description of the problem, we can identify the following data objects:

Object	Kind of Value	Type of Object	Name of Object
The current height	Variable	Real	*height*
The bounce number	Variable	Integer	*bounce*
A very small number	Constant	Real	*SMALL_NUMBER*

This list allows us to specify the problem as follows:

Input: The initial *height* of a ball

Output: For each rebound of the ball:
the number of the rebound and
the height of that rebound,
assuming that the height of each rebound is one-half the previous
height

Operations.   The operations that must be performed on these objects are:

i.   Input a real value (the original *height*)

ii.   Initialize *bounce* to zero

iii.   Divide the *height* by 2 (to compute the rebound height)

iv.   Increment *bounce*

v.   Display the current *bounce* number and *height*

vi.   Repeat operations iii–v as long as *height* is ⩾ SMALL_NUMBER

Algorithm.   Each of these operations is available through the operators and statements of C++. However, for the loop in vi we must ask where the termination condition should be placed. It should be clear that if *height* is initially less than *SMALL_NUMBER*, then none of the operations in iii–v should be performed. This suggests that we use a pretest loop as in the following algorithm:

Algorithm for Bouncing Ball Problem

1. Initialize *bounce* to 0.

2. Prompt for and read a value for *height*.

3. Display original *height* value with appropriate label.

4. Loop:

a. If *height* < *SMALL_NUMBER*, terminate the repetition.

b. Replace *height* with *height* divided by 2.

c. Add 1 to *bounce*.

d. Display *bounce* and *height*.

End Loop

Coding.   We could code this algorithm using a pretest form of a forever loop, but as we noted earlier, the C++ `while` loop has a simpler syntax. The program in Figure 6.4 implements this algorithm, using a `while` loop to implement the loop in step 4.

FIGURE 6.4   THE BOUNCING BALL.

```
/* bouncingball4.cpp calculates and displays the rebound heights
 * of a dropped ball.
 *
 *
 * Input:  a real height from which a ball is dropped.
 * Output: for each rebound of the ball from the pavement below:
 *            the number of the rebound and
 *            the height of that rebound
 *         assuming that the height of each rebound
 *         is one-half the previous height
 ************************************************************************/
```

```
#include <iostream.h>                    // <<, >>, cout, cin

int main()
{
    const double SMALL_NUMBER = 1.0e-3;     // 1 millimeter

    cout << "This program computes the number and height\n"
         << "of the rebounds of a dropped ball.\n";

    int bounce = 0;

    cout << "\nEnter the starting height (in meters): ";
    double height;
    cin >> height;

    cout << "\nStarting height: " << height << " meters\n";

    while (height >= SMALL_NUMBER)
    {
        height /= 2.0;
        bounce++;
        cout << "Rebound # " << bounce << ": "
             << height << " meters" << endl;
    }
}
```

Sample run:

```
This program computes the number and height
of the rebounds of a dropped ball.

Enter the starting height (in meters): 15

Starting height: 15 meters
Rebound # 1: 7.5 meters
Rebound # 2: 3.75 meters
Rebound # 3: 1.875 meters
Rebound # 4: 0.9375 meters
Rebound # 5: 0.46875 meters
Rebound # 6: 0.234375 meters
Rebound # 7: 0.117188 meters
Rebound # 8: 0.0585938 meters
Rebound # 9: 0.0292969 meters
Rebound # 10: 0.0146484 meters
Rebound # 11: 0.00732422 meters
Rebound # 12: 0.00366211 meters
Rebound # 13: 0.00183105 meters
Rebound # 14: 0.000915527 meters
```

THE while STATEMENT

While loops are implemented in C++ using a **while statement** of the following form.

THE while STATEMENT

Form

```
while (loop_condition)
    statement
```

where:

while is a C++ keyword;

`loop_condition` is a boolean expression; and

`statement` is a simple or compound statement.

Behavior

When execution reaches a while statement:

1. `loop_condition` is evaluated.

2. If `loop_condition` is true:

   a. The specified `statement`, called the **body** of the loop, is executed.

   b. Control returns to step 1.

   Otherwise

   Control is transferred to the statement following the while statement.

Like a for loop, a while loop has a loop condition that controls repetition. The placement of this loop condition before the body of the loop is significant because it means that a while loop is a pretest loop so that when it is executed, this condition is evaluated *before* the body of the loop is executed. This can be pictured as follows:

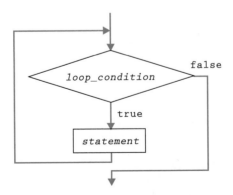

As this diagram indicates, execution of the specified statement is repeated as long as the loop condition remains true and terminates when it becomes false. For example, the following table provides a partial trace of the repetitions of the while loop in Figure 6.4, showing the values of the relevant data objects:

height	bounce	height >= SMALL_NUMBER	Action
15.0	0	true	Execute loop body
7.5	1	true	Execute loop body
3.75	2	true	Execute loop body
1.875	3	true	Execute loop body
.	.	.	.
.	.	.	.
.	.	.	.
0.00183105	13	true	Execute loop body
0.000915527	14	false	Terminate repetition

The preceding diagram indicates that the loop condition is evaluated before the loop body is executed, and thus if this condition is initially false, the body of the loop will not be executed. Stated differently, the body of a pretest loop will be executed *zero or more times,* and so these loops are said to exhibit **zero-trip behavior.** Thus, in the program in Figure 6.4, if the value entered for height is less than SMALL_NUMBER, the statements in the while loop will not be executed, because the condition height >= SMALL_NUMBER that controls the repetition will be false the first time it is evaluated. As we shall see, it is this zero-trip behavior that distinguishes the while loop from other noncounting C++ loops. It is important to keep this characteristic in mind when designing a solution to a problem, because it influences the decision of which loop to use.

LOOP CONDITIONS VS. TERMINATION CONDITIONS

A forever loop continues the repetition when its condition is false and terminates the repetition when that condition is true. A while loop behaves in the opposite manner, continuing the repetition as long as its condition is true and terminating the repetition when its condition is false. Put differently, the condition controlling a while loop must always be the *negation* of the condition controlling an equivalent forever loop.

```
for (;;)                        while (!condition)
{                               {
    if (condition) break;           statements
    statements                  }
}
```

To illustrate, the while loop in the bouncing-ball program in Figure 6.4 continues the repetition so long as height is greater than or equal to SMALL_NUMBER:

```
while (height >= SMALL_NUMBER)
{
    height /= 2.0;
    bounce++;
    cout << "Rebound # " << bounce << ": "
         << height << " meters" << endl;
}
```

The equivalent forever loop version would control the repetition by terminating when height is less than SMALL_NUMBER:

```
for (;;)
{
    if (height < SMALL_NUMBER) break;

    height /= 2.0;
    bounce++;
    cout << "Rebound # " << bounce << ": "
         << height << " meters" << endl;
}
```

WORDS OF WARNING

As with other loops, it is important to ensure that the body of a while loop will eventually cause its loop condition to become false, since otherwise an *infinite loop* will result. To illustrate, consider the while loop:

```
counter = 1;
while (counter < 100)
{
    cout << counter << endl;
    counter--;
}
```

Here, counter is initially less than 100, and since counter-- decrements counter by 1, the value of counter will always be less than 100.[4] Thus, the condition counter < 100 will always be true, resulting in an infinite loop, producing the output:

```
  1
  0
 -1
 -2
 -3
  .
  .
  .
```

Another common mistake is illustrated by the following code segment:

```
counter = 1;
while (counter < 100)
    cout << counter << endl;
    counter++;
```

This code segment will display the value 1 infinitely many times:

---

[4] In some environments, repetition will terminate when counter becomes MININT because the value of counter-- will then be MAXINT.

```
1
1
1
1
1
.
.
.
```

Errors of this kind can be fiendishly difficult to find, because the indentation of the statements makes them appear correct. The problem here is that the loop body is a single statement. Thus, in the absence of curly braces, only the statement

```
cout << counter << endl;
```

is in the body of the loop. To include the statement

```
counter++;
```

in the loop body, both statements must be enclosed within curly braces:

```
counter = 1;
while (counter < 100)
{
   cout << counter << endl;
   counter++;
}
```

6.4 REPETITION: THE do LOOP

In the last section, we saw that the `while` statement provides a loop that evaluates its loop condition prior to executing the statement it controls. We also saw that such pretest loops are useful in solving problems where zero-trip behavior is required.

There are some repetition problems, however, for which zero-trip behavior is not appropriate. For such problems, many languages provide a *posttest loop,* and in this section, we describe C++'s implementation of such loops.

EXAMPLE: HOW MANY DIGITS?

When we look at an integer, whether it be 45 or 2147483647, it is relatively easy to determine the number of digits in the integer simply by scanning through the number and counting the digits. However, a computer program cannot simply "scan and count" the number of digits in a number. The problem is to write a function that, given an integer value, will count the digits in that value.

OBJECT-CENTERED DESIGN

Behavior. The function should receive an integer value from its caller. It should count the digits in that integer and then return the count to its caller.

Specification. From the behavioral description, we can identify the following data objects in this problem:

Object	Kind	Type	Name
The integer value	varying	integer	*intValue*
The number of digits in the integer value	varying	integer	*numDigits*

This suggests the following specification for a function that solves this problem,

Receive: *intValue,* an integer value

Return: *numDigits,* the number of digits in *intValue*

and allows us to build a stub for the function, which we call `DigitsIn()`:

```
int DigitsIn(int intValue)
{
}
```

Operations. One way to solve this problem is to count how many times *intValue* must be divided by 10 to produce 0. For example, 45 has two digits, and two integer divisions by 10 are required to reach 0:

Repetition	Operation	*intValue*	*numDigits*	Action
0	None	45	0	Enter loop
1	45/10	4	1	Repeat execution
2	4/10	0	2	Terminate execution

Similarly, 5 has one digit, and one division by 10 gives 0:

Repetition	Operation	*intValue*	*numDigits*	Action
0	None	5	0	Enter loop
1	5/10	0	1	Terminate execution

In this approach, the operations that `DigitsIn()` must perform are

  i.   Integer division (*intValue* by 10)
  ii. Integer addition (Add 1 to *numDigits*)
  iii. Repetition of operations i and ii as long as *intValue* is not 0

Each of these operations is provided by a C++ operator or statement.
  There are two key observations in this solution:

  1. Since every number has at least one digit, we must perform operations i and ii *at least once.*
  2. We must *repeat* operations i and ii as long as *intValue* is not 0.

The second observation implies the need for a loop, but the first observation suggests that the loop should not exhibit zero-trip behavior. Putting the loop condition at the "bottom" of the loop, as in the following algorithm, will ensure this.

Algorithm to Count Digits

1. Initialize *numDigits* to 0.
2. Loop:
   a. Increment *numDigits.*
   b. Divide *intValue* by 10, storing the result in *intValue.*
   c. If *intValue* is 0, terminate the repetition.
   End Loop.
3. Return *numDigits.*

Coding. As we have seen before, loops like the one in this algorithm can be implemented using a forever loop:

```
for (;;)
{
   numDigits++;
   intValue /= 10;
   if (intValue == 0) break;
}
```

However, C++ provides a statement with a simpler syntax for such test-at-the-bottom loops. This is the do statement, and the function in Figure 6.5 illustrates its use:

FIGURE 6.5   FUNCTION DigitsIn().

```
/* DigitsIn counts the digits in an integer value.
 *
 * Receive:   intValue, an integer value
 * Return:    numDigits, the number of digits in intValue
 ************************************************************/

int DigitsIn(int intValue)
{
   int numDigits = 0;

   do
   {
      numDigits++;
      intValue /= 10;
   }
   while (intValue != 0);

   return numDigits;
}
```

Testing. A simple driver program to test function `DigitsIn()` is given in Figure 6.6.

FIGURE 6.6   DRIVER PROGRAM FOR FUNCTION `DigitsIn()`.

```
/* digits 6.cpp is a driver program to test function DigitsIn.
 *
 *  Input:  an integer value
 *  Output: the number of digits in that value
 ************************************************************/

#include <iostream.h>                 // cout, cin, , <<, >>

int DigitsIn(int intValue);

int main()
{
  int theValue;

  cout << "Enter an integer value: ";
  cin >> theValue;

  cout << theValue << " contains "
       << DigitsIn(theValue) << " digit(s).\n";
}

/*** Put definition of function DigitsIn() from Figure 6.5 here. ***/
```

Sample runs:

```
Please enter an integer value: 5
5 contains 1 digit(s).


Please enter an integer value: 12
12 contains 2 digit(s).


Please enter an integer value: 12345678
12345678 contains 8 digit(s).
```

The following table traces execution of the loop in `DigitsIn()` during the last sample run in Figure 6.6:

Repetition	intValue	numDigits	intVal != 0	Action
0	12345678	0	—	Enter loop
1	1234567	1	true	Execute loop body
2	123456	2	true	Execute loop body
3	12345	3	true	Execute loop body
4	1234	4	true	Execute loop body
5	123	5	true	Execute loop body
6	12	6	true	Execute loop body
7	1	7	true	Execute loop body
8	0	8	false	Terminate repetition

DigitsIn() returns the value of numDigits (8) after execution leaves the loop.

A POSTTEST LOOP

The function in Figure 6.5 uses a new C++ repetition statement, the **do statement,** which has the following form:

The do Statement

Form

```
do
    statement
while (loop_condition);
```

where:

do and while are C++ keywords;

loop_condition is a boolean expression;

statement is a simple or compound statement; and

a semicolon must follow the expression at the end of the statement.

Behavior

When execution reaches a do loop:

(1) *statement* is executed.

(2) *loop_condition* is evaluated.

(3) If *loop_condition* is true, then

    Control returns to step (1).

Otherwise

    Control passes to the first statement following the do loop.

Note that the loop condition in a do statement appears *after* the body of the loop, indicating that it is evaluated at the end, or "bottom," of the loop. The do loop is thus a **posttest** or **test-at-the-bottom loop,** in which execution flows as pictured in the following diagram:

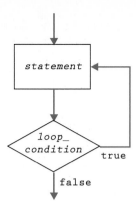

The fact that the loop condition is evaluated after the body of the loop has been executed guarantees that the body of the loop will be executed at least once. Thus, in contrast to the zero-trip behavior of pretest loops, posttest loops are said to exhibit **one-trip behavior.**

LOOP CONDITIONS VS. TERMINATION CONDITIONS

A do loop uses a loop condition that continues the repetition so long as the condition is true, and terminates the repetition when the condition becomes false. As with the while loop, the loop condition is the negation of the termination condition used in an equivalent forever loop.

To illustrate, the do loop in the `DigitsIn()` function in Figure 6.5 uses an *inequality* comparison in the loop condition:

```
do
{
    numDigits++;
    intValue /= 10;
}
while (intValue != 0);
```

An equivalent forever loop would use an *equality* comparison as a termination condition:

```
for (;;)
{
    numDigits++;
    intValue /= 10;
    if (intValue == 0) break;
}
```

WORDS OF WARNING

Do Not Forget the Semicolon. The syntax of the do statement differs from that of the while statement and is designed to indicate clearly that it is a posttest loop. However, there is another, less obvious, difference between while and do statements that is a common source of programming errors:

> *The* do *statement must be terminated with a semicolon, but it is an error to terminate a* while *statement with a semicolon.*

The reason is that the final component in each of the other loops is a statement, but the final component of a do loop is a boolean expression, which must be terminated with a semicolon.

Avoid Infinite Loops. As with while loops, it is important to ensure that the statements within a do loop will eventually cause repetition to terminate, because an infinite loop will result otherwise. For example, in the do loop

```
counter = 1;
do
{
   cout << counter << endl;
   counter--;
}
while (counter < 100);
```

the termination condition is always true because counter is initially less than 100 and counter-- decrements counter by 1, causing the value of counter to always be less than 100. Thus, this is an infinite loop, producing an unlimited amount of output:

```
 1
 0
-1
-2
-3
 .
 .
 .
```

✔ Quick Quiz 6.4

1. _____ loops execute a set of statements once for each value in a specified range and they are implemented in C++ by a _____ statement.

2. What are the four components of a counting for loop?

3. The terminating statement in a forever loop is usually a(n) _____ combination.

Answer questions 4–7 using "pretest" or "posttest".

4. A while loop is a _____ loop.

5. A do loop is a _____ loop.

6. The body of a _____ loop is always executed at least once.

7. A _____ loop has zero-trip behavior.

For questions 8–14, describe the output produced.

8. ```
for (int i = 0; i < 10; i++)
   cout << "2*" << i << " = " << 2*i << endl;
```
```

```
 9. for (int i = 0; i <= 5; i++)
        cout << 2*i + 1 << "   ";
    cout << endl;
10. for (int i = 1; i < 4; i++)
    {
        cout << i;
        for (int j = i; j >= 1; j--)
            cout << j << endl;
    }
11. i = 0;
    j = 0;
    for (;;)
    {
        k = 2 * i * j;
        if (k > 10) break;
        cout << i << j << k << endl;
        i++;
        j++;
    }
    cout << k << endl;
12. k = 5;
    i = -2;
    while (i <= k)
    {
        i += 2;
        k--;
        cout << i + k << endl;
    }
13. i = 4;
    while (i >= 0)
    {
        i--;
        cout << i << endl;
    }
    cout << "\n*****\n";
14. i = 0;
    do
    {
        k = i * i + 1;
        cout << i << ' ' << k << endl;
        i++;
    }
    while (k <= 10);
15. i = 4;
    do
    {
        k = i * i - 4;
        cout << i << ' ' << k << endl;
        i--;
    }
    while (k >= 0);
```

EXERCISES 6.4

For exercises 1–14, describe the output produced.

1.
```cpp
for (int i = 10; i > 0; i--)
    cout << i << " cubed = " << i*i*i << endl;
```

2.
```cpp
for (int i = 10; i > 0; i -= 2)
    cout << i << " squared = " << i*i << endl;
```

3.
```cpp
for (int i = 1; i <= 5; i++)
{
    cout << i << endl;
    for (int j = i; j >= 1; j -= 2)
    cout << j << endl;
}
```

4.
```cpp
k = 5;
for (int i = -2; i < 5; i += 2)
{
    cout << i + k << endl;
    k = 1;
}
```

5.
```cpp
for (int i = 3; i > 0; i--)
    for (int j = 1; j <= i; j++)
        for (int k = i; k >= j; k--)
            cout << i << j << k << endl;
```

6.
```cpp
for (int  i = 1; i <= 3; i++)
    for (int j = 1; j <= 3; j++)
    {
        for (int k = i; k <= j; k++)
            cout << i << j << k << endl;
        cout << endl;
    }
```

7.
```cpp
i = 5;
j = 1;
for (;;)
{
    k = 2 * i - j;
    if (k < 0) break;
    cout << i << j << k << endl;
    j++;
    i--;
}
cout << i << j << k << endl;
```

8.
```cpp
i = 0;
j = 10;
for (;;)
{
    k = 2 * i + j;
    if (k > 15) break;
    cout << i << j << k << endl;
    if (i + j < 10) break;
    i++;
    j--;
}
cout << i << j << k << endl;
```

9.
```
i = 0;
j = 10;
for (;;)
{
    k = 2 * i + j;
    if (k > 20) break;
    cout << i << j << k << endl;
    if (i + j < 10) break;
    i++;
    j--;
}
cout << i << j << k << endl;
```

10.
```
i = 5;
for (;;)
{
    cout << i;
    i -= 2;
    if (i < 1) break;
    j = 0;
    for (;;)
    {
        j++;
        cout << j;
        if (j >= i)  break;
    }
    cout << "###\n";
}
cout << "***\n";
```

11.
```
k = 5;
i = 32;
while (i > 0)
{
    cout << "base-2 log of " << i << " = " << k << endl;
    i /= 2;
    k--;
}
```

12.
```
i = 1;
while (i*i < 10)
{
    j = i;
    while (j*j < 100)
    {
        cout << i + j << endl;
        j *= 2;
    }
    i++;
}
cout << "\n*****\n";
```

13.
```
i = 0;
do
{
    k = i * i * i - 3 * i + 1;
    cout << i << k << endl;
    i++;
}
while (k <= 2);
```

14.
```
i = 0;
do
{
    j = i * i * i;
    cout << i;
    do
    {
        k = i + 2 * j;
        cout << j << k;
        j += 2;
    }
    while (k <= 10);
    cout << endl;
    i++;
}
while (j <= 5);
```

Each of the loops in the following program segment is intended to find the smallest value of number for which the product $1 \times 2 \times \cdots \times$ number is greater than limit. For each of exercises 15–17, make three trace tables, one for each loop, that display the values of number and product for the given value of limit.

```
/* A. Using a while loop */
    number = 0;
    product = 1;
    while (product <= limit)
    {
        number++;
        product *= number;
    }

/* B. Using a do loop */
    number = 0;
    product = 1;
    do
    {
        number++;
        product *= number;
    }
    while (product <= limit);

/* C. Using a test-in-the middle loop */
    number = 0;
    product = 1;
    for (;;)
    {
        number++;
        if (product > limit) break;
        product *= number;
    }
```

15.   limit = 20

16.   limit = 1

17.   limit = 0

For exercises 18–22, write a loop to do what is required.

18.   Display the value of x and decrease x by 0.5 as long as x is positive.

19. Display the squares of the first 50 positive even integers in increasing order.

20. Display the square roots of the real numbers 1.0, 1.25, 1.5, 1.75, 2.0, . . . , 5.0.

21. The sequence of *Fibonacci numbers* begins with the integers 1, 1, 2, 3, 5, 8, 13, 21, . . . where each number after the first two is the sum of the two preceding numbers. Display the Fibonacci numbers less than 500.

22. Repeatedly prompt for and read a real number until the user enters a positive number.

For exercises 23–27, write functions that will do what is required. To test these functions, you should write driver programs as instructed in Programming Problems 1–5 at the end of this chapter.

23. Given a real number x and a nonnegative integer n, use a loop to calculate x^n, and return this value.

24. Proceed as in exercise 23, but allow n to be negative. (x^{-n} is defined to be $1/x^n$, provided $x \neq 0$.)

25. Given a positive integer n, return the sum of the proper divisors of n, that is, the sum of the divisors that are less than n. For example, for $n = 10$, the function should return $1 + 2 + 5 = 8$.

26. Given an integer n, return true if n is prime and false otherwise. (A *prime number* is an integer $n > 1$ whose only divisors are 1 and n.)

27. Given a positive integer n, return the least nonnegative integer k for which $2^k \geq n$.

6.5 INPUT LOOPS

We saw in section 3.4 that one important use of loops is to input a collection of values into a program. Because the number of data values may not be known before repetition begins, we need some method to signal that the end of the data has been reached. In this section, we look at three different approaches: *sentinels, queries,* and *counting.* To illustrate how these three techniques are used, we will use each of them in solving the problem of calculating the average of a set of failure times.

RUNNING EXAMPLE: THE MEAN TIME TO FAILURE PROBLEM.

One important statistic that is used in measuring the reliability of a component in a circuit is the *mean time to failure,* which can be used to predict the circuit's lifetime. This is especially important in situations in which repair is difficult or even impossible, such as a computer circuit in a satellite. Suppose that an engineering laboratory has been awarded a contract by NASA to evaluate the reliability of a particular component for a future space probe to Mars. As part of this evaluation, an engineer at this laboratory has tested several of these circuits and recorded the time at which each failed. She now wishes to develop a program to process this data and determine the mean time to failure.

OBJECT-CENTERED DESIGN

Behavior. The program should display on the screen prompts for input and read a series of component failure times from the keyboard. It should count these failure times and compute their sum and the average failure time. The program should then display this average.

Objects.   In addition to the usual screen, keyboard, and prompts, we can identify the following objects in this problem:

Description	Kind	Type	Name
failure time	varying	double	*failureTime*
sum of the failure times	varying	double	*failureTimeSum*
number of components	varying	int	*numComponents*
average of the failure times	varying	double	*meanFailureTime*

Operations.   To solve this problem, we need the following operations:

   i.   Initialize an integer (*numComponents*)

   ii.   Display a string (prompt) and input a real (*failureTime*)

   iii.   Add a real (*failureTime*) to a real (*failureTimeSum*)

   iv.   Increment an integer (*numComponents*)

   v.   Repeat operations ii–iv once for each component

   vi.   Divide a real (*failureTimeSum*) by an integer (*numComponents*) and store the result in a real (*meanFailureTime*)

   vii.   Perform operation vi only if *numComponents* $\neq 0$

Algorithm.   We can organize these operations into the following algorithm:

> **Algorithm to Calculate Mean Time to Failure**
>
> **1.** Initialize *numComponents* to 0 and *failureTimeSum* to 0.0.
> **2.** Loop:
>> **a.** Prompt for and read a *failureTime*.
>> **b.** Add *failureTime* to *failureTimeSum*.
>> **c.** Increment *numComponents* by 1.
>
> End Loop
> **3.** If *numComponents* $\neq 0$
>> **a.** Calculate *meanFailureTime* = *failureTimeSum* / *numComponents*.
>> **b.** Display *meanFailureTime* and *numComponents*.
>
> Otherwise
>> Display a "No Data" message.

The question we must answer is this: Which of the loops provided in C++ should we use to implement the loop in step 2?

INPUT LOOPS: THE SENTINEL APPROACH

The first approach is the **sentinel approach** introduced in section 3.4. It uses a special value called an **end-of-data flag** or **sentinel** to mark the end of the data values to be processed.

Forever Loops and Sentinels.   The program in Figure 6.7, like the examples in section 3.4, uses a forever loop to implement the sentinel approach.

FIGURE 6.7   THE SENTINEL APPROACH IN A FOREVER LOOP.

```cpp
/* failuretime7.cpp uses a forever loop and a sentinel to process a
 * collection of failure times and find the mean time to failure.
 *
 * Input:        a collection of component failure times
 * Precondition: failure times >= 0
 * Output:       prompts and the average of the failure times
 ******************************************************************/

#include <iostream.h>                  // <<, >>, cout, cin

int main()
{
   cout << "Computing Component Mean Time to Failure\n\n";

   int numComponents = 0;
   double failureTime,
          failureTimeSum = 0.0;

   for (;;)                           // or while(true)
   {
      cout << "Enter a failure time (-1 to quit): ";
      cin >> failureTime;

      if (failureTime < 0) break;

      failureTimeSum += failureTime;
      numComponents++;
   }

   if (numComponents != 0)
      cout << "\nThe mean failure time of the "
           << numComponents << " components is "
           << failureTimeSum / numComponents << endl;
   else
      cerr << "\nNo failure times to process!\n";
}
```

Sample run:

```
Computing Component Mean Time to Failure

Enter a failure time (-1 to quit): 2.3
Enter a failure time (-1 to quit): 2.4
Enter a failure time (-1 to quit): 2.5
Enter a failure time (-1 to quit): 2.6
Enter a failure time (-1 to quit): 2.7
Enter a failure time (-1 to quit): -1

The mean failure time of the 5 components is 2.5
```

As the comment at the beginning of the forever loop indicates, a `while` statement could also be used to implement the input loop:

```
while(true)
{
    cout << "Enter a failure time (-1 to quit): ";
    cin >> failureTime;

    if (failureTime < 0) break;

    failureTimeSum += failureTime;
    numComponents++;
}
```

And as we noted earlier, a `do` statement could also be used, but this is not as common. The choice of which statement to use to implement an input loop is largely a matter of programmer preference. We will use the forever-loop version in this text because this has been the traditional way to write such loops in C, the parent language of C++.

If we examine this and earlier examples for similarities, we see the following pattern:

Pattern for Sentinel Input Loop (Indefinite Loop Version)

```
for (;;)                // or while(true)
{
```
Display a prompt (for a data value).
Read *theValue* to be processed.
If (*theValue* is the sentinel) terminate the repetition.
Process *theValue*.
```
}
```

This pattern provides a succinct and intuitive way to input any data set for which a sentinel value exists.

While Loops and Sentinels. Before indefinite loops and statements to exit from loops became common features of programming languages, the `while` loop as described in section 6.3 was the only loop available to implement the sentinel approach. It is still used by some programmers, and so we should understand how it works. The basic pattern is as follows:

Pattern for Sentinel Input Loop (`while` Loop Version)

Display a prompt for a data value.
Read *theValue* to be processed.

```
while (theValue is not the sentinel)
{

  Process theValue.
  Display a prompt for a data value.
  Read theValue to be processed.

}
```

For example, a `while` loop version of the sentinel loop used in the mean-time-to-failure program in Figure 6.7 would be written as follows:

```
int main()
{
        .
        .
        .

    cout << "Enter a failure time (-1 to quit): ";
    cin >> failureTime;

    while (failureTime >= 0)
    {
        failureTimeSum += failureTime;
        numComponents++;

        cout << "Enter a failure time (-1 to quit): ";
        cin >> failureTime;
    }
        .
        .
        .

}
```

Note the two input steps, one before the loop and one at the bottom of the loop. Obviously, the input step inside the loop is needed to read new data values. But one is also needed before the loop, because the `while` loop is a pretest loop and tests its condition before the body of the loop is executed. For this condition to compare an input value with the sentinel, a value must be input before the beginning of the loop.

In the past, when the `while` loop was the only noncounting loop provided in a language, a programmer had no choice but to do this extra coding when designing a sentinel loop, but the addition of indefinite loops and loop-exit statements in modern languages makes it possible to avoid this redundant code. Although the duplicate code is not a major violation of OOP's "don't-reinvent-the-wheel" tenet, it is not in the spirit of object-oriented programming, and we will therefore use the forever loop version of the sentinel approach in this text.

A Problem with Sentinels. To use the sentinel approach, there must be some value that is not a valid data value to use as a sentinel. For the mean-time-to-failure problem, all failure time are nonnegative numbers, and so any negative value can serve as the sentinel. For some problems, however, there may be no suitable value. For example, for a program that computes and displays the mean of an arbitrary set of real values, all real numbers are valid inputs, and so there is no value to use as a sentinel. Similarly, for a program that encrypts characters, it may not be possible to designate one character as a sentinel without limiting the usefulness of the program.

End-Of-File As a Sentinel Value. Recall from chapter 4 that `cin` is an object of type `istream` and that an `istream` has a number of status flags that indicate the state of the stream. One flag we skipped in that discussion is the *eof flag,* a special flag that is set when an input operation reads a special character called the **end-of-file** (or **eof**) **mark.**[5] For problems where there is no obvious sentinel value, we can use this eof mark as a sentinel.

As with the other status flags, the `istream` class provides a boolean function member to check the eof status flag. It is named `eof()` and returns `true` if the eof flag is set, `false` if it is clear. This function can be used like a sentinel test to check whether or not the eof mark was entered. To illustrate, Figure 6.8 presents a simple program that displays the numeric codes of characters the user enters from the keyboard. The eof character is used to signal the end of input. For the particular (UNIX) system used in the sample run, the eof mark is `Control-d`, and so entering it sets the eof flag in `cin`, causing the function member `cin.eof()` to return `true`, which terminates the repetition.

Figure 6.8   Displaying Character Codes.

```
/* charcodes8.cpp displays the numeric codes of whatever characters
 * the user enters, until the eof character is entered.
 *
 * Input:   a collection of characters
 * Output:  the (integer) numeric code of each character entered
 ***********************************************************************/

#include <iostream.h>                    // <<, cout, cin, get, eof()

int main()
{
    cout << "This program displays the numeric codes of whatever\n"
            "characters you enter.  (Type the eof character to quit.)\n";
```

---

[5] In the MS-DOS/Windows environment, the eof mark can be entered by typing `Control-z` followed by the `Enter` key. In the UNIX and Macintosh environments, `Control-d` is used.

```
    char ch;
    for (;;)
    {
        cin.get(ch);

        if (cin.eof()) break;

        cout << '\t' << int(ch) << endl;
    }
}
```

Sample run (UNIX System):

```
This program displays the numeric codes of whatever
characters you enter.   (Type the eof character to quit.)
a
        97
        10
b
        98
        10
c
        99
        10
ABC
        65
        66
        67
        10
^D
```

Note that for each sequence of characters that is entered, the program displays the numeric codes of those characters followed by the number 10. This happens because the `get()` function member of `cin` (unlike the input operator `>>`) reads all keystrokes, including white space. In particular, it reads the LF (line feed) character produced by the Enter key, whose ASCII code is 10.

There are two drawbacks to using the eof mark as a sentinel. The first is that it is **platform dependent,** that is, it depends on the particular operating system being used. The keystroke for the eof mark for one system may not be the same as that used for the eof mark on another system.

The second drawback is one that we discussed in section 4.3: Once any `istream` status flag other than *good* is set, no subsequent input actions have any effect until the status flags are cleared. In some versions of C++ it is possible to read values *after* the eof mark has been read by calling the `istream` function member `clear()` to reset the status flags. The simple program in Figure 6.9 illustrates how this is done. It reads two lists of numbers and computes the sum of the numbers in the first list and the product of the numbers in the second list. The end of each list is indicated by using the eof mark as a sentinel. As illustrated, this technique works in gnu C++; but it will not work in some other versions of C++.

FIGURE 6.9   PROCESSING TWO LISTS.

```
/* lists9.cpp processes two lists, summing the values in one,
 * and finding the product of the values in the other.
 *
 * Input:    two sequences of numbers
 * Output:   the sum of the numbers in the first sequence,
 *           the product of the numbers in the second sequence.
 ***********************************************************/

#include <iostream.h>              // <<, cout, cin, get, eof(), clear()

int main()
{
   cout << "This program reads two lists, summing the first\n"
           "and finding the product of the numbers in the second.\n\n"
           "Enter the list to be summed (end list with eof):\n";

   double number,
          sum = 0;

   for (;;)                                      // read 1st list
   {
      cin >> number;
      if (cin.eof()) break;
      sum += number;
   }
                                                 // eof flag is set,
   cin.clear();                                  //  so clear it
   //This may not work in some versions of C++

   cout << "\nEnter the list to be multiplied (end list with eof):\n";

   double product = 1;

   for (;;)                                      // read 2nd list
   {
      cin >> number;
      if (cin.eof()) break;
      product *= number;
   }

   cout << "\nThe sum of the first list is " << sum << endl
        << "and the product of the second list is " << product << endl;
}
```

Sample run (UNIX System using gnu C++):

```
This program reads two lists, summing the first
and finding the product of the numbers in the second.
```

```
Enter the list to be summed (end list with eof):
1 2 3 4 5 6
^D
Enter the list to be multiplied (end list with eof):
10 9 8 7
^D
The sum of the first list is 21
and the product of the second list is 5040
```

INPUT LOOPS: THE COUNTING APPROACH

Another way to process a set of input values is to first input the number of values in the data set and then use a counting loop to read and process that many values. Figure 6.10 is a modification of the mean-time-to-failure program in Figure 6.7 that uses this approach.

FIGURE 6.10   THE COUNTING APPROACH.

```cpp
/* failuretime10.cpp uses a counting loop to process a collection
 * of failure times and find the mean time to failure.
 *
 *  Input:   the number of component failure times and
 *           the collection of failure times
 *  Output: prompts and the average of the failure times
 ***************************************************************/

#include <iostream.h>                        // <<, >>, cout, cin

int main()
{
   cout << "Computing Component Mean Time to Failure\n\n";

   int numComponents;
   double failureTime,
          failureTimeSum = 0.0;

   cout << "How many failure times will be entered? ";
   cin >> numComponents;

   for (int count = 1; count <= numComponents; count++)
   {
      cout << "Enter failure time #" << count << ": ";
      cin >> failureTime;

      failureTimeSum += failureTime;
   }
```

```
  if (numComponents > 0)
     cout << "\nThe mean failure time of the "
          << numComponents << " components is "
          << failureTimeSum / numComponents << endl;
  else
     cerr << "\nNo failure times to process!\n";
}
```

Sample run:

```
Computing Component Mean Time to Failure

How many failure times will be entered? 5
Enter failure time #1: 2.3
Enter failure time #2: 2.4
Enter failure time #3: 2.5
Enter failure time #4: 2.6
Enter failure time #5: 2.7

The mean failure time of the 5 components is 2.5
```

Conceptually, this approach is quite simple. We ask the user how many values are to be entered and then use a `for` loop to read and process that many values. The general pattern is as follows:

Pattern for Counting Input Loop

Display a prompt for the number of values to be processed.

Read *numberOfValues* to be processed.

```
for (int var = 1; var <= numberOfValues; var++)
{
```
　　Display a prompt for a data value.

　　Read *theValue* to be processed.

　　Process *theValue*.
```
}
```

One disadvantage of this approach is its lack of flexibility. The number of data values entered must be exactly the number specified at the beginning of execution. If a user discovers during the input of the data values that there will be more (or fewer) values than were specified, there is no way out, except to abort the program and reexecute it. A related disadvantage is that the counting loop requires that we know in advance how many values will be entered. This may be difficult to determine for large data sets. The program is much more user-friendly if the computer, rather than the user, does the counting.

INPUT LOOPS: THE QUERY APPROACH

Each of the preceding kinds of input loops has its disadvantages. The sentinel approach can only be used in problems where there is a suitable value to use as the sentinel. The eof mark is platform dependent. The counting loop approach requires knowing in advance the number of values to be entered.

The final approach we consider is to **query the user** at the end of each repetition to determine whether there is more data to process. Although not without its disadvantages, this approach is the most broadly applicable.

The program in Figure 6.11 is a modification of the mean-time-to-failure programs in Figure 6.7 and 9.10 that uses this query approach. It asks the query

```
Do you have more data to enter (y or n)?
```

and then reads the user's response from the keyboard. Repetition continues until the user answers y or Y, and the loop condition

```
response == 'y' || response == 'Y'
```

then terminates the repetition.

 FIGURE 6.11   THE QUERY APPROACH.

```cpp
/* failuretime11.cpp uses a query-controlled loop to process a
 * collection of failure times and find the mean time to failure.
 *
 *   Input:   a collection of component failure times and
 *            user's response to "more data?" query
 *   Output:  prompts and the average of the failure times.
 ***************************************************************/

#include <iostream.h>                    // <<, >>, cout, cin

int main()
{
   cout << "Computing Component Mean Time to Failure\n";

   int numComponents = 0;
   double failureTime,
          failureTimeSum = 0.0;

   char response;

   do
   {
      cout << "\nEnter a failure time: ";
      cin >> failureTime;

      failureTimeSum += failureTime;
      numComponents++;

      cout << "Do you have more data to enter (y or n)? ";
      cin >> response;
   } while (response == 'y' || response == 'Y');
```

```
        cout << "\nThe mean failure time of the "
             << numComponents << " components is "
             << failureTimeSum / numComponents << endl;
}
```

Sample run:

```
Computing Component Mean Time to Failure

Enter a failure time: 2.3
Do you have more data to enter (y or n)? y

Enter a failure time: 2.4
Do you have more data to enter (y or n)? y

Enter a failure time: 2.5
Do you have more data to enter (y or n)? y

Enter a failure time: 2.6
Do you have more data to enter (y or n)? y

Enter a failure time: 2.7
Do you have more data to enter (y or n)? n

The mean failure time of the 5 components is 2.5
```

In problems where it is reasonable to assume that there is at least one data value to be entered and processed, the query and the corresponding loop condition are placed at the bottom of the loop, making it a posttest loop.[6] This suggests the following *pattern* for a query-controlled input loop:

---

[6] In problems where there might be no values to enter and process, a forever loop can be used:

```
for (;;)
{
    cout << "\nDo you wish to continue (y or n)? "
    char response;
    cin >> response;

    if (response == 'n' || response == 'N') break;

    cout << "\nEnter a value: ";
    double value;
    cin >> value;

    // process value
}
```

Pattern for Query-Controlled Input Loop

```
char response;
do
{

    Display a prompt for a data value.
    Input theValue to be processed.
    Process theValue.

    Display a query that asks if there is more data.
    Input the user's response (y or n).
}
while ((response != 'n') && (response != 'N'));
```

Query Functions. The code to perform a query tends to clutter a loop, and this may obscure the program's structure. One way to avoid this is by constructing a **query function** like the following to perform the query, read the user's response, and return true or false based on the response:

```
bool MoreValues()
{
    char answer;

    cout << "Do you have more values to enter (y or n)? ";
    cin >> answer;

    return (answer == 'y') || (answer == 'Y');
}
```

Since it returns a boolean value, a call to such a **query function** can be used as a loop condition. For example, we could modify the mean-time-to-failure program of Figure 6.11 to use the query function `MoreData()` to control the input loop:

```
int main()
{
         .
         .
         .
    do
    {
        cout << "\nEnter a failure time: ";
        cin >> failureTime;

        failureTimeSum += failureTime;
        numComponents++;

    } while (MoreValues());
         .
         .
         .
}
```

Each time execution reaches the loop condition, the function `MoreValues()` is called. It queries the user, reads the response, and returns true if the response was either `y` or `Y` and returns false otherwise. If `MoreValues()` returns true, the body of the `do` loop is repeated, but if it returns false, repetition is terminated.

This version of a query-controlled loop is easier to read than the earlier version in Figure 6.11 because the statements that perform the querying (including the declaration of a character variable to hold the response) are now hidden in the function `MoreValues()`.

Another advantage of this approach is that a query function can be stored in a library (e.g., `Queries`), from which it can be accessed by any program requiring a query-controlled loop. Since this particular query,

```
Do you have more values to enter (y or n)?
```

may be less appropriate for a different program, such a library might contain a variety of query functions such as:

`MoreValues():`   Asks if there are more values
`Continue():`   Asks if the user wants to continue
`Done():`   Asks if the user is finished

A program that uses the `#include` directive to insert the library's header file can use whichever query function is most appropriate.

The general pattern of a loop controlled by a query function is as follows:

Pattern for Input Loop Controlled by a Query Function

```
bool QueryFunction();        // or #include "QueryLibrary"
    .
    .
    .
do
{
    Display a prompt for a data value.
    Input theValue to be processed.
    Process theValue.
}
while (QueryFunction());
```

The Disadvantage of the Query Approach. The sentinel and counting approaches require one interaction by the user to enter each data value, but the query approach requires two—one for the data value, and one for the response to the query. This doubling of user effort may make the query approach too cumbersome for large data sets.

6.6 CHOOSING THE RIGHT LOOP

With so many different kinds of loops, it can be difficult for a programmer to decide which is best for a particular problem. One simple guideline is the following:

> *The choice of a loop should be determined by the nature of the problem.*

This means that choosing a loop is part of the design phase of program development. It should be done only after the algorithm has been developed in some detail, because the algorithm will provide clues as to which loop to use.

DECISION #1: USE A COUNTING LOOP OR A GENERAL LOOP?

The first question to ask is

> *Does the algorithm require counting through some fixed range of values?*

If the answer is yes, then a counting loop is needed, and a `for` loop is the appropriate choice. However, if solving the problem does not involve repeating the execution of statements a fixed number of times, then one of the more general loops— `while`, `do`, or forever—is a better choice.

DECISION #2: WHICH GENERAL LOOP?

If one of the general loops should be used, then the next question is: Which one? One way to proceed is to begin with a *generic loop* of the form

    Loop
        body-of-the-loop
    End Loop

in the algorithm. Then continue to develop the algorithm, adding any necessary initialization statements before the loop together with the statements that make up the body of the loop:

    initialization statements
    Loop
        statement$_1$
            .
            .
            .
        statement$_n$
    End Loop

Finally, formulate an appropriate termination condition and determine where it should be placed in the loop. This will determine which kind of loop to use:

> If the termination condition appears
>
> ▸ At the beginning of the loop, the loop is a pretest loop; choose a `while` loop;
>
> ▸ At the bottom of the loop, the loop is a posttest loop; choose a `do` loop;
>
> ▸ Within the list of statements, the loop is a test-in-the-middle loop; choose a forever loop with an `if-break` (or `if-return`) combination.

To illustrate, consider again the problem of designing an algorithm for the bouncing-ball problem of section 6.3. Using a generic loop, we write a first version of the algorithm as follows:

1. Initialize *bounce* to 0.
2. Enter a value for *height*.
3. Display original *height* value with appropriate label.
4. Loop

> Replace *height* with *height* divided by 2.
> Add 1 to *bounce*.
> Display *bounce* and *height*.

End Loop

Because repetition is to stop when *height* is less than some *SMALL_NUMBER*, the condition

> *height* < *SMALL_NUMBER*

can be used as a termination condition for the loop. However, the user could have entered zero or a negative value for *height*, in which case the body of the loop should not be executed. Thus, we should evaluate this condition immediately upon entering the loop:

1. Initialize *bounce* to 0.
2. Enter a value for *height*.
3. Display original *height* value with appropriate label.
4. Loop

> **a.** If *height* < *SMALL_NUMBER*, terminate the repetition.
> **b.** Replace *height* with *height* divided by 2.
> **c.** Add 1 to *bounce*.
> **d.** Display *bounce* and *height*.

End Loop

This is a pretest loop, and we should therefore use a `while` loop to implement it.

By contrast, if we reconsider the sentinel approach to reading a collection of values, we begin by constructing the generic loop

Loop
> Display a prompt for input.
> Input *theValue*.
> Process *theValue*.
End Loop

Since we are using the sentinel approach, an appropriate termination condition is

> *theValue* is the sentinel

Before this termination condition can be evaluated, *theValue* must have been read, which means that the termination condition must appear after the input statement. Also, a sentinel value must not be processed, which means that the termination condition should be placed before the processing statements:

Loop
    a. Display a prompt for input.
    b. Input *theValue.*
    c. If *theValue* is the sentinel, then terminate repetition.
    d. Process *theValue.*
End Loop

This is a test-in-the-middle loop, and we should therefore use a forever loop to implement it.

✔ Quick Quiz 6.6

1. Name the three kinds of input loops.
2. A special value used to signal the end of data is called a(n) _____ or _____.
3. (True or false) A disadvantage of using a `while` loop instead of a forever loop for sentinel-based input is that duplicate input steps are required.
4. The eof flag is set when a special character called the _____ mark is read.
5. The function member _____ from class `istream` is used to check the eof flag.
6. (True or false) One advantage of using the eof mark is that it is platform independent.
7. (True or false) The counting method of input is one of the most flexible methods.
8. A _____ is a question asked of the user to determine whether there are more data values.

6.7 EXAMPLE: CALCULATING DEPRECIATION

PROBLEM

Depreciation is a decrease in the value over time of some asset due to wear and tear, decay, declining price, and so on. For example, suppose that a company purchases a new computer system for $200,000 that will serve its needs for 5 years. After that time, called the *useful life* of the computer, it can be sold at an estimated price of $50,000, which is the computer's salvage value. Thus, the value of the computing equipment will have depreciated $150,000 over the 5-year period. The calculation of the value lost in each of several years is an important accounting problem, and there are several ways of calculating this quantity. We want to write one or more functions to calculate depreciation tables that display the depreciation in each year of an item's useful life.

OBJECT-CENTERED DESIGN

Behavior.   Each function should receive from its caller the amount to be depreciated and the number of years. The function should then display on the screen a depreciation table.

Objects.   The objects in this problem are straightforward:

Description	Kind	Type	Movement	Name
The amount to be depreciated	varying	real	received	*amount*
The item's useful life (in years)	varying	integer	received	*numYears*
The annual depreciation	varying	real	—	*depreciation*

Each function will have the same specification:

> **Receive:**   *amount* and *numYears*
>
> **Output:**   a depreciation table

Operations and Algorithms.   The operations in this problem depend on the method used to calculate the depreciation. There are several different methods, and we will consider two of them here.

One standard method is the **straight-line method,** in which the amount to be depreciated is divided evenly over the specified number of years. For example, straight-line depreciation of $150,000 over a 5-year period gives an annual depreciation of $150,000 / 5 = $30,000:

Year	Depreciation
1	$30,000
2	$30,000
3	$30,000
4	$30,000
5	$30,000

With this method, the value of an asset decreases a fixed amount each year.

The operations needed to calculate straight-line depreciation are all provided by C++ operations and statements:

   i.   Divide a real (*amount*) by an integer (*numYears*)

  ii.   Output an integer (the year) and a real (the depreciation)

 iii.   Repeat ii a specified number (*numYears*) of times.

Organizing them in an algorithm is straightforward.

Algorithm for Straight-Line Depreciation

1. Calculate *depreciation* = *amount* / *numYears*.

2. For *year* ranging from 1 through *numYears* do the following:
     Display *year* and *depreciation*.

Another common method of calculating depreciation is called the **sum-of-the-years'-digits method.** To illustrate it, consider again depreciating $150,000 over a 5-year period. We first calculate the "sum of the years' digits," $1 + 2 + 3 + 4 + 5 = 15$. In the first year, 5/15 of $150,000 ($50,000) is depreciated; in the second year, 4/15 of $150,000 ($40,000) is depreciated; and so on, giving the following depreciation table:

Year	Depreciation
1	$50,000
2	$40,000
3	$30,000
4	$20,000
5	$10,000

In addition to the operations for the straight-line method, the sum-of-the-years'-digits method requires:

iv.   Sum the integers from 1 through some given integer (*numYears*)

For this we can use the function Sum() in Figure 6.1.
    An algorithm for displaying annual depreciation values using this method is as follows:

Algorithm for Sum-of-the-Years'-Digits Depreciation

1. Calculate *sum* $= 1 + 2 + \ldots + numYears.$

2. For *year* ranging from 1 through *numYears* do the following:

    a. Calculate *depreciation* $= (numYears - year + 1) * amount / sum$

    b. Display *year* and *depreciation.*

Coding. The function StraightLine() in Figure 6.12 implements the algorithm for the straight-line method of depreciation and the function SumOfYears() implements the algorithm for the sum-of-the-years'-digits method. Because these functions are useful in a variety of problems, we would probably store them in a library with these function definitions along with that for function Sum() in an implementation file and the prototypes

```
void StraightLine(double amount, int numYears);

void SumOfYears(double amount, int numYears);
```

in the corresponding header file (e.g., Depreciation.h).

FIGURE 6.12   DEPRECIATION FUNCTIONS.

```
#include <iomanip.h>        // setprecision(), setw(), setiosflags()
#include <assert.h>         // assert()

/* StraightLine() displays a depreciation table for a given
 * amount over numYears years using the straight-line method.
 *
```

```
 * Receive: amount, a real
 *          numYears, an integer
 * Output:  a depreciation table
 * Uses:    format manipulators from iostream and iomanip
 ***************************************************************/

void StraightLine(double amount, int numYears)
{
   double depreciation = amount / numYears;

   cout << "\nYear -  Depreciation"
        << "\n--------------------\n";

   cout << fixed << showpoint << right      // set up format for $$
        << setprecision(2);

   for (int year = 1; year <= numYears; year++)
      cout << setw(3) << year
           << setw(13) << depreciation << endl;
}

/* SumOfYears() displays a depreciation table for a given
 * amount over numYears years using the sum-of-the-years'-digits
 * method.
 *
 * Receive: amount, a real
 *          numYears, an integer
 * Output:  a depreciation table
 * Uses:    function Sum() from Figure 6.1
 *          format manipulators from iostream and iomanip
 ***************************************************************/

void SumOfYears(double amount, int numYears)
{
   cout << "\nYear -  Depreciation"
        << "\n--------------------\n";

   double sum = Sum(numYears);

   double depreciation;

   cout << fixed << showpoint << right      // set up format for $$
        << setprecision(2);

   for (int year = 1; year <= numYears; year++)
   {
      depreciation = (numYears - year + 1) * amount / sum;
      cout << setw(3) << year
           << setw(13) << depreciation << endl;
   }
}
```

Testing. The program in Figure 6.13 uses these depreciation functions. It begins by defining a menu

```
Enter:
    a - to enter information about a new item
    b - to use the straight-line method
    c - to use the sum-of-the-years'-digits method
    d - to quit
-->
```

which it passes to the function `GetMenuChoice()` described in section 6.2. This function repeatedly displays a menu and reads the user's choice until the user enters a valid choice, which is then returned to the caller. For option `a`, the user enters an item's purchase price, its salvage value, and its useful life. Options `b` and `c` call the functions `StraightLine()` and `SumOfYears()`, respectively, to display the depreciation tables. The sentinel value `QUIT = 'd'` signals the end of input and a `switch` statement is used to process non-`QUIT` options.

 FIGURE 6.13   **METHODS OF DEPRECIATION.**

```
/*  depreciate13.cpp calculates and displays depreciation tables.
 *
 *  Input:   purchase price, salvage value, and useful
 *           life of an item
 *  Output: depreciation tables.
 *********************************************************************/

#include <iostream.h>        // <<, >>, cout, cin
#include <string>            // string
#include "Depreciation.h"

// or if not using this library,
// insert the prototypes of StraightLine() and SumOfYears() here and
// insert after main(), the function Sum() from Figure 6.1 and the
// #include directives and function definitions from Figure 6.12.

char GetMenuChoice(string MENU, char firstChoice, char lastChoice);

int main()
{
   const string MENU =
        "\nEnter:\n"
        "    a - to enter information for a new item\n"
        "    b - to use the straight-line method\n"
        "    c - to use the sum-of-the-years'-digits method\n"
        "    d - to quit\n"
        "--> ";
   const char QUIT = 'd';

   cout << "This program computes depreciation tables using\n"
        << "various methods of depreciation.\n";
```

```cpp
   char option;                            // menu option selected by user
   double purchasePrice,                   // item's purchase price,
          salvageValue,                    //     salvage value, and
          amount;                          //     amount to depreciate, and
   int usefulLife;                         //     useful life in years

   for (;;)
   {
      option = GetMenuChoice(MENU, 'a', QUIT);  // get user's choice

      if (option == QUIT) break;

      switch (option)                           // perform the option selected
      {
         case 'a':                              // get new item information
            cout << "What is the item's:\n"
                    "   purchase price? ";
            cin >> purchasePrice;
            cout << "   salvage value? ";
            cin >> salvageValue;
            cout << "   useful life? ";
            cin >> usefulLife;
            amount = purchasePrice - salvageValue;
            break;
         case 'b':                              // do straight-line method
            StraightLine(amount, usefulLife);
            break;
         case 'c':                              // do sum-of-years-digits method
            SumOfYears(amount, usefulLife);
            break;
         default:                               // execution should NEVER get here
            cerr << "*** Invalid menu choice: " << option << endl;
      }
   }
}

/* GetMenuChoice() repeatedly displays a MENU of choices in the
 * range firstChoice to lastChoice and reads a user's choice until
 * a valid choice is entered, which is then returned to the caller.
 *
 * Receive: MENU, a string
 *          firstChoice and lastChoice, chars
 * Return:  the choice entered by the user
 *************************************************************/

char GetMenuChoice(string MENU, char firstChoice, char lastChoice)
{
   char choice;                          // what the user enters

   for (;;)
   {
      cout << MENU;
      cin >> choice;
```

```
        if ((choice >= firstChoice) && (choice <= lastChoice))
            return choice;

        cerr << "\nI'm sorry, but " << choice
             << " is not a valid menu choice.\n";
    }
}
```

Sample run:

```
This program computes depreciation tables using
various methods of depreciation.

Enter:
   a - to enter information for a new item
   b - to use the straight-line method
   c - to use the sum-of-years'-digits method
   d - to quit
--> a

What is the item's
   purchase price? 2000.00
   salvage value? 500.00
   useful life? 5

Enter:
   a - to enter information for a new item
   b - to use the straight-line method
   c - to use the sum-of-years'-digits method
   d - to quit
--> b

Year -  Depreciation
--------------------
   1        300.00
   2        300.00
   3        300.00
   4        300.00
   5        300.00

Enter:
   a - to enter information for a new item
   b - to use the straight-line method
   c - to use the sum-of-years'-digits method
   d - to quit
--> c

Year -  Depreciation
--------------------
   1        500.00
   2        400.00
   3        300.00
   4        200.00
   5        100.00
```

```
Enter:
   a - to enter information for a new item
   b - to use the straight-line method
   c - to use the sum-of-years'-digits method
   d - to quit
--> x

I'm sorry, but x is not a valid menu choice

Enter:
   a - to enter information for a new item
   b - to use the straight-line method
   c - to use the sum-of-years'-digits method
   d - to quit
--> a

What is the item's
   purchase price? 1200.00
   salvage value? 200.00
   useful life? 3

Enter:
   a - to enter information for a new item
   b - to use the straight-line method
   c - to use the sum-of-years'-digits method
   d - to quit
--> b

Year -  Depreciation
--------------------
   1        333.33
   2        333.33
   3        333.33

Enter:
   a - to enter information for a new item
   b - to use the straight-line method
   c - to use the sum-of-years'-digits method
   d - to quit
--> d
```

Part of the Picture: Introduction to Algorithm Analysis

In the incident described in section 6.1, the student Gauss responded almost immediately when he was given the problem of summing the integers from 1 through 100. The simplicity and efficiency of his algorithm compared to the repetitive algorithm we used is an indication of his genius. We will describe his algorithm here and use it to introduce the area of computer science known as algorithm analysis.

To compute the sum of the integers from 1 through 100, Gauss perhaps observed that writing the sum forward,

$$sum = 1 + 2 + 3 + \cdots + 98 + 99 + 100$$

and then backward,

$$sum = 100 + 99 + 98 + \cdots + 3 + 2 + 1$$

and then adding corresponding terms in these two equations gives

$$2 \times sum = 101 + 101 + 101 + \cdots + 101 + 101 + 101$$
$$= 100 \times 101$$

Thus the sum is equal to

$$sum = \frac{100 \times 101}{2} = 5050$$

Applying his algorithm to the more general summation problem, we begin with the sum

$$sum = 1 + 2 + 3 + \cdots + (n - 2) + (n - 1) + n$$

reverse it,

$$sum = n + (n - 1) + (n - 2) + \cdots + 3 + 2 + 1$$

and then add these two equations to get

$$2 \times sum = (n + 1) + (n + 1) + (n + 1) + \cdots + (n + 1) + (n + 1) + (n + 1)$$
$$= n \times (n + 1)$$

Dividing by 2 gives

$$sum = \frac{n \times (n + 1)}{2}$$

This formula implies that function Sum() can be written without using a loop at all, as shown in Figure 6.14:

FIGURE 6.14   FUNCTION Sum() — NO-LOOP VERSION.

```
/* Sum(n) computes the sum of the integers from 1 to n
 * using Gauss' formula.
 *
 * Receive:      n, an integer
 * Precondition: n > 0
 * Return:       the sum 1 + 2 + ... + n
 **********************************************************/
int Sum(int n)
{
   return n * (n + 1) / 2;
}
```

This solution is better than one that uses a loop, because it solves the same problem *in less time*. To see why, suppose we want to compute the sum of the integers from 1 through 1000. A version of Sum() that uses a loop (such as that in Figure 6.1) must repeat the body of the loop 1,000 times. That means it must perform:

1,000 additions of count to runningTotal,

1,000 assignments of that result to runningTotal,

1,000 increments of count, and

1,000 comparisons of count to n,

for a total of 4,000 operations. For an arbitrary value of n, each of these operations would be performed n times for a total of 4n operations. We say that the number of operations performed by the loop version of Sum() **grows linearly** with the value of its parameter n.

By contrast, the final version of Sum() always does

1 addition,

1 multiplication, and

1 division,

for a total of 3 operations, *regardless of the value of* n. Thus the time taken by the last version of Sum() is **constant,** no matter what the value of its parameter n.

This is our first look at an important area of computer science called **analysis of algorithms.** We have seen two algorithms that solve the summation problem. To determine which of them is "better", we analyze the number of operations each requires to solve the problem. The algorithm using Gauss' formula solves the problem in constant time, while the algorithm using a loop solves the problem in time proportional to n, and consequently, Gauss' algorithm is to be preferred.

☞ *PROGRAMMING POINTERS*

✍ PROGRAM STYLE AND DESIGN

In this text, we use the following conventions for formatting loops:

1. *The statement in a* for, while, do, *and forever loop is indented. If the statement is compound, the curly braces are aligned with the* for, while, *or* do, *and the statements inside the block are indented. In a* do *loop,* do *is aligned with its corresponding* while.

```
for (...)                    for (...)
    statement                {
                                 statement₁

                                     .
                                     .
                                     .

                                 statementₙ
                             }


while(loop_condition)        while(loop_condition)
    statement                {
                                 statement₁

                                     .
                                     .
                                     .

                                 statementₙ
                             }
```

```
do                                  do
    statement                       {
while (loop_condition);                 statement₁

                                            .
                                            .
                                            .

                                        statementₙ
                                    }
                                    while (loop_condition);
```

2. *Anything that can be computed can be computed using (only) the three control structures: sequence, selection, and repetition.*

3. *Repetition structures can be implemented in C++ using the* for, while, *and* do *statements, and it is important to select the one that best implements the repetition structure required in a given problem.* Some guidelines for choosing the appropriate loop are as follows:

    ▶ *The* for *loop is most appropriate for performing repetition when the number of repetitions can be determined before the loop is entered.*

    ▶ *The* while *loop is most appropriate for performing repetition when zero-trip behavior is desired.* Since the loop condition appears at the top of the loop, the body of the loop will not be entered inadvertently if the loop condition is false initially.

    ▶ *The* do *loop is most appropriate for performing repetition when one-trip behavior is desired.* Since the loop condition appears at the bottom of the loop, the body of the loop will be executed at least once before repetition is terminated.

    ▶ *The forever loop can be used to perform repetition when neither zero-trip nor one-trip behavior is desired.* An if-break *or an* if-return combination is usually used to terminate repetition.

⚡ POTENTIAL PROBLEMS

1. *Care must be taken to avoid infinite looping.*

    ▶ The loop condition of a for loop must eventually become *false;* the body of a while loop or a do loop must contain statements that eventually cause its loop condition to become *false.* For example, the code fragment

    ```
    x = 0.0;
    do
    {
        cout << x << endl;
        x += 0.3;
    }
    while (x != 1.0);
    ```

    produces an infinite loop:

    ```
    0.0
    0.3
    0.6
    ```

```
0.9
1.2
1.5
1.8
 .
 .
 .
```

Since the value of x is never equal to 1.0, repetition is not terminated.

▸ The body of a forever loop should always contain an `if-break` or `if-return` combination and statements that ensure that the termination condition of the loop will eventually become *true*.

2. *In a* `while` *loop, the loop condition that controls repetition is evaluated before execution of the body of the loop. In a* `do` *loop, the loop condition that controls repetition is evaluated after execution of the body of the loop.* Thus, the body of a `while` loop will not be executed if the loop condition is false initially, but the statements in a `do` loop are always executed at least once.

3. *The* `for, while, do`, *and forever loops control a single statement.* For example, the following poorly-indented segment

```
for (int i = 1; i <= 10; i++)
   j = i*i;
   cout << j << endl;
```

will display only a single value,

```
100
```

since the output statement is outside the body of the loop. Likewise, the segment

```
int count = 1;
while (count <= 10)
   cout << count << '\t' << count*count << endl;
   count++;
```

will produce an infinite loop,

```
1       1
1       1
1       1
 .
 .
 .
```

because the statement that increments `count` is outside the body of the loop.

4. *In a* `do` *loop, the closing* `while (loop_condition)` *must be followed by a semicolon, or a syntax error will result.*

5. *In a* `for` *loop, neither the control variable nor any variable involved in the loop condition should be modified within the body of the loop, since it is intended to run through a specified range of consecutive values.* Strange and undesirable results may be produced otherwise. To illustrate, the statement

```
for (int i = 1; i <= 4; i++)
{
   cout << i << endl;
   i++;
}
```

produces the output

```
1
3
```

The statement

```
for (int i = 1; i <= 4; i++)
{
    cout << i << endl;
    i--;
}
```

results in an infinite loop, displaying the output

```
1
1
1
1
.
.
.
```

6. *Each use of the equality operator in a loop condition should be double-checked to make certain that the assignment operator is not being used.* Using = instead of == is one of the easiest errors to make. This error is illustrated by the following code fragment:

```
do
{
    // ... do some processing ...

    cout << "Do you wish to continue (y or n)? ";
    cin >> answer;
}
while (answer = 'y');
```

This loop will be executed infinitely many times, regardless of what the user enters, because:

1. The loop condition is an *assignment* that sets answer to y; it is not a *comparison;*
2. The assignment operator (=) produces the value that was assigned as its result;
3. This assignment thus produces the value 121 (the ASCII value of character y); and
4. C++ treats any nonzero value as true.

Similarly, the forever loop

```
for
{
    cout << "\nPlease enter an integer value (0 to quit): ";
    cin >> value;

    if (value = 0) break;

    // ... do something with value ...
}
```

is an infinite loop, because the termination condition in its if-break combination is an *assignment, not a comparison.* Because the result of that assignment is zero, and C++ uses zero to represent the value false, this termination condition will always be false, and so the break statement will never be executed.

Programming Problems

SECTIONS 6.1–6.4

1. Write a driver program to test the power function of exercise 23 of section 6.4.

2. Write a driver program to test the power function of exercise 24 of section 6.4.

3. Write a driver program to test the sum-of-divisors function of exercise 25 of section 6.4.

4. Write a driver program to test the prime-checker function of exercise 26 of section 6.4.

5. Write a driver program to test the power-of-two function of exercise 27 of section 6.4.

6. Write a program that displays the following multiplication table:

	1	2	3	4	5	6	7	8	9
1	1								
2	2	4							
3	3	6	9						
4	4	8	12	16					
5	5	10	15	20	25				
6	6	12	18	24	30	36			
7	7	14	21	28	35	48	49		
8	8	16	24	32	40	45	56	64	
9	9	18	27	36	45	54	63	72	81

7. A positive integer is said to be a *deficient, perfect,* or *abundant* number if the sum of its proper divisors is less than, equal to, or greater than the number, respectively. For example, 8 is deficient because its proper divisors are 1, 2, and 4, and $1 + 2 + 4 < 8$; 6 is perfect, because $1 + 2 + 3 = 6$; 12 is abundant, because $1 + 2 + 3 + 4 + 6 > 12$. Write a program that classifies n as being deficient, perfect, or abundant for $n = 20$ to 30, then for $n = 490$ to 500, and finally for $n = 8120$ to 8130. It should use the function from exercise 25 to find the sum of the proper divisors. *Extra:* Find the smallest odd abundant number. *Warning:* An attempt to find an odd perfect number will probably fail, because none has yet been found although it has not been proven that such numbers do not exist.

8. The Rinky Dooflingy Company currently sells 200 dooflingies per month at a profit of $300 per dooflingy. The company now spends $2000 per month on advertising and has fixed operating costs of $1000 per month that do not depend on the volume of sales. If the company doubles the amount spent on advertising, sales will increase by 20 percent. Write a program that displays under appropriate headings the amount spent on advertising, the number of sales made, and the net profit. Begin with the company's current status and successively double the amount spent on advertising until the net profit "goes over the hump," that is, begins to decline. The output should include the amounts up through the first time that the net profit begins to decline.

9. The *divide-and-average* algorithm for approximating the square root of any positive number a is as follows: take any initial approximation x that is positive, and then find a new approximation by calculating the average of x and a / x, that is, $(x + a / x) / 2$. Repeat this procedure with x replaced by this new approximation, stopping when x and a / x differ in absolute value by some specified error allowance, such as 0.00001. Write a program that reads values for x, a, and the small error allowance, and then uses this divide-and-average algorithm to find the approximate square root of x. Have the program display each of the successive approximations. Execute the program with $a = 3$ and error allowance $= 0.00001$, and use the following initial approximations: 1, 10, 0.01, and 100. Also execute the program with $a = 4$, error allowance $= 0.00001$, and initial approximations 1 and 2.

10. Write a program that accepts a positive integer and gives its prime factorization; that is, expresses the integer as a product of primes or indicates that it is a prime. (See exercise 26 of section 6.4 for the definition of a prime number.)

SECTIONS 6.5 & 6.6

11. Write a program to read a set of numbers, count them, and find and print the largest and smallest numbers in the list and their positions in the list.

12. Write a program that reads an exchange rate for converting English currency to U.S. currency and then reads several values in English currency and converts each amount to the equivalent U.S. currency. Display all amounts with appropriate labels. Use sentinel-controlled or end-of-file-controlled while loops for the input.

13. Proceed as in the preceding exercise, but convert several values from U.S. currency to English currency.

14. One method for finding the *base-b representation* of a positive integer given in base-10 notation is to divide the integer repeatedly by b until a quotient of zero results. The successive remainders are the digits from right to left of the base-b representation. For example, the binary representation of 26 is 11010_2, as the following computation shows:

$$
\begin{array}{r}
0 \text{ R } 1 \\
2\overline{)1} \text{ R } 1 \\
2\overline{)3} \text{ R } 0 \\
2\overline{)6} \text{ R } 1 \\
2\overline{)13} \text{ R } 0 \\
2\overline{)26}
\end{array}
$$

Write a program to accept various integers and bases and display the digits of the base-b representation (in reverse order) for each integer. You may assume that each base is in the range 2 through 10.

15. Proceed as in problem 14, but convert integers from base 10 to hexadecimal (base 16). Use a `switch` statement to display the symbols A, B, C, D, E, and F for 10, 11, 12, 13, 14, and 15, respectively.

16. Write a program that reads the amount of a loan, the annual interest rate, and a monthly payment and then displays the payment number, the interest for that month, the balance remaining after that payment, and the total interest paid to date in a table with appropriate headings. (The monthly interest is $r\,/\,12$ percent of the unpaid balance after the payment is subtracted, where r is the annual interest rate.) Use a function to display these tables. Design the program so it can process several different loan amounts, interest rates, and monthly payments, including at least the following triples of values: $100, 18 percent, $10, and $500, 12 percent, $25. (*Note:* In general, the last payment will not be the same as the monthly payment; the program should show the exact amount of the last payment due.)

17. Proceed as in exercise 16 but with the following modifications: During program execution, have the user enter a payment amount and a day of the month on which this payment was made. The monthly interest is to be calculated on the *average daily balance* for that month. (Assume, for simplicity, that the billing date is the first of the month.) For example, if the balance on June 1 is $500 and a payment of $20 is received on June 12, the interest will be computed on (500 * 11 + 480 * 19) / 30 dollars, which represents the average daily balance for that month.

18. Suppose that on January 1, April 1, July 1, and October 1 of each year, some fixed *Amount* is invested and earns interest at some annual interest rate R compounded quarterly (that is, $R / 4$ percent is added at the end of each quarter). Write a program that reads a number of years and that calculates and displays a table showing the year, the yearly dividend (total interest earned for that year), and the total savings accumulated through that year. Design the program to process several different inputs and to call a function to display the table for each input.

A possible modification/addition to your program: Instead of investing *Amount* dollars each quarter, invest *Amount* / 3 dollars on the first of each month. Then in each quarter, the first payment earns interest for three months ($R / 4$ percent), the second for two months ($R / 6$ percent), and the third for one month ($R / 12$ percent).

SECTION 6.7

19. A third method of calculating depreciation is the *double-declining balance method.* In this method, if an amount is to be depreciated over n years, $2 / n$ times the undepreciated balance is depreciated annually. For example, in the depreciation of $150,000 over a 5-year period using the double-declining balance method, 2/5 of $150,000 ($60,000) would be depreciated the first year, leaving an undepreciated balance of $90,000. In the second year, 2/5 of $90,000 ($36,000) would be depreciated, leaving an undepreciated balance of $54,000. Since only a fraction of the remaining balance is depreciated each year, the entire amount will never be depreciated. Consequently, it is permissible to switch to the straight-line method at any time. Develop an algorithm for this third method of calculating depreciation.

Modify the program in Figure 6.13 so that it includes this third method of calculating depreciation as one of the options. Also, modify the output so that the year numbers in all the depreciation tables begin with the current year rather than with year number 1.

Chapter 7

FUNCTIONS IN DEPTH

On two occasions I have been asked [by members of Parliament], 'Pray, Mr. Babbage, if you put into the machine wrong figures, will the right answers come out?' I am not able rightly to apprehend the kind of confusion of ideas that could provoke such a question.

CHARLES BABBAGE

"Fudd's Law states: 'What goes in must come out.' Aside from being patently untrue, Fudd's Law neglects to mention that what comes out need not bear any resemblance to what went in. "

V. OREHCK III   (fictitious)

So, Naturalists observe, a flea
Hath smaller fleas that on him prey;
And these have smaller fleas to bite 'em
and so proceed ad infinitum.

JONATHAN SWIFT

Before one can understand recursion, one must understand recursion.

V. OREHCK III   (fictitious)

Chapter Contents

7.1   Introductory Example: One-Step Integer Division

7.2   Parameters In Depth

7.3   Examples of Parameter Usage

7.4   Inline Functions

7.5   Scope, Overloading, and Templates

*7.6   Introduction to Recursion

      PART OF THE PICTURE: Numerical Methods

We have seen that designing a solution to a problem involves identifying the *objects* needed to solve the problem as well as the *operations* that must be applied to those objects. Thus far the problems we have examined have required operations that were either provided by C++ or were such that functions could easily be constructed to perform them. Functions are thus one mechanism to implement operations not provided in C++.

In this chapter, we study C++ functions in greater detail. We begin by introducing *reference parameters*, a new mechanism for passing values to and from functions. After presenting several examples that use reference parameters, we consider other properties of C++ functions and introduce recursion. We conclude the chapter with a PART OF THE PICTURE section that describes the area of computer science that studies numerical methods and how they are used to solve a variety of problems.

7.1 INTRODUCTORY EXAMPLE: ONE-STEP INTEGER DIVISION

PROBLEM

We saw in chapter 2 that C++ provides separate operators for calculating the quotient and the remainder that result when one integer is divided by another integer:

op1 / *op2* produces the *quotient* of the division of *op1* by *op2*; and

op1 % *op2* produces the *remainder* of the division of *op1* by *op2*.

Thus, the expression 5 / 3 produces 1, the quotient of the division, and 5 % 3 produces the remainder 2. Suppose that we want to perform both of these operations in a single step. Can we write a C++ function that, given two integer operands, returns both the quotient and the remainder?

OBJECT-CENTERED DESIGN

Behavior. Our function should receive two integer operands. It should compute and return the quotient and the remainder that result when the first integer is divided by the second, provided that the second operand is not zero.

Objects. Four data objects can be identified from our behavioral description:

Description	Type	Kind	Movement	Name
the first operand	int	varying	received (in)	*op1*
the second operand	int	varying	received (in)	*op2*
the quotient of their division	int	varying	returned (out)	*quotient*
the remainder of their division	int	varying	returned (out)	*remainder*

Note that two objects (*quotient* and *remainder*) are to be returned by the function. Technically, a C++ function cannot *return* two values because execution of a `return` statement immediately terminates execution of the function. Thus it will not work to write

```
int DivideInts(int op1, int op2)
{
    return op1 / op2;
    return op1 % op2;   // Execution won't get here!
}
```

because the second `return` statement will never be reached, since execution of the function will terminate when the first `return` statement is reached. Moreover, a function's `return` statement has the form

```
return expression;
```

and so only a single value can be returned to the caller using the `return` statement[1].

However, C++ provides **reference parameters** that make it possible for a function to *pass more than one value back* to its caller. Since we will use this mechanism, we should amend our object list as follows:

Description	Type	Kind	Movement	Name
the first operand	int	varying	received (in)	*op1*
the second operand	int	varying	received (in)	*op2*
the quotient of their division	int	varying	passed back (out)	*quotient*
the remainder of their division	int	varying	passed back (out)	*remainder*

This gives the following specification:

Receive: *op1*, an integer, and
                  op2, an integer

Precondition: *op2* $\neq$ 0

Pass back: *quotient*, an integer, and
                  remainder, an integer

The stub for a function satisfying this specification is as follows:

```
void DivideInts(int op1, int op2,
                int & quotient, int & remainder)
{
}
```

---

[1] The `return` statement can also be used without an expression; in this case, execution of the function terminates but no value is returned—the function is a `void` function.

The ampersand (&) in a parameter declaration specifies that the parameter is a reference parameter. Ordinary parameters (like op1 and op2) only pass values *into* a function, but reference parameters (like quotient and remainder) pass values both *into and out of* a function.

Operations.   From our behavioral description, we have the following operations:

   i.   Check that an integer (*op2*) is nonzero

   ii.   Compute the *quotient* from the division of two integers

   iii.   Compute the *remainder* from the division of two integers

   iv.   Pass *quotient* back to the caller

   v.   Pass *remainder* back to the caller

C++ provides all of these operations, and so we proceed to organize them into an algorithm.

Algorithm.   The reference parameter mechanism automatically performs iv and v, so our algorithm consists of only i–iii:

Algorithm for One-Step Integer Division

1. Check that *op2* is nonzero. If it is, terminate execution.

2. Compute *quotient = op1 / op2.*

3. Compute *remainder = op1 % op2.*

Coding. Figure 7.1 shows the complete definition of the function. Note that because values are passed back via reference parameters, void is used to indicate that the function returns no value (via a return statement).

FIGURE 7.1   1-STEP INTEGER DIVISION.

```
/* DivideInts performs integer division in 1 step.
 *
 * Receive:      op1 and op2, two integers
 * Precondition: op2 is nonzero
 * Pass back:    quotient and remainder, two integers
 * Uses:         assert()
 *******************************************************************/

void DivideInts(int op1, int op2, int & quotient, int & remainder )
{
   assert (op2 != 0);
   quotient = op1 / op2;
   remainder = op1 % op2;
}
```

Testing. Figure 7.2 presents a simple driver program that tests this function by displaying a table of division results obtained by repeatedly calling DivideInts().

FIGURE 7.2   DRIVER PROGRAM FOR DIVIDEINTS.

```
/* intdivision2.cpp displays a table of integer division results.
 *
 * Output: A table of the quotients and remainders produced by
 *         the divisions i/j with i and j running from 1 to 4.
 ***************************************************************/

#include <iostream.h>            // <<, cout, endl
#include <assert.h>              // assert()

void DivideInts(int op1, int op2, int & quotient, int & remainder);

int main()
{
   cout << "                 Division Table\n\n";

   int quot,                         // variables to hold the values
       rem;                          //  passed back from DivideInts()

   for (int j = 1; j <= 4; j++)
   {
      for (int i = 1; i <= 4; i++)
      {
         DivideInts(i, j, quot, rem);
         cout << i << " divided by " << j
              << " gives a quotient of " << quot
              << " and a remainder of " << rem << endl;
      }
      cout << endl;
   }
}

/*** Insert definition of DivideInts() from Figure 7.1 here. ***/
```

Sample run:

```
                   Division Table

1 divided by 1 gives a quotient of 1 and a remainder of 0
2 divided by 1 gives a quotient of 2 and a remainder of 0
3 divided by 1 gives a quotient of 3 and a remainder of 0
4 divided by 1 gives a quotient of 4 and a remainder of 0

1 divided by 2 gives a quotient of 0 and a remainder of 1
2 divided by 2 gives a quotient of 1 and a remainder of 0
3 divided by 2 gives a quotient of 1 and a remainder of 1
4 divided by 2 gives a quotient of 2 and a remainder of 0
```

```
1 divided by 3 gives a quotient of 0 and a remainder of 1
2 divided by 3 gives a quotient of 0 and a remainder of 2
3 divided by 3 gives a quotient of 1 and a remainder of 0
4 divided by 3 gives a quotient of 1 and a remainder of 1

1 divided by 4 gives a quotient of 0 and a remainder of 1
2 divided by 4 gives a quotient of 0 and a remainder of 2
3 divided by 4 gives a quotient of 0 and a remainder of 3
4 divided by 4 gives a quotient of 1 and a remainder of 0
```

Note that the driver program displays (among other things) the values of the arguments `quot` and `rem`. It should be evident from the sample run that each time function `DivideInts()` assigns values to its parameters `quotient` and `remainder`, the values of the corresponding arguments `quot` and `rem` are changed in the driver. Function `DivideInts()` is thus passing multiple values back to its caller, by changing the values of the two variables used as arguments.

Once tested, `DivideInts()` can be stored in a library (e.g., `MyMath`) for reuse by other programs. Such programs need only include the library's header file and then link in the object file produced by compiling its implementation file.

7.2 Parameters in Depth

The rule that governs the relationship between an argument (the value supplied when a function is called) and its corresponding parameter (the variable in the function's heading for storing the argument) is called a **parameter-passing mechanism.** In this section, we examine the various mechanisms available in C++ for passing parameters.

Value Parameters

The simplest parameter passing mechanism is the one that occurs by default. It is named **call-by-value,** and parameters whose values are passed using this mechanism are called **value parameters.** The rule governing them is:

Value Parameter

Form: *type parameter_name*

A value parameter is a distinct variable containing a copy of its argument.

Therefore, any modification of a value parameter within the body of a function *has no effect on the value of its corresponding argument.*

All of the parameters that we have seen in earlier chapters have been value parameters. For example, in the temperature-conversion function in Figure 3.2,

```
double FahrToCelsius(double tempFahr)
{
    return (tempFahr - 32.0) / 1.8;
}
```

the variable `tempFahr` is a value parameter. If `theHighTemp` is a `double` variable whose value is 92.0 and we call

```
celsTemp = FahrToCelsius(theHighTemp);
```

then a variable is allocated for parameter `tempFahr` and the value of `theHigh-Temp` (92.0) is *copied* into it. The function then is executed using this value.

Similarly, in the `Mascot()` function in Figure 5.1,

```
string Mascot(string university)
{
    if (university == "Illinois")
        return "Fighting Illini";
    else if (university == "Indiana")
        return "Hoosiers";
        .
        .
        .
}
```

the parameter `university` is a value parameter. If `school` is a `string` variable whose value is `"Michigan State"`, then when this function is called:

```
cout << Mascot(school) << endl;
```

a variable is allocated for parameter `university` and the value of `school` (`"Michigan State"`) is copied into it. The function is then executed using this value.

Because a value parameter is a distinct variable containing a copy of its argument, *any changes a function makes to a value parameter have no effect on the corresponding argument.* Thus, we could have written the factorial function from Figure 3.8 as follows:

```
int Factorial(int n)
{
    assert(n >= 0);

    double product = 1;

    while (n > 1)
    {
        product *= n;
        n--;
    }

    return product;
}
```

Because parameter `n` is a distinct variable containing a copy of whatever argument is passed, function `Factorial()` can freely change the value of `n` without changing the value of the corresponding argument in the caller.

REFERENCE PARAMETERS

If we examine the function `DivideInts()` in Figure 7.1,

```
void DivideInts(int op1, int op2,
                int & quotient, int & remainder )
{
    quotient = op1 / op2;
    remainder = op1 % op2;
}
```

we see that the parameters op1 and op2 are value parameters. However, the parameters quotient and remainder have an ampersand (&) between their type and their name. When used this way in a parameter declaration, the ampersand indicates that values should be passed to the parameter using the **call-by-reference** mechanism. Such parameters are thus called **reference parameters.** The rule governing them is as follows:

Reference Parameter

Form: *type & parameter_name*

Reference parameters are *aliases of* (alternate names for) their corresponding arguments.

Therefore, any change to the value of a reference parameter within the body of a function *changes the value of* its corresponding argument.

To illustrate, suppose i is 5 and j is 3 in the function call

```
DivideInts(i, j, quot, rem);
```

The value parameters op1 and op2 are distinct variables into which the arguments i and j are copied:

By contrast, quotient and remainder are reference parameters, and so they become aliases, or alternative names for their arguments quot and rem:

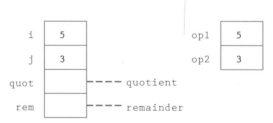

This means that when function DivideInts() assigns a value to its reference parameter quotient, the value of the corresponding argument quot is changed,

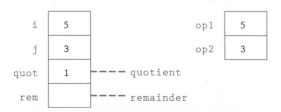

and when `DivideInts()` assigns a value to its reference parameter `remainder`, the value of the corresponding argument `rem` is changed:

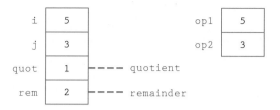

i	5
j	3
quot	1	---- quotient
rem	2	---- remainder

Thus, to design a function like `DivideInts()` that sends back more than one value to its caller, we can proceed as follows:

1. Define a reference parameter for each value to be passed back:

```
void DivideInts(int op1, int op2,
                int & quotient, int & remainder )
```

2. Assign to the reference parameters the values that must be sent back:

```
quotient = op1 / op2;
remainder = op1 % op2;
```

3. Call the function with a *variable* argument for each reference parameter:

```
DivideInts(i, j, quot, rem );
```

When the function terminates, the values of the argument variables will be changed to the values the function assigned to its reference parameters.

An Exam Analogy. Suppose that you are being given an exam by your instructor, and pretend for a moment that you are a function. If this is an oral exam, you are asked a question (an argument) by the instructor (the caller); you store it somewhere in your memory or write it down (a value parameter); and you respond by speaking the answer (the return value) to your instructor (the caller). By contrast, if this is a written exam, the instructor (the caller) might give you a sheet containing questions (call by value) and a blank blue book in which to write your answers (reference parameters) to give back to the instructor (the caller).

Common Errors. Because reference parameters can change the values of the corresponding arguments, these arguments must be objects whose values can be changed, that is, they must be variables. The argument corresponding to a value parameter can be a constant or literal, but *the argument corresponding to a reference parameter must be a **variable**.* For example, the function call

```
DivideInts(40, 3, 4, 5);
```

causes a compilation error because 4 and 5 are not variables. By contrast, if `quot` and `rem` are the `int` variables defined earlier, then the call

```
DivideInts(40, 3, quot, rem);
```

is valid, and following the call, the value of `quot` will be 13 and the value of `rem` will be 1.

The type of an argument corresponding to a reference parameter must match the type of that parameter. Thus, if `doubleQuot` and `doubleRem` are `double` variables and we call `DivideInts()` with them as arguments,

```
DivideInts(40, 3, doubleQuot, doubleRem);
```

a compilation error will result because their types do not match the types of their corresponding parameters.

const REFERENCE PARAMETERS

From the preceding discussion, it may seem that when an object's movement is *out of* (and perhaps also *into*) a function, it should be passed using the *call-by-reference* mechanism, and when it is *only into* a function, it should be passed using the *call-by-value* mechanism. However, there is an alternative to the call-by-value mechanism that is sometimes preferred.

A Problem with Value Parameters. As we have seen, a call-by-reference parameter is an alias of its argument, but a call-by-value parameter is a distinct variable into which the argument's value is copied. When the type of a value parameter is one of the fundamental types (e.g., `int`, `char`, `double`, . . .) the time needed to do this copying is usually negligible, but it might not be when the argument being passed is a *class object* (e.g., `string`, `ostream`, or `istream`).

To illustrate, recall that the `Mascot()` function in Figure 5.1 had a value parameter whose type was `string`:

```
string Mascot( string university )
{
    if (university == "Illinois")
        return "Fighting Illini";
    else if (university == "Indiana")
        return "Hoosiers";
          .
          .
          .
}
```

Suppose that `Mascot()` is called with `school` as an argument,

```
cout << Mascot(school) << endl;
```

where `school` is a `string` variable whose value is `"Penn  State"`. Before `Mascot()` can begin execution, two actions must occur:

1. Sufficient space must be allocated for the parameter `university` to hold its argument:

school	P	e	n	n		S	t	a	t	e

university										

2. The argument must be copied into this space:

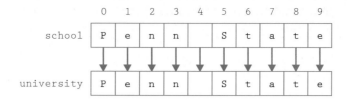

In this example, ten characters must be copied into the parameter's space, and the longer the argument, the greater the number of characters that must be copied. Such copying takes time, increasing the overall execution time of the function. In general, *if a parameter whose type is a class is a value parameter, then the corresponding class argument must be copied, which can be time-inefficient.*

Reference Parameters. Call by reference does not suffer this time-inefficiency because a reference parameter is an alias for its argument—no copying is required. To avoid the time-consuming copying of values required by call by value, many programmers in languages other than C++ always pass large arguments such as classes by reference, regardless of whether their movement is out of or into the function. To illustrate, suppose we make `university` a reference parameter in the function `Mascot()`:

```
string Mascot( string & university )
{
      .
      .
      .

}
```

Then, in a call like the following,

```
cout << Mascot(school) << endl;
```

the parameter `university` simply becomes an alias for its argument `school`:

| school | P | e | n | n | | S | t | a | t | e |---- university |

No copying occurs, avoiding the time-inefficiency of the call-by-value mechanism.

There is a danger with this approach, however. Suppose that the definition of function `Mascot()` contains the common error of using assignment (=) instead of comparison (==) in the `if` statement:

```
string Mascot( string & university )
{
   if (university = "Illinois")
      return "Fighting Illini";
         .
         .
         .

}
```

As explained in section 5.2, university will be assigned the string "Illinois". The result of this assignment is this string, and since it is nonzero, it will be treated as true in this context, causing "Fighting Illini" to be returned regardless of the original value of university. This is obviously an error. But a much more serious and much less obvious error occurs when this function is called as in

```
cout << Mascot(school) << endl;
```

where school has the value "Penn State". Since university is a reference parameter, it is an alias for its argument school, and so the change in the value of university also changes the value of school from "Penn State" to "Illinois", which compounds the error!

school | I | l | l | i | n | o | i | s ---- university

This is the problem with using reference parameters to avoid the inefficiency of the call-by-value mechanism: *If the function mistakenly changes the value of the parameter, the value of the corresponding argument is also changed, and the compiler cannot detect such mistakes.*

The Solution: const Reference Parameters. C++ provides a third method for passing parameters, called the **const reference mechanism,** that avoids both the time-inefficiency of the call-by-value mechanism and the potential for error of the call-by-reference mechanism. To illustrate, the parameter university in Mascot can be defined as a const reference parameter as follows:

```
string Mascot( const string & university )
{
    .
    .
    .
}
```

The effect of the const reference mechanism is twofold:

1. Like the reference mechanism, a const reference parameter is an *alias* of its corresponding argument, and so no time is wasted copying the argument.

school | P | e | n | n | | S | t | a | t | e ---- university

2. Unlike the reference mechanism, a const reference parameter is a **read-only** variable, which means that if the function tries to change the value of the parameter, the compiler will generate an error message, alerting the programmer to the mistake.

```
string Mascot(const string & university)
{
   if (university = "Illinois")
                        // COMPILATION ERROR (Good!)
```

```
      return "Fighting Illini";
          .
          .
          .

   }
```

 For these reasons, *the* `const` *reference mechanism is the preferred way to define parameters whose types are classes (or other large objects) and whose values are received but not passed back to their callers.*

USING PARAMETERS

Learning to use the three different kinds of parameters correctly is not difficult, but it does require us to expand the way we think about constructing functions. To define a function's parameters, a programmer must know precisely the *movement* of objects: What objects are received by the function (*in* objects) and what objects are returned to the caller (*out* objects). Jumping in and writing a C++ function without having a clear specification of the problem that includes a description of how values move into and out of the function often leads to wasted work.

Once the movement of a function's objects is known, the following guidelines can be used to decide what kind of parameters are needed.

P1. If an object is only received by a function from its caller and its type is a fundamental type, define a *value parameter* to receive that object.

P2. If an object is only received by a function from its caller and its type is a class (or other large object), define a `const` *reference parameter* to receive that object.

P3. If only one object must be sent back to its caller, then have the *function return* that object as its result.

P4. If more than one object must be sent back to its caller, use *reference parameters* for those objects to change argument variables in the caller.

In the next section, we present three examples that illustrate how these rules can be applied.

7.3 EXAMPLES OF PARAMETER USAGE

There are many problems that require passing more than one value back to the function's caller. In this section we consider three such problems: decomposing a name, designing a coin dispenser, and swapping the values of two variables. To save space, we will abbreviate the derivations of their solutions.

PROBLEM 1: DECOMPOSING A NAME

A person's full name has three parts: a first name, a middle name, and a last name. Our first problem is to write a function that, given a person's full name, passes back his or her first name, middle name, and last name.

In terms of behavior, such a function must receive from its caller a full name. The function must decompose this full name into a first name, a middle name, and a last name, and pass all of these back to the caller. We thus have the following objects:

Description	Type	Kind	Movement	Name
full name	string	varying	received (in)	*fullName*
the first name	string	varying	passed back (out)	*firstName*
the middle name	string	varying	passed back (out)	*middleName*
the last name	string	varying	passed back (out)	*lastName*

This gives the following specification:

Receive: *fullName*, a string value

Precondition: *fullName* contains a *firstName*, a *middleName*, and a *lastName*, separated by spaces

Pass back: *firstName, middleName, lastName*

Because *fullName* is a class object that is received from its caller, we define it as a const reference parameter, according to rule P2 in the preceding section. Because *firstName, middleName* and *lastName* are passed back to the caller, we define these objects as reference parameters, according to rule P4. This gives the following stub for our function:

```
void DecomposeName(const string & fullName, string & firstName,
                   string & middleName, string & lastName)
{
}
```

In order to decompose *fullName* into its three components, we must perform the following operations:

   i.   Extract and assign the first name in *fullName* to *firstName*

   ii.   Extract and assign the second name in *fullName* to *middleName*

  iii.   Extract and assign the third name in *fullName* to *lastName*

The string function member substr() can be used to do the extraction, but it requires the index at which to begin and the number of characters to be extracted. To see how to find these, we will work through an example.

Suppose that fullName is "John Quincy Doe":

For the first name, the index at which to begin is zero; the index for the middle name is one past the first blank (5); and for the last name, the index is one past the second blank (12). We thus need to find the index values of the first and second blanks, and for this we can use the `string` function member `find()`.

The number of characters to be extracted for the first name is equal to the index of the first blank (4). For the second name it is equal to the index of the second blank (11) minus the index of the first blank (4) minus one (= 6). The number of characters to be extracted for the last name is equal to the size of the `full-Name` (15) minus the index of the second blank (11) minus one (= 3). Note that, for simplicity, we are assuming that only one blank separates the first, middle, and last names.

We can organize these observations into the following algorithm:

Algorithm for Name Decomposition

1. Use `find()` to find the index of the first blank in *fullName*.
2. Use `substr()` to extract *firstName*.
3. Use `find()` to find the index of the second blank in *fullName*.
4. Use `substr()` to extract *middleName*.
5. Use `size()` and the result of 3 to find the number of characters in *lastName*.
6. Use `substr()` to extract *lastName*.

Given this algorithm, we can define our function as shown in Figure 7.3, which also contains a driver program to test it. Note that because a search can fail, it is always a good idea to check the value returned by `find()`, either with an `assert()` (as in `DecomposeName()`) or with an `if` statement.

FIGURE 7.3   NAME DECOMPOSITION.

```
/* name3.cpp is a driver program to test the function DecomposeName().
 *
 * Input:  a person's full name
 * Output: the person's first name, middle name, and last name
 *************************************************************/

#include <iostream.h>              // cout, cin, <<, >>
#include <string>                  // string, getline

void DecomposeName(const string & fullName, string & firstName,
                   string & middleName, string & lastName);

int main()
{
   cout << "Enter a full name: ";
   string fullName;
   getline(cin, fullName);

   string fName, mName, lName;
   DecomposeName(fullName, fName, mName, lName);
```

```
        cout << fName << endl
             << mName << endl
             << lName << endl;
}


/* DecomposeName breaks down a full name into its 3 parts.
 *
 *  Receive:       fullName, a string
 *  Precondition:  fullName contains 3 names separated by blanks
 *  Pass back:     the 3 parts: firstName, middleName and lastName
 *************************************************************/

#include <assert.h>          // assert()

void DecomposeName(const string & fullName, string & firstName,
                   string & middleName, string & lastName)
{
   int firstBlankIndex = fullName.find(' ', 0);
   assert(firstBlankIndex != NPOS);
   firstName = fullName.substr(0, firstBlankIndex);

   int secondBlankIndex = fullName.find(' ', firstBlankIndex + 1);
   assert(secondBlankIndex != NPOS);
   middleName = fullName.substr(firstBlankIndex + 1,
                                secondBlankIndex - firstBlankIndex - 1);

   int fullNameSize = fullName.size();
   lastName = fullName.substr(secondBlankIndex + 1,
                              fullNameSize - secondBlankIndex - 1);
}
```

Sample run:

```
Enter a full name: John Quincy Doe
John
Quincy
Doe
```

PROBLEM 2: DESIGNING A COIN DISPENSER

An automated cash register has two inputs: the amount of a purchase and the amount given as payment. It computes the number of dollars, quarters, dimes, nickels, and pennies to be given in change. The cashier returns the dollars to the customer, but the coins are returned by an automatic coin dispenser. Our problem is to write a function that, given the amount of a purchase and the amount given as payment, will compute and return the number of dollars to be returned by the cashier and the number of coins of each denomination to be returned by the coin dispenser.

Identifying the data objects in this problem is relatively easy:

Description	Type	Kind	Movement	Name
the amount of the purchase	real	varying	received (in)	*purchaseAmount*
the amount of the payment	real	varying	received (in)	*payment*
how many dollars in change	integer	varying	passed back (out)	*dollars*
how many quarters in change	integer	varying	passed back (out)	*quarters*
how many dimes in change	integer	varying	passed back (out)	*dimes*
how many nickels in change	integer	varying	passed back (out)	*nickels*
how many pennies in change	integer	varying	passed back (out)	*pennies*

Once we have identified these objects, we can specify the function as follows:

Receive: *purchaseAmount*, the (real) amount of the purchase
              payment, the (real) amount of the payment

Precondition: *payment* >= *purchaseAmount*

Pass back: *dollars*, the (integer) number of dollars in change
              quarters, the (integer) number of quarters in change
              dimes, the (integer) number of dimes in change
              nickels, the (integer) number of nickels in change
              pennies, the (integer) number of pennies in change

Using rule P1, we define *purchaseAmount* and *payment* as value parameters, and using rule P4, we define *dollars, quarters, dimes, nickels,* and *pennies* as reference parameters. We can then construct the following stub for the function MakeChange():

```
void MakeChange(double purchaseAmount,   // amount of purchase
                double payment,          // amount of payment
                int & dollars,           // dollars of change
                int & quarters,          // quarters of change
                int & dimes,             // dimes of change
                int & nickels,           // nickels of change
                int & pennies)           // pennies of change
{
}
```

To determine the sequence of operations needed to make change, we will work through a specific example. Suppose the amount of a purchase is $8.49 and we pay with a $10.00 bill. We clearly must begin by subtracting the purchase amount from the payment to get the total amount of change ($1.51). This is a real value, but our return values are integers, and so we must at some point convert this real value to an integer value. One approach would be to store the total amount of change (1.51) as a real value and perform a separate conversion as each return value is computed. However, this requires doing the same thing six times—an indication that there is probably a better way. Also, real values are not stored exactly (e.g., 1.51 might be stored as 1.50999...) and thus is it is better to convert the real amount

of change (1.51) into an integer value (151) at the outset, ensuring that no significant digits are lost. This can be done by multiplying the real amount of change by
100, adding 0.5, and then truncating the fractional part of the result. The following
examples illustrate this computation:

The result of this computation is the change in cents, and we will store this value in
a local (variable) object *change.*
    We can now construct the following algorithm to solve the problem:

Algorithm to Make Change

1. Compute *change* as the difference between *payment* and *purchaseAmount,* in
    cents.
2. If *change* is positive, then
    a. Compute *dollars* in *change* and remove *dollars* from *change.*
    b. Compute *quarters* in *change* and remove *quarters* from *change.*
    c. Compute *dimes* in *change* and remove *dimes* from *change.*
    d. Compute *nickels* in *change* and remove *nickels* from *change.*
    e. Compute *pennies* in *change.*
    Otherwise
       Set each of *dollars, quarters, dimes, nickels,* and *pennies* to zero.

Once *change* has been computed as the amount of change in cents, the number
of dollars of change can be computed using integer division, dividing the value of
change by 100:

```
dollars = change / 100;  // for change = 151, dollars equals 1
```

The remaining change is the remainder that results from this division:

```
change %= 100;            // for change = 151, change becomes 51
```

The number of quarters remaining in *change* can then be computed in a similar
manner by dividing *change* by 25,

```
quarters = change / 25;
```

The remainder of this division is then the amount of change remaining to be dis-
pensed as dimes, nickels, and pennies:

```
change %= 25;
```

Similar calculations are used to determine the number of dimes, nickels, and pennies. The complete function is given in Figure 7.4:

FIGURE 7.4   COMPUTING CHANGE.

```
/* MakeChange computes the dollars, quarters, dimes, nickels, and
 * pennies in change given the amount of a purchase and the amount paid.
 *
 * Receive:       purchaseAmount, the (real) amount of the purchase,
 *                payment, the (real) amount of the payment
 * Precondition: purchaseAmount <= payment.
 * Pass back:     dollars, the (integer) number of dollars,
 *                quarters, the (integer) number of quarters,
 *                dimes, the (integer) number of dimes,
 *                nickels, the (integer) number of nickels, and
 *                pennies, the (integer) number of pennies in change
 ************************************************************************/

void MakeChange(double purchaseAmount,   // amount of purchase
                double payment,          // amount of payment
                int & dollars,           // dollars of change
                int & quarters,          // quarters of change
                int & dimes,             // dimes of change
                int & nickels,           // nickels of change
                int & pennies)           // pennies of change
{
   int change = int(100.0 * (payment - purchaseAmount) + 0.5);

   if (change > 0)
   {
      dollars = change / 100;       // 100 pennies per dollar
      change %= 100;                // compute remaining change

      quarters = change / 25;       // 25 pennies per quarter
      change %= 25;                 // compute remaining change

      dimes = change / 10;          // 10 pennies per dime
      change %= 10;                 // compute remaining change

      nickels = change / 5;         // 5 pennies per nickel
      pennies = change % 5;         // pennies are all that's left
   }
   else
   {
      cerr << "*** Purchase amount: " << purchaseAmount
           << " exceeds payment: " << payment << endl;
      dollars = quarters = dimes = nickels = pennies = 0;
   }
}
```

It should be noted that we could write this function more succinctly using the DivideInts() function from section 7.1. We simply change the if statement in the function to

```
      if (change > 0)
      {
          DivideInts(change, 100, dollars, change);
          DivideInts(change, 25, quarters, change);
          DivideInts(change, 10, dimes, change);
          DivideInts(change, 5, nickels, pennies);
      }
      else
      {
          cerr << "*** Purchase amount: " << purchaseAmount
               << " exceeds payment: " << payment << endl;
          dollars = quarters = dimes = nickels = pennies = 0;
      }
```

We can test our function by writing a driver program that reads two amounts itemCost and amountPaid, calls MakeChange() to calculate the change that must be given, and then displays the amounts passed back by MakeChange(). Figure 7.5 presents a driver program that uses a sentinel-controlled loop to process several amounts.

 FIGURE 7.5   DRIVER PROGRAM FOR MakeChange().

```
/* changemaker5.cpp is a driver program that tests function MakeChange().
 *
 * Input:  the cost of an item, and the amount paid
 * Output: the change in terms of numbers of dollars, quarters,
 *         dimes, nickels, and pennies
 **************************************************************************/

#include <iostream.h>           // cout, cin, <<, >>
#include <string>               // string

void MakeChange(double purchaseAmount, double payment,
            int & dollars, int & quarters, int & dimes,
            int & nickels, int & pennies);

int main()
{
   const string SENTINEL = "a negative value";

   cout << "This program tests a change-making function...\n\n";

   double itemCost,         // a purchase
          amountPaid;       // what was paid

   int numDollars,         // variables for
       numQuarters,        //   the values
       numDimes,           //   to be output
       numNickels,
       numPennies;
```

```
      for (;;)
      {
         cout << "Enter item cost and amount paid ("
              << SENTINEL << " to quit): ";
         cin >> itemCost;

         if (itemCost < 0) break;

         cin >> amountPaid;

         MakeChange(itemCost, amountPaid, numDollars,
                    numQuarters, numDimes, numNickels, numPennies);

         cout << "The change from this purchase is:`n"
              << numDollars << " dollars,\n"
              << numQuarters << " quarters,\n"
              << numDimes << " dimes,\n"
              << numNickels << " nickels, and\n"
              << numPennies << " pennies\n\n";
      }
}
/*** Insert definition of MakeChange() from Figure 7.4 here ***/
```

Sample run:

```
This program tests a change-making function...

Enter item cost and amount paid (a negative value to quit): 1.01 2.00
The change from this purchase is:
0 dollars,
3 quarters,
2 dimes,
0 nickels, and
4 pennies

Enter item cost and amount paid (a negative value to quit): 1.34 5.00
The change from this purchase is:
3 dollars,
2 quarters,
1 dimes,
1 nickels, and
1 pennies

Enter item cost and amount paid (a negative value to quit): 9.99 10.00
The change from this purchase is:
0 dollars,
0 quarters,
0 dimes,
0 nickels, and
1 pennies

Enter item cost, and amount paid (a negative value to quit): -1
```

PROBLEM 3: INTERCHANGING THE VALUES OF TWO VARIABLES

There are certain problems in which it is necessary to interchange the values of two variables. For example, one approach to reverse the characters in a `string` is to interchange its first and last characters, interchange its second and next-to-last characters, and so on.

Because this "swapping" operation is useful in many problems, it is worthwhile to construct a function to perform it and store the function in a library. Given such a function, we can call

```
Swap(ch1, ch2);
```

to exchange the values of character variables `ch1` and `ch2`, or call

```
Swap(aString[i], aString[j]);
```

to exchange the values of the characters at indices `i` and `j` within `aString`.

If we assume for this example that two character variables are to have their values interchanged, then we can list the data objects needed to perform this operation as follows:

Description	Kind	Type	Movement	Name
the first variable	varying	char	received (in) and passed back (out)	*first*
the second variable	varying	char	received (in) and passed back (out)	*second*

Note the unusual movement of this function: because the value of *first* must be changed to the value of *second, first* must be passed back, and *second* must be received; and because the value of *second* must be changed to the value of *first, first* must be received and *second* passed back. Thus both have *in-out* movement, and we can specify the behavior as follows:

Receive: *first,* a (char) variable
             second, a (char) variable

Return: *first,* containing the value of *second,* and
            second, containing the value of *first.*

Since this specification indicates that two values are to be passed back, rule P4 can be applied with *first* and *second* as reference parameters because they are passed back, as well as received. This allows us to construct the following stub for the function `Swap()`:

```
void Swap(char & first, char & second)
{
}
```

To perform the swap operation, we cannot simply assign the value of `second` to `first` (or vice versa), because the value of `first` will be overwritten and lost.

Instead, the correct approach is to define an auxiliary variable and perform the interchange, as shown in Figure 7.6.

FIGURE 7.6   INTERCHANGING THE VALUES OF TWO VARIABLES.

```
/* Swap exchanges the values of two variables.
 *
 * Receive:    first, a (char) variable
 *             second, a (char) variable
 * Pass back: first, containing the value of second, and
 *             second, containing the value of first
 *************************************************************/

void Swap(char & first, char & second)
{
   char temporary = first;

   first = second;
   second = temporary;
}
```

Given such a function, other functions can use it to exchange the values of two character variables. For example, the following function receives a string and returns that string reversed:

```
string Reverse(const string & originalString)
{
   string resultString = originalString;
   int begin = 0,
       end = resultString.size() - 1;

   while (begin < end)
   {
      Swap(resultString[begin], resultString[end]);
      begin++;
      end--;
   }

   return resultString;
}
```

✔ Quick Quiz 7.3

1. The parameter-passing mechanism that occurs by default is call-by-_____

2. A _____ parameter contains a copy of the corresponding argument.

3. If a _____ parameter is changed in the body of the function, then the value of the corresponding argument is not changed.

4. If a _____ parameter is changed in the body of the function, then the value of the corresponding argument is also changed.

5. Placing a(n) _____ between a parameter's type and its name indicates that the parameter is a reference parameter.

Questions 6–11 assume the following function definition

```
void F(int x, int & y, int & z)
{
  z = y = x * x + 1;
}
```

and the following declarations in the calling function:

```
int a = 0, b = 1, c = 2, d = 3;
const int E  = 4;
```

6. (True or false) After `d = F(a, b, c);` is executed, d will have the value 1.

7. (True or false) After `F(a, b, c);` is executed, b and c will both have the value 1.

8. (True or false) After `F(c, d, E);` is executed, d will have the value 5.

9. (True or false) After `F(c+1, c-1, d);` is executed, d will have the value 10.

10. (True or false) The function call `F(c, d, E);` makes z a `const` reference parameter.

11. Rewrite the definition of `F()` so that x is a `const` reference parameter.

12. Given the function definition

```
void Change(int number, string & a, string & b, string & c)
{
    const string BAT = "bat";

    if (number < 3)
    {
        a = BAT;
        b = BAT;
    }
    else
        c = BAT;
}
```

What output will the following program segment produce?

```
string str1 = "cat", str2 = "dog", str3 = "elk";
Change(2, str1, str2, str3);
cout << "String = " << str1 << str2 < str3 << endl;
```

EXERCISES 7.3

Exercises 1–11 assume the following program skeleton:

```
void Calculate(double a, double & b,
              int m, int & k, int & n, char & c);
```

```
int main()
{
    const double PI = 3.14159;
    const int TWO = 2;
    const char INITIAL = 'N';

    int month, day, year, p, q;
    double hours, rate, amount, u, v;
    char code, dept;
}
```

Determine whether the given statement can be used to call the function `Calculate()`. If it cannot be used, explain why.

1. `Calculate(u, v, TWO, p, q, code);`

2. `Calculate(PI, u, TWO, p, v, dept);`

3. `Calculate(hours, PI, TWO, day, year, dept);`

4. `Calculate(13, hours, PI, 13, year, dept);`

5. `Calculate(PI * hours, PI, TWO, day, year, dept);`

6. `Calculate(PI, PI * hours, TWO, day, year, dept);`

7. `while (u > 0)`
   `    Calculate(u, v, TWO, p, q, code);`

8. `Calculate(0, hours, (p + 1) / 2, day, year, code)`

9. `Calculate(sqrt(amount), rate, 7, p, q, INITIAL);`

10. `while (amount > 0)`
    `    Calculate(TWO, amount, day, p + q, day, dept);`

11. `cout << Calculate(u, v, TWO, p, q, code);`

The following exercises ask you to write functions to compute various quantities. To test these functions, you should write driver programs as instructed in Programming Problems 1–3 at the end of this chapter.

12. Write a function that receives a weight in pounds and ounces and returns the corresponding weight in grams. (1 oz = 28.349527 g)

13. Write a function that receives a weight in grams and returns the corresponding weight in pounds and ounces. (1 g = 0.35274 oz)

14. Write a function that receives a measurement in yards, feet, and inches and returns the corresponding measurement in centimeters. (1 in = 2.54001 cm)

15. Write a function that receives a measurement in centimeters and returns the corresponding measurement in yards, feet, and inches. (1 cm = 0.3937 in)

16. Write a function that receives a time in the usual representation of hours, minutes, and a character value that indicates whether this is A.M. ('A') or P.M. ('P') and returns the corresponding military time.

17. Write a function that receives a time in military format and returns the corresponding time in the usual representation in hours, minutes, and A.M. / P.M. For example, a time of 0100 should be returned as 1 hour, 0 minutes, and 'A' to indicate A.M.; and a time of 1545 should be returned as 3 hours, 45 minutes, and 'P' to indicate P.M.

7.4 INLINE FUNCTIONS

We have seen that when one function F() calls another function G(), execution is transferred from F() to G(). When G() terminates, a second transfer of control is necessary to return execution back to F(). Each of these transfers takes time—a great deal of time in fact, compared to the speed at which a computer normally operates. *Each function call significantly increases the amount of time required for a program to execute.*

In many situations, the *overhead* associated with function calls is acceptable, but there are other problems in which time is so important that this overhead cannot be tolerated. For these problems, C++ provides *inlining* of functions.[2]

One of the details we omitted (for simplicity) in the description of function definitions in section 3.2 is that a definition can be preceded by a function specifier, which provides the compiler with special instructions about the function:

```
function_specifier return_type function_name
                              (parameter_declaration_list)
{
    statement_list
}
```

One such specifier is the **inline specifier,** which instructs the compiler to use the C++ inline mechanism to avoid the overhead of normal function calls.

To illustrate, suppose we want to inline the temperature-conversion function FahrToCelsius() in Figure 3.2. We can do so by preceding its prototype and its definition with the inline specifier:

```
inline  double FahrToCelsius(double tempFahr);
          .
          .
          .
inline  double FahrToCelsius(double tempFahr)
{
    return (tempFahr - 32.0) / 1.8;
}
```

When the function prototype and definition occur in the same file as in Figure 3.2, both must be labeled as inline. Otherwise, there will be a mismatch between the function's prototype and its definition, and a compiler error results.

The inline specifier suggests to the C++ compiler that it *replace each call to this function with the body of the function, with the arguments for that function call substituted for the function's parameters.*[3] For example, the compiler is being asked to effectively replace the function call in the statement

```
tempCelsius = FahrToCelsius(tempFahrenheit);
```

---

[2] The inline specifier effectively provides a fourth parameter passing mechanism that is known as *call-by-name,* or *macro-substitution.* See *Compilers: Principles, Techniques and Tools,* by Aho, Sethi and Ullman (Reading, Mass.: Addison-Wesley, 1986) for a discussion of the limitations of this mechanism.

---

[3] This *request* may be ignored by the compiler if it judges that the function definition is too complicated to be inlined efficiently.

with the body of the function, but with the argument `tempFahrenheit` substituted for parameter `tempFahr`:

```
tempCelsius = (tempFahrenheit - 32.0) / 1.8;
```

The effect of the `inline` specifier is to ask the compiler to take additional *compile time* to perform this substitution *for each call* to the function. This saves *run time,* because the elimination of each function call means that no transfers of execution need to be performed, eliminating the overhead incurred by those function calls.

INLINE FUNCTIONS AND LIBRARIES

The normal procedure for a function stored in a library is to put its prototype in the library's header file and its definition in the implementation file. This separation is not allowed, however, if we want to inline a function. *An* `inline` *library function must be defined in the header file.*

To illustrate, suppose that a library `MyMath` contains, among other mathematical functions, the function `Sum()` from Figure 6.14, with the prototype of `Sum()` in `MyMath.h` and its definition in `MyMath.cpp`. To designate `Sum()` as an inline function, we would remove its definition from the implementation file and replace its prototype in the header file with this definition, preceding it with the `inline` specifier, as shown in Figure 7.7.

 FIGURE 7.7   INLINE LIBRARY FUNCTIONS.

```
/* This header file provides an interface for library MyMath.
 * It contains prototypes and inline definitions of non-predefined
 * math functions.
 * ... remaining opening documentation omitted ...
 ****************************************************************/

int Factorial(int n);

inline  int Sum(int n)
{
    return n * (n + 1) / 2;
}

// ... other function prototypes and/or inline definitions
```

These steps are necessary because the only part of the library that the compiler sees when it compiles a program is the header file, which is inserted when it processes the `#include` directive. If the *compiler* (and not the *linker*) is to replace calls to a function with the function's definition, this definition must be available to the compiler, which means that it must be moved from the implementation file to the header file.

TO INLINE OR NOT TO INLINE: A SPACE-TIME TRADEOFF

Because inlined functions eliminate the overhead of function calls and make programs run faster, it may be tempting to make all functions inline. There is, however, a *space-time tradeoff:* a program that uses inlined functions may indeed run *faster* than its non-inlined equivalent, but it may also be much *larger* and thus require more memory.

To see why this happens, we must realize that, unlike the simple examples we have been using, functions written for real-world software projects typically (1) contain many statements, and (2) may be called at many different places in a program. When such a function is inlined, *each substitution of the function's body for its call replaces a single statement (the call) with many statements (the body),* which increases the overall size of the program.

More generally, suppose that we are working on a software project and write a function `F()` that is called at N different places in our program. Let S_{prog} denote the size of the program (including the definition and call of `F()`) and S_{fun} denote the size of function `F()`. If `F()` is not implemented as an inline function, the total space needed for the program is simply

$$S_{prog}$$

but if it is inlined, the program's total space will be approximately

$$S_{prog} + N \times S_{fun}$$

Thus, if the size of function `F()` is more than a few operations, and `F()` is called many times, then substituting the body of `F()` at each call will significantly increase the overall size of the program, a phenomenon known as **code bloat.**

 To avoid code bloat, we recommend that `inline` *be used with restraint:* If a function uses just a few operations (such as the `FahrToCelsius()` and `Sum()` functions), then designate it as `inline` to eliminate the overhead associated with calling the function. But if a function uses many operations, do not use `inline`.[4]

✔ Quick Quiz 7.4

1. (True or false) Function calls increase the execution time of a program.
2. The _____ specifier provides a way to avoid the overhead of function calls.
3. Describe what inlining a function suggests to the compiler.
4. For the function definition

   ```
   inline int F(int n)
   { return n * (n + 1) / 2; }
   ```

   how will the compiler modify the statement `cout << F(number);` ?

---

[4] There are situations where the use of `inline` will increase the size of a program without producing any gain in its execution speed. See *Effective C++,* by Scott Meyers (Reading, Mass.: Addison-Wesley, 1992), pp. 107–110.

5. If a library function is inlined, then the function must be defined in the _____ file of the library.

6. (True or false) Programs that use `inline` functions will usually run faster.

7. (True or false) Programs that use `inline` functions will usually require less memory.

7.5 SCOPE, OVERLOADING, AND TEMPLATES

As we have seen, identifiers are used to name the objects and functions in a program. For example, the library `MyMath` in Figure 7.7 might contain two summation functions, one to calculate sums of the form $1 + 2 + \cdots + n$ and another to calculate sums of the form $m + (m + 1) + \cdots + n$. Although we might use different names for the functions, this is not necessary. We can name them both `Sum()`:

```
inline int Sum(int n)
{
   return n * (n + 1) / 2;
}

inline int Sum(int m, int n)
{
   assert(m < n);
   return (n - m + 1) * (n + m) / 2;
}
```

As these definitions indicate

1. The same identifier can be used in different functions without conflict (e.g., parameter n).

2. Two functions can have the same name

However, if we try to use the same identifier to define two different objects in the same function as in

```
void F()
{
   int value;
   ...
   char value;        // ERROR!
   ...
}
```

a compilation error results.

These examples raise an important question:

What rules govern the use of and/or access to an identifier?

As we shall see, some rules govern access to identifiers in general and other rules govern access to identifiers that are names of functions. In this section we describe these rules.

The **scope** of an identifier is that portion of a program where that identifier is the name of an object or function that can be accessed. For example, consider again the definitions of the two summation functions. The identifier n is used in both definitions, but it has two distinct scopes. In the first function, n is the name of the first parameter, and any uses of n in the body of that function refer to that parameter:

```
int Sum(int n)
{
    return n * (n + 1) / 2;
}

int Sum(int m, int n)
{
    return (n - m + 1) * (n + m) / 2;
}
```

This is sometimes described by saying that *the body of the first function lies within the scope of its parameter* n.

In the second function, the identifier n is the name of the second parameter, and so any use of n in that function refers to that object:

```
int Sum(int n)
{
    return n * (n + 1) / 2;
}

int Sum(int m, int n)
{
    return (n - m + 1) * (n + m) / 2;
}
```

The body of the second function lies within the scope of its parameter n (and within the scope of its parameter m as well).

Any attempt to access an identifier outside its scope produces a compilation error. For example, if we changed the definition of the first function to

```
int Sum(int n)
{
    m = 1;
    return (n - m + 1) * (n + m) / 2;
}
```

then an error message like

```
Identifier 'm' is undeclared
```

would be generated when the function is compiled, because there is no identifier m whose scope reaches the body of that function. Understanding scope is important for understanding certain compilation errors.

Stated simply, the scope of an identifier depends on *where the identifier is declared.* The scopes of the identifiers we have seen thus far have been determined by four simple rules:[5]

S1. If an identifier is declared within a block,
    then its scope runs from its declaration to the end of the block.

S2. If an identifier is a declared outside all blocks,
    then its scope runs from its declaration to the end of the file.

S3. If an identifier is declared in the initialization expression of a `for` loop,
    then its scope runs from its declaration to the end of the loop.

S4. If an identifier is a parameter of a function,
    then its scope is the body of the function.

Note that an identifier's scope always begins at some point following its declaration. This observation can be summarized in the single rule:

An identifier must be declared before it can be used.

A Quick Example.   To illustrate how the compiler uses these rules, suppose that we were to rewrite the `GetMenuChoice()` function from section 6.2 as follows:

```
char GetMenuChoice(const string & MENU,
                   char firstChoice, char lastChoice)
{
   for (;;)
   {
      cout << MENU;
      char choice;
      cin >> choice;

      if (choice >= firstChoice && choice <= lastChoice)
         break;

      cerr << "\nI'm sorry, but " << choice
           << " is not a valid menu choice.\n";
   }

   return choice;               // ERROR!
}
```

When this function is compiled, the `return` statement generates an error message like

```
Identifier 'choice' is undeclared
```

(Before continuing, use the scope rules to try to find the cause of the error.)

---
[5] There is also a fifth rule that governs the scope of identifiers declared in classes as described in chapter 10.

The problem is that by declaring `choice` within the body of the loop, we have declared it inside a block, and by rule S1, its scope only runs through the last statement of the block:

```
char GetMenuChoice(const string & MENU,
                   char firstChoice, char lastChoice)
{
   for (;;)
   {
      cout << MENU;
      char choice;
      cin >> choice;

      if (choice >= firstChoice && choice <= lastChoice)
         break;

      cerr << "\nI'm sorry, but " << choice
           << " is not a valid menu choice.\n";
   }

   return choice;                  // ERROR!
}
```

Since the `return` statement appears after the block, it lies outside the scope of `choice`, and so the compiler generates an error when an attempt is made to access `choice`. The problem can be avoided by moving its declaration to the outermost block of the function, thus insuring that all statements that refer to `choice` lie within its scope:

```
char GetMenuChoice(const string & MENU,
                   char firstChoice, char lastChoice)
{
   char choice;

   for (;;)
   {
      cout << MENU;
      cin >> choice;

      if (choice >= firstChoice && choice <= lastChoice)
         break;

      cerr << "\nI'm sorry, but " << choice
           << " is not a valid menu choice.\n";
   }

   return choice;                  // Ok!
}
```

Objects Declared Outside All Blocks. Although we have not put any declarations of variables or constants outside all blocks, we have done so with prototypes of functions. For example, in Figure 7.3, the prototype of the function Decompose-Name() precedes the main function, so that the identifier DecomposeName is declared outside all blocks. By scope rule S2, its scope thus extends from its declaration to the end of the file:

```
#include <iostream.h>
#include <string>

void DecomposeName(const string & fullName,
                   string & firstName,
                   string & middleName, string & lastName)

int main()
{
   cout << "Enter a full name: ";
   string fullName;
   cin >> fullName;

   string fName, mName, lName;
   DecomposeName(fullName, fName, mName, lName);

   cout << fName << endl
        << mName << endl
        << lName << endl;
}.
 .
 .
```

This is the reason why a function prototype *must* precede calls to a function. Since a prototype is a declaration of the function, it begins the scope of the function. Calls to the function thus lie within its scope.

Identifiers that are declared in a library's header file, such as `cin`, `cout`, and `cerr` in `iostream.h` and the class `string` in the header file `string`, are also governed by rule S2. When the compiler processes a `#include` directive outside all blocks as in

```
#include <iostream.h>

int main()
{
   ...
}
```

then all objects in that file are inserted outside all blocks and thus fall under rule S2. The scope of such declarations thus extends from their declarations (i.e., from the `#include` directive) to the end of the file. Thus, if we were to write

```
#include <iostream.h>

int main()
{
   ...
}

void G()
{
   ...
}
```

then both `main()` and `G()` lie within the scope of `cin`, `cout`, and `cerr`. By contrast, if we write

```
int main()
{
   ...
}

#include <iostream.h>

void G()
{
   ...
}
```

then any attempt to access cin, cout, or cerr in main() will result in a compilation error, because main() does not lie within their scope.

Scopes of for-Loop Control Variables. Rule S3 that governs the scope of an identifier declared in the initialization expression of a for loop deserves special attention, because it is easy to make mistakes when using several for loops if this rule is not well understood. To illustrate, suppose that a programmer writes a program containing two for loops as follows:

```
int main()
{
   ...
   for (int i = 1; i <= someLimit; i++)
      // ... do something with i
   ...
   for (i = 1; i <= someLimit; i++)          // ERROR!
      // ... do something with i again
   ...
}
```

When the program is compiled, an error message like

```
Identifier 'i' is undeclared
```

is generated by the first line of the second for loop. The reason for this is that by rule S3, the scope of i begins at its declaration and ends at the end of the first for loop:

```
int main()
{
   ...
   for (int i = 1; i <= someLimits; i++)
      // ... do something with i
   ...
   for (i = 1; i <= someLimit; i++)          // ERROR!
      // ... do something with i again
   ...
}
```

As a result, the second loop lies outside the scope of i, so that when an attempt is made there to reuse i, it is no longer available, and the compiler generates an error.

Such an error can be corrected in several ways. One way is to redeclare i in the second loop, so that a new scope for i is present in that loop:

```
int main()
{
   ...
   for (int i = 1; i <= someLimit; i++)
      // ... do something with i
   ...
   for (int i = 1; i <= someLimit; i++)              // Ok!
      // ... do something with i again
   ...
}
```

Another solution is to move the declaration of i *before* the first loop, so that it is governed by rule S1 instead of rule S3, and both loops fall within its scope:

```
int main()
{
   ...
   int i;
   for (i = 1; i <= someLimit; i++)
      // ... do something with i
   ...
   for (i = 1; i <= someLimit; i++)              // Ok!
      // ... do something with i again
   ...
}
```

Name Conflicts. Our discussion of scope would not be complete without mentioning one final rule:

> *Within the scope of an identifier, no redeclaration of that identifier that results in an ambiguity for the compiler is permitted.*

As a simple illustration, suppose we write

```
int main()
{
   int value = 1;

   double value = 2.0;        // ERROR!

   cout << value << endl;
   return 0;
}
```

The redeclaration of value creates an *ambiguity* for the compiler, because in the output statement, it is unclear which value is to be displayed. From the standpoint of the compiler, value is declared as the name of an int object, starting the scope of the identifier value. When the compiler encounters a second declaration of the same name that it cannot distinguish from the first declaration, a **name conflict** arises,

```
int main()
{
    int value = 1;

    double value = 2.0;          // ERROR!

    cout << value << endl;
    return 0;
}
```

and so the compiler generates an error. By constrast, there is no name conflict in the following, because the scopes of the two versions of value do not overlap:

```
int main()
{
    ...
    if (x > 0)
    {
        int value = 1;
        cout << value << endl;
    }
    else
    {
        double value = 2.0;
        cout << value << endl;
    }
}
```

The compiler will eliminate ambiguity between names whenever it can. To illustrate, consider the following example:

```
int main()
{
    int value = 1;
    {
        double value = 2.3;
        cout << value << endl;
    }
    cout << value << endl;
}
```

The effect here is that the outer (int) version of value will be hidden from the statements within the scope of the nested object. Because value is redeclared in its own *nested block,* the compiler will assume that accesses within the scope of the nested declaration are to the local (double) version of value, and accesses outside of its scope are to the outer (int) version of value, and so the compiler will proceed to translate the code. The output produced will be

```
2.3
1
```

Since the outer object is accessible before and after this nested scope, but is not accessible within it, the nested object is sometimes described as creating **a**

hole in the scope of the outer object. Some compilers may generate a warning message like

```
Warning: redeclaration of 'value' hides previous declaration
```

to alert us to this hole.

FUNCTION SIGNATURES AND OVERLOADING

Earlier in this section, we considered two summation functions from the `MyMath` library:

```
int Sum(int n)
{
   return n * (n + 1) / 2;
}

int Sum(int m, int n)
{
   assert(m < n);
   return (n - m + 1) * (n + m) / 2;
}
```

It would seem that using the same name for two different functions in the same file should generate an error. However, no name conflict occurs when these definitions are compiled, even though there are two definitions for the same identifier! As we shall see, this is consistent with what we stated earlier:

> *Within the scope of an identifier, no redeclaration of that identifier that results in an ambiguity for the compiler is permitted.*

The key here is the phrase *an ambiguity for the compiler.* As we will now explain, the C++ compiler is in fact able to distinguish these functions from one another without ambiguity.

Signatures. The **signature** of a function is a list of the types of its parameters, including any `const` and reference parameter indicators (`&`). For example, the signature of the `DivideInts()` function in Figure 7.1 is

```
(int, int, int &, int &)
```

and the signature of the `DecomposeName()` function in Figure 7.3 is

```
(const string &, string &, string &, string &)
```

while the signature of the `MakeChange()` function in Figure 7.4 is

```
(double, double, int &, int &, int &, int &, int &)
```

and the signature of the `Swap()` function from Figure 7.6 is

```
(char &, char &)
```

Signatures are important, because the compiler essentially considers a function's signature to be a part of its name.

Overloading. If two different functions have the same name, that name is said to be **overloaded.** For example, when we use the same name for both of the summation functions

```
int Sum(int n)
{
   return n * (n + 1) / 2;
}

int Sum(int m, int n)
{
   assert(m < n);
   return (n - m + 1) * (n + m) / 2;
}
```

we are overloading the name Sum with two different definitions. The compiler is able to distinguish them from one another, because they have different signatures. If we call Sum() with

```
cout << Sum(100) << endl;
```

the call has one int argument, and so the compiler associates this call with the first definition of Sum() whose signature has one int type: However, if we write

```
cout << Sum(20, 40) << endl;
```

the function call has two int arguments, and so the compiler associates this call with the second definition of Sum() whose signature has two int types.

Signatures thus allow the C++ compiler to distinguish calls to different functions with the same name. As a result, we have the following rule governing overloading:

> The name of a function can be overloaded, provided *no two definitions of the function have the same signature.*

Note that the return type of a function is not a part of its signature. Thus, two functions with identical signatures but with different return types cannot have the same name.

Names should be overloaded only when it is appropriate. Otherwise the code you write may be very difficult to read and understand. Different functions that perform the same operation (e.g., summation, finding the minimum operation, finding the maximum) on different data types are prime candidates for overloading. But giving operations that have nothing to do with each other the same name simply because the language allows you to do so is an abuse of the overloading mechanism and is deplorable programming style.

It should be evident that overloading has been used since chapter 1. For example, the operators +, −, *, and / are all overloaded so that they can be applied to any of the numeric types. In the expression

```
2.0 / 5.0
```

the C++ compiler uses the real division operation (which produces the value 0.4), but in the integer expression

```
2 / 5
```

it uses the integer division operation (which produces the value 0). Many of the other operators, including <<, >>, =, +=, -=, *=, /=, <, >, ==, <=, >=, and !=, have also been overloaded with multiple definitions. For an expression of the form

$operand_1$ $operator$ $operand_2$

the compiler simply matches the types of $operand_1$ and $operand_2$ against the signatures of the available definitions of $operator$ to determine which definition to apply.

FUNCTION TEMPLATES

In section 7.3, we considered a function to interchange the values of two character variables:

```
void Swap(char & first, char & second)
{
   char temporary = first;

   first = second;
   second = temporary;
}
```

This function works well so long as the values we wish to exchange are two char values. But the swap operation is needed in many different problems such as sorting a list of strings, interchanging the smaller and larger of two integers, and interchanging two rows in a table of doubles. The preceding function, however, can be used only to exchange the values of two char objects and not string values, int values, double values, and so on.

One solution would be to create a library of overloaded Swap() functions, one for each type of values we may ever want to interchange:

```
/* This Swap library provides a collection of functions
 * for interchanging the values of two variables.
 * ...
 ***************************************************************/

inline void Swap(bool & first, bool & second)
{ bool temporary = first; first = second;
  second = temporary; }

inline void Swap(char & first, char & second)
{ char temporary = first; first = second;
  second = temporary; }

inline void Swap(short & first, short & second)
{ short temporary = first; first = second;
  second = temporary; }

inline void Swap(int & first, int & second)
{ int temporary = first; first = second;
  second = temporary; }
```

```
inline void Swap(long & first, long & second)
{ long temporary = first; first = second;
  second = temporary; }

inline void Swap(float & first, float & second)
{ float temporary = first; first = second;
  second = temporary; }

inline void Swap(double & first, double & second)
{ double temporary = first; first = second;
  second = temporary; }

inline void Swap(long double & first, long double & second)
{ long double temporary = first; first = second;
  second = temporary; }
```

Given such a library, we could interchange two values of any of the fundamental types simply by using the #include directive to insert this file and then calling a Swap() function:

```
...
#include "Swap.h"

int main()
{
   int i1 = 11,
       i2 = 22;
   double d1 = 11.1,
          d2 = 22.2;

   Swap(i1, i2);
   cout << i1 << ' ' << i2 << endl;

   Swap(d1, d2);
   cout << d1 << ' ' << d2 << endl;
}
```

The compiler will select the appropriate version of Swap() by matching the types of the arguments in the function call with the signatures of the functions in the library.

Suppose, however, we find that we need to exchange the values of two class (e.g., string) objects. We could add yet another definition to Swap.h,

```
inline void Swap(string & first, string & second)
{ string temporary = first; first = second;
  second = temporary; }
```

However, each definition of Swap() is doing exactly the same thing (on a different type of data). This should raise red flags, because we have said before that *any time we find ourselves repeating the same work, there is probably a better way.*

Parameters For Types. Here, the better way is to recognize that the only differences in any of these definitions are the three places where a type is specified. It would be nice if we could define the function and leave these types "blank ", to be filled in later,

```
inline void Swap(_____ & first, _____ & second)
{_____ temporary = first; first = second; second = temporary; }
```

and somehow *pass the type* to the function when we called it. Then we could replace all of these definitions with one.

This is effectively what C++ allows us to do, as shown in Figure 7.8.

 FIGURE 7.8   THE Swap() TEMPLATE.

```
/* This Swap library provides a template that generates functions
 * for interchanging the values of two variables.
 * ...
 ****************************************************************/

template<class Item>
inline void Swap(Item & first, Item & second)
{
    Item temporary = first;
    first = second;
    second = temporary;
}
```

Rather than specify that the function is to exchange two values of a particular type such as char, int, and so on, this definition uses the identifier Item as a "place-holder" for the type of the value to be exchanged. More precisely, the line

```
template<class Item>
```

informs the compiler of two things:

1. This definition is a **template:** *a pattern from which a function can be created.*
2. The identifier Item is the name of a **type parameter** for this definition that will be given a value when the function is called. (Remember, the word *class* means *type* in C++.)

The rest of the definition simply specifies the behavior of the function, using the type parameter Item in place of any specific type.

Using this version of the Swap library, we can now write

```
#include "Swap.h"

int main()
{
    int i1 = 11,
        i2 = 22;
    Swap(i1, i2);
    cout << i1 << ' ' << i2 << endl;

    double d1 = 33.3,
           d2 = 44.4;
    Swap(d1, d2);
    cout << d1 << ' ' << d2 << endl;
```

```
        string s1 = "Hi",
               s2 = "Ho";
        Swap(s1, s2);
        cout << s1 << ' ' << s2 << endl;
    }
```

When the compiler encounters the first call to `Swap()`,

```
    Swap(i1, i2);
```

in which the two arguments `i1` and `i2` are of type `int`, it uses the pattern given by our template to generate a *new* definition of `Swap()` in which the type parameter `Item` is replaced by `int`:

```
    inline void Swap( int  & first,  int  & second)
    {
        int  temporary = first;
        first = second;
        second = temporary;
    }
```

When it reaches the second call,

```
    Swap(d1, d2);
```

where the two arguments `d1` and `d2` are of type `double`, the compiler will use the same pattern to generate a second definition of `Swap()` in which the type parameter `Item` is replaced by `double`:

```
    inline void Swap( double  & first,  double  & second)
    {
        double  temporary = first;
        first = second;
        second = temporary;
    }
```

When the compiler reaches the final call,

```
    Swap(s1, s2);
```

in which the two arguments `s1` and `s2` are of type `string`, it will use the same pattern to generate a third definition of `Swap()` in which the type parameter `Item` is replaced by `string`:

```
    inline void Swap( string  & first,  string  & second)
    {
        string  temporary = first;
        first = second;
        second = temporary;
    }
```

We are spared from all of the redundant coding of the earlier approach because the compiler is providing multiple versions of the swap operation as they are needed.

Templates vs. Overloading. If there are several versions of the same operation to be encoded as functions, it may not be clear whether one should write several functions that overload the same name or write one function template. The following guideline helps with making this decision:

If each version of the operation behaves in exactly the same way,
   regardless of the type of data being used,
      then define a **function template** to perform the operation.

Otherwise, define a separate function for each operation
   and use **overloading** to give them the same name.

Thus, because each version of `Swap()` uses the three-way swap and behaves in exactly the same manner regardless of the type of values being interchanged, a function template is appropriate.

By contrast, the two summation functions we considered earlier use different formulas, and thus behave differently. These operations are therefore best performed by two separate functions that overload the name `Sum()`.

The reasoning behind this guideline should be clear. When the compiler creates a function definition from a template, it blindly replaces each occurrence of the type parameter with the type of the arguments. As a result, each definition created from a template must behave in exactly the same way, except for the type of data being operated upon. Overloading has no such restriction and so can be used for a wider variety of operations.

✔ Quick Quiz 7.5

1. The part of a program where an identifier refers to a particular object or function is called the _____ of that identifier.

2. (True or false). A compilation error results if an identifier is accessed within its scope.

3. The scope of an identifier declared within a block runs from its declaration to the _____.

4. The scope of a parameter is the _____.

5. What will the following statements produce?

```
for (int i = 0; i < 3; i++)
   cout << i << endl;
cout << "i is now " << i << endl;
```

6. A function's _____ is a list of the types of its parameters.

7. Two functions are said to be overloaded if they have the same _____.

8. A function's name can be overloaded provided no two definitions of the function have the same _____.

9. A _____ is a pattern from which a function can be constructed.

10. Templates may have _____ parameters, but ordinary functions may not.

11. Given the template definition

```
template<class something>
void Print(something x)
{ cout << "***" << x << "***\n"; }
```

describe what the compiler will do when it encounters the statements

```
int number = 123;
Print(number);
```

*7.6 INTRODUCTION TO RECURSION

All the examples of function calls considered thus far have involved one function F() calling a different function G() (with the calling function F() often being the main function). However, a function F() may also *call itself,* a phenomenon known as **recursion,** and in this section, we show how recursion is implemented in C++.

EXAMPLE 1:   THE FACTORIAL PROBLEM REVISITED

To illustrate the basic idea of recursion, we reconsider the problem of calculating the factorial function.

Objects. The objects and specification of this problem were given in section 3.4. The specification,

Receive: n, an integer.

Return: $n! = 1 \times 2 \times \cdots \times n$

gives rise to the following stub for the function:

```
int Factorial(int n)
{
}
```

Operations. Although the first definition of the factorial $n!$ of an integer n that one usually learns is

$$n! = \begin{cases} 1 & \text{if } n = 0 \\ 1 \times 2 \times \cdots \times n & \text{if } n > 0 \end{cases}$$

it would be foolish to use it to calculate a sequence of consecutive factorials; that is, to multiply together the numbers from 1 through n each time:

$$0! = 1$$
$$1! = 1$$
$$2! = 1 \times 2 = 2$$
$$3! = 1 \times 2 \times 3 = 6$$
$$4! = 1 \times 2 \times 3 \times 4 = 24$$
$$5! = 1 \times 2 \times 3 \times 4 \times 5 = 120$$

A great deal of the effort would be redundant, because it is clear that once a factorial has been calculated, it can be used to calculate the next factorial. For example, given the value 4! = 24, the value 5! can be computed simply by multiplying the value of 4! by 5:

$$5! = 5 \times 4! = 5 \times 24 = 120$$

This value of 5! can in turn be used to calculate 6!,

$$6! = 6 \times 5! = 6 \times 120 = 720$$

and so on. Indeed, to calculate $n!$ for any positive integer n, we need only know the value of 0!,

$$0! = 1$$

and the fundamental relation between one factorial and the next:

$$n! = n \times (n - 1)!$$

In general, a function is said to be **defined recursively** if its definition consists of two parts:

1.   An **anchor** or **base case,** in which the value of the function is specified for one or more values of the parameter(s)

2.   An **inductive** or **recursive step,** in which the function's value for the current value of the parameter(s) is defined in terms of previously defined function values and/or parameter values

For the factorial function we have:

$$0! = 1 \qquad \text{(the anchor or base case)}$$
$$\text{For } n > 0, n! = n \times (n - 1)! \quad \text{(the inductive or recursive step)}$$

The first statement specifies a particular value of the function, and the second statement defines its value for n in terms of its value for $n - 1$.

Algorithm.   This approach to calculating factorials leads to the following recursive definition of $n!$,

$$n! = \begin{cases} 1 & \text{if } n \text{ is } 0 \\ n \times (n -)! & \text{if } n > 0 \end{cases}$$

which can be used as an algorithm[6] for completing the stub of `Factorial()`. To see how it works, consider using it to calculate 5!. We must first calculate 4! because 5! is defined as the product of 5 and 4!. But to calculate 4! we must calculate 3! because 4! is defined as $4 \times 3!$. And to calculate 3!, we must apply the inductive step of the definition again, $3! = 3 \times 2!$, then again to find 2!, which is defined as $2! = 2 \times 1!$, and once again to find $1! = 1 \times 0!$. Now we have finally reached the anchor case:

---

[6] Note that a recursive definition with a slightly different anchor case can be constructed by observing that 0! and 1! are both 1. Although this alternative definition leads to a slightly more efficient implementation of `Factorial()`, we will use the simpler definition in this introduction to recursion.

$$5! = 5 \times 4!$$
$$\downarrow$$
$$4! = 4 \times 3!$$
$$\downarrow$$
$$3! = 3 \times 2!$$
$$\downarrow$$
$$2! = 2 \times 1!$$
$$\downarrow$$
$$1! = 1 \times 0!$$
$$\downarrow$$
$$0! = 1$$

Since the value of 0! is given, we can now backtrack to find the value of 1!,

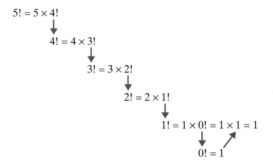

then backtrack again to find the value of 2!,

$$5! = 5 \times 4!$$
$$\downarrow$$
$$4! = 4 \times 3!$$
$$\downarrow$$
$$3! = 3 \times 2!$$
$$\downarrow$$
$$2! = 2 \times 1! = 2 \times 1 = 2$$
$$\downarrow \qquad \nwarrow$$
$$1! = 1 \times 0! = 1 \times 1 = 1$$
$$\downarrow \qquad \nearrow$$
$$0! = 1$$

and so on, until we eventually obtain the value 120 for 5!:

$$5! = 5 \times 4! = 5 \times 24 = 120$$
$$4! = 4 \times 3! = 4 \times 6 = 24$$
$$3! = 3 \times 2! = 3 \times 2 = 6$$
$$2! = 2 \times 1! = 2 \times 1 = 2$$
$$1! = 1 \times 0! = 1 \times 1 = 1$$
$$0! = 1$$

As this example demonstrates, a recursive definition may require considerable bookkeeping to record information at the various levels of the recursion, because this information is used *after* the anchor case is reached to backtrack from one level to the preceding one. Fortunately, most modern high-level languages (including C++) support recursion by automatically performing all of the necessary bookkeeping and backtracking.

Coding. Figure 7.9 shows a definition of `Factorial()` that implements this algorithm:

FIGURE 7.9 COMPUTING n! RECURSIVELY.

```
/* Factorial computes n! recursively.
 *
 * Receive:    n, an integer
 * Return:     n! (or -1 if n is negative)
 ******************************************/

int Factorial(int n)
{
    if (n == 0)
        return 1;                        // anchor case
    else if (n > 0)
        return n * Factorial(n-1);       // inductive step
    else                                 // invalid parameter
    {
        cout << "n! is not defined for negative n\n";
        return -1;
    }
}
```

When this function is called with an argument greater than zero, the inductive step

```
else if (n > 0)
    return n * Factorial(n-1);
```

causes the function to call itself repeatedly, each time with a smaller parameter, until the anchor case

```
if (n == 0)
   return 1;
```

is reached.

To illustrate, consider the statement

```
int fact = Factorial(4);
```

that calls the function `Factorial()` to calculate 4!. Since the value of n(4) is not 0, the inductive step executes

```
return n * Factorial(n-1);
```

which calls `Factorial(3)`. Before control is transferred to `Factorial(3)`, the current value (4) of the parameter n is saved so that the value of n can be restored when control returns. This might be pictured as follows:

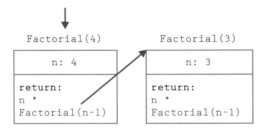

Since the value of n (3) in this function call is not 0, the inductive step in this second call to `Factorial()` generates another call `Factorial(n-1)` passing it the argument 2. Once again, the value of n (3) is saved so that it can be restored later:

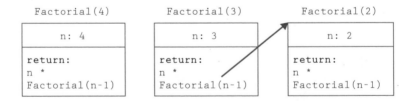

Since the value of n (2) in this function call is not 0, the inductive step in this third call to `Factorial()` generates another call `Factorial(n-1)` passing it the argument 1. Once again, the value of n (2) is saved so that it can be restored later. The call `Factorial(1)` in turn generates another call, `Factorial(0)`:

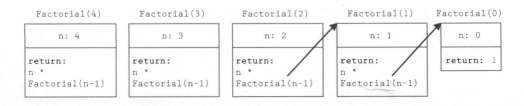

Because the anchor condition

```
if (n == 0)
    return 1;
```

is now satisfied in this last function call, no additional recursive calls are generated. Instead, the value 1 is returned as the value for Factorial(0):

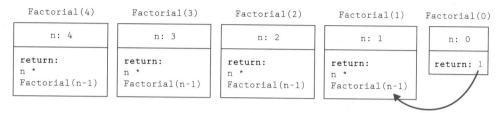

Now that Factorial(0) has been completed its computation, execution resumes in Factorial(1) where this returned value can now be used to complete the evaluation of

n * Factorial(n - 1) = 1 * Factorial(0) = 1 * 1 = 1

giving 1 as the return value for Factorial(1):

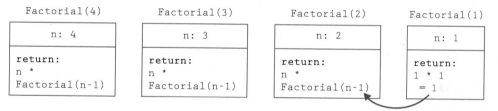

Once Factorial(1) has completed its computation, execution resumes in Factorial(2) where the return value of Factorial(1) can now be used to complete the evaluation of

n * Factorial(n - 1) = 2 * Factorial(1) = 2 * 1 = 2

giving 2 as the return value for Factorial(2):

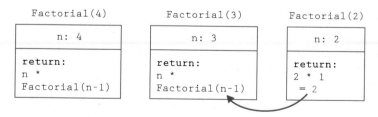

Since Factorial(2) has completed its computation, execution resumes in Factorial(3) where the return value of Factorial(2) is used to complete the evaluation of

n * Factorial(n - 1) = 3 * Factorial(2) = 3 * 2 = 6

giving 6 as the return value for Factorial(3):

```
Factorial(4)              Factorial(3)

    n: 4                      n: 3

return:                   return:
n *                       3 * 2
Factorial(n-1)              = 6
```

This completes the function call to `Factorial(3)`, and so execution resumes in the call to `Factorial(4)`, which computes and returns the value

```
n * Factorial(n - 1) = 4 * Factorial(3) = 4 * 6 = 24
```

giving 24 as the return value for `Factorial(4)`:

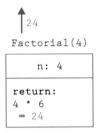

```
 ↑ 24
Factorial(4)

    n: 4

return:
4 * 6
  = 24
```

Note that in the definition `Factorial()` we test both of the conditions in our algorithm,

```
if (n == 0)
    return 1;                    // trivial case
else if (n > 0)
    return n * Factorial(n-1);   // inductive step
else                             // invalid parameter
{
    cout << "n! is not defined for negative n\n";
    return -1;
}
```

and use the final `else` to handle cases where the parameter `n` is a negative integer. To see the reason for this, consider what would happen if we had written the function without this `else` clause,

```
if (n == 0)
    return 1;
else
    return n * Factorial(n-1);
```

and the function were called with a negative integer, as in

```
int fact = Factorial(-1);
```

Since −1 is not equal to 0, the inductive step

```
else
   return n * Factorial(n-1);
```

would be performed, recursively calling `Factorial(-2)`. Execution of this call would begin, and since −2 is not equal to 0, the inductive step

```
else
   return n * Factorial(n-1);
```

would be performed, recursively calling `Factorial(-3)`. This behavior would continue until memory was exhausted, at which point the program would terminate abnormally, possibly producing an error message like

```
Stack overruns Heap.
```

Such behavior is described as **infinite recursion** and is obviously undesirable. To avoid it we programmed defensively by including the parameter-validity check.

EXAMPLE 2:   RECURSIVE EXPONENTIATION

Another classic example of a function that can be calculated recursively is the power function that calculates x^n, where x is a real value and n is a nonnegative integer. The first definition of x^n that one learns is usually an iterative (nonrecursive) one:

$$x^n = \underbrace{x \times x \times \cdots \times x}_{n \; x's}$$

and later one learns that x^0 is defined to be 1. (For convenience, we assume here that x^0 is 1 also when x is 0, although in this case, it is usually left undefined.)

 Objects. For this problem, we can identify two objects:

Description	Type	Kind	Movement	Name
the base value	double	varying	received (in)	x
the exponent	int	varying	received (in)	n
x raised to the power n	int	varying	returned (out)	none

This gives the specification

Receive: x, a real value;
　　　　　　　n, an integer
Return x^n, a real value

which suggests the following function stub:

```
double Power(double x, int n)
{
}
```

Operations. To solve a problem recursively, we must identify the anchor and inductive cases. The anchor step is clear: $x^0 = 1$. For the inductive case, we look at an example:

$$5.0^4 = 5.0 \times 5.0 \times 5.0 \times 5.0 = (5.0 \times 5.0 \times 5.0) \times 5.0 = 5.0^3 \times 5.0$$

In general,

$$x^n = x^{n-1} \times x$$

Algorithm. Combining our anchor and inductive steps provides the following recursive definition of x^n:

$$x^n = \begin{cases} 1 & \text{if } n \text{ is zero} \quad \text{(the anchor case)} \\ x^{n-1} \times x & \text{if } n \text{ is greater than 0} \quad \text{(the inductive case)} \end{cases}$$

As with the factorial function, this definition is an algorithm from which a recursive C++ function can be written, as shown in Figure 7.10:

FIGURE 7.10   PERFORMING EXPONENTIATION RECURSIVELY.

```
/* Power recursively computes x raised to the power n.
 * Receive:   x, a real value, and
 *            n, an integer
 * Return:    x raised to the power n
 ********************************************************/

double Power(double x, int n)
{
    if (n == 0)
        return 1.0;                      // anchor case
    else if (n > 0)
        return Power(x, n - 1) * x;     // inductive step (n > 0)
    else                                 // invalid parameter n
    {
        cerr << "*** Power has received a negative exponent.\n";
        return -1.0;
    }
}
```

The following diagram pictures the five levels of function calls generated when this function is called with `Power(3.0, 4)`:

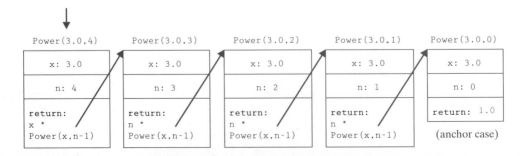

Because n is 0 in this last call, the anchor case has been reached, stopping the recursion. This sequence of recursive calls from an initial call to the anchor case is sometimes referred to as the *winding phase* of the recursion, because like a wind-up clock that is powered by winding a spring, the computation of a recursive function is powered by this sequence of calls that culminates in the anchor case.

Once the anchor case has been reached, the backtracking behavior begins that actually performs the computation, as shown in the following diagram:

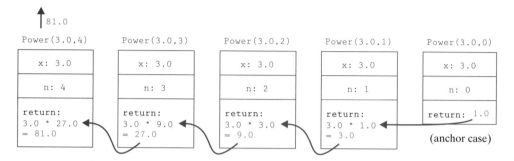

This phase in which values are returned from the anchor case back through each of the previous calls is sometimes referred to as the *unwinding phase* of the recursion, because like a wind-up clock performing its task as its spring unwinds, a recursive function performs its task by "unwinding" the recursive calls stacked up in its winding phase.

EXAMPLE 3:   DRY BONES!

The Old Testament book of Ezekiel is a book of vivid images that chronicle the siege of Jerusalem by the Babylonians and the subsequent forced relocation (known as the *exile*) of the Israelites following Jerusalem's fall. Chapter 37 describes a powerful vision of Ezekiel in which a valley of dry bones becomes reconnected as he prophesies. Tendons, muscle, and skin regrow on the reconnected bones and the dead skeletons return to life forming a vast army that fills the valley. This vision of new life arising from dry bones provided the homesick Israelites with hope that the "dry bones " of defeated Israel would "come back to life" and they could one day be free of their oppressors, the Babylonians.

Before the American Civil War, many black men and women in the United States found themselves in a situation similar to that of the Israelites, having been forcibly relocated from their homelands and brought to the United States to serve as slaves. One way that they were able to keep their hopes alive was through singing songs that spoke of freedom. However, songs that expressed such hopes directly could result in a beating for the singer, and so these sentiments had to be cleverly encoded in lyrics that would not catch the attention of the slaves' overseers.

One way this was done was by singing **spirituals** — songs whose lyrics referred to stories from the Bible that carried themes of hope and freedom. Songs like *Go Down Moses; Swing Low, Sweet Chariot;* and *Bright Canaan* are examples of spirituals that, in addition to their overt spiritual message, carried a second level of meaning that provided these men and women with the hope that they could one day be free of oppression.

One of the most subtle spirituals is *Dry Bones*. It makes no direct references to freedom, but uses the imagery of scattered bones being reconnected to encode the same message of hope conveyed in Ezekiel 37. With its message of freedom carefully hidden, such a song could be sung in the presence of even the harshest overseer:

```
Ezekiel cried, "Dem dry bones!"
Ezekiel cried, "Dem dry bones!"
Ezekiel cried, "Dem dry bones!"
Oh, hear the word of the Lord.

The foot bone connected to the leg bone,
The leg bone connected to the knee bone,
The knee bone connected to the thigh bone,
The thigh bone connected to the back bone,
The back bone connected to the neck bone,
The neck bone connected to the head bone,
Oh, hear the word of the Lord!

Dem bones, dem bones gonna walk aroun'
Dem bones, dem bones, gonna walk aroun'
Dem bones, dem bones, gonna walk aroun'
Oh, hear the word of the Lord.

The head bone connected to the neck bone,
The neck bone connected to the back bone,
The back bone connected to the thigh bone,
The thigh bone connected to the knee bone,
The knee bone connected to the leg bone,
The leg bone connected to the foot bone,
Oh, hear the word of the Lord!

Dem bones, dem bones gonna walk aroun'
Dem bones, dem bones, gonna walk aroun'
Dem bones, dem bones, gonna walk aroun'
Oh, hear the word of the Lord.
```

The structure of the song is interesting, because it can be partitioned into the following steps, which together comprise an algorithm for printing the song:

a. Print the `"Ezekiel cried"` variation of the chorus.

b. Print the *bone lyrics* from foot to head.

c. Print the `"Dem bones"` variation of the chorus.

d. Print the *bone lyrics* from toe to head.

e. Print the `"Dem bones"` variation of the chorus.

What makes the structure interesting is that while steps b and d are similar, they proceed in reverse order; that is, with the bones reversed. So in step b, the lines have the form

```
The X bone connected to the Y bone,
```

while in step d, the corresponding lines are in reverse order, with the bones reversed:

```
The Y bone connected to the X bone,
```

Because of this reversal, the actions performed in steps b-d can be described using recursion. More precisely, step c occurs in the middle, and so provides us with an anchor case:

X ==   "head"→ Print the "Dem bones" variation of the chorus

and every other case can be performed recursively, using this strategy :

1. Identify the next bone Y.
2. Print "The X bone connected to the Y bone,".
3. Recursively print the lyrics for bone Y.
4. Print "The Y bone connected to the X bone,".

The function `PrintBoneLyrics()` in Figure 7.11 encodes this recursive logic. The output statement

```
cout << "The " << bone              //  do 'downward' lyric
     << " bone connected to the "   //  before recursion
     << nextBone << " bone,\n";     //  (winding)
```

generates the lyrics for the current bone, and the function call

```
PrintBoneLyrics(nextBone);          //  do rest recursively
```

then recursively does the same for each of the bones "below" the current bone. Once the anchor case has been reached, the recursion then unwinds, executing the statement

```
cout << "\nThe " << nextBone        //  do 'upward' lyric
     << " bone connected to the "   //  after recursion
     << bone << " bone,";           //  (unwinding)
```

which generates the lyrics in the reverse order, with the bones reversed.

The first call to `PrintChorus()` in `main()` performs step a of the algorithm; the recursive function `PrintBoneLyrics()` performs steps b–d; and the second call to `PrintChorus()` performs the final step e.

 FIGURE 7.11   DRY BONES!

```
/* drybones11.cpp displays the lyrics of the song "Dry Bones."
 *
 * Output: lyrics of "Dry Bones"
 ****************************************************************/

#include <iostream.h>                    // cin, cout, <<, >>
#include <string>                        // string class

void PrintChorus(string variation);
void PrintLastLine();
void PrintBoneLyrics(const string & bone);
```

```
int main()
{
   PrintChorus("Ezekiel cried, \"Dem dry bones!\"\n");
   PrintBoneLyrics("foot");
   PrintLastLine();
   PrintChorus("Dem bones, dem bones gonna walk aroun'\n");
}

/* PrintChorus displays the lyrics of the chorus of the song, of
 * which there are two variations.
 *
 * Receive: variation, a string
 * Output:  the chorus with the specified variation.
 ***************************************************************/

void PrintChorus(string variation)
{
   cout << variation << variation << variation;
   PrintLastLine();
}

/* PrintLastLine displays the last line of each verse and the chorus.
 *
 * Output:  the last line
 ***************************************************************/

void PrintLastLine()
{
   cout << "Oh, hear the word of the Lord!\n\n";
}

/* PrintBoneLyrics displays the lyrics for a given bone.
 *
 * Receive: bone, a string.
 * Output:  the lyrics for that bone and (recursively) the lyrics
 *          for the bones "beneath" it (during winding) and then
 *          for the bones "above" it (during unwinding).
 ***************************************************************/

string GetNext(const string & aBone);

void PrintBoneLyrics(const string & bone)
{
   if (bone == "head")                          // Anchor: bone == head
                                                 //   sing chorus variation
      PrintChorus("Dem bones, dem bones gonna walk aroun'\n");

   else
   {                                             // Ind-Step: bone < head
      string nextBone = GetNext(bone);           //   find next body part
```

```
      cout << "The " << bone                // do 'upward' lyric
           << " bone connected to the "     // before recursion
           << nextBone << " bone,\n";        // (winding)

      PrintBoneLyrics(nextBone);             // do rest recursively

      cout << "The " << nextBone            // do 'downward' lyric
           << " bone connected to the "     // after recursion
           << bone << " bone,\n";            // (unwinding)
   }
}

/* GetNext gets the next bone.
 *
 * Receive:       aBone, a string.
 * Precondition: aBone is a valid bone (in the song).
 * Return:        the bone above aBone.
 ****************************************************************/

string GetNext(const string & aBone)
{
   if (aBone == "foot")
      return "leg";
   else if (aBone == "leg")
      return "knee";
   else if (aBone == "knee")
      return "thigh";
   else if (aBone == "thigh")
      return "back";
   else if (aBone == "back")
      return "neck";
   else if (aBone == "neck")
      return "head";
   else
      cerr << "\n*** GetNext(): "
           << aBone << " is unknown!" << endl;
   return "";
}
```

As this example illustrates, recursion is not limited to functions such as `Facto-rial()` and `Power()` that return values. Neither is it limited to numeric problems, but rather can be applied to solve any of the wide variety of problems whose solutions are inherently recursive. The Towers of Hanoi problem that we consider next is another example of such a problem.

EXAMPLE 4: TOWERS OF HANOI

The **Towers of Hanoi** problem is to solve the puzzle shown in the following figure, in which one must move the disks from the left peg to the right peg according to the following rules:

1. When a disk is moved, it must be placed on one of the three pegs.

2. Only one disk may be moved at a time, and it must be the top disk on one of the pegs.

3. A larger disk may never be placed on top of a smaller one.

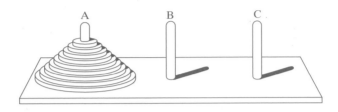

The following *game tree* shows the various configurations that are possible in the problem with two disks; the highlighted path in the tree shows a solution to the two-disk problem:

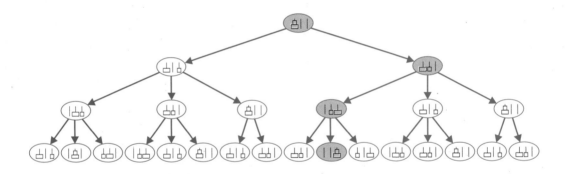

Legend has it that the priests in the Temple of Bramah were given a puzzle consisting of a golden platform with three diamond needles on which were placed sixty-four golden disks. The priests were to move one disk per day, following the preceding rules, and when they had successfully finished moving the disks to another needle, time would end. (*Question:* If the priests moved one disk per day and began their work in year 0, when would time end?)

Novices usually find the puzzle easy to solve for a small number of disks, but they have more difficulty as the number of disks grows to seven, eight, and beyond. To a computer scientist, however, the Towers of Hanoi puzzle is easy: We begin by identifying a base case, for which the problem is trivial to solve:

If there is one disk, then move it from Peg A to Peg C.

The puzzle is thus easily solved for $n = 1$ disk. We then seek an inductive solution for $n > 1$ disks, in which we assume that a solution exists for $n - 1$ disks:

1. *Move the topmost $n - 1$ disks from Peg A to Peg B, using Peg C for temporary storage.*

2. *Move the final disk remaining on Peg A to Peg C.*

3. *Move the n − 1 disks from Peg B to Peg C, using Peg A for temporary storage.*

This scheme is implemented by the recursive function `Move()` in Figure 7.12, which solves the Towers of Hanoi puzzle for *n* disks:

FIGURE 7.12   SOLVING THE TOWERS OF HANOI PROBLEM RECURSIVELY.

```
/* Move is a recursive function to solve the Hanoi Towers puzzle.
 *
 *  Receive:
 *    n, the number of disks to be moved;
 *    source, the needle the disks are to be moved from,
 *    destination, the needle the disks are to be moved to, and
 *    spare, the needle that can be used to store disks temporarily
 *************************************************************************/

void Move(int n, char source, char destination, char spare)
{
   if (n <= 1)                              // anchor
      cout << "Move the top disk from " << source << " to "
           << destination << endl;
   else
   {                                        // inductive case
      Move(n-1, source, spare, destination);
      Move(1, source, destination, spare);
      Move(n-1, spare, destination, source);
   }
}
```

Figure 7.13 presents a driver program that uses `Move()` to solve the Hanoi Towers problem, and an execution in which the problem is solved for 4 disks.

FIGURE 7.13   TOWERS OF HANOI DRIVER PROGRAM.

```
/* hanoitowers13.cpp solves the Towers of Hanoi puzzle recursively.
 *
 * Input:  numDisks, the number of disks to be moved
 * Output: a sequence of moves that solve the puzzle
 *************************************************************************/

#include <iostream.h>

void Move(int n, char source, char destination, char spare);
```

```
int main()
{
   const char PEG1 = 'A',           // the three pegs
             PEG2 = 'B',
             PEG3 = 'C';

   cout << "This program solves the Hanoi Towers puzzle.\n\n";

   cout << "Enter the number of disks: ";
   int numDisks;                    // the number of disks to be moved
   cin >> numDisks;
   cout << endl;

   Move(numDisks, PEG1, PEG2, PEG3);   // the solution
}

/*** Insert definition of Move() from Figure 7.12 here. ***/
```

Sample run:

```
This program solves the Hanoi Towers puzzle.

Rnter the number of disks: 4

Move the top disk from A to B
Move the top disk from A to C
Move the top disk from B to C
Move the top disk from A to B
Move the top disk from C to A
Move the top disk from C to B
Move the top disk from A to B
Move the top disk from A to C
Move the top disk from B to C
Move the top disk from B to A
Move the top disk from C to A
Move the top disk from B to C
Move the top disk from A to B
Move the top disk from A to C
Move the top disk from B to C
```

RECURSION OR ITERATION?

Many problems can be solved with equal ease using either a recursive or an iterative algorithm. For example, we implemented the factorial, power, and "dembones" functions in this section as recursive functions, but they can be written nonrecursively just as easily. What factors should determine the method to use?

Nonrecursive functions may execute more rapidly and use memory more efficiently than their recursive counterparts, unless the C++ compiler is instructed to perform **optimization** when compiling the function.[7] A good optimizing C++ com-

---

[7] Turning on optimization for GNU's g++ compiler is simply a matter of invoking g++ with the -O switch (for simple optimization) or -O2 (for highly optimized code). In the various GUI environments (e.g., Turbo, Visual C++, Symantec, CodeWarrior), programmers can customize their optimizations in an Optimizations dialogue box, accesssed via an Options menu choice.

piler can be thought of as an *expert system* in programming that will replace inefficient (but intuitive) recursive definitions with more efficient definitions that use loops. An optimizing compiler thus frees the programmer to write intuitive (if inefficient) source code, and leaves to the compiler the task of ensuring that the binary executable code is efficient.

Given a compiler capable of optimization, the following "rule-of-thumb" is one guideline for deciding whether to use recursion or iteration:

If there is little difference in the effort to define a function recursively or iteratively, then

    if time-efficiency is important and the C++ compiler will optimize recursion, then
        the recursive definition may be used;
    otherwise,
        the iterative definition should be used;
otherwise, if the function is significantly easier to implement recursively, then
    the recursive definition may be used;
otherwise,
    the iterative definition should be used.

Optimization, however, will increase compilation time, because the compiler must check the source program for inefficiencies and translate them into equivalent but more efficient binary statements. To minimize this increase in compilation time, the typical approach is to *compile programs without optimization during their development*. Once a program has been completely tested and is in its final form, then *compile the final version using optimization*. The added compile-time cost of optimization is then incurred only once.

For some problems, such as the Towers of Hanoi problem, recursion is the most natural and straightforward technique. For these problems, nonrecursive algorithms may not be obvious, may be more difficult to develop, and may be less readable than recursive ones. Recursion is also appropriate when the problem's data is organized in a data structure that is defined recursively. (Such data structures are typically studied in the second course in computer science.) In such circumstances, the simplicity of the recursive algorithms compensates for any inefficiency that might remain after optimization.

✔ Quick Quiz 7.6

1. _____ is the phenomenon of a function referencing itself.
2. Name and describe the two parts of a recursive definition of a function.
3. (True or false) A nonrecursive function for computing some value may execute more rapidly than a recursive function that computes the same value.

4. For the following recursive function, find `F(5)`.

```
int F(int n)
{
    if (n == 0)
        return 0;
    else
        return n + F(n - 1);
}
```

5. For the function in question 4, find `F(0)`.

6. For the function in question 4, suppose + is changed to * in the inductive step. Find `F(5)`.

7. For the function in question 4, what happens with the function call `F(-1)`?

Exercises 7.6

Exercises 1–12 assume the following function F:

```
void F(int num)
{
    if ((1 <= num) && (num <= 8))
    {
        F(num - 1);
        cout << num;
    }
    else
        cout << endl;
}
```

For exercises 1–3, tell what output is produced by the function call.

    1. `F(3);`   **2.** `F(7);`   **3.** `F(10);`

4–6. Tell what output is produced by the function calls in exercises 1–3 if `num - 1` is replaced by `num + 1` in the function definition.

7–9. Tell what output is produced by the function calls in exercises 1–3 if the `cout << num;` statement and the recursive call to `F()` are interchanged.

10–12. Tell what output is produced by the function calls in exercises 1–3 if a copy of the statement `cout << num;` is inserted before the recursive call to `F()`.

13. Given the following function `F()`, use the method illustrated in this section to trace the sequence of function calls and returns in evaluating `F(1, 5)`.

```
int F(int num1, int num2)
{
    if (num1 > num2)
        return 0;
    else if (num2 == num1 + 1)
        return 1;
    else
        return F(num1 + 1, num2 - 1) + 2;
}
```

14. Proceed as in exercise 13, but for `F(8, 3)`.

Exercises 15–17 assume the following function G():

```
void G(int num1, int num2)
{
   if (num2 <= 0)
      cout << endl;
   else
   {
      G(num1 - 1, num2 - 1);
      cout << num1;
      G(num1+1, num2-1);
   }
}
```

15. What output is produced by the function call G(14, 4)? (*Hint:* First try G(14, 2), then G(14, 3)).

16. How many letters are output by the call G(14, 10)?

17. If the cout << num1; statement is moved before the first recursive call to G(), what output will be produced by G(14, 4)?

For exercises 18–22, determine what is calculated by the given recursive function.

18.
```
void F(unsigned n)
{
   if (n == 0)
      return 0;
   else
      return n * F(n - 1);
}
```

19.
```
double F(double x, unsigned n)
{
   if (n == 0)
      return 0;
   else
      return x + F(x, n - 1);
}
```

20.
```
unsigned F(unsigned n)
{
   if (n < 2)
      return 0;
   else
      return 1 + F(n / 2);
}
```

21.
```
unsigned F(unsigned n)
{
   if (n == 0)
      return 0;
   else
      return F(n / 10) + n % 10;
}
```

22.
```
unsigned F(int n)
{
   if (n < 0)
      return F(-n);
```

```
      else if (n < 10)
        return n;
      else
        return F(n / 10);
  }
```

For exercises 23–27, write a nonrecursive version of the function.

  23. The function in exercise 18.
  24. The function in exercise 19.
  25. The function in exercise 20.
  26. The function in exercise 21.
  27. The function in exercise 22.

The following exercises ask you to write functions to compute various quantities. To test these functions, you should write driver programs as instructed in Programming Problems 8–11 at the end of this chapter.

  28. Write a recursive function that returns the number of digits in a nonnegative integer.
  29. Write a nonrecursive version of the function in exercise 28.
  30. Write a recursive function `PrintReverse()` that displays an integer's digits in reverse order.
  31. Write a nonrecursive version of the function `PrintReverse()` in exercise 30.
  32. Modify the recursive exponentiation function in the text so that it also works for negative exponents. One approach is to modify the recursive definition of x^n so that for negative values of n, division is used instead of multiplication and n is incremented rather than decremented:

$$x^n = \begin{cases} 1 & \text{if } n \text{ is zero} \\ x^{n-1}*x & \text{if } n \text{ is greater than 0} \\ x^{n+1}/x & \text{otherwise} \end{cases}$$

  33. For the function `Move()` in Figure 7.12, trace the execution of the function call `Move(4, 'A', 'B', 'C');` far enough to produce the first five moves. Does your answer agree with the program output in Figure 7.13?
  34. Proceed as in exercise 33 but for the call `Move(5, 'A', 'B', 'C');`

Part of the Picture: Numerical Methods

Mathematical models are used to solve problems in a wide variety of areas including science, engineering, business, and the social sciences. Many of these models consist of ordinary algebraic equations, differential equations, systems of equations, and so on, and the solution of the problem is obtained by finding solutions for these equations. Methods for solving such equations that can be implemented in a computer program are called **numerical methods,** and the development and analysis of such numerical methods is an important area of study in computer science.

Some of the major types of problems in which numerical methods are routinely used include the following:

1. *Curve fitting.* In many applications, the solution of a problem requires analyzing data consisting of pairs of values to determine whether the items in these pairs are related. For example, a sociologist might wish to determine whether there is a linear relationship between educational level and income level.

2. *Solving equations.* Such problems deal with finding the value of a variable that satisfies a given equation.

3. *Integration.* The solution of many problems such as finding area under a curve, determining total revenue generated by sales of an item, calculating probabilities of certain events, and calculating work done by a force, require the evaluation of an integral. Often these integrals can only be evaluated using numerical techniques.

4. *Differential equations.* Differential equations are equations that involve one or more derivatives of unknown functions. Such equations play an important role in many applications, and several effective and efficient numerical methods for solving these equations have been developed.

5. *Solving linear systems.* Linear systems consist of several equations, each of which has several unknowns. A solution of such a system is a collection of values for these unknowns that satisfies all of the equations simultaneously.

In this section, we present a simple but practical introduction to one of these areas: integration. Examples from some of the other areas are described in the exercises and in later chapters.

THE TRAPEZOID METHOD OF APPROXIMATING AREAS

One of the important problems in calculus is finding the area of a region having a curved boundary. Here we consider the simple case where the region is bounded below by the x-axis, above by the graph of a function $y = f(x)$, on the left by the vertical line $x = a$, and on the right by the vertical line $x = b$:[8]

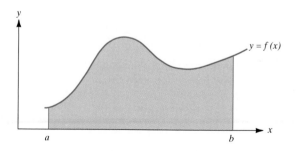

One commonly used method for approximating this area is to divide the region into strips and approximate the area of each strip by using a trapezoid. More precisely, we cut the interval $[a, b]$ into n parts, each of length $\Delta x = (b - a)/n$, using $n - 1$ equally spaced points $x_1, x_2, \ldots, x_{n-1}$. Locating the corresponding points on the curve and connecting consecutive points using line segments forms n trapezoids:

---

[8] More generally, the problem is to approximate the integral $\int_a^b f(x)dx$.

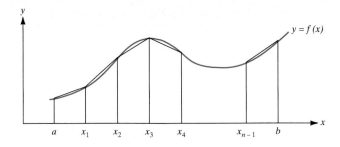

The sum of the areas of these trapezoids is approximately the area under the graph of f. The bases of the first trapezoid are $y_0 = f(a)$ and $y_1 = f(x_1)$, and thus its area is[9]

$$\frac{1}{2} \Delta x(y_0 + y_1)$$

Similarly, the area of the second trapezoid is

$$\frac{1}{2} \Delta x(y_1 + y_2)$$

where $y_2 = f(x_2)$, and so on. The sum of the areas of the n trapezoids is

$$\frac{1}{2} \Delta x(y_0 + y_1) + \frac{1}{2} \Delta x(y_1 + y_2) + \frac{1}{2} \Delta x(y_2 + y_3) + \cdots + \frac{1}{2} \Delta x(y_{n-1} + y_n)$$

where $y_0, y_1, \ldots, y_{n-1}, y_n$ are the values of the function f at $a, x_1, \ldots, x_{n-1}, b$, respectively. Combining terms, we can write this sum more simply as

$$\Delta x \left(\frac{y_0 + y_n}{2} + y_1 + y_2 + \cdots + y_{n-1} \right)$$

or, written more concisely using Σ (sigma) notation, as

$$\Delta x \left(\frac{y_0 + y_n}{2} + \sum_{i=1}^{n-1} y_i \right)$$

which is an approximation of the area under the curve.

   This formula can be treated as an algorithm for the trapezoidal method, which we can use to define a function, as shown in Figure 7.14. This particular definition reads the function values $y_0, y_1, \ldots, y_{n-1}, y_n$ from the keyboard.[10]

---

[9] The familiar formula from geometry for the area of a trapezoid with bases b_1 and b_2 and height h is $\frac{1}{2} h(b_1 + b_2)$. Note that in this problem, the bases are vertical and the "height" is horizontal.

---

[10] `TrapezoidalArea()` can be overloaded with other definitions that read the function values from a file, calculate them from an equation that defines the function, receive a `vector` of the function values from the caller (`vector` objects are discussed in chapter 9), and so on.

FIGURE 7.14   THE TRAPEZOIDAL METHOD (DEFINITION).

```
/* TrapezoidalArea computes the approximate area under a curve for
 * which a collection of y values at equally spaced x values are
 * entered from the keyboard.
 *
 *    Receive:       n, number of subintervals along the x axis
 *                   intLength, the length of the interval on the x axis
 *    Precondition: the y values correspond to equally-spaced x values
 *                   in the interval on the x axis.
 *    Return:        the approximate area under the curve
 ************************************************************************/

double TrapezoidalArea(int n, double intLength)
{
   double yValue;
   cout << "First y value? ";
   cin >> yValue;                        // the first y value
   double sum = yValue / 2.0;            // initialize sum to 1/2 of it

   for (int i = 1; i <= n - 1; i++)
   {
      cout >> "Next y value?  ";
      cin >> yValue;                     // i-th y value
      sum += yValue;                     // add it to sum
   }

   cout << "Last y value?  ";
   cin >> yValue;                        // the last y value
   sum += yValue/ 2.0;                   // add 1/2 of it to sum

   double deltaX = intLength / double(n);

   return deltaX * sum;                  // total area of trapezoids
}
```

Since there are many different problems to which the trapezoidal method can be applied, it makes sense to store this function in a library (e.g., our MyMath library) for easy reuse. Of course, the prototype of the function must be stored in the library's header file. There are also many other methods for approximating areas such as the rectangle method, the midpoint method, Gaussian quadrature, and Simpson's rule (see Programming Problem 20 at the end of this chapter). One could develop an entire library of functions that implement these various methods.

There are many problems where it is necessary to compute the area under a curve (or the more general problem of calculating an integral). We will now consider one such real-world problem and solve it using the trapezoidal method.

PROBLEM: ROAD CONSTRUCTION

A construction company has contracted to build a highway for the state highway commission. Several sections of this highway must pass through hills from which large amounts of dirt must be excavated to provide a flat and level roadbed. For example, one section that is 1000 feet in length must pass through a hill whose height (in feet) above the roadbed has been measured at equally spaced distances and tabulated as follows:

Distance	Height
0	0
100	6
200	10
300	13
400	17
500	22
600	25
700	20
800	13
900	5
1000	0

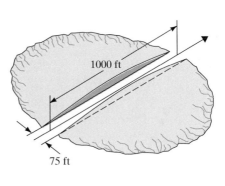

To estimate the construction costs, the company needs to know the volume of dirt that must be excavated from the hill.

OBJECT-CENTERED DESIGN

Preliminary Analysis.   To estimate the volume of dirt to be removed, we will assume that the height of the hill does not vary from one side of the road to the other. The volume can then be calculated as

(Volume = cross-sectional area of the hill) × (width of the road)

The cross-sectional area of the hill can be computed using the trapezoidal method.

Behavior. The program should display on the screen a prompt for the length of the roadway passing through the hill and the number of points at which the height was measured and read those values. The program should then pass these values to `Trapezoidal-Area()` to compute the cross-sectional area of the hill. It should then display a prompt for the width of the roadway, read this value from the keyboard, and then compute and display the volume of dirt to be removed.

Freeway construction (F3 Freeway, Oahu, Hawaii). (Photo courtesy of Tony Stone Images.)

Objects. From our behavioral description, we can identify the following objects:

Description	Kind	Type	Name
The length of roadway through the hill	varying	`double`	*roadLength*
The number of height measurements	varying	`int`	*numPoints*
The cross-sectional area of the hill	varying	`double`	*hillCrossSectionalArea*
The width of the road	varying	`double`	*roadWidth*
The volume of dirt	varying	`double`	*dirtVolume*

We can then specify the task of the program as follows:

Input: The length of a section of road
The number of height measurements at equally spaced points along this section
The collection of heights
The width of the road

Output: The volume of dirt to be removed

Operations. From our behavioral description, making a list of the operations is straightforward:

   i.   Read a double (*roadLength*) and an integer (*numPoints*) from the keyboard.

  ii.   Compute the cross-sectional area of the hill (`TrapezoidalArea()`).

 iii.   Initialize a real variable with a real value (*hillCrossSectionalArea, dirtVolume*).

 iv.   Multiply two real values.

Algorithm.   These operations can be organized into an algorithm, as follows:

Algorithm for Highway Construction Problem

1. Prompt for and read the length of the roadway through the hill into *roadLength*.
2. Prompt for and read the number of height measurements into *numPoints*.
3. Compute the approximate cross-sectional area of the hill in *hillCrossSectionalArea*.
4. Prompt for and read the width of the road into *roadWidth*.
5. Compute the volume of dirt to be removed:

$$dirtVolume = hillCrossSectionalArea \times roadWidth.$$

Coding and Testing.   The program in Figure 7.15 implements this algorithm.

FIGURE 7.15   ROAD CONSTRUCTION.

```
/* road15.cpp uses the trapezoidal method to find the volume of
 *  dirt that must be removed to construct a road through a hill.
 *
 *  Input:  the length of roadway through the hill,
 *          the width of the roadway
 *  Output: the approximate volume of dirt removed
 ***************************************************************/

#include <iostream>              // cin, cout. >>, <<

double TrapezoidalArea(int n, double totalLength);

int main()
{

   cout << "Enter the length of roadway through the hill: ";
   double roadLength;                            // get the road length
   cin >> roadLength;

   cout << "Enter the number of points at which hill elevation "
           "was measured: ";
   int numPoints;
   cin >> numPoints;

   cout << "Enter the hill elevations (y values) at the " << numPoints
        << " equally-spaced points.\n  The amount of dirt to be removed"
           " from the hill will be computed.\n\n";

                                         // compute X-sectional area
   double hillCrossSectionalArea = TrapezoidalArea(numPoints-1, roadLength);
```

```
    cout << "Enter the width of the roadway: ";
    double roadWidth;                               // get the road width
    cin >> roadWidth;
                                                    // compute volume
    double dirtVolume = roadWidth * hillCrossSectionalArea;
                                                    // display volume
    cout << "\n The volume of dirt to be removed is approximately "
         << dirtVolume << " cubic units." << endl;
}


/*** Insert definition of the function TrapezoidalArea()
     from Figure 7.14 here. ***/
```

Sample run:

```
Enter the length of roadway through the hill: 1000
Enter the number of points at which hill elevation was measured: 11
Enter the hill elevations (y values) at the 11 equally-spaced points.
The amount of dirt to be removed from the hill will be computed.

First y value? 0
Next y value?  6
Next y value?  10
Next y value?  13
Next y value?  17
Next y value?  22
Next y value?  25
Next y value?  20
Next y value?  13
Next y value?  5
Last y value?  0
Enter the width of the roadway: 75

The volume of dirt to be removed is approximately 1.09167e+06 cubic units
```

☞ PROGRAMMING POINTERS

✎ PROGRAM STYLE AND DESIGN

1. *Functions should be documented in the same way that programs are.* The documentation should include specifications and descriptions of

   - The *purpose* of the function
   - Any items that must be *received by* the function from its caller
   - Any items that must be *input to* the function
   - Any items that are *returned or passed back by* the function to its caller
   - Any items that are *output by* the function

2. *The layout of a program should clearly indicate the relationship of each line to its surrounding context.* In this text we do the following:

> ▸ Insert blank lines and documentation before each function definition to separate it from other functions

> ▸ Indent the declarations and statements within each function

> ▸ Follow the same stylistic standards for functions that we do for main programs

3. *Declare variable objects as close as possible to their first use.* This practice increases the readability of a program by keeping the use of an object and its declaration close together. It also aids with debugging because it delays the scope of an identifier as late as possible, which minimizes the number of variables to keep track of at any given point in the program.

   The primary exception is that *variables should not be casually declared within loops,* because such variables must be constructed anew on every repetition of the loop, and this slows execution.

4. *Parameters should be declared as determined by the* **specification** *of a function: If the specification for a function stipulates that*

> ▸ *The function* **receives and does not return** *a non-class value, then define a* **value** *parameter to hold that value*

> ▸ *The function* **receives and does not return** *a class value, then define a* **const reference** *parameter to hold that value*

> ▸ *The function* **returns** *a single value, then use a* `return` *statement in the function*

> ▸ *The function* **returns** *(and perhaps also receives) more than one value, then define a* **reference** *parameter to hold each of these values*

5. *All variables that are used within a function should be defined within that function, either as parameters (if named in the specification) or as local variables (if required by the algorithm but not named in the specification).* Following this guideline keeps functions self-contained, increases their generality, and hence their reuseability.

6. *Only simple functions should be specified as being inline functions.* Substitution of an inline function's body for each of its calls can increase a program's size considerably if the function is nontrivial and/or it is called at several places in the program.

7. *Recursive functions should be clearly marked as such.* For clarity and readability, the anchor case and inductive steps of a recursive function should be marked with comments.

8. *Unless optimized, recursive functions typically execute slower than their nonrecursive counterparts.* Because of this, a file containing a recursive function definition should be compiled with optimization turned on.

⚡ POTENTIAL PROBLEMS

1. *When a function is called, the number of arguments should be the same as the number of parameters in the function heading.*[11] For example, consider the function prototype

---

[11] An exception is when one or more parameters at the end of the parameter list have *default argument* (see the website described in the preface); for example,

```
void f(int x, int y = 0, double z = 3.5);
```

As the following examples show, this function may be called with 1, 2, or 3 arguments:

```
f(1, 2, 4.9);    Within f, x will have the value 1, y the value 2, and z the value 4.9
f(1, 2);         Within f, x will have the value 1, y the value 2, and z the value 3.5
f(1);            Within f, x will have the value 1, y the value 0, and z the value 3.5
```

```
int Maximum(int number1, int number2);
```

If i, j, and k are integer variables, the function call

```
larger1 = Maximum(i, j, k);
```

will generate an error, because the number of arguments does not match the number of parameters.

2. *The type of an argument corresponding to a value parameter should be compatible with the type of that parameter.* For example, for the function Maximum() in Potential Problem 1, the statement

```
larger2 = Maximum(someValue, 3.75);
```

is incorrect, because a real value such as 3.75 should not be passed to the integer parameter number2, since a loss of precision will occur.

3. *An argument that corresponds to a reference parameter must be a variable whose type matches the type of that parameter; it may not be a constant or an expression.* For example, the function with prototype

```
void FindTaxes(double income,
               double & netIncome, double & tax);
```

cannot be called by the statement

```
FindTaxes(salary, 3525.67, incomeTax);
```

because the constant 3525.67 cannot be associated with the reference parameter netIncome.

4. *A function's parameters (and non-static local variables) are allocated memory only during execution of that function; there is no memory associated with them either before or after execution of that function.* Any attempt to use these parameters outside the function will thus generate an error.

5. *An identifier must be declared before it can be used.* For example, if the function FindTaxes() calls the function Calculate(), then a prototype (or definition) of Calculate() must precede the definition of FindTaxes().

```
void Calculate(parameter_list));
      .
      .
      .

void FindTaxes();
{
      .
      .
      .

   Calculate(argument_list);
      .
      .
      .

}
```

Programming Problems

SECTION 7.3

1. Write a driver program to test the weight-conversion functions of exercises 12 and 13.

2. Write a driver program to test the length-conversion function of exercises 14 and 15.

3. Write a driver program to test the time-conversion function of exercises 16 and 17.

4. With **polar coordinates** (r, θ) of a point P, the first polar coordinate r is the distance from the origin to P, and the second polar coordinate θ is the angle from the positive x axis to the ray joining the origin with P.

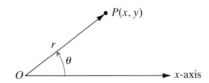

The formulas that relate polar coordinates of a point to its **rectangular coordinates** (x, y) are

$$x = r \cos \theta$$
$$y = r \sin \theta$$

Write a function `Convert()` that converts polar coordinates to rectangular coordinates. Use it in a program that reads the polar coordinates for several points and calls `Convert()`, which calculates and returns the rectangular coordinates for each point. The program should display both pairs of coordinates.

5. Write a function `CalculateTaxes()` that calculates and returns the amount of city income tax and the amount of federal income tax to be withheld from an employee's pay for one pay period. Assume that city income tax withheld is computed by taking 1.15 percent of gross pay on the first $40,000 earned per year, and that federal income tax withheld is computed by taking the gross pay less $50 for each dependent claimed and multiplying by 20 percent.

    Use this function in a program that for each of several employees reads the employee's number, number of dependents, hourly pay rate, city income tax withheld to date, federal income tax withheld to date, and hours worked for this period, and then calls function `CalculateTaxes()` to find the amount of taxes to be withheld. The program should then display the employee number, gross pay, and net pay for this pay period, the amount of city income tax and the amount of federal income tax withheld for this pay period, and the total amounts withheld through this pay period.

6. The **greatest common divisor** of two integers a and b, GCD(a, b), not both of which are zero, is the largest positive integer that divides both a and b. The **Euclidean algorithm** for finding this greatest common divisor of a and b is as follows: Divide a by b to obtain the integer quotient q and remainder r, so that $a = bq + r$. (If $b = 0$, GCD(a, b) = a.) Then GCD(a, b) = GCD(b, r). Replace a with b and b with r, and repeat this procedure. Since the remainders are decreasing, eventually a remainder of 0 will result. The last nonzero remainder is GCD(a, b). For example,

$$
\begin{array}{ll}
1260 = 198 \times 6\ + 72 & \text{GCD}(1260, 198) = \text{GCD}(198, 72) \\
198 = 72 \times 2 + 54 & \phantom{\text{GCD}(1260, 198)} = \text{GCD}(72, 54) \\
72 = 54 \times 1 + 18 & \phantom{\text{GCD}(1260, 198)} = \text{GCD}(54, 18) \\
54 = 18 \times 3 + 0 & \phantom{\text{GCD}(1260, 198)} = 18
\end{array}
$$

(*Note:* If either *a* or *b* is negative, replace it with its absolute value.) The **least common multiple** of *a* and *b*, LCM(*a*, *b*), is the smallest nonnegative integer that is a multiple of both *a* and *b*, and can be calculated using

$$\text{LCM}(a, b) = \frac{|a \times b|}{\text{GCD}(a, b)}$$

Write a program that reads two integers and then calls a function that calculates and passes back the greatest common divisor and the least common multiple of the integers. The program should then display the two integers together with their greatest common divisor and their least common multiple.

7. The graph of a person's emotional cycle $y = f(x)$ is a sine curve having an amplitude of 1 and a period of 28 days. On a given day, the person's emotional index is $f(age)$, where *age* is his or her age in days. Similarly, the physical and intellectual cycles are sine curves having an amplitude of 1 and periods of 23 and 33 days, respectively. Write a function that receives a person's age and returns his or her physical, intellectual, and emotional indices for the current day. Write another function to compute a person's biorhythm index, which is the sum of the the physical, intellectual, and emotional cycles. Write a driver program to test your functions.

SECTION 7.6

8. Write a driver program to test the digit-counting functions of exercises 28 and 29.

9. Write a driver program to test the reverse-printing functions of exercises 30 and 31.

10. Write a driver program to test the modified exponentiation function of exercise 32.

11. Write a test driver for one of the functions in exercises 18–22. Add output statements to the function to trace its actions as it executes. For example, the trace displayed for F(21) for the function F in exercise 20 should have a form like

```
F(21)  = 1 + F(10)
   F(10)  = 1 + F(5)
      F(5)  = 1 + F(2)
         F(2)  = 1 + F(1)
            F(1) returns 0
         F(2) returns 1
      F(5) returns 2
   F(10) returns 3
F(21) returns 4
```

where the indentation level reflects the depth of the recursion. (*Hint:* This can be accomplished by declaring a variable `level` outside all blocks, initially zero, that is incremented when the function is entered and decremented just before exiting the function.)

12. Proceed as in exercise 11 but for the function `PrintReverse()` of exercise 30. The trace for the function call `PrintReverse (9254)` should have a form like:

```
PrintReverse (9254):  Output 4, then call PrintReverse (925).
   PrintReverse (925):  Output 5, then call PrintReverse (92).
      PrintReverse (92):  Output 2, then call PrintReverse (9).
         PrintReverse (9):  Output 9 and \n.
         PrintReverse (9) returns.
      PrintReverse (92) returns.
   PrintReverse (925) returns.
PrintReverse (9254) returns.
```

13. Write a recursive function that prints the lyrics of the song *Bingo:*

Verse 1:   There was a farmer had a dog,
And Bingo was his name-o.
B-I-N-G-O!
B-I-N-G-O!
B-I-N-G-O!
And Bingo was his name-o!

Verse 2:   Same as verse 1, but lines 3, 4, and 5 are:

(Clap)-I-N-G-O!

Verse 3:   Same as verse 1, but lines 3, 4, and 5 are:

. . .
(Clap, clap)-N-G-O!

Verse 4:   Same as verse 1, but lines 3, 4, and 5 are:

(Clap, clap, clap)-G-O!

Verse 5:   Same as verse 1, but lines 3, 4, and 5 are:

(Clap, clap, clap, clap)-O!

Verse 6:   Same as verse 1, but lines 3, 4, and 4 are:

(Clap, clap, clap, clap, clap)

Also write a driver program to test your function.

14.   Write a recursive function that prints a nonnegative integer with commas in the correct locations. For example, it should print 20131 as 20,131. Write a driver program to test your function.

15.   The Euclidean algorithm for finding the greatest common divisor of two integers (not both zero) is described in problem 6. Write a recursive function that calculates the greatest common divisor of two integers using the Euclidean algorithm. Write a driver program to test your function.

16.   The sequence of *Fibonacci numbers,* 1, 1, 2, 3, 5, 8, 13, 21, . . . , (see Programming Problem 23 in chapter 3) can be defined recursively by:

$$f_1 = f_2 = 1 \qquad \text{(anchor)}$$
$$\text{For } n \geq 3, f_i = f_{i-1} + f_{i-2} \quad \text{(inductive step)}$$

A recursive function seems like a natural way to calculate these numbers. Write such a function and then write a driver program to test your function. (*Note:* You will probably find that this function is very inefficient. See if you can figure out why by tracing some function calls as was done in the text.)

17.   Write a recursive function to find the prime factorization of a positive integer, that is, to express the integer as a product of primes or indicate that it is a prime. Display the prime factors in descending order. Write a driver program to test the function.

18.   Consider a network of streets laid out in a rectangular grid, for example,

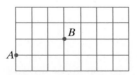

In a *northeast path* from one point in the grid to another, one may walk only to the north (up) and to the east (right). For example, there are four northeast paths from A to B in the preceding grid:

Write a recursive function to count the number of northeast paths from one point to another in a rectangular grid. Write a driver program to test your function.

Part of the Picture: Numerical Methods

19. Another method of numerical integration that generally produces better approximations than the trapezoidal method is based on the use of parabolas and is known as *Simpson's rule*. In this method, the interval $[a, b]$ is divided into an even number n of subintervals, each of length Δx, and the sum

$$\frac{\Delta x}{3}(y_0 + 4y_1 + 2y_2 + 4y_3 + 2y_4 + \cdots + 2y_{n-2} + 4y_{n-1} + y_n)$$

is used to find the area under the graph of f over the interval $[a, b]$. Write a function `SimpsonArea()` like `TrapezoidalArea()` in Figure 7.14 but use Simpson's rule. Then modify the program in Figure 7.15 to use this function to find the volume of dirt removed.

20. The work done (in joules) by a force (in newtons) that is applied at an angle θ (radians) as it moves an object from $x = a$ to $x = b$ on the x axis (with meters as units) is given by

$$W = \cos\theta \int_a^b F(x)\,dx$$

where $F(x)$ is the force applied at point x. That is, the work done is the area under the graph of $y = F(x)$ from $x = a$ to $x = b$ multipled by $\cos\theta$. Modify the program in Figure 7.15 to compute the work done for $\theta = 0.35$ radians, $a = 10.0$ m, $b = 40.0$ m, and the following forces measured at equally-spaced points from a to b: 0.0, 4.5, 9.0, 13.0, 14.0, 10.5, 12.0, 7.8, 5.0 (all in newtons).

21. Repeat problem 20 but use Simpson's rule (see Problem 19).

22. Overload the function `TrapezoidalArea()` in Figure 7.15 with a definition that has as parameters the endpoints a and b of the interval and the number n of subintervals, and which calls some given function `F()` to calculate the function values rather than input them. Test your function with a driver program and function `F()` that calculates x^2. (Note: The area under the graph of $y = x^2$ from $x = a$ to $x = b$ is $(b^3 - a^3)/3$.)

23. Another area of numerical methods is equation solving. One method for finding an approximate solution of an equation $f(x) = 0$ for some function f is the *bisection method*. In this method, we begin with two numbers a and b, where the function values $f(a)$ and $f(b)$ have opposite signs. If f is continuous between $x = a$ and $x = b$— that is, if there is no break in the graph of $y = f(x)$ between these two values—then the graph of f must cross the x-axis at least once between $x = a$ and $x = b$; thus, there must be at least one solution of the equation $f(x) = 0$ between a and b. To locate one of these solutions, we first bisect the interval $[a, b]$ and determine in which half f changes sign, thereby locating a smaller subinterval containing a solution of the equation. We bisect this subinterval and determine in which half f changes sign; this gives a still smaller subinterval containing a solution.

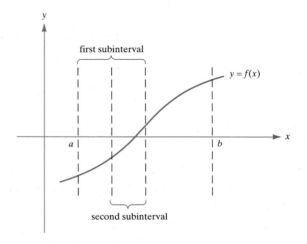

Repeating this process gives a sequence of subintervals, each of which contains a solution of the equation and whose length is one-half that of the preceding interval. Write a function to implement the bisection method and use it to find a solution of the equation $x^3 + x - 5 = 0$.

Chapter 8

FILES AND STREAMS

I can only assume that a "Do Not File" document is filed in a "Do Not File" file.

SENATOR FRANK CHURCH

The goal is information at your fingertips.

BILL GATES

The next best thing to knowing something is knowing where to find it.

SAMUEL JOHNSON

. . . it became increasingly apparent to me that, over the years, Federal agencies have amassed vast amounts of information about virtually every American citizen. This fact, coupled with technological advances in data collection and dissemination, raised the possibility that information about individuals conceivably could be used for other than legitimate purposes and without the prior knowledge or consent of the individuals involved.

PRESIDENT GERALD R. FORD

The rights of the people to be secure in their persons, houses, papers, and effects against unreasonable searches and seizures, shall not be violated. . . .

FOURTH AMENDMENT OF THE U. S. CONSTITUTION

Chapter Contents

8.1   Introductory Example: Weather Data Analysis

8.2   `ifstream` and `ofstream` Objects

8.3   Example: Scanning for a Virus

8.4   Additional Fstream Operations

PART OF THE PICTURE: Database Systems

461

Many computer users have had the unfortunate experience of having their word processor (or text editor) unexpectedly fail while they were editing a document. This is especially annoying because all of the information entered since the last save operation is lost. This happens because a word processor is an executable program, and the information being edited (documents, programs, input data, etc.) is stored in the section of main memory allocated to the word processor. When the word processing program terminates, this memory is deallocated and its contents are lost.

To minimize this problem, many word processors and text editors provide an **autosave** feature that saves the information being edited in some *stable* location (such as a secondary memory) so that information is not lost, even if a power outage should occur. Examples of secondary memory include hard disks, floppy disks, floptical disks, and magnetic tapes.

Information that is saved in secondary memory must be stored in such a way that:

1. It can be retrieved in the future
2. It is kept separate from all other documents, programs, and so on, that are saved

To achieve these goals, secondary memory is organized into distinct containers called **files,** in which information can be stored. When a document must be edited, the word processor *loads* it from secondary memory to main memory by *reading* from the file in which it is stored. The operation of *saving* information to secondary memory involves *writing* the information to a file.

Files can be classified by the kind of data stored in them. Those that contain textual characters (such as the source code for a program, numbers entered with a text editor, etc.) are called **text files.** By contrast, files that contain non-ASCII/EBCDIC characters (such as the binary code for a compiled program, or the control codes for a word processor) are called **binary files.** In this chapter, we will discuss input and output using text files.

In addition to providing a stable place to store *programs* indefinitely, files can also be used to store *data.* If a large set of data values is to be processed, then those values can be stored in a file, and a program can be written to read these values from the file and process them. This capability is especially useful in testing and debugging a program because the data does not have to be reentered each time the program is executed. In this chapter, we will examine the file-processing features of C++.

8.1 INTRODUCTORY EXAMPLE: WEATHER DATA ANALYSIS

Until now our programs have been *interactive,* meaning that the user entered data directly from the keyboard in response to prompts and/or queries displayed on the screen. There are many problems, however, in which the sheer volume of data to be processed makes it impractical to enter it from the keyboard. For such problems, the data can be stored in a file and the program designed to read data values from that file. In this section we look at one such problem.

PROBLEM: PROCESSING METEOROLOGICAL DATA

A meteorologist must record and process large amounts of weather-related data. One part of this data consists of thousands of atmospheric pressure readings that were recorded every 15 minutes for the past year. This data has been stored in a file named `pressure.dat`, and the minimum, the maximum, and the average of these readings must be computed. A program is needed to read this data, calculate these statistics, and write the results to an output file.

OBJECT-CENTERED DESIGN

Behavior. For maximum flexibility, our program should display on the screen a prompt for the name of the input file containing the pressure readings to be processed and then read this filename from the keyboard. It should then read an arbitrary number of values from that file, compute the minimum, maximum, and average of those values. The program should display on the screen a prompt for the name of the output file, which is entered from the keyboard. It must then write the minimum, maximum, and average to that output file.

Objects. In addition to the objects identified in the preceding behavior, the program must maintain a count of how many values have been read and their sum, because these values are needed to compute the average of a collection of values. This gives the following list of objects needed to solve the problem:

Description	Kind	Type	Name
The name of the file in which the pressure readings are stored	varying	string	*inputFileName*
A pressure reading	varying	double	*reading*
The number of readings	varying	int	*count*
The minimum reading	varying	double	*minimum*
The maximum reading	varying	double	*maximum*
The sum of the readings	varying	double	*sum*
The average reading	varying	double	none (*sum/count*)
The name of the file to which the results are to be written	varying	string	*outputFileName*

From this list we can specify the problem as follows:

Input(keyboard):	*inputFileName,* a string naming an input file
Input(*inputFileName*):	a sequence of pressure readings
Input(keyboard):	*outputFileName,* a string naming an output file
Output(*outputFileName*):	the minimum, maximum, and average of the input values

Operations. From our behavioral description, the following operations are needed:

i. Prompt for and read a string (*inputFileName* and *outputFileName*) from the keyboard

ii. Initialize *count, sum, maximum,* and *minimum* to specific values

iii. Read a real value (*reading*) stored in a file

iv. Increment an integer variable (*count*) by 1

    v.   Add a real value (*reading*) to a real value (*sum*)

   vi.   Update *minimum* with *reading,* if necessary

  vii.   Update *maximum* with *reading,* if necessary

 viii.   Repeat operations iii–vii until the end of the file is reached

   ix.   Write real values *(minimum, maximum, sum/count)* to an output file

All of these operations can be performed by C++ operations, functions, and statements we have studied except those that involve files (iii, viii, and ix). These (and other) file-processing operations are the topic of study in this chapter.

As we shall see, there are three additional administrative operations required to read from or write to a file.

> ▶ In order for a program to read from a file, C++ requires that a special object called an **ifstream** be **opened** to connect that file with the program

> ▶ In order for a program to write to a file, a special object called an **ofstream** must be **opened** to connect the program and that file

> ▶ When a program is done using a file, the ifstream or ofstream to that file should be **closed**

This adds two more objects to our list of objects,

Description	Kind	Type	Name
Stream from program to input file	varying	ifstream	*inStream*
Stream from program to output file	varying	ofstream	*outStream*

and two more operations to our list of operations:

    x.   *Open* a stream to a file

  xi.   *Close* a stream to a file

Algorithm.   The preceding operations can be organized into the following algorithm:

Algorithm for Processing Meteorological Data

1. Prompt for and read the name of the input file into *inputFileName.*

2. Open an ifstream named *inStream* to the file whose name is in *inputFile-Name.* (If this fails, display an error message and terminate the algorithm.)

3. Initialize *count* to 0; *sum* to 0.0; *maximum* to the smallest possible (real) value; and *minimum* to the largest possible (real) value.

4. Loop:

    a. Read a (real) value for *reading* from *InStream.*

    b. If the end-of-file mark was read, exit the loop.

    c. Increment *count.*

    d. Add *reading* to *sum.*

    e. If *reading* is less than *minimum*
        Set *minimum* to *reading.*

      f. If *reading* is greater than *maximum*
           Set *maximum* to *reading*.

    End Loop

5. Close *inStream*.
6. Prompt for and read the name of the output file into *outputFileName*.
7. Open an `ofstream` named *outStream* to the file whose name is in *outputFile-Name*. (If this fails, display an error message and terminate the algorithm.)
8. Write *count* to *outStream*.
9. If *count* is greater than zero

    Write *minimum, maximum,* and *sum/count* to *outStream*.

10. Close *outStream*.

Coding. Once one is familar with the file-processing capabilities of C++, encoding the preceding algorithm in a program like that in Figure 8.1 is straightforward. The file-processing features used in this program will be described in the following sections.

FIGURE 8.1   READING A FILE OF METEOROLOGICAL DATA.

```
/* meteorology1.cpp reads meteorological data stored in a file,
 * computes the minimum, maximum, and average of the readings,
 * and writes these statistics to an output file.
 *
 *   Input(keyboard): names of the input and output files
 *   Input(file):     a sequence of meterological readings
 *   Output(file):    the number of readings, the minimum reading,
 *                    the maximum reading, and the average reading
 ****************************************************************/

#include <iostream.h>              // cin, cout
#include <fstream.h>               // ifstream, ofstream
#include <string>                  // string, getline()
#include <assert.h>                // assert()
#include <float.h>                 // DBL_MIN and DBL_MAX

int main()
{
   cout << "This program computes the number, maximum, minimum, and\n"
           "average of an input list of numbers in one file,\n"
           "and places its results in another file.\n\n";

   // ---------- Input Section ------------------------------------

   cout << "Enter the name of the input file: ";
   string inputFileName;
   getline(cin, inputFileName);              // get name of input file
                                             // open an input stream to
   ifstream inStream;                        //   the input file,
   inStream.open(inputFileName.data());      //   establish connection,
   assert( inStream.is_open() );             //   check for success
```

```
int count = 0;                          // number of values
double reading,                         // value being processed
       maximum = DBL_MIN,               // largest seen so far
       minimum = DBL_MAX,               // smallest seen so far
       sum = 0.0;                       // running total

for (;;)                                // loop:
{
   inStream >> reading;                 //    read a value

   if ( inStream.eof() ) break;         //    if eof, quit

   count++;                             //    update: count,
   sum += reading;                      //            sum,
   if (reading < minimum)
       minimum = reading;               //            minimum, and
   if (reading > maximum)
       maximum = reading;               //            maximum.
}                                       // end loop

inStream.close();                       // close the connection

// ------------ Output Section --------------------------------

cout << "Enter the name of the output file: ";
string outputFileName;
getline(cin, outputFileName);
                                        // open an output stream to
ofstream outStream(outputFileName.data());// the output file,
                                        //    establish connection,
assert( outStream.is_open() );          //    and check for success
                                        // write results to file
outStream << "\n--> There were " << count << " values.";

if (count > 0)
    outStream << "\n\tranging from " << minimum
              << " to " << maximum
              << "\n\tand their average is " << sum / count
              << endl;

outStream.close();                      // close the stream

cout << "Processing complete.\n";
}
```

By allowing the user to enter the name of the input file to be processed, the program provides a convenient way to process the data values in *any* input file, which simplifies testing its correctness. Note that we use the `string` library function `getline()` to read the name of the file. This permits the user to enter multi-word file names, as allowed by some operating systems. If we had used the input operator (>>), then only single-word names could be entered.

Testing. To test the correctness of the program, we construct several **test files,** in which we place a small set of data values that will be used to check whether or not the program is performing correctly. For example, we might place an ascending sequence of numbers

```
11
12
13
14
15
```

in one file `test1.dat`, a descending sequence

```
99 98 97 96 95 94 93 92 91
```

in another file `test2.dat`, two sets of numbers separated by a blank line

```
4 5 6
1 2 3

9 8
7
```

in yet another file `test3.dat`, and so on. We thus create test files that *exercise* the program, looking for conditions under which it fails. Figure 8.2 shows sample runs of the program using the first two files. Once the program has been thoroughly tested, we can execute it using the original data file (`pressure.dat`) and have confidence in the results it produces.

FIGURE 8.2   TESTING THE PROGRAM IN FIGURE 8.1.

Sample run #1:

```
This program computes the number, maximum, minimum, and
average of an input list of numbers in one file,
and places its results in another file.

Enter the name of the input file: test1.dat
Please enter the name of the output file: test1.out
Processing complete.
```

Listing of `test1.out`:

```
--> There were 5 values.
    ranging from 11 to 15
    and their average is 13.
```

Sample run #2:

```
This program computes the number, maximum, minimum, and
average of an input list of numbers in one file,
and places its results in another file.
```

```
Enter the name of the input file: test2.dat
Please enter the name of the output file: test2.out
Processing complete.
```

Listing of test2.out:

```
--> There were 9 values.
    ranging from 91 to 99
    and their average is 95.
```

Note that in these sample runs of the program, the only output that appears on the screen are the opening message, the prompts for the names of the input and output files, and a termination message. The rest of the output is written to the output file specified by the user. The only data that is input from the keyboard are the two filenames. All other input data is read from the input file.

8.2 ifstream AND ofstream OBJECTS

In this section, we examine the types and operations provided by the fstream library for performing file I/O.

DECLARING FSTREAM OBJECTS

Recall that with interactive I/O, the iostream library automatically establishes the following connections (among others) between programs executing in main memory and I/O devices:

1. An istream object named cin connects the program and the keyboard
2. An ostream object named cout connects the program and the screen.[1]

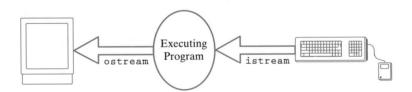

These streams are constructed automatically for interactive programs, but if a program is to perform input from and/or output to a text file, it must construct streams for this purpose. This operation is called **opening** the streams. Opening a stream creates a connection between a program (in main memory) and a text file (stored on some secondary memory device such as a disk drive).

---

[1] The ostream object cerr is also established as a second connection between the program and the screen.

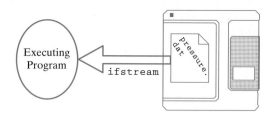

As illustrated in the program in Figure 8.1, a program that is to read from a file must open an **ifstream** to that file, and a program that is to write to a file must open an **ofstream** to that file. We will use the generic term *fstream* to refer to these classes. They are declared in the fstream library, so that any program wishing to use these classes must contain the #include <fstream.h> directive.[2]

Declaring an Fstream Object. Before a program can read values from a text file, it must construct an ifstream object to act as a connection from the file to the program. This can be done with a declaration of the form

```
ifstream input_stream_name;
```

Similarly, a program that writes values to a text file must first construct an ofstream object to act as a connection from the program to the file. This can be accomplished with

```
ofstream output_stream_name;
```

For example, the program in Figure 8.1 uses the declaration

```
ifstream inStream;
```

to construct an ifstream object named inStream.

Once an fstream object has been constructed, various operations can be applied to that fstream. We will examine these operations in the remainder of this section.

THE BASIC FSTREAM OPERATIONS

It is important to understand that the classes ifstream and ofstream are *derived from* the classes istream and ostream, respectively, which means that these classes have been constructed as *extensions* of the istream and ostream classes. As a result, all of the operations on istream and ostream objects can also be performed on ifstream and ofstream objects, respectively, along with several new operations that are limited to fstream objects. Some of the most commonly used operations are:

open()   A function that establishes a connection between a program and
            a file

is_open()   A boolean function that returns true if a file was opened suc-
            cessfully and returns false otherwise

---

[2] As noted before, a recent change in the C++ standard allows fstream in place of <fstream.h> and adding the statement using namespace std; after all the #include directives.

>>   An operator that inputs an object from a file that has been
              opened for input

getline()   A function that reads a line of text from a file into a `string`
              object

<<   An operator that outputs an object to a file that has been
              opened for output

eof()   A boolean function that returns true if the last input operation
              read the end-of-file mark and returns false otherwise

close()   A function that terminates a connection between a program and
              a file

We now examine each of these operations in more detail.

The open() Member. Just as the declaration

```
int i;
```

declares object `i` as an uninitialized variable, the declarations

```
ifstream inStream;
ofstream outStream;
```

declare the objects `inStream` and `outStream` as uninitialized fstreams—as *potential* connections between a program and files. These potential connections become *actual* connections by using the `open()` function member. In the program in Figure 8.1, the statement

```
inStream.open(inputFileName.data());
```

initializes the `ifstream` object `inStream` by establishing it as a connection between the program and the file whose name is stored in the `string` object `inputFileName`. So if `inputFileName` contains the string `"pressure.dat"`, then the program is connected to the file `pressure.dat`:

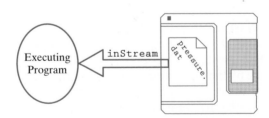

Note that when the file name is stored in a `string` object, the `string` function member `data()` must be used to extract the character string literal from the string.

To illustrate, consider a small version of the file `pressure.dat`:

```
11.1 22.2 33.3 44.4
55.5 66.6 77.7
88.8 99.9
```

It is important to realize that a **text file** like this is simply a *sequence of characters*. Such files are created by the operating system, which automatically places a special **end-of-file mark** at the end of the file. If we use the symbol ⅋ to represent a blank, the symbol ⏐ to represent a newline, and the symbol ◊ to represent the end-of-file mark, then after the statement

```
inStream.open(inputFileName.data());
```

has been executed, `inStream` may be visualized as

```
11.1⅋22.2⅋33.3⅋44.4⏐55.5⅋66.6⅋77.7⏐88.8⅋99.9⏐◊
```

inStream

where the down-arrow (↓) indicates the **read position,** denoting the next character to be read.

The `open()` function member can also be used to open `ofstream` objects as connections to output files. For example, given the declaration

```
ofstream outStream;
```

the statement

```
outStream.open("NewFile.out");
```

creates a new file named `NewFile.out` containing only the end-of-file mark, and then establishes `outStream` as a connection between the program and the file:

outStream

In this diagram, the down-arrow (↓) represents the **write position**—the position at which the next output value will be placed in the stream.

A (simplified) general form of the `open()` member is as follows:

The open() Member

Form

fstream_name.open(*file_name*);

where:

fstream_name is the name of the fstream being initialized;

file_name is the (character string literal) name of a data file .

Action

The object *fstream_name* is initialized as a connection between the executing program and the file named *file_name* .

By default, opening an `ofstream` to a file is *destructive*. That is, if a file named `NewFile.out` exists and the statement

```
outStream.open("NewFile.out");
```

is executed, any old contents of `NewFile.out` will be destroyed.

For situations where this destruction is undesirable, the `open()` function member can be used with a second **mode argument,** which can be any of the following.[3]

Mode	Description
`ios::in`	The default mode for `ifstream` objects. Open a file for input, nondestructively, with the read position at the file's beginning.
`ios::trunc`	Open a file and delete any contents it contains (i.e., *truncate* it).
`ios::out`	The default mode for `ofstream` objects. Open a file for output, using `ios::trunc`.
`ios::app`	Open a file for output, but nondestructively, with the write position at the file's end (i.e., for *appending*).
`ios::ate`	Open an existing file with the read position (`ifstream` objects) or write position (`ofstream` objects) at the end of the file.
`ios::nocreate`	Open a file only if it already exists.
`ios::noreplace`	Open a file only if it does not already exist.
`ios::binary`	Open a file in binary mode.

To illustrate, to open an `ofstream` to a file named `ExistingFile.out` and add data at the end of the file, we can use `ios::app` as a second argument, as follows:

```
outStream.open("ExistingFile.out", ios::app);
```

This second argument makes the `open()` function *nondestructive* so that the old contents of `ExistingFile.out` are preserved, and any additional values written to the file will be *appended* to it.

Initialization at Declaration. In practice, the `open()` function member is rarely used, because C++ provides an alternative means of initializing an fstream object *when it is declared.* Just as we can initialize a variable in its declaration,

```
int sum = 0;
```

we can initialize the fstream when we declare it. For example, instead of using

```
fstream outStream;
outStream.open(outputFileName.data());
```

the program in Figure 8.1 opened the second (output) fstream with

```
ofstream outStream(outputFileName.data());
```

This statement both declares `outStream` as an `ofstream` and opens it as a connection to the file whose name is stored in `outputFileName`.

---

[3] In fact, these modes can be combined using the bitwise-OR (|) operator.

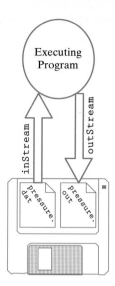

The general form of an initializing declaration of an fstream is :

Fstream Initializing Declaration

Forms

```
ifstream fstream_name(file_name, mode);
```

or

```
ofstream fstream_name(file_name, mode);
```

where:

  fstream_name is the name of the fstream being initialized;

  file_name is the (character string literal) name of a data file; and

  mode is the optional mode argument described above.

Action

The object *fstream_name* is initialized as a connection between the executing program and the file named *file_name*.

 The tradeoffs in the two initialization mechanisms are:

▶ Using the open() function is perhaps more readable than using the initializing declaration since it explictly states the operation being performed. Also, an open operation is common in programming languages.

▶ Initializing an fstream object is an easily forgotten detail since we do not need to initialize cin or cout before we use them. Initializing such objects at their declaration is thus perhaps less error-prone because it eliminates having to remember to use the open() operation.

The two mechanisms are functionally equivalent, however, and the choice is largely a matter of programming style.

Programming Defensively—the `is_open()` Member. There are a number of errors that can occur in opening an fstream to a file. To illustrate, consider the following attempt to initialize an `ifstream` to an input file:

```
ifstream inStream(file_name);
```

If the file *file_name* does not exist or cannot be found, then the open operation fails. Obviously, if this happens, any subsequent attempts to read from that file will also fail. Consequently,

> *The success or failure of a call to open a file should always be **tested** before proceeding with any additional operations on the file.*

This testing is easily done using the boolean function member `is_open()` whose form is as follows.[4]

The `is_open()` Member

Use

```
fstream_name.is_open();
```

where:

fstream_name is the name of an fstream that serves as a connection to some file.

Action

`is_open()` returns:

`true` if *fstream_name* was successfully opened;

`false` if the open operation failed.

In the program in Figure 8.1, we used the `assert()` mechanism to check for successful opens:

```
assert(inStream.is_open());
```

and

```
assert(outStream.is_open());
```

This provides a succinct way to test each fstream and terminate the program if it failed to open. If we wish to display a more user-friendly diagnostic message, we could use an `if` statement instead:

```
if (!inStream.is_open())
{
    cerr << "Unable to open: " << inputFileName << endl;
    exit(1);
}
```

If failure to open should not be treated as a fatal error, the call to `exit()` may be omitted.

---

[4] Some compilers that are not fully ANSI-C++ compliant may not provide the `is_open()` function. In this case, the success or failure of the open operation can be tested using the `good()` or `fail()` functions; for example, `assert(inStream.good());` or `assert(!inStream.fail());`.

An **InteractiveOpen()** **Function.** Quite often when an fstream is opened to a file, the user must be queried for the name of the file, which must be stored in a string and then used to open the file. The details of carrying out these steps tend to clutter the code and can be hidden by encapsulating them in a function. Figure 8.3 gives a pair of such functions that overload the name InteractiveOpen() to allow both ifstream and ofstream objects to be conveniently opened. These two functions might be stored in a library—for example, in a Query library that also contains the interactive query functions from section 6.5—to simplify the task of opening an ifstream to a file.

FIGURE 8.3   **InteractiveOpen().**

```
#include <iostream.h>            // cin, cout, >>, <<
#include <fstream.h>             // ifstream, ofstream
#include <string>                // string, getline()

// --- Open an ifstream interactively ---------------------

void InteractiveOpen(ifstream & theIFStream)
{
   cout << "Enter the name of the input file: ";
   string inputFileName;
   getline(cin, inputFileName);

   theIFStream.open(inputFileName.data());

   if (!theIFStream.is_open())
   {
      cerr << "\n***InteractiveOpen(): unable to open "
           << inputFileName << endl;
      exit(1);
   }
}

// --- Open an ofstream interactively ---------------------

void InteractiveOpen(ofstream & theOFStream)
{
   cout << "Enter the name of the output file: ";
   string outputFileName;
   getline(cin, outputFileName);

   theOFStream.open(outputFileName.data());

   if (!theOFStream.is_open())
   {
      cerr << "\n***InteractiveOpen(): unable to open "
           << outputFileName << endl;
      exit(1);
   }
}
```

The Input Operator. One of the most elegant features of C++ is its *consistency* — its use of the same operators to perform tasks that are functionally similar. The task of performing input from a file is an example of this consistency, because input from an ifstream is performed in the same manner as input from an istream. That is, once an ifstream has been established as a connection to some file, the same input operator (>>) we have used to input data from the keyboard using an istream (i.e., cin) can now be used to input data from a file via the ifstream to that file. Thus, in the program in Figure 8.1, the statement

```
inStream >> reading;
```

gets the next value from the file connected to the program through the ifstream object inStream and stores it in the variable reading. For example, given inStream as described earlier,

```
11.1b22.2b33.3b44.4↵55.5b66.6b77.7↵88.8b99.9↵ ◊
```
                              inStream

execution of this input statement reads the characters '1', '1', '.', '1', and then stops upon encountering the blank. The characters are then converted to the real value 11.1, which is stored in variable reading:

```
11.1          11.1b22.2b33.3b44.4↵55.5b66.6b77.7↵88.8b99.9↵ ◊
reading                        inStream
```

In the next repetition of the loop, execution of the statement

```
inStream >> reading;
```

skips the blank, reads the characters '2', '2', '.', '2', and then stops upon encountering the next blank. The characters are converted to the real value 22.2, which is stored in variable reading.

```
22.2          11.1b22.2b33.3b44.4↵55.5b66.6b77.7↵88.8b99.9↵ ◊
reading                        inStream
```

In subsequent repetitions of the loop, the value 33.3 is read in exactly the same way,

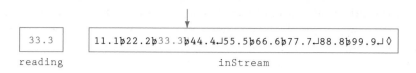

as is the value 44.4, except that reading stops at the newline character instead of at a blank:

(Recall that any *white space* character—blank, tab, or newline—serves to delimit numbers.) Subsequent repetitions of the loop read the remaining values in the same way until only the 99.9 remains unread:

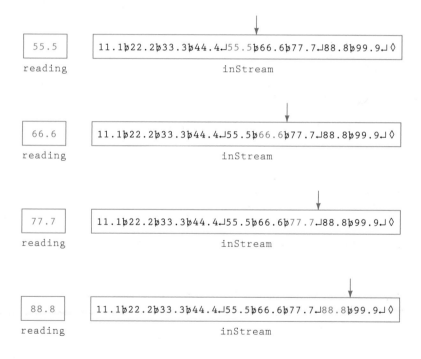

The next repetition skips the blank, reads the four characters '9', '9', '.', '9', and stops when the newline is encountered:

On the final trip through the loop, the input statement attempts to read a value but finds no data before the end-of-file mark. This causes the member function `eof()` to return the value `true`, which terminates the loop. (See the discussion of `eof()` later in this section.)

Note that this is similar to what would happen if we were to use the statement

```
cin >> reading;
```

to get the next `double` value from the keyboard and store it in `reading`. The only difference is that the input operator would extract values from the `istream` named `cin` instead of from the `ifstream` named `inStream`.

Input is consistent in the `iostream` library because the same operator (`>>`) is used to input a `double` value from an `istream` object such as `cin` and to input a `double` value from an `ifstream` object such as `inStream`. The only difference in these operations is the type of their first operand. As we saw in section 7.5, when the same operator (such as `>>`) can be applied to operands of different types, that operator is said to be **overloaded.** Just as we overloaded the function `Swap()` by defining its behavior for a variety of types, the designer(s) of the fstream library overloaded the `>>` operator so that it can be applied to `ifstream` objects as well as `istream` objects.

The `getline()` Function. As we saw in chapter 4, the `string` library provides a utility function named `getline()` that, given an `istream` object and a `string` object, fills the `string` object with a line of input from the `istream`. Since an `ifstream` is a specialized kind of `istream`, we can also use `getline()` for input from an `ifstream`.

This function is most commonly used in files that are organized into lines. For example, if `nameStream` is an `ifstream` to a file containing a list of names,

nameStream

we can either use the input operator `>>`

```
inStream >> firstName >> lastName;
```

to read the individual name components into `string` objects `firstName` and `lastName`:

                nameStream   firstName   lastName

or we can use the `getline()` function

```
getline(inStream, name);
```

and read the entire first line into a `string` object name:

nameStream   name

We can thus describe the getline() function as follows:

The getline() Function

Use

getline(*stream_object*, *string_object*);

where:

stream_object is an istream or ifstream connected to a file; and

string_object is a variable string object.

Action

Reads characters from *stream_object*, storing them in *string_object*, until a newline character is read (but is not stored in *string_object*).

Note the difference in how the input operator and the getline() function treat the newline character: >> leaves it unread in the stream (and will skip it as leading white space on the next read), whereas getline() reads it, but does not add it to the end of the string object.

This difference between >> and getline() can cause difficulty if calls to them are carelessly intermixed. To illustrate, suppose that empStream is an ifstream connected to a file containing employee numbers and employee names, each on a separate line:

```
101
Al Smith
102
Betty Smith
...
```

Then empStream can be visualized as follows:

empStream

Now, consider the following input loop:

```
int empNumber;
string empName;
```

```
for (;;)
{
    empStream >> empNumber;
    getline(empStream, empName);

    if (empStream.eof()) break;

    // Process empNumber and empName
}
```

The problem here is that when the input operation has read the employee number,

it leaves the newline unread in the stream. Since the character at the read position is a newline and `getline()` stops when it reads a newline, it will stop immediately, leaving `empName` empty:

`empNumber` and `empName` will then not be processed in the way we expect, which is clearly a problem. Even worse, when control returns to the top of the loop and the input statement tries to extract a value for `empNumber`, the read position is at the `"A"` in `"Al Smith"`:

Since `"A"` is not an integer, this will set the *fail* and/or *bad* status bits of `empStream`, but not the *eof* bit. Once a bit other than *good* is set, no subsequent input operations will succeed, and so no progress is made towards the end-of-file mark. This, combined with `eof()` being `false`, means that execution is stuck in an infinite loop!

The solution to the problem is to follow the input operation with a call to the stream function member `get()` to explicitly consume the newline character following each extraction of a value for `empNumber`:

```
int empNumber;
string name;
char theNewLine;
```

```
for (;;)
{
   empStream >> empNumber;         // this leaves an unread newline
   empStream.get(theNewLine);      //   at the read position, so get() it
   getline(empStream, name);       //   and getline() won't trip on it

   if (empStream.eof()) break;

   // Process empNumber and name
}
```

Now, when our input loop executes, 101 is read into empNumber,

after which the call to get() moves the read position past the newline,

and the call to getline() correctly reads "Al Smith" into empName:

Both values are now available to be processed, and the stream is left in the correct state for the next repetition.

The eof() Member. We saw in section 6.5 that the end-of-file mark can be used as a sentinel value to control an input loop as follows:

```
for (;;)
{
   cin >> inputValue;

   if (cin.eof()) break;

   // ... process inputValue
}
```

Such a loop will continue to execute until the user enters an end-of-file mark as a sentinel to indicate that no more data is to be entered.

In the program in Figure 8.1, the main processing loop has a similar form:

```
for (;;)
{
    inStream >> reading;

    if (inStream.eof()) break;

    // ...process reading
}
```

Here, the function call

```
inStream.eof()
```

behaves exactly like

```
cin.eof()
```

except that the user need not enter an end-of-file mark to make the function return `true`, because the file from which we are reading already contains such a mark:

```
11.1♭22.2♭33.3♭44.4⏎55.5♭66.6♭77.7⏎88.8♭99.9⏎ ◊
```
inStream

`inStream.eof()` returns `true` following execution of the statement

```
inStream >> reading;
```

provided there is no data between the read position and the end-of-file mark.

The `eof()` Member

Use

  `fstream_name.eof()`

where:

  `fstream_name` is the name of an fstream that serves as a connection to some file.

Action

`eof()` returns:

  `true`, if the last input operation on `fstream_name` failed because the end of file mark was encountered;

  `false`, otherwise.

Again, we see a pleasing consistency in the I/O facilities of the `iostream` library, because `eof()` is a function member of `ifstream` objects just as it is of `istream` objects. This is an example of the usefulness of the C++ *inheritance* mechanism—`eof()` is actually a member of the class `ios`, from which other I/O-stream classes are derived. These other classes (`istream` and `ifstream`) thus inherit `eof()` from the base class `ios` (which all of them hold in common) and thus avoid redundant redefinitions of their own `eof()` functions.

The Output Operator. Just as the input operator is overloaded to perform consistently with both `istream` and `ifstream` objects, the output operator (`<<`) is overloaded to behave consistently with both `ostream` and `ofstream` objects. For example, as we saw in Figure 8.1, we can declare

```
ofstream outStream(outputFileName.data());
```

to open an output connection between a program and a file whose name is stored in the `string` object `outputFileName`. The `ofstream` object `outStream` is initially empty, containing only the end-of-file mark:

outStream

The program in Figure 8.1 contains statements to write results to an output file via `outStream`:

```
outStream << "\n--> There were a total of " << count << " values.";

if (count > 0)
    outStream << "\n\tranging from " << minimum
              << " to " << maximum
              << "\n\tand their average is " << sum / count
              << endl;
```

Execution of the first statement inserts the appropriate characters into `outStream`,

outStream

and execution of the output statement within the `if` statement inserts the remaining characters:

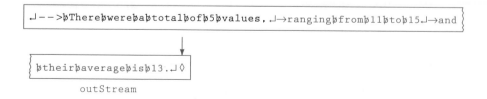

outStream

Here we have used the right-arrow symbol (→) to represent a tab character.

Execution of the program simply displays the introductory message on the screen, prompts for the names of the input and output files, and then displays a `Processing complete` message; all other output has been sent to the output file via `outStream` instead of to the screen via `cout`.

The `close()` Member. We have seen that the initialization of an fstream establishes that object as a connection between a program and a file. As an object declared within a function, an fstream is disconnected when execution leaves that function (i.e., leaves the scope of the fstream), just as a local variable's value is lost when execution leaves the scope of that variable.

Nevertheless, it is considered good programming practice to disconnect an fstream explicitly, using the `close()` member function. In the program in Figure 8.1, the statements

```
inStream.close();
```

and

```
outStream.close();
```

sever the connection between the program and the input file and the output file, respectively. We can describe the `close()` operation as follows:

The `close()` Member

Use

  fstream_name`.close();`

where:

  fstream_name is the name of an fstream that serves as a connection to some output file.

Action

The executing program and the output file are disconnected, and *fstream_name* becomes undefined.

In the program in Figure 8.1, the effect of the statement

```
outStream.close();
```

is to write the contents of the `ofstream` named `outStream`

```
⏎-->bTherebwerebabtotalbofb5bvalues, ⏎→rangingbfromb11btob15⏎→and
```

```
btheirbaveragebisb13.⏎◊
```

        `outStream`

to the output file (e.g., `test1.out`), which we might visualize as

```
-->There were a total of 5 values,
   ranging from 11 to 15
   and their average is 13.
```

Using the `close()` function is most important when a program uses many different files, because many operating systems place a limit on the number of files a

program may have open simultaneously.[5] This means that if a program tries to open more files than allowed, the operating system will terminate the program abnormally. This problem can be avoided by always using the `close()` function to sever the connection between a program and a file when the program is done using it. This keeps the number of open files associated with the program from growing beyond the limit allowed by the operating system.

FSTREAMS AS PARAMETERS

Fstreams, like any other types of objects, may be used as arguments to user-defined functions. In this case, however, *the parameters corresponding to fstream arguments must be reference parameters,* because:

- ▶ As we have seen, reading from an `ifstream` alters the read position in that `ifstream`
- ▶ Writing to an `ofstream` alters the write position in that `ofstream`

The fstream parameter must be defined as a reference parameter so that these changes to the fstream in the function are propagated back to the caller of the function.

SUMMARY

The following points summarize some of the important points regarding file I/O in C++.

- ▶ A text file is simply a container for characters stored on a secondary memory device.
- ▶ A file cannot be accessed directly from a program, but must be accessed indirectly through an fstream—an abstract conduit between the program and the file through which the program can perform input from and/or output to the file.
- ▶ Either the initialization-at-declaration mechanism or the `open()` function member can be used to connect an fstream to a file.
- ▶ If an `ifstream` is opened to a file, then the fstream is initialized with the contents of that file and the read position at the first character in the fstream.
- ▶ If an `ofstream` is opened to a file, then the fstream is initialized as empty (containing only the end-of-file mark) with the write position at the end-of-file mark. Any previous contents of the file are destroyed.
- ▶ If an `ofstream` is opened to a file using the mode `ios::app`, then the file must exist and the fstream is initialized with the contents of that file with the write position at the end of the file.
- ▶ The input operator (`>>`) can be used to extract the first value following the read position in an `ifstream`. The read position is advanced to the first character past the input value. Any initial white space characters are skipped. Numeric values are delimited by nonnumeric characters.
- ▶ The `string` library `getline()` function can be used to extract the line of input beginning at the read position in an `ifstream` and store the extracted

---

[5] For example, the original UNIX systems allowed a program to have a maximum of 15 files open simultaneously.

characters in a `string` variable. The function stops storing characters as soon as it reads a newline character, and it leaves the read position at the first character beyond that newline. Care must be taken when intermixing calls to `getline()` and calls to the input operator.

▶ The output operator (`<<`) can be used to insert a value into an `ofstream` at the write position. The write position is advanced to the point immediately following the value.

▶ The `close()` function member should be used to disconnect an fstream from a file when that file is no longer needed.

✔ Quick Quiz 8.2

1. The `iostream` library establishes a(n) _____ object named _____ that connects a program and the keyboard.

2. The `iostream` library establishes a(n) _____ object named _____ that connects a program and the screen.

3. In order for a program to read data from a file, a(n) _____ object must connect the program to that file.

4. In order for a program to write output to a file, a(n) _____ object must connect the program to that file.

5. The types of fstreams needed to connect a program and a file are declared in the _____ library.

6. (True or false) Almost none of the operations on iostreams can be performed on fstreams.

7. Write a statement to declare an fstream named `inputStream` that will be used for input from a file and another statement that uses the `open()` function to connect the program to a file named `EmployeeInfo`.

8. Repeat question 7 but use the initialization-at-declaration mechanism.

9. Repeat question 7 but for an fstream named `outputStream` that will be used for output to a file named `EmployeeReport`.

10. Repeat question 9 but use the initialization-at-declaration mechanism.

11. Modify your answers to questions 7 and 8 so that the user inputs the name of the file into a `string` variable `inputFileName`.

12. (True or false) The declaration `ifstream inStream("data");` will destroy the contents of the file named `data`.

13. (True or false) The declaration `ofstream outStream("data");` will destroy the contents of the file named `data`.

14. Write a statement that will stop program execution if an attempt to open the `ifstream inputStream` fails.

15. Write a statement that will extract an entire line from the `ifstream` in question 14.

16. Write a statement that will display the message `"End of file"` for the `ifstream` in question 14 when the end-of-file mark is reached.

17. Write a statement to disconnect the `ifstream` in question 14.

EXERCISES 8.2

1. Using both the (a) open() function and (b) the initialization-at-declaration mechanism, write statements to declare and open an fstream named inputStream as a connection to an input file named InData.

2. Proceed as in exercise 1 but open an fstream named outputStream as a connection to an output file named OutData.

3. Proceed as in exercise 1 but declare a string variable inputFileName and read the name of the input file into it.

4. Proceed as in exercise 2 but declare a string variable outputFileName and read the name of the output file into it.

For exercises 5–7, assume that num1, num2, num3, and num4 are integer variables, and that inStream is an istream connected to a file containing the following data:

```
1  -2 3↵
4 -5 6↵
7        -8        9↵
```

Tell what values will be assigned to these variables when the statements are executed.

5. inStream >> num1 >> num2 >> num3 >> num4;

6. inStream >> num1 >> num2;
   inStream >> num3;
   inStream >> num4;

7. inStream >> num1 >> num2;
   inStream >> num3 >> num4;

For exercises 8–12, assume that inStream has been opened as a connection to an input file that contains the following data

```
123   45.6↵
X78 -909.8 7↵
-65 $  432.10↵
```

and that the following declarations are in effect:

```
int
    n1, n2, n3;
double
    r1, r2, r3;
char
    c1, c2, c3, c4;
```

List the values that are assigned to each of the variables in the input list, or explain why an error occurs:

8. inStream >> n1 >> r1 >> c1 >> n2 >> r2
            >> c2 >> n3 >> c3 >> c4 >> r3;

9. inStream >> n1 >> c1 >> c2 >> r1 >> r2
            >> n2 >> n3 >> c3;

10. inStream >> n1 >> r1 >> c1 >> c2 >> c3
            >> n2 >> r2 >> c4 >> r3 >> n3;

11. inStream >> c1 >> n1 >> r1 >> r2
            >> n2 >> c2 >> c3 >> r3;

12.
```
inStream >> n1 >> r1 >> c1 >> c2
        >> c3 >> n2 >> c4;
```

For exercises 13–17, assume that `inStream` has been opened as a connection to an input file that contains the following data

```
♭54♭32E1⏎—6.78♭$90⏎⏎♭1⏎ ◊
```
inStream

and that the following declarations are in effect:

```
int
    n1, n2, n3, n4;
double
    r1, r2, r3;
char
    c1, c2, c3, c4;
```

List the values that are assigned to each of the variables in the input list, or explain why an error occurs. Also, show the location of the read position after each of the statements is executed.

13. `inStream >> n1 >> r1 >> r2 >> c1 >> n2 >> n3;`

14. `inStream >> n1 >> r1 >> r2 >> c1 >> c2 >> n2 >> n3;`

15.
```
inStream >> n1 >> n2 >> c1 >> c2 >> c3
        >> r1 >> c4 >> n2 >> r2;
```

16. `inStream >> r1 >> r2 >> r3 >> c1 >> n1 >> n2;`

17. `inStream >> n1 >> n2 >> c1 >> n3 >> c2 >> r1 >> c3 >> n4 >> r2;`

8.3 EXAMPLE: SCANNING FOR A VIRUS

A computer **virus** is a piece of software that, when executed, attempts to hide itself within other executable programs. When it succeeds, the executable program becomes a **host** for the virus, so that when it is executed, the virus tries to "infect" other programs. That is, if the programs on one computer are infected with a virus and a user copies one of those programs onto a floppy disk and then takes the floppy disk to another computer to execute that program, the virus will try to replicate itself by infecting the programs on that computer. A computer virus can thus spread quickly among a community of computer users if they share infected software applications.

There are a number of organizations that write software products to combat viruses. These products utilize two basic approaches:

▶ Virus *detection & recovery* to identify viruses in a system and remove them (hopefully without damaging their hosts)

▶ Virus *prevention* to keep new viruses from infecting a computer's programs, by watching for behavior characteristic of viruses

A virus can be very malicious. An example is the infamous Michelangelo virus, which is programmed to do nothing (but replicate itself) until March 6 (the birthday of Michelangelo) when it erases the hard disk of the computer whose software it infects. By contrast, the CODE 252 virus activates whenever an infected system or application is executed, and displays the annoying message:

```
You have a virus
Ha Ha Ha Ha Ha Ha Ha
Now erasing all disks...
Ha Ha Ha Ha Ha Ha Ha
P.S. Have a nice day
Ha Ha Ha Ha Ha Ha Ha
(Click to continue...)
```

Fortunately, this message is a "practical joke" as the virus does not actually delete any files or directories.

For viruses that display such messages, the character string displayed is typically stored within the virus as a constant. That means that to identify whether or not a program is a host for a virus, a virus-detection program can simply scan the suspected host for the appropriate string. This is the approach used to detect the ANTI virus; virus-detection programs simply scan executable programs suspected of being hosts for the string "ANTI".

The program in Figure 8.4 simulates this detection technique. It uses the capabilities provided by the `string` class and an end-of-file controlled loop to repeatedly:

- ▶ Read a line from a file,
- ▶ Scan that line for a given string of text,
- ▶ If the string of text is found, display a message to that effect.

The sample run in Figure 8.4 uses a text file named `binary.sim`, in which we have simulated the appearance of a binary file infected with the ANTI virus.[6]

FIGURE 8.4   SCANNING FOR A VIRUS.

```
/* virus4.cpp simulates the behavior of a virus detection program.
 *
 * Input:  the name of the input file; the string to be checked
 * Output: a message indicating whether the input string occurs
 *         in the input file
 **********************************************************************/

#include <iostream.h>              // cin, cout, <<, >>
#include <fstream.h>               // ifstream, open(), close(), eof()
#include <string>                  // string, getline(), find(), NPOS

void InteractiveOpen(ifstream & theIFStream);
```

---

[6] Since viruses embed themselves in executable programs, an actual virus-detection program would have to scan a *binary* file instead of a text file. The stream to the file would thus have to be opened using the `ios::binary` mode. Since binary files are not line-oriented, a somewhat more complicated scanning technique would be required.

```
int main()
{
   cout << "This program searches a file for a given string.\n";

   ifstream inStream;
   InteractiveOpen(inStream);
                                        // get the search string
   cout << "Enter the string being sought: ";
   string searchString;
   getline(cin, searchString);

   string lineOfText;

   for (;;)
   {
      getline(inStream, lineOfText);         // get a line from the file

      if (inStream.eof()) break;             // quit, if at eof
                                             //  display a "found" msg.
      if (lineOfText.find(searchString, 0) != NPOS)
         cout << "\n*** " << searchString
              << " found in this file." << endl;
   }

   cout << "\nProcessing complete.\n";       // message to user
   inStream.close();                         // close the file
}

/*** Insert the definition of the function
     InteractiveInput() from Figure 8.3 here. ***/
```

Listing of simulated virus-infected file:

```
aisjdfklasdjfklasjfljasdfljasdas;l
zzmANTIkladfklajsdfklajsdfkjasdljaslkdfj
kasjfklasdjfklajsdfkljasdflkalskdf
kjavjdfjoiwjefmm,.xmcjeoieCewmp.EM
,mckwjoaejcccnmeyquvhi hnrefnnfhDKFa
nacjksnfhean, ae lcajwefawefmaklmefl;m
ckmadjeoiemaamcl;maelalskmclamsl;k
```

Sample run:

```
This program searches a file for a given string.
Enter the name of the input file: binary.sim
Please enter the string being sought: ANTI

*** ANTI found in this file.

Processing complete.
```

8.4 ADDITIONAL FSTREAM OPERATIONS

In addition to the basic operations of `open()`, `is_open()`, `<<`, `>>`, `getline()`, `eof()`, and `close()`, there are many other operations that can be used with fstreams. Several of these have already been discussed in previous chapters, including:

- the function member `get()`, which reads a character from a stream without skipping white space
- the stream-status function members `good()`, `bad()`, and `fail()`
- the function member `clear()` to reset the status bits of a stream
- the function member `ignore()` to skip a specified number of characters
- the various stream manipulators

In fact, most of the operations that can be applied to the `istream` object `cin` can be applied to an `ifstream` object, and most of the operations that can be applied to the `ostream` object `cout` can be applied to an `ofstream` object. The table that follows lists some of the stream function members that can be applied to both `istream` and `ifstream` objects, or to both `ostream` and `ofstream` objects. Functions that we have not seen before are highlighted in color.

Function Member	Description
`good()`	Return `true` if and only if the *good* bit is set (1)
`fail()`	Return `true` if and only if the *fail* bit is set (1)
`bad()`	Return `true` if and only if the *bad* bit is set (1)
`eof()`	Return `true` if and only if the *eof* bit is set (1)
`clear()`	Reset the *good* bit to 1, all other status bits to 0
`setstate(sBit)`	Set the status bit `sBit` to 1, where `sBit` is one or more of `ios::badbit, ios::failbit, ios::eofbit`
`get(ch)`	Read the next character (including white space) into `ch`
`seekg(offset, base)`	Move the read position `offset` bytes from `base`
`seekp(offset, base)`	Move the write position `offset` bytes from `base` `base` is one of `ios::beg, ios::cur`, or `ios::end`
`tellg()`	Return the offset of the read position within the stream
`tellp()`	Return the offset of the write position within the stream
`peek()`	Return the next character in the stream, but leave it unread
`putback(ch)`	Modify the stream so that `ch` will be the next character read
`ignore(n, stopChar)`	Skip `n` characters, or until `stopChar` is encountered, where `n` defaults to 1 and `stopChar` defaults to eof

This is not an exhaustive list; the iostream library is extensive and the list above does little more than scratch the surface of its capabilities.

In addidition to the stream function members, there are a variety of **manipulators** that can be used to affect the formatting of an `ostream` or an `ofstream`. In this section, we will discuss some of the stream operations and manipulators that we have not seen before.

THE `seekg()`, `tellg()`, `seekp()`, AND `tellp()` MEMBERS

The file-processing programs we have considered thus far have used **sequential access,** which means that the values in the file are accessed and processed sequentially, from beginning to end. To access any item in the file, one must pass through all the items that precede it. It obviously takes more time, therefore, to access a value near the end of the file than one near the beginning.

For a given `ifstream`, sequential input is accomplished by:

- ▶ Initializing the read position to the first character in the file;
- ▶ Ensuring that an input operation always begins at the read position; and
- ▶ After each input operation, advancing the read position to the first character after the input value.

Similarly, sequential processing in an `ofstream` is accomplished by:

- ▶ Initializing the write position to the end-of-file mark;
- ▶ Ensuring that an output operation inserts characters at the write position; and
- ▶ After each output operation, advancing the write position to the first position after the output value (i.e., back to the end-of-file mark).

It should be clear that sequential I/O is accomplished simply by ensuring that the read/write positions are advanced in the stream and are never moved backward.

Sequential processing is sufficient to solve most problems involving files, but there are some problems whose solutions require that the data in a file be accessed and processed in a nonsequential manner. Such nonsequential access is called **direct** or **random access** because an item can be accessed directly by specifying its offset from the beginning of the file.

Example: Two-Pass File Processing. Consider the following problem: Given a file of numbers, calculate the average of the numbers in the file and then display the difference between each number and this average.

Two passes must be made through the file to solve this problem; one pass to accumulate the information needed to compute the average,

```
for (;;)
{
   inStream >> newValue;
   if (inStream.eof()) break;
   sum += newValue;
   count++;
}

if (count > 0) average = sum / count;
```

and a second pass to calculate and display the difference between each number and this average:

```
for (;;)
{
   inStream >> newValue;
   if (inStream.eof()) break;
   cout << newValue - average << endl;
}
```

The problem is, once we have read the contents of the file in the first pass, how do we reset the read position back to the beginning of the file for the second pass?

For such situations, the iostream library provides the function members seekg(), tellg(), seekp(), and tellp(), which make it possible to manipulate a stream's read and write position directly rather than sequentially. The program in Figure 8.5 uses the seekg() function to solve our problem. Recall from chapter 4 that the function member clear() must be used to clear the *eof* status bit between the two passes because no more input operations on that stream will succeed until this bit is cleared.

FIGURE 8.5   A TWO-PASS FILE-PROCESSING PROGRAM.

```
/* twopass5.cpp illustrates making two passes through a file:
 * one pass to find the average of the numbers in the file, and
 * a second pass to find the difference between each number and
 * the average.
 *
 * Input:  a series of values from a file named "Data5"
 * Output: each value and its difference from the average value
 *************************************************************/

#include <iostream.h>    // cout, <<
#include <fstream.h>     // instream, is_open(), eof(), clear(), seekg(),  >>
#include <assert.h>      // assert

int main()
{
   ifstream inStream("Data5");
   assert(inStream.is_open());

   double newValue,
          sum = 0.0,
          average = 0.0;
   int count = 0;

   for (;;)
   {
      inStream >> newValue;
      if (inStream.eof()) break;
      sum += newValue;
      count++;
   }

   if (count > 0) average = sum / count;

   inStream.clear();                   // clear eof bit
   inStream.seekg(0, ios::beg);        // reset read position
```

```
for (;;)
{
    inStream >> newValue;
    if (inStream.eof()) break;
    cout << newValue << ": " << newValue - average << endl;
}

inStream.close();
}
```

---

seekg(). For an `ifstream` named `inStream`, the function call

```
inStream.seekg(offset, base);
```

alters the read position within `inStream`.[7] Here *base* is one of the following:

- ► `ios::beg` causes the read position to move *offset* bytes from the **beginning** of the stream
- ► `ios::cur` causes the read position to move *offset* bytes from its **current position**
- ► `ios::end` causes the read position to move *offset* bytes from the **end** of the stream

The arguments `ios::beg` and `ios::end` provide positioning of the read position relative to the beginning and end of the stream, respectively, whereas `ios::cur` provides positioning of the read position relative to its current position.

To illustrate, suppose that `inStream` has the following contents:

inStream

Then the call

```
inStream.seekg(-2, ios::end);
```

can be used to move the read position 2 bytes before the end-of-file mark in `inStream`:

inStream

---

[7] The `'g'` in `seekg()` and `tellg()` refers to the fact that one *gets* values from the stream being manipulated (i.e., that it is an input stream).

The function call

```
inStream.seekg(0, ios::beg);
```

will reset the read position to the first character in `inStream`:

inStream

After this, the call

```
inStream.seekg(3, ios::cur);
```

will advance the read position by three bytes from its current position:

inStream

The subsequent call

```
instream.seekg(-1, ios::cur);
```

will move the read position backward one byte from its current position:

inStream

This ability to move the read position is useful when it is necessary for a program to reread some earlier value in the stream.

The `seekg()` function is most useful when a file consists of a series of lines or records, each having a fixed length. As a simple example, suppose that a file named `Friends` contains the first names of some friends, one per line, and padded with blanks so that each line is eight characters long:

Friends

The statement

```
ifstream friendStream("Friends");
```

initializes `friendStream` as a connection to this file:

If `LINE_LENGTH` has been defined by

```
const int LINE_LENGTH = 8;
```

we can move the read position to the beginning of the first line with the statement

```
friendStream.seekg(0 * LINE_LENGTH, ios::beg);
```

to the beginning of the second line with

```
friendStream.seekg(1 * LINE_LENGTH, ios::beg);
```

and in general, to the beginning of the `i`th line with the statement:

```
friendStream.seekg((i-1) * LINE_LENGTH, ios::beg);
```

Thus, the statement

```
friendStream.seekg(2*LINE_LENGTH, ios::beg);
```

will move the read position 16 bytes from the beginning of the file:

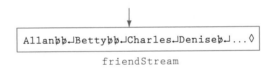

Similarly, the statement

```
friendStream.seekg(LINE_LENGTH, ios::cur);
```

can be used to move the read position from the beginning of one line to the beginning of the next line:

The function `seekg()` thus allows us to adjust the read position in any way that is useful in solving a particular problem.

It should be apparent that seeking with a negative offset from the base `ios::beg`, or seeking with a positive offset from the base `ios::end` is not desirable. Such operations will set the stream-status *fail* bit, disabling all subsequent operations on the stream until the status bits are reset using the `clear()` function member.

tellg(). It is sometimes convenient to think of a stream as a *list* of characters, in which each position has its own number or *index*, similar to a string object:

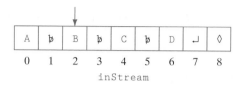

The tellg() function can be used to find the index of the read position. For example, the statements

```
inStream.seekg(0, ios::end);
long lastPosition = inStream.tellg();
```

will (1) move the read position to the end-of-file mark

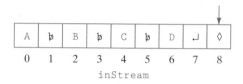

and (2) store the index of the end-of-file mark (i.e., 8) in lastPosition. Note that because the index of the first character is always zero, the index of the end-of-file mark is always the number of characters in the file (not counting the end-of-file mark). A text-processing program could use this fact to determine how many characters are in a file, rather than counting them one at a time.

Knowing the index of the last character allows us to find the middle of a file. For example, the statements

```
inStream.seekg(0, ios::end);

long lastPosition = inStream.tellg(),
     middlePosition = (lastPosition + 1) / 2;

inStream.seekg(middlePosition, ios::beg);
```

can be used to move the read position to the middle character in inStream:

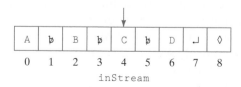

It should be evident that like seekg(), tellg() is most useful for files that are organized into lines or records of fixed lengths. To illustrate, suppose that in the earlier example using the file `Friends`, the read position has moved away from the beginning of a line,

and we want to advance it to the next line. Because `friendStream.tellg()` returns the index of the current read position (11), the statement

```
long offBy = friendStream.tellg() % LINE_LENGTH;
                              // how far past beginning of line
```

can be used to to compute the number of characters (`offBy = 3`) that the read position is past the beginning of the current line; and the statement

```
friendStream.seekg(LINE_LENGTH - offBy, ios::cur);
                              // go to beginning of next line
```

can then be used to move the read position forward to the beginning of the next line.

seekp() and tellp(). The functions `seekg()` and `tellg()` can only be used with input streams, because they only manipulate the read position within a stream. The write position within an `ostream` or `ofstream` can be manipulated by using the functions `seekp()` and `tellp()`.[8] These functions behave in the same manner as `seekg()` and `tellg()`, respectively, but must be applied to output streams.

The `peek()` and `putback()` Members.

Two other function members allow the programmer to do some useful, if unconventional, operations on an input stream. These functions are named `peek()` and `putback()`, and their names describe the operations they perform.

peek(). The `peek()` function allows the programmer to *look ahead* in an input stream. This operation is similar to the `get()` function, in that both return the next character in the stream, but `get()` advances the read position and `peek()` does not.

To illustrate, consider a problem that the C++ compiler has when reading a C++ program from a stream. One of the tasks of a compiler is **lexical analysis,** which breaks the source program down into a sequence of indivisible symbols, called **tokens.** This task is accomplished by a special function called the **lexical analyzer,** which the compiler calls whenever it needs the next token. For each identifier, each keyword, each operator, and each punctuation mark, the compiler has a distinct token. For example, the compiler might refer to the + operator as PLUS_TOKEN, the ++ operator as INCREMENT_TOKEN, and the += operator as PLUS_EQUALS_TOKEN.

---

[8] The `'p'` in `seekp()` and `tellp()` refers to the fact that one *puts* values into the stream being manipulated (i.e., that it is an output stream).

One problem for the compiler is to distinguish the three tokens that begin with the + character. Suppose, for example, that the compiler's input stream is named inStream and appears as follows:

inStream

Suppose further that the compiler requests the next token from its lexical analyzer, which executes the statement:

```
inStream.get(ch);
```

Clearly, this will retrieve the value ' + ' and advance the read position:

inStream

In order to determine which operation the programmer specified, the lexical analyzer needs more information: if the next character is an equal sign (=), then the operator is +=; if the next character is another +, the operator is the increment operator ++; and if the next character is a letter, a digit, or a white-space character, then the operator is simply the addition operator +. The peek() function makes it possible to look ahead at the next character without actually moving the read position.[9]

```
nextCh = inStream.peek();              // look ahead at next char

if (nextCh == '=')                     // if it's an =
{
    inStream.get(nextCh);              //    get the char
    return PLUS_EQUALS_TOKEN;          //    and return +=
}
else if (nextCh == '+')                // else if it's another +
{
    inStream.get(nextCh);              //    get the char
    return INCREMENT_TOKEN;            //    and return ++
}
else if (isalnum(nextCh)              // else if it's a letter
        || isspace(nextCh))            //    digit, or whitespace,
    return ADDITION_TOKEN;             //    just return +
else                                   // else
    // ... generate error message      //    illegal token
```

---

[9] Recall from chapter 2 that the ctype library function isalnum(ch) returns true if and only if its argument ch is an alphanumeric character. Similarly, isspace(ch) returns true if and only if its argument ch is a white-space character.

Thus, if

```
inStream.peek()
```

returns the character y, then the lexical analyzer can infer that inStream contains

inStream

indicating that the addition operator + was specified, and not ++ or +=. The y is left in the stream where it can be subsequently processed in the normal fashion the next time the compiler asks the lexical analyzer for a token.

putback(). An alternative approach is provided by the putback() function, whose effect is to cause its character argument to be put back into the input stream, so that the next call to get() will input that character.

As an example, consider again the compiler problem, where the lexical analyzer has used get() to retrieve the character + from inStream:

inStream

An alternative to using peek() would be to use get() to retrieve the next character,

```
inStream.get(nextCh);
```

and then use putback() to return it to inStream, if necessary:

```
if (nextCh == '=')                      // if it's an =
    return PLUS_EQUALS_TOKEN;           //    just return +=
else if (nextCh == '+')                 // else if it's another +
    return INCREMENT_TOKEN;             //    just return ++
else if (isalnum(nextCh)                // else if it's a letter
        || isspace(nextCh))             //    digit, or whitespace,
{
    inStream.putback(nextCh);           //    put it back for now
    return ADDITION_TOKEN;              //    and return +
}
else                                    // else
    // ...generate error message        //    illegal token
```

Thus, if the value of nextCh were y, the putback() function would return that character to the stream so that the next time the compiler asks the lexical analyzer for a token, its call to get() will retrieve that character.

THE setstate() MEMBER

The clear() function can be used to reset the status bits of a stream. In addition to clearing the stream-status bits, it is sometimes useful to be able to *set* them. This can be done using the stream function member setstate().

To illustrate, suppose that we have a problem involving the seven colors red, orange, yellow, green, blue, indigo and violet, and we want to write a `GetColor()` function to input a color, similar to the `getline()` function provided by the `string` library. Our function will read a word from a stream into a `string` variable, which it then passes back to the caller via a reference parameter.

But what do we do if the user enters an invalid value, a word that is not one of the seven colors? If we wish to handle this situation in a way that is consistent with the `iostream` library, then our function should set the *fail* status bit in the stream from which we attempted to read. Figure 8.6 shows how the stream function member `setstate()` can be used to do this:

FIGURE 8.6   SETTING STREAM-STATUS FLAGS.

```cpp
void GetColor(istream & theStream, string & theColor)
{
  string theWord;
  theStream >> theWord;

  if (theWord == "red" || theWord == "orange" ||
      theWord == "yellow" || theWord == "green" ||
      theWord == "blue" || theWord == "indigo" ||
      theWord == "violet")
    theColor = theWord;
  else
  {
    theStream.seekg(-theWord.size(), ios::cur);   // unread the word
    theStream.setstate(ios::failbit);             // indicate failure
  }
}
```

By setting the *fail* status bit in the stream, this function leaves the handling of the error up to its caller. For example, a programmer wishing to treat this as a fatal error can write

```cpp
string aColor;
GetColor(cin, aColor);
assert(cin.good());
```

and if the user enters any word other than a valid color value, the call to `assert()` will terminate the program. By contrast, a programmer who wishes to treat this occurrence as a non-fatal error and have the user try again, can write

```cpp
string aColor;
for (;;)
{
  GetColor(cin, aColor);
  if (cin.good()) break;
  cout << "Try again: ";
  cin.clear();
  cin.ignore(80, '\n');
}
```

and the user will be given more chances to enter a valid value. Such flexibilty is a hallmark of good design, because it leaves the decision of how to handle the problem up to users of the function, allowing them to choose the approach they prefer.

The `setstate()` function member can be used to set the status bits in a stream, which are referred to by the following names:

Status Bit	Description
`ios::badbit`	The *bad* bit: 1 if an unrecoverable error occurred, 0 otherwise.
`ios::failbit`	The *fail* bit: 1 if a recoverable error occurred, 0 otherwise.
`ios::eofbit`	The *eof* bit: 1 if the end-of-file mark was read, 0 otherwise.

In practice, `setstate()` is rarely passed `ios::eofbit`, since that is set by the input operations.

THE FORMATTING MANIPULATORS

As we saw in chapter 4, the `iostream` library and its companion library `iomanip` provide manipulators for controlling the format of `ostream` and `ofstream` objects. Manipulators can be divided into two categories: those without arguments and those that require arguments.[10]

Manipulators Without Arguments. The manipulators that do not require arguments are available in the `iostream` library. Some of these manipulators are given in the following table:

Manipulator	Description
`boolalpha` `noboolalpha`	Use strings `true` and `false` for I/O of boolean values Use integers `1` and `0` for I/O of boolean values
`scientific` `fixed`	Use floating-point (scientific) notation Use fixed-point notation
`showpoint` `noshowpoint`	Show decimal point and trailing zeros for whole real numbers Hide decimal point and trailing zeros for whole real numbers
`showpos` `noshowpos`	Display positive values with a + sign Display positive values without a + sign

`dec`
`oct`
`hex`
	Display integer values in base 10
	Display integer values in base 8
	Display integer values in base 16

`showbase` `noshowbase`	Display integer values indicating their base (e.g., `0x` for hex). Display integer values without indicating their base
`uppercase` `nouppercase`	In hexadecimal, use symbols A–F; in scientific, use E In hexadecimal, use symbols a–f; in scientific, use e

---

[10] The manipulators are those specified in the ANSI Standard C++ draft standard. As noted in chapter 4, if your compiler is not fully ANSI-compatible, some of them may not be provided.

Manipulator	Description
skipws	Skip white space on input
noskipws	Don't skip white space on input
flush	Write contents of stream to screen (or file)
endl	Insert newline character and flush the stream
left	Left-justify displayed values, pad with fill character on right
right	Right-justify displayed values (except strings), pad with fill character on left
internal	Pad with fill character between sign or base and value

MANIPULATORS WITHOUT ARGUMENTS

As we saw in chapter 4, manipulators are inserted into the stream, but instead of appending values to the stream (except for endl), they affect the format of values that are subsequently inserted into the stream. For example, if we were to write

```
int i = 17;

cout << showbase
        << oct << i << endl
        << dec << i << endl
        << hex << i << endl;
```

then the following values would be displayed

```
021
17
0x11
```

because $21_8 = 17_{10} = 11_{16}$.

Manipulators Requiring Arguments. To use the manipulators that require arguments, the file <iomanip.h> must be included. The table below gives some of these manipulators.

Manipulator	Description
setprecision(num)	Set the number of decimal digits to be displayed to num
setw(num)	Display the next value in a field whose width is num
setfill(ch)	Set the fill character to ch (blank is the default)

MANIPULATORS THAT TAKE ARGUMENTS

When a real number is inserted into a stream, the number of digits that are displayed to the right of the decimal point is called the **precision** of the number. As we have seen before, this characteristic can be controlled with the setprecision() manipulator.

We have also seen that when a number is inserted into a stream, it is first placed into a **field,** which is then inserted into the stream. The size of this field is controlled by the setw() manipulator. If the size of the field is less than the size of the value being displayed, the field is automatically expanded to the same size as the value. If the size of the field exceeds the size of the value being displayed, then the empty positions in the field are filled with the **fill character** (by default, a blank), whose value is set by the `setfill()` manipulator.

Here is a simple code fragment that illustrates the use of these manipulators:

```
cout << fixed << showpoint            // show decimal point and zeros
     << setprecision(2)               // 2 decimal places
     << setfill('*') << left          // pad with *, left-justify
     << setw(6) << 1.0 / 3.0 << endl
     << setfill('$') << right         // pad with $, right-justify
     << setw(6) << 1.0 / 3.0 << endl;
```

When executed, this statement produces the following output:

```
0.33**
$$0.33
```

Note that unlike `setprecision()`, `setw()` affects only the next value inserted into the stream, so `setw()` must precede *each* insertion of a value whose field width we wish to specify.

To display a column of figures with their decimal points aligned, the `right` manipulator can be used with `setprecision()` and `setw()`. For example, to display a table of square roots to seven decimal places, we could write this code segment:

```
cout << fixed << showpoint << right
     << setprecision(7) << setfill('.');

for (int i = 1; i <= 10; i++)
   cout << setw(2) << i << setw(12) << sqrt(i) << endl;
```

Executing these statements produces the output

```
 1....1.0000000
 2....1.4142136
 3....1.7320508
 4....2.0000000
 5....2.2360680
 6....2.4494897
 7....2.6457513
 8....2.8284271
 9....3.0000000
10....3.1622777
```

✔ Quick Quiz 8.4

1. (True or false) Sequential access refers to being able to access an item in a file directly by specifying its sequential position in the file.

2. (True or false) Direct access refers to being able to access an item in a file directly by specifying its offset from the beginning of the file.

3. Another name for direct access is _____ access.

4. The _____ function can be used to find the location of the read position in an `istream` and the _____ function can be used to move to that position.

5. Write a statement that moves the read position in the `ifstream inputStream` to the third character from the beginning of the stream.

6. Proceed as in question 5 but move the read position to the third character past the current position.

7. Proceed as in question 5 but move the read position to the last character in the stream.

8. Write statements to display the next character in the fstream of question 5 and remove it from the fstream.

9. Write statements to display the next character in the fstream of question 5 without removing it from the fstream. Do this in two different ways.

10. _____ can be used to control the format of `ofstream` objects.

Part of the Picture: Database Systems

BY KEITH VANDER LINDEN

One of our local supermarket chains keeps detailed records of its products, sales, customers, and supplies. They can tell you the current price of any item in any of their stores, who supplied it, and how long it's been on the shelf. They can tell you how many people bought tortilla chips at the rock-bottom sale price last weekend and whether they also bought salsa and bean dip to go with them. Not surprisingly, this level of record keeping produces a staggering volume of information, commonly called **data.** Why do they go to all this trouble? The answer—they have to make business decisions and these decisions are based on data. The more accurate and detailed the data, the better the decisions can be. Was the rock-bottom sale price for the chips too high, or too low? Did they make an overall profit? How many units of chips should they buy next time? The data can help answer these questions, and thus are critical to business in a competitive market.

This use of data is not unique to the grocery business. Banks keep records of our accounts and our transactions, universities and colleges keep records of our tuition costs and our performance, airlines keep records on which planes are flying where and who has paid to ride on them. As in the case of the supermarket, these data sets can become very large, and must be maintained for long periods of time. Furthermore, they must be conveniently accessible to many people. It is useful, therefore, to store and maintain them on computers. The data sets themselves, when stored on a computer, are commonly called **databases,** and the programs designed to maintain them are called **database management systems.**

The current chapter has discussed files, and it is not hard to see that their ability to store large amounts of data in a persistent manner is important for database systems. Section 8.1 gave an example of how files can be used to maintain a small meteorological database. As we work with that database, however, a problem arises: The database will change, as all realistic databases do. We may, for example, want to add temperature readings to the pressure readings already contained there. Adding this information to the file is easy enough, but we must also modify the code by adding an additional variable to store the temperature, an extra input command to read the value, and we must know the order in which the pressure and temperature readings are stored in the file. Another complication would arise if we wanted to add information on the particular instruments used to collect the readings. This would probably require a separate file of information for each of the instruments, new code to read and process this file, and some additional code allowing us to record which readings were taken with which instruments.

What started as a fairly simple problem, with a small driver program and a single data file, has become much more complex. In addition, this complexity is likely to increase as the database grows, and as more and more people want to access it. Database systems are designed to address these problems. Although varied, they tend to provide a number of common facilities.

- ▶ *High-level views of the data*—Databases allow programmers to view the data at a higher level, ignoring some of the details of the location and format of the files.

- ▶ *Access routines*—A high-level view of the data wouldn't be of much use if the programmer couldn't retrieve and manipulate the data. Database systems, therefore, provide what is called a **query language,** which provides a set of operations that a programmer can use when accessing and manipulating a database.

- ▶ *Support for large databases*—Databases tend to be large, frequently too large to fit into a computer's main memory. For example, the supermarket database mentioned earlier maintains approximately one *terabyte* of data, that's 10^{12} bytes or 1,000 gigabytes. Database systems are designed to manipulate large databases such as this without reading them into memory all at once.

- ▶ *Security*—It is frequently important to restrict access to sensitive or proprietary data in a database. Most database systems provide this capability.

- ▶ *Data sharing*—The data stored in a database is often of interest to many different people. Several people may, therefore, want to retrieve or modify the data at the same time. Database systems typically provide a check-in/check-out protocol for the data, much like the protocol for checking out books at a public library. This ensures that only one person can manipulate the data at a time.

THE RELATIONAL MODEL

Different models may be used to design a database system, each of which attempts to provide the features just mentioned. One particular model, called the **relational model,** has become an industry standard. In this model, the database is viewed as a set of tables with one row for each entry. For instance, the data from a simple employee database would be viewed as follows:

Name	ID Number	Pay Rate	Department
Jon	45678	7.50	Accounting
Mark	56789	8.75	Accounting
Paul	67891	9.35	Marketing
Matthew	78912	10.50	Accounting
Gabriel	89123	6.35	Marketing
Joe	91234	10.50	Development
Naomi	98765	7.15	Development
Jamie	12345	9.15	Development
April	23456	8.75	Accounting
Jodi	34567	10.50	Service

In this set of data, called a **table,** the top row specifies the contents of each column of data. In this case we have the employee's name, ID number, pay rate, and department. The table has one row, called a **record,** for each employee, and each record has one entry for each column, called a **field.** We will call this table the `Employee` table. Note that there is no mention here of the files that contain the data, or in what format the data is represented. The database system takes care of these details so the programmer doesn't have to.

One popular query language for the relational model is called **SQL** (for "Structured Query Language"). SQL provides commands to add data for tables, retrieve data from tables, and modify data in tables. For example, consider the following command:

```
SELECT *
FROM Employee
WHERE Rate = 10.5;
```

This command will retrieve, or *select,* all the records (specified by the "*") from the Employee table that have a pay rate of $10.50. The resulting records are as follows:

Name	ID Number	Pay Rate	Department
Matthew	78912	10.50	Accounting
Joe	91234	10.50	Development
Jodi	34567	10.50	Service

Note that the result is itself a table. This elegant feature allows the output of one SQL command to be used as the input to another.

AN EXAMPLE: THE SELECT COMMAND

To gain a better understanding of the relationship between file manipulation and database management, we will build a simple relational database system with a scaled-down implementation of the select command. This implementation will go in a library so we'll be able to see the differences between the file manipulation used to implement the select command (in the library), and the use of the command itself (in a driver program).

The select command assumes a relational view of the database, so we must implement one. Recall that the relational data model views a database as a table or set of tables where the structure of each table can be specified by indicating the fields it will contain, and the type of data stored in each field. This structure is called a **schema.** The schema for the Employee table is as follows[11]:

```
Name       string
ID         int
Rate       double
Department string
```

This schema says that Employee will contain a record for each employee and that each record will contain the employee's name (a string), the employee's ID number (an int), his or her pay rate (a double), and a department name (a string). We will store this schema in a schema file named Employee.schema.

The actual data for Employee will be stored in a separate data file named Employee.data. The contents of this file for the Employee table are as follows:

```
Jon      45678   7.50   Accounting
Mark     56789   8.75   Accounting
Paul     67891   9.35   Marketing
Matthew  78912  10.50   Accounting
Gabriel  89123   6.35   Marketing
Joe      91234  10.50   Development
```

---

[11] Note that a full database system would maintain a considerably more complex schema than this, but this will serve our current needs.

```
Naomi    98765    7.15    Development
Jamie    12345    9.15    Development
April    23456    8.75    Accounting
Jodi     34567   10.50    Service
```

Notice how the columns in `Employee.data` match the rows in `Employee.schema`. The first column is the name (a `string`), second column is the ID number (an `int`), and so forth.

The representation of the `Employee` table, therefore, consists of two files: `Employee.schema` and `Employee.data`. We can now implement a `select()` function which makes use of these files. The function will have four parameters:

- ▶ the name of a table to operate on (e.g., `Employee`);
- ▶ the name of a field on which to select (e.g., `Rate`);
- ▶ the relational operator to use (we'll assume `==` for now);
- ▶ the field value to check (e.g., `10.5`).

It will return all the records in the given table whose specified field is equal to the specified value. So, for example, the *C++* function call equivalent to the select command given would be:

```
select("Employee", "RATE", "=", "10.50");
```

The simple driver for this function, shown in Figure 8.6, prompts the user of the system for the name of a table, a field name, a relational operator, and an appropriate value for that field. The input format is very similar to that of the SQL select command shown. It then calls the `select()` function.

FIGURE 8.6   A DRIVER PROGRAM TO TEST THE SELECT FUNCTION

```cpp
int main()
{
  string
    tableName,           // the table name, not the associated filenames
    selectedFieldName,   // the field whose value you want to restrict
    selected Operator,   // the relational operator for the restriction
    selectedFieldValue;  // the value that the field should have

  // Get the specifics of the select command from the user (using a
  //    format similar to the SQL select statement.
  cout << "\nWelcome to SelectBase, a simple database system\n\n"
          "Please complete the following query: "
          "\n\nSELECT *"
          "\nFROM ";
  cin >> tableName;
  cout << "WHERE ";
  cin >> selectedFieldName >> selectedOperator >> selectedFieldValue;

  // Execute the Select command.
  select(tableName, selectedFieldName, selectedOperator, selectedFieldValue);
}
```

Sample run:

```
Welcome to SelectBase, a simple database system

Please complete the following query:
```

```
SELECT *
FROM Employee
WHERe Rate = 10.5

Matthew   78912   10.50   Accounting
Joe       91234   10.50   Development
Jodi      34567   10.50   Service
```

This driver function illustrates the level of database programming. There are no file manipulation commands here, no `for` loops, no I/O streams, and the programmer doesn't know anything about the `.schema` and `.data` files or their format. All of these things are maintained by the implementation of `select()`, and thus do not concern the database programmer.

To see inside the implementation of `select()`, consider the code segment shown in Figure 8.7. This is where we place the nested loop that reads each field (as specified in `Employee.schema`) for each record (as contained in `Employee.data`). To make the implementation more general, the order and types of the fields are specified by the contents of the `.schema` file, rather than being hard-coded. This way, `select()` can manipulate many different tables, so long as they have consistent schema and data files.

FIGURE 8.7   NESTED **for** LOOPS FOR THE **select()** FUNCTION

```
for (;;)  // for each record in the data file
  {
    outputLine = "";    // We'll add to this one field at a time.
    selectLine = false; // Assume that the record is not selected.

    for (;;) // for each field in the schema file
      {
        // Get the next field specification from the schema file.
        schemaFile >> currentFieldName >> currentFieldType;
        if (schemaFile.eof()) break;

        dataFile >> currentFieldValue;
        if (dataFile.eof())
          {
            schemaFile.close();
            dataFile.close();
            return;
          }

        // Check if the current record satisfies the selection criterion
        if (recordSelected(selectedFieldName, currentFieldName,
                           selectedFieldValue, currentFieldValue,
                           currentFieldType))
          selectLine = true;

        // Add the new field to the output string.
        outputline += currentFieldValue + "\t ";
      }
```

```
    // Output the current record if it has been selected.
    if (selectLine)
      cout << outputLine << endl;

    // Prepare to do a second pass through the schema file.
    schemaFile.seekg(0, ios::beg);
    schemaFile.clear();
  }
```

FURTHER READING

The field of database systems is active, both in research and in applications. If you are interested in reading additional material, consider going to the following sources:

▶ Ullman and Widom's text *A First Course in Database Systems,* Prentice Hall, 1997 — This is a good, current overview of the field of database systems. It covers the relational model, and also deals with newer object-oriented approaches to database modeling.

▶ E. F. Codd's original paper, "A Relational Model of Data for Large Shared Data Banks," *Communications of the ACM,* 1970, 13(6), pages 377–387 — This is a classic paper on the relational database model.

▶ For information on some current database systems, try visiting the Oracle or Sybase corporation web sites: www.oracle.com; www.sybase.com.

EXERCISES

1. Because the driver program discussed in this section reads relational tables based on a schema, you can perform many useful database operations without modifying the code. Try some of the following:

   (a) Add a field to the database for the employee's last name. Remember that you'll have to modify both the schema and the data file in a consistent manner.

   (b) Create a new table for a college bookstore that maintains information on books (e.g., the title, author, ISBN number, and price).

   (c) Create a new table for your class, including fields for student names, ID numbers, and grades for the various projects you've done.

2. Modify the program in this section to add column headers to the table output. The headers should be based on the names of the fields given in the schema file.

3. The implementation of `select()` given in this section always uses the `==` operator. Modify the program to implement the other relational operators as well (i.e., `<`, `>`, `<=`, `>=`, and `!=`).

4. Modify the program from exercise 3 to write the results of the select command to a file rather than writing them to `cout`. The program should prompt the user for an output file name. It should then write the results to this file, or to `cout` if no filename is given. Now, use this program to select the following records:

   (a) Find the employees in `Employee` with a pay rate equal to $10.50 and a Department of "Accounting".

   (b) Find the employees in `Employee` with a pay rate greater than $8.00 and less than $10.00.

5. The relational model also supports a command that returns a specified column (or columns) from a table rather than returning the full record. This command, called **project,** is implemented in SQL by allowing the programmer to replace the `"*"` in the `SELECT` clause of the select command with a field name (or names).

Modify the program in this section to support this. You should allow the user to enter either a "*" in the SELECT clause, or a specific field name. For example, if the user enters * in the SELECT clause, the full records will be returned:

```
Welcome to SelectBase, a simple database system

Please complete the following query:

SELECT *
FROM Employee
WHERE Department = Development

Joe     91234  10.50  Development
Naomi   98765   7.15  Development
Jamie   12345   9.15  Development
```

If, on the other hand, the user enters a field name in the SELECT clause, only the value of that field will be returned:

```
Welcome to SelectBase, a simple database system

Please complete the following query:

SELECT Name
FROM Employee
WHERE Department = Development

Joe
Naomi
Jamie
```

☞ *PROGRAMMING POINTERS*

✍ PROGRAM STYLE AND DESIGN

1. *If a program is to read data from a file, an* ifstream *must be declared and initialized as a connection between the program and the file. If it is to write data to a file, an* ofstream *must be declared and initialized as a connection between the program and the file.* The three basic steps for file-processing programs are thus:
   a. Declare and open an ifstream object for each input file and an ofstream object for each output file to establish connections between the program and the files
   b. Perform the desired processing with the file via the fstreams
   c. Close each fstream object, severing the connection with the file
2. *A forever loop controlled by the* ifstream *function member* eof() *can be used to read data from a file via an* ifstream:

```
ifstream theStream("SomeFile");

for (;;)
{
   // read a value from theStream
   if (theStream.eof()) break;
   // Process the value.
}
```

Some programmers prefer the while loop version:

```
// read a value from theStream
while (!theStream.eof())
{
    // Process the value
    // read a value from theStream
}
```

⚡ POTENTIAL PROBLEMS

1. *Before an fstream can be used, it must be opened as a connection to a particular file.* There are two ways to do this. The simplest way is to initialize the fstream with the name of the file in the fstream's declaration:

    ```
    ofstream outStream("OutputFile.TXT");
    ```

    Alternatively, the stream can be declared and opened separately, using the open() function member:

    ```
    ofstream outStream;
    outStream.open("OutputFile.TXT");
    ```

2. *When opening a stream to a file, the name of the file must be given as a character string literal.* For example, to open an ifstream named inStream to a file named Text, we can write

    ```
    ifstream inStream("Text");
    ```

    because "Text" is a character string literal. However, if the name of the file is stored in a string variable named fileName, then the string function member data() must be used to extract the character string literal stored in fileName:

    ```
    ifstream inStream( fileName.data() );
    ```

3. *The operations performed on an fstream must be consistent with the mode by which it was initialized.* Applying the input operator to an ofstream or applying the output operator to an ifstream will generate a compilation error.

4. *When inputting character values, the extraction operator (>>) skips over any leading white-space characters (blanks, tabs, and newlines); the member functions* get() *and* getline() *do not.* For example, if the user enters:

    ```
    A↵
    B↵
    C↵
    ```

    then the istream named cin can be visualized as follows:

    cin

    Now, if the following statements are executed:

    ```
    cin >> letter1;
    cin >> letter2;
    cin >> letter3;
    ```

then 'A' is read and stored in `letter1`,

the newline (as white space) is skipped and the value 'B' is read and stored in `letter2`,

and the newline (as white space) is skipped and the value 'C' is read and stored in `letter3`,

leaving the final newline unread. By contrast, if the following statements are executed:

```
cin.get(letter1);
cin.get(letter2);
cin.get(letter3);
```

then the value 'A' is read and stored in `letter1` as before,

but the newline value '\n' is read and stored in `letter2`,

and the value 'B' is read and stored in `letter3`,

leaving the second newline, 'C', and third newline unread.

5. *Care must be taken when mixing calls to* >> *and* `getline()`. If a call to >> precedes a call to `getline()` and the values being read are separated by a newline character, then an additional call to `get()` should be inserted between >> and `getline()` to consume the newline character. Otherwise, `getline()` will halt when it reads that newline, and pass back an empty string.

6. *Every numeric input value in a data file should be followed by white space or an end-of-file mark.* When a value is read for a numeric variable, all characters up to the next blank, tab, end-of-line mark, or end-of-file mark are read. If those characters cannot be converted to a numeric value of the appropriate type, an error occurs and execution terminates.

7. *If an end-of-file mark is encountered while attempting to read a value for a numeric variable, the value of that variable is undefined.* For this reason, *the* `eof()` *function should always be evaluated following an input statement* to prevent the use of such a variable.

8. *An fstream should always be closed using the member* `close()` *once use of that fstream has been completed.*

9. *The parameters to hold fstream arguments must be **reference parameters,** because an input or output operation changes the stream's read or write position, respectively*

10. *Once the eof, bad, or fail state bits have been set in a stream, no subsequent operations can be performed on that stream until those bits have been cleared (using the* `clear()` *member).*

Programming Problems

SECTIONS 8.1–8.3

1. Write a program to concatenate two files; that is, to append one file to the end of the other.

2. Write a program that reads a text file and counts the vowels in the file.

3. Write a program that reads a text file and counts the occurrences in the file of a specified string entered during execution of the program.

4. Write a program that reads a text file and counts the characters in each line. The program should display the line number and the length of the shortest and longest lines in the file, as well as the average number of characters per line.

5. Write a program to copy one text file into another text file in which the lines are numbered 1, 2, 3, . . . with a number at the left of each line.

6. Write a program that reads a text file and writes it to another text file, but with leading blanks and blank lines removed. Run this program using as input files the last two C++ programs you have written, and comment on whether you think indenting C++ programs makes them more readable.

7. Write a file pagination program that reads a text file and prints it in blocks of 20 lines. If after printing a block of lines, there still are lines in the file, the program should allow the user to indicate whether more ouput is desired; if so, the next block should be printed; otherwise, execution of the program should terminate.

8. People from three different income levels, A, B, and C, rated each of two different products with a number from 0 through 10. Construct a file in which each line contains the income level and product rankings for one respondent. Then write a program that reads this information and calculates

(a) For each income bracket, the average rating for Product 1

(b) The number of persons in Income Bracket B who rated both products with a score of 5 or higher

(c) The average rating for Product 2 by persons who rated Product 1 lower than 3

Label all output and design the program so that it automatically counts the respondents.

9. Write a program to search the file Users (see descriptions following this problem set) to find and display the resources used to date for specified users whose identification numbers are entered during execution of the program.

10. Write a program to search the file Inventory (see descriptions following this problem set) to find an item with a specified item number. If a match is found, display the item number and the number currently in stock; otherwise, display a message indicating that it was not found.

11. At the end of each month, a report is produced that shows the status of each user's account in Users (see descriptions following this problem set). Write a program to accept the current date and produce a report of the following form:

```
                    USER ACCOUNTS--mm/dd/yy
                       RESOURCE            RESOURCES
     USER-ID             LIMIT                USED
     ------------------------------------------------------
     10101               $750                 $381
     10102               $650                 $599***
       .                  .                     .
       .                  .                     .
       .                  .                     .
```

where mm/dd/yy is the current data and the three asterisks (***) indicate that the user has already used 90 percent or more of the resources available to him or her.

12. Write a program that reads a text file, counting the nonblank characters, the nonblank lines, the words, and the sentences, and then calculates the average number of characters per word and the average number of words per sentence. You may assume the following: The file contains only letters, blanks, commas, periods, semicolons, and colons; a word is any sequence of letters that begins a line or is preceded by one or more blanks and that is terminated by a blank, comma, semicolon, colon, period, or the end of a line; and a sentence is terminated by a period.

13. (Project) Write a menu-driven program that uses the files Student and Student-Update (see descriptions following this problem set) and allows (some of) the following options. For each option, write a separate function so that options and corresponding functions can be easily added or removed.

(1) Locate a student's permanent record when given his or her student number, and print it in a nicer format than that in which it is stored.

(2) Same as option 1, but locate the record when given the student's name.

(3) Print a list of all student names and numbers in a given class (1, 2, 3, 4, 5).

(4) Same as option 3 but for a given major.

(5) Same as option 3 but for a given range of cumulative GPAs.

(6) Find the average cumulative GPAs for (a) all females, (b) all males, (c) all students with a specified major, and (d) all students.

(7) Produce updated grade reports with the following format (where *xx* is the current year):

```
                GRADE REPORT  --  SEMESTER 2    5/29/xx

                        DISPATCH UNIVERSITY

        10103          James L. Johnson

                            GRADE                  CREDITS
                            =====                  =======
        ENGL 176              C                       4
        EDUC 268              B                       4
        EDUC 330              B+                      3
        P E 281               C                       3
        ENGR 317              D                       4


        Cumulative Credits:     28
        Current GPA:           1.61
        Cumulative GPA:        2.64
```

Here, letter grades are assigned according to the following scheme: A = 4.0, A− = 3.7, B+ = 3.3, B = 3.0, B− = 2.7, C+ = 2.3, C = 2.0, C− = 1.7, D+ = 1.3, D = 1.0, D− = 0.7, and F = 0.0. (See Programming Problem 5 in chapter 2 for details on the calculation of GPAs.)

(8) Same as option 7, but instead of producing grade reports, produce a new file containing the updated total credits and new cumulative GPAs.

(9) Produce an updated file when a student (a) drops or (b) adds a course.

(10) Produce an updated file when a student (a) transfers into or (b) withdraws from the university.

SECTION 8.4

14. Suppose that each line of a file contains a student's last name and exam scores. Write a program that reads and counts the scores, then calculates the mean score and reads through the file again to calculate the variance and standard deviation. Display how many numbers there are and their mean, variance, and standard deviation with appropriate labels. If $\bar{x}$ denotes the mean of the numbers $x_1, \ldots, x_n$, the *variance* is the average of the squares of the deviations of the numbers from the mean:

$$\text{variance} = \frac{1}{n} \sum_{i=1}^{n} (x_i - \bar{x})^2$$

and the *standard deviation* is the square root of the variance.

15. Letter grades are sometimes assigned to numeric scores by using the grading scheme commonly called *grading on the curve*. In this scheme, a letter grade is assigned to a numeric score, according to the following table:

x = Numeric Score	Letter Grade
$x < m - \dfrac{3}{2}\sigma$	F
$m - \dfrac{3}{2}\sigma \le x < m - \dfrac{1}{2}\sigma$	D
$m - \dfrac{1}{2}\sigma \le x < m + \dfrac{1}{2}\sigma$	C
$m + \dfrac{1}{2}\sigma \le x < m + \dfrac{3}{2}\sigma$	B
$m + \dfrac{3}{2}\sigma \le x$	A

where m is the mean score and σ is the standard deviation. Extend the program of problem 14 to read the student information in the file, calculate the mean and standard deviation of the scores, and produce another file containing each student's name, exam score, and the letter grade corresponding to that score.

16. Information about computer terminals in a computer network is maintained in a file. The terminals are numbered 1 through 100, and information about the nth terminal is stored in the nth line of the file. This information consists of a terminal type (string), the building in which it is located (string), the transmission rate (integer), an access code (character), and the date of last service (month, day, year). Write a program to read terminal numbers from the keyboard and directly access the line in the file for each terminal by moving the read position directly to that line. The program should retrieve and display the information about that terminal.

17. Extend the program of problem 16 to accept a date of service along with each terminal number and in addition to displaying terminal information on the screen, produce a new updated file containing the terminal number and date of service for each terminal processed during execution.

18. Extend the program of problem 17 to close the input file and output file, reopen them for input, and then produce a new file containing the information of the original file but with the dates of service updated with the information from the update file.

DESCRIPTIONS OF DATA FILES

The following describe the contents of data files used in exercises in the text. Listings of them are available at the web site described in the preface.

Inventory:
Item number: an integer
Number currently in stock: an integer (in the range 0 through 999)
Unit price: a real value
Minimum inventory level: an integer (in the range 0 through 999)
Item name: a character string
File is sorted so that item numbers are in increasing order.

`Student:`

This is a file of student records organized as follows: They are arranged so that student numbers are in increasing order.

Student number: an integer
Student's name: two character strings (last, first) and a character (middle initial)
Hometown: two character strings of the form city, state
Phone number: a character string
Gender: a character (M or F)
Year: a 1-digit integer (1, 2, 3, 4, or 5 for special)
Major: a character string
Total credits earned to date: an integer
Cumulative GPA: a real value

`StudentUpdate:`

This is a file of student grade records organized as follows. They are sorted so that student numbers are in increasing order. There is one update record for each student in the file Student.

Student number: an integer (same as those used in the file `Student`)
For each of five courses:
  Course name: a seven-character string (e. g., CPSC131)
  Letter grade: a two-character string (e. g., A−, B+, Cb/)
  Course credit: an integer

`Users:`

This is a file of computer system records organized as follows. They are arranged so that identification numbers are in increasing order.

Identification number: an integer
User's name: Two strings of the form last-name, first-name
Password: a string
Resource limit (in dollars):   an integer with up to four digits
Resources used to date: a real value

`LeastSquaresFile:`

This is a text file in which each line contains a pair of real numbers representing the x coordinate and the y coordinate of a point.

Chapter 9

ARRAYS AND
`vector<T>`s

With silver bells, and cockle shells,
And pretty maids all in a row.

MOTHER GOOSE

I've got a little list, I've got a little list.

GILBERT AND SULLIVAN, *The Mikado*

Get your ducks in a row and then cook their goose. (Pause). Gooses. (Pause).
Geese. (Pause). Whatever they're called, cook 'em!

V. OREHCK III (fictitious)

Chapter Contents

9.1   Introductory Example: Quality Control

9.2   C-Style Arrays

9.3   Example: Sorting Employee Information

9.4   The `vector<T>` Class Template

9.5   Example: Processing Test Scores

PART OF THE PICTURE: Component Programming

In this chapter, we combine two ideas that may, at first glance, seem unrelated. The first is the idea of *processing sequences* of values. For example, in section 8.1, we considered the problem of finding the minimum, maximum, and mean of a sequence of atmospheric pressure readings. The second idea is that of *indexed* (or *subscripted*) *variables*. In chapter 4 we presented the string class that makes it possible to store a collection of characters in a single object. A string object aString is an *indexed* object, which means that aString[i] can be used to access the character of aString whose index is i.

As we will see in this chapter, these two ideas can be combined to give a powerful mechanism for solving problems that involve processing sequences of non-character data (such as atmospheric pressure readings). This processing can often be done most efficiently if the entire sequence can be stored in an indexed variable valueSequence so that the value stored in any location i can be accessed directly by using the expression valueSequence[i].

An **array** is such a variable. It is more general than a string object, because it is not limited to storing char values. An array can be declared to store values of any type: char, int, and double values, as well as values of class objects such as string. In short, an array can be defined to store values of any type that has been declared prior to the declaration of the array.

In the first two sections of this chapter, we introduce **C-style arrays** that C++ inherits from its parent language C. For these arrays, the programmer must specify the size of the array in its declaration, and once the program is compiled, this size cannot be changed without changing the array declaration and recompiling the program. Consequently, such arrays are called **fixed-size arrays.** In later sections, we will introduce **vector<T>,** a C++ standard class template that eliminates many of the limitations of C-style arrays.

9.1 INTRODUCTORY EXAMPLE: QUALITY CONTROL

We begin with a problem that can be solved using C-style arrays.

PROBLEM: MEAN TIME TO FAILURE

An electronics company uses a robot to manufacture circuit boards that have five different components. A quality control engineer monitors the robot by checking each circuit board and recording in a file the number of defective components on that board:

```
0  0  1  0  0  0  2  0  4  0  0  0  1  0  0  0  0  2  0  0  0  0  1  0
0  3  0  0  0  0  0  0  2  0  0  0  3  0  0  0  0  0  0  0  1  0  0
0  0  0  0  0  2  0  0  0  0  1  0  0  0  0  0  1  0  0  0  0  0  1  0
```

To analyze the overall performance of the robot, a program that generates a **frequency distribution** is needed. The frequency distribution should show the number of boards in which there were no defective components, one defective component, two defective components, three defective components, four defective components and five defective components:

```
58 had 0 failed components (80.6%)
7 had 1 failed components (9.7%)
```

```
4 had 2 failed components (5.6%)
2 had 3 failed components (2.8%)
1 had 4 failed components (1.4%)
0 had 5 failed components (0%)
```

Such an analysis may help a company decide whether to upgrade its equipment. Weighing the cost of a new robot (that presumably makes fewer mistakes) against the cost of repairing or discarding 19.4 percent of the circuit boards helps in making an informed decision.

OBJECT-CENTERED DESIGN

Behavior.   The program should display on the screen a prompt for the name of the input file, read this name from the keyboard, and then open an fstream to that file. It should then use an input loop to read the data values from the fstream, counting the occurrences of each 0, 1, 2, 3, 4, and 5. It should then display the number and percentages of occurrences of each 0, 1, 2, 3, 4, and 5.

Objects.   The objects in this problem are as follows:

Description	Kind	Type	Name
The name of the input file	varying	string	*inputFileName*
An fstream to the input file	varying	ifstream	*inStream*
The number of circuit boards	varying	int	*numCircuitBoards*
Each data value	varying	int	*numFailures*
The number of 0s	varying	int	*count*[0]
The number of 1s	varying	int	*count*[1]
The number of 2s	varying	int	*count*[2]
The number of 3s	varying	int	*count*[3]
The number of 4s	varying	int	*count*[4]
The number of 5s	varying	int	*count*[5]

Operations.   The operations needed to solve the problem are

   i.   Display a string on the screen

  ii.   Read a string from the keyboard

 iii.   Open an fstream to a file whose name is stored in a string

 iv.   Read data values from the fstream, counting occurrences of 0, 1, 2, 3, 4, and 5

  v.   Display the number and percentage of occurrences of 0, 1, 2, 3, 4, and 5

Each of these operations is either predefined in C++ or is easily implemented using only a few statements.

Algorithm.   The program must read from the data file and count the number of occurrences of each number in the file. One approach would be to declare 6 different counter variables,

```
int count0 = 0,
    count1 = 0,
    count2 = 0,
    count3 = 0,
    count4 = 0,
    count5 = 0;
```

and then use a switch statement to select the appropriate counter to be incremented:

```
inStream >> score;
if (inStream.eof()) break;
switch (score)
{
    case 0: count0++;
            break;
    case 1: count1++;
            break;
    case 2: count2++;
            break;
    case 3: count3++;
            break;
    case 4: count4++;
            break;
    case 5: count5++;
            break;
}
```

However, such a solution is clumsy, because it requires that we declare and manage 6 different counters. Moreover, it is *not scalable:* if the company creates a new product with 10 components or 100 components, then the program must be modified extensively.

A **C-style array** provides a better solution. We define a single array object with space for 6 different integer values:

```
const int SIZE = 6;
int count[SIZE] = {0};
```

This definition creates an indexed variable named count that can store 6 integers. Each of these integers has a different index in the range 0 to 5. That is, the first integer in count has index 0, the second integer in count has index 1, . . . , and the last integer in count has the index 5. The definition also initializes each of these integers to 0. We can visualize such an object as follows:

count | 0 | 0 | 0 | 0 | 0 | 0 |
      [0] [1] [2] [3] [4] [5]

Because count has index values ranging from 0 to 5 and these values coincide with the number of components on the circuit board, we can use this one array to count the occurrences of each of the values 0 through 5. We can write statements like the following

```
inStream >> numFailures;
if (inStream.eof()) break;
count[numFailures]++;
```

to add 1 to the integer in `count` whose index is `numFailures`. For example, if `numFailures` is 2, then execution of

```
count[numFailures]++;
```

will increment the integer in `count` whose index is 2:

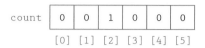

$$\text{count} \quad \boxed{0} \; \boxed{0} \; \boxed{1} \; \boxed{0} \; \boxed{0} \; \boxed{0}$$

[0] [1] [2] [3] [4] [5]

The following algorithm for solving the quality-control problem uses this approach.

Algorithm for Quality Control Analysis

1. Prompt for and read the name of the input file into *inputFileName*.
2. Open an `ifstream` named *inStream* to the file whose name is in *inputFile-Name*. (If this fails, display an error message and terminate the algorithm.)
3. Initialize *numCircuitBoards* to 0.
4. Initialize each integer in the array *count* to 0.
5. Loop:
   a. Read an integer *numFailures* from *inStream*.
   b. If the end-of-file mark was read, exit the loop.
   c. Increment the element of *count* indexed by *numFailures*.
   d. Increment *numCircuitBoards*.

   End loop
6. Close *inStream*.
7. For each *index* in the range 0 through 5:

   Display *index* and *count*[*index*] with appropriate labels.

Coding. The program in Figure 9.1 implements this algorithm. It uses the function `InteractiveOpen()` from Figure 8.3 to open the file containing the failure data.

FIGURE 9.1   QUALITY CONTROL FAILURE FREQUENCY DISTRIBUTION.

```
/* qualitycontrol1.cpp shows the distribution of component failure rates
 * that are stored in an input file.
 *
 *   Input(file):     a sequence of failure rates
 *   Output(screen):  the number and percentage of occurrences
 *                    of each failure rate
 ******************************************************************************/

#include <iostream.h>          // cout, <<, fixed, showpoint
#include <fstream.h>           // ifstream, >>, eof(), close()
#include <iomanip.h>           // setprecision()
#include <string>              // string, getline()
```

```
void InteractiveOpen(ifstream & theIFStream);

const int CAPACITY = 6;                       // # of array elements

int main()
{
   cout << "Quality Control: Component Failure Frequency Distribution.\n\n";

   ifstream inStream;
   InteractiveOpen(inStream);
   int count[CAPACITY] = {0},                 // array of counters
       numFailures,                           // input variable
       numCircuitBoards = 0;                  // # of input values

   for (;;)                                   // loop:
   {
      inStream >> numFailures;                //   read input value
      if (inStream.eof()) break;              //   if done, quit
      count[numFailures]++;                   //   increment its counter
      numCircuitBoards++;                     //   one more input value
   }                                          // end loop
   inStream.close();                          // close the stream

   cout << "\nOut of " << numCircuitBoards << " circuit boards:\n"
        << setprecision(1) << fixed << showpoint;

   for (int i = 0; i < CAPACITY; i++)         // output counters
      cout << count[i] << " had " << i
           << " failed components ("          // and percentages
           << double(count[i]) / numCircuitBoards * 100
           << "%)" << endl;
}

/*** Insert the definition of the function
     InteractiveInput() from Figure 8.3 here. ***/
```

Sample run:

```
Quality Control: Component Failure Frequency Distribution.

Enter the name of the input file: failures.dat

Out of 72 circuit boards:
58 had 0 failed components (80.6%)
7 had 1 failed components (9.7%)
4 had 2 failed components (5.6%)
2 had 3 failed components (2.8%)
1 had 4 failed components (1.4%)
0 had 5 failed components (0.0%)
```

9.2 C-STYLE ARRAYS

The program in Figure 9.1 uses the definitions

```
const int CAPACITY = 6;          // # of array elements
    .
    .
    .
int count[CAPACITY] = {0},        // array of counters
    .
    .
    .
```

to construct `count` as an array of 6 integers, with each integer being initialized to 0. The first part of the definition

```
int count[CAPACITY] = {0};        // array of counters
```

instructs the compiler to reserve a block of memory large enough to hold 6 integer values and associates the name `count` with this block. Since `count` has room for 6 integers, its **capacity** is said to be 6. The integer-sized spaces in `count` are called **elements** and are indexed from 0 through 5:

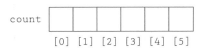

```
count  │   │   │   │   │   │   │
        [0] [1] [2] [3] [4] [5]
```

Unlike some languages, *the index of the first element of any C++ array is always zero.* The second part of the definition,

```
int count[CAPACITY]  = {0};        // array of counters
```

initializes the first element of `count` to zero, and as described later, the remaining elements are initialized to zero by default:

```
count  │ 0 │ 0 │ 0 │ 0 │ 0 │ 0 │
        [0] [1] [2] [3] [4] [5]
```

Whereas the capacity of an array is the number of values that it can store, its **size** is *the number of values it actually contains.* Both the capacity and the size of `count` are 6.

In this example, `count` is an array of integers, but the elements of an array may be of any type. For example, the declarations

```
const int NUM_ELEMENTS = 4;
char charArray[NUM_ELEMENTS];      // array of 4 char elements
long intArray[NUM_ELEMENTS];       // array of 4 long elements
string stringArray[NUM_ELEMENTS];  // array of 4 string elements
```

construct three arrays, each having four elements, (i.e., having *capacity* 4), but each containing no values (i.e., each having *size* 0). `charArray` has space for 4 characters (stored in 4 bytes):

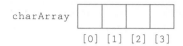

$$\text{charArray} \quad \boxed{\ \ |\ \ |\ \ |\ \ }$$

[0] [1] [2] [3]

intArray has space for 4 long-integers (stored in 4 × 4 bytes = 16 bytes):

intArray

[0]   [1]   [2]   [3]

stringArray has space for 4 string objects, for which the storage requirements vary according to the lengths of the string values being stored.

These declarations are examples of the following (simplified) general form of an array declaration:

Array Declaration (simplified)

Form

```
type array_name[CAPACITY];
```

where:

   type is any defined type (predefined, or programmer-defined);

   array_name is the name of the array object being defined; and

   CAPACITY is the number of values the object can contain.

Purpose

Instructs the compiler to reserve sufficient storage to hold *CAPACITY* objects of type *type*, and associates the name *array_name* with that storage.

To understand the implications of an array declaration, it is useful to contrast a char array and a string object:

```
const int CAPACITY = 16;
char charArray[CAPACITY];
string aString;
```

charArray is a 16-byte **fixed-capacity array,** whose capacity cannot change during program execution. By contrast, the object aString can be thought of as a **varying-capacity array** (initially of capacity zero) that will automatically grow as needed, according to the number of characters stored in it.

It is important to remember this property of C-style arrays: Unlike a string object, *the capacity of a C-style array is fixed when the program is compiled.* If we try to enter the capacity at run-time as in

```
cout << "Enter the number of components: ";
int arrayCapacity;
cin >> arrayCapacity;
int count[arrayCapacity];              // ERROR!
```

then a compilation error will result. The reason is that the memory for a C-style array is allocated by the compiler, and so the size of the array must be available when its definition is compiled.

Define Capacity With a Constant, Not a Literal. It is good programming practice to use constants to specify the capacity of arrays as in

```
const int CAPACITY = 5;
double int[CAPACITY];
      .
      .
      .
for (int i = 0; i < CAPACITY; i++)
    cout << count[i];
```

rather than using literals:

```
int count[5];
      .
      .
      .
for (int i = 0; i < 5; i++)
    cout << count[i];
```

This makes the program more flexible. It is often necessary to adjust the capacity of an array several times before the final version of a program is completed or to modify the capacity after the program has been in use for some time. If literals are used, making these modifications requires finding and changing each literal throughout the entire program:

```
double count[100];
      .
      .
      .
for (int i = 0; i < 100; i++)
    cout << count[i];
```

But if a named constant (such as CAPACITY) is used throughout the program, then modifying the capacity of the array requires only a single modification—change the declaration of the named constant:

```
const int CAPACITY = 100;
double count[CAPACITY];
      .
      .
      .
for (int i = 0; i < CAPACITY; i++)
    cout << count[i];
```

When the program is recompiled, the compiler will update all uses of CAPACITY with the new value, saving time and ensuring consistent capacities in all array accesses.

ARRAY INITIALIZATION

As we have noted, simple array declarations of the form

```
type array_name[capacity];
```

specify no initialization for the array. Because no initial values are supplied, such arrays will usually contain whatever "garbage" values remain from prior use of the memory block allocated to the array.

Because an array can store different values, it cannot be initialized with a single value:

```
int intArray[CAPACITY] = 0;      //  ERROR!
```

Instead, a sequence of initializing values must be listed between curly braces, { and }, and separated by commas; for example,

```
const int CAPACITY = 10;

int intArray[CAPACITY] = {9,8,7,6,5,4,3,2,1,0};
```

The first value in the list is stored in the first array element, the second value in the second element, and so on, resulting in an object that can be pictured as follows:

intArray	9	8	7	6	5	4	3	2	1	0
	[0]	[1]	[2]	[3]	[4]	[5]	[6]	[7]	[8]	[9]

If the number of initial values listed is less than than the capacity of the array, then those elements for which no initial values were provided are each set to zero. For example, the declarations

```
const int CAPACITY = 10;

double intArray[CAPACITY] = {9,8,7,6,5,4};      // Okay!
```

will construct intArray as follows:

intArray	9	8	7	6	5	4	0	0	0	0
	[0]	[1]	[2]	[3]	[4]	[5]	[6]	[7]	[8]	[9]

The program in Figure 9.1 used this feature to initialize the array of counters:

```
int count[CAPACITY] = {0};
```

This definition explicitly initializes the first element to 0 and implicitly initializes the remaining elements to the zero default value. This sort of initialization is needed for an array of counters, because *if no initialization is supplied in an array definition, then the values in the array will be undefined and will likely contain "garbage" values.*

Character Arrays. C-style arrays are a legacy from C++'s parent language. Because C has no class mechanism, it has no standard `string` class for storing character strings. As a result, strings are stored in character arrays. For compatibility, C++ retains this and other features of C for storing character strings.

One of these features is to support a different form of initialization for character arrays. An array of characters can be initialized in the normal way:

```
const int NAME_CAPACITY = 10;

char name[NAME_CAPACITY] = {'J', 'o', 'h', 'n', ' ', 'D', 'o', 'e'};
```

However, typing all of the commas and single quotes is tedious. Thus, for convenience, an array of characters can also be initialized with a character string literal:

```
char name[NAME_CAPACITY] = "John Doe";
```

Both definitions construct `name` as an array object whose *capacity* is 10 and whose *size* is 8 because there are eight characters in `"John Doe"`.

Behind the scenes, things are more complicated: this initialization sets the elements of `name` to the individual characters in `"John Doe"` and adds an invisible **null character,** the NUL character `'\0'` whose numeric code is 0, which C uses as an *end-of-string* mark:[1]

String-processing functions can use this NUL character to find the end of the string. For example, the following statements can be used to output the characters stored in `name`:

```
for (int i = 0; name[i] != '\0'; i++)
    cout << name[i];
```

The array elements are output, starting at index 0 and terminating when the character being examined is the NUL character.

To provide room for the NUL character, the capacity of a character array must always be at least 1 more than the size of the largest string to be stored in the array. If we forget this and define the array to have the same size as the character strings to be stored, the behavior of the standard C string-processing functions will be unpredictable and may produce run-time errors that can be very difficult to find.

In languages such as C that have no classes, such difficulties cannot be avoided. However, C++ provides a `string` class that eliminates such problems. For this reason, many C++ programmers use the standard `string` class and avoid character arrays altogether.

---

[1] `\0` is the escape sequence for the NUL character just as `\n` is the escape sequence for the new-line character. Since its octal numeric code is 000, it could also be written as `\000`. We will use the customary short version `\0` in this text.

THE SUBSCRIPT OPERATION

In chapter 4, we saw that the individual characters in a string object can be accessed using the subscript operator and an index. More precisely, the character at index i within string object aString can be accessed by using aString[i]. In the same way, the value at index *i* in an array named *array_name* can be accessed using

```
array_name[i]
```

The program in Figure 9.1 gives examples of this **subscript operation.** The statements

```
inStream >> numFailures;
if (inStream.eof()) break;
count[numFailures]++;
```

inside the input loop, read a value from inStream into numFailures, and (after testing for the end-of-file condition) increment the element of count whose index is equal to the value of numFailures. Because there are 58 zeros in the data file, count[0] is incremented 58 times; since there are 7 ones in the file, count[1] is incremented 7 times; and so on. After input is complete, count contains the following values:

The for loop that generates the program's output also uses the subscript operator:

```
for (int i = 0; i < CAPACITY; i++)              // output counters
   cout << count[i] << " had " << i
        << " failed components ("               // and percentages
        << double(count[i])/ numCircuitBoards * 100
        << "%)" << endl;
```

In the first pass through the loop, i is 0, so count[i] accesses the value 58, producing the output

```
58 had 0 failed components (80.6%)
```

In the second pass, i is 1, so count[i] accesses the value 7, producing the output

```
7 had 1 failed components (9.7%)
```

The remaining lines of output are generated in a similar way.

It is worth noting that any operation that is defined for a given type can be applied to an array element of that type. For example, any operation that can be applied to the type double can be applied to an element of a double array named realArray, as in

```
#include <math.h>                          // sqrt()
    .
    .
    .
for (int i = 0; i < CAPACITY; i++)
   cout << sqrt(realArray[i]);      // sqrt() takes a double argument
```

Similarly, any operation that is defined for the type char can be applied to any of the elements of a char array named name:

```
#include <ctype.h>                         // islower(), toupper()
    .
    .
    .
for (int i = 0; name[i] != '\0'; i++) // Each of these char
   if (islower(name[i]))                 //    functions takes
      name[i] = toupper(name[i]);        //    a char argument
```

PROCESSING ARRAYS WITH for LOOPS

A for loop is useful for implementing many array operations, because its loop-control variable can be used to count through the index values of the array. The indices of an array declared by

```
someType someArray[CAPACITY];
```

range from 0 through $CAPACITY - 1$. Thus, each element of an array can be accessed in turn by using the subscript operation with the loop-control variable in the body of a for loop that counts from 0 to $CAPACITY - 1$:

```
for (int i = 0; i < CAPACITY; i++)
   // ... do something with someArray[i]
```

We have seen, for example, that the program in Figure 9.1 uses a for loop to display the elements of the array count in order.

```
for (int i = 0; i < CAPACITY; i++)                      // output counters
   cout << count[i] << " had " << i
        << " failed components ("                       // and percentages
        << double( count[i] )/ numCircuitBoards * 100
        << "%)" << endl;
```

Similarly, if dubArray is an array of real numbers and we wish to sum the first numValues values stored in it, we can write

```
double sum = 0.0;

for (int i = 0; i < numValues; i++)
   sum += dubArray[i];
```

In mathematical formulas, notation like V_i has historically been used to denote the ith element in a subscripted variable V. Because arrays are subscripted variables, single-letter identifiers like i, j, and k are commonly used as names for array indices. This is one of the few cases where single-letter identifiers are acceptable as names of objects.

ARRAYS AS PARAMETERS

Functions can be written that accept arrays via parameters and then operate on the arrays by operating on individual array elements. For example, we could encapsulate the preceding statements for adding the elements of a double array in the following function:

```
/* ArraySum() computes the sum of the first itsSize
 *    double values stored in an array.
 *
 * Receive: theArray, an array of double values
 *          itsSize, an integer
 * Return:  the sum of the values
 ***************************************************************/

double ArraySum(const double theArray[], int itsSize)
{
   double sum = 0.0;              // sum of the array elements

   for (int i = 0; i < itsSize; i++)
      sum += theArray[i];

   return sum;
}
```

As this example illustrates, placing a pair of brackets ([]) after the name of a parameter indicates that the parameter is an array, and that it is not necessary to specify the capacity of the array. In this case, *there is no restriction on the capacity of the array that is passed to the function.*

It is also important to remember that *arrays are automatically passed by reference.* That is, simply specifying that a parameter is an array makes it a reference parameter, without having to use the usual ampersand (&) notation. If the function modifies the array, then the corresponding argument will also be modified. This can be prevented by declaring the array as a constant reference parameter, as we did with theArray in the function ArraySum().

THE typedef MECHANISM

C++ has inherited another mechanism from its parent language C that can be used to *increase the readability of a program and to make some types easier to use.* This is the **typedef mechanism,** so named because its declarations have the form

```
typedef ExistingTypeName NewTypeName;
```

for an existing type, and

```
typedef element_type NewTypeName[CAPACITY];
```

for an array. The first declaration makes the name *NewTypeName* a *synonym* for *ExistingTypeName*, which is some existing type. The second typedef declaration associates the name *NewTypeName* with arrays whose capacity is *CAPACITY* (which may be omitted) and whose elements are of type *element_type*. For example, if we wish to use the type identifier real instead of double, we could write

```
typedef double real;
```

and the word `real` then becomes a synomym for `double` and may be used any place that the word `double` is used. The `typedef` declaration

```
typedef double DoubleArray[100];   // an array type
```

associates the name `DoubleArray` with arrays whose elements are `double` values and whose capacity is 100. The declarations

```
const int CAPACITY = 6;                // # of array elements
typedef int IntegerArray[CAPACITY];  // an array type
```

associate the name `IntegerArray` with arrays whose elements are integers and whose capacity is 6.

These new type identifiers can be used to declare the types of variables, constants, and the return types of functions. For example, if we inserted the preceding `typedef` declaration of `IntegerArray` after the definition of `CAPACITY` in the program in Figure 9.1, we could then use `IntegerArray` to declare the array `count`:

```
IntegerArray count = {0};
```

Such `typedef`s are usually placed outside all blocks (typically after the `#include` directives) so that they have global scope and can be used to declare objects in all the functions that follow. The following code segment illustrates:

```
#include <iostream.h>

typedef double DoubleArray[100];
double ArraySum(DoubleArray theArray, int itsSize);

int main ()
{
   . . .
   DoubleArray tempReadings;   // array of temperature readings
   int numReadings;            // number of readings
   . . .
   // calculate the mean temperature
   double meanTemp =
            ArraySum(tempReadings, numReadings) / numReadings;
   . . .
}

/* Function ArraySum . . .
          . . .                  */
double ArraySum(DoubleArray theArray, int itsSize)
{
   // . . . definition of ArraySum given earlier
}
```

Here the type identifier `DoubleArray` is used to declare the array `tempReadings` in the main program and to specify the type of the parameter `dubArray` in the prototype and in the definition of the function `ArraySum`. This makes these declarations easier to read than if we had used the array declarations everywhere (and this is especially true for multidimensional arrays as described in chapter 12.)

OUT-OF-RANGE ERRORS

It is important to note that *no checking is done to ensure that indices stay within the range determined by an array's declaration* and that strange results may be obtained when an index is allowed to get out of bounds. This is illustrated by the program in Figure 9.2.[2]

FIGURE 9.2   WHY ARRAY INDICES MUST STAY IN BOUNDS.

```
/* outofrange.cpp demonstrates aberrant behavior
 * resulting from out-of-range errors.
 ***********************************************/

#include <iostream.h>              // cout, <<

const int CAPACITY = 4;
typedef int IntArray[CAPACITY];

void PrintArray(char name, IntArray x, int numElements);

int main()
{

    IntArray a = {0, 1, 2, 3},
             b = {4, 5, 6, 7},
             c = {8, 9, 10, 11};
    int below = -3,
        above = 6;

    PrintArray('a', a, 4);
    PrintArray('b', b, 4);
    PrintArray('c', c, 4);

    b[below] = -999;
    b[above] = 999;

    cout << endl;
    PrintArray('a', a, 4);
    PrintArray('b', b, 4);
    PrintArray('c', c, 4);
}
```

[2] The output on your system may not agree exactly with that shown in the sample run. For example, some systems allocate memory from higher addresses to lower and the output in this case will probably appear as follows:

```
a =     0    1     2     3
b =     4    5     6     7
c =     8    9    10    11

a =     0    1   999     3
b =     4    5     6     7
c =     8 -999    10    11
```

```
#include <iomanip.h>                  // setw()

/* PrintArray() displays an int array.
 *
 * Receives:  name, a character, and x, an int array
 * Output:    name of array, and 4 values stored in it
 ************************************************************/

void PrintArray(char name, IntArray x, int numElements)
{
    cout << name << " = ";
    for (int i = 0; i < numElements; i++)
        cout << setw(5) << x[i];
    cout << endl;
}
```

Sample run:

```
a =       0     1     2     3
b =       4     5     6     7
c =       8     9    10    11

a =       0  -999     2     3
b =       4     5     6     7
c =       8     9   999    11
```

We see that even though there are no statements of the form a[i] = *value*; or c[i] = *value*; to change values stored in a and c, the second element of a was changed to -999 and the third element of c was changed to 999.

This happens because the memory location being accessed is typically determined by simply counting forward or backward from the **base address** of the array—the address of the first element in the array. Thus, the illegal array references b[-3] and b[6] accessed the memory locations associated with a[1] and c[2]:

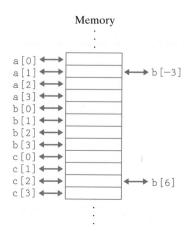

Thus modifying b[-3] and b[6] changed a[1] and c[2], respectively. This change is obviously undesirable! An array reference such as b[500] that is very much out of range will likely cause the program to "crash."

As this example demonstrates, it is important to check that the index is not out of range. See the function in Figure 9.3 for an example of how this is done.

PREDEFINED ARRAY OPERATIONS

The C++ string class provides a rich set of predefined operations on string objects. This raises the question: *What predefined operations are there for arrays?*

C++ has inherited from C the **C standard library,** which provides a variety of functions for processing character arrays. These functions are divided among several different libraries, including <string.h>, <stdlib.h>, and <stdio.h>.[3] Also, the iostream operators have been overloaded to operate on char arrays, allowing us to write

```
char name[CAPACITY];
     .
     .
     .
cin >> name;
```

to fill a character array name with characters from the keyboard. Similarly, we can simply write

```
cout << name;
```

to display the contents of a character array name.

However, there are virtually *no* similar operations or libraries of standard predefined functions for operating on numeric (or other) arrays. For example, there is no operation or function to input or output a numeric array. We must implement all such operations ourselves.

One of the reasons for this disparity is that functions typically use loops to process arrays. As we saw earlier, these loops begin processing with the value at index 0 and terminate after processing the final value in the array. A character-array-processing function "knows" that it has processed the final value in a character array when it reaches the NUL character that marks the end of the string:

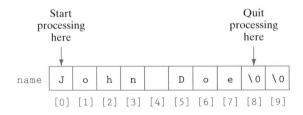

Even though the capacity and size of name differ, a function can still determine when to quit processing.

---

[3] The string class eliminates the need for most of these functions in C++. They are described in appendix D.

However, there is no numeric equivalent of the NUL character that can be used to mark the end of a sequence of numbers. For example, if we want to process the integers in the following `intArray`,

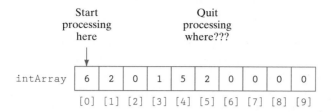

we have no way of knowing how many data values to process, because we do not know which of the last four zeros are values stored in the array and which are default zeros used to fill the array.

A NON-OOP APPROACH

Because there is no end-of-sequence value comparable to the NUL character, a function that processes an array of numbers must use some alternative mechanism to determine when the final number has been processed. One solution is to pass both the array and its size to the function, and then use this size in the computation, as in the `ArraySum()` function:

```
double ArraySum(DoubleArray theArray, int itsSize)
{
    double sum = 0.0;           // sum of the array elements

    for (int i = 0; i < itsSize ; i++)
        sum += theArray[i];

    return sum;
}
```

Unfortunately, this means that passing a sequence of values to `ArraySum()` requires two arguments instead of one, which is *not consistent with the aims of object-oriented programming*. That is, if we wish to treat a sequence of values as a single object (which is the reason for storing the values in an array), then it should only be necessary to pass that one object to the function.

The Deeper Problem. One of the principles of object-oriented programming is that *an object should be self-contained*, which means that it should carry within itself all of the information necessary to describe and operate on it. A fundamental problem with C-style arrays is that they violate this principle. In particular, they carry neither their size nor their capacity within them, and so *C-style arrays are not self-contained objects*. For this reason, functions to operate on C-style arrays usually require two (and sometimes three) arguments just to characterize the array being processed, as the following examples illustrate.

Array Input. As we have noted, C and C++ provide no predefined array-input operation (except for char arrays), and so values must be read and stored into an array one at a time. When the number of values is exactly the same as the capacity of the array, a for loop can be used to perform this task. For example, if we have exactly 10 homework scores to input, we can define an array whose capacity is 10 and then use a for loop to count through the index values 0 through 9:

```
const int NUM_SCORES = 10;
double score[NUM_SCORES];

for (int i = 0; i < NUM_SCORES; i++)
{
    cout << "Enter score "       // display prompt for score #
        << (i + 1) << ':';       //   1, 2, ..., NumScores
    cin >> score[i];             // store score in array
}
```

In this loop, the first value read is stored in score[0], the second value in score[1], the third in score[2], and so on.

In general, however, the actual number of values entered may be less than or equal to the capacity of the array. A general purpose array-input function cannot therefore assume that the size and capacity of the array will be the same. Since the number of values to be entered is not known in advance, the function should count the number of values entered and pass this information back to the caller, along with the values themselves.

Figure 9.3 presents such a function. It assumes that the type identifier DoubleArray has been declared using typedef as described earlier:

```
const int CAPACITY = . . .;
typedef double DoubleArray[CAPACITY];
```

For maximum reusability, it receives the istream from which the values are to be extracted, so that the array can be input from the keyboard or from a file. Also, it uses the eof mark as a sentinel to control the input loop. Note that because C-style arrays are not self-contained, three different parameters—theArray, ITS_CAPACITY, itsSize—are needed to characterize what is conceptually a single object.

FIGURE 9.3   C-STYLE ARRAYS: INPUT.

```
/* Read reads a sequence of double values from the keyboard.
 * and stores them in an array.
 *
 * Receive:      in, an istream containing input values
 *               theArray, an empty array of double values
 *               ITS_CAPACITY, the number of values it can hold
 * Input:        a sequence of numbers
 * Precondition: There is at least one number in the sequence.
 * Pass back:    the modified istream in,
 *               theArray, containing the sequence of numbers
 *               itsSize, the number of values in theArray
 *****************************************************************/
```

```
void Read(istream & in, DoubleArray theArray,
          int ITS_CAPACITY,  int & itsSize)
{
   itsSize = 0;

   for (;;)
   {
      in >> theArray[itsSize];

      if (in.eof()) break;

      itsSize++;
      if (itsSize >= ITS_CAPACITY)  // prevent out-of-range error
      {
         cerr << "\nRead warning: array is full!\n;
         return;
      }
   }
}
```

Remember that *an array is automatically passed using the call-by-reference mechanism* so no ampersand (`&`) is placed between `DoubleArray` and `theArray`.
   Given this function and the earlier `typedef` declaration, statements like

```
int numberOfValues;

cout << "Enter the sequence of values (eof to quit):\n";
Read(cin, anArray, CAPACITY, numberOfValues);
```

can be used to fill `anArray` with values from the keyboard; or the call

```
Read(anIFStream, anArray, CAPACITY, numberOfValues);
```

can be used to fill `anArray` with values from a file, if *anIFStream* is connected to that file. When the function terminates, `numberOfValues` will contain the number of input values and `anArray` will contain those values.

Array Output. As with input, C and C++ provide no predefined array-output operation (except for `char` arrays), and so a function to perform this operation must display the values in the array one at a time. The basic algorithm is quite simple:

   For each value in the array:
      Display that value.

As we saw previously, a function can access each value in the array by using a `for` loop that counts from 0 through one less than the size of the array. The function should thus receive not only the array but also its size. The function in Figure 9.4 illustrates this approach.

FIGURE 9.4   C-STYLE ARRAYS: OUTPUT.

```
/* Print displays the values in an array of doubles.
 *
 *   Receive: out, the ostream being written to
 *            theArray, an array of double values
 *            itsSize, the number of values it holds
 *   Output:  each value in theArray, on a separate line, to
 *                the ostream out
 *   Return:  the modified ostream out
 *************************************************************/

void Print(ostream & out, DoubleArray theArray, int itsSize)
{
   for (int i = 0; i < itsSize; i++)   // for each value in theArray:
      out << theArray[i] << endl;      //   display it via out
}
```

Given this function and the declarations we saw earlier, the call

```
Print(cout, anArray, numberOfValues);
```

can be used to display the values in anArray on the screen; and a call like

```
Print(anOFStream, anArray, numberOfValues);
```

can be used to write the values in anArray to a file to which anOFStream
is connected.

AN OBJECT-ORIENTED APPROACH

We have seen two significant problems with C-style arrays:

1. The capacity of a C-style array cannot change during program execution
2. C-style arrays are not self-contained objects, since an operation on a C-style
    array needs at least two pieces of information: the array and some way to
    identify its final value (e.g., its size)

With respect to the first problem, C++ provides a way to allocate arrays at run-
time. A description of the mechanism for this is somewhat beyond the level of this
text and we defer it to Chapter 13. In the next section, we will discuss the vec-
tor<T> class template, which uses (and effectively hides) this mechanism. When
we use vector<T> we will in fact be using this mechanism indirectly.

With respect to the second problem, we have seen that the C++ class mechanism
allows different data members to be stored within a single object. This provides
a solution to the second problem—by storing an array, its capacity, and its size
within a class structure, a single class object can encapsulate all three pieces of information. This is the approach used by the vector<T> class template that we describe next.

✔   **Quick Quiz 9.2**

Questions 1–16 assume the following definitions:

```
double a[5],
       b[5] = {0},
       c[5] = {1},
       d[5] = {0,0,0,0,0},
       e[5] = {1,2,3,4,5};
char f[5] = {'a', 'b'},
     g[5] = "abcde";
typedef int alpha[5];
alpha beta;
```

1. (True or false) a is an array indexed 0, 1, 2, 3, 4, 5.
2. (True or false) All elements of a are initialized to 0.
3. (True or false) All elements of b are initialized to 0.
4. (True or false) All elements of c are initialized to 1.
5. (True or false) The definition of d could be shortened to `double d[5] = {0};`.
6. (True or false) The definition of b could be shortened to `double b[5] = 0;`.
7. (True or false) `e[3] == 3`.
8. The capacity of a is _____ .
9. (True or false) `f[2]` is the NUL character.
10. (True or false) The definition of f could also be written `char f[5] = "ab";`.
11. (True or false) `g[5]` contains an end-of-string mark.
12. (True or false) alpha is an array indexed 0, 1, 2, 3, 4.
13. (True or false) beta is an array indexed 0, 1, 2, 3, 4.
14. The address of `a[0]` is called the _____ address of a.
15. (True or false) The output produced by `cout << e << endl;` will be `12345`.
16. (True or false) The output produced by `cout << f << endl;` will be `ab`.
17. (True or false) C-style arrays are self-contained.
18. Arrays are passed as _____ parameters.

For Questions 19–22, assume the declarations:

```
int number[5] = {1};
typedef double Dubber[5];
Dubber xValue;
```

Tell what values will be assigned to the array elements.

19. ```
    for (int i = 0; i <= 4; i++)
        xValue[i] = double(i) / 2.0;
    ```
20. ```
    for (int i = 0; i < 5; i++)
        if (i % 2 == 0)
            number[i] = 2 * i;
        else
            number[i] = 2 * i + 1;
    ```
21. ```
    for (int i = 1; i < 5; i++)
        number[i] = 2 * number[i - 1];
    ```
22. ```
    for (int i = 3; i >= 0; i--)
        number[i] = 2 * number[i + 1];
    ```

Exercises 9.2

For exercises 1–8, assume that the following declarations have been made:

```
const int LITTLE = 6,
            MEDIUM = 10,
            BIG = 128;
int i, j, n = 9;
    temp,
    number[MEDIUM] = {99, 33, 44, 88, 22, 11, 55, 66, 77};
char ch,
     letterCount[BIG];
typedef double LittleDouble[LITTLE];
LittleDouble value;
```

Tell what value (if any) will be assigned to each array element, or explain why an error occurs:

1.
```
for (i = 0; i < MEDIUM; i++)
    number[i] = i / 2;
```

2.
```
for (i = 0; i < LITTLE; i++)
    number[i] = i * i;
for (i = LITTLE; i < MEDIUM; i++)
    number[i] = number[i - 5];
```

3.
```
for (i = 0; i < 3; i++)
    LittleDouble[i] = 0;
for (i = 3; i < LITTLE; i++)
    LittleDouble[i] = 1;
```

4.
```
for (i = 1; i < LITTLE; i += 2)
{
    value[i - 1] = double(i) / 2.0;
    value[i] = 10.0 * value[i - 1];
}
```

5.
```
i = 0;
while (i != 10 )
{
    if (i % 3 == 0)
        number[i] = 0;
    else
        number[i] = i;
    i++;
}
```

6.
```
number[1] = 1;
i = 2;
do
{
    number[i] = 2 * number[i - 1];
    i++;
}
while (i < MEDIUM);
```

7.
```
for (ch = 'A'; ch <= 'F'; ch++)
    if (ch == 'A')
        letterCount[ch] = 1;
    else
        letterCount[ch] = letterCount[ch - 1] + 1;
```

8.
```
for (i = 0; i < n - 1; i++)
{
    for (j = i; j < n - 1; j++)
        if (number[j] > number[j + 1])
        {
            temp     = number[j];
            number[j] = number[j + 1];
            number[j + 1] = temp;
        }
}
```

For exercises 9–15 write definitions of the given arrays in two ways: (a) without using `typedef` and (b) using `typedef`.

9. An array with capacity 10 in which each element is an integer.

10. An array whose indices are integers from 0 through 10 and in which each element is a real value.

11. An array with capacity 10 in which each element is an integer, all of which are initially 0.

12. An array that can store 5 strings.

13. An array that can store 5 characters and is initialized with the vowels a, e, i, o, and u.

14. An array that can store 100 values, each of which is either `true` or `false`.

15. An array whose indices are the decimal ASCII values (0–127), such that the value stored in an element is `true` if the index is that of a vowel, and `false` otherwise.

For exercises 16–18, write definitions and statements to construct the given array.

16. An array whose indices are the integers from 0 through 99 and in which the value stored in each element is the same as the index.

17. An array whose indices are the integers from 0 through 99 and in which the values stored in the elements are the indices in reverse order.

18. An array of capacity 50 in which the value stored in an element is true if the corresponding index is even and false otherwise.

Exercises 19–25 ask you to write functions to do various things. Also, include any `typedef` declarations that are needed. To test these functions, you should write driver programs as instructed in Programming Problems 1–6 at the end of this chapter.

19. Return the smallest value stored in an array of integers.

20. Return the largest value stored in an array of integers.

21. Return the range of values stored in an array of integers; that is, the difference between the largest value and the smallest value.

22. Return `true` if the values stored in an array are in ascending order and `false` otherwise.

23. Insert a value into an array of integers at a specified position in the array.

24. Remove a value from an array of integers at a specified position in the array.

25. Perform a *linear search* of a sequence of integers stored in an array for a given value—start at index 0 and examine successive elements until either the value is found or the end of the sequence is reached. It should return the index at which the value is found or −1 if it is not found.

9.3 EXAMPLE: SORTING EMPLOYEE INFORMATION

PROBLEM

The Yoyodyne Corporation keeps track of employee seniority and salaries in a file employees.dat, in which the first line in the file describes the employee with the most seniority, the second line describes the employee with next highest seniority, and so on. Each line contains an employee's name in last-name, first-name order, followed by his or her weekly salary:

```
Somebody, Jane      950.00
Yahyah, Noah        845.00
Newman, Alfred      735.00

        .
        .
        .
```

The problem is that the company paymaster uses this file to write the paychecks in order of seniority, but the company mailboxes are in alphabetical order. As a result, putting the paychecks into the mail boxes takes an inordinate amount of time. A program is needed to read the information in employee.dat and create a second file in which the employees are listed in alphabetical order.

OBJECT-CENTERED DESIGN

Behavior. The program should open an fstream to the file named employees.dat. It should then read a sequence of employee records from the stream, and close it. After this, it should sort this sequence so that the last names are in alphabetical order. Next, it should open an fstream to a file named payroll.dat, write the sorted sequence of employee records to the fstream, and then close the fstream.

Objects. From the statement of the problem and our behavioral description, we have the following objects:

Description	Type	Kind	Name
the stream to the input file	ifstream	varying	*inStream*
name of the input file	string	constant	"employee.dat"
a line of employee info	string	varying	*empLine*
a sequence of employee records	vector<string>	varying	*empVector*
the stream to the output file	ofstream	varying	*outStream*
name of the output file	string	constant	"payroll.dat"

As we shall see, the C++ vector<T> class template provides a convenient way to store an arbitrarily long sequence of values of type T. We therefore use a vector<string> object to store the sequence of lines of text from the input file.

Operations. From the behavioral description, we find the following operations:

   i.   Open an fstream to an input file

   ii. Read a sequence of employee records from an fstream

iii. Close an fstream

iv. Sort a sequence of employee records

v. Open an fstream to an output file

vi. Write a sequence of employee records to an fstream

As we shall see, each of these operations is either predefined in C++ or is easily implemented with a few simple statements. In particular, C++ provides a `sort()` function template that works on a wide variety of objects, including `vector<T>` objects. Our task is further simplified by the format of the input file: because an employee's last name is the first item on each line, we can simply read the file a line at a time and then sort these lines.

Algorithm.   Our algorithm is thus as follows:

Algorithm for Sorting Problem

1. Open an `ifstream` named *inStream* to "employees.dat".
   (If this fails, display an error message and terminate the algorithm.)
2. Loop:
     a. Read a line from *inStream* into *empLine.*
     b. If the eof mark was read, terminate repetition.
     c. Append *empLine* to *empVector.*
   End loop
3. Close *inStream.*
4. Sort the lines in *empVector.*
5. Open an `ofstream` named *outStream* to "payroll.dat".
   (If this fails, display an error message and terminate the algorithm.)
6. For each index *i* of *empVector:*
     Write *empVector*[*i*] to *outStream.*
7. Close *outStream.*

Note that because we do not know at the outset how many employee records are in `employees.dat`, we must use an indefinite loop to perform step 2. Once this step is finished, the number of employees is known, and so we can use a `for` loop in step 6.

Coding. The program in Figure 9.5 is a complete implementation of this algorithm in C++. It uses two new features of C++: the `vector<T>` class template and the `sort()` algorithm template, each of which is a standard component of C++.

FIGURE 9.5   SORTING A FILE OF EMPLOYEE RECORDS.

```
/* emprecords5.cpp sorts a sequence of employee records stored in a file
 * so they are arranged with the last names in alphabetical order.
 *
 * Input (file):    employee records
 * Output (screen): user messages
 * Output (file):   sorted employee records
 ******************************************************************************/
```

```
#include <iostream.h>                    // cout, <<, >>
#include <fstream.h>                     // ifstream, ofstream
#include <string>                        // string
#include <assert.h>                      // assert()
#include <vector>                        // vector<T>
#include <algorithm>                     // sort()

int main()
{
   cout << "This program sorts the data in a file"
        << " named 'employees.dat'.\n";

   ifstream inStream("employees.dat");      // input stream
   assert(inStream.is_open());

   vector<string> empVector;                // sequence-holder

   string empLine;                          // input variable

   for (;;)                                 // loop:
   {
      getline(inStream, empLine);           //    read a name
      if (inStream.eof()) break;            //    quit if eof
      empVector.push_back(empLine);         //    append name
   }                                        // end loop

   inStream.close();                        // close stream

   sort(empVector.begin(), empVector.end());  // sort vector

   ofstream outStream("payroll.dat");       // output stream
   assert(outStream.is_open());

   for (int i = 0; i < empVector.size(); i++) // display
      outStream << empVector[i] << endl;    //   vector

   outStream.close();

   cout << "\nProcessing complete.\n";
}
```

Listing of input file employees.dat:

```
Somebody, Jane      950.00
Yahyah, Noah        845.00
Newman, Alfred      735.00
Bigfoot, Ben        425.00
Valyou, Mary        300.00
Smith, Nancy        195.00
Juan, John          175.00
Doe, John           150.00
Buck, John          150.00
Deere, John         150.00
```

Sample run:

```
This program sorts the data in a file named 'employees.dat'.

Processing complete.
```

Listing of output file `payroll.dat`:

```
Bigfoot, Ben        425.00
Buck, John          150.00
Deere, John         150.00
Doe, John           150.00
Juan, John          175.00
Newman, Alfred      735.00
Smith, Nancy        195.00
Somebody, Jane      950.00
Valyou, Mary        300.00
Yahyah, Noah        845.00
```

In the next section, we examine the vector<T> class template in depth.

9.4 THE vector<T> CLASS TEMPLATE

A QUICK REVIEW OF FUNCTION TEMPLATES

In section 7.5 we introduced **function templates,** which are *patterns* for functions from which the compiler can create actual function definitions. A template typically has a **type parameter** that is used as a place holder for a type that will be supplied when the function is called. For example, we considered the following function template:

```
template <class Item>
void Swap(Item & first, Item & second)
{
    Item temporary = first;
    first = second;
    second = temporary;
}
```

When Swap() is called with

```
Swap(int1, int2);
```

the compiler creates an instance of Swap() in which the type-parameter Item is replaced by int —the type of the variables whose values are being exchanged. But when Swap() is called with

```
Swap(char1, char2);
```

the compiler creates an instance of Swap() in which Item is replaced by char. Function templates thus allow a programmer to create **generic functions** — functions that are *type independent.*

CLASS TEMPLATES

In addition to function templates, C++ also allows **class templates,** which are type-independent patterns from which actual classes can be defined. These are useful for building **generic container classes**—objects that store other objects. In the early 1990s, Alex Stepanov and Meng Lee of Hewlett Packard Laboratories extended C++ with an entire library of class and function templates, which has come to be known as the **Standard Template Library (STL).** In 1994, the ANSI/ISO standards committee adopted STL as a standard part of the C++ language.

The simplest container in STL is the `vector<T>` class template, which can be thought of as a type-independent pattern for a self-contained array class whose capacity may vary. Its declaration has the form

```
template <class T>
class vector
{
    // details of vector omitted...
};
```

where `T` is a parameter for the type of values to be stored in the container. To illustrate its use, consider the following definitions:

```
vector< double > realVector;
vector< string > stringVector;
```

When it processes the first definition, the compiler will create a definition of class `vector` in which each occurrence of `T` is replaced by `double`, and will use this class to construct an object named `realVector`. When it processes the second definition, the compiler will create a second definition of class `vector` in which each occurrence of `T` is replaced by `string`, and use this class to define an object named `stringVector`.[4]

Because a class template is a parameterized pattern from which a class can be built and not an actual class itself, its name includes its `<T>` parameter, as in `vector<T>`, to distinguish it from an actual class, which is not parameterized.

DEFINING vector<T> OBJECTS

The definition

```
vector<string> empVector;
```

in the program of Figure 9.5 creates an **empty vector<string>,** meaning a `vector` that can store `string` values and whose size and capacity are both zero. As the program demonstrates, having a capacity of zero is not a problem, because a `vector<T>` object can increase its capacity as necessary during program execution.

Preallocating a vector<T> Object. Sometimes it is useful to *preallocate* the capacity of a `vector<T>` (see the discussion of `push_back()` later). This can be

---

[4] Since class names must be unique, whenever the compiler builds an actual class from a class template, it gives the new class a unique name formed by combining the name of the class and its parameterized type(s), a process known as **name mangling.** For example, `vector<double>` and `vector<string>` might be mangled to `vector_d` and `vector_s`, respectively.

done by passing the desired capacity as an argument to the object being constructed. For example, if we write

```
vector<string> empVector(10);
```

then `empVector` will be constructed as a `vector` of `string` values whose capacity is 10. Its size will also be 10 since these string values will be initialized (by default) to strings of length 0 that contain no characters:

empVector

Unlike C-style arrays whose capacity must be known at compile-time, the space for `vector<T>` objects is allocated during program execution. This allows us to write code like the following that provides *interactive control* over the capacity of a `vector<T>`:

```
int numberOfEmployees
cin >> numberOfEmployees;
vector<string> empVector(numberOfEmployees);
```

Whatever value the user enters for `numberOfEmployees` will be the initial capacity (and size) of `empVector`.

Preallocating and Initializing a `vector<T>` Object.   A third form of a `vector<T>` definition can be used both to preallocate the capacity of a `vector<T>` object and to initialize each element to a specified value. For example, the definition

```
vector<double> realVector(10, 0.0);
```

will construct `realVector` as a `vector` of `double` values, with capacity 10, and containing 10 zeros (making its size also 10):

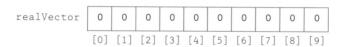

Similarly, the definition

```
vector<string> names(4, "Jane Doe");
```

will construct `names` as a `vector` of 4 `string` values, each initialized to `"Jane Doe"`:

names	Jane Doe	Jane Doe	Jane Doe	Jane Doe
	[0]	[1]	[2]	[3]

The three forms of `vector<T>` definitions can be summarized as follows:

> ## vector<T> Definition
>
> **Forms**
>
> ```
> vector<element_type> object_name;
> vector<element_type> object_name(initial_capacity);
> vector<element_type> object_name(initial_capacity,
>                                  initial_value);
> ```
>
> where:
>
>   *element_type* is any known type;
>
>   *object_name* is the name of the vector object being defined;
>
>   *initial_capacity* is an integer expression; and
>
>   *initial_value* is an object of type *element_type*.
>
> **Purpose**
>
> Define a varying-capacity object capable of storing values of type *element_type*.
>
> Form 1 constructs *object_name* with capacity and size 0.
>
> Forms 2 and 3 both construct *object_name* with capacity *initial_capacity* and with size *initial_capacity*. Form 2 initializes the elements to default values of type *element_type*. Form 3 initializes each element to *initial_value*.

vector<T> FUNCTION MEMBERS

The Standard Template Library provides a rich set of operations for vector<T>. As we shall see, these operations allow a vector<T> to be treated much like an array, but without the limitations of C-style arrays. The following table lists some of these operations:

Function Member	Description
`vector<Type> v;`	Construct *v* as a vector<Type> of capacity 0
`vector<Type> v(n);`	Construct *v* as a vector<Type> of capacity *n*, size *n*, and each element initialized to a default *Type* value
`vector<Type> v(n, initVal);`	Construct *v* as a vector<Type> of capacity *n*, size *n*, and each element initialized to *initVal*
`v.capacity()`	Return the number of values *v* can store
`v.size()`	Return the number of values *v* currently contains
`v.empty()`	Return true if and only if *v* contains no values (i.e., *v*'s size is 0)
`v.reserve(n);`	Grow *v* so that its capacity is *n* (does not affect *v*'s size)
`v.push_back(value);`	Append *value* at *v*'s end
`v.pop_back();`	Erase *v*'s last element
`v.front()`	Return a reference to *v*'s first element
`v.back()`	Return a reference to *v*'s last element

The Constructors. The first group of member functions shows the three major ways to construct a `vector<T>`. We have already described these in some detail.

Checking Size and Capacity. The second group group of member functions show how much more self-contained `vector<T>` objects are than C-style arrays:

- ▶ The `v.size()` function member returns the number of values in v. As with C-style arrays, *the index of the first value of a* `vector<T>` *is always 0;* but unlike a C-style array, which provides no way to identify its final value, *the index of the final value in a* `vector<T>` *object v is always* `v.size()-1`.

- ▶ `v.empty()` is a simpler alternative to the boolean expression `v.size() == 0`.

- ▶ `v.capacity()` returns the current capacity of v.

- ▶ `v.reserve()` can be used to increase the capacity of v, but this is more often done implicitly using `v.push_back()`.

To illustrate the use of these function members, suppose we write

```
vector<double> realVector;
cout << realVector.capacity() << ' '
     << realVector.size() << endl;
```

The output produced will be

```
0  0
```

because `realVector` is an empty container. But if we write

```
vector<double> realVector(3);
cout << realVector.capacity() << ' '
     << realVector.size() << endl;
```

the values

```
3  3
```

will be displayed, because `realVector` has space for 3 values and contains 3 default `double` values (0). The same output will be produced if we write

```
vector<double> realVector(3, 4.0);
cout << realVector.capacity() << ' '
     << realVector.size() << endl;
```

because `realVector` has space for 3 values and contains 3, each of which is 4.0:

realVector	4.0	4.0	4.0
	[0]	[1]	[2]

Appending and Removing Values. The third group of function members shows how values can be appended to or removed from a `vector<T>`. A statement of the form

```
v.push_back(value);
```

appends `value` to the end of v, and increases its size by 1. If necessary, the capacity of v is increased to accommodate the new value. The amount by which the capacity is increased depends on the operating system of a particular machine. Because memory allocation takes time, a large block of elements (typically 4K bytes) is allocated all at once.

To illustrate, execution of the statements

```
vector<double> realVector;
cout << realVector.capacity() << ' '
     << realVector.size() << endl;

for (int i = 0; i < 1024; i++)
{
    realVector.push_back(i);
    cout << realVector.capacity() << ' '
         << realVector.size() << endl;
}
```

on one machine produced

```
0 0
512 1
512 2
 .
 .
 .
512 511
512 512
1024 513
1024 514
 .
 .
 .
1024 1022
1024 1023
```

On this particular machine, blocks of size 4K (= 4096) bytes are allocated at a time, which increases the capacity of the vector<double> object realArray by 512 elements because each double value requires 8 bytes of storage.

Obviously, if a program only requires a few elements, this allocation of large blocks can waste both space and time. However, if a vector<T> object is defined with a preallocated capacity, a very different behavior results. Execution of the statements

```
vector<double> realVector(3, 4.0);
cout << realVector.capacity() << ' '
     << realVector.size() << endl;

for (int i = 0; i < 1024; i++)
{
    realVector.push_back(i);
    cout << realVector.capacity() << ' '
         << realVector.size() << endl;
}
```

by the same machine produced

```
3  3
6  4
6  5
6  6
12 7
12 8
 .
 .
 .
```

Here, we see that the capacity is initially 3, as expected, but when a fourth value is appended to the full realVector, its capacity doubles in size from 3 to 6. Similarly, when the capacity of realVector is 6 and we add a seventh value, its capacity doubles again (to 12).

This behavior is a nice compromise between allocating many small blocks of memory (which wastes time) and allocating only a few large blocks of memory (which wastes space). It can be produced by declaring the vector<T> as non-empty or by using the function member reserve() to set the capacity of an empty vector<T>.

The function v.pop_back() can be used to remove the last value in v. This will decrease the size of v by 1, but it does not change its capacity.

Accessing the First and Last Values. The front() and back() function members can be used to access the first and last values in a vector<T>. More precisely, if realVector is the vector

realVector	4.3	7.2	5.9
	[0]	[1]	[2]

then front() and back() can be used to retrieve the first and last values, as in

```
cout << realVector.front() << ' '
     << realVector.back() << endl;
```

which will display

```
4.3 5.9
```

These member functions can also be used to change the first and last values, as in

```
realVector.front() = 1.1;
realVector.back()  = 9.0;
```

which will modify realVector as follows:

realVector	1.1	7.2	9.0
	[0]	[1]	[2]

vector<T> OPERATORS

There are four basic **operators** defined in vector<T>:

Operator	Description
v[i]	Access the element of v whose index is i
v1 = v2	Assign a copy of v2 to v1
v1 == v2	Return true if and only if v1 has the same values as v2, in the same order
v1 < v2	Return true if and only if v1 is lexicographically less than v2

The Subscript Operator. The first operator is the familiar subscript operator that provides convenient access to the element with a given index. As with C-style arrays, the index of the first element of a vector<T> is always 0, and the expression *vectorName*.size()-1 is always the index of the final value in *vectorName*. This allows all of the elements in a vector<T> to be processed using a for loop and the subscript operator, as we saw in the program in Figure 9.5:

```
for (int i = 0; i < empVector.size(); i++)    // display
   outStream << empVector[i] << endl;          //   vector
```

The vector<T> subscript operation is thus similar to that of string and C-style array objects.

When Not to Use Subscript.   There is one important difference between vector<T>s and C-style arrays. To illustrate this difference, suppose we modified the Read() function in Figure 9.3 to read values into a vector<T> as follows:

```
template <class T>
void Read(istream & in, vector<T> & theVector)
{
   int itsSize = 0;

   for (;;)
   {
      in >> theVector[itsSize];    // LOGIC ERROR:
      if (in.eof()) break;         //   size, capacity not updated!
      itsSize++;
   }
}
```

This does not work correctly, however, because *if the subscript operator is used to append values to a* vector<T>, *neither its size nor its capacity is modified. The function member* push_back() *should always be used to append values to a* vector<T>, because it updates the vector's size (and if necessary, its capacity).[5] Figure 9.6 shows the correct way to write a generic vector<T> input function.

---

[5] The push_back() function also correctly updates the iterator returned by the end() function member, while the subscript operator does not. STL algorithms will thus not work properly if subscript is used to append values to a vector<T>.

FIGURE 9.6   VECTOR<T> INPUT FROM AN `istream`.

```
/* Read fills a vector<T> with input from a stream.
 *
 * Receives:       type parameter T,
 *                 an istream and a vector<T>
 * Precondition: operator >> is defined for type T
 * Passes back:  the modified istream and the modified vector<T>
 ***************************************************************/

template <class T>
void Read(istream & in, vector<T> & theVector)
{
   T inputValue;

   for (;;)
   {
      in >> inputValue;
      if (in.eof()) break;
      theVector.push_back(inputValue);
   }
}
```

Given this function template, the statements

```
vector<double> realVector;
Read(cin, realVector);
```

will cause the compiler to create a definition of Read() in which each occurrence of T has been replaced by double, and the call to Read() will be linked to this definition. If in the same program we write

```
vector<string> stringVector;
Read(cin, stringVector);
```

then the compiler will create a second definition of Read() in which each occurrence of T is replaced by string, and this second call to Read() will be linked to this definition. A function template to fill a vector<T> from a file is similar.

When to Use Subscript. Once a vector<T> contains values, *then and only then* should the subscript operator be used to access (or change) those values. For example, Figure 9.7 presents a generic output function that uses a for loop and the subscript operator to display the values in a vector<T>:

FIGURE 9.7   `vector<T>` OUTPUT.

```
/* Print writes a vector<T> to a stream.
 *
 * Receives:       type parameter T
 *                 an ostream and a vector<T>
 * Precondition: operator << is defined for type T
 * Passes back:  the modified ostream
 ***************************************************************/
```

```
template <class T>
void Print(ostream & out, const vector<T> & theVector)
{
   for (int i = 0; i < theVector.size(); i++)
      out << theVector[i] << ' ';
}
```

Given this function template and the statements

```
vector<double> realVector(5, 1.1);
Print(cout, realVector);
```

the compiler will generate a definition of `Print()` in which each occurrence of T is replaced by `double`. When executed, it will produce the output

```
1.1 1.1 1.1 1.1 1.1
```

Because all three of these functions are useful in many problems, they would probably be stored in a library (e.g., `MyVector.h`) so that any program can easily reuse them.

The Assignment Operator. The assignment operator (=) is straightforward, behaving exactly as one would expect. For example, the definitions

```
vector<int> v1;
vector<int> v2(5, 1);
```

create v1, an empty `vector<int>`, and v2, a non-empty `vector<int>`:

A subsequent assignment statement

```
v1 = v2;
```

changes v1 to a copy of v2:

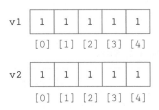

The Equality Operator. The equality operator (==) is also straightforward. It compares its operands element by element and returns true if and only if they are identical; that is, their sizes match and their values match. For example, the definitions

```
vector<int> v1(4, 1);
vector<int> v2(5, 1);
```

produce two similar but not identical vector<int> objects:

```
v1 | 1 | 1 | 1 | 1 |
    [0] [1] [2] [3]


v2 | 1 | 1 | 1 | 1 | 1 |
    [0] [1] [2] [3] [4]
```

When these are compared using the equality operator,

```
if (v1 == v2)
// ... do something appropriate
```

the expression produces the value false, because v1 and v2 are not identical.

The Less-Than Operator. The less-than operator (<) is also defined for vector<T> objects. It behaves much like the string less-than operation, performing an element-by-element comparison until a mismatch (if any) occurs. If the mismatched element in the left operand is less than the corresponding element in the right operand, the operation returns true; otherwise it returns false. If all the elements of both vector<T> objects are compared and no mismatch is found, the operation returns false.

To illustrate, suppose the two vector<int> objects v1 and v2 have the following values:

```
v1 | 1 | 1 | 1 | 1 | 1 |
    [0] [1] [2] [3] [4]


v2 | 1 | 1 | 2 | 3 |
    [0] [1] [2] [3]
```

When these are compared using the less-than operator:

```
if (v1 < v2)
// ... do something appropriate
```

the values at index 0 are compared first:

```
v1 | 1 | 1 | 1 | 1 | 1 |
    [0] [1] [2] [3] [4]


v2 | 1 | 1 | 2 | 3 |
    [0] [1] [2] [3]
```

Because they are equal, the function moves on and examines the values at index 1:

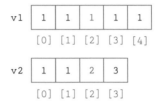

Because they are equal, it moves on and examines the values at index 2:

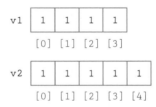

Because the value (1) at index 2 in v1 is less than the value (2) at index 2 in v2, the < operation returns true.

If the values of v1 and v2 are

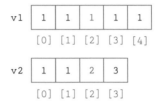

the values at index 0 are compared. Because they match, the values at index 1 are compared. This continues through the values at index 2 and the function moves on and examines the values at index 3. Because we have reached the end of v1 and no mismatch has occurred, the operation returns true.

THE STANDARD TEMPLATE LIBRARY

There are several other operations that can be performed on vector<T> objects. However, to understand them, we need to know more about the Standard Template Library (STL).

The Organization of STL. The Standard Template Library has three different kinds of components:

1. **Containers:** A group of class templates that provide standardized, generic, off-the-shelf structures for storing data
2. **Iterators:** A generic means of accessing, finding the successor of, and finding the predecessor of a container element

3.   Algorithms: A group of function templates that provide standardized, generic, off-the-shelf functions for performing many of the most common operations on container objects.

In order for the algorithms in STL to be truly generic, they must be able to operate on any container. To make this possible, each container provides iterators for the algorithms to use. Iterators thus provide the interface that is needed for STL algorithms to operate on STL containers.

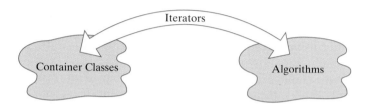

The program in Figure 9.5 gives an illustration of this when it calls

```
sort(empVector.begin(), empVector.end());
```

The `sort()` function is a generic STL algorithm that requires two iterators: one to the first element, and one to the end of the sequence. As we shall see, because `vector<T>` is a container, `empVector.begin()` returns an iterator that points to its first element, and `empVector.end()` returns an iterator that points beyond its last element.

STL Container Class Templates. The Standard Template Library provides a rich variety of containers. The following table gives a brief description of these containers and indicates how they differ from one another. Like `vector<T>`, each container has properties and operations that make it particularly useful for a large category of problems. A detailed study of these containers is beyond the scope of this introductory text, however, and is left for the sequel.

Containers	Description
`vector<T>`	Linear, contiguous storage; fast inserts only at the end
`list<T>`	Linear, non-contiguous storage; fast inserts anywhere
`deque<T>`	Linear, non-contiguous storage; fast inserts at both the beginning and the end
`set<T, less<T> >`	Set of T objects, fast associative lookup, with no duplicates allowed
`multiset<T, less<T> >`	Same as `set<T>`, but duplicates are allowed
`map<T₁, T₂, less<T₁> >`	Map T_1 objects to T_2 objects in a 1-to-1 manner (a no-duplicate associative array)
`multimap<T₁, T₂, less<T₁> >`	Map T_1 objects to T_2 objects in a 1-to-many manner (associative array with duplicates)

Containers	Description
stack<C>	Last-In-First-Out container; built from container C (a vector<T>, a list<T>, or a deque<T>)
queue<C>	First-In-First-Out container; built from container C (a list<T> or a deque<T>)
priority_queue<C>	First-In-First-Out sorted container; built from container C (a vector<T> or a deque<T>)

STL Iterators. The elements of a vector<T> can be accessed using an index and the subscript operator, but this is not true for other containers such as list<T>. Stated differently, using the subscript operator and indices is not a generic way to access an element in a container.

In order for a Standard Template Library algorithm to work on *any* STL container, some truly generic means of accessing the elements in a container is required. For this purpose, STL provides objects called **iterators** that can "point at" an element, access the value within that element, and move from one element to another.

Each STL container provides its own group of iterator types and (at least) two function members that return iterators:

- begin(): returns an iterator positioned at the first element in the container
- end():   returns an iterator positioned at the element following the last value in the container

To illustrate, suppose the following statements are executed:

```
vector<int> vec;           // empty vector
vec.push_back(9);          // append 9
vec.push_back(8);          // append 8
vec.push_back(7);          // append 7
```

The expressions vec.begin() and vec.end() produce iterators that can be visualized as follows:

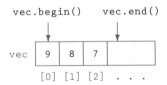

A function like sort() then uses these iterators

```
sort(vec.begin(), vec.end());
```

to access (and rearrange) the values that lie between the two iterators:

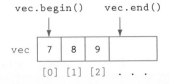

Defining Iterator Objects. Each STL container also declares an `iterator` type that can be used to define iterator objects. To ensure that the right type is used, the identifier `iterator` must be preceded by the name of its container and the **scope operator** (`::`). For example, the statements:

```
vector<double> vec;          // empty vector
vec.push_back(9.0);          // append 9
vec.push_back(8.0);          // append 8
vec.push_back(7.0);          // append 7
vector<double>::iterator vecIter = vec.begin();
```

define `vecIter` as an `iterator` object positioned at the first element of `vec`:

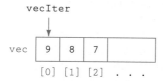

Iterator Operations. Among the operators that can be applied to an iterator are:

► The **increment operator** (`++`). Applied as a prefix or postfix operator to an iterator, `++` moves the iterator from its current position to the next element of the container.

► The **decrement operator** (`--`). Applied as a prefix or postfix operator to an iterator, `--` moves the iterator from its current position to the previous element of the container.

► The **dereferencing operator** (`*`). Applied as a prefix operator to an iterator, `*` accesses the value stored at the position to which the iterator points.

Other operators that can be applied to `vector<T>::iterator` objects include assignment (`=`), equality comparisons (`==` and `!=`), addition (`+`), subtraction (`-`), the corresponding shortcuts (`+=`, `-=`), and the subscript operator (`[]`).

The increment, decrement, and arithmetic operators can be used to *change the position* of an iterator variable. The dereferencing operator can be used to *access the value* at the iterator's current position.

The following example illustrates the use of these operators. It is an alternative way to write the function template `Print()` of Figure 9.7, using an iterator and two of these operators:

```
template <class T>
void Print(ostream & out, const vector<T> & theVector)
{
   vector<T>::iterator vecIter = theVector.begin();

   while(vecIter != theVector.end())
   {
      out << *vecIter << ' ';
      vecIter++;
   }
}
```

On each pass through the while loop, the * operator is used to access the value at the iterator's current position, and the ++ operator then advances the iterator to the next element.

Unlike the function in Figure 9.7 (which requires the subscript operator), this function template can be made into a generic Print() *algorithm template* that allows the values in almost *any* STL container to be output to an ostream:

```
template <class Container>
void Print(ostream & out, const Container & theContainer)
{
    Container::iterator conIter = theContainer.begin();

    while(conIter != theContainer.end())
    {
        out << *conIter << ' ';
        conIter++;
    }
}
```

In summary, iterators provide a mechanism for moving among and accessing the values in a container that is independent of any particular container (i.e., a *generic* mechanism). Understanding the preceding introduction to iterators should enable you to use the STL containers and algorithms effectively.

STL Algorithms. Like sort(), most of the algorithms in the Standard Template Library are function templates designed to operate on *a sequence of elements*, rather than on a specific container. The STL way of designating a sequence for an algorithm is by using two iterators:[6]

► An iterator positioned at the first element in the sequence
► An iterator positioned *after* the last element in the sequence

In the discussion that follows, we will refer to these two iterators as *begin* and *end*, respectively.

The Standard Template Library provides over 80 algorithm templates. An in-depth examination of these algorithms is beyond the scope of this text,[7] but the table that follows provides a brief introduction to what is available.

Algorithm	Description
accumulate(*begin*, *end*, *init*)	Return the sum of the values in the sequence; *init* is the initial value for the sum (e.g., 0 for integers, 0.0 for reals)

---

[6] If an entire container were passed to an algorithm, then the algorithm would affect the entire container. Passing iterators to the beginning and end of the sequence allows an algorithm to act on a subset of the container's elements.

[7] For complete coverage, see *The STL <Primer>*, by Graham Glass and Brett Schumacher, Prentice Hall, 1996.

Algorithm	Description
binary_search(*begin, end, value*)	Return `true` if *value* is in the sorted sequence; if not present, return `false`
find(*begin, end, value*)	Return an iterator to *value* in the unsorted sequence; if not present, return *end*
count(*begin, end, value, 0*)	Return how many times *value* occurs in the sequence
fill(*begin, end, value*);	Assign *value* to every element in the sequence
iota(*begin, end, firstVal*);	Fill the sequence with monotonically increasing values, starting with *firstVal*
for_each(*begin, end, F*);	Apply function *F* to every element in the sequence
lower_bound(*begin, end, value*);	Return an iterator to the *first* position at which *value* can be inserted and the sequence remain sorted
upper_bound(*begin, end, value*);	Return an iterator to the *last* position at which *value* can be inserted and the sequence remain sorted
max_element(*begin, end*)	Return an iterator to the maximum sequence value
min_element(*begin, end*)	Return an iterator to the minimum sequence value
next_permutation(*begin, end*);	Shuffle the sequence to its next permutation, and return `true` (If there is none, return `false`)
prev_permutation(*begin, end*);	Shuffle the sequence to its previous permutation, and return `true` (If there is none, return `false`)
random_shuffle(*begin, end*);	Shuffle the values in the sequence randomly
replace(*begin, end, old, new*);	In the sequence, replace each value *old* with *new*
reverse(*begin, end*);	Reverse the order of the values in the sequence
sort(*begin, end*);	Sort the sequence into ascending order
unique(*begin, end*);	In the sequence, replace any consecutive occurrences of the same value with one instance of that value

The function in Figure 9.8 illustrates the use of these algorithms. It finds the mean of the values in a vector<double>, using the accumulate() algorithm:

FIGURE 9.8   FINDING THE MEAN OF A VECTOR<DOUBLE>.

```
/* Mean finds the mean value in a vector<double>.
 *
 * Receive:      vec, a vector<double>
 * Precondition: vec is not empty
 * Return:       the mean of the values in vec
 ***********************************************************/
```

```
double Mean(const vector<double> & vec)
{
   if (vec.size() > 0)
      return accumulate(vec.begin(), vec.end(), 0.0) / vec.size();
   else
   {
      cerr << "\n***Mean: empty vector received!\n" << endl;
      return 0.0;
   }
}
```

The accumulate() algorithm eliminates the need to write a for loop to sum the values in a vector (or any of the other STL containers), and also eliminates the need to define a variable to store that sum. Familiarity with the algorithms provided by STL can save time and effort, and allow us to write functions that are more streamlined and efficient.

vector<T> FUNCTION MEMBERS INVOLVING ITERATORS

Now that we have been introduced to the Standard Template Library and its concept of iterators, we have the background needed to understand a group of vector<T> function members that utilize iterators. The following table presents a few of these functions:

Function Member	Description
v.begin() v.end()	Return an iterator positioned at v's first value Return an iterator positioned 1 element past v's last value
v.rbegin() v.rend()	Return a reverse iterator positioned at v's last value Return a reverse iterator positioned 1 element before v's first value
v.insert(pos, value); v.insert(pos, n, value);	Insert value into v at iterator position pos Insert n copies of value into v at iterator position pos
v.erase(pos); v.erase(pos1, pos2);	Erase the value in v at iterator position pos Erase the values in v from iterator positions pos1 to pos2

Note that whereas the push_back() and pop_back() function members add or remove values at the end of a vector<T>, the insert() and erase() functions can be used to add or remove values at any position in a vector<T>.

To illustrate, consider the following vector<double> named scores, containing a sequence of ten test scores given by judges in some competition:

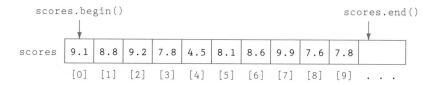

To reduce the effect of bias, the high score (9.9) and the low score (4.5) are to be thrown out and the mean of the remaining scores computed.

Eliminating the low score can be done in one step using the STL min_element() algorithm to position an iterator at the 4.5 and then pass this iterator to the vector<T> function member erase(),

```
scores.erase(min_element(scores.begin(), scores.end()));
```

or divide the operation into two separate steps:

```
vector<int>::iterator it = min_element(scores.begin(), scores.end());
scores.erase(it);
```

The maximum score can be erased using the same approach with the max_element() algorithm. The result is that the 4.5 and 9.9 are erased from scores, the remaining values are shifted to the left to fill their spaces, and scores.size() and scores.end() are appropriately updated:

The resulting vector can then be passed to the function Mean() in Figure 9.8 to compute the average score.

DECISION MAKING: USE A vector<T> OR A C-STYLE ARRAY?

We have now seen two different ways to store a sequence of values of the same type: the C-style array and the C++ vector<T> class template. This raises the question:

> When should a C-style array be used and when should a C++ vector<T> be used?

Whereas the C-style array is a legacy of programming in the early 1970s, the C++ vector<T> was designed in the early 1990s, and thus incorporates over 20 years of additional programming wisdom. This design of vector<T> (along with the other class templates in STL) gives it some definite advantages over C-style arrays, making it the preferred choice in almost every situation:

- ▶ The capacity of a vector<T> can change during execution; the capacity of a C-style array is fixed at compile-time, and cannot be changed without recompiling the program.

- ▶ A vector<T> is a self-contained object; the C-style array is not. If the same operation can be implemented with either container, the array version will require more parameters.

- ▶ A vector<T> is a class template, and its function members (augmented with the STL algorithms) provide ready-to-use implementations of many common operations. The C-style array requires that we reinvent the wheel for most operations.

ARRAY AND vector<T> LIMITATIONS

One weakness of both the C-style array and the C++ vector<T> is that the insertion and deletion operations can be quite time-consuming, especially for large sequences. For example, consider the following ordered sequence of ten integers

$$23, 25, 34, 48, 61, 79, 82, 89, 91, 99$$

If these values are stored in an array or vector<int> and we wish to insert the value 56 into its proper position, then the fifth through the tenth values must be shifted one position to the right to make room for the new value:

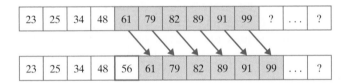

Erasing a value from the sequence also requires moving values; for example, to remove the second number, we must shift the third through the eleventh values one position to their left to "close the gap":

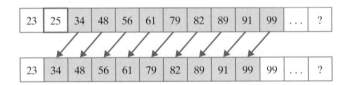

If insertions and erasures are restricted to the ends of the sequence, then array and vector<T> implementations that do not require moving array elements are possible. Two important special cases are stacks and queues. A **stack** is a sequence in which values may be inserted **(pushed)** and removed **(popped)** at only one end, called the **top** of the stack.[8] If elements may be inserted only at one end (the **rear**) and removed only at the other (the **front**), the sequence is called a **queue.** STL provides standardized *adaptor* class templates for building such objects out of other containers.

---

[8] This is the source of the names push_back() and pop_back() for the vector<T> class template function members.

In summary, arrays and `vector<T>` objects work well for storing sequences in which insertions and deletions are infrequent or are restricted to the ends of the list. **Dynamic** sequences whose sizes may vary greatly during processing and those in which items are frequently inserted and/or deleted anywhere in the sequence are better stored in a varying-size STL `list<T>` container, which is described in chapter 13.

9.5 EXAMPLE: PROCESSING TEST SCORES

PROBLEM

Professor von Neuperson has a file containing the class roster for each class she teaches. To help with processing the grades for her classes, she would like a program that will allow her to: enter a test score for each student in the file; calculate the mean of the scores, excluding the lowest and the highest score; and then display each person's name and score and the difference between that score and the mean. For example, if the mean score is 75, the program should display something like

```
... 82 (+7)
```

for a score of 82, and

```
... 69 (-6)
```

for a score of 69.

OBJECT-CENTERED DESIGN

Behavior.   The program should display on the screen a prompt for the name of the class roster file and read its name from the keyboard. It should then read a sequence of names from the input file. The program should then read a sequence of test scores from the keyboard, prompting for them using the sequence of names. It should eliminate the outliers of this sequence—the high and low scores—and then compute the mean of the sequence of test scores. Finally, the program should display this mean value, and then display the sequences of names and test scores, along with the difference of each test score from the mean.

Objects.   Although most of the objects in our behavioral description are familiar, two of them require special attention: the sequence of names and the sequence of scores. A `vector<T>` can be used to store these sequences.

Description	Type	Kind	Name
name of the class roster file	`string`	varying	*inputFileName*
the sequence of names	`vector<string>`	varying	*names*
the sequence of scores	`vector<double>`	varying	*scores*
the outliers of the sequence	`double, double`	varying	none
the mean score	`double`	varying	*meanScore*
the difference of a score and the mean score	`double`	varying	none

Operations. The operations specified in our behavioral description are as follows:

    i.   Read a `string` from the keyboard

    ii.   Open an fstream to an input file

    iii.   Read a sequence of `string` values from the fstream into a `vector<string>`

    iv.   Read a sequence of `double` values from the keyboard into a `vector<double>`, using a sequence of `string` values stored in a `vector<string>` as prompts

    v.   Eliminate the outliers of a sequence of double values

    vi.   Compute the mean of a sequence of `double` values stored in a `vector<double>`

    vii.   Display a `double`

    viii.   Display the sequence of `string` values stored in a `vector<string>`, a corresponding sequence of `double` values stored in a `vector<double>`, and the difference of two `double` values

Operations, i, ii, and viii are predefined, and a straightforward modification of the `Read()` function of Figure 9.6 can be used for operation iii. In the last section we saw that operation v can be done with two statements, and the `Mean()` function from Figure 9.8 provides operation vi. We will need to write a function `PromptAndRead()` to perform operation iv and another function `Print-Results()` for operation viii.

Behavior of `PromptAndRead()`. This function should receive a sequence of names from its caller. For each name in that sequence, it should display on the screen a prompt for that name's score, read the score from the keyboard, and append it to a sequence of double values. The resulting sequence of double values should be passed back to the caller.

Objects for `PromptAndRead()`. The objects in this subproblem are as follows:

Description	Type	Kind	Movement	Name
a sequence of names	vector<string>	constant	received (in)	*names*
a name in the sequence	string	varying	none	*names[i]*
a double value	double	varying	none	*aScore*
a sequence of doubles	vector<double>	varying	passed back (out)	*scores*
for-loop-control variable	int	varying	none	*i*

Operations for `PromptAndRead()`. The operations for this function are:

    i.   Receive a sequence of names from the caller

    ii.   Access one string from a sequence of string values

    iii.   Display a string on the screen

    iv.   Read a double from the keyboard

v. Append a double to a sequence of double values

vi. Repeat operations ii–v once for each string in a sequence of string values

vii. Pass a sequence of double values back to the caller

Each of these operations is predefined.

Algorithm for `PromptAndRead()`. We can organize these operations into the following algorithm for the function `PromptAndRead()`:

Algorithm for `PromptAndRead()`

1. Receive *names,* a sequence of names from the caller.

2. For each index *i* in *names*:
   a. Display *names[i]* in a prompt for a score.
   b. Read a double from `cin` into *aScore*.
   c. Append *aScore* to a sequence of double values named *scores.*

3. Pass *scores* back to the caller.

Coding and Testing of `PromptAndRead()`. The function in Figure 9.9 encodes the preceding algorithm in C++.

FIGURE 9.9   **PROMPTING AND READING TEST SCORES.**

```
/* PromptAndRead reads a sequence of test scores from the keyboard.
 *
 * Receive:       names, a vector of strings,
 *                scores, a vector of doubles
 * Precondition:  names is not empty AND scores is empty
 * Output:        prompts for test scores, using names
 * Input:         a sequence of test scores
 * Pass back:     scores containing the input values
 ***************************************************************/

void PromptAndRead(const vector<string> & names, vector<double> & scores)
{
   double aScore;                          // input variable
   for (int i = 0; i < names.size(); i++)  // for each index in sequence
   {
      cout << "Enter the score for "
           << names[i] << ": ";            //    prompt,
      cin >> aScore;                        //    read, and
      scores.push_back(aScore);             //    append
   }
}
```

Once `PromptAndRead()` has been thoroughly tested, we continue to the function `PrintResults`, which is to perform the following operation in the original problem:

viii. Display the sequence of `string` values stored in a `vector<string>`, a corresponding sequence of `double` values stored in a `vector<double>`, and the difference of two `double` values

Behavior of `PrintResults()`. This function should receive from its caller a sequence of string values (names), a sequence of scores, and a mean score. It should display the mean value on the screen, and then for each name in the sequence of names, it should display that name, the corresponding entry in the sequence of scores, and the difference of that score and the mean.

Objects for `PrintResults()`. The objects in this subproblem are as follows:

Description	Type	Kind	Movement	Name
a sequence of names	`vector<string>`	constant	received (in)	*names*
a sequence of scores	`vector<double>`	constant	received (in)	*scores*
the mean score	`double`	constant	received (in)	*meanScore*
a name in the sequence	`string`	varying	none	*names[i]*
the corresponding score	`double`	varying	none	*scores[i]*
the loop-control variable	`int`	varying	none	*i*

Operations for `PrintResults()`. The operations in this function are

  i. Receive a `double`, a sequence of `string` values, and a sequence of `double` values from the caller

 ii. Display a `double` on the screen, with appropriate formatting for a test score

iii. Access a `string` in a sequence of `string` values

 iv. Access the corresponding `double` in a sequence of `double` values

  v. Display the accessed `string` and `double` on the screen

 vi. Display the difference of two doubles, showing the sign

vii. Repeat operations iii–vi once for each string in a sequence of string values

Each of these operations is predefined in C++.

Algorithm for `PrintResults()`. We can organize these operations into the following algorithm:

Algorithm for `PrintResults()`

1. Receive *meanScore,* a `double`; *names,* a sequence of `string` values; and *scores,* a sequence of `double` values from the caller.

2. Display *meanScore* via `cout`.

3. For each index *i* in *names:*
  a. Display *names[i]*, *scores[i]*, and *scores[i]* − *meanScore,* with appropriate formatting.

Coding and Testing of `PrintResults()`. Figure 9.10 shows an encoding of the preceding algorithm in C++.

FIGURE 9.10   DISPLAYING NAMES, TEST SCORES, AND MEAN DIFFERENCE.

```cpp
/* PrintResults() displays names, test scores, and differences between
 * the scores and the mean score.
 *
 *   Receive: meanScore, a double,
 *            names, a vector of strings,
 *            scores, a vector of doubles
 *   Output:  each name in names, each score in scores
 *            and the difference of each score and meanScore
 ************************************************************************/

#include <iomanip.h>                          // setprecision()

void PrintResults(double meanScore, const vector<string> & names,
                  const vector<double> & scores)
{
   cout << "\nThe mean score is "
        << right << fixed << showpoint     // format for test scores
        << setprecision(1) << meanScore    // show mean score
        << " (ignoring max and min).\n"
        << endl;

   for (int i = 0; i < names.size(); i++)  // for each index in sequence:
      cout << setw(20) << names[i]         //    display name,
           << noshowpos << setw(5)
           << scores[i] << "\t("           //        score, and
           << showpos << setw(5)
           << scores[i] - meanScore        //        difference from mean
           << ')' << endl;
}
```

Algorithm for Original Problem.   Once we have functions to perform each of the operations needed for our problem, we are ready to organize those operations into an algorithm.

Algorithm for Score-Processing Problem

1. Prompt for and read the name of the class roster file into *inputFileName*.
2. Open an `ifstream` named *inStream* to the file whose name is in *inputFile-Name*. (If this fails, display an error message and terminate the algorithm.)
3. Read a sequence of names from *inputFileName* into *roster*.
4. Using *roster* to prompt, read a sequence of test scores into *scores*.
5. Save a copy of *scores* in *originalScores*.
6. Eliminate the outliers from *scores*.
7. Compute the mean of the values in *scores*, and store it in *meanScore*.
8. Via `cout`, display *meanScore*, each name in *names*, the corresponding score from *originalScores*, and the difference of that score from *meanScore*.

Coding. The program in Figure 9.11 implements the preceding algorithm. It uses the vector<T> class template.

FIGURE 9.11   TEST SCORE PROCESSING.

```
/* testscores11.cpp processes a sequence of test scores, using a class
 * roster stored in a file.
 * Input(keyboard): the name of the roster file and
 *                  a sequence of test scores
 *  Input(file):    a sequence of names
 *  Precondition:   the sequence of names is not empty
 *  Output:         the mean of the sequence of test scores,
 *                     each student's name, the score for that student,
 *                     and the difference between the score and the mean
 ***************************************************************/

#include <iostream.h>                      // cout, cin, <<, >>
#include <fstream.h>                       // ifstream
#include <string>                          // string
#include <vector>                          // vector<T>
#include <algorithm>                       // max, min_element()
#include "MyVector.h"                      // Read()

double Mean(const vector<double> & vec);

void PromptAndRead(const vector<string> & names, vector<double> & scores);

void PrintResults(ostream & out, double meanScore,
                  const vector<string> & names,
                  const vector<double> & scores);

int main()
{
   cout << "This program requires a roster of student names.\n"
        << "Enter the name of the roster file: ";
   string inputFileName;
   cin >> inputFileName;

   vector<string> roster;                  // the class roster
   Read(inputFileName, roster);            // -- read it

   vector<double> scores;                  // the score sequence
   PromptAndRead(roster, scores);          // -- read it

   vector<double> originalScores = scores; // save a copy
                                           // remove extreme values
   scores.erase(min_element(scores.begin(), scores.end()));
   scores.erase(max_element(scores.begin(), scores.end()));

   double meanScore = Mean(scores);        // find mean w/o extremes
                                           // output w/ extremes
```

```
        PrintResults(cout, meanScore, roster, originalScores);

        return 0;
}

/* Read() fills a vector<T> with input from an ifstream.
 *
 * Receives:      type parameter T, an ifstream, and a vector<T>
 * Precondition: operator >> is defined for type T
 * Passes back:  the modified ifstream and the modified vector<T>
 ****************************************************************/

template <class T>
void Read(ifstream & inStream, vector<T> & theVector)
{
    T inputValue;

    for (;;)
    {
        in >> inputValue;
        if (in.eof()) break;
        theVector.push_back(inputValue);
    }
}

/*** Insert the definitions of:
         Mean() from Figure 9.8,
         PromptAndRead() from Figure 9.9, and
         PrintResults() from Figure 9.10 here. ***/
```

Listing of file `names.txt` used in sample run:

```
Jack_Sprat
Jill_Tumbling
Mary_HattaLamb
Peter_Pumpkin
Jack_B_Nimble
Cinderella_Slipper
Prince_Charming
```

Sample run:

```
This program requires a roster of student names.
Enter the name of the roster file: names.txt
Enter the score for Jack_Sprat: 100
Enter the score for Jill_Tumbling: 5
Enter the score for Mary_HattaLamb: 70
Enter the score for Peter_Pumpkin: 75
Enter the score for Jack_B_Nimble: 80
Enter the score for Cinderella_Slipper: 73
Enter the score for Prince_Charming: 77
```

The mean score is 75.0 (ignoring max and min).

```
Jack_Sprat              100.0    (+25.0)
Jill_Tumbling             5.0    (-70.0)
Mary_HattaLamb           70.0    ( -5.0)
Peter_Pumpkin            75.0    ( +0.0)
Jack_B_Nimble            80.0    ( +5.0)
Cinderella_Slipper       73.0    ( -2.0)
Prince_Charming          77.0    ( +2.0)
```

✔ **Quick Quiz 9.5**

Questions 1–15 assume that the following statements have been executed:

```
vector<int> a, b(5), c(5, 1), d(5);
d.push_back(77);
d.push_back(88);
```

1. The type of values stored in a is _____.
2. The capacity of a is _____ and its size is _____.
3. The capacity of b is _____ and its size is _____.
4. The capacity of c is _____ and its size is _____.
5. The capacity of d is _____ and its size is _____.
6. What output is produced by

   ```
   cout << c.front() << ' ' << c.back() << endl;
   ```

7. What output is produced by

   ```
   cout << d.front() << ' ' << d.back() << endl;
   ```

8. (True or false) a.empty().
9. (True or false) c < d.
10. (True or false) c[1] == 1.
11. What output is produced by

    ```
    for (int i = 0; i < c.size(); i++)
        cout << c[i] << ' ';
    ```

12. What output is produced by

    ```
    d.pop_back();
    for (int i = 0; i < d.size(); i++)
        cout << d[i] << ' ';
    ```

13. d.begin() returns an iterator positioned at _____ in d.
14. d.end() returns an iterator positioned at _____ in d.
15. (True or false) vector<T> objects are self-contained.

For questions 16–19, assume the declarations

```
vector<double> xValue(5);
vector<int> number(5, 1);
```

Describe the contents of the vector<T> after the statements are executed.

16.
```
for (int i = 0; i <= 4; i++)
    xValue.push_back(double(i) / 2.0)
```

17.
```
for (int i = 0; i < 5; i++)
    if (i % 2 == 0)
        number.push_back(2 * i);
    else
        number.push_back(2 * i + 1);
```

18.
```
for (int i = 1; i < 5; i++)
    number.push_back(2 * number[i - 1]);
```

19.
```
for (int i = 1; i <= 3; i++)
    number.pop_back();
for (int i = 1; i <= 3; i++)
    number.push_back(2);
```

20. When, where, and by whom was the Standard Template Library (STL) developed?

21. What are the three kinds of components in the STL?

22. _____ provide the interface between STL algorithms and STL containers.

23. A(n) _____ is a sequence in which values may be inserted and removed at only one end.

24. A(n) _____ is a sequence in which values may be inserted only at one end and removed only at the other end.

EXERCISES 9.5

For exercises 1–12, assume that the following declarations have been made,

```
vector<int> number,
            v(10, 20),
            w(10);
int num;
```

and that for exercises that involve input, the following values are entered:

```
99 33 44 88 22 11 55 66 77 -1
```

Describe the contents of the given vector<T> after the statements are executed.

1.
```
for (int i = 0; i < 10; i++)
    number.push_back(i / 2);
```

2.
```
for (int i = 0; i < 6; i++)
    w.push_back(i / 2);
```

3.
```
for (;;)
{
    cin >> num;
    if (num < 0) break;
    number.push_back(num);
}
```

4.
```
for (int i = 0; i <= 5; i++)
    number.push_back(i);
for (int i = 0; i < 2; i++)
    number.pop_back();
for (int i = 0; i <= 5; i++)
    number.push_back(i);
```

For exercises 5–12 assume that the loop in exercise 3 has been executed.

5.
```
for (int i = 0; i < number.size() - 1; i += 2)
    number[i] = number[i + 1];
```

6.
```
number.pop_back();
number.push_back(number.front());
```

7.
```
int temp = number.front();
number.front() = number.back();
number.back() = temp;
```

8.
```
sort(number.begin(), number.end());
```

9.
```
for (int i = 0; i < number.size(); i++)
    w.push_back(number[i] + v[i]);
```

10.
```
while (v < number)
{
    v.erase(v.begin());
    number.erase(number.begin());
}
```

11.
```
vector<int>::iterator iter = number.begin();
while (*iter > 25)
{
    number.erase(iter);
    iter++;
}
```

12.
```
for (vector<int>::iterator iter = number.begin();
        iter != number.end(); iter++)
    w.push_back(*iter + 1);
```

For exercises 13–17 write a definition for a vector<T> having the given properties.

13. Can store long int values.

14. Capacity 10 and each element is a long int.

15. Capacity 10 and each element is a long int, all of which are initially 0.

16. Capacity 5, size 5, and each element contains a string, initially "xxx".

17. Capacity 100 and each element is either true or false.

For exercises 18–20, write definitions and statements to construct a vector<T> with the required properties.

18. Stores the sequence of integers from 0 through 99.

19. Stores the sequence of integers from 0 through 99 in reverse order.

20. Has capacity 50 and the value stored in an element is true if the corresponding index is even and is false otherwise.

Exercises 21–27 ask you to write functions to do various things. To test these functions, you should write driver programs as instructed in Programming Problems 18–20 at the end of this chapter.

21. Returns `true` if the values stored in a `vector<double>` are in ascending order and `false` otherwise.

22. Finds the range of values stored in a `vector<double>`, that is, the difference between the largest value and the smallest value.

Exercises 23–27 deal with operations on *n-dimensional vectors,* which are sequences of n real numbers and which are studied and used in many areas of mathematics and science. They can obviously be modeled in C++ by `vector<double>`s of capacity n. In the description of each operation, A and B are assumed to be *n*-dimensional vectors:

$$A = (a_1, a_2, \ldots, a_n)$$
$$B = (b_1, b_2, \ldots, b_n)$$

23. Compute and return the sum of two *n*-dimensional vectors:

$$A + B = (a_1 + b_1, a_2 + b_2, \ldots, a_n + b_n)$$

24. Compute and return the difference of two *n*-dimensional vectors:

$$A - B = (a_1 - b_1, a_2 - b_2, \ldots, a_n - b_n)$$

25. Compute and return the product of a scalar (real number) and an *n*-dimensional vector:

$$cA = (ca_1, ca_2, \ldots, ca_n)$$

26. Compute and return the magnitude of an *n*-dimensional vector:

$$|A| = \sqrt{a_1^2 + a_2^2 + \cdots + a_n^2}$$

27. Compute and return the inner (or dot) product of two *n*-dimensional vectors (which is a scalar):

$$A \cdot B = a_1 * b_1 + a_2 * b_2 + \cdots + a_n * b_n = \sum_{i=1}^{n} (a_i * b_i)$$

Part of the Picture: Component Programming

Before the Industrial Revolution, a *smith* was an important part of nearly every community. His job was to manufacture whatever metal components the members of the community might need. For example, if a horse lost a shoe, the owner of the horse would pay the smith to make a new horseshoe that was the correct size. In the absence of factories to mass-produce horseshoes and other common items in standard sizes, each new shoe had to be made from scratch.

This all changed with the Industrial Revolution. Once entrepreneurs identified markets for standard items such as horseshoes and built factories to produce them, these items could be mass-produced much less expensively than if they were made by hand.

A second result of the Industrial Revolution was the advent of interchangeable components. No two horseshoes made by a smith were exactly alike; each was simply close enough to the correct size to do the job. By contrast, mass-produced items were virtually identical and were thus interchangeable. This made possible the assembly lines that make consumer products such as automobiles out of standardized components—pistons, axles, wheels, and so on. If a car's axle broke, no smith was needed to laboriously manufacture a new one. Instead, a replacement that was virtually identical could be ordered from the manufacturer.

COMPUTER HARDWARE

The same revolution occurred in computer hardware during the 1970s. The processors in early computers were built by hand and cost thousands or millions of dollars, but the invention of the microprocessor in the early 1970s made it possible to mass-produce the processor in a chip, some of which cost less than $100.

With the mass production of computer components has come interchangeability. When one memory or processor chip wears out, it can be unplugged from its circuit board and replaced by another chip that is functionally identical, even if the replacement is made by a different manufacturer. By using inexpensive, functionally identical components that connect in a standardized way, the cost of manufacturing and repairing computing systems has decreased dramatically since 1970.

COMPUTER SOFTWARE

The same revolution is just beginning in computing software. Historically, programmers have worked like the preindustrial smith, manually building from scratch the objects and operations needed to solve particular problems.

A step forward occurred in 1988 with the standardization of the C language and its many function libraries. Once the functions in these libraries were standardized, they became like software components that could be "plugged in" as needed, reducing programming effort and cost. However, such libraries only provided standardized operations, not objects.

With the publication of the ANSI/ISO draft standard for C++ in 1995 and its embrace of the Standard Template Library, standardized objects such as istream, ostream, string, vector<T>, list<T>, set<T>, map<T>, and so on, are becoming a reality. Because such objects have a well-defined set of operations that can be applied to them, they can be "plugged in" to programs as needed, an approach called **component programming.** By eliminating the need to build such objects from scratch, component programming increases programmer productivity, which reduces the cost of software.

To use such objects effectively, a programmer must be familiar with the operations they provide. For example, in the phone-number problem from section 4.5, it was necessary to check that each character in parameter aString was a digit. If a programmer simply knew that C++ had a string class, without investigating the operations it provides, he or she might be tempted to write the following code to do this checking:

```
for (int i = 0; i < aString.size(); i++)
   if (aString[i] != '0' && aString[i] != '1' && aString[i] != '2' &&
       aString[i] != '3' && aString[i] != '4' && aString[i] != '5' &&
       aString[i] != '6' && aString[i] != '7' && aString[i] != '8' &&
       aString[i] != '9')
      PhoneError("A phone number must consist of all digits");
```

This approach is the programming equivalent of manually beating a horseshoe out of a bar of metal. It is far more costly in terms of time and effort than using the standardized operation:

```
if (aString.find_first_not_of("0123456789", 0) != NPOS)
    PhoneError("A phone number must consist of all digits");
```

In the same fashion, a programmer needing to locate an item named value within a sequence might begin correctly by storing the sequence in a vector<T>, but then unnecessarily write a function to search the vector<T> for the value:

```
template <class T>
int Search(const vector<T> & theVec, const T & searchVal)
{
    for (int i = 0; i < theVec.size(); i++)
        if (theVec[i] == searchVal)
            return i;

    return -1;
}
        .
        .
        .
int index = Search(vec, value);
```

The STL `find()` algorithm provides an efficient, standardized way to solve this problem:

```
vector<T>::iterator it = find(vec.begin(), vec.end(), value);
```

and requires far less work. STL thus provides both standardized objects and algorithms.

Of course, practice is required to become familiar with the standardized components and their capabilities. Much of learning to program is becoming familiar with what standard objects are available and what operations can be performed on them. We hope that our introduction to STL objects and algorithms will whet your appetite to explore them further.

☞ *PROGRAMMING POINTERS*

✍ PROGRAM STYLE AND DESIGN

1. *C-style arrays and* `vector<T>`*s can be used to store sequences of values* since the elements of an array or `vector<T>` all have the same type.

2. *If a problem involves a sequence of unknown or varying length, or requires the use of an operation that is predefined for a* `vector<T>`, *store the sequence in a* `vector<T>` *instead of in a C-style array.* The `vector<T>` class template provides a standardized, variable-capacity, self-contained object for storing sequences of values, and STL provides many predefined `vector<T>` operations.

3. *Do not reinvent the wheel.* When a problem requires an operation on a `vector<T>`, thoroughly review the `vector<T>` function members and STL algorithms to see if the operation is already defined or if there are other operations that make yours easier to implement.

4. *When using C-style arrays, always define their capacity using a constant, not a literal.* Such a constant can be used to control `for` loops, passed to functions, and so on, which simplifies program maintenance if the array must be resized.

⚡ POTENTIAL PROBLEMS

1. *In C++, the subscript operator is a pair of square brackets, not a pair of parentheses.* An attempt to access element i of an array A by using `A(i)` will be interpreted by the C++ compiler as a call to a function named A, passing it the argument i. A compile-time error will result unless such a function exists, in which case a logical error will result.

2. *The first element of a C++ array or* `vector<T>` *has the index value 0 — not 1, as in many programming languages.* Forgetting this can produce some puzzling results. To illustrate, suppose that a programmer attempts to fill and output a character array named `anArray` as follows:

```
cout >> "? ";                          // prompt for input
for (int i = 1, i < CAPACITY; i++)     // read in elem-by-elem
   cin.get(anArray[i]);
//...
cout << anArray;                       // display A
```

If the user enters

    WXYZ

no output will be produced. The reason for this is that the contents of anArray are

because all the array elements were initialized to the NUL character. Because the first element of the array contains the NUL character (which is used to terminate character strings), all predefined operations will treat that array as though it contains the empty string.

3.   *No checking is performed to ensure that array or* vector<T> *indices stay within the range of valid indices.* As the program in Figure 9.2 demonstrates, out-of-range indices can produce obscure errors whose source can be very difficult to find.

4.   *A character string literal is invisibly terminated with the NUL character* '\0', *and a character array must leave room for this character.* Most of the standard operations for processing character arrays use the NUL character as an end-of-string marker. If a program mistakenly constructs a character array containing no terminating character or somehow overwrites the terminating character of a string with some non-null value, the results are unpredictable, but can easily produce a run-time error.

5.   *Array arguments are automatically passed by reference.* If a function has an array parameter through which a value is being passed back to its caller, it is a mistake to declare the array as a reference parameter. If a function has an array parameter that is being received but not returned, that parameter should be declared as a const parameter.

6.   *Always append new values to a* vector<T> *using its* push_back() *function member.* The size, capacity, and iterators of a vector<T> are all correctly updated by push_back(). None of these are updated by the subscript operator, however, so it should never be used to append values to (or insert values beyond the size of) a vector<T>.

7.   *The iterator returned by the* vector<T> *function member* end() *is positioned **beyond** the final value, not **at** the final value.* A common mistake is to forget this and write code like:

```
for (iter = vec.begin(); iter <= vec.end(); iter++)
// ... do something with *iter
```

The result will likely be a run-time error during the final repetition of the loop, because the value of *iter is undefined when iter is positioned beyond the final value in vec. The correct way is to *use the inequality operator when comparing iterators,*

```
for (iter = vec.begin(); iter != vec.end(); iter++)
// ... do something with *iter
```

which will terminate the repetition when iter moves beyond the final value in vec.

8. *When nesting STL templates (or using the STL* `stack`, `queue`, *or* `priority_queue` *adaptors), leave a space between the two* > *symbols.* A common mistake is to forget this and write

    ```
    vector<vector<int>> myGrid;
    ```

    to define `myGrid` as a vector of vectors. The compiler will read the >> as the output operator, and since this makes no sense in this context, a compilation error will result. The proper approach is to leave a space:

    ```
    vector<vector <int > > myGrid;
    ```

Programming Problems

SECTION 9.2

1. Write a driver program to test the min and max functions of exercises 19 and 20.

2. Write a driver program to test the range function of exercise 21.

3. Write a driver program to test the ascending-order function of exercise 22.

4. Write a driver program to test the insert function of exercise 23.

5. Write a driver program to test the remove function of exercise 24.

6. Write a driver program to test the linear-search function of exercise 25.

7. The Rinky Dooflingy Company records the number of cases of dooflingies produced each day over a four-week period. Write a program that reads these production numbers and stores them in an array. The program should then accept from the user a week number and a day number, and should display the production level for that day. Assume that each week consists of five workdays.

8. The Rinky Dooflingy Company maintains two warehouses, one in Chicago and one in Detroit, each of which stocks at most 25 different items. Write a program that first reads the product numbers of items stored in the Chicago warehouse and stores them in an array `Chicago`, and then repeats this for the items stored in the Detroit warehouse, storing these product numbers in an array `Detroit`. The program should then find and display the *intersection* of these two lists of numbers; that is, the collection of product numbers common to both sequences. The lists should not be assumed to have the same number of elements.

9. Repeat problem 8 but find and display the *union* of the two lists, that is, the collection of product numbers that are elements of at least one of the sequences of numbers.

10. The Rinky Dooflingy Company manufactures different kinds of dooflingies, each identified by a product number. Write a program that reads product numbers and prices, and stores these values in two arrays, `number` and `price`; `number[0]` and `price[0]` are the product number and unit price for the first item, `number[1]` and `price[1]` are the product number and unit price for the second item, and so on. The program should then allow the user to select one of the following options:

    (a) Retrieve and display the price of a product whose number is entered by the user. (Use the linear search procedure developed in problem 6 to determine the index of the specified item in the array `number`.)

    (b) Print a table displaying the product number and the price of each item

11. Suppose that a row of mailboxes are numbered 1 through 150 and that, beginning with mailbox 2, we open the doors of all the even-numbered mailboxes. Next, beginning with mailbox 3, we go to every third mail box, opening its door if it is closed and

closing it if it is open. We repeat this procedure with every fourth mailbox, then every fifth mailbox, and so on. Using an array to model the mailboxes, write a program to determine which mailboxes will be open when this procedure is completed.

12. If $\bar{x}$ denotes the mean of a sequence of numbers $x_1, x_2, \ldots, x_n$, the *variance* is the average of the squares of the deviations of the numbers from the mean,

$$variance = \frac{1}{n} \sum_{i=1}^{n} (x_i - \bar{x})^2$$

and the *standard deviation* is the square root of the variance. Write functions to calculate the mean, variance, and standard deviation of the values stored in an array, and a driver program to test your functions.

13. Letter grades are sometimes assigned to numeric scores by using the grading scheme commonly called *grading on the curve*. In this scheme, a letter grade is assigned to a numeric score according to the following table, where m is the mean score and σ (sigma) is the standard deviation.

x = Numeric Score	Letter Grade
$x < m - \dfrac{3}{2}\sigma$	F
$m - \dfrac{3}{2}\sigma \leq x < m - \dfrac{1}{2}\sigma$	D
$m - \dfrac{1}{2}\sigma \leq x < m + \dfrac{1}{2}\sigma$	C
$m + \dfrac{1}{2}\sigma \leq x < m + \dfrac{3}{2}\sigma$	B
$m + \dfrac{3}{2}\sigma <= x$	A

Write a program that reads a list of real numbers representing numeric scores, stores them in an array, calls the functions from problem 12 to calculate their mean and standard deviation, and then calls another function to display the letter grade corresponding to each numeric score.

14. A prime number is an integer greater than 1 whose only positive divisors are 1 and the integer itself. The Greek mathematician Eratosthenes developed an algorithm, known as the *Sieve of Eratosthenes*, for finding all prime numbers less than or equal to a given number n; that is, all primes in the range 2 through n. Consider the list of numbers from 2 through n. Two is the first prime number, but the multiples of 2 (4, 6, 8, . . .) are not, and so they are crossed out in the list. The first number after 2 that was not crossed out is 3, the next prime. We then cross out from the list all higher multiples of 3 (6, 9, 12, . . .). The next number not crossed out is 5, the next prime, and so we cross out all higher multiples of 5 (10, 15, 20, . . .). We repeat this procedure until we reach the first number in the list that has not been crossed out and whose square is greater than n. All the numbers that remain in the list are the primes from 2 through n. Write a program that uses this sieve method and an array to find all the prime numbers from 2 through n. Run it for $n = 50$ and for $n = 500$.

15. One way to sort a list of values stored in an array is called *simple selection sort:* Find the largest entry in the list and move it to the end of the list; find the next largest entry in the list and move it to the next-to-the-end position; find the third largest entry in the list and move it to the second-from-the-end position; and so on. Write a function to sort a list of items stored in an array using this simple selection sort method, and then a driver program to test its correctness.

16.   *Insertion sort* is an efficient sorting method for small data sets. It begins with the first item, x_1, then inserts x_2 into this one-item list in the correct position to form a sorted two-element list, then inserts x_3 into this two-element list in the correct position, and so on. For example, to sort the list 7, 1, 5, 2, 3, 4, 6, 0, the steps are as follows (the element being inserted is highlighted):

List

7

1, 7   (shift 7 one position to the right)

1, 5, 7   (shift 7 to the right again)

1, 2, 5, 7   (shift 5 and 7 to the right)

1, 2, 3, 5, 7   (shift 5 and 7 to the right)

1, 2, 3, 4, 5, 7   (shift 5 and 7 to the right)

1, 2, 3, 4, 5, 6, 7   (shift 7 to the right)

0, 1, 2, 3, 4, 5, 6, 7   (shift all of 1 through 7 to the right)

Write a function to sort a list of items stored in an array using this insertion sort method, and then a driver program to test its correctness.

17.   The investment company of Pickum & Loozem has been recording the trading price of a particular stock over a 15-day period. Write a program that reads these prices and sorts them into increasing order, using the insertion sort scheme described in the preceding exercise. The program should display the trading range; that is, the lowest and the highest prices recorded, and also the median price.

SECTION 9.3–9.5

18.   Write a driver program to test the ascending-order function of exercise 21 of section 9.5.

19.   Write a driver program to test the range function of exercise 22 of section 9.5.

20.   Write a menu-driven calculator program that allows a user to perform the operations on *n*-dimensional vectors in exercises 23–27 of section 9.5.

21.   Proceed as in problem 7 for retrieving production levels, but use a vector<T> to store the production numbers.

22.   Proceed as in problem 8 for finding the intersection of two lists, but use a vector<T> to store the lists.

23.   Proceed as in problem 9 for finding the union of two lists, but use a vector<T> to store the lists.

24.   Proceed as in problem 10 for processing product numbers and prices, but use vector<T>s instead of arrays.

25.   Proceed as in problem 11, but use a vector<T> to model the mailboxes.

26. Proceed as in problem 12 for calculating the mean, variance, and standard deviation of a sequence of scores, but use a vector<T> to store the scores.

27. Proceed as in problem 13 for grading on the curve, but use vector<T>s instead of arrays.

28. Proceed as in problem 14 for finding prime numbers using the Sieve Method of Eratosthenes, but use a vector<T> instead of an array.

29. Proceed as in problem 17 for finding the range of stock prices, but store the prices in a vector<T> and use the sort algorithm to sort the prices.

30. Write a function to perform addition of large integers, for which there is no limit on the number of digits. (*Suggestion:* Treat each number as a sequence, each of whose elements is a block of digits of the number. For example, the integer 179,534,672,198 might be stored with Block[0] = 198, Block[1] = 672, Block[2] = 534, and Block[3] = 179. Then add the integers (lists) element by element, carrying from one element to the next when necessary.) Write a driver program to test your function.

31. Proceed as in problem 30, but for subtraction of large integers.

32. Proceed as in problem 30, but for multiplication of large integers.

33. Proceed as in problem 30, but for division of large integers.

34. Write a big-integer calculator program that allows the user to enter two large integers and the operation to be performed, and which calls the appropriate function from problems 30–33 to carry out that operation.

35. Develop a recursive function to generate all of the $n!$ permutations of the set $\{1, 2, \ldots, n\}$. (*Hint :* The permutations of $\{1, 2, \ldots, k\}$ can be obtained by considering each permutation of $\{1, 2, \ldots, k - 1\}$ as an ordered list and inserting k into each of the k possible positions in this list, including at the front and at the rear.) For example, the permutations of $\{1, 2\}$ are $(1, 2)$ and $(2, 1)$. Inserting 3 into each of the three possible positions of the first permutation yields the permutations $(3, 1, 2)$, $(1, 3, 2)$, and $(1, 2, 3)$ of $\{1, 2, 3\}$, and using the second permutation gives $(3, 2, 1)$, $(2, 3, 1)$, and $(2, 1, 3)$. Write a driver program to test your function.

Chapter 10

BUILDING CLASSES

The old order changeth, yielding place to new.

ALFRED, LORD TENNYSON

. . . All manner of things—everything that begins with an M . . . such as mousetraps, and the moon, and memory, and muchness—you know you say things are "much of a muchness."

THE DORMOUSE IN LEWIS CARROLL'S
ALICE'S ADVENTURES IN WONDERLAND

I'd never join a club that would accept someone like me as a member.

GROUCHO MARX

Chapter Contents

10.1   Introductory Example: Modeling Temperatures

10.2   Designing a Class

10.3   Implementing Class Attributes

10.4   Implementing Class Operations

10.5   `friend` Functions

10.6   Example: Retrieving Student Information

PART OF THE PICTURE: Artificial Intelligence

We have seen that designing a C++ program involves identifying the objects in a problem and then using types to create software representations of those objects. Once these objects are created, programming consists of applying to those objects the operations needed to solve the problem.

We have also seen that when there is no predefined type that suffices to model an object, the C++ class can be used to create a new type to represent the object. Classes thus provide a way to extend the C++ language, allowing it to represent an ever-increasing number of objects.

Until now, we have simply *used* classes that someone else built. In this chapter, we learn how to *build* them ourselves and study the ideas of encapsulation and information hiding that underlie class design.

10.1 INTRODUCTORY EXAMPLE: MODELING TEMPERATURES

As usual, we begin with a problem.

PROBLEM: TEMPERATURE CONVERSION

Write a program that, given a temperature in Fahrenheit, Celsius, or Kelvin, will display the equivalent temperature in each of the scales.

PRELIMINARY ANALYSIS

In chapter 3 we saw that a Fahrenheit temperature could be modeled using a `double` variable,

```
double tempFahrenheit = 0.0;    // Brrrrr!
```

because such an object has only a single attribute—its number of degrees. However, the problem here is to model a temperature having two attributes—its *number of degrees* and its *scale* (Fahrenheit, Celsius, or Kelvin). Of course, we could model this using two variables:

```
char myScale = 'F';
double myDegrees = 0.0;
```

But this requires two data items (`myScale` and `myDegrees`) to model a single object (a temperature). To apply some function `G()` to a temperature, we would have to pass it each of the data items used in our model,

```
G(myScale, myDegrees);
```

instead of being able to pass a single object:

```
G(theTemperature);
```

Similarly, displaying a temperature would require an output statement like

```
cout << myDegrees << myScale;
```

instead of simply

```
cout << theTemperature;
```

This approach is not too inconvenient for objects that can be described with two attributes, but it quickly becomes unmanageable as the complexity of the object being modeled increases. Just think how many data items would be needed to represent a tax form like that shown in Figure 10.1.

Copy C For EMPLOYEE'S RECORDS (See Notice on back.)		**1996**	OMB No. 1545-0008
a Control number ABC-123	**1** Wages, tips, other comp. 1111.11		**2** Federal income tax withheld .00
b Employer's ID number 123456789	**3** Social security wages		**4** Social security tax withheld 11.22
	5 Medicare wages and tips		**6** Medicare tax withheld 22.11
c Employer's name, address, and ZIP code Dinoville Rock Quarry 1212 T-Rex Ave. Bedrock, Prehistoria 00001			
d Employee's social security number 987-675-4321			
e Employee's name, address, and ZIP code Fred Flintstone 123 Cave A Bedrock, Prehistoria 00002			
7 Social security tips	**8** Allocated tips		**9** Advance EIC payment
10 Dependent care benefits	**11** Nonqualified plans		**12** Benefits included in box 1
13 See instrs. for box 13		**14** Other	
15	Statutory Deceased employee	Pension Legal Hshld. Subtotal Deferred plan rep. emp.	compensation
PR	123456789	1111.11	.00
16 State Employer's state I.D. #	**17** State wages, tips, etc.		**18** State income tax
19 Locality name Bedrock	**20** Local wages, tips, etc. 1111.11		**21** Local income tax .00

Form W-2 Wage and Tax Statement   Dept. of the Treasury -- IRS
This information is being furnished to the IRS. If you are required to file a tax return, a negligence penalty/other sanction may be imposed on you if this income is taxable and you fail to report it.

FIGURE 10.1 A W-2 Income Tax Form.

EXTENDING OBJECT-CENTERED DESIGN

In chapter 3 we extended object-centered design to situations where some operation needed to solve a problem is not predefined:

1. Identify the behavior required to solve the problem
2. Identify the objects
3. Identify the operations

   For each operation that is not predefined:

   a. Define a function to perform that operation

   b. If that operation is reusable, store it in a library

4. Organize the objects and operations into an algorithm

5. Encode the algorithm in C++

6. Test and maintain the program

In the temperature problem, however, we have a situation that is not covered by these rules: the object (a `Temperature`) has a *type* that is not predefined. In chapter 4, we suggested that when an object has multiple attributes, making it impossible to represent it with predefined types, a C++ class can be used to create a new type that has those attributes. Thus we need to extend object-centered design again to cover this new situation:

1. Identify the behavior required to solve the problem

2. Identify the objects

    For each object that cannot be directly represented with the existing types:

        a. Design and build a class to represent such objects

        b. Store it in a class library

3. Identify the operations

    For each operation that is not predefined:

        If the operation is an operation on a class object from step 2a,

            Design and build a class function member to perform that operation

        Otherwise

        a. Design and build a non-member function to perform that operation

        b. If the operation is reusable, store it in a library

4. Organize the objects and operations into an algorithm

5. Encode the algorithm in C++

6. Test and maintain the program

For the temperature problem, therefore, we should create a `Temperature` class containing both the scale and degrees of an arbitrary temperature and function members to perform temperature conversions. Given such a class, solving the problem is straightforward.

OBJECT-CENTERED DESIGN

Behavior.   Our program should display on the screen a prompt for a temperature (degrees and scale), and should then read a temperature from the keyboard. It should then display the Fahrenheit, Celsius, and Kelvin equivalents of that temperature.

Objects.   We can identify the following objects in our problem:

Description	Kind	Type	Name
A temperature	varying	Temperature	*the Temperature*
Its Fahrenheit equivalent	varying	Temperature	none
Its Celsius equivalent	varying	Temperature	none
Its Kelvin equivalent	varying	Temperature	none

Operations. The operations needed to solve this problem are as follows:

i. Display a string on the screen

ii. Read a *Temperature* from an `istream`

iii. Determine the Fahrenheit equivalent of a *Temperature*

iv. Determine the Celsius equivalent of a *Temperature*

v. Determine the Kelvin equivalent of a *Temperature*

vi. Display a *Temperature* to an `ostream`

Here, only operation i is predefined. The `Temperature` class will have function members that perform operations ii–vi.

Algorithm. Assuming the availability of a `Temperature` class that provides operations ii–vi, we can organize the preceding operations into the following algorithm:

Algorithm for Temperature Conversion

1. Via `cout`, display a prompt for a temperature.

2. From `cin`, read a temperature into *theTemperature*.

3. Via `cout`, display:
    a. the Fahrenheit equivalent of *theTemperature*
    b. the Celsius equivalent of *theTemperature*
    c. the Kelvin equivalent of *theTemperaure*

Coding. Given a `Temperature` class (stored in a header file `Temperature.h`) that provides the required operations, we can encode this algorithm in C++ as shown in Figure 10.2.

FIGURE 10.2   A TEMPERATURE CONVERSION PROGRAM.

```
/* tempconversion2.cpp displays a temperature in Fahrenheit, Celsius,
 * and Kelvin, using class Temperature.
 *
 *  Input:  an arbitrary Temperature
 *  Output: its Fahrenheit, Celsius and Kelvin equivalents
 ******************************************************************/

#include <iostream.h>                     // >>, <<, cin, cout
#include "Temperature.h"                  // Temperature

int main()
{
   cout << "This program shows the Fahrenheit, Celsius, and\n"
           "Kelvin equivalents of a temperature.\n\n";

   char response;
   Temperature theTemperature;            // construction
```

```
      do
      {
         cout << "Enter a temperature (e.g., 98.6 F): ";

         cin >> theTemperature;                    // input

         cout << "-->"                             // output
              << theTemperature.Fahrenheit()       // its F equivalent
              << " = "
              << theTemperature.Celsius()          // its C equivalent
              << " = "
              << theTemperature.Kelvin()           // its K equivalent
              << endl;          // output

         cout << "\nDo you have more temperatures to convert? ";
         cin >> response;
      }
      while (response == 'Y' || response == 'y');
   }
```

Sample run:

```
This program shows the Fahrenheit, Celsius, and
Kelvin equivalents of a temperature.

Enter a temperature (e.g., 98.6 F): 212 F
-->212 F = 100 C = 373.15 K

Do you have more temperatures to convert? Y
Enter a temperature (e.g., 98.6 F): 0 C
-->32 F = 0 C = 273.15 K

Do you have more temperatures to convert? Y
Enter a temperature (e.g., 98.6 F): 100 K
-->-279.67 F = -173.15 C = 100 K

Do you have more temperatures to convert? N
```

We will design and build the Temperature class in the following sections, and use it to illustrate the principles of class design.

10.2 DESIGNING A CLASS

As with programs, creating a class consists of two phases:

1. The design phase in which we plan the class
2. The implementation phase in which we encode this design in C++.

This section explores the first phase. Sections 10.3 and 10.4 will examine the implementation phase.

CLASS DESIGN

Designing a class consists of identifying two things:

▶ its **behavior:** the *operations* that can be applied to a class object

▶ its **attributes:** the *data* that must be stored to characterize a class object

The behavior is usually identified first, because it is often not obvious what the attributes of the class should be, and identifying the class behavior can sometimes clarify them. Also, if the behaviors are identified first, before any of the attribute details are fixed, they will be independent of any particular details of how the attributes are implemented. This *independence from implementation details* is very important in good class design.

THE EXTERNAL AND INTERNAL PERSPECTIVES

Up to now, our approach to programming has been that of an observer looking from outside the program into its details. Since we reside outside the program, this is a natural way to begin, and as long as we are merely *using* predefined classes, this **external perspective** is adequate.

One of the basic ideas in class design is **object autonomy,** embodied in **the I-can-do-it-myself principle,** which means that an object should carry within itself the ability to perform its operations. That is, rather than viewing a class operation as manipulation of an object by a program, object autonomy views a class operation as an object taking an action. To incorporate the I-can-do-it-myself principle into the design of a class, we must shift our perspective from that of an external observer to that of the object being designed. More precisely, we want to think through our design as though *we are the object.* The resulting approach describes an object in first person terminology, and is called the **internal perspective.**

As a simple illustration of the difference, rather than referring to the `Temperature` data members as *its* degrees and *its* scale (which imply we are outside, looking in), we will refer to them as *my* degrees and *my* scale (indicating that we are the object, looking out). This approach leads to a natural implemention of the I-can-do-it-myself principle, resulting in an autonomous object.

In the sections that follow, we will use *both* perspectives. When working in a program and using a class, we will use the external perspective. When working inside a class or building its function members, we will use the internal perspective.

Temperature BEHAVIOR

From an internal perspective, a `Temperature` object must provide the following operations if the program in Figure 10.2 is to work:

1. Define myself *implicitly* by initializing my degrees and scale with default values
2. Read a temperature from an `istream` and store it in my data members
3. Compute the Fahrenheit temperature equivalent to me
4. Compute the Celsius temperature equivalent to me
5. Compute the Kelvin temperature equivalent to me
6. Display my degrees and scale using an `ostream`

Although these operations suffice to solve the problem at hand, designing a reuseable class involves identifying other operations that a user of the class is likely to need. To that end, we might extend our list with the following operations:

7. Define myself *explicitly* by initializing my degrees and scale with specified values
8. Identify my number of degrees
9. Identify my scale
10. Compute my temperature plus a given number of degrees
11. Compute my temperature minus a given number of degrees
12. Compare myself to another `Temperature` object using any of the six relational operators ($==, !=, <, >, <=, >=$)
13. Assign another `Temperature` value to me using the assignment operator ($=$)

This is not an exhaustive list, but it is a good start and will serve to introduce the details of class implementation. Other operations can be added later.

The last operation, assignment, is already provided. For any class we define, the C++ compiler creates a *default assignment operation,* so that a statement like

```
temp2 = temp1;
```

can be used to copy the data members of `temp1` into `temp2`. We must implement the other operations ourselves as function members, as described in section 10.4.

Temperature ATTRIBUTES

To identify a class' attributes, it is a good idea to go through the list of behaviors and identify what information each of them requires. If the same information is required by several different operations, then such information is probably one of the object's attributes.

For example, if we examine the first twelve operations in our list, operations i and vi–xi indicate that, from an internal perspective, a `Temperature` object has the following attributes:

1. my degrees, and
2. my scale.

In fact, these are the only attributes needed for class `Temperature`. For other classes, a complete set of attributes may not be evident at the outset. In this case, others can be added later, when the implementation of an operation requires an attribute not on the list.

10.3 IMPLEMENTING CLASS ATTRIBUTES

Once we have a design for a class, we can use it as a blueprint for implementing the class. Since we want the class to be reuseable, it is declared in a library header file (e.g., `Temperature.h`) and the nontrivial operations are usually defined in a separately-compiled implementation file (e.g., `Temperature.cpp`). As suggested in chapter 3, the documentation for the class and its function members are commonly put in a separate documentation file (e.g., `Temperature.doc`).

Given a class design that includes its attributes, the first task is to define objects to represent those attributes. For our `Temperature` class, we can represent the number of degrees with a real object, and the scale with a character object. Thus, in `Temperature.h`, we write:

```
/* Temperature.h is the header file for class Temperature.
 * ...
 ************************************************************/

double myDegrees;
char    myScale;        // 'F', 'C', or 'K'
```

These will become the **data members** of our `Temperature` class. We will begin the names of data members with the prefix `my` to indicate that these are attributes of the class, and to reflect our internal perspective. And as with all identifiers, the name of a data member should be *self-documenting,* describing the attribute being stored.

Implementation Decisions. We could have used `string` to define `myScale` if we wanted to store the entire name of the scale, but we chose `char` instead because temperatures are usually written using a single character for the scale (e.g., 98.6 F, 100 C, 273 K). The best choice in some situations may not be clear, but a decision must be made before we can proceed. Such implementation decisions can always be revised later if they prove unwise.

ENCAPSULATION

Once we have defined objects for the data members of our class, we can actually create the class by wrapping these objects in a **class declaration** (again, in `Temperature.h`):

```
class Temperature
{
 public:

                                        // to be filled in later
 private:

    double myDegrees;
    char    myScale;                    // 'F', 'C', or 'K'
};
```

Don't forget the semicolon after the closing curly brace. Like all declarations, a class declaration must be terminated by a semicolon.

This declaration creates a new type named `Temperature`. If we use this type to declare objects as in

```
#include "Temperature.h"
      .
      .
      .
Temperature temp1,
            temp2;
```

then `temp1` and `temp2` are two distinct `Temperature` objects, each containing two data members: a `double` named `myDegrees` and a `char` named `myScale`. We might picture these objects as follows:

temp1   myDegrees [   ]   temp2   myDegrees [   ]
          myScale [ ]   myScale [ ]

Wrapping the data members in a class declaration and then using the class as a type to declare an object makes it possible for an object to store values of different types. In the vocabulary of programming languages, we say that class `Temperature` **encapsulates** the `double` data member `myDegrees` and the `char` data member `myScale`. Encapsulation allows a single object to store values of different types.

INFORMATION HIDING

We have defined `myScale` as a `char`, but we might decide in the future to define it as a `string` so it could store the name of a temperature scale instead of only its first letter. The possibility that a class' data members may be revised is the reason for preceding the data members with the keyword `private`. If we omit the `private` specifier, a program can directly access the data member `myScale` as in

```
if ( temp1.myScale  == 'F')
    // do something with Fahrenheit temp1
```

However, if we were to later change the type of `myScale`, this revision would *break* that program, making it necessary to rewrite some of it as well. In some situations, the required revisions may be so extensive that software is not ready on time and/or is more expensive than was predicted, the obvious result of which is a loss of sales.

The root of the problem is allowing a programmer to access a class' data members. By making them *private*, we prevent such direct access. If, for example, `myScale` is private and a program tries to access it as above, then an error message such as

```
Member 'myScale' of class 'Temperature' is private
```

will be generated.

This aspect of class design is called **information hiding.** By preventing a program from directly accessing the data members of a class, we hide that information, thus removing the temptation to access the data members directly.

> *It is good programming style to hide all data members of a class by making them **private.***

Once we have the data members encapsulated and hidden, we are almost ready to begin implementing the class operations.

CLASS INVARIANTS

Before defining class operations, we should identify any restrictions on the values of the data members of our class. For example, we might stipulate that the only valid values for the data member `myScale` will be the characters F, C, or K. If we identify and specify such restrictions at the outset, then we can implement the various class operations in a way that ensures that they are observed.

To document such limitations concisely, we usually define a condition (i.e., a boolean expression) that describes the restriction. For example, we might write

```
myScale == 'F' || myScale == 'C' || myScale == 'K'
```

to describe our restriction on the value of `myScale`.

Once we have a description of each restriction governing the data members, we then want to make certain that nothing we write violates that condition—we want it to be `true`, both before and after each call to a class operation. Because this condition will be true throughout the class, it is called a **class invariant.** When such an invariant can be defined, it is good practice to record it in both the class documentation file and in the header file near the data member(s) involved.

CONDITIONAL COMPILATION AND THE CLASS "WRAPPER"

Whenever a program stored in a file is compiled, it is first examined by a special program called the **preprocessor.** The preprocessor scans through the file doing some preliminary analysis before the file is passed on to the compiler itself. For example, the preprocessor strips all comments from the program so that the compiler need not spend time finding them, only to ignore them. Another task of the preprocessor is to process all **preprocessor directives,** which are lines that begin with a # character such as

```
#include FileName
```

When it encounters this directive, the preprocessor finds the file named `FileName` and inserts it at that point in the program.

For large projects consisting of many library files, it is customary for each file to include whatever class declarations it needs. This means that the same class could be declared in several different places in a project, and this results in an error because C++ does not permit a class to be declared more than once.

However, no error results if the header file `<iostream.h>` is included more than once. Why? Because the contents of `<iostream.h>` are wrapped in directives that basically tell the preprocessor, *"If this is the first time you have seen this class, go ahead and process the declaration. If you have seen it before, skip the declaration."*

Thus, before we proceed to implement the class operations, we need to surround the class `Temperature` with directives that tell the preprocessor to do the same for class `Temperature`:

```
#ifndef TEMPERATURE
#define TEMPERATURE

class Temperature
{
 public:
                            // to be filled in later

 private:
    double myDegrees;
    char    myScale;        // 'F', 'C', or 'K'
};
```

```
#endif
```

These are called **conditional-compilation directives** because of what they do. The directive

```
#ifndef TEMPERATURE
```

instructs the preprocessor, *"If* `TEMPERATURE` *is not defined, then continue processing as usual. Otherwise, skip everything between here and the first* `#endif` *directive you encounter."*[1] Because `TEMPERATURE` is undefined the first time the preprocessor examines the file, it proceeds on to the next line. Here it encounters the directive

```
#define TEMPERATURE
```

which defines the identifier `TEMPERATURE`. The preprocessor then continues and processes the class declaration and passes it on to the compiler.

If the preprocessor should encounter `Temperature.h` a second time, the first thing it sees is the directive

```
#ifndef TEMPERATURE
```

This time, however, `TEMPERATURE` is defined, and so the preprocessor skips everything between that point and the `#endif` directive.

 The result is that *the class declaration is only processed once, regardless of how many different files include* `Temperature.h`. Every class should be wrapped in these directives to prevent redeclaration errors if the header file is included more

---

[1] The compiler will also stop skipping text if it encounters a `#else` or `#elif` directive, which behave like the `else` or the `else if` in an `if` statement.

than once in a project. Customarily, the identifier used with the `#ifndef` and `#define` directives (`TEMPERATURE` in this case) is the name of the class in all uppercase letters.

10.4 IMPLEMENTING CLASS OPERATIONS

Once a class' attributes are defined, encapsulated, hidden, and wrapped, we are ready to begin implementing the class operations. This is done using **function members.** We will begin our study of how they are defined by looking at a simple example: an output function that displays a `Temperature` via an `ostream` (operation vi in our list). It is a good practice to define such output functions early, because displaying the data members of a class object can help with checking the correctness of the remaining operations.

Temperature OUTPUT

From an external perspective, the purpose of an output function `Print()` is to allow a programmer to display the values that make up a class object. In our case, a programmer should be able to write

```
temp1.Print(cout);
```

to display the degrees and scale in a `Temperature` object `temp1`, and write

```
temp2.Print(cout);
```

to display the degrees and scale of `temp2`.

As an autonomous object, a `Temperature` should be able to display itself. From an internal perspective, a call to `Print()` can thus be viewed as a **message** the program is sending to *you* (a `Temperature` object), with `cout` as an argument—like someone else telling you

>   *"Hey you! Print yourself using* `cout`.*"*

The definition of `Print()` must therefore provide the instructions that I (a `Temperature` object) apply to my data members to perform the operation.

Applying object-centered design from the internal perspective gives the following specification for the operation's behavior:

Receive: *out,* the `ostream` to which information is to be written

Output: `myDegrees` followed by a space and then `myScale`

Pass back: *out,* with `myDegrees`, a space, and `myScale` inserted into it

It is important that the specification of a function member be phrased from the internal perspective, because we want our operations to reflect the I-can-do-it-myself approach: As a `Temperature` object, when I receive a `Print(out)` message, I insert the values stored in `myDegrees` and `myScale` into *out.*

Figure 10.3 shows a definition of this operation. Because of the simplicity of this function, we define it as an `inline` function. This definition is stored in the header file `Temperature.h`, after the class declaration.

FIGURE 10.3   DISPLAYING A `Temperature`.

```
// ...  Class declaration goes here ...


// -------- Output function member -------------------------------------

inline void Temperature::Print(ostream & out) const
{
    out << myDegrees << ' ' << myScale;
}
```

From an external perspective, calling this function will display the data members `myDegrees` and `myScale` of the `Temperature` object to which the `Print()` message is being sent, so the call

```
temp1.Print(cout);
```

will display the data members of `temp1` via `cout`, while the call

```
temp2.Print(cout);
```

will display the data members of `temp2`. At the end of this section, we will see how to overload the output operator (`<<`) to display a `Temperature` value in the usual manner.

Note that as a `Temperature` function member, `Print()` must be called using **dot notation.** Put differently, `Print()` must be sent as a message to a `Temperature` object. If we attempt to call `Print()` without using dot notation,

```
Print(cout);            // ERROR!
```

the compiler will generate an error, because we have not specified a `Temperature` object to receive the message.

In this first look at the definition of a function member, we introduced a number of new features, and we will now look at each of these in more detail.

Full Function Names. The first new feature is the name of the function member:

```
inline void  Temperature::Print (ostream & out) const
```

In the definition of a function member, *preceding the name of the function by the name of a class and the* **scope operator** (`::`) *informs the compiler that a function member of that class is being defined.* The resulting name is called the **fully-qualified name** of the function (or **full name** for short).

 It is important to use the full name in the definition of function members, because *function members can access the private data members of their class, but normal functions cannot.* If the full name is not used in a function member's definition, as in

```
inline void Print(ostream & out) const   // Not a function member
{
    out << myDegrees << ' ' << myScale;   // ERROR!
}
```

the compiler views this as a normal (non-member) function, and errors like

```
Identifier 'myDegrees' is not defined
Identifier 'myScale' is not defined
```

will be generated, since the private data members of a class are invisible to a non-member function.

Full names are also important because they permit function members of different classes to have the same name and signature. For example, we might declare classes X, Y, and Z, each having its own Print() function member. By using the full name to define each Print() function, the compiler can distinguish one function definition from another:

```
void X::Print(ostream & out)
{
     // send data members of X to out...
}
void Y::Print(ostream & out)
{
     // send data members of Y to out...
}
void Z::Print(ostream & out)
{
     // send data members of Z to out...
}
```

Constant Function Members. The next new feature in Print() is the keyword const at the end of the function heading:

```
inline void Temperature::Print(ostream & out) const
```

This informs the compiler that Print() is a **constant function member** of class Temperature, which means that it may not change any of the data members. Any attempt to modify a data member in this function will be caught by the compiler as an error. *All function members that do not alter the data members of the class should be declared as* const *functions.*

Before a function member's definition will compile correctly, a prototype of that function must be stored inside the class declaration. If the function member is to be visible outside of the class, this prototype must be stored in the public section of the class. Also, since the Print() prototype refers to the type ostream, we must include the iostream header file:

```
#include <iostream.h>                      // ostream, ...

class Temperature
{
 public:
   void Print(ostream & out) const;
 private:
   double myDegrees;
   char   myScale;                         // 'F', 'C', or 'K'
};
```

Note that it is not necessary to specify `inline` or the full name of the function within the class itself because *prototypes within a class are, by default, both* `inline` *and function members.* Keeping these prototypes simple reduces clutter within the class declaration and thus increases readability. For the same reason, the function members of a class should be documented in a separate file. To complete our function `Print()`, therefore, we add documentation for it to the library's documentation file (`Temperature.doc`).

Of course, before the `Print()` function is of any use, the data members `myDegrees` and `myScale` must contain values. We therefore turn our attention to two functions that can be used to initialize these data members.

THE DEFAULT-VALUE CONSTRUCTOR

As we have seen, a `Temperature` definition

```
Temperature temp1,
             temp2;
```

defines `temp1` and `temp2` as objects that might be pictured as follows:

```
temp1                           temp2
      myDegrees [         ]           myDegrees [         ]
        myScale [  ]                    myScale [  ]
```

The data members of these objects remain undefined, because the compiler has no way (yet) of knowing what initial values to provide for them. What we would like is for such definitions to define `temp1` and `temp2` with some default initial value (e.g., 0 degrees Celsius):

```
temp1                           temp2
      myDegrees [0.0]                 myDegrees [0.0]
        myScale [C]                     myScale [C]
```

Constructor Functions. C++ allows such initialization behavior to be performed by a function member. More precisely, to initialize the data members of a class, C++ allows us to define special function members called **constructor functions.** *The name of a constructor function is always the same as the name of the class.*

To be autonomous, a `Temperature` object should be able to initialize itself. Applying the I- can-do-it-myself principle, a constructor function defines the sequence of actions that I (a `Temperature` object) take to initialize my data members when I am defined. Applying object-centered design from this internal perspective gives the following specification for the behavior of this default-value constructor:

Postcondition: `myDegrees == 0.0 && myScale == 'C'`

We specify the behavior of a constructor function using a **postcondition,** a boolean expression that must be `true` when the function terminates. A postcondition is needed to specify the behavior, because *a constructor function cannot return anything to its caller.*

Figure 10.4 shows the definition of a default-value constructor for class `Temperature`. Because of the simplicity of this function, we define it as `inline`, and place its definition in `Temperature.h`, after the declaration of class `Temperature`.

FIGURE 10.4   THE `Temperature` DEFAULT-VALUE CONSTRUCTOR.

```
// -------- Default-value constructor ---------------------------------

inline Temperature::Temperature()
{
    myDegrees = 0.0;
    myScale = 'C';
}
```

Here again, we see some new features. The first is that there is no return type between `inline` and the function's full name because *constructor functions have no return type,* not even `void`. As an initialization function, a constructor never returns anything to its caller. Its sole purpose is to initialize the class' data members.

Next comes the full name of the function, in which the first `Temperature` is the name of the class of which the function is a member, `::` is the scope operator, and then follows the name of the function.

```
inline  Temperature::Temperature()
```

Since the name of a constructor is always the same as the name of its class, the name of the function is also `Temperature`.

Because a constructor function modifies the data members of the class (by initializing them), it is not a constant function member, so there is no `const` following its heading. From the external perspective, the body of the function simply assigns initial values to the data members of the object to which this message is being sent.

We also store a prototype of this function in the public section of the class declaration:

```
class Temperature
{
 public:
   Temperature();
   void Print(ostream & out) const;
 private:
   double myDegrees;
   char   myScale;        // 'F', 'C', or 'K'
};
```

As before, we omit the `inline` and use the normal name of the function instead of its full name. We also add its documentation to `Temperature.doc`.

Given this much, a programmer can now write a short program to test the class declaration and function member definitions:

```
#include <iostream.h>
#include "Temperature.h"

int main()
{
    Temperature temp1;        // the compiler sends temp1 the
                              //  'initialize yourself' message
    temp1.Print(cout);
}
```

When this program is executed, it will display the values

```
0 C
```

This output is produced because whenever the C++ compiler processes the definition of a class object, it searches the class for a constructor it can use to initialize that object. If it finds such a constructor, it uses a call to that function to initialize the object.[2] *The constructor function is automatically called by the compiler whenever a class object is defined.* For this reason, *always provide one or more constructor functions when building a class.*

EXPLICIT-VALUE CONSTRUCTORS

The constructor function we just defined only allows us to initialize a `Temperature` object to the value 0 degrees Celsius. It would be more useful to allow initializations to arbitrary temperatures. This can be accomplished by overloading the constructor with a second definition that receives the initial values via its parameters. From the internal perspective, object-centered design gives us the following specification for the operation's behavior:

Receive: *initialDegrees,* a `double`
                  initialScale, a `char`

Precondition: *initialScale* is one of {'f', 'c', 'k', 'F', 'C', 'K'}

Postcondition: `myDegrees` == *initialDegrees* && `myScale` == *initialScale* in uppercase

Unlike the default-value constructor, this function receives its initialization values from the caller, and so our constructor must supply parameters to hold those values. For user convenience, we will allow the scale to be in either upper or lower case, making six valid values for `myScale`: `'f'`, `'c'`, `'k'`, `'F'`, `'C'`, `'K'`. Since there is the possibility of the caller passing an invalid value for *initialScale* and violating the precondition, the function must check the validity of *initialScale* before proceeding with the initialization. To simplify this checking and to assure that the class invariant holds, our function will first convert *initialScale* to uppercase, if necessary.

---

[2] In the case of an `inline` constructor, it actually inserts statements to perform the initialization specified by the body of the constructor:

```
temp1.myDegrees = 0.0;
temp1.myScale = 'C';
```

Figure 10.5 presents a definition of this function. Because of its complexity, it should *not* be designated `inline`. Instead, its definition should be stored in the class implementation file (`Temperature.cpp`) so that it can be compiled separately. Note that the full name of this constructor is exactly the same as the full name of the default-value constructor in Figure 10.4. Like any function, a constructor can be overloaded with multiple definitions, so long as the signature of each definition is distinct.

 FIGURE 10.5   THE `Temperature` EXPLICIT-VALUE CONSTRUCTOR.

```
/* Temperature.cpp contains the definitions of Temperature operations.
 *   ...
 ***************************************************************/

#include "Temperature.h"                  // class Temperature

// -------- Explicit-value constructor --------------------------------

#include <ctype.h>                         // islower(), toupper()
#include <stdlib.h>                        // exit()

Temperature::Temperature(double initialDegrees, char initialScale)
{
   if (islower(initialScale))             // if scale is lowercase
   initScale = toupper(initialScale);     //   convert it to uppercase

   switch (initialScale)
   {
      case 'F': case 'C': case 'K':        // if scale is valid
         myDegrees = initialDegrees;       //   proceed with
         myScale = initialScale;           //   initialization
         break;
      default:                             // otherwise, error msg
         cerr << "\n*** Temperature constructor received invalid scale "
              << initialScale << endl;
         exit(1);
   }
}
```

Note also that although 0 degrees Kelvin (absolute zero) is the lowest possible temperature, we have neglected to check that the temperature received from the caller is at least this great. Adding this check is left as an exercise.

To use this function, we must place its prototype in the public portion of class Temperature:

```
class Temperature
{
 public:
   Temperature();
   Temperature(double initialDegrees, char initialScale);
   void Print(ostream & out) const;
```

```
   private:
     double myDegrees;
     char   myScale;        // 'F', 'C', or 'K'
};
```

We also add its documentation to Temperature.doc.

Given this prototype, a programmer can now write

```
#include <iostream.h>
#include "Temperature.h"

int main()
{
    Temperature temp1(98.6, 'F'),
                temp2;

    temp1.Print(cout);
    temp2.Print(cout);
}
```

When this program is compiled and linked to the Temperature object file, the values

```
98.6 F
0 C
```

will be displayed when the program is executed. In the definitions

```
Temperature temp1(98.6, 'F'),
            temp2;
```

the object temp1 is constructed using the explicit-value constructor, and temp2 is constructed using the default-value constructor. These objects are thus initialized as follows:

Class Object Initialization. The syntax of the explicit-value constructor deserves comment. As noted earlier, when the C++ compiler processes the definition of a class object, it searches the class for a constructor it can use to initialize the object. When it sees a "normal" class object definition (without arguments),

```
Temperature temp2;
```

the compiler searches the class for a constructor function that has no parameters. Finding one, it uses that constructor to perform the initialization.

When the compiler sees a class object definition for which arguments are specified,

```
Temperature temp1(98.6, 'F');
```

it searches the class for a constructor function whose signature (i.e., list of parameter types) matches the types of the arguments. When it finds such a function, the compiler uses that constructor to perform the initialization.

This syntax should not seem completely unfamiliar. In chapter 8, we saw that an `ifstream` object can be initialized with the name of a file; for example,

```
ifstream inStream("weather.dat");
```

Such a statement is using an `ifstream` explicit-value constructor to open the stream to the file whose name it is passed as an argument.

According to the C++ standard, any object can be initialized in this way. Instead of writing

```
double sum = 0.0;
char middleInitial = 'C';
```

we could instead write

```
double sum(0.0);
char middleInitial('C');
```

The C++ standard actually suggests that the latter approach is the *preferred* way to initialize an object. The synax using = is simply provided as a convenient shorthand to this approach.

Now that we have constructors that allow `Temperature` objects to be initialized, we proceed to build the two simplest function members of class `Temperature`.

ACCESSOR FUNCTIONS

An **accessor function** is a function member that allows a programmer to read, but not modify, some attribute of the class. From an external perspective, a programmer should be able to send the message

```
temp1.Degrees()
```

to access the number of degrees in a `Temperature` object `temp1`, and send the message

```
temp1.Scale()
```

to access the scale of `temp1`.

An autonomous `Temperature` object will know how many degrees it has. From an internal perspective, when I (a `Temperature`) receive the `Degrees()` message, I should return the number of degrees I have. We thus have this simple specification for the behavior of `Degrees()`:

> **Return:** `myDegrees`

The specification of the behavior of `Scale()` is similar:

> **Return:** `myScale`

Figure 10.6 shows the definitions of these function members. Because of the simplicity of these functions, we define them as `inline` functions and store their definitions in the class header file `Temperature.h`. Because these function members read, but do not modify the data members, they are designated as `const` function members.

FIGURE 10.6   Temperature ACCESSOR FUNCTIONS.

```
// -------- Degrees extractor ----------------------------------------

inline double Temperature::Degrees() const
{
   return myDegrees;
}


// -------- Scale extractor ------------------------------------------

inline char Temperature::Scale() const
{
   return myScale;
}
```

As with all function members, prototypes of these functions must be stored in the class declaration:

```
class Temperature
{
 public:
   Temperature();
   Temperature(double initialDegrees, char initialScale);

   double Degrees() const;
   char Scale() const;

   void Print(ostream & out) const;
 private:
   double myDegrees;
   char myScale;          // 'F', 'C', or 'K'
};
```

 It is our practice to group function prototypes within a class declaration according to purpose, with blank lines separating each group. For example, constructors, accessors, and I/O functions all have distinct purposes, so we group their prototypes accordingly.

From an external perspective, when the `Degrees()` message is sent to a `Temperature` object, it will return the `myDegrees` data member of that object. To illustrate, given the declarations

```
Temperature temp1(98.6, 'F'),
            temp2;
```

the expression

```
temp1.Degrees()
```

will access the value of the `myDegrees` data member of `temp1` (i.e., 98.6), while the expression

```
temp2.Degrees()
```

will access the value of the `myDegrees` data member of `temp2` (i.e., 0.0). The `Scale()` function behaves in a similar manner using the `myScale` data member.

Temperature INPUT

Next, we provide a function member to read a `Temperature` value from an `istream`. We want a statement such as

```
temp2.Read(cin);
```

that will read a number and a character from `cin` and store them in `temp2.my-Degrees` and `temp2.myScale`, respectively.

From an internal perspective, the definition of `Read()` contains the instructions that I (as an autonomous `Temperature` object) must follow to input a temperature. From this perspective, object-centered design gives the following specification:

Receive:	*in,* an `istream` containing a `double` and a `char`
Input:	*inDegrees,* the `double` value, and *inScale,* the `char` value
Precondition:	*inScale* is one of {'f', 'c', 'k', 'F', 'C', 'K'}
Pass back:	*in,* with *inDegrees* and *inScale* extracted from it
Postcondition:	`myDegrees == ` *inDegrees* `&& myScale == ` *inScale*

For user convenience, we accept the scale in either upper or lowercase, and convert lowercase entries to uppercase to satisfy the class invariant. To guard against an invalid scale being entered, we must check that the entered scale satisfies the precondition before modifying the data members. If the scale is invalid, we will set the fail bit in the `istream`, and leave further corrective action up to the caller.

Due to the complexity of this function, we do not define it as `inline`, and so this definition should be stored in `Temperature.cpp`, for separate compilation. Since this function modifies the `Temperature` function members, it is not defined as a constant function member. Figure 10.7 presents an implementation of this function.

FIGURE 10.7   **Temperature INPUT.**

```
// -------- Temperature Input ------------------------------------------

void Temperature::Read(istream & in)
{
   double inDegrees;                    // temporary variables to
   char inScale;                        //  store the input values

   in >> inDegrees >> inScale;          // read the values from the stream

   if (islower(inScale))                // if scale is lower case
      inScale = toupper(inScale);       //   convert it to upper case
```

```
switch(inScale)
{
   case 'F': case 'C': case 'K':   // if scale is valid
      myScale = inScale;           //    assign input values
      myDegrees = inDegrees;       //    to data members
      break;
   default:                        // otherwise
      in.set_state(ios::fail);     //    set fail bit in stream, and
}                                  //    leave data members unchanged
}
```

As with the explicit-value constructor, we leave checking that the temperature entered is at least 0 degrees Kelvin (absolute zero) as an exercise.

As a function member, a prototype of this function must be added to the class declaration:

```
class Temperature
{
 public:
    Temperature();
    Temperature(double initialDegrees, char initialScale);

    double Degrees() const;
    char Scale() const;

    void Read(istream & in);
    void Print(ostream & out) const;
 private:
    double myDegrees;
    char   myScale;        // 'F', 'C', or 'K'
};
```

We finish by adding the documentation for this function to the library documentation file.

Given this function prototype, a programmer can now use Read() to input temperatures from an istream or from an ifstream. For example, to build an input loop, we could use any temperature with an invalid scale as a sentinel value:

```
Temperature temp1;

for (;;)
{
   cout << "Enter a temperature, as in 98.6 F (0 A to quit): ";
   temp1.Read(cin);

   if (cin.fail()) break;

   // ... process the temperature in temp1 ...
}
```

Once this fragment is compiled and linked to the Temperature object file, a series of temperature values can be read from the keyboard and processed. At the end of this section, we will see how to overload the input operator (>>) to read `Temperature` values in the usual manner.

CONVERSION FUNCTIONS

Next, we examine the function members that produce equivalent temperatures in different scales. We begin with the `Fahrenheit()` function member.

From the internal perspective, I (an autonomous `Temperature` object) should be able to compute the Fahrenheit `Temperature` equivalent to myself. Object-centered design produces the following specification for this behavior:

Return: The Fahrenheit temperature equivalent of myself

Since the particular formula used to compute the return value depends on the current value of `myScale`, a selection statement is needed to select the appropriate formula. The resulting function is sufficiently complex that it is not defined as `inline`. Since the function accesses but does not modify any of the data members, it is defined as a constant function member. Figure 10.8 presents an implementation of this function.

FIGURE 10.8 THE `Fahrenheit()` FUNCTION MEMBER.

```
// -------- The equivalent Fahrenheit temperature ----------------------

Temperature Temperature::Fahrenheit() const
{
   switch (myScale)
   {
      case 'F':
         return Temperature(myDegrees, 'F');
      case 'C':
         return Temperature(myDegrees * 1.8 + 32.0, 'F');
      case 'K':
         return Temperature((myDegrees - 273.15) * 1.8 + 32.0, 'F');
   }
}
```

Note how this function constructs the `Temperature` value to be returned. It calls the explicit-value `Temperature` constructor to build the appropriate value in each case of the `switch` statement. For example, in the first case, the function call

```
Temperature(myDegrees, 'F')
```

passes the arguments `myDegrees` and `'F'` to the explicit-value constructor, which constructs a `Temperature` object from these values and returns it to `Fahrenheit()`. The function `Fahrenheit()` then uses this `Temperature` object as its return value for this case. Note also that because the class invariant ensures that `myScale` is one of `'F'`, `'C'`, or `'K'`, we need not check for other cases.

As always, we must place a prototype of this function member in the class declaration:

```
class Temperature
{
 public:
   Temperature();
   Temperature(double initialDegrees, char initialScale);

   double Degrees() const;
   char Scale() const;

   Temperature Fahrenheit() const;

   void Read(istream & in);
   void Print(ostream & out) const;
 private:
   double myDegrees;
   char   myScale;        // 'F', 'C', or 'K'
};
```

We also add the documentation for this function to the class library documentation file.

A programmer can now write

```
Temperature temp1;                    // default value: 0 C
Temperature temp2 = temp1.Fahrenheit();

temp2.Print(cout);
```

and the Fahrenheit equivalent of 0 degrees Celsius will be displayed:

```
32 F
```

The function members `Celsius()` and `Kelvin()` are similar, and are left as exercises.

OVERLOADING OPERATORS

Each of the preceding operations has been implemented as a "normal" function member, in that its name was an identifier. For some operations (addition, subtraction, relational comparisons, and I/O), it is more convenient to define an *operator* to perform them. Just as normal functions can be overloaded, C++ allows operators to be overloaded for classes. Such **operator overloading** is the topic we examine next.

Temperature Addition (and Subtraction). If `Temperature` objects `temp1` and `temp2` are constructed as

```
Temperature temp1(95.0, 'F'),
            temp2;
```

it would be convenient if we could use the + operator in a statement like

```
temp2 = temp1 + 3.6;
```

to add an amount to `temp1`. Similarly, it would be convenient if we could use the – operator to subtract a specified amount from a `Temperature`.

To add an amount to a temperature using +, we need to overload the + operator. To do this, we define a `Temperature` function member with the name `operator+`. Similarly, to overload the - operator, we define a function member with the name `operator-`. In general, *we can overload an arbitrary operator whose symbol is* Δ *by defining a function with the name* **operatorΔ**, provided it has a signature distinct from that of any existing definition of `operator`Δ.

If `operator+()` is defined as a `Temperature` function member, an expression like

```
temp1 + 3.6
```

is treated by the C++ compiler as a call to this function member:

```
temp1.operator+(3.6)
```

Put differently, such an expression sends the `operator+` message to `temp1` with 3.6 as an argument.

Using object-centered design, we can specify the behavior of `operator+` as follows:

Receive: *rightOperand,* a `double` value

Return: *resultTemp,* a `Temperature` such that
  resultTemp.`myScale == myScale`, and
  resultTemp.`myDegrees == myDegrees +` *rightOperand*

With no precondition to verify, this function is simple enough to write as an `inline` function. Since the function changes the values of the data members in the `Temperature` receiving the message, it should not be defined as a constant function member.

Figure 10.9 presents an implementation of this function. It uses the explicit-value `Temperature` constructor to build the return value.

FIGURE 10.9   OVERLOADING OPERATOR +.

```
// -------- Add a double to a Temperature -----------------------

inline Temperature Temperature::operator+(double rightOperand)
{
   return Temperature(myDegrees + rightOperand, myScale);
}
```

We then add the function prototype to the class declaration,

```
class Temperature
{
 public:
   Temperature();
   Temperature(double initialDegrees, char initialScale);
```

```
      double Degrees() const;
      char Scale() const;

      Temperature Fahrenheit() const;
      // other conversion functions omitted ...

      Temperature operator+(double rightOperand);

      void Read(istream & in);
      void Print(ostream & out) const;
   private:
      double myDegrees;
      char   myScale;        // 'F', 'C', or 'K'
   };
```

and finish by adding documentation to the class library documentation file.
   The definition of the subtraction operation is similar and is left as an exercise.

The Relational Operators. As we noted earlier, it would be useful if we could compare two `Temperature` objects using relational operators. This would allow a computerized thermometer to be programmed with statements like

```
   if (yourTemperature > Temperature(98.6, 'F'))
      cout << "You have a fever!\n";
```

or a computer-controlled thermostat to be programmed with statements like

```
   while (houseTemperature < Temperature(20, 'C'))
      RunFurnace();
```

To permit such operations, we must overload the relational operators for class `Temperature`. We will do this for two of them, the less-than operator (<) and the equality operator (==). The others are similar and are left as exercises.
   As we saw with operator +, if we define `operator<()` as a function member of class `Temperature`, then an expression of the form

```
   houseTemperature < Temperature(20, 'C')
```

will be treated by the compiler as a call to this function member:

```
   houseTemperature.operator<(Temperature(20, 'C'))
```

Intuitively, such a call is sending the less-than message to `houseTemperature`, along with a `Temperature` argument (20 degrees Celsius in this case). From the internal perspective, I (an autonomous `Temperature`) should return `true` if and only if I am less than that `Temperature` argument.
   Using object-centered design, we can specify the behavior of `operator<` as follows:

Receive: *rightOperand,* a `Temperature` value
Return: `true` if and only if I am less than *rightOperand*

Note that an expression like

```
   Temperature(0, 'C') < Temperature(32, 'F')
```

should return `false`, since these two temperatures are in fact equal! The implementation of `operator<` is thus complicated by the possibility that `myScale` and *rightOperand*.`myScale` are not the same. Figure 10.10 shows one way that this function can be implemented:

FIGURE 10.10   OVERLOADING OPERATOR <.

```
// -------- less-than ------------------------------------------------

bool Temperature::operator<(const Temperature & rightOperand) const
{
   Temperature localTemp;              // the equivalent of rightOperand,
                                       //  but in my scale
   switch (myScale)
   {
      case 'C': localTemp = rightOperand.Celsius();
                break;
      case 'F': localTemp = rightOperand.Fahrenheit();
                break;
      case 'K': localTemp = rightOperand.Kelvin();
                break;
   }

   return myDegrees < localTemp.Degrees();
}
```

This implementation of the function resolves the problem of mismatched scales by using a local `Temperature` object `localTemp`, which it sets to the equivalent of `rightOperand` in the same scale as the `Temperature` object receiving the message. Once we have two temperatures in the same scale, we can simply compare their `myDegrees` members using the less-than operation.[3]

The equality (`==`) operator can be overloaded using much the same approach, as shown in Figure 10.11:

FIGURE 10.11   OVERLOADING OPERATOR ==.

```
// -------- equality ------------------------------------------------

bool Temperature::operator==(const Temperature & rightOperand) const
{
   Temperature localTemp;              // the equivalent of rightOperand,
                                       //  but in my scale
```

[3] A class function member can directly access the private data members in class objects it receives as parameters. For readability, we use an object's accessor function, rather than directly accessing its data members.

```
    switch (myScale)
    {
        case 'C': localTemp = rightOperand.Celsius();
                break;
        case 'F': localTemp = rightOperand.Fahrenheit();
                break;
        case 'K': localTemp = rightOperand.Kelvin();
                break;
    }

    return myDegrees == localTemp.Degrees();
}
```

Both of these functions are sufficiently complicated that they should not be defined as `inline`,[4] but should instead be stored in `Temperature.cpp` where they can be separately compiled.

Prototypes for these operations must be placed in the class declaration:

```
class Temperature
{
 public:
    Temperature();
    Temperature(double initialDegrees, char initialScale);

    double Degrees() const;
    char Scale() const;

    Temperature Fahrenheit() const;
    // other conversion prototypes omitted ...

    Temperature operator+(double rightOperand) const;
    // operator- prototype omitted ...

    bool operator<(const Temperature & rightOperand) const;
    bool operator==(const Temperature & rightOperand) const;
    // other relational operator prototypes omitted ...

    void Read(istream & in);
    void Print(ostream & out) const;
 private:
    double myDegrees;
    char    myScale;        // 'F', 'C', or 'K'
};
```

---

[4] The version on our web site presents an alternative, more space-efficient approach. The redundant code is eliminated by isolating it in a private auxiliary `Compare()` function member that, given a `Temperature` *rightOperand*, returns -1 if I am less than *rightOperand*, 0 if we are equal, and $+1$ if I am greater than *rightOperand*. Each relational operator can then be defined in one statement using `Compare()`:

```
inline bool Temperature::operator<(const Temperature & rightOperand)
{
    return Compare(rightOperand) < 0;
}
```

Documentation for these functions is placed in `Temperature.doc`.

The remaining relational operators can be overloaded in a similar fashion and are left as exercises.

The I/O Operators. We have already seen that the function members `Read()` and `Print()` provide a way to perform `Temperature` I/O. However, these functions do not coordinate well with the normal iostream I/O operators. For example, to use `Read()` and `Print()`, we would have to rewrite the program in Figure 10.2 as follows:

```
int main()
{
   cout << "This program shows the Fahrenheit, Celsius, and\n"
           "Kelvin equivalents of a temperature.\n";

   char response;
   Temperature theTemperature;                    // construction

   do
   {
      cout << "\nEnter a temperature (e.g., 98.6 F): ";
      theTemperature.Read(cin);                    // input

      cout << "\n-->";                             // output
      theTemperature.Fahrenheit().Print(cout);   // its F equivalent
      cout << " = ";
      theTemperature.Celsius().Print(cout);       // its C equivalent
      cout << " = ";
      theTemperature.Kelvin().Print(cout);        // its K equivalent
      cout << endl;

      cout << "Do you have more temperatures to convert? ";
      cin >> response;

   }
   while (response == 'Y' || response == 'y');
}
```

Note the **chaining** of function member calls in the statement

```
theTemperature.Fahrenheit().Print(cout);
```

The chained function calls are processed from left to right. First, the `Fahrenheit()` message is sent to `theTemperature`, which returns a `Temperature` object. The `Print()` message is then sent to this `Temperature` object, which displays itself.

This method of outputting `Temperature` values works correctly, but it is far less elegant than the approach in Figure 10.2, which used the output operator (`<<`) to insert a `Temperature` into an `ostream`. We will now overload `operator<<` using our `Print()` function, and overload `operator>>` using `Read()`. Doing so does not require much code, but some subtle issues must be addressed.

The first issue is that we cannot define `operator<<` as a function member of a class. To see why, recall that if an operator whose symbol is Δ is defined as a function member of a class, and *object* is an object of that class, then the expression

    object Δ *Operand*

is treated by the compiler as

    object.operatorΔ(*Operand*)

If this observation is applied to the output expression

    cout << someTemperature

then it should be evident that operator<< must be defined as a function member of class ostream, not class Temperature. This requires that we add a new prototype for operator<< to the declaration of ostream, but on most platforms, users are not permitted to modify the header files that come with the system.

Fortunately, C++ provides a way around this problem. If the operator whose symbol is Δ is defined as a normal function—one that acts upon its operands via parameters—and not as a function member of the class, then the expression

    object Δ *operand*

is treated by the compiler as the function call

    operatorΔ(*object*, *operand*)

More precisely, if we wish to call

    cout << temp1;

then we need to define a non-member function operator<< that the compiler can call as

    operator<<(cout, temp1);

We can thus define operator<< as a non-member function, using an external perspective. Using object-centered design gives the following specification of the function's behavior:

Receive:	*out,* the ostream to which values are being written
	theTemp, the Temperature object whose value is being written
Output:	*theTemp*.myDegrees and *theTemp*.myScale
Pass back:	*out,* containing the inserted values
Return:	*out,* for use by a subsequent output operation

Figure 10.12 presents the implementation of operator<<. Because most of the work is done by the Print() function member of parameter theTemp, the function is simple enough to define as inline, and so we store it in the class header file Temperature.h. Because it is a normal (i.e., non-member) function, no prototype is placed within the class declaration.

FIGURE 10.12 OVERLOADING OPERATOR <<.

```
// -------- ostream output ------------------------------------------

inline ostream & operator<<(ostream & out, const Temperature & theTemp)
{
    theTemp.Print(out);   // tell theTemp to print itself
    return out;
}
```

This function is deceptively simple. It seemingly just receives the `ostream` and `Temperature` operands, and calls the `Print()` function of the `Temperature` operand. Because `Print()` inserts values into its `ostream` operand `out`, `out` is defined as a reference parameter.

However, the function also returns `out` and we see that the return type of the function is `ostream &`, something we have not seen before. These are the two subtle parts of the function, and we will deal with them separately.

The `<<` operator returns *out* so that output operations can be chained. That is, when we insert two `Temperature` objects `temp1` and `temp2` into `cout`,

```
cout << temp1 << temp2;
```

there are two different calls to `operator<<`, and these are executed from left to right. To distinguish them, suppose we number the output operators as follows:

```
cout <<₁ temp1 <<₂ temp2;
```

In executing these functions from left to right, the compiler treats them as nested function calls, with $<<_1$ being performed first, as the "inner" call:

```
operator<<₂( operator<<₁(cout, temp1), temp2);
```

The return-value from $<<_1$ is thus used as the left argument to $<<_2$:

```
operator<<₂ ( operator<<₁'s return_value, temp2);
```

The subtle point is that since the left operand of `operator<<` is the `ostream` into which values are inserted, $<<_2$ will try to insert `temp2` into whatever value $<<_1$ returns.

From this, it should be apparent that $<<_1$ must return an `ostream` for use by $<<_2$. Moreover, the `ostream` that $<<_1$ returns should be the same `ostream` into which $<<_1$ inserted its value, and so it should return its parameter `out`, rather than a particular `ostream` such as `cout`. If `operator<<` were to explicitly return `cout`,

```
inline ostream & operator<<(ostream & out,
                            const Temperature & theTemp)
{
    theTemp.Print(out);
    return cout;              // LOGIC ERROR!
}
```

then a code fragment like

```
ifstream dataStream("datafile");

dataStream << temp1 << temp2;
```

would correctly insert `temp1` into the `ifstream` named `dataStream`, but would incorrectly insert `temp2` into `cout`. To avoid this, `operator<<` must return its parameter `out`, which, as an alias for the stream into which values are being inserted, returns the appropriate stream.

The other subtle point has to do with the return type of `operator<<`. Why did we define its return type as `ostream &`? The reason is that when a C++ function returns a value in the usual fashion, it actually returns a *copy* of the value to the caller of the function.[5] That is, if we had defined the function to simply return an `ostream`,

```
inline ostream  operator<<(ostream & out,
                           const Temperature & theTemp)
{
   theTemp.Print(out);
   return out;
}
```

then the `return` statement would create a copy of parameter `out`, which, as a reference parameter, would create a copy of its argument. That means that in an output expression like

```
cout << temp1 << temp2;
```

`temp1` would be inserted into `cout`, but `temp2` would be inserted into a copy of `cout`, the result of which is unpredictable.

To avoid such copying, C++ allows a function to be defined with a **reference return type.** The effect is to "turn off" the copying mechanism and return the actual object. Thus, when we write

```
inline ostream & operator<<(ostream & out,
                            const Temperature & theTemp)
{
   theTemp.Print(out);
   return out;
}
```

we are telling the compiler, "Don't return a copy of `out`, but instead return the actual `ostream` for which it is an alias."[6]

---

[5] The caller maintains this copy, called a *temporary,* as long as it is needed and then discards it.

[6] The reference return type cannot be used to circumvent the scope rules—if you try to use a reference return type to return an object defined within the function (i.e., a local), the compiler will generate an error message.

Figure 10.13 presents a definition of the input operator, which is similar.

FIGURE 10.13   OVERLOADING OPERATOR >>.

```
// -------- istream input --------------------------------------------

inline istream & operator>>(istream & in, Temperature & theTemp)
{
   theTemp.Read(in);
   return in;
}
```

Note that since the output operator does not modify the Temperature being displayed, it was declared a constant reference parameter. The input operator, however, does modify its Temperature parameter, so it is declared as a reference parameter.

This completes our implementation of the various Temperature operations.

SUMMARY: THE Temperature CLASS

Figure 10.14 presents a final version of the Temperature class declaration.

FIGURE 10.14   THE TEMPERATURE CLASS DECLARATION.

```
/* This file contains the interface for class Temperature.
 *  ...
 ************************************************************/

#ifndef TEMPERATURE
#define TEMPERATURE

#include <iostream.h>                    // istream, ostream

class Temperature
{
 public:                                // The class interface
   Temperature();
   Temperature(double initialDegrees, char initialScale);

   double Degrees() const;
   char Scale() const;

   Temperature Fahrenheit() const;
   Temperature Celsius() const;
   Temperature Kelvin() const;

   void Print(ostream & out) const;
   void Read(istream & in);
```

```
         bool operator==(const Temperature & rightOperand) const;
         bool operator!=(const Temperature & rightOperand) const;
         bool operator<(const Temperature & rightOperand) const;
         bool operator>(const Temperature & rightOperand) const;
         bool operator<=(const Temperature & rightOperand) const;
         bool operator>=(const Temperature & rightOperand) const;

         Temperature operator+(double rightOperand) const;
         Temperature operator-(double rightOperand) const;

      private:                          // The hidden details
         double myDegrees;
         char myScale;                  // 'F', 'C' or 'K'
    };

    // ... Definitions of inline functions, operator<<, and
           operator>> go here ...

    #endif
```

Class Structure. As Figure 10.14 illustrates, every class has two parts:

- ► The **public** portion of the class, consisting of those components (data or operations) that are accessible outside of the class; and
- ► The **private** portion of the class, consisting of those components (data or operations) that can only be accessed inside the class.

As mentioned earlier, most class operations are declared in the public section and data members in the private portion of the class. This makes the data members inaccessible to programs using the class, preventing programmers from writing programs that depend upon those particular details.

The Class Interface. The benefit of keeping data members private is that it forces programs to interact with a class object through its public function members. The set of public operations can thus be thought of as an **interface** between the class and programs that use it. Since the interface provides the sole means of operating on class objects, it is important that it be well-designed—a good interface must provide all of the functionality needed to operate on a class object. *Designing a good interface thus requires much time and thought, and should not be hurried.*

One reason for designing the interface carefully is that a class interface must be *stable.* If it changes frequently, then programs that use the class must be revised often to accommodate the changes. Programmers will eventually tire of revising their programs and stop using the class. A stable interface is only possible if it is carefully designed from the outset.

If an interface is stable, then any program that uses the class solely through the interface will not break even if the private portion of the class (its data members) is modified extensively. Such extensive modifications are common in maintaining or upgrading many real-world systems. Data members of a class are replaced by others that more efficiently represent the object being modeled. If the interface is stable, the time required to upgrade such a system is only the time to modify the data members. This in turn means that such systems can be maintained more easily, which saves time and money.

Although most classes will have this simple 2-part structure, C++ does allow classes to have multiple public and private sections. Thus the general structure of a class is as follows:

Class Declaration Statement

Form

```
class ClassName
{
    PublicPart₁
    PrivatePart₁
    PublicPart₂
    PrivatePart₂
        .
        .
        .
    PublicPartₙ
    PrivatePartₙ
};
```

where:

ClassName is an identifier naming the class,

each *PublicPart_i* consists of the keyword `public:` and a list of declarations of members (or friends) of the class; and

each *PrivatePart_i* consists of the keyword `private:` and a list of declarations of members (or friends) of the class.

Purpose

Define a new data type *ClassName*, which is a class consisting of the specified private and public parts. Each component (data or function) declared in a private part is accessible only within the class. Each component (data or function) declared in a public part is accessible outside the class.

The public section of a class need not come first, but we will usually place it there so that it is easy to find. Since it provides the class interface, most readers are more interested in it than in the private details.

10.5 friend FUNCTIONS

Although most operations on a class object can be defined as function members, there are some occasions when this is not possible. For example, we saw in Figure 10.12 that the iostream insertion operator ($<<$) could not be defined as a

`Temperature` function member because its left operand is an `ostream`, not a `Temperature`:

```
cout << "The temperature is " << temp1 << endl;
```

Our solution was to define a non-member version of `operator<<` that used the public function member `Print()` to perform its task:

```
inline ostream & operator<<(ostream & out,
                            const Temperature & theTemp)
{
   theTemp.Print(out);
   return out;
}
```

Now, suppose we want to define `operator<<` without calling `Print()`. If `operator<<` attempts to access the data members of its parameter `theTemp` directly,

```
inline ostream & operator<<(ostream & out,
                            const Temperature & theTemp)
{
   out << theTemp.myDegrees << ' '
       << theTemp.myScale;   // ERROR!
   return out;
}
```

the compiler will generate error messages like

```
Member 'myDegrees' is private in class 'Temperature'
Member 'myScale' is private in class 'Temperature'
```

By not allowing the function to access the data members, the compiler is enforcing the class' information-hiding mechanism.

But suppose that the only reasonable way to define some operation requires that a non-member function be able to access the private data members. In such rare situations, C++ allows a class to grant this special access privilege to the function by specifying that it is a **friend.**

To illustrate, suppose we replace the `Print()` prototype in class `Temperature` with a prototype of `operator<<` preceded by the keyword `friend`:

```
class Temperature
{
 public:                                    // The class interface

         .
         .
         .

    friend ostream & operator<<(ostream & out,
                                const Temperature & theTemp);
    void Read(istream & in);

         .
         .
         .
```

```
  private:                        // The hidden details
    double myDegrees;
    char myScale;                 // 'F', 'C' or 'K'
};
```

If we define `operator<<` as a non-member function,

```
inline ostream & operator<<(ostream & out,
                            const Temperature & theTemp)
{
   out << theTemp.myDegrees << ' '
       << theTemp.myScale;    // Ok now!
   return out;
}
```

then this function will compile correctly. By naming `operator<<` as a `friend`, the class grants this function access to its private section. Note that this does not allow a programmer to circumvent the information-hiding mechanism, because only a person able to alter the class declaration can insert a `friend` prototype.

Note also that `operator<<` is not designated as a `const` function. This is because it is not a function member and `const` *can only be applied to function members.*

We can also replace the `Read()` prototype with a `friend` prototype of `operator>>`:

```
class Temperature
{
 public:                                // The class interface

           .
           .
           .

    friend ostream & operator<<(ostream & out,
                                const Temperature & theTemp);
    friend istream & operator>>(istream & in,
                                Temperature & theTemp);

           .
           .
           .

  private:                        // The hidden details
    double myDegrees;
    char myScale;                 // 'F', 'C' or 'K'
};
```

We can then define `operator>>` as a non-member function that directly accesses the data members of its parameter `theTemp`. Because of the relative complexity of this definition, it should not be designated as `inline` and should be stored in `Temperature.cpp` for separate compilation.

```
istream & operator>>(istream & in, Temperature & theTemp)
{
   double inDegrees;              // temporary variables to
   char inScale;                  //  store the input values

   in >> inDegrees >> inScale;    // read the values from the stream

   if (islower(inScale))          // if scale is lower case
      inScale = toupper(inScale); //   convert it to uppercase

   switch(inScale)
   {
      case 'F': case 'C': case 'K':   // if scale is valid
         theTemp.myScale = inScale;   //   assign input values
         theTemp.myDegrees = inDegrees; //   to data members
         break;
      default:                        // otherwise
         in.setstate(ios::failbit);   //   set fail bit instream, and
      }                               //   leave data members unchanged

   return in;
}
```

Use of friend. The `friend` mechanism is rarely needed to define class operations. As we saw with class `Temperature`, most operations on a class object can be defined as function members, so the `friend` mechanism is not needed for them.

When the left operand of an operation is of a type different from the class being built, then a function member cannot be used and a non-member function must be defined. But even in such infrequent cases, a public intermediary function (like `Print()` or `Read()`) can be defined which the non-member function can call. The only circumstances where the `friend` mechanism is an absolute necessity are when the left operand of the operation is of some type different from the class being built and the operation *must* directly access the data members of the class. Because it embodies the external approach to defining class operations (in which a function manipulates an object from outside) instead of the I-can-do-it-myself principle of the internal approach, we will use the `friend` mechanism only in those rare circumstances where it is a necessity.

✔ Quick Quiz 10.5

1. For an object that cannot be directly represented with existing types, we design and build a _____ to represent it and store it in a _____.
2. The behavior of a class object is the collection of _____ that can be applied to the object.
3. The attributes of a class object consist of the _____ that must be stored to characterize the object.
4. (True or false) The attributes of a class are usually identified before the behavior.
5. Object autonomy is embodied in the _____ principle.
6. _____ allows a single object to store values of different types.

7. What is the purpose of hiding data members in a class?

8. Data members are hidden by declaring them to be _____ .

9. Before a program is compiled it is first examined by the _____ .

10. All lines that begin with a _____ character are preprocessor directives.

11. Directives of the form

```
#ifndef name
#define name

    .
    .
    .

#endif
```

are called _____ directives.

12. Class operations are implemented using _____ members.

13. (True or false) Specifications of function members should usually be formulated from an external perspective.

14. In the definition of a function member, the name of the function is preceded by the _____ and the _____ operator.

15. A function member that does not alter the data members of the class should be declared as a _____ function by attaching the keyword _____ at the end of its heading.

16. A constructor in a class `Student` will be named _____ .

17. Name and describe two kinds of constructors.

18. The _____ (public or private) portion of a class acts as an interface between the class and programs that use it.

19. A class can give a non-member function access to the class' data members by specifying that the function is a _____ .

20. Write a declaration for a class `Student` that has two data members, `myID` of type `int`, and `myName` of type `string`, an output function member, and an input function member.

Exercises 10.5

For exercises 1 and 2, add functions to class `Temperature` to implement the specified operation.

1. Add functions to class `Temperature` that convert a `Temperature` value to (a) Celsius (b) Kelvin.

2. Add a function to class `Temperature` that decreases a `Temperature` value by a numeric value.

For exercises 3-8, define the private portion of a class to model the given item.

3. Cards in a deck of playing cards.

4. Time measured in hours, minutes, and seconds.

5. A telephone number as area code, local exchange, and number.

6. Position of a checker on a board.

7. A point (x, y) in a Cartesian coordinate system.

8. A point (r, θ) in a polar coordinate system.

For exercises 9–14, completely implement a class for the specified objects, supplying a complete set of operations for the class. You should write a driver program to test your class as Programming Problems 1–6 at the end of the chapter ask you to do.

9. Exercise 3

10. Exercise 4

11. Exercise 5

12. Exercise 6

13. Exercise 7

14. Exercise 8

For exercises 15–17, develop a class for the given information, and then write operations appropriate for an object of that type. You should write a driver program to test your class as Programming Problems 7–9 at the end of the chapter ask you to do.

15. Information about a person: name, birthday, age, gender, social security number, height, weight, hair color, eye color, and marital status.

16. Statistics about a baseball player: name, age, birthdate, position (pitcher, catcher, infielder, outfielder).

17. Weather statistics: date; city and state, province, or country; time of day; temperature; barometric pressure; weather conditions (clear skies, partly cloudy, cloudy, stormy).

For exercises 18–20, write appropriate class declarations to describe the information in the specified file. See the end of Chapter 8 for descriptions of these files.

18. `Student`

19. `Inventory`

20. `Users`

10.6 EXAMPLE: RETRIEVING STUDENT INFORMATION

Once we can create classes, we can represent complex objects in software. In this section, we build an information retrieval system that a university registrar might use to maintain student records.

PROBLEM: INFORMATION RETRIEVAL

The registrar at IO University has a data file named `student.dat` that contains student records:

```
111223333 Bill Board
Freshman    16.0  3.15

666554444 Jose Canusee
Sophomore   16.0  3.25
```

```
777889999 Ben Dover
Junior      16.0   2.5

333221111 Stan Dupp
Senior      8.0   3.75

444556666 Ellie Kat
Senior      16.0   3.125

999887777 Isabelle Ringing
Junior      16.0   3.8
         .
         .
         .
```

Each pair of lines in this file has the form

> *studentNumber firstName lastName*
> *studentYear credits gradePointAverage*

where

> *studentNumber* is a 9-digit (integer) student ID number,
> *firstName, lastName,* and *studentYear* are character strings,
> *credits* is the (real) number of credits this student carried this semester, and
> *gradePointAverage* is the (real) grade point average of this student this semester.

The registrar at IOU needs a program that will let her enter student numbers, and that will retrieve and display the information for those students.

OBJECT-CENTERED DESIGN

Behavior. The program should read a sequence of students from the input file `student.dat`. It should then repeatedly prompt for and read a student ID number from the keyboard, search the sequence of students for the position of the student with that student ID number, and if found, display the information for that student.

Objects. An abbreviated list of the objects in this problem is as follows:

Description	Kind	Type	Name
A sequence of students	varying	`vector<Student>`	*studentVec*
Name of the input file	constant	`string`	*INPUT_FILE*
A student ID number	varying	`long`	*studentID*
The position of the student	varying	`vector<T>::iterator`	*position*
A student	varying	`Student`	none

As we saw in chapter 9, we can use a `vector<T>` to store a sequence of objects of type `T`. However, we need to store a sequence of students. Since there is no predefined type that allows us to represent a student object, we will build a `Student` class for this.

Operations. The operations needed to solve this problem are as follows:

   i.   Read a sequence of students from the input file
   ii.   Display a prompt
  iii.   Read a long integer from the keyboard
   iv.   Search a sequence of students for one with a particular ID number
   v.   Display a student
   vi.   Repeat steps ii–v an arbitrary number of times

The Standard Template Library's `find()` algorithm requires that the relational operators `<` and `==` be defined for objects being compared, so we add these operations to our list:

 vii.   Compare two `Student` objects using `<`
viii.   Compare two `Student` objects using `==`

Algorithm. Given a `Student` class that provides the appropriate operations, we can organize these operations into the following algorithm:

Algorithm for Student Information Retrieval

1. Read a sequence of students from *INPUT_FILE* into *studentVec*.
2. Repeatedly do the following:
    a. Prompt for and read *studentID*.
    b. Search *studentVec* for the student with *studentID,* returning its *position*.
    c. If the search was successful
        Display the student at *position*.
      Otherwise
        Display an error message.

Before we can code this algorithm, we must build a `Student` class. From an internal perspective, the behaviors required of a `Student` include:

- Initialize myself with default values
- Initialize myself with explicitly supplied values
- Read my attributes from an `istream` and store them in me
- Display my attributes using an `ostream`
- Compare myself and another `Student` using the `<` and `==` relational operators

These are the minimal operations needed to solve the problem. To make the class truly reuseable, we should add (at least) the following operations:

- Access any of my attributes
- Compare myself and another `Student` using the `!=`, `>`, `<=`, and `>=` operators

The Student attributes required to solve this problem include the attributes stored in the input file:

my id number, my first name, my last name, my year, my credits, and *my GPA*

Figure 10.15 presents the class declaration containing prototypes for these operations and data members for these attributes:

FIGURE 10.15   **THE HEADER FILE FOR CLASS Student.**

```
/* Student.h contains the interface for class Student.
 * ...
 ****************************************************** /

#ifndef STUDENT                          // compile-once
#define STUDENT                          //  wrapper

#include <iostream.h>                    // istream, ostream
#include <string>                        // string

class Student
{
 public:                                 // The Interface
    //  constructors
    Student();
    Student(long idNumber, const string & firstName,
            const string & lastName, const string & year,
            double credits, double gpa);

  //  accessors
   long IDNumber() const;
   string FirstName() const;
   string LastName() const;
   string Year() const;
   double Credits() const;
   double GPA() const;

   //  relational ops
   bool operator==(const Student & rightOperand) const;
   bool operator!=(const Student & rightOperand) const;
   bool operator<(const Student & rightOperand) const;
   bool operator>(const Student & rightOperand) const;
   bool operator<=(const Student & rightOperand) const;
   bool operator>=(const Student & rightOperand) const;

   //  I/O
   void Read(istream & in);              //   called by operator>>
   void Print(ostream & out) const;      //   called by operator<<
```

```
  private:                              // Implementation Details
                                        // Examples:
    long    myIDNumber;                 //    123456789
    string myFirstName,                 //    Jane
           myLastName,                  //    Doe
           myYear;                      //    Senior
    double myCredits,                   //    15.0
           myGPA;                       //    3.75
};


// ******** Non-member Operations *****************************
// -------- insertion (input) ---------------------------------
inline istream& operator>>(istream & in, Student & theStudent)
{
   theStudent.Read(in);
   return in;
}

// -------- extraction (output) -------------------------------
inline ostream& operator<<(ostream & out, const Student & theStudent)
{
   theStudent.Print(out);
   return out;
}

// ******** Member Operations *********************************
// -------- Accessor functions --------------------------------
inline long Student::IDNumber() const
{
   return myIDNumber;
}

inline string Student::FirstName() const
{
   return myFirstName;
}

inline string Student::LastName() const
{
   return myLastName;
}

inline string Student::Year() const
{
   return myYear;
}

inline double Student::Credits() const
{
   return myCredits;
}
```

```cpp
inline double Student::GPA() const
{
   return myGPA;
}


// -------- relational operators --------------------------------
inline bool Student::operator==(const Student & rightOperand) const
{
   return myIDNumber == rightOperand.IDNumber();
}


inline bool Student::operator!=(const Student & rightOperand) const
{
   return myIDNumber != rightOperand.IDNumber();
}


inline bool Student::operator<(const Student & rightOperand) const
{
   return myIDNumber < rightOperand.IDNumber();
}


inline bool Student::operator>(const Student & rightOperand) const
{
   return myIDNumber > rightOperand.IDNumber();
}


inline bool Student::operator<=(const Student & rightOperand) const
{
   return myIDNumber <= rightOperand.IDNumber();
}


inline bool Student::operator>=(const Student & rightOperand) const
{
   return myIDNumber >= rightOperand.IDNumber();
}

#endif
```

The more complicated operations are defined in the implementation file `Student.cpp`, for separate compilation. Figure 10.16 shows the definitions of these functions.

FIGURE 10.16   THE IMPLEMENTATION FILE FOR CLASS Student.

```cpp
/* Student.cpp implements the non-trivial Student operations.
 * ...
 ****************************************************************/

#include "Student.h"                          // class Student
```

```
// -------- default-value constructor -------------------------
Student::Student ()
{
   myIDNumber = 0;
   myFirstName = "";
   myLastName = "";
   myYear = "";
   myCredits = 0.0;
   myGPA = 0.0;
}


// -------- explicit-value constructor --------------------
Student::Student (long idNumber, const string & firstName,
                  const string & lastName, const string & year,
                  double credits, double GPA)
{
   myIDNumber = idNumber;
   myFirstName = firstName;
   myLastName = lastName;
   myYear = year;
   myCredits = credits;
   myGPA = GPA;
}


// -------- input (function member) ----------------------------
void Student::Read(istream & in)
{
   in >> myIDNumber >> myFirstName >> myLastName
      >> myYear >> myCredits >> myGPA;
}


// -------- output (function member) --------------------------
#include <iomanip.h>                          // setw, setprecision
void Student::Print(ostream & out) const
{
   out << setw(9) << myIDNumber << '\t'
       << myFirstName << ' ' << myLastName
       << '\n' << myYear
       << setprecision(4) << showpoint
       << fixed << setw(8) << myCredits
       << setw(8) << myGPA << endl;
}
```

Note that the layout of the input file determines the arrangement of the data members in the input statement in function Read(). In particular, Read() assumes that the student's ID number comes first, followed by the student's name (first, then last), followed by the remainder of the student's data (year, semester hours, and GPA) on the next line. The output function produces output having a similar format.

Coding. Given class `Student` and the Standard Template Library, our algorithm is relatively easy to implement. The basic idea is to define a `vector<Student>` object named `studentVec` to store the sequence of `Student` values from the input file:

```
vector<Student> studentVec;
```

The effect of this is to create a vector of student objects that we can visualize as follows:

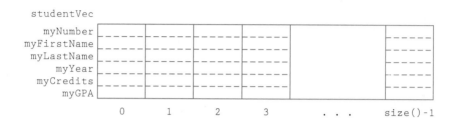

We can then apply any of the `vector<T>` operations described in chapter 9 and the STL algorithms such as `sort()` or `find()` to `studentVec`.

Figure 10.17 gives the implementation of our algorithm using this approach.

FIGURE 10.17 STUDENT INFORMATION RETRIEVAL.

```cpp
/* registrar.cpp retrieves a student's data from a file
 *   using their id #.
 * Input (file):     a sequence of Students
 * Input (keyboard): one or more student numbers
 * Output:           that student's data
 *****************************************************************/

#include <iostream.h>          // cin, cout
#include <fstream.h>           // ifstream, ofstream
#include <assert.h>            // assert()
#include <vector>              // vector<T>
#include <algorithm>          // find
#include "Student.h"           // Student
#include "MyVector.h"          // Read()

int main()
{
  const string INPUT_FILE = "students.dat";

  cout << "This program provides an information retrieval system\n"
          "  by reading a series of student records from "
       << '\'' << INPUT_FILE << '\''
       << "\n  and then allowing retrieval of any student's data.\n";

  vector<Student> studentVec;
  Read(INPUT_FILE, studentVec);
```

```
   long studentID;                            // the student we seek
   vector<Student>::iterator position;        // position of the student

   for (;;)                                   // repeat:
   {
      cout << "\nEnter the ID # of a student (eof to quit): ";
      cin >> studentID;                       //  get the student

      if (cin.eof()) break;                   //  if finished, quit

      position = find(studentVec.begin(),     //  search
                      studentVec.end(),       //   the vector for
                      Student(studentID,      //   this student id #
                            "", "",           //   using placeholder
                            "", 0, 0));       //   arguments

      if (position != studentVec.end())       //   if found
         cout << endl << *position << endl;   //     display student
      else                                    //   otherwise, tell user
         cerr << "\nThere is no student with ID # "
              << studentID  << ".\n";
   }
}
```

Listing of input file `students.dat`:

```
111223333 Bill Board
Freshman   16.0 3.15

666554444 Jose CanuSee
Sophomore 16.0 3.25

777889999 Ben Dover
Junior     16.0  2.5

333221111 Stan Dupp
Senior     8.0 3.75

444556666 Ellie Kat
Senior     16.0 3.125

999887777 Isabelle Ringing
Junior     16.0  3.8
```

Sample run:

```
This program provides an information retrieval system
  by reading a series of student records from 'students.dat'
  and then allowing retrieval of any student's data.
```

```
Enter the ID # of a student (eof to quit): 333221111

 333221111 Stan Dupp
       Senior 16.0000  3.7500

Enter the ID # of a student (eof to quit): 123456789

There is no student with ID # 123456789.

Enter the ID # of a student (eof to quit): 999887777

 999887777 Ringing, Isabelle
       Junior  8.0000  3.8000

Enter the ID # of a student (eof to quit): ^D
```

Taking the time to implement an object as a class is an *investment for the future*—if the registrar subsequently asks us to write a program to create a list of all students who will be graduating with honors, our Student class makes this easy:

```cpp
// ...open inStream and outStream...

cout << "Seniors whose GPA is 3.5 or greater:\n";
for (;;)
{
   inStream >> aStudent;

   if (inStream.eof()) break;

   if (aStudent.Year() == "Senior" && aStudent.GPA() >= 3.5)
      outStream << aStudent << endl;
}

// ... close inStream and outStream ...
```

By planning for the future when we design a class, we save ourselves and others a great deal of time and effort.

EXERCISES 10.6

1. Suppose that a Student value *s1* will be considered to be less than another Student value *s2* if:

> the myLastName member of *s1* is less than the myLastName member of *s2*; or
> the myLastName member of *s1* is equal to the myLastName member of *s2* and
> the myFirstName member of *s1* is less than the myFirstName member of *s2*.

A rule for the greater-than relationship between two Student values is similar. Provide definitions for operator< and operator> that implement these relationships.

2.   Suppose that a `Student` value *s1* can be described as "equal to" another `Student` value *s2* if the `myLastName` member of *s1* is equal to the `myLastName` member of *s2* and the `myFirstName` member of *s1* is equal to the `myFirstName` member of *s2*. A rule for the inequality relation of two `Student` values is similar. Provide definitions for `operator==` and `operator!=` that implement these relationships, being sure to clearly state the assumptions they make.

3.   An alternative approach to equality of `Student` objects is to describe a `Student` value *s1* as "equal to" another `Student` value *s2* if the `myIDNumber` member of *s1* is equal to the `myIDNumber` member of *s2*. A rule for the inequality relation of two `Student` values is similar. Provide definitions for `operator==` and `operator!=` that implement these relationships. What advantages are there to implementing these operations in this way rather than as described in exercise 2? What disadvantages? (*Hint:* Consider the problem of searching for a particular student in the registrar's file.)

4.   Using the functions defined in exercises 1 and 2 (or 3), provide definitions for `operator<=` and `operator>=` that implement the less-than-or-equal and greater-than-or-equal relations on two `Student` values.

Part of the Picture: Artificial Intelligence

BY KEITH VANDER LINDEN

Just over an hour into the sixth game of their chess match, Garry Kasparov, the reigning world champion, conceded defeat to Deep Blue, a chess-playing computer developed by IBM corporation. Kasparov lost the match, held in May of 1997, 3.5 games to 2.5 games. It marked the first time a computer program had defeated a world chess champion in anything approaching tournament conditions.

Although this result came as a surprise to many, it has been clear for some time that a computer would eventually beat a world champion player. Since their introduction to tournament play in the late 1960's, chess programs have made steady progress, defeating a chess master in 1983, a grandmaster in 1988, and now the world champion. This is by no means the end of the story, however. There are reservations concerning the validity of this most recent match: it was not really a tournament setting with multiple players, Kasparov was not allowed to study Deep Blue's previous matches, and he was under considerable pressure to hold off a perceived "attack on humanity" by computer programs. Nevertheless, another milestone has been passed.

The construction of game-playing programs such as Deep Blue is part of a subfield of Computer Science known as **Artificial Intelligence** or **AI.** Roughly speaking, AI is an attempt to program computers to perform intelligent tasks. Giving a precise definition of AI is difficult, however, and most AI textbooks spend a laborious opening chapter attempting to characterize the field. This difficulty comes about for two reasons: (1) because intelligent behavior is complex and hard to define; and (2) because the styles of programming used to implement this behavior are diverse.

INTELLIGENCE

We all have a general notion of what intelligence is. We presume to know who has it and who doesn't. Garry Kasparov, for example, is intelligent by any measure. He is the world champion of chess, a game long seen as a pinnacle of human intellectual achievement. But what about Deep Blue? Is it intelligent? It beat Garry Kasparov in a chess match; this must mean something.

Clearly, Deep Blue has performed an intelligent feat. It has done so, however, in a very narrow domain. This is one thing that distinguishes its accomplishment from general human intelligence. Intelligent behavior, the "I" in AI, is diverse. Humans display profoundly complex behavior in many areas, all of which have been topics of study in AI, including:

- *Reasoning and problem solving*—Humans are able to reason about their world and to plan their own actions accordingly. This encompasses a variety of activities, including game playing, mathematical theorem proving, and the planning of actions. Examples of systems which perform these tasks include Deep Blue, the game-playing system just discussed; EQP, a system which, in 1996, proved a theorem that no human has successfully proven; and SPIKE, a system which plans observation schedules for the Hubble space telescope.

- *Memory*—Humans are able to remember things about their world. In AI, the study of this area is called **knowledge representation.** It serves as the foundation of all reasoning and problem solving. Deep Blue, for example, represents considerable knowledge about chess but, it must be said, little or nothing about anything else.

- *Motion and manipulation*—Humans are able to perform actions in their world. The area of AI which deals with this is called **robotics.** This area, much popularized in science fiction, includes the development of robotic arms for assembly lines, or of fully mobile agents such as Robosoft's Auto VacC, an autonomous vacuum cleaner.

- *Perception*—Humans are able to see and to hear. The areas of AI concerned with these behaviors are called **computer vision** and **speech recognition.** They have been successful in fielding systems, which convert written characters into ASCII characters, called optical character recognition systems, and systems which convert spoken words into ASCII words, called speech-to-text dictation systems.

- *Language processing*—Humans are able to process natural, human languages. In AI, the behaviors studied include the ability to understand language **(natural language understanding),** the ability to produce language **(natural language generation),** and the ability to translate from one language to another **(machine translation).** Examples of this include Météo, a system which generates weather reports in English and French, and Systran, a machine translation system used by the European Commission.

- *Learning*—Humans are also able to learn from past experiences. In AI, the study of this phenomenon is called **machine learning.** One practical application of this involves **data mining.** Data mining tools attempt to find consistent patterns in large amounts of data. One such tool, ISL's Clementine, has been trained to predict the audience-share for prospective new television shows on the BBC.

Deep Blue can play chess well, but doesn't exhibit any of the other behaviors just given. It can't even move its own chess pieces. At first glance, however, many of these other areas don't appear to be all that difficult, particularly when compared with chess. My four-year old son, for example, can't play chess very well yet, but he does exhibit all the other behaviors with relative ease. He remembers things, he perceives and manipulates things, he processes language, and he learns. These have all come naturally to him. Surely with a little extra work, Deep Blue could do them as well. This is a critical misconception. Just because a task is easy for people doesn't necessarily means that it is *simple.* In fact, some of the things humans find extremely easy to perform have turned out to be among the hardest to program. For example, in the area of natural language processing, we have not succeeded in producing a system capable of engaging in meaningful conversation except in narrowly defined contexts. Conversely, some of the greatest successes in AI have been in areas seen as requiring great skill such as chess playing, calculus, and medical diagnosis.

This paradox of sorts is part of the reason that early researchers in AI grossly underestimated the difficulties in AI programming. Indeed, the field of AI has been greatly damaged by overly-ambitious expectations. In the mid-to-late 50's, for example, many people felt that machine translation programs were just around the corner. In retrospect, this was an extraordinary claim given that at the time we barely knew how to translate FORTRAN into assembly language.

PROGRAMMING TECHNIQUES

Another point that distinguishes Deep Blue's accomplishment from general human intelligence is the mechanism by which it operates, the "A" in its AI. As there is a wide range of intelligent behavior, there is also a wide range of programming techniques used to implement them "artificially." These techniques include:

- *Heuristic search*—AI programs are frequently designed to consider a number of choices. This is called **search** because the program is said to search through a space of possible choices and their consequences. For example, before making a choice, Deep Blue considers many moves and what their consequences might be many steps into the future. It uses a 256-processor architecture to do this, considering on the order of 200 million board positions per second. Search alone is seldom sufficient, however. The nature of chess, for example, dictates that Deep Blue be selective in what moves it considers, and how far down the road it considers them. There are simply too many alternatives to consider them all. It, therefore, tends to ignore the less promising ones, and to focus on a few options. These options are chosen based on **heuristics,** or rules of thumb, such as "first, consider moves that gain control of the center of the board."

- *Logic programming*—This approach involves representing knowledge in a well-defined format and performing logical inferences on it. For example, EQP, the theorem-proving program mentioned earlier, uses such an approach to prove theorems. It takes a set of given knowledge, and attempts to derive the theorem logically from this knowledge. The programming language **Prolog** has been specifically designed to support logic programming.

- *Expert systems*—Expert systems encode knowledge elicited from an expert in some domain. Many of these systems have become commercial successes, including XCON (a system which configures computer components for DEC equipment), and SBDS (a system which diagnoses electrical problems in Ford automobile engines).

- *Neural networks*—The techniques given so far are programmed on computers which are built with digital circuitry. The human brain, on the other hand, is very different. It is constructed of very simple brain cells, called neurons, which are highly interconnected with one another. Computer models of this structure are called **neural networks** or **connectionist systems.** They display radically different characteristics from traditional programming techniques.

These techniques are not mutually exclusive, and may be used individually or in combinations to implement the intelligent behaviors discussed.

EXAMPLE: THE NOT-ONE GAME

Early researchers in AI frequently used games such as chess as a vehicle for their research. Games tend to be limited in scope and to have well-defined rules. Chess, for example, has a 12 × 12 board with a finite set of pieces, where each piece has a well-defined set of possible moves. This allowed the researchers to avoid the problems involved in modeling the other areas of intelligent behavior. We, too, will take advantage of this and implement a program that plays **not-one,** a simple dice game for two players.

In not-one, each player takes a turn in which they roll two dice and remember the sum of the values as their first roll. They may roll again as many times as they would like, with the object of getting the highest roll possible. The only stipulation is that they are forced to quit with a score of 0 for the turn if they roll the same sum as they did for their first roll. The player with the highest score after 12 turns wins.

We'll start by implementing a turn-taking driver program (see Figure 10.18[1]). This driver runs a 12-turn game, printing out the scores at the end of each turn:

FIGURE 10.18   A DRIVER FOR NOT-ONE.

```cpp
int main()
{
  cout << "\nReady to play some Not-One!\n" << endl;

  Player1 player1;                       // john
  Player2 player2;                       // jane

  int player1Score = 0,                  // initialize
      player2Score = 0,                  //  counters
      player1LastRoll = 0,
      player2LastRoll = 0;

  for (int i = 1; i <= 12; i++)          // play 12 rounds
    {
                                         //  the 1st player's turn
      cout << "----------------------------------------\n"
           << player1.Name() << ", turn " << i;
      player1LastRoll = player1.TakeTurn(player2LastRoll);
      player1Score += player1LastRoll;
                                         //   the 2nd player's turn
      cout << "----------------------------------------\n"
           << player2.Name() << ", turn " << i;
      player2LastRoll = player2.TakeTurn(player1LastRoll);
      player2Score += player2LastRoll;
                                         //   summarize round
      cout << "****************************************\n"
           << " Turn " << i << " - "
           << player1.Name() << ": " << player1Score << "; "
           << player2.Name() << ": " << player2Score
           << "\n****************************************\n"
           << endl;
    }
}
```

Notice that this driver makes use of two user-defined classes, `Player1` and `Player2`, which implement the methods `TakeTurn()` and `Name()`. We have created two classes

---

[1] This driver program was written by Joel Adams.

rather than one so that the player that goes first may have a different strategy from the player that goes second. The TakeTurn() member function for Player1 is as follows:

FIGURE 10.19 A TURN-TAKING MEMBER FUNCTION FOR NOT-ONE.

```
int Player1::TakeTurn(int opponentsLastRoll)
{
  RandomInt die1(1, 6);            // Declare the random dice.
  RandomInt die2(1, 6);

  myCurrentRoll = 0;
  myFirstRoll = die1 + die2;
  int scoreThisTurn = myFirstRoll;
  cout << "\n First Roll: " << die1 << " + " << die 2
          << " = " << die1 + die2;

  UpdateData(opponentsLastRoll));  // Keep track of opponent if desired.

  for (;;)                         // Continue rolling until Stop() returns
    {                              // true.
      if (Stop())
        {
          cout << ". Stopping.\n" << endl;
          break;
        }
      else
          cout << ". Continuing . . . ";

      myCurrentRoll = die1.Generate() + die2.Generate();
      cout << "\n Next Roll: " << die1 << " + " << die2
          << " = " << die1 + die2;

      if (myCurrentRoll == myFirstRoll)
        {
          cout << ". OOOOPS!\n" << endl;
          scoreThisTurn = 0;
          break;
        }
      else
        scoreThisTurn = Max(scoreThisTurn, myCurrentRoll);
    }

  RaiseScore (scoreThisTurn);
  return scoreThisTurn;
}
```

The TakeTurn() function declares two dice of type RandomInt (see the website described in the preface) and implements the player's turn with a loop that continues until either the player decides to stop, as determined by the Stop() member function, or the player rolls the first roll again. The appropriate score is then returned.

There are many strategies which may be implemented for this game. Recall that Deep Blue used heuristic search in its strategy. That was appropriate in chess, but it is not as useful here because not-one decisions are, for the most part, made independently of what the other player is likely to do in the future. We will, therefore, use a scaled-down expert system approach in which we encode knowledge from expert players. The simplest strategy is to encode the somewhat dubious "knowledge" that a player should always accept his or her first roll. This strategy has the virtue of simplicity, and also the advantage that it never gets a 0 for a turn because it never risks re-rolling. It is implemented with the following `Stop()` member function for `Player1`:

```cpp
bool Player1::Stop() const

{

   return true;

}
```

Another simple strategy is to randomly determine whether to go on or not. This is implemented in the following `Stop()` member function for `Player2`:

```cpp
bool Player2::Stop() const

{

   RandomInt choice(0,1);     // Declare a random coin.

   if (choice)

      return true;

   else

      return false;

}
```

A partial output for a game between these two strategies is shown here. This output shows the first three turns and uses the names "Fast" and "Random" for the two strategies.

FIGURE 10.20   A SAMPLE OUTPUT OF A NOT-ONE GAME.

```
Ready to play some Not-One!

-----------------------------------------
Fast, turn 1
  First Roll: 2 + 2 = 4.  Stopping.
-----------------------------------------
random, turn 1
  First Roll: 2 + 4 = 6.  Continuing . . .
  Next Roll: 4 + 4 = 8.  Continuing . . .
  Next Roll: 4 + 4 = 8.  Continuing . . .
  Next Roll: 3 + 3 = 6.  OOOOPS!
```

```
*********************************************
 Turn 1 - Fast: 4; random: 0
*********************************************


-------------------------------------------
Fast, turn 2
 First Roll: 1 + 1 = 2.   Stopping.


-------------------------------------------
random, turn 2
 First Roll: 4 + 4 = 8.   Stopping.


*********************************************
 Turn 2 = Fast: 6; random: 8
*********************************************


-------------------------------------------
Fast, turn 3
 First Roll: 4 + 4 = 8.   Stopping.


-------------------------------------------
random, turn 3
 First Roll: 6 + 1 = 7.   Continuing . . .
 Next Roll: 1 + 2 = 3.   Continuing . . .
 Next Roll: 1 + 2 = 3.   Stopping.


*********************************************
  Turn 3 - Fast: 14; random: 15
*********************************************
```

There are clearly more effective strategies for this game, which would most likely include additional expert knowledge about how to act in certain specific situations. Expert players, for example, might likely take more risks if they are far behind near the end of a game, or they might become more conservative if they have a "comfortable" lead. Other approaches might involve a statistical analysis of "optimal" choice. Implementing this additional knowledge is left as an exercise.

FURTHER READING

If you are interested in reading further on Artificial Intelligence, consider going to the following sources:

- ▶ Russell and Norvig's text *Artificial Intelligence, A Modern Approach,* Prentice Hall, 1995 — This is a good, comprehensive introduction to the field, which discusses not only the computer science in AI, but also the influence of other disciplines such as philosophy, psychology, and linguistics. They also discuss many of the concepts and example systems mentioned in this section.

- ▶ Some of the early papers in AI are still as incisive today as they were when they first came out — Turing wrote a landmark paper on the nature of AI, "Computing Machinery and Intelligence," *Mind,* 59:433–460, 1950. Searle wrote an oft-cited critique of Turing's vision, "Minds, Brains and Programs," *Behavioral and Brain Sciences,* 3:417–424, 1980.

▶ There are also extensive materials available on the internet—Carnegie Mellon's AI repository at

> `http://www.cs.cmu.edu/Groups/AI/html/repository.html`

has an extensive collection of documents and systems. The Kasparov vs. Deep Blue chess match is discussed at length at IBM's site,

> `http://www.chess.ibm.com/`

EXERCISES

1. Using the not-one skeleton given in this section, program the not-one game with better heuristic functions for player 1 and player 2. Try pitting your strategy against those of your colleagues.

2. Write a strategy that allows the user to play manually against other strategies.

☞ *PROGRAMMING POINTERS*

✍ PROGRAM STYLE AND DESIGN

1. *When an object in a program cannot be represented directly using predefined types, define a class to represent such objects.* The class is the central mechanism for defining new types in C++. Remember, the language was originally called "C with classes."

2. *Use classes to define new types whose values consist of multiple attributes of arbitrary types.* One of the purposes of the class is to permit different data types to be encapsulated in a single object. For example, to model an address, we might declare:

```
class Address
{
   public:
           // ... Interface omitted ...
   private:
      int    myHouseNumber;
      string myStreet;
      string myCity;
      string myState;
      long   myZipCode;
};
```

3. *Use indentation to reflect the structure of your class, since this increases its readability.*

4. *Use descriptive identifiers for the data members that reinforce the I-can-do-it-myself principle.* For example, begin each name of a data member with the prefix my.

5. *Place the class interface first in the class declaration so that it is easy to find.* Then users of your class can find the class interface without wading through all of its private details.

6. *Keep all data members of a class private and provide accessor functions to retrieve the values of those members.* One purpose of a class is to hide implementation details from programs that use an object. By providing a carefully designed set of interface functions and preventing programs from accessing the data members except through this interface, the class simplifies program maintenance.

7. *If a class function member does not modify the data members of the class, then the function should be declared and defined as a constant function by placing the key-*

word `const` *at the end of its heading.* **Make a practice of defining** `const` **function members as often as appropriate, since doing so lets the compiler help you find logic errors if such functions inadvertently change the value of a data member (or call a function that does so).**

8. *Define trivial function members in the same file as the class (i.e., in the header file) using the* `inline` *specifier.* **C++ does allow trivial functions to be defined within the class declaration, but doing so clutters the declaration, reducing its readability, so this practice should be avoided.**

9. *Define nontrivial function members in a separately-compiled implementation file.* **If a definition is stored in the header file, it will be recompiled every time a program that includes that definition is compiled, which wastes time. Storing a function in a separately-compiled implementation file eliminates this extra work.**

10. *Only overload an operator to perform an operation that is consistent with its symbol.* **For example, the standard** `string` **class overloads + to perform concatenation, which is the equivalent of adding two** `string` **values. Avoid being cute and abusing the overloading mechanism by giving operators counter-intuitive definitions since this reduces the readability of the code.**

⚡ POTENTIAL PROBLEMS

1. *Members of a class that are declared following the keyword* `private`: *are not accessible outside of the class.* **Private members of a class can only be accessed by function members and friend functions.**

2. *In definitions of the member functions of a class, the function's name must be qualified with the name of the class and the scope operator (* `::` *).* **For example, given a class declaration**

```
class Point
{
 public:
    void Print(ostream & out) const;
    // ...
 private:
    double myX,
           myY;
};
```

the `Print()` function for this class could be defined as:

```
inline void Point::Print(ostream & out)
{
    out << '(' << myX << ',' << myY << ')';
}
```

3. *The name of the constructor is the same as the name of the class, and the constructor has no return type.* **For example, given a class declaration**

```
class Point
{
 public:
    Point(double xVal, double yVal);
    // ...
 private:
    double myX,
           myY;
};
```

the constructor for this class could be defined as:

```
Point::Point(double xVal, double yVal)
{
    myX = xVal;
    myY = yVal;
}
```

4. *Member functions that do not modify the object containing them should be declared and defined as constant functions.* This is accomplished by placing the keyword const after the closing parentheses that follows the parameter list. For example, given a class declaration

```
class Point
{
 public:
    double X() const;
    // ...
 private:
    double myX,
           myY;
};
```

the accessor function X() could be defined as:

```
inline double Point::X() const
{
    return myX;
}
```

5. *It is good practice to surround a class declaration with conditional compilation pre-processor directives*

```
#ifndef CLASSNAME
#define CLASSNAME

ClassDeclaration

#endif
```

to avoid generating errors if multiple files insert that declaration using the #include *directive.* To see why, suppose that the class Point described previously has been declared, and we use it to create two new classes, Line and Rectangle:

```
#include "Point.h"                    #include "Point.h"

class Line                           class Rectangle
{                                    {
 public:                              public:
   // ...                               // ...
 private:                             private:
   double mySlope;                      Point myUpperLeft,
   Point myYIntercept;                        myLowerRight;
};                                   };
```

Now if a graphing program should use the #include directive to insert both Line.h and Rectangle.h, then Point is declared twice, generating an error. By surrounding Point as follows,

```
#ifndef POINT
#define POINT

class Point
{
   // ...
};

#endif
```

the code declaring class `Point` will be processed in whichever header file is processed first, but skipped in the header file that is processed second, eliminating the error.

6.   A `friend` *function must be named as such by the class of which it is a* `friend`. *This is accomplished by preceding its declaration with the keyword* `friend` *in the class declaration. However, the* `friend` *mechanism should only be used in situations where a function member cannot be used and direct access to the data members of a class object are required.*

Programming Problems

Section 10.5

1.   Write a driver program to test the playing-cards class of exercise 9.

2.   Write a driver program to test the time class of exercise 10.

3.   Write a driver program to test the phone-number class of exercise 11.

4.   Write a driver program to test the checker-board class of exercise 12.

5.   Write a driver program to test the Cartesian-coordinate class of exercise 13.

6.   Write a driver program to test the polar-coordinate class of exercise 14.

7.   Write a driver program to test the personal-information class of exercise 15.

8.   Write a driver program to test the baseball-player class of exercise 16.

9.   Write a driver program to test the weather-statistics class of exercise 17.

10. The *point-slope equation* of a line having slope m and passing through point P with coordinates (x_1, y_1) is

$$y - y_1 = m(x - x_1)$$

(a) Write a class for a `CartesianPoint`, described by its x and y coordinates, with all appropriate operations on such objects.

(b) Write a `LineSegment` class, described by two `CartesianPoint` endpoints. In addition to the usual operations, this class should provide operations to compute:
   (i) The midpoint of the line segment joining two points
   (ii) The equation of the perpendicular bisector of this line segment

(c) Write a class for a `Line`, described by its slope and a point on the line, with functions that
   (i) Find the point-slope equation of the line
   (ii) Find the slope-intercept equation of the line

(d) Write a program to read the point and slope information for two lines and to determine whether they intersect or are parallel. If they intersect, find the point of intersection and also determine whether they are perpendicular.

11. Write a program that accepts a time of day in military format and finds the corresponding standard representation in hours, minutes, and A.M/P.M., or accepts the time in the usual format and finds the corresponding military representation. For example, the input 0100 should produce 1:00 A.M. as output, and the input 3:45 P.M. should give 1545. Use a class to store the time, and provide extraction or conversion functions to display the time in either format.

12. A *rational number* is of the form a/b, where a and b are integers with $b \neq 0$. Write a program to do rational number arithmetic, storing each rational number in a record that has a numerator field and a denominator field. The program should read and display all rational numbers in the format a/b, or simply a if the denominator is 1. The following examples illustrate the menu of commands that the user should be allowed to enter:

Input	Output	Comments
3/8 + 1/6	13/24	$a/b + c/d = (ad + bc)/bd$ reduced to lowest terms
3/8 − 1/6	5/24	$a/b − c/d = (ad − bc)/bd$ reduced to lowest terms
3/8 * 1/6	1/16	$a/b * c/d = ac/bd$ reduced to lowest terms
3/8 / 1/6	9/4	$a/b / c/d = ad/bc$ reduced to lowest terms
3/8 I	8/3	Invert a/b
8/3 M	2 + 2/3	Write a/b as a mixed fraction
6/8 R	3/4	Reduce a/b to lowest terms
6/8 G	2	Greatest common divisor of numerator and denominator
1/6 L 3/8	24	Lowest common denominator of a/b and c/d
1/6 < 3/8	true	$a/b < c/d$?
1/6 <= 3/8	true	$a/b \leq c/d$?
1/6 > 3/8	false	$a/b > c/d$?
1/6 >= 3/8	false	$a/b \geq c/d$?
3/8 = 9/24	true	$a/b = c/d$?
2/3 X + 2 = 4/5	X = − 9/5	Solution of linear equation $(a/b)X + c/d = e/f$

13. A *complex number* has the form $a + bi$ where a and b are real values and $i^2 = -1$. The standard C++ library includes a class `complex` for processing complex numbers. Examine the structure of this class to find the operations it provides and what data members it uses. (See the website described in the preface for a link to the ANSI/ISO C++ standard.)

14. Using the `complex` type, write a program to find the roots (real or complex) of a quadratic equation. (See Programming Problem 16 of Chapter 3.)

Chapter 11

ENUMERATIONS

God created the integers; all the rest is the work of man.

LEOPOLD KRONECKER

Roses are 0, violets are 3 ???

(orig.)

This guy Roy G. Biv — now he was one COLORFUL character . . .

V. OREHCK III (fictitious)

Chapter Contents

11.1   Introductory Example: Wavelengths of Colors
11.2   C-Style Enumerations
11.3   Object-Oriented Enumerations
11.4   Example: Geological Classification
        PART OF THE PICTURE: The C++ Type Hierarchy

The *fundamental types* provided in C++ make it possible to represent objects whose values are integers, reals, characters, and so on. The C++ *class types* make it possible to represent complex objects having multiple attributes, and in the objects we have examined thus far, these attributes have been represented using the fundamental types. Some real-world objects, however, may have attributes that cannot be modeled in a natural and efficient way using only the fundamental types; for example:

▶ A person's gender: *female* or *male*

▶ An automobile's manufacturer: *Buick, Chevrolet, Chrysler, Ferrari, Ford, Mercedes Benz, Oldsmobile, Saab, Toyota, Volkswagen, . . .* (to name just a few)

▶ A craftsman's expertise: *apprentice, journeyman, master*

▶ Athletic shoes designed for specific sports: *running shoes, tennis shoes, cross trainers, volleyball shoes, basketball shoes, . . .* (another long list)

Each of these attributes could be represented using the `string` type, but this can result in very inefficient programs. To see why, suppose that an object has an attribute named `hue`, whose value is one of the seven colors: *RED, ORANGE, YELLOW, GREEN, BLUE, INDIGO,* and *VIOLET*. One approach is to use a `string` object to represent these colors:

```
string hue;  // "RED", "ORANGE", ..., "VIOLET"
```

The object `hue` can then be assigned a character `string` color value, can be compared using the `string` relational operators, and so on. The problem is that using a `string` can be very time-inefficient, since a seemingly simple assignment such as

```
hue = "ORANGE";
```

may actually require six assignments—one for each character being assigned. Comparisons can be time-consuming for the same reason. The boolean expression in the `if` statement

```
if (hue == "VIOLET")
   DoSomethingWith(hue);
```

may require 6 comparisons, one for each character in *VIOLET*.

An alternative approach is to represent such attributes using the `int` type, but this is clumsy and results in programs that are hard to read. For example, if we represent `hue` as an integer,

```
int hue;   // 1 - RED, 2 - ORANGE, ..., 7 - VIOLET
```

we avoid the inefficiency of the `string` type, because the assignment

```
hue = 2;
```

requires just one integer assignment. Similarly, a comparison

```
if (hue == 4)
   DoSomethingWith(hue);
```

involves only one integer comparison.

The difficulty with this approach is remembering which integer is associated with which color. Is *RED* represented by zero or one? What is the fourth color?

The programmer is forced to remember this object-to-integer mapping and use it consistently. This is annoying, because maintaining such a mapping is a mechanical process and could just as well be done by the computer. It would be much more convenient to simply write

```
hue = ORANGE;
```

or

```
if (hue == GREEN)
    DoSomethingWith(hue);
```

Fortunately, C++ provides a mechanism for doing this, allowing the programmer to construct objects whose values are names of real-world entities like colors, genders, days, and so on. In this chapter we will examine this mechanism, called the *enumeration*.

11.1 INTRODUCTORY EXAMPLE: WAVELENGTHS OF COLORS

As usual, we begin with an example to introduce this chapter's topic.

PROBLEM

Botanist Dan N. Baum studies conifers and how their needles absorb light. To help with his research, he has hired us to write a program that, given one of the colors red, orange, yellow, green, blue, indigo, or violet, will display the wavelength of light associated with that color.

OBJECT-CENTERED DESIGN

Behavior. The program should display on the screen a prompt for a color and then read the color from the keyboard. It should then compute and display on the screen the wavelength of light associated with that color.

Objects. In addition to the usual screen, keyboard, and prompt objects, this problem involves the following objects:

Description	Kind	Type	Name
A color	varying	Color	*theColor*
The associated wavelength	varying	double	*wavelength*

As we saw in the introduction to this chapter, using the type string to represent *theColor* would not be very efficient. We will instead create a new type named Color that avoids these inefficiencies.

Operations. Solving this problem involves the following operations:

  i.   Output a string via an ostream
  ii.   Read a Color value via an istream

> **iii.** Compute the (double) wavelength associated with a given Color value
>
> **iv.** Display a double via an ostream

Of these operations, i and iv are predefined, but we will need to write functions to perform operations ii and iii.

Algorithm. Given functions to perform each of these operations, we can organize them into the following algorithm:

Algorithm for color wavelengths

1. Via cout, display a prompt for a color.
2. From cin, read a color into *theColor*.
3. Compute *wavelength*, the wavelength associated with *theColor*.
4. Via cout, display *wavelength*.

Coding. The program in Figure 11.1 implements the preceding algorithm. It uses the type Color defined in Color.h. In the next section, we will see how to build this type Color in a way that is both efficient and readable.

FIGURE 11.1   A Color–WAVELENGTH PROGRAM.

```
/* rainbow1.cpp computes the wavelength of light for a given Color.
 *
 * Input:        theColor, a Color value
 * Precondition: theColor is one of RED, ORANGE, YELLOW,
 *                  GREEN, BLUE, INDIGO, VIOLET
 * Output:       the wavelength of light corresponding to theColor
 ***************************************************************/

#include <iostream.h>                    // cin, cout
#include "Color.h"                       // Color

int main()
{
   cout << "To compute the wavelength corresponding to a given color,\n"
        << "enter a color (e.g., RED): ";
   Color theColor;
   cin >> theColor;

   double wavelength = Wavelength(theColor);
   cout << "\nThe corresponding wavelength is " << wavelength << endl;
   return 0;
}
```

Sample run:

```
To compute the wavelength corresponding to a given color,
enter a color (e.g., RED): BLUE

The corresponding wavelength is 4.7e-07
```

11.2 C-STYLE ENUMERATIONS

The declaration

```
enum Color {RED, ORANGE, YELLOW, GREEN, BLUE, INDIGO, VIOLET};
```

creates a new type named `Color` whose values are the seven colors listed between the curly braces. Because the valid values are explicitly listed or *enumerated* in the declaration, this kind of type is called an **enumeration.**

ENUMERATION DECLARATIONS

The declaration of an enumeration must:

1. Provide a name for the enumeration, which becomes the name of a new type

2. Explicitly list all of the values (called **enumerators**) of this new type

In the example above, `Color` is the name of the enumeration, and its enumerators are the identifiers

```
RED, ORANGE, YELLOW, GREEN, BLUE, INDIGO, VIOLET
```

When the compiler encounters such a declaration, it performs the object-to-integer mapping referred to earlier, associating the integer 0 with the first identifier in this list, the integer 1 with the second, and so on. Thus, for the preceding declaration, the compiler makes the following associations:

As another example, the declaration

```
enum Gender {FEMALE, MALE};
```

declares a new type `Gender` whose values are the identifiers `FEMALE` and `MALE`; the compiler will associate the integer 0 with `FEMALE` and the integer 1 with `MALE`. Similarly, the declaration

```
enum HandTool {HAMMER, PLIERS, SAW, SCREWDRIVER};
```

constructs a new type `HandTool` whose values are `HAMMER`, `PLIERS`, `SAW`, and `SCREWDRIVER`, and associates the integers 0, 1, 2, and 3 with these identifiers, respectively. By contrast, neither of the declarations

```
enum Zipcodes {12531, 14405, 21724, 30081};   // ERROR!
enum LetterGrades {A, A-, B+, B, B-, C+, C,   // ERROR!
                   C-, D+, D, D-, "FAIL" };
```

is a valid enumeration, because each contains items that are not valid identifers.

C++ also allows the programmer to specify explicitly the values given to the enumerators. For example, the declaration

```
enum NumberBase {BINARY = 2,
                 OCTAL = 8,
                 DECIMAL = 10,
                 HEX = 16, HEXADECIMAL = 16};
```

associates the identifiers BINARY, OCTAL, DECIMAL, HEX, and HEXADECIMAL with the values 2, 8, 10, 16, and 16, respectively. Similarly, if we wished to have the values 1, 2, . . . , 7 associated with the seven colors given earlier (instead of 0 through 6), we could use the declaration

```
enum Color {RED = 1, ORANGE = 2, YELLOW = 3, GREEN = 4,
            BLUE = 5, INDIGO = 6, VIOLET = 7};
```

or more compactly,

```
enum Color {RED = 1, ORANGE, YELLOW, GREEN, BLUE, INDIGO, VIOLET};
```

because the integer associated with an enumerator is, by default, one more than the integer associated with the preceding enumerator. The iostream library uses an enumeration declaration something like

```
enum Flag {GOOD_BIT = 1, BAD_BIT, FAIL_BIT = 4, EOF_BIT = 8};
```

which associates 1 with GOOD_BIT, 2 with BAD_BIT, 4 with FAIL_BIT, and 8 with EOF_BIT.[1]

These examples illustrate the flexibility of C++—the integers associated with the names need not be distinct nor must they be given in ascending order, although it is good programming style to do so.

The general form of an enumeration declaration is as follows:

Form

    enum *TypeName* { *List* };

where:

    TypeName is an identifier naming a new type; and
    List is a list of the values for the new type, separated by commas, each of which is a valid

      IDENTIFIER

or an initialization expression of the form

      IDENTIFIER = integer_constant

Purpose

Define a new data type whose values are the identifiers in *List*. Each identifier is associated with an integer as follows:

    If an item in *List* has the form *IDENTIFIER = integer_constant*, then *integer_constant* is associated with *IDENTIFIER*;

---

[1] Because each enumerator is a power of 2, each has a 1 at a different position in its binary representation. Such enumerators are called **bit masks,** and make it possible to efficiently store a boolean value such as an iostream status attribute using only a single bit of memory.

> otherwise if it is the first item in the list,
>
>   0 is associated with the *IDENTIFIER*;
>
> otherwise,
>
>   1 + (the integer associated with the preceding identifier) is associated with the *IDENTIFIER*.

Because the compiler essentially treats an enumeration as a series of constant integer declarations, we will use the same uppercase naming convention for enumerators that we use for constant objects.

DEFINING ENUMERATION OBJECTS

To illustrate how enumerations are used, consider the following expansion of enumeration `Color`:

```
enum Color {COLOR_UNDERFLOW = -1,          // too-low error
            RED, ORANGE, YELLOW, GREEN,    // 0-3
            BLUE, INDIGO, VIOLET,          // 4-6
            COLOR_OVERFLOW,                // too-high error
            NUMBER_OF_COLORS = 7};
```

Here, we added the identifiers `COLOR_UNDERFLOW` and `COLOR_OVERFLOW` as values to indicate error conditions. As we will see later, these values can be used to keep from "falling off the ends of the list." We also added the identifier `NUMBER_OF_COLORS`, whose value is the number of values in the list, because this count is often useful.

If it is worthwhile to define a new type, it is usually worth taking the time to store that type in a library so that it can be easily reused. We thus store this declaration of type `Color` in a header file `Color.h` so that programs like that in Figure 11.1 can include it and avoid reinventing the wheel.

Given this type, we can declare a `Color` object named `theColor` as in Figure 11.1. If appropriate, an enumeration object can also be initialized when it is declared:

```
Color theColor = YELLOW;
```

USING ENUMERATIONS

In addition to defining enumeration objects, an enumeration can be used as the index of an array. For example, suppose we define `colorArray` as follows:

```
double colorArray[NUMBER_OF_COLORS] = {0.0};
```

This definition builds the object `colorArray` as a fixed-size array with index values 0 through 6. Because the C++ compiler treats the identifiers `RED` through `VIOLET` as the integer values 0 through 6, we can visualize `colorArray` as follows:

colorArray	0.0	0.0	0.0	0.0	0.0	0.0	0.0
	[RED]	[ORANGE]	[YELLOW]	[GREEN]	[BLUE]	[INDIGO]	[VIOLET]

The `Color` enumerators can then be used with the subscript operator to access the array elements.

In the same way, an extra enumerator like `NUMBER_OF_COLORS` can be used to provide a `vector<T>` with an initial size:

```
vector<double> colorVector(NUMBER_OF_COLORS);
```

This defines `colorVector` as a varying-sized object, initially with seven elements:

colorVector	0.0	0.0	0.0	0.0	0.0	0.0	0.0
	[RED]	[ORANGE]	[YELLOW]	[GREEN]	[BLUE]	[INDIGO]	[VIOLET]

C-Style Enumeration Operations

Many enumeration operations are predefined. For example, an enumeration object can be assigned a value, used as a parameter, compared using the relational operators, and so on. But other operations must be defined by the creator or user of the enumeration. For example, the program in Figure 11.1 requires computing the wavelength corresponding to a `Color` value. Since there is no predefined operation to do this, one must be provided. The function in Figure 11.2 shows one way to do this. Because this `Color` operation is nontrivial, its definition should be stored in the library's implementation file `Color.cpp` and its prototype in the header file `Color.h`.

 FIGURE 11.2   COMPUTING `Color` WAVELENGTH.

```
// ------- Wavelength of a Color ------------------------------------------

double Wavelength(Color aColor)
{
   switch(aColor)
   {
      case RED:
                return 6.5E-7;
      case ORANGE:
                return 6.0E-7;
      case YELLOW:
                return 5.8E-7;
      case GREEN:
                return 5.2E-7;
      case BLUE:
                return 4.7E-7;
      case INDIGO:
                return 4.4E-7;
      case VIOLET:
                return 4.1E-7;
      default:
                cerr << "\n*** Wavelength: invalid color received!\n";
                return 0.0;
   }
}
```

A program like that in Figure 11.1 can call this function,

```
double wavelength = Wavelength(theColor);
```

and the argument `theColor` will be passed to the function via parameter `aColor`. The function's `switch` statement will then select and return the appropriate wavelength.

The program in Figure 11.1 also requires that we be able to read a `Color` value from the keyboard using `operator>>`, which is not predefined. As we saw in section 10.4, overloading the input function is a bit complicated; therefore, we will derive it in more detail.

Function Behavior. The function `operator>>()` should receive `istream` and `Color` parameters from its caller. Because an `istream` is a stream of characters, this function should read a sequence of characters from the `istream` into a `string` object. For user convenience, we will allow these characters to be either upper- or lowercase and design the function to convert the characters in this string to uppercase, if necessary. Based upon the value of that string, the function must assign the corresponding `Color` enumerator to the `Color` parameter. If the string does not correspond to any valid `Color` enumerator, the *fail* bit should be set in the `istream`. Finally, the function should return its `istream` parameter (so that input operations can be chained).

Function Objects. The objects in this problem are as follows

Description	Type	Kind	Movement	Name
An `istream`	`istream`	varying	received (in), passed back (out), and returned	`in`
A `Color`	`Color`	varying	received (in) and passed back (out)	*aColor*
A `string`	`string`	varying	none	*colorString*

The specification of the operation is thus:

Receive:	*in*, an `istream`
	aColor, a `Color` object
Precondition:	*in* contains a string corresponding to a `Color` value
Input:	a string from *in*
Pass back:	*in* with the string removed
	aColor, containing the `Color` corresponding to the string read from *in*
Return:	*in* (for chaining)

From this, we can write the following stub for the function:

```
istream & operator>>(istream & in, Color & aColor)
{
   // ... to be filled in shortly ...
   return in;
}
```

Function Operations. The operations in this problem are as follows:

i.   Receive arguments from the caller

ii. Read a `string` from an `istream`

iii. Convert the characters in a `string` to uppercase, if necessary

iv. Assign to the `Color` parameter `aColor` the enumerator corresponding to the `string` (or set the *fail* bit in the `istream` if there is no such `Color` enumerator)

Function Algorithm. We can organize these operations into the following algorithm:

Algorithm for color input

0. Receive *in* and *aColor* from the caller.

1. From *in*, read a string into *colorString*.

2. For each index *i* in *colorString:*

   If *colorString*[*i*] is lowercase, convert it to uppercase.

3. If *colorString* == "RED"

   Assign enumerator RED to *aColor.*

   Else if *colorString* == "ORANGE"

   Assign enumerator ORANGE to *aColor.*

   Else if *colorString* == "YELLOW"

   Assign enumerator YELLOW to *aColor.*

   Else if *colorString* == "GREEN"

   Assign enumerator GREEN to *aColor.*

   Else if *colorString* == "BLUE"

   Assign enumerator BLUE to *aColor.*

   Else if*colorString* == "INDIGO"

   Assign enumerator INDIGO to *aColor.*

   Else if *colorString* == "VIOLET"

   Assign enumerator VIOLET to *aColor.*

   Else

   Set the *fail* bit in stream *in.*

4. Return *in.*

Function Coding. Given this algorithm, we can fill in the function's stub as shown in Figure 11.3. Because this is a nontrivial function, we store its definition in the `Color` library's implementation file, `Color.cpp`, and place its prototype in `Color.h`.

Note that we must perform selection using the `string` object `colorString`. Because the selector in a `switch` statement cannot be based on a string value, we must use a multibranch `if` statement to perform the selection.

FIGURE 11.3   Color INPUT.

```
// ------- Color Input -----------------------------------------------
#include <string>                    // string
#include <ctype.h>                   // is lower(), toupper()

istream & operator>>(istream & in, Color & aColor)
{
   string colorString;
   in >> colorString;

   for (int i = 0; i < colorString.size(); i++)
      if (islower(colorString[i]))
         colorString[i] = toupper(colorString[i]);
   if (colorString == "RED")
      aColor = RED;
   else if (colorString == "ORANGE")
      aColor = ORANGE;
   else if (colorString == "YELLOW")
      aColor = YELLOW;
   else if (colorString == "GREEN")
      aColor = GREEN;
   else if (colorString == "BLUE")
      aColor = BLUE;
   else if (colorString == "INDIGO")
      aColor = INDIGO;
   else if (colorString == "VIOLET")
      aColor = VIOLET;
   else
      in.setstate(ios::failbit);

   return in;
}
```

Given this function, the program in Figure 11.1 can now contain the statements

```
Color theColor
cin >> theColor;
```

and since `theColor` is of type `Color`, the compiler will search for a version of `operator>>` whose signature is `(istream &, Color &)`. Finding its prototype in `Color.h`, the compiler will allow the call to proceed. The linker will then search for a definition with this signature. Upon finding it in `Color.cpp`, the linker will bind the function call to this definition.

OTHER ENUMERATION OPERATIONS

Because we are building a `Color` library, it makes sense to provide additional `Color` operations that might be useful.

Output. As we saw in Figure 11.3, all I/O is performed at the character level, and the input function basically reads `string` values and maps them to `Color` values.

The output function must therefore perform the opposite Color-to-string mapping and write the resulting string to an ostream. Figure 11.4 gives a definition of this function which, because of its complexity, should be defined in Color.cpp.

FIGURE 11.4   Color OUTPUT.

```
// ------- Color Output -----------------------------------------

ostream & operator<<(ostream & out, Color aColor)
{
   switch(aColor)
   {
      case RED:
                  out << "RED";
      case ORANGE:
                  out << "ORANGE";
      case YELLOW:
                  out << "YELLOW";
      case GREEN:
                  out << "GREEN";
      case BLUE:
                  out << "BLUE";
      case INDIGO:
                  out << "INDIGO";
      case VIOLET:
                  out << "VIOLET";
      default:
                  cerr << "\n*** operator<<: invalid color received!\n";
   }
   return out;
}
```

As described earlier, the compiler treats an enumeration as a special kind of integer. This has two implications for this function:

1. If a function receives but does not pass back an enumeration value, the value should be passed using the call-by-value mechanism. That is, since an enumeration is not a class, an enumeration value should not be passed using the const reference mechanism.

2. Because we are using an enumeration (as opposed to a string), we may use a switch statement to perform the selection.

Once the function is defined and its prototype stored in Color.h, a programmer can write

```
cout << "Color me " << theColor << endl;
```

and if the value of theColor is BLUE, then

```
Color me BLUE
```

will be displayed.

Successor. A *successor function* is a function that, given a value *v*, returns the value that follows *v* in the list of enumerators. For example, given RED, a successor function will return ORANGE; given ORANGE, it will return YELLOW; and so on; given VIOLET, however, it will return COLOR_OVERFLOW, one of our "illegal" Color enumerators.

Figure 11.5 presents a function Next() that provides this operation for our Color enumeration. As usual, the complexity of this function implies that it be stored in Color.cpp.

 FIGURE 11.5   **Color SUCCESSOR.**

```
// ------- Color Successor ------------------------------------------------

Color Next(Color aColor)
{
   switch (aColor)
   {
      case RED:
                    return ORANGE;
      case ORANGE:
                    return YELLOW;
      case YELLOW:
                    return GREEN;
      case GREEN:
                    return BLUE;
      case BLUE:
                    return INDIGO;
      case INDIGO:
                    return VIOLET;
      case VIOLET:
                    return COLOR_OVERFLOW;
      default:
                    cerr << "\n*** Next(): invalid color received!\n";
                    return COLOR_OVERFLOW;
   }
}
```

This function shows why the enumerators COLOR_UNDERFLOW and COLOR_OVER-FLOW were added. By providing these extra "invalid" values at each end of the enumerator list, we provide an error value for the function to return when there is no valid return value.

We can use this function to drive a for loop that iterates through the Color values:

```
for (Color aColor = RED; aColor <= VIOLET; aColor = Next(aColor))
   cout << aColor << ' ';
```

On each repetition, the call to Next() returns the successor to aColor, and so this statement produces

```
RED ORANGE YELLOW GREEN BLUE INDIGO VIOLET
```

For the final repetition (when `aColor` is `VIOLET`), the call to `Next()` returns `COLOR_OVERFLOW`. Because the compiler treats `VIOLET` as 6 and `COLOR_OVER-FLOW` as 7, the condition

```
aColor <= VIOLET
```

is evaluated as

```
COLOR_OVERFLOW <= VIOLET
```

which is `false`, terminating the repetition.

Predecessor. Whereas a successor function returns the next value in a sequence, a predecessor function returns the previous value in the sequence. A predecessor function is similar to the successor function and is left as an exercise.

LIBRARIES AND TYPES

As we saw with classes, the true purpose of a library is as follows:

> The purpose of a library is to store
> 1. a type declaration; and
> 2. the operations on objects of that type.

That is, a library is intended to be a container for a type, including the collection of functions that form the basic operations on that type. In the case of type `Color`, we would define a library named `Color`. In its interface file `Color.h`, we would store the declarations of `Color` and the various `Color` operations, as shown in Figure 11.6:

FIGURE 11.6   **THE `Color` INTERFACE FILE.**

```
/* Color.h contains the interface for enumeration Color.
 *  ...
 **************************************************************/


// --- The type
enum Color {COLOR_UNDERFLOW = -1,          // too-low error
            RED, ORANGE, YELLOW, GREEN,    // 0-3
            BLUE, INDIGO, VIOLET,          // 4-6
            NUMBER_OF_COLORS,              // 7
            COLOR_OVERFLOW = 7};           // too-high error

// --- Its interface
#include <iostream.h>                         // istream, ostream

istream & operator>>(istream & in, Color & aColor);
ostream & operator<<(ostream & out, Color aColor);
Color Next(Color aColor);
Color Previous(Color aColor);
double Frequency(Color aColor);
double Wavelength(Color aColor);
// ... additional Color operations ...
```

The corresponding definitions of the `Color` operations would then be stored in the library's implementation file `Color.cpp` and documentation for the library in its documentation file `Color.doc`.

Given this library, a program can now use the type `Color` and its operations simply by including the library's header file (`Color.h`) as in Figure 11.1. After the program is compiled, the resulting object file must be linked with the definitions in the implementation object file.

✔ ## Quick Quiz 11.2

1. The compiler treats an enumerator as a special kind of _____.
2. (True or false) `enum T {1, 2, 3, 4};` is a valid enumeration declaration.
3. (True or false) `enum T {FORTY, FIFTY, SIXTY};` is a valid enumeration declaration.
4. (True or false) `enum T {FORTY-ONE, FIFTY-ONE, SIXTY-ONE};` is a valid enumeration declaration.

Questons 5–14 use the following declarations;

```
enum English {ZERO, ONE, TWO, THREE, FOUR};
enum German {EIN = 1, ZWEI, DREI, VIER};
enum PigLatin {EROZAY, EETHRAY = 3, IVEFAY = 5, IXSAY};
enum Nonsense {FEE, FI = 6, FO, FUM, FOO = 3, BAR};
```

5. What value is associated with `THREE`?
6. What value is associated with `DREI`?
7. What value is associated with `IXSAY`?
8. What value is associated with `FEE`?
9. What value is associated with `FUM`?
10. What value is associated with `BAR`?
11. What type is defined by the last declaration?
12. In the last declaration, `FUM` is called a(n) _____.
13. (True or false) `EETHRAY < IVEFAY`.
14. (True or false) `FOO > BAR`.
15. (True or false) An enumeration parameter should not be declared using the `const` reference mechanism.
16. (True or false) Enumerations may be used as array indices.
17. Write an enumeration declaration for the names of the days of the week.
18. What is the main purpose of a library?

EXERCISES 11.2

1. Write an enumeration `MonthAbbrev`, whose values are abbreviations of the months of the year and consist of the first three letters of the months' names.

Exercises 2–7 assume the enumerated type `MonthAbbrev` of exercise 1. For each, find the value of the given expression.

2. `Jan < Aug`
3. `Sep <= Sep`
4. `Sep + 1`
5. `Apr - 1`
6. `Aug + 2`
7. `Aug - 2`

Exercises 8–13 ask you to develop a library for the enumerated type `MonthAbbrev` of exercise 1. To test this library, you should write driver programs as instructed in Programming Problem 1 at the end of this chapter.

8.   Construct a header file for the type `MonthAbbrev` that defines it together with (at least) I/O operations and a successor operation.

9.   Construct an implementation file for the header file of exercise 8.

10.   Write a documentation file to complete the library for the type `MonthAbbrev` of exercises 8 and 9.

11.   Write a function whose parameter is the number of a month and whose value is the corresponding value of type `MonthAbbrev`. Add this function—its prototype, definition, and documentation—to the appropriate files in the library for the type `MonthAbbrev` of exercises 8–10

12.   Write a function whose parameters are a nonnegative integer n and a month abbreviation `Abbrev` and that finds the "nth successor" of `Abbrev`. The 0th successor of `Abbrev` is `Abbrev` itself; for n > 0, the nth successor of `Abbrev` is the nth month following `Abbrev`. For example, the fourth successor of `Aug` is `Dec`, and the sixth successor of `Aug` is `Feb`. Add this function—its prototype, definition, and documentation—to the appropriate files in the library for the type `MonthAbbrev` of exercises 8–10.

13.   Proceed as in exercise 12, but define the function recursively.

Exercises 14–16 ask you to develop a library for an enumerated type `Day` for the names of the days of the week. To test this library, you should write driver programs as instructed in Programming Problem 2 at the end of this chapter.

14.   Construct a header file for type `Day`. It should at least have I/O operations and a successor operation.

15.   Construct an implementation file for the type `Day` of exercise 14.

16.   Write a documentation file to complete the library for the type `Day` of exercises 14 and 15.

11.3 OBJECT-ORIENTED ENUMERATIONS

Because C-style enumerations are not classes, they suffer from two drawbacks:

1.   The operations on a C-style enumeration cannot be defined as function members, and so C-style enumerations are not consistent with the I-can-do-it-myself principle

2.   Because there is no class invariant, operations on a C-style enumeration cannot assume that valid values will be passed to an enumeration parameter

Both of these deficiencies can be overcome by replacing a C-style enumeration with a class.

DECLARING ENUMERATION CLASSES

As we saw in chapter 10, building a class consists of carefully designing the class and then using that design as a blueprint to implement the class.

Class Design.   Recall that the first step in designing a class is to list the operations it should provide. Applying the internal perspective to the design of a `Color` class, we might list the following:

- Initialize myself to a default color value
- Initialize myself to an explicitly supplied color value
- Return my wavelength
- Return my frequency
- Display my value on a given `ostream`
- Read a color value from a given `istream` into me
- Compare myself with another `Color` using any of the relational operators
- Increment myself to the color value that follows mine
- Decrement myself to the color value that precedes mine

Again, this is not an exhaustive list, but it will be adequate to illustrate the use of enumerations with classes.

Class Implementation.   Once we have identified what operations the class is to provide, we are ready to begin implementing its data members. From our list of operations, it should be evident that the class needs to store a color value. To represent a color value, we begin by declaring an enumeration named `ColorValue`, in the class header file `Color.h`:

```
enum ColorValue {COLOR_UNDERFLOW = -1,
                 RED, ORANGE, YELLOW, GREEN,
                 BLUE, INDIGO, VIOLET,
                 COLOR_OVERFLOW,
                 NUMBER_OF_COLORS = 7};
```

We can then declare an object that can store a `ColorValue`:

```
ColorValue myColorValue;
```

This will be the only data member of the class and so we wrap it, but not the declaration of `ColorValue`, within a declaration of class `Color`:

```
enum ColorValue {COLOR_UNDERFLOW = -1,
                 RED, ORANGE, YELLOW, GREEN,
                 BLUE, INDIGO, VIOLET,
                 COLOR_OVERFLOW,
                 NUMBER_OF_COLORS = 7};
class Color
{
 public:
   // ... to be filled in later ...
 private:
   ColorValue myColorValue;
};
```

We thus have *two* types: `ColorValue`, which is the name of an enumeration of color values, and `Color`, which is the name of a class that contains a data member of type `ColorValue`. However, no operations will be defined for type

ColorValue; its sole purpose is to support the declaration of the data member myColorValue. Instead, all operations will be defined as function members (or friends) of class Color. By declaring ColorValue outside of class Color, the various ColorValue enumerators (RED, ORANGE, . . .) can be used as is, both by the class and by any program that uses this class.[2]

To finish our class declaration, we wrap it and the declaration of ColorValue inside preprocessor directives that prevent it from being compiled more than once:

```
#ifndef COLOR
#define COLOR

enum ColorValue {COLOR_UNDERFLOW = -1,
                 RED, ORANGE, YELLOW, GREEN,
                 BLUE, INDIGO, VIOLET,
                 COLOR_OVERFLOW,
                 NUMBER_OF_COLORS = 7};
class Color
{
 public:
   // ... to be filled in later ...
 private:
   ColorValue myColorValue;
};

#endif
```

Given this much, a definition

```
Color hue;
```

will define hue as a Color object that we might visualize as follows:

Of course, to provide hue with an initial value, we need to supply a Color constructor function, so we proceed to the implemention of the Color operations.

DEFINING COLOR OPERATIONS

The Class Invariant. The value of the class' data member myColorValue must be one of the ColorValue enumerators that names a color. Thus, an invariant for the class Color is

```
myColorValue == RED || myColorValue == ORANGE ||
myColorValue == YELLOW || myColorValue == GREEN ||
myColorValue == BLUE || myColorValue == INDIGO ||
myColorValue == VIOLET
```

---

[2] If ColorValue were declared publicly within class Color, then any use of an enumerator outside of the class would have to be qualified with the name of the class and the scope operator (e.g., Color::RED, Color::ORANGE, etc.).

Our implementations of the class constructors and other operations that can modify this data member must ensure that this invariant is never violated. Other operations that use the data member can then be assured that its value satisfies this condition.

The Default-Value Constructor.   As a default color value, we might choose any of the colors. Here we will use the first valid color value RED. Applying object-centered design from the internal perspective gives the following specification of the behavior of the default-value constructor:

> **Postcondition:**   `myColorValue == RED`

Figure 11.7 gives a `Color` constructor that guarantees this postcondition. Because this function is so simple, we define it as an `inline` function in `Color.h` (following class `Color`). We store its prototype in the public section of class `Color`, as shown in Figure 11.14.

FIGURE 11.7   **THE `Color` DEFAULT VALUE CONSTRUCTOR.**

```
// ------- Default Value Constructor -----------------------------------

inline Color::Color()
{
    myColorValue = RED;
}
```

A programmer can now write

```
Color hue;
```

and `hue` will be auto-initialized to the color RED:

The Explicit Value Constructor.   If we wish to initialize a `Color` object with any value other than RED, we must, of course, supply a second constructor. Applying object-centered design from an internal perspective gives the following specification of its behavior:

> **Receive:**   *initialColorValue*, a `ColorValue`
> **Precondition:**   *initialColorValue* is one of RED, . . . , VIOLET
> **Postcondition:** `myColorValue ==` *initialColorValue*

Figure 11.8 presents a `Color` constructor that ensures that the precondition and postcondition are satisfied and thus guarantees that the class invariant remains true. As before, we define this explicit-value constructor as an `inline` function in `Color.h`, following the declaration of the class `Color`.

FIGURE 11.8 THE Color EXPLICIT VALUE CONSTRUCTOR.

```
// ------- Explicit Value Constructor ----------------------------------

#include <assert.h>                                        // assert()

inline Color::Color(ColorValue initialColorValue)
{
   assert(RED <= initialColorValue && initialColorValue <= VIOLET);
   myColorValue = initialColorValue;
}
```

The declaration

```
    Color hue(BLUE);
```

will construct hue and initialize it with the color value BLUE:

Color Wavelength. Next on our list of operations is a function to "return my wavelength." We can specify its behavior as follows:

Return: the (double) wavelength corresponding to myColorValue.

The function in Figure 11.9 satisfies this specification. Because this operation should not alter any of the class data members, it is defined as a const function member. Note that it also need not include a default case in the switch statement because of the class invariant. Because of the relative complexity of this function, we put its prototype in the public section of class Color (see Figure 11.14) and its definition in a separately-compiled implementation file Color.cpp.

FIGURE 11.9 Color WAVELENGTH.

```
/* Color.cpp provides the implementation of class Color operations
 * ...
 ***********************************************************************/

#include "Color.h"                                         // class Color

// ------- Wavelength ------------------------------------------------

double Color::Wavelength() const
{
   switch (myColorValue)
   {
     case RED:
                 return 6.5E-7;
     case ORANGE:
                 return 6.0E-7;
```

```
          case YELLOW:
                    return 5.8E-7;
          case GREEN:
                    return 5.2E-7;
          case BLUE:
                    return 4.7E-7;
          case INDIGO:
                    return 4.4E-7;
          case VIOLET:
                    return 4.1E-7;
     }
}
```

A programmer can now write

```
cout << hue.Wavelength() << endl;
```

and the appropriate wavelength for the color in `hue` will be displayed. A function member to compute the frequency of a `Color` is straightforward and is left as an exercise.

Color I/O. As we saw in section 10.4, the extraction operator (>>) should not be defined as a function member of a class other than `istream`. We will therefore use the same approach as we did there: define a public `Read()` function member and then overload `operator>>` as a non-member function that uses `Read()`. The behavior of this `Read()` function can be specified as follows:

Receive:	*in,* an `istream`
Input:	*colorString,* a character string
Precondition:	*colorString* is one of "RED", "ORANGE", . . . ,"VIOLET"
Postcondition:	`myColorValue` contains the `ColorValue` corresponding to *colorString*
Pass back:	*in* with the character string literal removed

Figure 11.10 gives a definition of `Read()` that satisfies this specification. Because the function can modify `myColorValue`, it must ensure that the class invariant remains true. And because it is relatively complicated, it is defined in `Color.cpp`. The prototype of this function must, of course, be stored in the public section of class `Color`, as shown in Figure 11.14.

FIGURE 11.10   Color INPUT (FUNCTION MEMBER).

```
// ------- Input Function Member -----------------------------------------

#include <string>                          // string
#include <stdlib.h>                        // exit()
#include <ctype.h>                         // islower(), toupper
void Color::Read(istream & in)
{
   string colorString;                                          // read string
   in >> colorString;
```

```
for (int i = 0; i < colorString.size(); i++)        // convert case
   if (islower(colorString[i]))                       // if needed
      colorString[i] = toupper(colorString[i]);

if (colorString == "RED")                             // map to ColorValue
   myColorValue = RED;
else if (colorString == "ORANGE")
   myColorValue = ORANGE;
else if (colorString == "YELLOW")
   myColorValue = YELLOW;
else if (colorString == "GREEN")
   myColorValue = GREEN;
else if (colorString == "BLUE")
   myColorValue = BLUE;
else if (colorString == "INDIGO")
   myColorValue = INDIGO;
else if (colorString == "VIOLET")
   myColorValue = VIOLET;
else
{
   cerr << "\n*** Read: invalid color received!\n";
   exit(1);
}
}
```

A programmer can now write

```
hue.Read(cin);
```

to read a color value for `hue`.

Of course, it would be more convenient if we could use the operator `>>` to read a `Color`. Because this operation must be defined as a non-member function, its specification is as follows:

Receive:	*in,* an `istream`, *theColor,* a `Color`
Input:	*colorString,* a character string
Precondition:	*colorString* is one of "RED", "ORANGE", . . . , "VIOLET"
Pass back:	*in,* with the character string literal removed; *theColor,* containing the `ColorValue` corresponding to *colorString*
Return:	*in,* for chaining of input operations

Although this specification is somewhat complicated, the definition of the function is quite simple, thanks to the `Read()` function member. We can therefore inline `operator>>` in `Color.h`, as shown in Figure 11.11. Because `operator>>` is not a function member of class `Color`, no prototype is placed in the declaration of class `Color`.[3]

---

[3] If `operator>>` were to directly assign a `ColorValue` to the private member `theColor.myColor-Value`, instead of using the public `theColor.Read()` function member to do so indirectly, then it would be necessary for class `Color` to contain a prototype of `operator>>` naming it as a `friend`.

FIGURE 11.11   COLOR INPUT (NON-MEMBER FUNCTION).

```
// -------- Non-member Input ------------------------------------

inline istream & operator>>(istream & in, Color & theColor)
{
   theColor.Read(in);
   return in;
}
```

Given this definition, a statement like

```
cin >> hue;
```

can be used to read a color value from the keyboard into `hue`. A `Color` output operation can be provided using a similar two-function approach and is left as an exercise.

Relational Operators. Unlike `operator<<` and `operator>>`, the relational operators `==`, `!=`, `<`, `>`, `<=`, and `>=` can be overloaded as function members of class `Color`. However, if we do so, then a boolean expression like

```
someColor == RED
```

will be valid, but an expression

```
RED == someColor
```

will not be valid, because such an expression sends `RED` (a `ColorValue` object) the `==` message with a `Color` argument, and there is no definition of `operator==` with such a signature. Put differently, the equality operation will not be symmetric if we define `operator==` as a `Color` function member.

This problem can be circumvented by defining `operator==` as a non-member function. Its behavior can be specified by:

Receive: *left,* a `Color`, and *right,* another `Color`

Return: `true`, if and only if *left*.myColorValue `==` *right*.myColorValue

The other relational operators have similar specifications. For example,

Receive: *left,* a `Color`, and *right,* another `Color`

Return: `true`, if and only if *left*.myColorValue `<` *right*.myColorValue

is a specification for the less-than operation.

Figure 11.12 presents definitions of `operator==`, `operator<`, and `operator<=` satisfying these specifications. Because they are relatively simple, we define them as inline in `Color.h`.

FIGURE 11.12   COLOR RELATIONAL OPERATORS.

```
// -------- Equality --------------------------------------------

inline bool operator==(const Color & left, const Color & right)
{
   return left.myColorValue == right.myColorValue;
}
```

```
// -------- Less-than ------------------------------------------

inline bool operator<(const Color & left, const Color & right)
{
   return left.myColorValue < right.myColorValue;
}


// -------- Less-than-or-equal ----------------------------------

inline bool operator<=(const Color & left, const Color & right)
{
   return left.myColorValue <= right.myColorValue;
}


// ... remaining relational operators omitted
```

If we try to compile these functions, an error message is generated because they are non-member functions trying to access the private myColorValue data members of their operands. Either the class must provide a public accessor function member to access myColorValue or it must specify that these functions are friend functions, as shown in Figure 11.14. Once this is done, a programmer can write

```
if (hue1 == hue2)
   // ... do whatever is appropriate for equal colors
```

or

```
if (hue1 < hue2)
   // ... do whatever is appropriate
```

to compare two Color objects.

Although it is less obvious, we can also compare a Color and a ColorValue:

```
if (hue == VIOLET)
   // ... do something appropriate
```

or

```
if (ORANGE < hue)
   // ... do something appropriate
```

Even though there are no definitions of operator== or operator< with the signature (Color, ColorValue) or (ColorValue, Color), such comparisons still work. When the compiler encounters the comparison

```
hue == VIOLET
```

it searches for a definition of operator== whose signature is (Color, ColorValue). Because there is none, it uses the explicit-value constructor to build a Color out of a ColorValue and then uses the definition of operator== whose signature is (Color, Color). The compiler thus uses the explicit-value constructor to build VIOLET into a Color, which it then passes to the definition of operator== whose signature is (Color, Color).

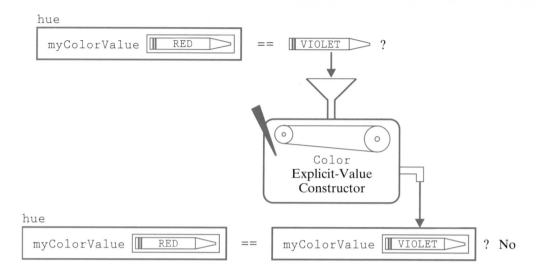

In the same way, when the C++ compiler encounters an expression like

```
ORANGE < hue
```

it uses the explicit-value constructor to build a `Color` having `ORANGE` as its value, which it then supplies as the left operand to `operator<`.

Using this approach streamlines our class considerably. Without it, we would have to explicitly overload each of the six relational operators with *three* definitions: one with the signature (`Color`, `Color`), one with the signature (`Color`, `ColorValue`), and one with the signature (`ColorValue`, `Color`), a total of eighteen different functions.

One way to think of what is happening in these examples is that the compiler is using the explicit-value constructor to perform an **automatic type conversion** of `ORANGE` from `ColorValue` to `Color`.[4] Because the only relational operators in the interface of class `Color` have the signature (`Color`, `Color`), it may not be obvious to a programmer examining the class interface that a `Color` and a `ColorValue` can be compared. For this reason, behaviors that rely on this automatic type conversion must be well documented.

The Increment and Decrement Operators. Overloading the increment operator is complicated by having two forms: the prefix form

```
++x;
```

and the postfix form

```
x++;
```

Recall that these two forms have different behaviors, which we can specify as follows:

---

[4] Any time we define an explicit-value constructor for a class, the compiler may use it to perform such an automatic type conversion without alerting us.

Prefix:

Precondition:	$myColorValue_{Original}$ <= VIOLET
Return:	the Color that follows me
Postcondition:	myColorValue == the ColorValue following $myColorValue_{Original}$

Postfix:

Precondition:	$myColorValue_{Original}$ <= VIOLET
Return:	my original Color
Postcondition:	myColorValue == the ColorValue following $myColorValue_{Original}$

Although the value of myColorValue is the same in both versions, the two versions return different values, as we saw in section 2.6. In order for ++ to elicit two different behaviors, operator++ must be overloaded with two different definitions, one for the prefix form and one for the postfix form. In keeping with the I-can-do-it-myself principle, both versions should be function members of class Color.

How to do this is not obvious. As we saw in section 10.4, overloading a function definition requires that its signature be different from the signatures of all other definitions of the function. But how can the expression

```
++aColor
```

be distinguished from the expression

```
aColor++
```

when neither has any operands other than aColor?

The answer is that the C++ compiler will translate the prefix version as a call

```
aColor.operator++()
```

but it will translate the postfix version as a call

```
aColor.operator++(0)
```

Put differently, the C++ compiler treats calls to the prefix version of operator++ as though they have the signature (), but it treats calls to the postfix version as though they have the signature (int). We can use these differences in signature to define two different versions of operator++, as shown in Figure 11.13. Note that it is not necessary to name the int parameter in the postfix version, since it is not used anywhere in the function—its sole purpose is to provide that version of operator++ with a different signature.

The difference in the behavior of the two functions is clear when viewed from an internal perspective. In the prefix version I increment myself and then return a Color with my new value; but in the postfix version I save my original Color, increment myself, and then return the saved Color.

FIGURE 11.13   Color INCREMENT OPERATORS.

```
// -------- Prefix Increment ----------------------------------------

Color Color::operator++()
{
   switch(myColorValue)
   {
      case RED:
                  myColorValue = ORANGE;
                  break;
      case ORANGE:
                  myColorValue = YELLOW;
                  break;
      case YELLOW:
                  myColorValue = GREEN;
                  break;
      case GREEN:
                  myColorValue = BLUE;
                  break;
      case BLUE:
                  myColorValue = INDIGO;
                  break;
      case VIOLET:
                  myColorValue = COLOR_OVERFLOW;
                  break;
   }

   return Color(myColorValue);
}

// -------- Postfix Increment ---------------------------------------

Color Color::operator++(int)
{
   Color myOriginalColor(myColorValue);

   switch(myColorValue)
   {
      case RED:
                  myColorValue = ORANGE;
                  break;
      case ORANGE:
                  myColorValue = YELLOW;
                  break;
      case YELLOW:
                  myColorValue = GREEN;
                  break;
      case GREEN:
                  myColorValue = BLUE;
                  break;
```

```
            case BLUE:
                        myColorValue = INDIGO;
                        break;
            case INDIGO:
                        myColorValue = VIOLET;
                        break;
            case VIOLET:
                        myColorValue = COLOR_OVERFLOW;
                        break;
        }

    return myOriginalColor;
}
```

Prototypes of these functions are placed in the `Color` declaration, as shown in Figure 11.14. Either version of `operator++` can then be applied to a `Color` object. For example, to display a list of the colors, we can write

```
    for (hue = RED; hue <= VIOLET; hue++)
        cout << hue << ' ';
```

and the values

```
    RED ORANGE YELLOW GREEN BLUE INDIGO VIOLET
```

will be displayed.

The decrement operator (`--`) can be overloaded in a similar manner for `Color` values. Doing this is left as an exercise.

Array Indices. As we saw in section 11.2, the enumerators in a `Color` enumeration can be used as the indices of an array or `vector<T>`. However, class `Color` cannot be used in this way in its present form, because the compiler will not treat a `Color` class object as an `int`.

For such situations, C++ permits a **type conversion function member.** The name of such a function is the type being converted to, which also serves as the return type of the function. A `Color-to-int` converter can be defined as follows:

```
    inline Color::operator int() const
    {
        return int(myColorValue);
    }
```

The function simply uses the C++ typecast mechanism to return the integer corresponding to `myColorValue`. The corresponding prototype in class `Color` is

```
    operator int() const;
```

Given such a function, a `Color` class object may be used in a context that is undefined for the `Color` class but is defined for `int` values (e.g., as an array subscript), and the compiler will use this function to map the `Color` object into the `int` corresponding to its `myColorName` member.

The problem with defining a `Color-to-int` converter is that doing so implicitly defines *all* int-compatible functions for Color objects, regardless of how appropriate or inappropriate.[5] Because such conversions are performed automatically and invisibly by the compiler, logic errors that are extremely difficult to find can result. To avoid such errors, we tend to avoid defining automatic type-conversion function members for classes.

THE COLOR HEADER FILE

Figure 11.14 contains the final declaration of class Color. The implementations of the non-inline functions given earlier would be collected together in the implementation file.

 FIGURE 11.14   CLASS Color DECLARATION.

```
/* Color.h presents the declaration of class Color.
 *
 * Class Invariant:
 *      myColorValue == RED || myColorValue == ORANGE ||
 *      myColorValue == YELLOW || myColorValue == GREEN ||
 *      myColorValue == BLUE || myColorValue == INDIGO ||
 *      myColorValue ==  VIOLET
 ******************************************************************/

#ifndef COLOR
#define COLOR

#include <iostream.h>                           // istream, ostream

enum ColorValue {COLOR_UNDERFLOW = -1,
                 RED, ORANGE, YELLOW, GREEN,
                 BLUE, INDIGO, VIOLET,
                 NUMBER_OF_COLORS,
                 COLOR_OVERFLOW = 7};

class Color
{
 public:
   Color();                                     // constructors
   Color(ColorValue initialColorValue);

   double Wavelength() const;                   // properties
   double Frequency() const;

   void Read(istream & in);                     // I/O
   void Print(ostream & out) const;

                                                // relationals
```

---

[5] For example, sqrt() is defined for double values, and an int can be promoted to a double. If we define a Color-to-int converter, then it becomes permissible to pass a Color to sqrt(), which does not make sense.

```
      friend bool operator==(const Color & left, const Color & right);
      friend bool operator!=(const Color & left, const Color & right);
      friend bool operator<(const Color & left, const Color & right);
      friend bool operator>(const Color & left, const Color & right);
      friend bool operator<=(const Color & left, const Color & right);
      friend bool operator>=(const Color & left, const Color & right);

      Color operator++();                              // prefix ++
      Color operator++(int);                           // postfix ++

      Color operator--();                              // prefix --
      Color operator--(int);                           // postfix --

   private:
      ColorValue myColorValue;
   };

   // ... inline definitions go here ...

   #endif
```

Given this class, we can now redo the program in Figure 11.1 as shown in Figure 11.15.

FIGURE 11.15   AN O-O Color–WAVELENGTH PROGRAM.

```
/* rainbow15.cpp computes the wavelength of light for a given Color.
 *
 * Input:        theColor, a Color value.
 * Precondition: theColor is one of RED, ORANGE, YELLOW,
 *                   GREEN, BLUE, INDIGO, VIOLET.
 * Output:       the wavelength of light corresponding to theColor.
 ********************************************************************/

#include <iostream.h>                         // cin, cout
#include "Color.h"                            // Color

int main()
{
   cout << "\nTo compute the wavelength of a given color,\n"
        << "enter a color (e.g., RED): ";
   Color theColor;
   cin >> theColor;

   double wavelength = theColor.Wavelength();

   cout << "\nThe corresponding wavelength is " << wavelength << endl;
   return 0;
}
```

The behavior of this program is identical to that of Figure 11.1, but the `Color` used by this program is a class, not a C-style enumeration, and is thus more consistent with the I-can-do-it-myself principle. That is, the program in Figure 11.1 uses the external approach by applying `Wavelength()` as a function to a `Color`, but the program in Figure 11.15 uses the internal approach by sending a `Wavelength()` message to a `Color` object, which then responds to that message.

This completes our introduction to enumerations in classes. In the next section, we present a simple application using this approach.

✔ Quick Quiz 11.3

1. What are two of the main drawbacks of C-style enumerations?
2. (True or false) If a class is used to provide operations on an enumeration, it is customary to place the enumeration declaration outside of the class declaration.
3. Why is it important that class operations do not violate the class' invariants?
4. The compiler may use a(n) _____ constructor in a class `C` to perform automatic conversion of a type to type `C`.
5. For prefix ++, the signature of `operator++` is _____, and for postfix ++, the signature of `operator++` is _____.

EXERCISES 11.3

1. Redesign the type `MonthAbbrev` described in exercises 1–12 of Section 11.2 so that it is a class instead of an enumeration type.
2. Redesign the type `Day` described in exercises 14–16 of section 11.2 so that it is a class instead of an enumeration type.
3. Design a `Date` class to model dates consisting of a month name, a day number, and a year number. Operations should at least include input and output.
4. Design a class for doing simple arithmetic with names of numbers; for example, zero, one, two, . . . , nine, ten. Operations should at least include input, output, and some of the relational operators.
5. Design a `PlayingCard` class to model playing cards. Operations should at least include input and output. Also formulate appropriate class invariants.

11.4 EXAMPLE: GEOLOGICAL CLASSIFICATION

Objects are often organized into groups that share similar characteristics. To illustrate:

▶ A doctor might be described as an internist, a pediatrician, a surgeon, a gynecologist, a family practitioner, or some other specialty, according to his or her area of training.

▶ Members of the animal kingdom are organized into groups (called phyla) according to whether or not they have vertebrae, the relative positions of their nervous and digestive systems, and their outer covering.

▶ The elements are organized into groups according to the number of electrons in the outermost shell of one of their atoms.

These are just a few of the many situations in which we **classify** objects. By classifying objects into groups according to their characteristics, objects that are in some way similar become *related* by their group membership.

In this section, we implement a simple library that illustrates how enumerations can be used to create software simulations of classifications from the real world. The problem we will consider is a simplified rock-classification problem.

In geology, rocks are classified according to the nature of their origin. More precisely, a given rock is described as:

▶ *Igneous,* if it is volcanic in origin (i.e., formed as the result of solidifying magma);

▶ *Metamorphic,* if the rock was formed under conditions of high temperature and pressure; and

▶ *Sedimentary,* if the rock was formed from the laying down of deposits of sediment.

Igneous rocks include basalt, granite, and obsidian. Metamorphic rocks include marble, quartzite, and slate. Sedimentary rocks include dolomite, limestone, sandstone, and shale.

Knowing the different categories of rocks can make outdoor activities (such as backpacking and canoeing) more interesting. For example, if one is hiking through a valley whose walls contain layers of sandstone, then one can conclude that the walls of the valley were probably once under water and may contain fossils of water creatures. By contrast, a valley whose walls consist of granite means that there was once a volcano in the vicinity, and finding it can make for an interesting diversion in the hike.

It is relatively easy to write a program that, given the name of a rock, describes some of its characteristics. Figure 11.16 gives an example of such a program.

FIGURE 11.16   **A ROCK CLASSIFICATION PROGRAM.**

```
/* geology16.cpp allows a user to retrieve information about rocks.
 *
 * Receive: the name of a rock
 * Output:  the known information about that rock
 *************************************************************/

#include <iostream.h>                    // cin, cout

#include "Rock.h"                        // class Rock

int main()
{
   cout << "This program provides information about "
           "specific rocks.\n";

   Rock aRock;                           // input variable
   char response;                        // query response
   do
   {
      cout << "\nEnter the name of a rock: ";
      cin >> aRock;
      if (cin.fail()) break;
```

```
            cout << endl << aRock
                 << " is classified as a(n) " << aRock.Kind()
                 << " rock, and\n its texture is " << aRock.Texture()
                 << endl;

            cout << "\nEnter 'c' to continue, anything else to quit: ";
            cin >> response;
        }
    while (response == 'c');
    return 0;
}
```

Sample run:

```
This program provides information about specific rocks.

Enter the name of a rock: sandstone

Sandstone is classified as a(n) SEDIMENTARY rock, and
 its texture is COARSE.

Enter 'c' to continue, anything else to quit: c

Enter the name of a rock: obsidian

Obsidian is classified as a(n) IGNEOUS rock, and
 its texture is FINE.

Enter 'c' to continue, anything else to quit: q
```

The interesting thing about the preceding program is that it allows the user to communicate in real-world terms (the names of rocks), rather than through some artificial mechanism (such as a menu). This is accomplished by using the techniques of the last section to create the type Rock as a class that uses an enumeration RockName whose values are the names of common rocks,

Because it might be useful for other geological programs to be able to use the class Rock, it should be stored in a library to facilitate its reuse. Figure 11.17 gives a header file for such a library:

 FIGURE 11.17   CLASS ROCK HEADER FILE.

```
/* Rock.h provides the declaration of class Rock.
 *
 * Class Invariant:
 *     The value of myRockName is one of the following:
 *         BASALT, DOLOMITE, GRANITE, LIMESTONE, MARBLE,
 *         OBSIDIAN, QUARTZITE, SANDSTONE, SHALE, SLATE
 ***************************************************************/

#ifndef ROCK
#define ROCK
```

682   CHAPTER 11   ENUMERATIONS

```cpp
#include <iostream.h>                              // istream, ostream

#include "RockKind.h"                              // class RockKind
#include "RockTexture.h"                           // class RockTexture

enum RockName {ROCK_UNDERFLOW = -1,
               BASALT, DOLOMITE, GRANITE,          // recognized
               LIMESTONE, MARBLE, OBSIDIAN,        //   names of
               QUARTZITE, SANDSTONE, SHALE, SLATE, //   rocks
               NUMBER_OF_ROCKS,
               ROCK_OVERFLOW = NUMBER_OF_ROCKS};

class Rock
{
 public:                                           // constructors:
   Rock();                                         //   default value
   Rock(RockName initialRock);                     //   explicit value

   void Read(istream & in);                        // input
   void Print(ostream & out) const;                // output

   RockKind Kind() const;                          // igneous, ...
   RockTexture Texture() const;                    // coarse, ...

   Rock operator++();                              // prefix ++
   Rock operator++(int);                           // postfix ++
   Rock operator--();                              // prefix --
   Rock operator--(int);                           // postfix --

                                                   // relationals
   friend bool operator==(const Rock & left, const Rock & right);
   friend bool operator!=(const Rock & left, const Rock & right);
   friend bool operator<(const Rock & left, const Rock & right);
   friend bool operator>(const Rock & left, const Rock & right);
   friend bool operator<=(const Rock & left, const Rock & right);
   friend bool operator>=(const Rock & left, const Rock & right);

 private:
   RockName myRockName;
};

// -------- Non-member input ---------------------------------------
inline istream & operator>>(istream & in, Rock & theRock)
{
   theRock.Read(in);
   return in;
}

// -------- Non-member output --------------------------------------
inline ostream & operator<<(ostream & out, const Rock & theRock)
{
   theRock.Print(out);
   return out;
}
```

```
// -------- Initialize me (default value) --------------------------
inline Rock::Rock()
{
   myRockName = BASALT;
}

// -------- Initialize me (explicit-value) -----------------------
#include <assert.h>
inline Rock::Rock(RockName initialRock)
{
   assert(BASALT <= initialRock && initialRock < NUMBER_OF_ROCKS);
   myRockName = initialRock;
}

//--------- Compare me and anotherRock using equality -------------
inline bool operator==(const Rock & left, const Rock & right)
{
   return left.myRockName == right.myRockName;
}

// ---   Inline definitions for operators !=, <, >, <=, and >= are
// ---   essentially the same and are omitted here to save space.

#endif
```

Note that this class depends upon the classes RockKind and RockTexture, each of which has its own header file. Since there are three real-world kinds of rocks, a RockKind class can be created with an enumeration of its own, whose values are the various kinds of rocks as shown in Figure 11.18.

FIGURE 11.18   CLASS RockKind HEADER FILE.

```
/* RockKind.h declares class RockKind.
 *
 *     The value of myRockKindName is one of the following:
 *        IGNEOUS, METAMORPHIC, SEDIMENTARY,
 *****************************************************************/

#ifndef ROCK_KIND
#define ROCK_KIND

enum RockKindName {KIND_UNDERFLOW = -1,
                   IGNEOUS, METAMORPHIC, SEDIMENTARY,
                   NUMBER_OF_KINDS,
                   KIND_OVERFLOW = NUMBER_OF_KINDS};

#include <iostream.h>                       // istream, ostream
```

```
class RockKind
{
 public:                              // constructors:
   RockKind();                        //   default value
   RockKind(RockKindName initialRock); //  explicit value

   void Read(istream & in);           // input
   void Print(ostream & out) const;   // output

   RockKind operator++();             // prefix ++
   RockKind operator++(int);          // postfix ++
   RockKind operator--();             // prefix --
   RockKind operator--(int);          // postfix --

   friend bool operator==(const RockKind & left, const RockKind & right);
   friend bool operator!=(const RockKind & left, const RockKind & right);
   friend bool operator<(const RockKind & left, const RockKind & right);
   friend bool operator>(const RockKind & left, const RockKind & right);
   friend bool operator<=(const RockKind & left, const RockKind & right);
   friend bool operator>=(const RockKind & left, const RockKind & right);

 private:
   RockKindName myRockKindName;
};

// -------- Non-member input -------------------------------------
inline istream & operator>>(istream & in, RockKind & theRockKind)
{
   theRockKind.Read(in);
   return in;
}

// -------- Non-member output ------------------------------------
inline ostream & operator<<(ostream & out, const RockKind & theRockKind)
{
   theRockKind.Print(out);
   return out;
}

// -------- Initialize me (default-value) ------------------------
inline RockKind::RockKind()
{
   myRockKindName = IGNEOUS;
}

// -------- Initialize me (explicit-value) -----------------------
#include <assert.h>
inline RockKind::RockKind(RockKindName initialRockKindName)
{
   assert(IGNEOUS <= initialRockKindName &&
          initialRockKindName < NUMBER_OF_KINDS);
   myRockKindName = initialRockKindName;
}
```

```cpp
// --------- Compare me and anotherRockKind using == --------------
inline bool operator==(const RockKind & left, const RockKind & right)
{
   return left.myRockKindName == right.myRockKindName;
}

// ---   Inline definitions for operators !=, <, >, <=, and >= are
// ---   essentially the same and are omitted here to save space.

#endif
```

A class RockTexture can be created using a similar RockTextureName enumeration and is left as an exercise.

The implementation file for class RockKind contains the definitions of the nontrivial RockKind function members. Figure 11.19 shows part of this file.

FIGURE 11.19   CLASS RockKind IMPLEMENTATION FILE.

```cpp
/* RockKind.cpp defines the nontrivial members of class RockKind.
   ********************************************************/

#include <string>
#include <ctype.h>

#include "RockKind.h"

// -------- Read a value into me from in ----------------------------
void RockKind::Read(istream & in)
{
   string rockKindString;
   in >> rockKindString;

   for (int i = 0; i < rockKindString.size(); i++)
      if (islower(rockKindString[i]))
         rockKindString[i] = toupper(rockKindString[i]);

   if (rockKindString== "IGNEOUS")
      myRockKindName = IGNEOUS;
   else if (rockKindString== "METAMORPHIC")
      myRockKindName = METAMORPHIC;
   else if (rockKindString== "SEDIMENTARY")
      myRockKindName = SEDIMENTARY;
   else
   {
      cerr << "\n*** Read: Rock kind is unknown\n"
           << endl;
      in.setstate(ios::failbit);
   }
}
```

```cpp
// -------- Display me via out --------------------------
void RockKind::Print(ostream & out) const
{
   switch(myRockKindName)
   {
      case IGNEOUS:
                       out << "IGNEOUS";
                       break;
      case METAMORPHIC:
                       out << "METAMORPHIC";
                       break;
      case SEDIMENTARY:
                       out << "SEDIMENTARY";
                       break;
   }
}

// -------- Increment me (prefix) --------------------------
RockKind RockKind::operator++()
{
   switch(myRockKindName)
   {
      case IGNEOUS:
                       myRockKindName = METAMORPHIC;
                       break;
      case METAMORPHIC:
                       myRockKindName = SEDIMENTARY;
                       break;
      case SEDIMENTARY:
                       myRockKindName = KIND_OVERFLOW;
                       break;
   }
   return RockKind(myRockKindName);
}

// -------- Increment me (postfix) --------------------------
RockKind RockKind::operator++(int)
{
   RockKindName savedRockKindName = myRockKindName;
   switch(myRockKindName)
   {
      case IGNEOUS:
                       myRockKindName = METAMORPHIC;
                       break;
      case METAMORPHIC:
                       myRockKindName = SEDIMENTARY;
                       break;
      case SEDIMENTARY:
                       myRockKindName = KIND_OVERFLOW;
                       break;
   }
   return RockKind(savedRockKindName);
}
```

```
// -------- Decrement me (prefix) ------------------------------------
// ------- Decrement me (postfix) ------------------------------------

// Definitions of operator--() and operator--(int) are similar to those
// of operator++() and perator++(int) and are omitted to save space.
```

An implementation file for class RockTexture is similar, and left as an exercise.

Figure 11.20 shows part of the implementation file Rock.cpp containing definitions of several of the nontrival Rock function members.

FIGURE 11.20   CLASS ROCK IMPLEMENTATION FILE.

```
/* Rock.cpp defines the nontrivial members of class Rock.
   **************************************************************/

#include "Rock.h"

// ------- Read a value into me from in -------------------------
#include <ctype.h>
#include <string>

void Rock::Read(istream & in)
{
   string rockString;
   in >> rockString;

   for (int i = 0; i < rockString.size(); i++)
      if (islower(rockString[i]))
         rockString[i] = toupper(rockString[i]);

   if (rockString == "BASALT")
      myRockName = BASALT;
   else if (rockString == "DOLOMITE")
      myRockName = DOLOMITE;
                  .
                  .
                  .

   else if (rockString == "SLATE")
      myRockName = SLATE;
   else
   {
      cerr << "\n*** Read:Rock " << rockString
           << " is not recognized!\n" << endl;
      in.setstate(ios::failbit);
   }
}
```

```cpp
// -------- Display my value via out ----------------------------
void Rock::Print(ostream & out) const
{
   switch(myRockName)
   {
      case BASALT:     out << "BASALT";
                       break;
      case DOLOMITE:   out << "DOLOMITE";
                       break;

                              .
                              .
                              .

      case SLATE:      out << "SLATE";
                       break;
   }
}
// -------- My kind (igneous, metamorphic, ...) ---------------
RockKind Rock::Kind() const
{
   switch (myRockName)                  // if the rock is...
   {
      case BASALT: case GRANITE:     //   any of these, then
      case OBSIDIAN:                 //       its an igneous rock
         return RockKind(IGNEOUS);
      case MARBLE: case QUARTZITE:   //   any of these, then
      case SLATE:                    //     it's a metamorphic rock
         return RockKind(METAMORPHIC);
      case DOLOMITE: case LIMESTONE: //   any of these, then
      case SANDSTONE: case SHALE:    //     it's a sedimentary rock
         return RockKind(SEDIMENTARY);
      }
   }
}


// -------- My texture (coarse, fine, ...) ------------------
RockTexture Rock::Texture() const
{
   // ... See Programming Problems ...
}


// -------- Increment my value (prefix) ---------------------
Rock Rock::operator++()
{
   switch(myRockName)
   {
      case BASALT:
                     myRockName = DOLOMITE;
                     break;
      case DOLOMITE:
                     myRockName = GRANITE;
                     break;
```

```
                         .
                         .
                         .

        case SLATE:
                        myRockName = ROCK_OVERFLOW;
    }
    return Rock(myRockName);
}


// -------- Increment my value (postfix) --------------------
Rock Rock::operator++(int)
{
    RockName savedRockName = myRockName;

    switch(myRockName)
    {
        case BASALT:
                        myRockName = DOLOMITE;
                        break;
        case DOLOMITE:
                        myRockName = GRANITE;
                        break;

                         .
                         .
                         .

        case SLATE:
                        myRockName = ROCK_OVERFLOW;
                        break;
    }

    return Rock(savedRockName);
}

// -------- Decrement me (prefix) -------------------------------
// -------- Decrement me (postfix) ------------------------------

// Definitions of operator--() and operator--(int) are similar to those
// of operator++() and operator++(int) and are omitted to save space.
```

By planning for the future and providing useful functions like ++ and -- (even though they are not needed to solve the problem at hand) we produce a first class data type that is useful in other problems. For example, this extra functionality makes it quite easy to display a table of the recognized rocks and their kinds:

```
for (Rock aRock = BASALT; aRock <= SLATE; aRock++)
    cout << aRock << ": " << aRock.Kind() << endl;
```

As the examples of this chapter illustrate, enumeration-based classes, together with functions that provide useful operations on them, allow objects from the real world to be represented using their real-world names, both by *programmers* as they write programs, and by *users* as they execute programs.

Part of the Picture: The C++ Type Hierarchy

At this point, we have examined many of the types available in C++. Figure 11.21 presents a diagram in which these types are organized into a **type hierarchy** that shows their relationships to one another:

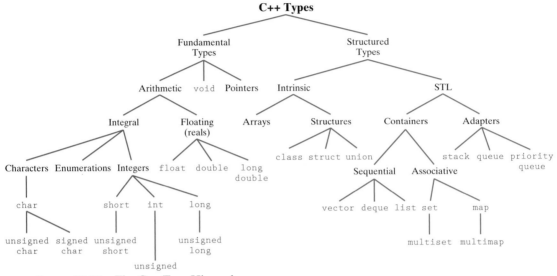

FIGURE 11.21   The C++ Type Hierarchy.

The hierarchy provides a map of the richness of the C++ language that shows where we have been, and where we have not yet explored. A second volume of this text is planned, which will explore those types not examined in this text.

📖 PROGRAMMING POINTERS

✍ PROGRAM STYLE AND DESIGN

1. *Use enumerations to improve program readability and to make the program easier to understand and use.* For example, using enumerated values such as

    ```
    enum Color {BLACK, BLUE, RED, ORANGE, YELLOW, GREEN,
                BROWN, VIOLET, GRAY, WHITE};
    ```

    to represent colors in a program, instead of cryptic codes 0, 1, 2, 3, 4, 5, 6, 7, 8, and 9, obviously makes the program easier to read and understand.

2. *Use uppercase letters for enumerators.* Enumerators are similar to constant objects, so we use the same stylistic conventions.

3. *Pad enumerations with* underflow/overflow *values at the ends of the identifier list.* This provides "illegal" values that functions can return in error situations or that can be used as sentinel values.

4. *Wrap enumerations within a class so that*
    a. *objects of that type are self-contained, and*
    b. *class invariants can be enforced.*

Doing so results in a class of objects that reflects the I-can-do-it-myself principle.

5. *For classes that wrap enumerations, define the relational operators as non-member functions to preserve the symmetric property of the relation.* For example, if an expression of the form e == c is valid, then the expression c == e should also be valid. With enumeration classes, this is somewhat tricky because e and c may not have the same type. If e is an enumeration object and c is an enumeration class object, then one way to resolve this is for the enumeration class to (1) name the relational operators as `friend` functions that compare two enumeration class objects, and (2) supply an explicit-value constructor to perform automatic type conversion. This allows the compiler to transparently construct e into an enumeration class object, allowing it to be compared to c.

6. *Declare **every** class in its own header file.* By doing so, a program that wants to use a class can include its header file without having to include classes that are not being used.

⚡ POTENTIAL PROBLEMS

1. *Values listed in an enumeration must be legal identifiers and may not be overloaded.* For example, the declaration

    ```
    enum PassengerType {FIRST-CLASS,
                        COACH, STANDBY};     // ERROR!
    ```

    is not allowed because `FIRST-CLASS` is not a legal identifier. The declarations

    ```
    enum Weekday {MONDAY, TUESDAY, WEDNESDAY,
            THURSDAY, FRIDAY};
    enum VacationDay {FRIDAY, SATURDAY, SUNDAY}; // ERROR!
    ```

    are not allowed because the same identifier (`FRIDAY`) may not be used in two declarations.

2. *Values of an enumerated data type cannot be input or output unless the I/O operators are overloaded.*

Programming Problems

SECTION 11.2

1. Write a driver program to test the library for the enumerated type `MonthAbbrev` of exercises 1–12.

2. Write a driver program to test the library for the enumerated type `Day` of exercises 14–16.

SECTIONS 11.3

3. Write a driver program to test the enumeration class `MonthAbbrev` of exercise 1.

4. Use the type `MonthAbbrev` of exercise 1 in a program that prompts for and reads the rainfall for each month and then calculates and displays the average monthly rainfall for the year.

5. Add a function member to class `MonthAbbrev` of exercise 1 whose parameter is a year in the range from 1538 through 1999 and that returns the number of days in the month. Remember that February has 28 days, except in a leap year, when it has 29. A leap year is one in which the year number is divisible by 4 except for centesimal years (those ending in 00); these centesimal years are not leap years unless the year

number is divisible by 400. Thus 1950 and 1900 are not leap years, but 1960 and 1600 are. Test the new function with a driver program.

6. Use the function of exercise 5 in a program that reads two dates (month and a day) in the same year and then calculates and displays the number of days between these two dates.

7. Write a driver program to test the enumeration class `Day` of exercise 2.

8. Use the type `Day` of exercise 2 in a program that first reads an employee's name and hourly pay rate, and then for each weekday (Monday through Friday) prompts for and reads the number of hours worked by that employee. Display the total hours worked and the pay for each employee. (Assume that hours above 40 are paid at the overtime rate of 1.5 times the regular hourly rate.)

9. Use the type `Day` of exercise 2 in a program that first reads a customer's account number and current balance, and then for each weekday (Monday through Friday) prompts for and reads a series of transactions by that customer of the form D (deposit) or W (withdrawal), followed by an amount, and updates the balance with this amount. Display the new balance after all transactions for the week have been processed.

10. Write a driver program to test the enumeration class `Date` of exercise 3.

11. Modify the program in problem 6 so that it uses the type `Date` of exercise 3 and determines the number of days between any two dates.

12. Use the type `Date` of exercise 3 to develop a class `Event` to model events scheduled for specified dates. Use this class in a program that reads several events and stores these in a vector (or array) of `Event`s. After all the events have been entered, the program should display a schedule of events in chronological order.

13. Write a driver program to test the name-of-number enumeration class of exercise 4.

14. Add some simple arithmetic operations to the name-of-number enumeration class of exercise 4. Use the modified class in a program that models a simple calculator in which the user "speaks" the names of the numbers.

15. Write a driver program to test the enumeration class `PlayingCard` of exercise 5.

16. Use the type `PlayingCard` of exercise 5 in a program that deals random hands of cards, making certain that none of them have been dealt already. (For more of a challenge, design the program to play a simple card game such as Go Fish!).

17. (*Project*) Design a class `PeriodicTable` to model the periodic table of elements, using an enumeration whose values are the element abbreviations (e.g. H, He, Li, . . .). Construct I/O operations for and add functions that return: the atomic number of the element, the atomic weight of the element, the number of protons (and/or neutrons) in the nucleus of the element, the period of the element, the group of the element, and any other useful operations that represent standard information that can be extracted from the periodic table. Then write a menu-driven program that allows a user to obtain the information about any element whose symbol they input.

18. (*Project*) Design an enumeration class `Sword` in which the enumerators are SHORT, BROAD, LONG, and TWOHANDED, and which has the following operations: I/O; a function `Reach()` that returns the length of a `Sword` object (e.g., 18 inches, 24 inches, 36 inches, and 48 inches, respectively); and a function `Speed()` that returns the time required to swing a `Sword` object as a value proportional to its length. Write a program that allows its user to pick the weapons of two duelists and then provides a blow-by-blow account of a simulated duel.

19. (*Group Project*) Have one group member proceed as in problem 18, but have a second group member build another library that defines the type `Armor` with enumerators NONE, LEATHER, CHAIN, and PLATE with the following operations: I/O; a function Protection() that returns the degree to which the Armor object protects its wearer (e.g. 0.0, 0.50, 0.75, and 0.95, respectively); a function Weight() that returns the degree to which a wearer of the Armor object is slowed in swinging a weapon (e.g. 0, 2, 4, 8). Write the duel-simulation program in such a way that the user can choose both the duelists' weapons and armor, and that both are considered in the simulation.

SECTION 11.4

20. Implement the class RockTexture, that supports the use of the three real-world rock textures: COARSE, INTERMEDIATE, and FINE.

21. Implement the Rock function member Texture(), assuming the following:

> granite, sandstone, dolomite, and limestone are coarse in texture
>
> basalt, shale, slate, and quartzite are intermediate in texture
>
> obsidian and marble are fine in texture.

Chapter 12

MULTIDIMENSIONAL ARRAYS

We are columns left alone
  of a temple once complete.

CHRISTOPHER CRANCH

A teacher who can arouse a feeling for one single good action,
  for one single good poem,
    accomplishes more than he who fills our memory with row on row
    of natural objects, classified with name and form.

JOHANN WOLFGANG VON GOETHE

Would someone please wake the person in row 3 seat 6?

V. OREHCK III (during a lecture on matrices)

Chapter Contents

12.1   Introductory Example: Mileage between Cities

12.2   C-Style Multidimensional Arrays

12.3   Multidimensional `vector<T>` Objects

12.4   A `vector<T>`-Based Matrix Library

        PART OF THE PICTURE: Computer Graphics

In chapter 9 we introduced C-style arrays and `vector<T>` class templates and used them to store sequences of values. Each of the containers considered in that chapter had one *dimension:* its **length,** which is the number of values in the sequence.

C++ also allows arrays and vectors of more than one dimension. As we shall see, a two-dimensional array or vector can be used to store a data set whose values are arranged in **rows** and **columns.** Similarly, a three-dimensional array or vector is an appropriate storage structure when the data can be arranged in **rows, columns,** and **ranks.** When there are several characteristics associated with the data, still higher dimensions may be useful, with each dimension corresponding to one of these characteristics. In this chapter we consider the use of multidimensional arrays in C++ programs.

12.1 INTRODUCTORY EXAMPLE: MILEAGE BETWEEN CITIES

PROBLEM

The German transportation tycoon Otto Bonn is expanding his trucking business into Florida, with shipping centers in Daytona Beach, Gainesville, Jacksonville, Miami, Tallahassee, and Tampa. He has hired us as software consultants to create a computerized mileage chart for his truck drivers. Given any two of these cities, our program must display the approximate mileage between them.

PRELIMINARY ANALYSIS

From a road atlas, we can find the following mileages between Florida cities:

	Daytona Beach	Gainesville	Jacksonville	Miami	Tallahassee	Tampa
Daytona Beach	0	97	90	268	262	130
Gainesville	97	0	74	337	144	128
Jacksonville	90	74	0	354	174	201
Miami	268	337	354	0	475	269
Tallahassee	262	144	174	475	0	238
Tampa	130	128	201	269	238	0

The basic idea is to create a software representation of such a chart, and then use it to look up the distance between any two of the cities.

OBJECT-CENTERED DESIGN

Behavior.   For simplicity, our program will begin by displaying on the screen a numbered menu of the cities. It should then read the numbers of two cities from the keyboard. Next, it should look up the mileage between those cities in a software mileage chart. Finally, it should display that mileage.

Objects

Description	Kind	Type	Name
A menu of cities	constant	`string`	*CITY_MENU*
The number of a city	varying	`int`	*city1*
The number of another city	varying	`int`	*city2*
A mileage chart	constant	`int[][]`	*MILEAGE_CHART*
The mileage	varying	`int`	*mileage*

As we shall see, the type `int[][]` refers to a two-dimensional array of integers, which provides a convenient way to represent our mileage chart.

Operations.   Our behavioral description gives the following set of operations:

   i.   Define a two-dimensional array with initial values

  ii.   Display a string on the screen

 iii.   Read two integers from the keyboard

 iv.   Look up an entry in the two-dimensional array

  v.   Output an integer

Algorithm.   These operations are easily organized into the following algorithm:

Algorithm for City Mileages

0. Define *MILEAGE_CHART*, a two-dimensional array of city mileages, and *CITY_MENU*, a menu of the supported cities.

1. Via `cout`, display *CITY_MENU*.

2. From `cin`, read two integers into *city1* and *city2*.

3. Compute *mileage*, by looking up *MILEAGE_CHART*[*city1*][*city2*].

4. Via `cout`, display *mileage*.

Coding.   The preceding algorithm is easily encoded in C++, as shown in Figure 12.1.

FIGURE 12.1   A MILEAGE CALCULATOR.

```
/* findmileage1.cpp computes the mileage between two cities.
 *
 * Input:        city1 and city2, two integers representing cities
 * Precondition: for n cities, city1 and city2 are in the range 0..n-1
 * Output:       the mileage between city1 and city2
 ****************************************************************/

#include <iostream.h>              // cin, cout, <<, >>
#include <string>                  // string
```

```cpp
int main()
{
   const int NUMBER_OF_CITIES = 6;
   const int MILEAGE_CHART[NUMBER_OF_CITIES][NUMBER_OF_CITIES]
      = { {   0,  97,  90, 268, 262, 130 },      // Daytona Beach
          {  97,   0,  74, 337, 144, 128 },      // Gainesville
          {  90,  74,   0, 354, 174, 201 },      // Jacksonville
          { 268, 337, 354,   0, 475, 269 },      // Miami
          { 262, 144, 174, 475,   0, 238 },      // Tallahassee
          { 130, 128, 201, 269, 238,   0 } };    // Tampa

   const string CITY_MENU
         = "To determine the mileage between two cities,\n"
           "please enter the numbers of 2 cities from this menu:\n\n"
           "    0 for Daytona Beach,   1 for Gainesville\n"
           "    2 for Jacksonville,    3 for Miami\n"
           "    4 for Tallahassee,     5 for Tampa\n\n"
           "--> ";

   cout << CITY_MENU;
   int city1, city2;
   cin >> city1 >> city2;

   int mileage = MILEAGE_CHART[city1][city2];

   cout << "\nThe mileage between those 2 cities is "
        << mileage << " miles.\n";
   return 0;

}
```

Sample run:

```
To determine the mileage between two cities,
please enter the numbers of 2 cities from this menu:

    0 for Daytona Beach,   1 for Gainesville
    2 for Jacksonville,    3 for Miami
    4 for Tallahassee,     5 for Tampa

--> 2 5

The mileage between those 2 cities is 201 miles.
```

12.2 C-Style Multidimensional Arrays

There are many problems in which the data being processed can be naturally organized as a *table*. The mileage problem in the preceding section is such a problem since mileage charts are commonly given in tabular form. For these problems, two-dimensional arrays provide a way to build a software model of a table.

DEFINING A TWO-DIMENSIONAL ARRAY

The program in Figure 12.1 illustrates how a two-dimensional array can be defined and initialized. The statements

```
const int NUMBER_OF_CITIES = 6;
const int MILEAGE_CHART[NUMBER_OF_CITIES][NUMBER_OF_CITIES]
  = { {   0,  97,  90, 268, 262, 130 },     // Daytona Beach
      {  97,   0,  74, 337, 144, 128 },     // Gainesville
      {  90,  74,   0, 354, 174, 201 },     // Jacksonville
      { 268, 337, 354,   0, 475, 269 },     // Miami
      { 262, 144, 174, 475,   0, 238 },     // Tallahassee
      { 130, 128, 201, 269, 238,   0 } };   // Tampa
```

define the object `MILEAGE_CHART` as a constant two-dimensional array of integers, consisting of six rows and six columns, which we might visualize as follows:

	[0]	[1]	[2]	[3]	[4]	[5]
[0]	0	97	90	268	262	130
[1]	97	0	74	337	144	128
[2]	90	74	0	354	174	201
[3]	268	337	354	0	475	269
[4]	262	144	174	475	0	238
[5]	130	128	201	269	238	0

As with one-dimensional arrays, each dimension of a two-dimensional array is indexed starting with zero, so the six rows are indexed from zero to five as are the six columns. As we shall see, these row and column indices are used to uniquely identify each element in the array.

This example shows how a two-dimensional array object can be initialized by listing the initial values in curly braces. Although not required, the values for each row are often enclosed in their own pair of curly braces, because this can make the declaration more readable by delimiting the values of each row.

Two-dimensional arrays like `MILEAGE_CHART` that have the same number of rows as columns are called *square* arrays. But non-square arrays are needed for some problems. For example, consider the monitor screen of a computer being used in a command-line (text-only) mode. Typically, such a screen can display 24 lines, with 80 characters on each line. The standard way to describe the screen is in terms of horizontal rows and vertical columns, with the rows numbered from 0 through 23 and the columns numbered from 0 through 79. The position at row 0 and column 0 is usually in the upper left corner of the screen, giving the screen the following layout:

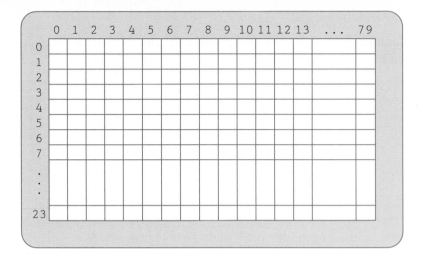

Such a screen can be modeled in software using a two-dimensional array of characters, declared as follows:

```
const int ROWS = 24,
          COLUMNS = 80;

char screen[ROWS][COLUMNS];
```

Note that this definition creates `screen` as a two-dimensional array *variable* object, whereas `MILEAGE_CHART` in Figure 12.1 is a two-dimensional array *constant* object.

The `typedef` mechanism introduced in chapter 9 to define an identifier as a synonym for a one-dimensional array type can also be used for multidimensional arrays. For example, to declare the identifier `MileageTable` as a synonym for an array of double values representing mileages, we would write

```
const int NUMBER_OF_CITIES = 6;
typedef double MileageArray[NUM_CITIES][NUM_CITIES];
```

We can then use this new type to define the two-dimensional array `MileageArray` object:

```
const MileageArray MILEAGE_CHART
  = { {   0,  97,  90, 268, 262, 130 },     // Daytona Beach
      {  97,   0,  74, 337, 144, 128 },     // Gainesville
      {  90,  74,   0, 354, 174, 201 },     // Jacksonville
      { 268, 337, 354,   0, 475, 269 },     // Miami
      { 262, 144, 174, 475,   0, 238 },     // Tallahassee
      { 130, 128, 201, 269, 238,   0 } };   // Tampa
```

Similarly, we might define the type `MonitorScreen` by

```
const int ROWS = 24,
          COLUMNS = 80;
```

```
typedef char MonitorScreen[ROWS][COLUMNS];
```

and then use this new type to declare the variable `screen` by

```
MonitorScreen screen;
```

PREDEFINED TWO-DIMENSIONAL ARRAY OPERATIONS

As with one-dimensional arrays, the central predefined operation for two-dimensional arrays is the **subscript operation** used to access the elements of an array. A one-dimensional array uses a single subscript operator to access an element:

```
double aOneDimensionalArray[10];
       .
       .
       .
aOneDimensionalArray[0] = 2.5;
```

Objects like `MILEAGE_CHART` and `screen` are two-dimensional objects and require two subscript operators, one for each dimension. The element in row 0, column 0, of `MILEAGE_CHART` can be accessed using

```
MILEAGE_CHART[0][0]
```

The element of `MILEAGE_CHART` in the second column of the first row can be accessed using

```
MILEAGE_CHART[0][1]
```

the first element of the third using

```
MILEAGE_CHART[2][0]
```

and the element at row 4, column 3 using

```
MILEAGE_CHART[4][3]
```

and so on. In general, the notation

```
MILEAGE_CHART[r][c]
```

can be used to access the value at row `r` and column `c`. The program in Figure 12.1 looked up the mileage between `city1` and `city2`,

```
int mileage = MILEAGE_CHART[city1][city2];
```

by accessing the element at row `city1` and column `city2`.

Because `MILEAGE_CHART` is a constant object, we are only permitted to read (i.e., look up) its values. If we try to change one of `MILEAGE_CHART`'s elements as in

```
cin >> MILEAGE_CHART[r][c];
```

the compiler will generate an error because we may not alter the value of a constant object.

By contrast, the object `screen` described earlier is a *variable* object, so values can be assigned to it. For example, the statement

```
screen[0][0] = 'X';
```

assigns the character `'X'` to the element in row 0 and column 0.

DEFINING TWO-DIMENSIONAL ARRAY OPERATIONS

If we wish to perform operations other than subscript on a two-dimensional array, we must write functions to perform them. Operations on one-dimensional arrays typically use a `for` loop to count through the index values:

```
for (int i = 0; i < howManyValues; i++)
   // ... do something with oneDimensionalArray[i]
```

Operations that access the values stored in a two-dimensional array use two nested `for` loops: an outer loop counting through the rows, and an inner loop counting through the columns:

```
for (int r = 0; r < howManyRows; r++)
   for (int c = 0; c < howManyColumns; c++)
      // ... do something with twoDimensionalArray[r][c]
```

For example, to fill the object `screen` with blanks, we can use a function like the following:

```
void ClearScreen(MonitorScreen theScreen,
                 int numRows, int numColumns)
{
   for (int row = 0; row < numRows; row++)
      for (int col = 0; col < numColumns; col++)
         theScreen[row][col] = ' ';
}
```

To display `screen` via `cout`, we could use

```
void Display(MonitorScreen theScreen,
             int numRows, int numColumns)
{
   for (int row = 0; row < numRows; row++)
   {
      for (int col = 0; col < numColumns; col++)
         cout << theScreen[row][col];
      cout << endl;
   }
}
```

Each pass through the inner loop displays all the characters in one row of theScreen and then moves to a new line before displaying the characters in the next row.

Primitive graphics functions can also be designed using this technique. For example, here is a simple function that can be used to draw a box of arbitrary size at an arbitrary position on a MonitorScreen:

```
void DrawBox(MonitorScreen theScreen,        // 2-D array
             int numRows, int numColumns, // its size
             int topRow, int leftCol,      // upper left corner
             int bottomRow, int rightCol, // bottom right   "
             char drawChar)               // outline character
{
    assert(0 <= topRow && topRow < numRows);
    assert(0 <= leftCol && leftCol < numColumns);
    assert(0 <= bottomRow && bottomRow < numRows);
    assert(0 <= rightCol && rightCol < numColumns);

    // draw top & bottom edges
    for (int col = leftCol; col <= rightCol; col++)
       theScreen[topRow][col] =
          theScreen[bottomRow][col] = drawChar;

    // draw left & right edges
    for (int row = topRow; row <= bottomRow; row++)
       theScreen[row][leftCol] =
          theScreen[row][rightCol] = drawChar;
}
```

Other functions can use primitive graphics functions like DrawBox() to draw more complex patterns on screen. For example, the following function can be used to fill screen with nested boxes:

```
void DrawNestedBoxes(MonitorScreen theScreen,
                     int numRows, int numColumns,
                     char drawChar)
{
    for (int offset = 0; offset < numRows/2; offset += 2)
       DrawBox(theScreen, numRows, numColumns, offset, offset,
               numRows - offset - 1, numColumns - offset - 1,
               drawChar);
}
```

Given the object named screen defined previously, the following sequence of function calls can be used to initialize, draw on, and display screen:

```
ClearScreen(screen, ROWS, COLUMNS);
DrawNestedBoxes(screen, ROWS, COLUMNS, 'X');
Display(screen, ROWS, COLUMNS);
```

When executed, the output from function Display() appears as follows:

```
XXXXXXXXXXXXXXXXXXXXXXXXXXXXXXXXXXXXXXXXXXXXXXXXXXXXXXXXXXXXXXXXXXXXXXXXXXXXXXXX
X                                                                            X
X XXXXXXXXXXXXXXXXXXXXXXXXXXXXXXXXXXXXXXXXXXXXXXXXXXXXXXXXXXXXXXXXXXXXXXXXXXXX X
X X                                                                        X X
X X XXXXXXXXXXXXXXXXXXXXXXXXXXXXXXXXXXXXXXXXXXXXXXXXXXXXXXXXXXXXXXXXXXXXXXXX X X
X X X                                                                    X X X
X X X XXXXXXXXXXXXXXXXXXXXXXXXXXXXXXXXXXXXXXXXXXXXXXXXXXXXXXXXXXXXXXXXXX X X X
X X X X                                                                X X X X
X X X X XXXXXXXXXXXXXXXXXXXXXXXXXXXXXXXXXXXXXXXXXXXXXXXXXXXXXXXXXXXXXX X X X X
X X X X X                                                            X X X X X
X X X X X XXXXXXXXXXXXXXXXXXXXXXXXXXXXXXXXXXXXXXXXXXXXXXXXXXXXXXXX X X X X X
X X X X X X                                                        X X X X X X
X X X X X X                                                        X X X X X X
X X X X X XXXXXXXXXXXXXXXXXXXXXXXXXXXXXXXXXXXXXXXXXXXXXXXXXXXXXXXX X X X X X
X X X X X                                                            X X X X X
X X X X XXXXXXXXXXXXXXXXXXXXXXXXXXXXXXXXXXXXXXXXXXXXXXXXXXXXXXXXXXXXXX X X X X
X X X X                                                                X X X X
X X X XXXXXXXXXXXXXXXXXXXXXXXXXXXXXXXXXXXXXXXXXXXXXXXXXXXXXXXXXXXXXXXXXX X X X
X X X                                                                    X X X
X X XXXXXXXXXXXXXXXXXXXXXXXXXXXXXXXXXXXXXXXXXXXXXXXXXXXXXXXXXXXXXXXXXXXXXXXX X X
X X                                                                        X X
X XXXXXXXXXXXXXXXXXXXXXXXXXXXXXXXXXXXXXXXXXXXXXXXXXXXXXXXXXXXXXXXXXXXXXXXXXXXX X
X                                                                            X
XXXXXXXXXXXXXXXXXXXXXXXXXXXXXXXXXXXXXXXXXXXXXXXXXXXXXXXXXXXXXXXXXXXXXXXXXXXXXXXX
```

Using Enumerations. As a second application of two-dimensional arrays, suppose that four times a day, water temperatures are recorded at each of three discharge outlets of the cooling system of a nuclear power plant. These temperature readings can be arranged in a table having four rows and three columns:

Time	Location		
	Outlet1	Outlet2	Outlet3
12 A.M.	65.5	68.7	62.0
6 A.M.	68.8	68.9	64.5
12 P.M.	70.4	69.4	66.3
6 P.M.	68.5	69.1	65.8

In this table, the three temperature readings at 12 A.M. are in the first row, the three temperatures at 6 A.M. are in the second row, and so on. We might model such a table by first declaring an enumeration for the row indices,

```
enum Row {ROW_UNDERFLOW = -1, MIDNIGHT, SIX_AM, NOON, SIX_PM,
          NUM_TIMES, ROW_OVERFLOW = 4};
```

and another enumeration for the indices of the columns:

```
enum Column {COLUMN_UNDERFLOW = -1, OUTLET1, OUTLET2, OUTLET3,
             NUM_OUTLETS, COLUMN_OVERFLOW = 3};
```

Recall that the C++ compiler treats MIDNIGHT, SIX_AM, NOON, SIX_PM, and NUM_TIMES as equivalent to 0, 1, 2, 3, and 4, respectively; and OUTLET1, OUTLET2, OUTLET3, and NUM_OUTLETS as equivalent to 0, 1, 2, and 3, respectively. This means that the declaration:

```
double temperatureGrid[NUM_TIMES][NUM_OUTLETS];
```

defines temperatureGrid as a two-dimensional array, consisting of four rows and three columns. The C++ compiler thus reserves 12 memory locations for this object and associates `temperatureGrid` with these memory locations. We can visualize this as follows:

temperatureGrid:	[OUTLET1]	[OUTLET2]	[OUTLET3]
[MIDNIGHT]			
[SIX_AM]			
[NOON]			
[SIX_PM]			

The notation

    temperatureGrid[NOON][OUTLET2]

thus refers to the element in row NOON and column OUTLET2 of temperature-Grid. In general, the notation

    temperatureGrid[r][c]

refers to the entry in row r and column c, that is, to the temperature recorded at time r, location c.

As before, the `typedef` mechanism can be used to declare the name `Table_of_Temperatures` as a type denoting a two-dimensional array of real values,

    typedef double Table_of_Temperatures[NUM_TIMES][NUM_OUTLETS];

and this type can then be used to declare `temperatureGrid` to be an object whose type is `Table_of_Temperatures`:

    Table_of_Temperatures temperatureGrid;

DECLARING THREE-DIMENSIONAL ARRAYS

To illustrate the use of an array with more than two dimensions, suppose that the temperatures in the last example are recorded for 1 week, so that seven such tables are collected:

Saturday

Time	Location		
	Outlet1	Outlet2	Outlet3
12 A.M.	66.5	69.4	68.4
6 A.M.	68.4	71.2	69.3
12 P.M.	70.1	71.9	70.2
6 P.M.	69.5	70.0	69.4

Monday

Time	Location		
	Outlet1	Outlet2	Outlet3
12 A.M.	63.7	66.2	64.3
6 A.M.	64.0	66.8	64.9
			66.3
			65.8

Sunday

Time	Location		
	Outlet1	Outlet2	Outlet3
12 A.M.	65.5	68.7	62.0
6 A.M.	68.8	68.9	64.5
12 P.M.	70.4	69.4	66.3
6 P.M.	68.5	69.1	65.8

The collection of these tables can be modeled with a **three-dimensional array** object, declared by

```
enum DayName {DAY_UNDERFLOW = -1, SUNDAY, MONDAY, TUESDAY,
              WEDNESDAY, THURSDAY, FRIDAY, SATURDAY,
              NUM_DAYS, DAY_OVERFLOW = 7};

enum Row {ROW_UNDERFLOW = -1, MIDNIGHT, SIX_AM, NOON, SIX_PM,
          NUM_TIMES, ROW_OVERFLOW = 4};

enum Column {COLUMN_UNDERFLOW = -1, OUTLET1, OUTLET2, OUTLET3,
             NUM_OUTLETS, COLUMN_OVERFLOW = 3};

typedef double
   ThreeDimTemperatureArray[NUM_DAYS][NUM_TIMES][NUM_OUTLETS];

ThreeDimTemperatureArray temperature;
```

The object `temperature` can then be used to store these 84 temperature readings.

OPERATIONS ON THREE-DIMENSIONAL ARRAYS

Subscript. A single subscript operator is needed to access an element in a one-dimensional array and two subscript operators are needed to access an element in a two-dimensional array, so it seems reasonable that three subscript operators are needed to access an element in a three-dimensional array. For example,

```
temperature[MONDAY][MIDNIGHT][OUTLET3]
```

refers to the temperature recorded on Monday at 12 A.M. at the third outlet; that is, the value 64.3 in the second table, first row, and third column. In general,

```
temperature[d][t][o]
```

is the temperature recorded on day `d` at time `t` for outlet `o`.

Other Operations. Other operations on three-dimensional arrays can be encoded as functions. Typically, these use three nested `for` loops to run through the elements of the array. For example, if a file contains a week's 84 temperature readings, the following function can be used to read the values from that file into `temperature`:

```
void Read(ifstream & in, ThreeDimTemperatureArray temperature,
          int numDays, int numTimes, int numOutlets)
{
   for (int d = 0; d < numDays; d++)
      for (int t = 0; t < numTimes; t++)
         for (int o = 0; o < numOutlets; o++)
            in >> temperature[d][t][o];
}
```

Functions can be defined to perform any non-subscript operation we need on a three-dimensional array.

HIGHER-DIMENSIONAL ARRAYS

In some problems, arrays with even more dimensions may be useful. For example, suppose that a retailer maintains an inventory of jeans. She carries several different brands of jeans and for each brand she stocks a variety of styles, waist sizes, and inseam lengths. A four-dimensional array can be used to record the inventory, with each element of the array being the number of jeans of a particular brand, style, waist size, and inseam length currently in stock. The first index represents the brand; thus it might be of type

```
enum BrandType {LEVI, WRANGLER, CALVIN_KLEIN,
                LEE, BIG_YANK, NUM_BRANDS};
```

(We will omit the *underflow* and *overflow* enumerators in this example, to save space.) The second index represents styles and is of type

```
enum StyleType {BAGGY, TAPERED, STRAIGHTLEG, DESIGNER, NUM_STYLES};
```

The third and fourth indices represent waist size and inseam length, respectively. For waist sizes ranging from 28 through 48 and inseam lengths ranging from 26 through 36, we might declare enumerations as follows:

```
enum WaistType {W28, W29, W30, W31, W32, W33, W34, W35, W36,
                W37, W38, W39, W40, W41, W42, W43, W44, W45,
                W46, W47, W48, NUM_WAIST_SIZES};
enum InseamType {I26, I27, I28, I29, I30, I31, I32, I33, I34,
                 I35, I36, NUM_INSEAM_SIZES};
```

A program to maintain the inventory can then declare the type

```
typedef int
   JeansArray[NUM_BRANDS][NUM_STYLES]
             [NUM_WAIST_SIZES][NUM_INSEAM_SIZES];
```

and then use this type to define a four-dimensional array `jeans` having indices of the types just described:

```
JeansArray jeans;
```

The value of the expression

```
jeans[LEVI][DESIGNER][W32][I31]
```

is the number of Levi's designer 32×31 jeans that are in stock. The statement

```
jeans[brand][style][waist][inseam]--;
```

can be used to record the sale (i.e., decrement the inventory) of one pair of jeans of a specified `brand`, `style`, `waist` size, and `inseam` length.

As these examples illustrate, *n*-dimensional arrays can be defined and subscript operators can be used to access the array elements. C++ places no limit on the number of dimensions of an array, but the number of values in each dimension must be specified. The general form of an array declaration is as follows:

Form

$ElementType$ $arrayName[DIM_1][DIM_2] \ldots [DIM_n];$

where:

$ElementType$ is any known type;

$arrayName$ is the name of the array being defined; and

each DIM_i must be a nonnegative integer (constant) value.

Purpose

Defines an n-dimensional object whose elements are of type $Element-Type$, in which DIM_1, DIM_2, . . . , DIM_n are the number of elements in each dimension.

Array of Arrays Declarations. One way to view a multidimensional array is as an **array of arrays;** that is, an array whose elements are other arrays. For example, consider the nuclear power plant's temperature grid described earlier:

```
double temperatureGrid[NUM_TIMES][NUM_OUTLETS];
```

Since NUM_TIMES is 4, this table can be thought of as a one-dimensional array, whose four elements are its rows:

Of course, each of the rows in temperatureGrid is itself a one-dimensional array of three real values:

A table can thus be viewed as a one-dimensional array whose components are also one-dimensional arrays.

C++ allows array declarations to be given in a form that reflects this perspective.

If we first declare the type identifier `TemperatureList` as a synonym for an array of outlet readings,

```
enum Column {OUTLET1, OUTLET2, OUTLET3, NUM_OUTLETS};

typedef double TemperatureList[NUM_OUTLETS];
```

the objects of type `TemperatureList` are one-dimensional arrays of `double` values. We can then use this new type to declare a second type `TemperatureTable` as an array whose elements are `TemperatureList` objects:

```
enum Row {MIDNIGHT, SIX_AM, NOON, SIX_PM, NUM_TIMES};

typedef TemperatureList TemperatureTable[NUM_TIMES];
```

This declares the name `TemperatureTable` as a new type, whose objects are two-dimensional arrays of double values. The resulting type can then be used to define a two-dimensional array object `temperatureGrid`, as before:

```
TemperatureTable temperatureGrid;
```

Regardless of which approach is used, the notation

```
temperatureGrid[SIX_AM]
```

refers to the second row of temperatures in the table,

and the notation

```
temperatureGrid[SIX_AM][OUTLET2]
```

to the second entry in this row.

This idea can be extended to higher-dimensional arrays. For example, the three-dimensional array of temperature tables considered earlier can also be thought of as an array of arrays. In particular, since one temperature table was recorded for each day, the entire three-dimensional array can be viewed as an array of temperature tables, meaning a one-dimensional array whose components are two-dimensional arrays. If we adopt this point of view, we might declare the three-dimensional array `temperature` by adding the declarations

```
enum Days {SUNDAY, MONDAY, TUESDAY, WEDNESDAY,
           THURSDAY, FRIDAY, SATURDAY, SUNDAY, NUM_DAYS};

typedef TemperatureTable ThreeDimTemperatureArray[NUM_DAYS];

ThreeDimTemperatureArray temperature;
```

to the preceding declarations. This may make it clearer that the notation

```
temperature[MONDAY]
```

refers to the entire temperature table that was recorded on Monday; that is, `temperature[MONDAY]` is the two-dimensional array corresponding to the following temperature table:

Time	Location Outlet1	Outlet2	Outlet3
12 A.M.	63.7	66.2	64.3
6 A.M.	65.0	66.8	64.9
12 P.M.	72.7	69.9	66.3
6 P.M.	66.6	68.0	65.8

As in the previous example, each row in a temperature table can be viewed as a one-dimensional array of temperatures, and each table can therefore be viewed as a one-dimensional array of the temperature arrays. The doubly-indexed expression

`temperature[MONDAY][MIDNIGHT]`

refers to the first row in the temperature table for `Monday`,

```
63.7   66.2   64.3
```

and the triply-indexed expression

`temperature[MONDAY][MIDNIGHT][OUTLET3]`

accesses the third temperature in this row:

```
64.3
```

DRAWBACKS OF C-STYLE ARRAYS

The drawbacks of C-style arrays can be summarized in one sentence:

C-style arrays are not self-contained objects.

When we define a function to implement an array operation, we must pass not only the array, but also the bound on each of its dimensions. To illustrate, the function `Read()` to read values from a file into a `ThreeDimTemperatureArray` must receive not only the `ifstream` to the file and the `ThreeDimTemperatureArray`, but also the number of days, number of times, and number of outlets:

```
void Read(ifstream & in, ThreeDimTemperatureArray temperature,
          int numDays, int numTimes, int numOutlets)
{
   for (int d = 0; d < numDays; d++)
      for (int t = 0; t < numTimes; t++)
         for (int o = 0; o < numOutlets; o++)
            in >> temperature[d][t][o];
}
```

The reason is that an array is not a class and thus does not have data members in which these attributes can be stored. In the next section, we will see how the Standard Template Library `vector<T>` class template can be used to get around this drawback.

✔ Quick Quiz 12.2

1. A(n) _____ array is useful for storing data arranged in rows and columns.
2. A(n) _____ array is useful for storing data arranged in rows, columns, and ranks.
3. Arrays with the same number of rows as columns are said to be _____ arrays.

Questions 4–14 refer to the following two-dimensional array:

	[0]	[1]	[2]	[3]
[0]	11	22	0	43
[1]	1	-1	0	999
[2]	-5	39	15	82
[3]	1	2	3	4
[4]	44	33	22	11

mat:

Find the value of each expression in questions 4–9.

4. `mat[2][3]`   5. `mat[4][1]`   6. `mat[1][1]`
7. `mat[0][0] + mat[0][1]`   8. `mat[0][0] + mat[1][0]`   9. `mat[3]`

Find the value of x in each of questions 10–14:

10.
```
int x = 0;
for (int i = 0; i <= 4; i++)
   x += mat[i][1];
```

11.
```
int x = 0;
for (int j = 0; j < 4; j++)
   x += mat[1][j];
```

12.
```
int x = 0;
for (int k = 0; k <= 3; k++)
   x += mat[k][k];
```

13.
```
int x = 0;
for (int i = 0; i < 5; i++)
   for (int j = 0; j < 4; j++)
      x += mat[i][j];
```

14.
```
int x = 0;
for (int j = 0; j < 4; j++)
   for (int i = 0; i < 5; i++)
      x += mat[i][j];
```

15. The main drawback of C-style arrays is that they are not _____ objects.

EXERCISES 12.2

Exercises 1–6 assume that the following declarations have been made:

```
enum Color {RED, YELLOW, BLUE, GREEN, WHITE, BLACK, NUM_COLORS};

typedef int BigTable[50][100];
typedef char CharTable[26][26];
typedef bool BooleanTable[2][2];
typedef bool BitArray[2][2][2][2];
typedef int Shirt[NUM_COLORS][10][20];
typedef Shirt ShirtStock[5];
```

How many elements can be stored in an array of each type?

1. BigTable   2. CharTable   3. BooleanTable

4. BitArray   5. Shirt   6. ShirtStock

Exercises 7–10 assume that the following declarations have been made:

```
typedef int Array3x3[3][3];

Array3X3 mat;
```

Tell what value (if any) is assigned to each array element, or explain why an error occurs.

```
7.  for (int i = 0; i < 3; i++)
        for (int j = 0; j < 3; j++)
            mat[i][j] = i + j;

8.  for (int i = 0; i < 3; i++)
        for (int j = 2; j >= 0; j--)
            if (i == j)
                mat[i][j] = 0;
            else
                mat[i][j] = 1;

9.  for (int i = 0; i < 3; i++)
        for (int j = 0; j < 3; j++)
            if (i < j)
                mat[i][j] = -1;
            else if (i == j)
                mat[i][j] = 0;
            else
                mat[i][j] = 1;

10. for (int i = 0; i < 3; i++)
    {
        for (int j = 0; j < i; j++)
            mat[i][j] = 0;
        for (j = i; j < 3; j++)
            mat[i][j] = 2;
    }
```

Exercises 11–14 assume that the following declarations have been made:

```
char logo[2][9] = {"Computers", "and More!"};
```

Tell what output will be produced or explain why an error occurs.

11.
```
for (int i = 0, i < 2; i++)
{
    for (int j = 0; j < 9; j++)
        cout << logo[i][j];
    cout << endl;
}
```

12.
```
for (int j = 0; j < 9; j++)
{
    for (int i = 0; i < 2; i++)
        cout << logo[i][j];
    cout << endl;
}
```

13.
```
for (int i = 0; i < 2; i++)
{
    for (int j = 0; j < 9; j++)
        cout << logo[j][i];
    cout << endl;
}
```

14.
```
for (int i = 0; i < 2; i++)
{
    for (int j = 8; j >= 0; j--)
        cout << logo[i][j];
    cout << endl;
}
```

15. Write a function that, given a `TemperatureTable` (as declared in section 12.2), will calculate and return the average temperature at each of the three locations.

16. Construct two enumerations: `AutoModel`, whose values are ten different automobile models, and `EmployeeName`, whose values are the names of eight employees of an auto dealership. Using these types, overload the I/O operators with definitions to perform input and output of sales tables. The output operator should display the sales table with the rows labeled with the automobile models and the columns labeled with the employee's names.

17. Like one-dimensional arrays, multidimensional arrays are stored in a block of consecutive memory locations, and address translation formulas are used to determine the location in memory of each array element. To illustrate, consider a 3×4 array a of integers, and assume that an integer can be stored in one memory word. If a is allocated memory in a row-wise manner and b is its base address, then the first row of a, `a[0][0]`, `a[0][1]`, `a[0][2]`, `a[0][3]`, is stored in words b, $b + 1$, $b + 2$, $b + 3$; the second row in words $b + 4$ through $b + 7$; and the third row in words $b + 8$ through $b + 11$.

Address	Memory	Array Element
	⋮	
b		a[0][0]
$b+1$		a[0][1]
$b+2$		a[0][2]
$b+3$		a[0][3]
$b+4$		a[1][0]
$b+5$		a[1][1]
$b+6$		a[1][2]
$b+7$		a[1][3]
$b+8$		a[2][0]
$b+9$		a[2][1]
$b+10$		a[2][2]
$b+11$		a[2][3]
	⋮	

In general, a[i][j] is stored in word $b + 4i + j$.

(a) Give a similar diagram and formula if a is a 3 × 3 array of integer values.

(b) Give a similar diagram and formula if a is a 3 × 4 array of double values, where double values require two words for storage.

12.3 MULTIDIMENSIONAL vector<T> OBJECTS

In chapter 9, we considered the vector<T> class template provided by the Standard Template Library (STL). As a pattern for a class, vector<T> can be used to create self-contained objects that do not suffer from the drawbacks associated with C-style arrays. Moreover, many common operations are already implemented by the function members provided in vector<T> and by applying the STL algorithms to vector<T> objects. This means that a programmer need not reinvent the wheel for these operations.

Among the function members provided by vector<T> are three constructors whose prototypes (in simplified form) are as follows:

```
vector();
vector(int n);
vector(int n, T initialValue);
```

The first constructs an empty vector<T> object; the second constructs a vector<T> object with capacity n and fills it with a default value of type T; and the third constructs a vector<T> object with capacity n and fills it with the specified initialValue. For example, the declarations

```
vector<double> aVector;

const int INITIAL_CAPACITY = 10;
vector<double> bVector(INITIAL_CAPACITY);

vector<double> cVector(INITIAL_CAPACITY, 1.0);
```

construct aVector as a vector of doubles, initially empty; bVector as a vector of 10 `doubles`, all initialized to some default value (e.g., 0.0); and `cVector` as a vector of 10 `doubles`, all initialized to 1.0:

aVector

bVector	0.0	0.0	0.0	0.0	0.0	0.0	0.0	0.0	0.0	0.0

cVector	1.0	1.0	1.0	1.0	1.0	1.0	1.0	1.0	1.0	1.0

It is the last two types of constructor that make it possible to build multidimensional `vector<T>` objects.

TWO-DIMENSIONAL `vector<T>` OBJECTS

A Two-Step Approach. Suppose that we want to build a two-dimensional object named `table` consisting of three rows and four columns. We might begin by defining a one-dimensional `vector<T>` object named `initialRow` whose capacity is the desired number of columns (4), and fill it with some initial value:

```
const int COLUMNS = 4;
vector<double> initialRow(COLUMNS, 0.0);
```

This builds a one-dimensional vector named `initialRow`, whose size and capacity are each 4:

	[0]	[1]	[2]	[3]
initialRow:	0.0	0.0	0.0	0.0

Because a vector is a one-dimensional object, a **vector of vectors** is a two-dimensional object. We can thus define a two-dimensional object named `table` as a vector of vectors, using the desired number of rows (3) as its capacity, and with the object `initialRow` as its initial value:

```
const int ROWS = 3;
vector< vector<double> > table(ROWS, initialRow);
```

Note the space separating `double>` and `>`. *It is important to remember the space between the angle brackets (> >),* because if we write

```
vector< vector<double >>  table(ROWS, initialRow);      // ERROR!
```

the compiler will mistake `>>` for the input operator, which will result in a compilation error.

Because each element of `table` is a `vector<double>`, and `initialRow` is a `vector<double>`, the compiler will use `initialRow` to initialize each element of `table`. The result is that `table` is constructed as a 3 × 4 vector of vectors, in which each of the three rows is a copy of `initialRow`:

```
table:    [0]   [1]   [2]   [3]
     [0]  0.0 | 0.0 | 0.0 | 0.0
     [1]  0.0 | 0.0 | 0.0 | 0.0
     [2]  0.0 | 0.0 | 0.0 | 0.0
```

A single-subscript expression such as

```
table[0]
```

refers to one row of `table`,

```
table:    [0]   [1]   [2]   [3]
     [0]  0.0 | 0.0 | 0.0 | 0.0
```

and a double-subscript expression such as

```
table[0][2]
```

refers to an element within the specified row of `table`:

```
table:    [0]   [1]   [2]   [3]
     [0]  0.0 | 0.0 | 0.0 | 0.0
```

In general, the expression

```
table[r][c]
```

can be used to access the value stored in column `c` of row `r`.

A One-Step Approach. We can define the same vector of vectors in one step by using a more concise (although somewhat less readable) form that avoids the need to define the object `initialRow`:

```
const int ROWS = 3;
const int COLUMNS = 4;
vector< vector<double> > table(ROWS,
                          vector<double>(COLUMNS, 0.0));
```

This uses the `vector<T>` constructor *twice:* an "outer" call,

```
vector< vector<double> > table( ROWS,

                          vector<double>(COLUMNS, 0.0) );
```

and nested within it, an "inner" explicit call to the same constructor:

```
vector< vector<double> > table(ROWS,
                          vector<double>(COLUMNS, 0.0) );
```

This inner constructor builds a nameless `vector<double>` object containing four zeros (like `initialRow` in the two-step approach). This nameless vector of `double` values is then passed as the initial value to the outer call to the constructor, which uses it to initialize each of its three vector elements. The result is the same 3×4 vector of vectors of `double` values we obtained earlier.

```
table:   [0]   [1]   [2]   [3]

 [0]    0.0   0.0   0.0   0.0

 [1]    0.0   0.0   0.0   0.0

 [2]    0.0   0.0   0.0   0.0
```

Using `typedef` for Readability. The `typedef` mechanism can be used to improve the readability of this one-step approach:

```
typedef vector<double> TableRow;
typedef vector<TableRow> Table;
```

The first `typedef` declares the name `TableRow` as a type that is a synonym for a one-dimensional vector of `double`s. The second `typedef` then declares the name `Table` as a synonym for a two-dimensional vector of `TableRow` values; that is, a vector of vectors of `double`s.

For reusability, we would put these `typedef` declarations for two-dimensional vectors in a header file `Table.h` as shown in Figure 12.2.

FIGURE 12.2   A HEADER FILE FOR TYPE `Table`.

```
/* Table.h contains the declarations for type Table.
 *  ...
 *****************************************************/

#include <vector>

typedef vector<double> TableRow;
typedef vector<TableRow> Table;

// ... prototypes of Table operations
```

A program that includes `Table.h` can then use

```
Table aTable;
```

to define an object `aTable` as an empty two-dimensional `Table`. To define a non-empty `Table`, we can use

```
const int ROWS = 3,
          COLUMNS = 4;
Table theTable(ROWS, TableRow(COLUMNS, 0.0));
```

The result is a definition that is more readable than those that explicitly use the type `vector< vector<double> >`. This approach also eliminates the compiler error described earlier that is caused by forgetting a space between the two `>` symbols.

Two-Dimensional `vector<T>` Operations

We have already seen that double-subscript expressions of the form

```
theTable[r][c]
```

can be used to access the element at row `r` and column `c` in `theTable`. In addition to the subscript operator, other `vector<T>` function members can be applied to two-dimensional vectors. We will look briefly at two of these functions.

The `size()` Function. Suppose that we want to determine the number of rows in a two-dimensional vector. If `theTable` is the 3×4 two-dimensional vector described earlier, then the expression

```
theTable.size()
```

returns 3, the number of rows in `theTable`. The expression

```
theTable[r].size()
```

can be used to find the number of columns in row `r`, because `theTable[r]` returns the vector of `double` values in `theTable` whose index is `r`, and applying `size()` to that vector returns the number of values in it. If `theTable` is rectangular, then each row will have the same size allowing us to apply `size()` to any row. If `theTable` is not rectangular, then the size of each row may be different, and so `size()` must be applied to each row separately.

The `push_back()` Function. Suppose that we need to add a new (fourth) row to `theTable`. This can be done by using the `vector<T>` function member `push_back()`:

```
theTable.push_back(TableRow(COLUMNS, 0.0));
```

Since `TableRow` has been declared as a synonym for `vector<double>`, the expression

```
TableRow(COLUMNS, 0.0)
```

is a call to the `vector<T>` constructor to build a nameless vector of zeros. The `push_back()` function then appends this vector to the existing rows in `theTable`:

theTable:	[0]	[1]	[2]	[3]
[0]	0.0	0.0	0.0	0.0
[1]	0.0	0.0	0.0	0.0
[2]	0.0	0.0	0.0	0.0
[3]	0.0	0.0	0.0	0.0

To add a column to theTable, push_back() can be used to append a double value to each row of theTable, because each row in theTable is itself a vector of double values:

```
for (int row = 0; row < theTable.size(); row++)
    theTable[row].push_back(0.0);
```

Execution of this loop will add a fifth column to theTable:

```
theTable:   [0]  [1]  [2]  [3]  [4]
```

	[0]	[1]	[2]	[3]	[4]
[0]	0.0	0.0	0.0	0.0	0.0
[1]	0.0	0.0	0.0	0.0	0.0
[2]	0.0	0.0	0.0	0.0	0.0
[3]	0.0	0.0	0.0	0.0	0.0

Note that push_back() makes it easy to build non-rectangular tables. For example, consider the following code fragment:

```
Table aTable;

for (int cols = 1; cols <= 3; cols++)
    aTable.push_back(TableRows(cols, 0.0) );
```

Initially, aTable is constructed as an empty vector. The first pass through the for loop constructs a nameless vector containing one zero and appends it to aTable:

```
aTable:   [0]
```

	[0]
[0]	0.0

The second pass through the for loop constructs and appends another nameless vector containing two zeros:

```
aTable:   [0]  [1]
```

	[0]	[1]
[0]	0.0	
[1]	0.0	0.0

The third pass through the for loop constructs and appends a third nameless vector of three zeros:

```
aTable:   [0]  [1]  [2]
```

	[0]	[1]	[2]
[0]	0.0		
[1]	0.0	0.0	
[2]	0.0	0.0	0.0

Two-dimensional vectors thus need not be square, nor even rectangular. Such non-rectangular two-dimensional tables are sometimes called **jagged tables** or **jagged arrays.**

DEFINING TWO-DIMENSIONAL vector<T> FUNCTIONS

The subscript and other vector<T> operations can be used as "building blocks" for operations that are not predefined for two-dimensional vectors. The following examples illustrate how this is done.

Two-Dimensional vector Output. We can use the vector size() function and subscript operations to display a two-dimensional vector via an ostream as shown in Figure 12.3. For reusability, we define this function in a separately-compiled implementation file Table.cpp and place a prototype in Table.h (see Figure 12.2).

FIGURE 12.3   A Table OUTPUT OPERATION.

```
/* Table.cpp defines various Table operations.
 *  ...
 ************************************************************/

#include "Table.h"

void Print(ostream & out, const Table & aTable)
{
   for (int row = 0; row < aTable.size(); row++)
   {
      for (int col = 0; col < aTable[row].size(); col++)
         out << aTable[row][col] << '\t';
      out << endl;
   }
}
```

If theTable is the Table object we defined previously, then the call

```
Print(cout, theTable);
```

will display theTable as follows:

```
0     0     0     0
0     0     0     0
0     0     0     0
```

In the outer loop, the expression

```
aTable.size()
```

returns the number of rows in the argument corresponding to parameter aTable. Since each row in aTable is itself a vector of double values, the inner loop expression

```
aTable[row].size()
```

returns the number of columns in aTable[row].

Because `size()` is applied separately to each row, the function in Figure 12.3 can be used to display any table, whether square, rectangular, or jagged. Thus, if `aTable` is the jagged table described earlier,

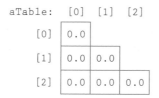

the call

```
Print(cout, aTable);
```

will display

```
0
0    0
0    0    0
```

Two-Dimensional vector Input. The data for a table is often stored in a file, and an operation to fill a two-dimensional vector from a file is thus a useful operation. There are several ways such an operation can be implemented. The approach used by the function `Fill()` in Figure 12.4 resembles the way C-style arrays are input. The number of rows and number of columns in the table are read from the first line of the file and these values are used to preallocate a local two-dimensional vector of the appropriate dimensions, which is then filled with values from the file. Again, for reusability, we would store this function in `Table.cpp` and put a prototype in `Table.h`.

FIGURE 12.4   A `Table` INPUT OPERATION.

```
void Fill(const string & fileName, Table & aTable)
{
   ifstream in(fileName.data());            // open stream to file
   assert(in.is_open());                    // verify

   int rows,                                // input variables
       cols;                                //   for dimensions
   in >> rows >> cols;                      // read dimensions

   Table locTable(rows, TableRow(cols));    // construct local table with
                                            //   correct # rows and columns
   for (int r = 0; r < rows; r++)           // for each row
      for (int c = 0; c < cols; c++)        //   input cols values into row
         in >> locTable[r][c];

                                            // assign locTable to aTable so
   aTable = locTable;                       //   it has correct dimensions
   in.close();                              // close stream
}
```

This function constructs a local `Table locTable` that has the correct number of rows and columns. A pair of nested `for` loops is then used to fill this table with values from the file. Assigning this table to the reference parameter `aTable` destroys the corresponding `Table` argument and constructs a new one whose capacity will match exactly the dimensions of the table stored in the file when `Fill()` terminates.

An alternative approach is to leave the number of rows and columns unspecified; read values from the file and use `push_back()` to append them to a vector that stores a row of the table; and at the end of the row, use `push_back()` again to append that vector to the vector of vectors. The function `Load()` in Figure 12.5 uses this approach.

FIGURE 12.5   A `Table` INPUT OPERATION.

```
void Load(const string & fileName, Table & aTable)
{
    ifstream in(fileName.data());          // open stream to file
    assert(in.is_open());                  // verify

    Table locTable;                        // empty local table
    double aValue;                         // input variable
    char separator;                        // to test for '\n'

    for (;;)                               // loop:
    {
        TableRow aRow;                     //    start with an empty row
        for (;;)                           //    loop:
        {
            separator = in.peek();         //        peek at the next char
            if (separator == '\n') break;  //        if at end of row, exit
            in >> aValue;                  //        read a value
            if (in.eof()) return;          //        if eof, quit
            aRow.push_back(aValue);        //        append value to row
        }                                  //    end loop
        in.get(separator);                 //    consume the newline
        locTable.push_back(aRow);          //    append row to table
    }                                      // end loop

    aTable = locTable;                     // assign locTable to aTable
    in.close();                            // close stream
}
```

The advantage of this approach is its generality. The input file need not contain the table's dimensions, only the table data. Also, because each row corresponds to one line from the input file, `Load()` can be used to read square, rectangular, or jagged tables, and it requires no information in the input file other than the table's data. Its disadvantage is that a significant portion of the vector's memory may be wasted, because when `push_back()` expands the capacity of a vector, memory is allocated in large blocks, rather than an element at a time.

✔ Quick Quiz 12.3

1. (True or false) A vector of vectors is a two-dimensional object.
2. (True or false) The declaration

   ```
   vector<vector<int>> intTable(3, vector<int>(4, 0));
   ```

   will cause a compile-time error.

Questions 3–8 assume the following declarations:

```
typedef vector<double> TableRow;
typedef vector<TableRow> Table;
Table qqTab(5, TableRow(4, 0.0));
```

3. qqTab will have _____ rows and _____ columns
4. Write an expression to change the element in the second row and third column of qqTab to 1.1.
5. What is the value of qqTab.size()?
6. What is the value of qqTab[0].size()?
7. Write a statement to append the value 99.9 at the end of the second row of qqTab.
8. Write statements to append a row containing 4 zeros at the bottom of qqTab.

Exercises 12.3

For each of the following exercises, write a function for type Table to do what is required.

1. A function SetElem() that, for a given row r, column c, and double value element, sets the value in row r, column c to element.
2. A function RowSum() that sums the values in a given row of a Table.
3. A function ColumnSum() that sums the values in a given column of a Table.
4. A function RowAverage() that, given a row number, computes the average of the values in that row.
5. A function RowStdDeviation() that, given a row number, computes the standard deviation of the values in that row (see Programming Problem 12 at the end of chapter 9).
6. A function ColumnAverage() that, given a column number, computes the average of the values in that column.
7. A function ColumnStdDeviation() that, given a column number, computes the standard deviation of the values in that column (see Programming Problem 12 at the end of chapter 9).

12.4 A vector<T>-Based Matrix Library

A two-dimensional numeric array having *m* rows and *n* columns is called an ***m × n*** **matrix.** In this section, we briefly examine how to build a Matrix class, together with one very useful Matrix operation: **matrix multiplication.** There are many other matrix operations, and some of these are described in the exercises. We will also describe one of the many important applications that involve the manipulation of matrices.

MATRIX MULTIPLICATION

Suppose that *Mat1* is an $m \times n$ matrix and *Mat2* is an $n \times p$ matrix. The product *Mat3* of *Mat1* and *Mat2* is an $m \times p$ matrix with the entry $Mat3[i][j]$, which appears in the ith row and the jth column, given by

$$Mat3[i][j] = \text{The sum of the products of the entries in row } i \text{ of}$$
$$Mat1 \text{ with the entries of column } j \text{ of } Mat2$$
$$= Mat1[i][1] * Mat2[1][j] + Mat1[i][2] * Mat2[2][j]$$
$$+ \cdots + Mat1[i][n] * Mat2[n][j]$$

Note that the number of columns (n) in *Mat1* must equal the number of rows in *Mat2* for the product of *Mat1* with *Mat2* to be defined.

As an example, suppose that *Mat1* is the 2×3 matrix

$$\begin{bmatrix} 1 & 0 & 2 \\ 3 & 0 & 4 \end{bmatrix}$$

and that *Mat2* is the 3×4 matrix

$$\begin{bmatrix} 4 & 2 & 5 & 3 \\ 6 & 4 & 1 & 8 \\ 9 & 0 & 0 & 2 \end{bmatrix}$$

Because the number of columns (3) in *Mat1* equals the number of rows in *Mat2*, the product matrix *Mat3* is defined. The entry in the first row and first column is

$$1 * 4 + 0 * 6 + 2 * 9 = 22$$

Similarly, the entry in the first row and second column is

$$1 * 2 + 0 * 4 + 2 * 0 = 2$$

The complete product matrix *Mat3* is the 2×4 matrix given by

$$\begin{bmatrix} 22 & 2 & 5 & 7 \\ 48 & 6 & 15 & 17 \end{bmatrix}$$

In general, the algorithm for multiplying matrices is as follows:

Matrix Multiplication Algorithm

1. If the number of columns in *Mat1* $\neq$ the number of rows in *Mat2*, then the product *Mat3* = *Mat1* * *Mat2* is not defined; terminate the algorithm.
2. For each row i in *Mat1*, do the following:

   For each column j in *Mat2* do the following:

   a. Set *Sum* equal to 0.
   b. For each column k in *Mat1* (= the number of rows in *Mat2*):
      Add $Mat1[i][k] * Mat2[k][j]$ to *Sum*.
   c. Set $Mat3[i][j]$ equal to *Sum*.

This is the general algorithm for matrix multiplication. However, before we can encode it, we need a `Matrix` class in which to store this operation.

BUILDING A `Matrix` CLASS: THE EXTERNAL APPROACH

If we take the external approach to implementing matrix multiplication, then building a `Matrix` class is quite easy, because a matrix can be thought of as a vector of vectors of numbers. We can simply use a `typedef` statement to declare the name `Matrix` as an alias for `vector< vector<double> >`, as shown in Figure 12.6. To make this declaration reusable, we would place it in a `Matrix` library header file.

FIGURE 12.6   BUILDING `Matrix` USING `typedef`.

```
/* Matrix.h provides the type Matrix and its operation prototypes.
 * ...
 ***********************************************************************/

#include <vector>
#include "Table.h"                              // Table prototypes

typedef vector<double> MatrixRow;
typedef vector< MatrixRow > Matrix;

// ... Matrix operation prototypes go here
```

The primary advantage of this approach is *convenience,* because a program that includes this header file can now define an empty `Matrix` object as follows:

```
Matrix aMatrix;
```

A non-empty `Matrix` can be defined using the approach we saw in the preceding section:

```
const int ROWS = 3,
          COLS = 4;
Matrix theMatrix(ROWS, MatrixRow(COLS, 0.0));
```

This definition builds `theMatrix` as a 3 × 4 matrix, and sets each of its elements to zero.

theMatrix:	[0]	[1]	[2]	[3]
[0]	0.0	0.0	0.0	0.0
[1]	0.0	0.0	0.0	0.0
[2]	0.0	0.0	0.0	0.0

`Matrix` OPERATIONS

Because the identifier `Matrix` is an alias for `vector< vector<double> >`, any operation defined for `vector< vector<double> >` can be applied to a `Matrix` object. For example, the double-subscript operation can be used to access a particular element of a `Matrix`. Similarly, the `size()` function can be used to determine the number of rows in a `Matrix`. The statements

```
for (int r = 0; r < theMatrix.size(); r++)
   for (int c = 0; c < theMatrix[r].size(); c++)
      theMatrix[r][c] = r + c + 1;
```

will modify `theMatrix` as follows:

theMatrix:	[0]	[1]	[2]	[3]
[0]	1.0	2.0	3.0	4.0
[1]	2.0	3.0	4.0	5.0
[2]	3.0	4.0	5.0	6.0

In addition, because `Matrix` is an alias for `vector< vector<double> >` and `Table` is also an alias for `vector< vector<double> >`, the operations defined for `Table` (e.g., `Fill()` from Figure 12.4) can also be applied to `Matrix` objects.

Operations that are specific to `Matrix` objects and that are not predefined for `vector< vector<double> >` and `Table` must be defined as functions. For example, Figure 12.7 shows the implementation of the matrix multiplication operation by overloading `operator*`. Because this is a reasonably complicated operation, we define it in a separately compiled implementaton file `Matrix.cpp` and place its prototype in `Matrix.h`.

 FIGURE 12.7   Matrix MULTIPLICATION.

```
/* Matrix.cpp defines the Matrix operations.
 *  ...
 ***************************************************************/

#include "Matrix.h"                          // type Matrix
#include <assert.h>                          // assert()

Matrix operator*(const Matrix & mat1, const Matrix & mat2)
{
   const int ROWS1 = mat1.size(),
             ROWS2 = mat2.size();
   assert(ROWS1 > 0 && ROWS2 > 0);           // verify nonzero

   const int COLS1 = mat1[0].size(),
             COLS2 = mat2[0].size();
   assert(COLS1 == ROWS2);                   // check precondition

   Matrix mat3(ROWS1, MatrixRow(COLS2, 0.0)); // define result Matrix
```

```
   for (int i = 0; i < ROWS1; i++)            // for each row in mat1:
      for (int j = 0; j < COLS2; j++)         //  for each col in mat2:
      {
          double sum = 0;
          for (int k = 0; k < COLS1; k++)     //     for each column in mat1:
              sum += mat1[i][k] * mat2[k][j];  //        sum the products
          mat3[i][j] = sum;                    //        put sum in result Matrix
      }

   return mat3;                               // return the result Matrix
}
```

Once `Matrix` operations have been defined, a program can make use of these operations in the same manner as those of any other class, as illustrated in Figure 12.8:

 FIGURE 12.8   PROGRAM TO DEMONSTRATE `Matrix` MULTIPLICATION.

```
/* matmult8.cpp illustrates use of the matrix multiplication function.
 *
 *  Input (keyboard): names of files containing matrices
 *  Input (files):    two matrices
 *  Precondition:     the first line of each file == rows & columns
 *  Output (screen):  the matrices together with their product
 **************************************************************************/

#include <iostream.h>                    // cin, cout, <<, >>
#include <string>                        // string type
#include "Table.h"                       // Fill(), Print()
#include "Matrix.h"                      // Matrix, operator *

int main()
{
  cout << "\nThis program demonstrates matrix multiplication,\n"
          "by multiplying two matrices stored in separate files.\n"
          "\nA file must list the # of rows and columns of its "
          "matrix.\n";
                                         // get file names
  cout << "\nPlease enter the name of the first file: ";
  string file1;
  cin >> file1;

  cout << "and the name of the second file: ";
  string file2;
  cin >> file2;

  Matrix matrix1,
         matrix2;
```

```
    Fill(file1, matrix1);                   // load Matrix1 from File1
    Fill(file2, matrix2);                   // load Matrix2 from File2
                                            // Display the matrices
    cout << "\n- Matrix1 -------------------------------------\n";
    Print(cout, matrix1);
    cout << "\n- Matrix2 -------------------------------------\n";
    Print(cout, matrix2);

    Matrix matrix3 = matrix1 * matrix2;     // perform multiplication
                                            // display Matrix3
    cout << "\n- Matrix3 -------------------------------------\n";
    Print(cout, matrix3);
    return 0;
}
```

Listing of Input File mat2x3.dat

```
2 3
1 0 2
3 0 4
```

Listing of Input File mat3x4.dat

```
3 4
4 2 5 3
6 4 1 8
9 0 0 2
```

Sample run:

```
This program demonstrates matrix multiplication,
by multiplying two matrices stored in separate files.

A file must list the # of rows and columns of its matrix.

Please enter the name of the first file: mat2x3.dat
and the name of the second file: mat3x4.dat

- Matrix1 -------------------------------------
1       0       2
3       0       4

- Matrix2 -------------------------------------
4       2       5       3
6       4       1       8
9       0       0       2

- Matrix3 -------------------------------------
22      2       5       7
 3      6       15      17
```

It is important to understand that the statement

```
Matrix matrix1,
       matrix2;
```

builds `matrix1` and `matrix2` as empty vectors of vectors of numbers. The statements

```
Fill(file1, matrix1);
Fill(file2, matrix2);
```

use function `Fill()` from the `Table` library we defined in the previous section, and the statements

```
Print(cout, matrix1);
Print(cout, matrix2);
```

apply the function `Print()` from the same `Table` library. The declaration of the result matrix

```
Matrix matrix3 = matrix1 * matrix2;
```

constructs `matrix3` as a `Matrix`, and initializes it with the `Matrix` returned by `operator*`, rather than using the default assignment mechanism. The definition of `Print()` from the `Table` library is then used a final time to display `matrix3`.

BUILDING A Matrix CLASS: THE INTERNAL APPROACH

The preceding approach to building a `Matrix` library reflects the external approach: We used `typedef` to declare the name `Matrix` as a type, and then defined non-member functions to act as operations on a `Matrix`. This approach does not reflect the I-can-do-it-myself philosophy of the internal approach of object-centered design; operations like `Fill()` and `Print()` are functions that manipulate their `Matrix` parameter, rather than messages being sent to a `Matrix` object.

To build a `Matrix` that reflects the I-can-do-it-myself approach, we must somehow declare the name `Matrix` as the name of a class, and then define operations like `Fill()` and `Print()` as function members of that class. To do this, we must use a new feature of C++ called its **inheritance** mechanism.

Using Inheritance. Just as a child inherits characteristics such as eye and hair color from his parents, C++ provides a mechanism whereby a class can be declared to inherit the data and function members of another class. We can use this inheritance mechanism to build a `Matrix` class that inherits the data and function members of a vector of vectors of `double` values, and then add our specialized `Matrix` operations to the new class. Figure 12.9 shows the C++ syntax for this.

FIGURE 12.9   DERIVING Matrix FROM vector.

```
/* Matrix.h derives class Matrix from the STL vector class template.
 * ...
 ************************************************************************/

#include <vector>

typedef vector<double> OneDimVector;
typedef vector<OneDimVector> TwoDimVector;
```

```
class Matrix : public TwoDimVector
 {
  public:
    Matrix(unsigned rows, unsigned columns);
    unsigned Rows() const;
    unsigned Columns() const;
    void Matrix::Print(ostream & out) const;
    void Matrix::Read(istream & in);
    Matrix operator*(const Matrix & Mat1);
    // ... additional operations omitted ...

  private:
    unsigned myRows,
             myColumns;
 };

// ... definitions of simple Matrix operations go here as inline...
```

The key to the inheritance mechanism is the first line of the class declaration:

```
class Matrix : public TwoDimVector
```

This line declares that the class `Matrix` *is a* `TwoDimVector`, a vector of vectors of `double` values. The class `TwoDimVector`, which is just a synonym for `vector< vector<double> >`, is called the **parent class** (or **base class** or **superclass**), and the class `Matrix` is called the **child class** (or **derived class** or **subclass**). The word `public` indicates that any function member that is public in `TwoDimVector` will also be public for our `Matrix` class.[1] That is, if `aMatrix` is an object of type `Matrix`,

```
Matrix aMatrix;
```

then because a `Matrix` is a `TwoDimVector`, a vector function member such as `empty()` can be applied to `aMatrix`:

```
if (aMatrix.empty()) // ... aMatrix is empty
```

Even though there is no prototype for an `empty()` function member within class `Matrix`, `empty()` can still be applied, because `Matrix` inherits it from `TwoDimVector`. Similarly, `push_back()` can be used, as in

```
const int COLUMNS = 10;
aMatrix.push_back(OneDimVector(COLUMNS, 0.0));
```

to append a row of ten zeros to `aMatrix`, because class `Matrix` inherits the `push_back()` function member from `TwoDimVector`. And once a `Matrix` has been given a set of values, the subscript operator can be used to access those values

```
aMatrix[r][c]
```

---
[1] With the exception of constructors and the destructor.

because Matrix also inherits this vector operation. In short, any message that can be sent to a TwoDimVector can be sent to a Matrix (but it must have the proper arguments).

Inheritance thus saves a great deal of work by allowing vector operations to be applied to a Matrix object without redefining those operations. It is one more tool that can be used to avoid reinventing the wheel.

In general, the C++ inheritance mechanism can be described as follows:

The C++ Inheritance Mechanism

Form

```
class Child : public Parent
{
  // ... members of Child
};
```

where *Child* and *Parent* are valid C++ identifiers.

Purpose

Child inherits:

▸ the function members of *Parent*, except for its constructors and destructor;

▸ the data members of *Parent*, provided the keyword private: is replaced by **protected:** in *Parent*;

public members of *Parent* are public in *Child* and protected members of *Parent* are private in *Child*;

Child may contain additional data or function members, as needed.

Any time we encounter a situation where we need to build a class that **is a** specialized occurrence of some existing class, this inheritance mechanism can be applied.

Constructor. Unlike most function members, the constructors of a parent class are not inherited by a child class, and so the child class must provide its own constructor functions. However, the child class constructors can use the parent class constructors to initialize the data members the child inherits from the parent. Figure 12.10 shows the definition of the constructor for class Matrix that uses this approach. Because of its simplicity, we define it in the header file Matrix.h, following the declaration of class Matrix.

FIGURE 12.10   THE **Matrix m × n** CONSTRUCTOR.

```
inline Matrix::Matrix(unsigned rows, unsigned columns)
   : TwoDimVector( rows, OneDimVector(columns) )
{
   myRows = rows;
   myColumns = columns;
}
```

In a nutshell, this syntax tells the compiler to construct a `Matrix` by first calling the constructor for class `TwoDimVector` to allocate any storage required and to initialize any data members that `Matrix` inherits from `TwoDimVector`. Then the statements in the body of the `Matrix` are executed to initialize the new data members `myRows` and `myColumns`.

To illustrate, consider the following declaration of the `Matrix` object `theMatrix`:

```
Matrix theMatrix(3, 4);
```

When it is encountered, the `Matrix` constructor calls the `TwoDimVector` constructor, passing it the desired number of rows (3) and columns (4), which allocates space for the 3 × 4 two-dimensional vector that will store the elements of `theMatrix` and initializes all of these elements to 0:

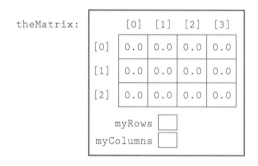

The `Matrix` constructor then assigns the value 3 and 4 to the data members `myRows` and `myColumns`, respectively.

Similarly, we can write

```
cout << "Enter the number of rows and columns in the matrix: ";
int numRows, numColumns;
cin >> numRows >> numColumns;

Matrix aMatrix(numRows, numColumns);
```

and `aMatrix` will be constructed as a `Matrix` whose dimensions are `numRows` by `numColumns` and whose elements are initialized to zero.

This definition of the `Matrix` constructor in Figure 12.10 illustrates the **member initialization list** mechanism that a child class constructor can use to invoke the constructor of its parent class. Its general form is

```
Child::Child(ChildConstructorParameterList)
   : Parent(ParentConstructorArgumentList)
{ StatementList }
```

where *Child* is the name of the child class, and *Parent* is the name of the parent class. When such a function executes, the first thing that occurs is a call to the constructor for class *Parent*, passing it the arguments in *ParentConstructor-ArgumentList*, which uses these values to construct a *Parent* object. When the constructor function of class *Parent* terminates, the *StatementList* in the *Child* constructor is executed, which initializes any new data members defined within the *Child* class.

Note that the constructor in Figure 12.10 is sufficiently short to be defined as `inline`. This is frequently the case when using the inheritance mechanism, because most of the initialization work is done by the parent class constructor. The inheritance mechanism thus provides a way to reuse the work done for one class in designing another class and thus avoid redundant coding.

The `Rows()` and `Columns()` Operations. In addition to the `Matrix` constructors, we must define its specialized operations. We begin with functions that return the dimensions of the matrix, that is, the number of rows and columns. These are member functions that simply return the values stored in the data members `myRows` and `myColumns`, as shown in Figure 12.11. The functions `Rows()` and `Columns()` are so simple that we define them as an inline function in the `Matrix` header file.

FIGURE 12.11   **`Rows()` AND `Columns()` OF A `Matrix`.**

```
// Number of rows in a Matrix
inline unsigned Matrix::Rows() const
{
   return myRows;
}


// Number of columns in a Matrix
inline unsigned Matrix::Columns() const
{
   return myColumns;
}
```

Given these functions, a programmer can now write

```
aMatrix.Rows()
```

to determine the number of rows in `aMatrix`, and

```
aMatrix.Columns()
```

to determine the number of columns.

The Output Operation. Because an output function is helpful in debugging other operations, we will define it next. Our approach will be that described in chapter 10:

(1)   Define an output member function `Print()`, and then

(2)   Overload `operator<<()` as an external function that calls `Print()`.

A specification for the `Print()` function member (from an internal perspective) is:

Receive: *out*, an `ostream`

Output: My values, each row on a separate line

Pass back: *out*, containing the output values

Figure 12.12 shows a definition of `Print()` that satisfies this specification. Given the complexity of `Print()`, we define it in a separately compiled implementation file `Matrix.cpp` and prototype it inside the declaration of class `Matrix`.

FIGURE 12.12   THE `Matrix Print()` OPERATION.

```
void Matrix::Print(ostream & out) const
{
   for (int i = 0; i < myRows; i++)
   {
      for (int j = 0; j < myColumns; j++)
         out << (*this)[i][j] << '\t';
      out << endl;
   }
}
```

This function uses a special feature that C++ provides to allow objects to refer to themselves. *Every class object contains a predefined local variable named* **this** *whose value is the address of the object so that the value of the dereferenced variable* ***this** *is the object itself.* Thus, in `Print()`, *this will be the `Matrix` object containing this function, and since the class `Matrix` inherits the vector subscript operator, it can be applied to *this.

There is an alternative way to define `Print()` that does not use this. It is shown in Figure 12.13.

FIGURE 12.13   ALTERNATIVE `Matrix Print()` OPERATION.

```
void Matrix::Print(ostream & out) const
{
   TwoDimVector::iterator rowIt = begin();
   OneDimVector::iterator columnIt;

   while (rowIt != end())
   {
      columnIt = (*rowIt).begin();
```

```
      while (columnIt != (*rowIt).end())
      {
         out << *columnIt << '\t';
         columnIt++;
      }
      out << endl;
      rowIt++;
   }
}
```

This version of `Print()` begins by defining `rowIt` as a `TwoDimVector` iterator, using the `begin()` function inherited from vector to position it at the beginning of the `Matrix`. Dereferencing it (`*rowIt`) produces a `OneDimVector` iterator positioned at the first row. The function also defines the `OneDimVector` iterator `columnIt` to traverse each row.

The outer `while` loop moves `rowIt` through the rows of the `Matrix` until it moves beyond the last row and the condition `rowIt != end()` becomes false causing repetition to terminate. (Note that the `end()` function member is also inherited from `TwoDimVector`.) On each pass through this loop, `columnIt` is positioned at the first element of the current row pointed to by `*rowIt` and the inner `while` loop then moves `columnIt` along this row, dereferencing it to access each element in that row and displaying that element. This inner `while` loop terminates when `columnIt` reaches the end of the current row and the condition (`columIt != *rowIt.end()`) becomes false. This process is then repeated with the next row.

Given one of these versions of the `Print()` function, it is easy to overload `operator<<()` as shown in Figure 12.14. This function makes it possible to write statements such as

```
cout << aMatrix;
```

to display the value of a `Matrix`.

FIGURE 12.14   OUTPUT OPERATOR << FOR **Matrix**

```
inline ostream & operator<<(ostream & out, const Matrix & theMatrix)
{
   theMatrix.Print(out);
   return out;
}
```

The Input Operation. In a similar way we can define an input operation for the class `Matrix`. We first define a function member `Read()` operation to input the entries of a `Matrix` from an istream and then overload `operator>>()` to call `Read()`. Figure 12.15 shows the definitions of `Read()`. It is defined in `Matrix.cpp` and prototyped inside the class. The inlined definition of `operator>>()` in Figure 12.16 would be placed in `Matrix.h` following the class declaration.

FIGURE 12.15   THE **Matrix Read()** OPERATION.

```
void Matrix::Read(istream & in)
{
    for (int i = 0; i < myRows; i++)
        for (int j = 0; j < myColumns; j++)
            in >> (*this)[i][j];
}
```

FIGURE 12.16   INPUT OPERATOR **>>** FOR **Matrix**

```
inline istream & operator>>(istream & in, Matrix & theMatrix)
{
    theMatrix.Read(in);
    return in;
}
```

Matrix Multiplication. The final operation we will define for our Matrix class is multiplication. The function in Figure 12.17 implements the matrix multiplication algorithm given earlier. Because it is sufficiently complicated, we define it in the implementation file Matrix.cpp and prototype it inside the class Matrix. Note that the Matrix constructor function is used to define the object mat3 and to initialize all of its elements to zero.

FIGURE 12.17   **Matrix** MULTIPLICATION.

```
Matrix Matrix::operator*(const Matrix & mat2)
{
    assert (myColumns == mat2.Rows());          // check dimensions

    Matrix mat3(myRows, mat2.Columns());        // build result Matrix

    for (int i = 0; i < myRows; i++)            // for each of my rows:
        for (int j = 0; j < mat2.Columns(); j++)  //   for each col in mat2:
        {
            double sum = 0;
            for (int k = 0; k < myColumns; k++)   //    for each of my columns:
                sum += (*this)[i][k] * mat2[k][j];  //       sum the products
            mat3[i][j] = sum;                     //       put sum in result Matrix
        }
    return mat3;                                 // return result matrix
}
```

Additional matrix operations, such as addition, subtraction, and transposition are similar to the ones we have defined, and are described in the exercises.

OBJECT-CENTERED DESIGN

In chapter 10, we saw that creating classes plays a central role in object-oriented design. Inheritance plays a key role in creating classes, and thus is important in object-oriented design. It can be incorporated into our approach to OCD as follows:

1. Identify the behavior required to solve the problem
2. Identify the objects:
   For each object that cannot be directly represented with the existing types:
      a. Design and build a class to represent such objects
      b. If the new class is is an extension of an existing class, make the relationship explicit using inheritance
      c. Store it in a class library
3. Identify the operations:
   For each operation that is not predefined:
      If the operation is an operation on a class object from step 2a,
         Design and build a class function member to perform that operation
      Otherwise
         a. Design and build a non-member function to perform that operation
         b. If the operation is reusable, store it in a library
4. Organize the objects and operations into an algorithm
5. Encode your algorithm in C++
6. Test and maintain your program

APPLICATION: SOLVING LINEAR SYSTEMS

A linear system is a set of linear equations, each of which involves several unknowns; for example,

$$5x_1 - x_2 - 2x_3 = 11$$
$$-x_1 + 5x_2 - 2x_3 = 0$$
$$-2x_1 - 2x_2 + 7x_3 = 0$$

is a linear system of three equations involving the three unknowns x_1, x_2, and x_3. A solution of such a system is a collection of values for these unknowns that satisfies all of the equations simultaneously.

One method for solving a linear system is called **Gaussian elimination.** In this method, we first eliminate x_1 from the second equation by adding $\frac{1}{5}$ times the first equation to the second equation and, from the third equation, by adding $\frac{2}{5}$ times the first equation to the third equation. This yields the linear system

$$5x_1 - x_2 - 2x_3 = 11$$
$$4.8x_2 - 2.4x_3 = 2.2$$
$$-2.4x_2 + 6.2x_3 = 4.4$$

which is equivalent to the first system because it has the same solution as the original system. We next eliminate x_2 from the third equation by adding $2.4 / 4.8 = \frac{1}{2}$ times the second equation to the third, giving the new equivalent linear system:

$$5x_1 - x_2 - 2x_3 = 11$$
$$4.8x_2 - 2.4x_3 = 2.2$$
$$5x_3 = 5.5$$

Once the original system has been reduced to such a *triangular* form, it is easy to find the solution. It is clear from the last equation that the value of x_3 is

$$x_3 = \frac{5.5}{5} = 1.100$$

Substituting this value for x_3 in the second equation and solving for x_2 gives

$$x_2 = \frac{2.2 + 2.4(1.1)}{4.8} = 1.008$$

and substituting these values for x_2 and x_3 in the first equation gives

$$x_1 = \frac{11 + 1.008 + 2(1.100)}{5} = 2.842$$

The original linear system can also be written as a single matrix equation

$$Ax = b$$

where A is the 3×3 **coefficient matrix,** b is the 3×1 **constant vector,** and x is the 3×1 **vector of unknowns:**

$$A = \begin{bmatrix} 5 & -1 & -2 \\ -1 & 5 & -2 \\ -2 & -2 & 7 \end{bmatrix}, \quad x = \begin{bmatrix} x_1 \\ x_2 \\ x_3 \end{bmatrix}, \quad b = \begin{bmatrix} 11 \\ 0 \\ 0 \end{bmatrix}$$

The operations used to reduce the original linear system to triangular form use only the coefficient matrix A and the constant vector b. Thus, if we combine these into a single matrix by adjoining b to A as a last column,

$$Aug = \begin{bmatrix} 5 & -1 & -2 & 11 \\ -1 & 5 & -2 & 0 \\ -2 & -2 & 7 & 0 \end{bmatrix}$$

we can carry out the required operations on this new matrix, called the **augmented matrix,** without writing down the unknowns at each step. Thus we add $-Aug[1][0] / Aug[0][0] = 1/5$ times the first row of Aug to the second row, and $-Aug[2][0] / Aug[0][0] = 2/5$ times the first row of Aug to the third row, to obtain the new matrix:

$$Aug = \begin{bmatrix} 5 & -1 & -2 & 11 \\ 0 & 4.8 & -2.4 & 2.2 \\ 0 & -2.4 & 6.2 & 4.4 \end{bmatrix}$$

Then adding $-Aug[2][1] / Aug[1][1] = 1/2$ times the second row to the third row gives the following *triangular* matrix, which corresponds to the final triangular system of equations:

$$Aug = \begin{bmatrix} 5 & -1 & -2 & 11 \\ 0 & 4.8 & -2.4 & 2.2 \\ 0 & 0 & 5 & 5.5 \end{bmatrix}$$

From this example, we see that the basic row operation performed at the ith step of the reduction process is:

For $k = i + 1, i + 2, \ldots, n$

Replace row_k by $\text{row}_k - \dfrac{Aug[k][i]}{Aug[i][i]} \times \text{row}_i$

Clearly, for this to be possible, the element $Aug[i][i]$, called a **pivot** element, must be nonzero. If it is not, we must interchange the ith row with a later row to produce a nonzero pivot.

An algorithm and a program for solving linear systems using Gaussian elimination can be found at the website described in the preface. To minimize the effect of roundoff error in the computations, it selects as a pivot at each stage in the reduction the candidate that is largest in absolute value.

✔ Quick Quiz 12.4

1. A two-dimensional numeric array having m rows and n columns is called a(n) _____ .

Questions 2–4 assume the following matrices:

$$A = \begin{bmatrix} 1 & 2 & 0 \\ 3 & 1 & 3 \end{bmatrix}, \quad B = \begin{bmatrix} 1 & 0 \\ 2 & -1 \\ 1 & 3 \end{bmatrix}$$

2. $A * B$ will be a(n) _____ × _____ matrix.
3. Calculate $A * B$.
4. Calculate $B * A$ or explain why it is not defined.

Questions 5–8 assume the following declaration:

```
class XXX : public YYY;
```

5. Class XXX is called a _____ class of class YYY.
6. Class YYY is called a _____ class of class XXX.
7. (True or false) All of the members of class XXX are also members of class YYY.
8. YYY can invoke XXX's constructor by using the _____ mechanism.
9. Every class object contains a predefined local variable named _____ whose value is the address of the object; the value of _____ will be the object itself.

EXERCISES 12.4

1.   Add a constructor function to class Matrix that, upon receiving a vector of double values, builds a Matrix containing one row containing the elements of that vector.

2. Add a constructor function to class `Matrix` that, upon receiving a vector of `double` values, builds a `Matrix` containing one column containing the elements of that vector.

3. Add a + operation to class `Matrix`. The sum of two matrices is defined as follows: If A_{ij} and B_{ij} are the entries in the *i*th row and *j*th column of $m \times n$ matrices A and B, respectively, then $A_{ij} + B_{ij}$ is the entry in the *i*th row and *j*th column of the sum, which will also be an $m \times n$ matrix. For example,

$$\begin{bmatrix} 1 & 0 & 2 \\ -1 & 3 & 5 \end{bmatrix} + \begin{bmatrix} 4 & 2 & 1 \\ 7 & 0 & 3 \end{bmatrix} = \begin{bmatrix} 5 & 2 & 3 \\ 6 & 3 & 8 \end{bmatrix}$$

4. Add a − operation to class `Matrix`. The definition of the difference of two matrices is the same as that for the sum in exercise 3 except that the entries of the second matrix B are subtracted from the first matrix A.

5. Add a function member to class `Matrix` to find the transpose of a matrix, which is defined as follows: Suppose that A is an $m \times n$ matrix, and that A_{ij} is the entry in the *i*th row and *j*th column of A. The transpose of A is an $n \times m$ matrix T in which $T_{ji} = A_{ij}$, for all indices *i* and *j*. For example, if A is the 2×3 matrix

$$\begin{bmatrix} 1 & 0 & 2 \\ -1 & 3 & 5 \end{bmatrix}$$

the transpose of A is the 3×2 matrix

$$\begin{bmatrix} 1 & -1 \\ 0 & 3 \\ 2 & 5 \end{bmatrix}$$

Part of the Picture: Computer Graphics

Computer graphics is the area of computing that studies how information can be modeled and manipulated using pictures on a computer screen. To provide graphics capabilities, a computer screen is usually organized as a two-dimensional array (e.g., 480 × 640) of picture elements, called **pixels.** Primitive graphics operations include the ability to set a particular pixel to a given color (black or white on a monochrome screen). From these primitive operations, higher-level graphics operations can be implemented to draw lines, boxes, circles, text, and so on.

Functions that perform graphics operations are typically stored in *graphics libraries* so they are easy to access. However, in order for such functions to be as efficient as possible, they are often written as low-level (e.g., assembly language) functions. Because of this, graphics functions cannot usually be ported between different hardware platforms or operating systems. Implementations of C++ for different platforms thus have different graphics libraries:

▶ For C++ implementations on most UNIX systems, the X-windows environment provides graphics libraries such as *Xlib* and *Xt*, that provide low-level and high-level graphics functions, respectively.

▶ On the Macintosh, Symantec C++ and CodeWarrior each provide libraries that provide a rich set of graphics objects (e.g., *Window, Pane, Button, Scroll-Bar, CheckBox,* and so on), and functions to manipulate them.

▶ On PCs running MS-DOS, Turbo/Borland C++ provides a library
  (GRAPHICS.LIB) that provides a graphics window (e.g., a *viewport*) and an
  assortment of functions to draw graphics objects (e.g., *arc, circle, polygon,
  ellipse, line, rectangle,* and so on) within that window.

▶ On PCs running MS-Windows, Turbo/Borland C++ and Visual C/C++ provide
  libraries (*ObjectWindows* and the *MS Foundation Classes,* respectively) that
  provide graphics objects and operations similar to those available on the
  Macintosh.

Unfortunately, none of these libraries is compatible with the others, and so C++ programs
that employ them are limited to that particular environment. A standard C++ graphics library is sorely needed.

   To illustrate the use of a graphics library, we have implemented a class named CartesianSystem, whose source code can be found at the website described in the preface.
Graphics operations (e.g., DrawAxes(), Graph(), DensityPlot(), and so on) are provided as member functions of class CartesianSystem.

EXAMPLES: FUNCTION GRAPHING AND DENSITY PLOTS

Function Graphing. The number and quality of software packages and hand-held calculators that can be used to generate high-resolution graphs of functions are increasing
rapidly. For example, Figure 12.18(a) shows the graph of $y = x * \cos(x)$ for $-8 \leqslant x \leqslant 8$
as plotted on a graphing calculator, and Fig-ure 12.18(b) shows the same graph as produced by the powerful software package Mathematica™.

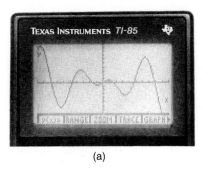

(a)

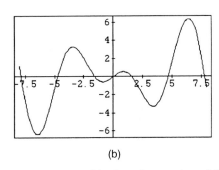

(b)

FIGURE 12.18   (a) Plot of $y = x * \cos(x)$ on a graphing calculator. (b) Plot of $y = x * \cos(x)$
produced by Mathematica.

   The window containing each of the plots shown in Figure 12.18 is similar to the two-
dimensional character array screen presented in section 12.1 in that it is simply a two-
dimensional array of points (pixels), some of which (those corresponding to points on the
graph of the function) are "on" (black) and the rest of which are "off" (white). The following
enlarged view of the portion of the graphics window near the origin shows clearly the grid
structure of this part of the window:

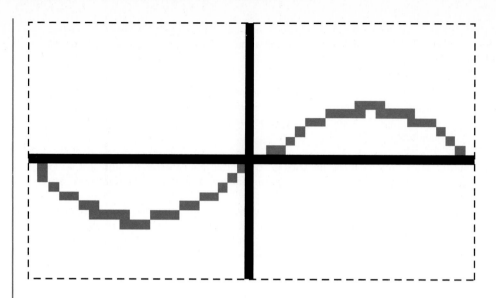

Class `CartesianSystem` contains a member function `Graph()` that, given a function $f(x)$, draws the graph of $f(x)$. To plot a function $y = f(x)$, `Graph()` uses a loop to iterate through the x values. For each such x value, the y value nearest the actual function value $y = f(x)$ is determined, and the point (x, y) is mapped into the appropriate pixel in the window. This pixel is then set to a color different from the background by using a primitive graphics command.

The program in Figure 12.19 uses the `Graph()` member of class `CartesianSystem` to plot graphs of some functions in the Turbo C++ environment.

Figure 12.19   Plotting a Function.

```
/* plotter19.cpp can be used to graph an arbitrary function(s)
   using class CartesianSystem.

   Output: prompts for input
   Input:  values for the endpoints of the x and y axes
   Output: the graphs of f(x) and g(x)

   Note:   In this example, two functions f(x) and g(x) are plotted.
----------------------------------------------------------------*/

#include <iostream.h>                // cin, cout, >>, <<
#include <math.h>                    // cos()

#include "CartSys.h"                 // declaration of CartesianSystem

double f(double x)                   // a function to be plotted
{
    return x * cos(x);
}
```

```
double g(double x)                 // another function to be plotted
{
    return x;
}

int main()
{
    cout << "\nThis program plots some functions..."
            "\n(currently y = x*cos(x) and y = x.)\n";

    double xMin, xMax,             // endpoints of the axes
           yMin, yMax;
    char returnChar;                // the newline

    do                             // get the x bounds
    {
        cout << "\nPlease enter the minimum and maximum x values: ";
        cin >> xMin >> xMax;
    }
    while (xMin >= xMax);

    do                             // get the y bounds
    {
        cout << "\nPlease enter the minimum and maximum y values: ";
        cin >> yMin >> yMax;
    }
    while (yMin >= yMax);

    cin.get(returnChar);           // clean out the newline
                                   // construct a Cartesian system
    CartesianSystem CoordinateSys(xMin, xMax, yMin, yMax);

    CoordinateSys.DrawAxes();      // draw the axes

    CoordinateSys.Graph(f);        // graph f

    CoordinateSys.Graph(g, CYAN);  // graph g in a different color
}
```

Sample run:

```
This program plots some functions...
 (currently y = x*cos(x) and y = x.)

Please enter the minimum and maximum x values: -8 8

Please enter the minimum and maximum y values: -7 7
```

The sample run of that program produced the following output:

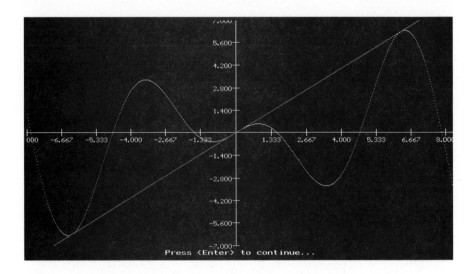

Density Plots. We have just seen how a function $y = f(x)$ of a single variable x can be plotted. Graphs of functions $z = f(x, y)$ of two variables x and y are surfaces in three dimensions and are considerably more difficult to display on a two-dimensional screen. Some software packages are able to generate good two-dimensional representations of many three-dimensional surfaces. For example, Mathematica produced the following graph of the surface defined by

$$z = e^{-(x^2 + y^2)}$$

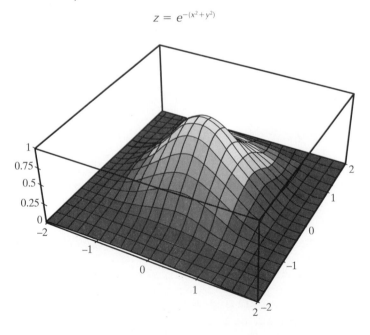

Note that in this representation, shading is used to represent the height of the function, with lighter shades for larger values and darker shades for smaller values. This shading, together with the curved grid lines and the enclosing box produces a visual illusion of a three-dimensional surface.

Another representation of a surface that uses shading but not perspective is a **density plot** obtained by projecting onto a plane a representation like the preceding one. The following is the density plot generated by Mathematica for this surface. The various densities of gray again indicate different heights of the function.

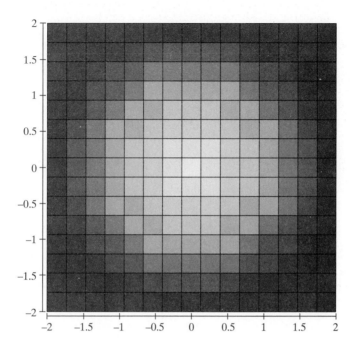

To generate a density plot, class CartesianSystem provides a member function named DensityPlot(). This function sets each pixel to a color, based on the value of z (i.e., lesser z values produce darker colored pixels and greater z values produce lighter colored pixels). The program in Figure 12.20 uses this function to produce the density plot of the function $z = e^{-(x^2+y^2)}$.

FIGURE 12.20   PLOTTING A DENSITY PLOT.

```
/* densityplot20.cpp can be used to draw a density plot of an
   arbitrary function z = f(x, y) using class CartesianSystem.

   Output: prompts for input
   Input:  values for the endpoints of the x and y axes
   Output: the graphs of f(x) and g(x)

-------------------------------------------------------------*/

#include <iostream.h>            // cin, cout, >>, <<
#include <math.h>                // exp()

#include "CartSys.h"             // declaration of CartesianSystem
```

```
double f(double x, double y)        // f(x,y)
{
    return exp( -(x*x + y*y) );
}
int main()
{
    cout << "\nThis program does a density plot of a function..."
            "\ncurrently z = e^(-x^2 + y^2).\n";

    double xMin, xMax,                // axes endpoints
           yMin, yMax,
           zMin, zMax;
    char returnChar;                  // the newline

    do                                // get x-axis endpoints
    {
        cout << "\nPlease enter the minimum and maximum x values: ";
        cin >> xMin >> xMax;
    }
    while (xMin >= xMax);

    do                                // get y-axis endpoints
    {
        cout << "\nPlease enter the minimum and maximum y values: ";
        cin >> yMin >> yMax;
    }
    while (yMin >= yMax);

    do                                // get z-axis endpoints
    {
        cout << "\nPlease enter the minimum and maximum z values: ";
        cin >> zMin >> zMax;
    }
    while (zMin >= zMax);

    cin.get(returnChar);              // clean out the newline
                                      // construct the cartesian system
    CartesianSystem CoordinateSys(xMin, xMax, yMin, yMax, zMin, zMax);

    CoordinateSys.DensityPlot(f); // plot the function
}
```

Sample run:

```
This program does a density plot of a function...
  (currently z = e^(-x^2 + y^2).)

Please enter the minimum and maximum x values: -2 2

Please enter the minimum and maximum y values: -2 2

Please enter the minimum and maximum z values: 0 1
```

The sample run shown produced the following output for the function $f(x, y) = e^{-(x^2 + y^2)}$:

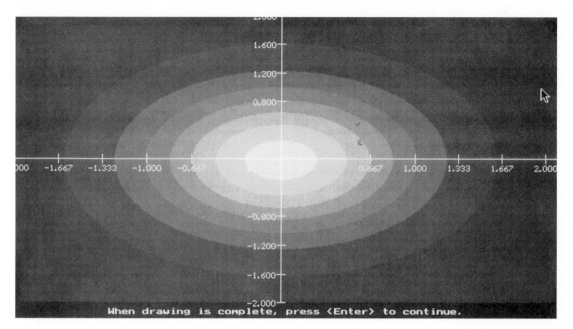

The ideas in these examples can be modified to display an image that is represented in digitized form and to enhance this image. This digitized representation might be a table of light intensities transmitted from a remote sensor such as a camera in a satellite. This problem of visual image processing and enhancement is described in the programming problems at the end of the chapter.

GUI WINDOWS APPLICATION PROGRAMMING

In a *command-line environment*, programs are *text-oriented*, in that they communicate with their users primarily by writing text to the screen; and a user communicates with the program by typing text at the keyboard.

By contrast, when a program (called a *Windows application*) is written to take advantage of the capabilities of a **graphical user interface (GUI)** environment like MS-Windows, the program must coordinate the construction and destruction of screen graphics objects such as windows, menus and dialogue boxes. In addition to user activity at the keyboard, it must also respond to the user clicking the mouse buttons, and the same user action may require different responses, depending on where the mouse is pointing. Windows applications thus entail considerably more complexity than text-oriented programs.

Figure 12.21 illustrates this with a simple Windows application program. It uses the Turbo C++ ObjectWindows library, whose header file is <owl.h>. It simply constructs a SampleApplication object named exampleApp, calls its Run() function member, and when that function terminates, returns the value of the Status data member of exampleApp.

FIGURE 12.21   A WINDOWS APPLICATION PROGRAM.

```
#include "SampApp.h"                        // our SampleApplication class

int PASCAL WinMain(HANDLE hInstance, HANDLE hPrevInstance,
                LPSTR lpCmdLine, int nCmdShow)
```

```
{
    SampleApplication exampleApp(          //  An application object
         "Sample Windows Application",     //    with this Name
         hInstance,                        //    with this process
         hPrevInstance,                    //    with this parent process
         lpCmdLine,                        //    with these cmdline args
         nCmdShow);                        //    and displayed this way

    exampleApp.Run();

    return exampleApp.Status;
}
```

When executed, this program displays a blank window, and then waits for the user to take an action:

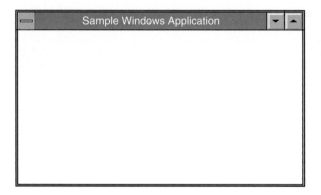

Note that this window has the usual button for the control menu, with *Move, Size, Maximize, Minimize, Close* and *Next* choices. This button and its actions are provided automatically by the ObjectWindows library, ensuring uniform behavior and saving us work.

If the left mouse button is clicked within the window, the coordinates to which the mouse is pointing are displayed at that position, as illustrated in the next screen shot:

If the right mouse button is clicked, a dialogue box that allows the user to clear the window is displayed:

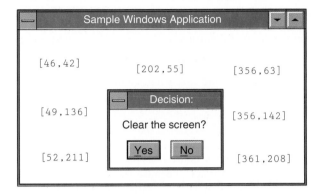

Execution terminates when the user selects *Close* from the window's control menu.

Given the simplicity of the main function, it should be evident that much of the application's functionality is supplied by class `SampleApplication` (and the `SampleWindow` class it uses). In fact, all of the non-application-specific functionality of these classes is inherited from the ObjectWindows `TApplication` and `TWindow` classes, providing a good illustration of the power of inheritance. For descriptions of these classes see the website described in the preface.

☞ PROGRAMMING POINTERS

Many of the programming pointers given for one-dimensional arrays at the end of chapter 9 also apply to multidimensional arrays, and the reader should refer to those for an expanded discussion.

✍ PROGRAM STYLE AND DESIGN

1. *Like one-dimensional arrays, multidimensional array objects should be stored within a class, so that*

    ▶ *the number of elements in each dimension, and*

    ▶ *the operations on the object*

    can be encapsulated within a single package. This makes it easier to reuse the work that was invested in building that object and its operations.

2. *Use of a multidimensional array or vector is appropriate when a table of data values, a list of tables, and so on must be stored in main memory for processing.* Using a multidimensional array or vector when it is not necessary, however, can tie up a large block of memory locations. The amount of memory required to store a multidimensional array/vector may be quite large, even though each index is restricted to a small range of values. For example, the three-dimensional array `threeD` declared by

    ```
    typedef int ThreeDimArray[20][20][20];
    ThreeDimArray threeD;
    ```

    requires $20 \times 20 \times 20 = 8000$ memory locations.

3. *Design classes as generally as possible, so that they can be used as base classes from which more specialized classes can be derived.* This can save much time and effort, because the members of the base class are *inherited* by the derived class, and thus need not be recoded. The keys to designing a good base class are as follows:

   1. Try to anticipate special purpose instances of a class that may be needed later

   2. Identify the *attributes* these special purpose instances have *in common*

   These common attributes indicate what should appear in the *base* class; attributes that are not common to all instances are specialized, and so should appear in *derived* classes.

4. *If a function must receive a class object that contains an array or vector member, then the parameter to hold that object should be declared as a reference parameter.* It is especially important that class objects be passed as constant reference parameters, rather than as value parameters, because the time and memory required to copy class objects as value parameters can greatly slow the execution of a function.

5. *Do not reinvent the wheel.* When a problem requires an operation on a multidimensional vector, thoroughly review the `vector<T>` function members and STL algorithms to see if the operation is already defined, or if there are other operations that make yours easier to implement.

⚡ POTENTIAL PROBLEMS

1. *In C++, multiple indices are each enclosed in brackets ([and]) and attached to the array/vector object.* In some languages, a single pair of brackets (or parentheses) is used to enclosed a list of indices. However, attempting to access the value in row `i` and column `j` of a two-dimensional array `A` in C++ by using

   ```
   A[i,j]
   ```

   will cause a compile-time error.

2. *The first element of a C++ array or `vector<T>` has the index value 0, not 1 as in many programming languages.*

3. *No checking is performed to ensure that array or `vector<T>` indices stay within the range of valid indices.*

4. *Assignment of one array to another is not permitted.* This is another significant reason for using vectors instead of arrays.

5. *Arrays and vectors cannot be input/output simply by including the array name in an input/output list.*

6. *Array arguments are automatically passed by reference.*

7. *When using vectors of vectors, leave a space between the two > symbols.* A common mistake is to forget this and to define a vector of vectors with a statement like

   ```
   vector<vector<int>> myGrid;
   ```

   The compiler will read the `>>` as the output operator, and since this makes no sense in this context, a compilation error will result. The proper approach is to leave a space:

   ```
   vector< vector<int> > myGrid;
   ```

8. *When processing the elements of a multidimensional array/vector using nested loops, the loops must be arranged so that the indices vary in the appropriate order.* To illustrate, suppose that the two-dimensional array `table` is declared by

```
typedef int Array3x4[3][4];
Array3x4 table;
```

and the following data values are to be read into the array:

```
11  22  27  35  39  40  48  51  57  66  67  92
```

If these values are to be read and assigned in a rowwise manner so that the value is the matrix

```
11  22  27  35
39  40  48  51
57  66  67  92
```

then the following nested `for` loops are appropriate:

```
for (int row = 0; row < 3; row++)
    for (int col = 0; col < 4; col++)
        cin >> table[row][col];
```

If the order of these loops is reversed,

```
for (int col = 0; col < 4; col++)
    for (int row = 0; row < 3; row++)
        cin >> table[row][col];
```

then `table` will be loaded column-by-column, instead of row-by-row,

```
11  35  48  66
22  39  51  67
27  40  57  92
```

and operations applied to `table` will produce incorrect results.

Programming Problems

SECTIONS 12.1–12.3

1. Write a program to calculate and display the first ten rows of Pascal's triangle. The first part of the triangle has the form

```
        1
      1   1
    1   2   1
  1   3   3   1
1   4   6   4   1
```

in which each row begins and ends with 1, and each of the other entries in a row is the sum of the two entries just above it. If this form for the output seems too challenging, you might display the triangle as

```
1
1  1
1  2  1
1  3  3  1
1  4  6  4  1
```

2. A demographic study of the metropolitan area around Dogpatch divided it into three regions: urban, suburban, and exurban, and published the following table showing the annual migration from one region to another (the numbers represent percentages):

↗	Urban	Suburban	Exurban
Urban	1.1	0.3	0.7
Suburban	0.1	1.2	0.3
Exurban	0.2	0.6	1.3

For example, 0.3 percent of the urbanites (0.003 times the current population) move to the suburbs each year. The diagonal entries represent internal growth rates. Using a two-dimensional array with an enumerated type for the indices to store this table, write a program to determine the population of each region after 10, 20, 30, 40, and 50 years. Assume that the current populations of the urban, suburban, and exurban regions are 2.1, 1.4, and 0.9 million, respectively.

3. The famous mathematician G. H. Hardy once mentioned to the brilliant young Indian mathematician Ramanujan that he had just ridden in a taxi whose number he considered to be very dull. Ramanujan promptly replied that, on the contrary, the number was very interesting because it was the smallest positive integer that could be written as the sum of two cubes (that is, written in the form $x^3 + y^3$, with x and y integers) in two different ways. Write a program to find the number of Hardy's taxi.

4. A certain professor has a file containing a table of student grades, where the first line of the file contains the number of students and the number of scores in the table; each row of the table represents the exam scores of a given student and each column represents the scores on a given exam. The maximum possible score on each exam was 100 points. Write a program that, given the name of such a file, generates a report summarizing the overall percentage for each student, and the average score on each exam.

5. The group CAN (Citizens Against Noise) has collected some data on the noise level (measured in decibels) produced at seven different speeds by six different models of cars. This data is summarized in the following table:

	Speed (MPH)						
Car	**20**	**30**	**40**	**50**	**60**	**70**	**80**
0	88	90	94	102	111	122	134
1	75	77	80	86	94	103	113
2	80	83	85	94	100	111	121
3	68	71	76	85	96	110	125
4	77	84	91	98	105	112	119
5	81	85	90	96	102	109	120

Write a program that will display this table in easy-to-read format, and that will calculate and display the average noise level for each car model, the average noise level at each speed, and the overall average noise level.

6. Suppose that a certain automobile dealership sells ten different models of automobiles and employs eight salespersons. A record of sales for each month can be represented by a table in which each row contains the number of sales of each model by a given salesperson, and each column contains the number of sales of each model by a given salesperson. For example, suppose that the sales table for a certain month is as follows:

```
0 0 2 0 5 6 3 0
5 1 9 0 0 2 3 2
0 0 0 1 0 0 0 0
1 1 1 0 2 2 2 1
5 3 2 0 0 2 5 5
2 2 1 0 1 1 0 0
3 2 5 0 1 2 0 4
3 0 7 1 3 5 2 4
0 2 6 1 0 5 2 1
4 0 2 0 3 2 1 0
```

Write a program to produce a monthly sales report, displaying the monthly sales table in the form:

```
                        Salesperson
   Model :   1   2   3   4   5   6   7   8:  Totals
   -----------------------------------------------
     1  :    0   0   2   0   5   6   3   0  :   16
     2  :    5   1   9   0   0   2   3   2  :   22
     3  :    0   0   0   1   0   0   0   0  :    1
     4  :    1   1   1   0   2   2   2   1  :   10
     5  :    5   3   2   0   0   2   5   5  :   22
     6  :    2   2   1   0   1   1   0   0  :    7
     7  :    3   2   5   0   1   2   0   4  :   17
     8  :    3   0   7   1   3   5   2   4  :   25
     9  :    0   2   6   1   0   5   2   1  :   17
    10  :    4   0   2   0   3   2   1   0  :   12
   -----------------------------------------------
  Totals :  23  11  35   3  15  27  18  17
```

As indicated, the report should also display the total number of automobiles sold by each salesperson and the total number of each model sold by all salespersons.

7. Suppose that the prices for the ten automobile models in problem 6 are as follows:

Model #	Model Price
0	$17,450
1	$19,995
2	$26,500
3	$25,999
4	$10,400
5	$18,885
6	$11,700
7	$14,440
8	$17,900
9	$19,550

Write a program to read this list of prices and the sales table given in problem 6, and calculate the total dollar sales for each salesperson and the total dollar sales for all salespersons.

8. A certain company has a product line that includes five items that sell for $100, $75, $120, $150, and $35. There are four salespersons working for this company, and the following table gives the sales report for a typical week:

Salesperson	Item Number				
Number	1	2	3	4	5
1	10	4	5	6	7
2	7	0	12	1	3
3	4	9	5	0	8
4	3	2	1	5	6

Write a program to

(a) Compute the total dollar sales for each salesperson

(b) Compute the total commission for each salesperson if the commission rate is 10 percent

(c) Find the total income for each salesperson for the week if each salesperson receives a fixed salary of $500 per week in addition to commission payments

9. A number of students from several different engineering sections performed the same experiment to determine the tensile strength of sheets made from two different alloys. Each of these strength measurements is a real number in the range 0 through 10. Write a program to read several lines of data, each consisting of a section number and the tensile strength of the two types of sheets recorded by a student in that section, and store these values in a two-dimensional array. Then calculate

(a) For each section, the average of the tensile strengths for each type of alloy

(b) The number of persons in a given section who recorded strength measures of 5 or higher

(c) The average of the tensile strengths recorded for alloy 2 by students who recorded a tensile strength lower than 3 for alloy 1

10. A magic square is an $n \times n$ table in which each of the integers 1, 2, 3, . . . , n^2 appears exactly once and all column sums, row sums, and diagonal sums are equal. For example, the following is a 5 × 5 magic square in which all the rows, columns, and diagonals add up to 65:

17	24	1	8	15
23	5	7	14	16
4	6	13	20	22
10	12	19	21	3
11	18	25	2	9

The following is a procedure for constructing an $n \times n$ magic square for any odd integer n. Place 1 in the middle of the top row. Then after integer k has been placed, move up one row and one column to the right to place the next integer $k + 1$, unless one of the following occurs:

(i) If a move takes you above the top row in the jth column, move to the bottom of the jth column and place the integer $k + 1$ there

(ii) If a move takes you outside to the right of the square in the ith row, place $k + 1$ in the ith row at the left side

(iii) If a move takes you to an already filled square or if you move out of the square at the upper right-hand corner, place $k + 1$ immediately below k

Write a program to construct an $n \times n$ magic square for any odd value of n.

11. Consider a square grid, with some cells empty and others containing an asterisk. Define two asterisks to be *contiguous* if they are adjacent to each other in the same row or in the same column. Now suppose we define a *blob* as follows:

(a) A blob contains at least one asterisk

(b) If an asterisk is in a blob, then so is any asterisk that is contiguous to it

(c) If a blob has more than two asterisks, then each asterisk in it is contiguous to at least one other asterisk in the blob

For example, there are four blobs in the partial grid

seven blobs in

and only one in

Write a program that uses a recursive function to count the number of blobs in a square grid. Input to the program should consist of the locations of the asterisks in the grid, and the program should display the grid and the blob count.

12. The game of *Life*, invented by the mathematician John H. Conway, is intended to model life in a society of organisms. Consider a rectangular array of cells, each of which may contain an organism. If the array is assumed to extend indefinitely in both directions, each cell will have eight neighbors, the eight cells surrounding it. Births and deaths occur according to the following rules:

(a) An organism is born in an empty cell that has exactly three neighbors

(b) An organism will die from isolation if it has fewer than two neighbors

(c) An organism will die from overcrowding if it has more than three neighbors

The following display shows the first five generations of a particular configuration of organisms:

Write a program to play the game of *Life* and investigate the patterns produced by various initial configurations. Some configurations die off rather quickly; others repeat after a certain number of generations; others change shape and size and may move across the array; and still others may produce "gliders" that detach themselves from the society and sail off into space.

13. The game of Nim is played by two players. There are usually three piles of objects, and on his or her turn, each player is allowed to take any number (at least one) of objects from one pile. The player taking the last object loses. Write a program that allows the user to play Nim against the computer. You might have the computer play a perfect game, or you might design the program to "teach" the computer. One way for the computer to "learn" is to assign a value to every possible move, based on experience gained from playing games. The value of each possible move is stored in some array; initially, each value is 0. The value of each move in a winning sequence of moves is increased by 1, and those in a losing sequence are decreased by 1. At each stage, the computer selects the best possible move (that having the highest value).

14. Write a program that allows the user to play tic-tac-toe against the computer.

SECTION 12.4

15. Write a driver program to test the `Matrix` constructor in exercise 1.

16. Write a driver program to test the `Matrix` constructor in exercise 2.

17. Write a driver program to test the `Matrix` addition operator in exercise 3.

18. Write a driver program to test the `Matrix` subtraction operator in exercise 4.

19. Write a driver program to test the `Matrix` transpose function in exercise 5.

20. A certain company manufactures four electronic devices using five different components that cost $10.95, $6.30, $14.75, $11.25, and $5.00, respectively. The number of components used in each device is given in the following table:

Device Number	Component 1	2	3	4	5
1	10	4	5	6	7
2	7	0	12	1	3
3	4	9	5	0	8
4	3	2	1	5	6

Write a program that uses matrix multiplication to

(a) Calculate the total cost of each device

(b) Calculate the total cost of producing each device if the estimated labor cost for each device is 10 percent of the cost in part (a)

21. The vector-matrix equation

$$\begin{bmatrix} N \\ E \\ D \end{bmatrix} = \begin{bmatrix} \cos\alpha & -\sin\alpha & 0 \\ \sin\alpha & \cos\alpha & 0 \\ 0 & 0 & 1 \end{bmatrix} \begin{bmatrix} \cos\beta & 0 & \sin\beta \\ 0 & 1 & 0 \\ -\sin\beta & 0 & \cos\beta \end{bmatrix} \begin{bmatrix} 1 & 0 & 0 \\ 0 & \cos\gamma & -\sin\gamma \\ 0 & \sin\gamma & \cos\gamma \end{bmatrix} \begin{bmatrix} I \\ J \\ K \end{bmatrix}$$

is used to transform local coordinates (I, J, K) for a space vehicle to inertial coordinates (N, E, D). Write a program that reads values for α, β, and γ and a set of local coordinates (I, J, K) and then uses matrix multiplication to determine the corresponding inertial coordinates.

22. A Markov chain is a system that moves through a discrete set of states in such a way that when the system is in state i there is probability P_{ij} that it will next move to state j. These probabilities are given by a transition matrix P, whose (i, j) entry is P_{ij}. It is easy to show that the (i, j) entry of P^n then gives the probability of starting in state i and ending in state j after n steps.

To illustrate, suppose there are two urns A and B containing a given number of balls. At each instant, a ball is chosen at random and is transferred to the other urn. This is a Markov chain if we take as a state the number of balls in urn A and let P_{ij} be the probability that a ball is transferred from A to B if there are i balls in urn A. For example, for four balls, the transition matrix P is given by

$$\begin{bmatrix} 0 & 1 & 0 & 0 & 0 \\ \frac{1}{4} & 0 & \frac{3}{4} & 0 & 0 \\ 0 & \frac{1}{2} & 0 & \frac{1}{2} & 0 \\ 0 & 0 & \frac{3}{4} & 0 & \frac{1}{4} \\ 0 & 0 & 0 & 1 & 0 \end{bmatrix}$$

Write a program that reads a transition matrix P for such a Markov chain and calculates and displays the value of n and P^n for several values of n.

23. A directed graph, or digraph, consists of a set of vertices and a set of directed arcs joining certain of these vertices. For example, the following diagram pictures a directed graph having five vertices numbered 1, 2, 3, 4, and 5, and seven directed arcs joining vertices 1 to 2, 1 to 4, 1 to 5, 3 to 1, 3 to itself, 4 to 3, and 5 to 1:

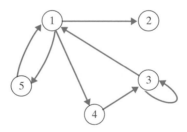

A directed graph having n vertices can be represented by its adjacency matrix, which is an $n \times n$ matrix, with the entry in the ith row and jth column 1 if vertex i is joined to vertex j, and 0 otherwise. The adjacency matrix for this graph is

$$\begin{bmatrix} 0 & 1 & 0 & 1 & 1 \\ 0 & 0 & 0 & 0 & 0 \\ 1 & 0 & 1 & 0 & 0 \\ 0 & 0 & 1 & 0 & 0 \\ 1 & 0 & 0 & 0 & 0 \end{bmatrix}$$

If A is the adjacency matrix for a directed graph, the entry in the ith row and jth column of A^k gives the number of ways that vertex j can be reached from the vertex i by following k edges. Write a program to read the number of vertices in a directed graph and a collection of ordered pairs of vertices representing directed arcs, construct the adjacency matrix, and then find the number of ways that each vertex can be reached from every other vertex by following k edges for some value of k.

24. A company produces three different products. They are processed through four different departments, A, B, C, and D, and the following table gives the number of hours that each department spends on each product:

Product	A	B	C	D
1	20	10	15	13
2	18	11	11	10
3	28	0	16	17

The cost per hour of operation in each of the departments is as follows:

Department	A	B	C	D
Cost per hour	$140	$295	$225	$95

Write a program that uses matrix multiplication to find the total cost of each of the products.

25. The inverse of an $n \times n$ matrix A is a matrix A^{-1} for which both the products $A * A^{-1}$ and $A^{-1} * A$ are equal to the identity matrix having 1s on the diagonal from the upper left to the lower right and 0s elsewhere. The inverse of matrix A can be calculated by solving the linear systems $Ax = b$ for each of the following constant vectors b:

$$\begin{bmatrix} 1 \\ 0 \\ 0 \\ \vdots \\ 0 \end{bmatrix} \begin{bmatrix} 0 \\ 1 \\ 0 \\ \vdots \\ 0 \end{bmatrix} \begin{bmatrix} 0 \\ 0 \\ 1 \\ \vdots \\ 0 \end{bmatrix} \cdots \begin{bmatrix} 0 \\ 0 \\ 0 \\ \vdots \\ 1 \end{bmatrix}$$

These solutions give the first, second, third, . . . , nth column of A^{-1}. Write a program that uses Gaussian elimination to solve these linear systems and thus calculates the approximate inverse of a matrix.

Part of the Picture: Computer Graphics

26. Add a member function to class `CartesianSystem` to plot graphs of parametric equations of the form

$$x = x(t), \quad y = y(t), \quad a \le t \le b$$

27. A *scatter plot* of a set of data pairs (x, y) of real numbers is obtained simply by plotting these points. Add a member function to class `CartesianSystem` to produce a scatter plot of a set of data pairs read from a file. Execute your program using `LeastSquaresFile` (see the description at the end of Chapter 8).

28. We noted that the ideas in this section can be modified to carry out *visual image processing* and *enhancement*. Make a file that represents light intensities of an image in digitized form; say, with intensities from 0 through 9. Write a program that reads these intensities from the file and then reconstructs and displays them using a different character for each intensity. This image might then be enhanced to sharpen the contrast. For example, gray areas might be removed by replacing all intensities in the range 0 through some value by 0 (light) and intensities greater than this value by 9 (dark). Design your program to accept a threshold value that distinguishes light from dark and then enhances the image in the manner described.

29. An alternative method for enhancing an image (see problem 28) is to accept three successive images of the same object and, if two or more of the intensities agree, to use that value; otherwise, the average of the three values is used. Modify the program of problem 28 to use this technique for enhancement.

POINTERS AND RUN-TIME ALLOCATION

[P]ointers] are like jumps, leaping wildly from one part of a data structure to another. Their introduction into high-level languages has been a step backward from which we may never recover.

C. A. R. HOARE

He's making a list, and checking it twice, gonna' find out who's naughty or nice . . .

CHRISTMAS CAROL: *Santa Claus Is Coming To Town*

. . . is the sort of person who keeps a list of all of his lists.

V. OREHCK III (fictitious)

Chapter Contents

13.1   Introduction to Pointer Variables

13.2   Run-Time Allocation Using `new` and `delete`

13.3   The STL `list<T>` Class Template

PART OF THE PICTURE: The TCP/IP Communications Architecture

*13.4   Pointers and Command-Line Arguments

PART OF THE PICTURE: Data Structures

In chapters 9 and 12, we saw two different data structures that C++ provides for storing sequences of values: arrays and `vector<T>`s. One significant difference between these two kinds of objects is the way in which they are defined. To define an array object named `anArray`, its capacity *must* be known at *compile time:*

```
const int CAPACITY = 50;
int anArray[CAPACITY];
```

While a `vector<T>` object can be defined in this way,

```
const int CAPACITY = 50;
vector<int> aVector(CAPACITY);
```

its capacity can also be specified at *run time:*

```
cout << "Enter the number of values to be stored: ";
int capacity;
cin  >> capacity;
vector<int> aVector(capacity);
```

This is the basic difference between the two kinds of objects: an array's storage is determined (and is fixed) when the program is compiled, but the storage of a `vector<T>` object is determined (and can change) while the program executes. The `string` class is similar to `vector<T>` in that a `string` object's storage automatically adjusts to the number of characters being stored.

To build objects whose storage can grow (and shrink) at run time, C++ provides a way to request and return memory during program execution. To understand this feature and how to use it, we must first study *pointers* and *indirecton.*

13.1 INTRODUCTION TO POINTER VARIABLES

As usual, we begin with a program. The purpose of the program in Figure 13.1 is only to introduce the basics of pointers and indirection. It is not intended to show how pointers are typically used in programs.[1]

FIGURE 13.1   USING INDIRECTION.
_____

```
/* indirection1.cpp illustrates indirection and pointer variables.

   Output: addresses of memory locations and the integers
           stored there
   ---------------------------------------------------------------*/

#include <iostream.h>

int main()
{
    int i = 11,
        j = 22,
        k = 33;
```

_____

[1]For some versions of C++ it may be necessary to use `(void*)pointerVariable` in an output statement for addresses to display correctly.

```
int * iPtr = &i,
    * jPtr = &j,
    * kPtr = &k;

cout << "\nAt address " << iPtr
     << ", the value " << *iPtr << " is stored.\n"
     << "\nAt address " << jPtr
     << ", the value " << *jPtr << " is stored.\n"
     << "\nAt address " << kPtr
     << ", the value " << *kPtr << " is stored.\n";
}
```

Sample run:

```
At address 0x0053AD78, the value 11 is stored.

At address 0x0053AD7C, the value 22 is stored.

At address 0x0053AD80, the value 33 is stored.
```

DECLARING AND INITIALIZING POINTERS

We begin with the declarations in the program in Figure 13.1. The declarations of integer variables i, j, and k are straightforward, so we proceed to the next set of declarations:

```
int * iPtr = &i,
    * jPtr = &j,
    * kPtr = &k;
```

There are two new items in this declaration statement:

1. An asterisk (*) before the name of an object in a declaration of the form

    ```
    Type * variableName;
    ```

    declares that *variableName* is an object that can store *the address of* an object of the specified *Type*. Such variables are often called **pointer variables,** or simply **pointers.** Thus, the declarations

    ```
    int * iPtr,
        * jPtr,
        * kPtr;
    ```

    declare that iPtr, jPtr, and kPtr are pointer variables, each of which can store the address of an integer variable. The type of each of these variables is int *.

2. The ampersand operator (&) can be used as a unary prefix operator that, when applied to an object,

    ```
    &variable_name
    ```

    returns the address with which *variableName* is associated, and so & is called the **address-of operator.** Thus, the expressions &i, &j, and &k

return the addresses (or references[2]) associated with variables i, j, and k, respectively.

Combining these two pieces of information, we see that the declarations

```
int * iPtr = &i,
    * jPtr = &j,
    * kPtr = &k;
```

declare iPtr, jPtr, and kPtr as pointer variables, each of which can store the address of an integer, and they initialize iPtr to the address of variable i, jPtr to the address of variable j, and kPtr to the address of variable k. In the sample run in Figure 13.1, the address associated with variable i is the hexadecimal value 0x0053AD78, the address of j is 0x0053AD7C, and the address of k is 0x0053AD80. We can visualize the layout of the program's data in memory as follows:[3]

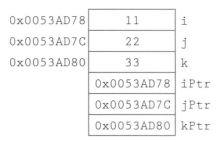

It is important to remember that:

> *In a declaration, the asterisk operator * must precede each identifier that is to serve as a pointer.*

Thus,

```
double * ptr1,
       * ptr2;
```

---

[2] The word *reference* is used as a synonym for *address*. In fact, this is the origin of the phrase *reference parameter*—the value of a reference parameter is actually the address of its argument, rather than a copy of the argument.

---

[3] Note that (using hexadecimal arithmetic)

```
0x0053AD7C - 0x0053AD78 = 4
```

and

```
0x0053AD80 - 0x0053AD7C = 4
```

which indicates that the size of an int on this particular machine is 4 bytes (32 bits).

is a correct declaration of `ptr1` and `ptr2` as pointers to `double`s. Had we written

```
double * ptr1,
         ptr2;
```

only `ptr1` would be a pointer variable; `ptr2` would be an ordinary `double` variable.

Another example of a pointer is the predefined data member `this` in a class object. In section 12.4 we described `this` as a predefined local variable whose value is the address of the object that contains it. In other words, `this` is a pointer to the object that contains it.

Using `typedef` for Readability. An alternative notation that does not require the repeated use of the asterisk in pointer declarations is to use `typedef` to rename a pointer type. For example, we could first declare

```
typedef double * DoublePointer;
```

and then use `DoublePointer` to declare `ptr1` and `ptr2`:

```
DoublePointer ptr1,
              ptr2;
```

Similarly, to declare the pointers in Figure 13.1, we could write:

```
typedef int * IntPointer;

IntPointer iPtr = &i,
           jPtr = &j,
           kPtr = &k;
```

Such declarations improve the readability of pointer declarations, especially when pointer parameters are being declared.

BASIC POINTER OPERATIONS

C++ supports a variety of operations on pointers, including initialization, dereferencing, I/O, assignments, comparisons, and arithmetic. We examine each of these in turn.

Initialization. When a pointer variable is initialized to an address, as in

```
int * iPtr = &i;
```

that address must be the address of an object whose type is the same as the type to which the pointer points. The pointer is said to be **bound** to that type. For example, the declarations

```
double doubleVar;

int * iPtr = &doubleVar;        // ERROR
```

will cause a compiler error, because an integer pointer may only store addresses of integer objects.

One important exception is that 0 can be assigned to any pointer variable. The value that results is called the **null pointer value** for that type and 0 is often called the **null address.** Thus, the declarations

```
char * cPtr = 0;
int * iPtr = 0;
double * dPtr = 0;
```

are all valid initializations using the null address.

A null pointer value is often depicted graphically using the electrical engineering *ground* symbol

For example, the pointer iPtr can be pictured as

The null address can also be used in a boolean expression to indicate whether or not a pointer is pointing to anything:

```
if (dPtr == 0)
    // dPtr is not currently pointing to anything
else
    // dPtr is pointing to a memory location
```

As we shall see, such comparisons are especially important when pointers are used to store the addresses of blocks of memory allocated at run time.

Indirection and Dereferencing. Pointer variables not only store addresses but also provide access to the values stored at those addresses. An expression of the form

    *pointerVariable

can be used to access the value at the address stored in *pointerVariable*. It can be thought of as going to the reference (address) stored in *pointerVariable* and accessing the value stored at that address. To illustrate, in the sample run of Figure 13.1, the value of the expression

    iPtr

is 0x0053AD78, and the value of the expression

    *iPtr

is 11, because 11 is the value stored at address 0x0053AD78. We can visualize this situation as follows:

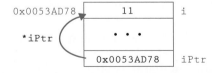

For the same reason, the values of the expressions *jPtr and *kPtr are 22 and 33, respectively. Thus, the value of variable i can be accessed via the expression `*iPtr`, the value of `j` via `*jPtr`, and the value of `k` via `*kPtr`. In general, the value of a variable `v` can be *accessed indirectly* by applying the `*` operator to a pointer variable `vPtr` whose value is the address of `v`. For this reason, the `*` operator is called the **indirection operator.** Since *reference* is another term for *address* and applying the indirection operator to a pointer variable accesses the value at the address stored in that pointer variable, applying the indirection operator to a pointer variable is called **dereferencing** that pointer variable.

We have already used this indirect access technique in the preceding chapter (see section 12.4). As we saw there, each class object contains a pointer variable `this` whose value is the address of the object that contains it. This means that dereferencing `this` provides a way to (indirectly) access that object. We might picture this as follows:

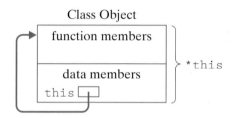

The indirection operator can be used on either side of an assignment statement. If the statement

```
i = *jPtr;
```

were added to the program in Figure 13.1, the value of `i` would be changed from 11 to 22, because dereferencing `jPtr` produces the value 22 stored at address `0x0053AD7C` and this value would be assigned to `i`. The statement

```
*iPtr = j;
```

would produce the same result. Dereferencing `iPtr` gives the memory location whose address is `0x0053AD78` and the assignment operator would then copy the value of `j` (22) into this memory location. Since this address is associated with the variable `i`, the effect is to change the value of `i`.

As we noted earlier, the purpose of the program in Figure 13.1 was to introduce the basics of pointers and indirection. Pointers are not often used to store addresses that are associated with names. Instead, as we shall see, pointers are used to store and retrieve values in memory locations with which *no name* has been associated.

To summarize what we have seen thus far, the value of an expression

```
pointerVariable
```

is simply the address stored within *pointerVariable*; the expression

```
*pointerVariable
```

uses the address stored in the pointer to access (indirectly) the contents of the memory location at that address.

Pointers to Class Objects. Although the program in Figure 13.1 does not do so, we can also declare pointers to class objects and use them to store the addresses of class objects. For example, in chapter 10 we built a `Temperature` class that can be used to define `Temperature` objects such as

```
Temperature temp1(98.6, 'F');
```

Given such an object, we could declare a pointer to a `Temperature` and use it to store the address of that object,

```
Temperature * tempPtr = & temp1;
```

which can be pictured as follows:

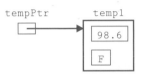

The members of `temp1` can be accessed (indirectly) via `tempPtr`. For example, `temp1` has a `Scale()` function member that returns the value (`'F'`) of its `myScale` data member. `Scale()` can be called using `tempPtr`, and this can be done in two ways. One way is combine the indirection operator with the dot operator and write

```
(*tempPtr).Scale()
```

In this expression, the pointer `tempPtr` is first dereferenced to access the object to which it points (i.e., `temp1`), and the dot operator is then used to send that object the `Scale()` message.

This notation is rather cumbersome, however, because it involves two operators and the indirection operation must be parenthesized because it has lower priority than the dot operator. For this reason, C++ provides a more convenient notation that accomplishes the same thing in one operation:

```
tempPtr->Scale()
```

Here `->` is the **class pointer selector operator** whose left operand is a *pointer* to a class object and whose right operand is a *member* of the class object. This operator provides a convenient way to access that object's members, and the "arrow" notation clearly indicates that the member is being accessed through a pointer.

I/O. In the program in Figure 13.1, we displayed the addresses of `i`, `j`, and `k`, by using an output statement to display the values of `iPtr`, `jPtr`, and `kPtr`:[4]

```
cout << "\nAt address " << iPtr        // &i
     . . .
     << "\nAt address " << jPtr        // &j
     . . .
     << "\nAt address " << kPtr        // &k
     . . .
```

---

[4] See footnote 2 re the use of `void*`.

Similarly, to find the particular addresses associated with `iPtr`, `jPtr`, and `kPtr`, we could write:

```
cout << "\n iPtr is stored at address " << &iPtr
     << ",\n jPtr is stored at address " << &jPtr
     << ", and\n kPtr is stored at address " << &kPtr
     << endl;
```

The address-of operator allows us to determine the exact memory address at which an object is stored, whereas pointer variables allow us to store these addresses.

Just as the value of a pointer can be output using `<<`, an address could be input and stored in a pointer variable using `>>`. However, this is rarely done, because we usually are not interested in the address of the memory location storing a value, only in the value itself. In fact, it is dangerous to input address values because an attempt to access a memory address outside the space allocated to an executing program will result in a fatal run-time error.

Assignment. Although the program in Figure 13.1 does not illustrate it, pointer variables can be assigned the values of other pointer variables that are *bound to the same type*. For example, if we were to add the statement

```
jPtr = iPtr;
```

to the program, then the value of `iPtr` would be copied to `jPtr` so that both have the same memory address as their value; that is, both point to the same memory location, as the following diagrams illustrate:

Before the assignment:

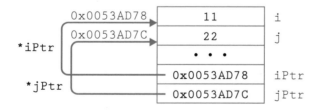

After the assignment `jPtr = iPtr;`:

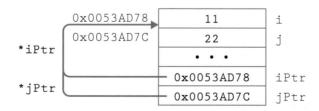

After the assignment statement is executed, jPtr no longer points to j, but now points to i. Thus, applying the indirection operator to jPtr will access the memory location associated with i. For example, an output statement

```
cout << *jPtr;
```

will display the value 11 instead of 22, and the statement

```
*jPtr = 44;
```

will change the value at address 0x0053AD78 (i.e., the value of i) from 11 to 44:

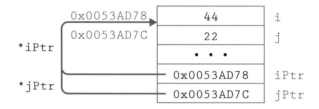

    We have included this example to show that pointers are a very powerful (and dangerous) feature of programming languages. Statements that change the value of a variable in a statement in which that variable is not named are generally considered to be poor programming practice, because they make programs more difficult to debug by hiding such changes. In the preceding example, the expressions *iPtr and *jPtr are alternate names for variable i, and are sometimes called **aliases** for i. A function that changes a variable's value through an alias for that variable is said to exhibit **the aliasing problem.**

Comparison. The relational operators can be used to compare two pointers that are *bound to the same type.* The most common operation is to use == and != to determine if two pointer variables both point to the same memory location. For example, the boolean expression

```
iPtr == jPtr
```

is valid and returns true if and only if the address in iPtr is the same as the address in jPtr. However, if pointers nPtr and dPtr are declared by

```
int * nPtr;
double * dPtr;
```

the comparison

```
nPtr == dPtr    // ERROR!
```

will result in a compilation error, because iPtr and jPtr are bound to different types.

The *null address may be compared with any pointer variable.* For example, the conditions

```
nPtr != 0
```

and

```
dPtr == 0
```

are both valid boolean expressions.

Pointer Arithmetic. To explain arithmetic operations on pointers, it is helpful to make use of a C++ operator that we have not used up to now. This is the **sizeof operator,** which may be applied to any type T or to any object o, and returns:

- ▶ the number of bytes required to store an object of type T, or
- ▶ the number of bytes allocated by the compiler for object o.

The `sizeof` operator can thus be applied to either objects or types:

```
sizeof(type-specifier)
sizeof object-expression
```

Note that in the first case, the type specifier is enclosed within parentheses, but no parentheses are used to enclose the expression in the second form.

To illustrate, the expression

```
sizeof(char)
```

evaluates to 1, because objects of type `char` are allocated one byte. Similarly, if `longVar` is declared by

```
long int longVar;
```

the expression

```
sizeof longVar
```

will evaluate to 4, because `long int` objects are stored in four bytes.

Understanding the `sizeof` operator makes it easier to understand pointer arithmetic. We consider the increment and decrement operations first because they are probably the most commonly used arithmetic operations on pointer variables. For a pointer variable `ptr` declared by

```
Type * ptr;
```

the increment statement

```
ptr++;
```

adds the value `sizeof(Type)` to the address in `ptr`. Similarly, a decrement statement

```
ptr--;
```

subtracts the value `sizeof(Type)` from the address in `ptr`. If *intExpr* is an integer expression, a statement of the form

```
ptr += intExp;
```

adds the value *intExp* `* sizeof(Type)` to `ptr`, and

```
ptr -= IntExp;
```

subtracts the value *IntExp* * sizeof(*Type*) from ptr.

To illustrate how these operations are used, suppose that ptr is a pointer whose value is the address of the first element of an array of double elements:

```
double dArray[10],          // array of 10 doubles
    * ptr = &(dArray[0]);   // pointer to first element of dArray
```

or equivalently,

```
double dArray[10],          // array of 10 doubles
    * ptr = dArray;         // pointer to first element of dArray
```

Now consider the following loop:

```
for (int i = 0; i < 10; i++)
{
    *ptr = 0;
    ptr++;
}
```

On the first pass through the loop, ptr is dereferenced and the value 0 is assigned to the memory location at that address. ptr is then incremented, which adds sizeof(double) to its value, effectively making ptr point to the second element of the array:

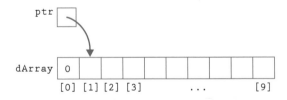

The next pass again dereferences ptr, sets that memory location to zero, and increments ptr:

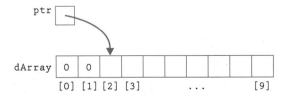

This continues with each subsequent iteration. On the final pass, the last element of the array is set to zero and `ptr` is again incremented, so that it points to the first address past the end of the array:

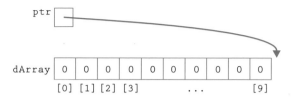

A pointer can thus be used to move through consecutive blocks of memory, accessing them in whatever way a particular problem requires.

Pointers as Arguments and Parameters.   Pointers may also be passed as arguments to functions. The parameters corresponding to such arguments may be either value or reference parameters, but the pointer argument and the corresponding parameter must be bound to the same type. The return type of a function may also be a pointer.

✔ Quick Quiz 13.1

1. A pointer variable stores a(n) _____ .
2. _____ is the address-of operator.
3. _____ is the dereferencing operator.
4. _____ is the indirection operator.
5. _____ is the class pointer selector operator.

Questions 6–18 assume the following declarations:

```
double * x,
        y = 1.1;
```

and that `double` values are stored in 8 bytes of memory. Answer each of questions 6–12 with (a) address or (b) `double` value:

6. The value of x will be a(n) _____.
7. The value of y will be a(n) _____
8. The value of &y will be a(n) _____.
9. The value of &x will be a(n) _____.
10. The value of *x will be a(n) _____.
11. The value of (*x) * y will be a(n) _____.
12. The word reference is a synonym for a(n) _____.
13. In the assignment x = 0; , 0 is called the _____ address.
14. The output produced by the statements x = &y; cout << *x; is _____.
15. The output produced by the statements x = &y; *x = 3.3; cout << y; is _____.
16. (True or false) sizeof(double) == sizeof y.

17. (True or false) `sizeof(double) == sizeof(*x)`.

18. If the output produced by `cout << x;` is `0x12a30`, the value of `x + 4` is _____.

EXERCISES 13.1

Exercises 1–9 assume the following declarations:

```
int i1 = 11,
    i2 = 22;
double d1 = 3.45,
       d2 = 6.78;
class Point
{ double x() { return xCoord; }
  double y() { return yCoord; }
 private:
  double xCoord, yCoord;
};
```

1. Write declarations for variables `p1` and `p2` whose values will be addresses of memory locations in which a `double` can be stored.

2. Write a statement to assign the address of `d1` to the variable `p1` in exercise 1, or explain why this is not possible.

3. Write a statement to assign the address of `i2` to the variable `p2` in exercise 1, or explain why this is not possible.

4. Write declarations for a variable `q` whose value will be a memory location in which a `Point` object can be stored.

5. Write declarations that initialize variables `ptr1` and `ptr2` with the addresses of `11` and `12`, respectively.

6. Write a statement that will make variables `p1` and `p2` of exercise 1 point to the same memory location.

7. Write a statement that will copy the value stored in the memory location pointed to by `ptr2` into the memory location pointed to by `ptr1`, for `ptr1` and `ptr2` as in exercise 5.

8. Write a statement to output the *x* coordinate and the *y* coordinate of the point in the memory location pointed to by the variable `q` of exercise 4.

9. Write statements that use the variables `p1` and `p2` of exercise 2 but *not* the variables `d1` and `d2` to interchange the values of `d1` and `d2`.

For exercises 10–16, use the `sizeof` operator to find how many bytes your C++ compiler allocates for the given data type:

10.	`int`	**11.**	`float`
12.	`double`	**13.**	`short int`

14. A `string` whose value is `"Bye!"`

15. A `string` whose value is `"Auf Wiedersehen!"`

16. Pointers to the types in exercises 10–15.

17.   Using the address-of operator, find the starting addresses your C++ compiler assigns to each of the objects in the following declarations:

```
const int SIZE = 10;
char charArray[SIZE];
int intArray[SIZE];
double doubleArray[SIZE];
char charVar;
```

18.   Use the `sizeof` operator to find the number of bytes your C++ compiler allocates for each object defined in exercise 17.

19.   Suppose that the starting address of the first object in a block is b. Using b, the `sizeof` operator, and the results from exercises 17 and 18, construct an expression that can be used to find the address of any subsequent object declared in that same block.

20.   Using `typedef`, create an alias type `CharPointer` for pointers to type `char`.

Exercises 21–23 assume an array declaration like the following:

```
double anArray[10];
```

21.   Use the address-of operator to find the address of the first element of `anArray`.

22.   Find the value associated with the name `anArray`.

23.   What inference can you make from the results of exercises 21 and 22?

13.2 RUN-TIME ALLOCATION USING new AND delete

In the first part of chapter 9, we saw that the definition of a C-style array

```
const int CAPACITY = 10;
double arrayName[CAPACITY];
```

causes the compiler to allocate a block of memory large enough to hold ten double values and associate the starting address of that block with the name *arrayName*. Such fixed-size arrays have two drawbacks:

- ▶ If the size of the array exceeds the number of values to be stored in it, then memory is wasted by the unused elements
- ▶ If the size of the array is smaller than the number of values to be stored in it, then the problem of array overflow may occur

At the root of these problems is the fact that the size of a C-style array is fixed when the program is *compiled*. In our example, the size of the block of memory allocated for *arrayName* cannot be changed, except by editing the declaration of CAPACITY and then recompiling the program.

In chapter 9, we saw that both of these problems are solved by the STL vector<T> class template, which allocates memory to a vector<T> object as the program executes (i.e., **run-time allocation**) instead of when it is compiled (i.e., compile-time allocation). In the rest of this section, we examine the mechanism C++ provides for run-time memory allocation.

At its simplest, a run-time memory allocation mechanism requires two operations:

1. Acquire additional memory locations as they are needed
2. Release memory locations when they are no longer needed

C++ provides the predefined operations `new` and `delete` to perform these two operations of memory allocation and deallocation during program execution.

THE new OPERATION

The `new` operation is used to request additional memory from the operating system during program execution. The general form of such a request is:

The new Operation

Form

```
new Type
```

Purpose

Issue a run-time request for a block of memory that is large enough to hold an object of the specified `Type`. If the request can be granted, `new` returns the address of the block of memory; otherwise, it returns the null address.

Since the `new` operation returns an address and addresses can be stored in pointer variables, this operation is almost always used in conjunction with a pointer. For example, when the statements

```
int * intPtr;

intPtr = new int;
```

are executed, the expression `new int` issues a request to the operating system for a memory block large enough to store an integer value (that is, for `sizeof(int)` bytes of memory). If the operating system is able to grant the request, `intPtr` will be assigned the address of this memory block. Otherwise, if all available memory has been exhausted, `intPtr` will be assigned the null address 0. Because of this possiblity, the value returned by `new` should always be tested before it is used:

```
assert(intPtr != 0);
```

or

```
if (intPtr == 0)
{
    cerr << "\n*** No more memory!\n";
    exit(1);
}
```

If `intPtr` is assigned a nonzero value, the newly allocated memory location is an **anonymous variable;** that is, it is an allocated memory location that has no name associated with it. For example, suppose `new` returns the address `0x020`:

```
            intPtr
          ┌──────────┐
          │  0x020   │      0x020 ┌──────────────────┐
          └──────────┘            └──────────────────┘
```

Because there is no name associated with this newly allocated memory, it *cannot be accessed directly* in the same way other variables are accessed. However, its address is stored in intPtr, so this anonymous variable can be *accessed indirectly* by dereferencing intPtr:

Statements such as the following can be used to operate on this anonymous variable:

```
cin >> *intPtr;        // store input value in the new integer

if (*intPtr < 100)  // apply relational ops to new integer
   (*intPtr)++;        // apply arithmetic ops to new integer
else
   *intPtr = 100;   // assign values to the new integer
```

In short, anything that can be done with an "ordinary" integer variable can be done with this anonymous integer variable by accessing it indirectly via intPtr.

Allocating Arrays with new. In practice, new is rarely used to allocate space for scalar values like integers. Instead, it is used to allocate space for either arrays or for anonymous class objects. To illustrate the former, consider an integer array object anArray declared by

```
int anArray[10];
```

The value associated with the name anArray is the **base address** of the array, that is, the address of the first element of the array.[5] The type of object anArray is int[10].

A type such as int[10] can be used with new to allocate the memory for an array at run time. For example, the statements

```
int * arrayPtr;

arrayPtr = new int[10];
```

allocate space for an array of ten integers. Until the second statement is executed, arrayPtr is simply a pointer variable whose value is undefined. After it is exe-

---

[5] This is one reason that the assignment operator cannot be used to copy a "normal" array—the statement

```
alpha = beta;
```

would attempt to copy the starting address of beta into alpha, as opposed to copying the elements of beta.

cuted (assuming that sufficient memory is available), `arrayPtr` contains the base address of the *newly allocated* array. If that address is `0x032`, we might picture the situation as follows:

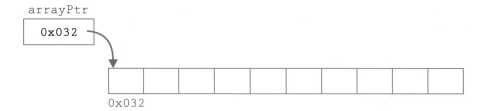

But we have seen previously that the value associated with the name of a compile-time allocated array is its base address. This means that:

> *If the base address of a run-time allocated array is stored in a pointer variable, then the elements of that array can be accessed via the pointer in exactly the same way that the elements of a compile-time allocated array are accessed via its name, by using the subscript operator* (`[]`).

That is, the first element of the new array can be accessed using the notation `arrayPtr[0]`, the second element using `arrayPtr[1]`, the third element using `arrayPtr[2]`, and so on:

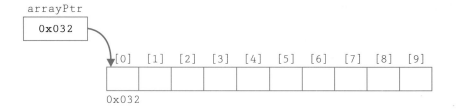

Note that this is consistent with our description of array-address mapping described in section 9.2. The value of the pointer variable `arrayPtr` is the base address of the array, and for a given index `i`, the subscript operator

```
arrayPtr[i]
```

simply accesses the memory location `arrayPtr + i`.

The advantage of run-time allocation is that it is not necessary to know the size of the array at compile time. For example, we can write:

```
cout << "How many entries? ";        // find how big the
cin >> numEntries;                   //    array should be

double *dPtr =                       // allocate an array
       new double[numEntries];       //    exactly that size
assert(dPtr != 0)                    // check for success
```

```
cout << "Enter your values.\n";      // fill it with values
for (int i = 0; i < numEntries; i++)
   cin >> dPtr[i];
...
```

Unlike arrays whose memory is allocated at compile time, arrays whose memory is allocated at run time can be tailored to the exact size of the list to be stored in them. The wasted memory problem is solved because the array will not be too large. The overflow problem is solved because the array will not be too small.

This is the approach used by the vector<T> class template, which might be implemented as follows:

```
template<class T>
class vector
{
 public:
   vector();
   vector(int n);
   ...
 private:
   T * tPtr;
   int mySize;
   ...
};
```

This version of vector<T> contains a data member that is a pointer to an object of type T. The first vector<T> constructor simply initializes this pointer to the null address to signify an empty vector:

```
template<class T>
vector<T>::vector()
{
   tPtr = 0;
   mySize = 0;
   ...
}
```

But the second vector<T> constructor uses new to dynamically allocate an array of n elements, each of which is of type T:

```
template<class T>
vector<T>::vector(int n)
{
   tPtr = new T[n];
   mySize = n;
   ...
}
```

The definition of a vector object

```
vector<int> intVector(10);
```

uses this second constructor to build `intVector` as follows:

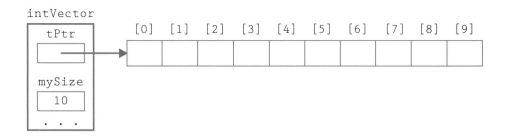

The other `vector<T>` operations simply access the elements of this anonymous array via the `tPtr` data member.

In summary, the `new` operator can be used to allocate anonymous array variables at run time, and the capacities of these arrays can be tailored to the number of values being stored in the arrays. By storing the base address of an array in a pointer variable, most things that can be done with a compile-time allocated array can be done with the run-time allocated array using the pointer.[6]

The Copy Constructor. There are situations in which the compiler needs to create a copy of an object. For example, when an argument is passed to a function via a value parameter, the compiler must construct the parameter as a copy of the argument. Similarly, when a function returns a local object, the function terminates, ending the lifetime of that object, so the compiler builds an (anonymous) copy of the object called a *temporary* to transmit the return value back to the caller.

To make copies of a class object, the compiler supplies a **default copy constructor,** which simply copies the members of the object byte by byte. This default copy constructor works fine, except when the object being copied contains a data member that is a pointer. To see why, suppose that the compiler uses it to make a copy of the following object named `intVector`:

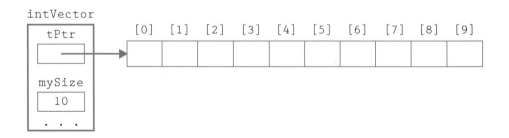

---

[6] While doing so is a bit simplistic, some programmers like to think of the name of a compile-time allocated array as a *constant pointer,* because like a pointer, the evaluation of such a name produces the array's base address, and like a constant, C++ does not allow that value to be altered.

When the default copy constructor copies the data members of intVector, it blindly copies the data members of intVector. Although it correctly copies mySize and it copies tPtr, it does not copy the run-time allocated array, because that array is not a data member of intVector. The result can be pictured as follows:

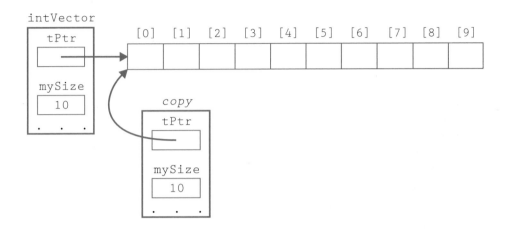

 That is, when a class contains a data member that is a pointer, the default copy constructor *does not make a distinct copy* of the object pointed to by that pointer. This can be a problem. For example, if *copy* is a value parameter in a function that modifies its value parameter's anonymous array, these modifications will simultaneously change the anonymous array of intVector. This should not happen with a value parameter!

To make a distinct copy of a class object containing a pointer data member, C++ allows a class to have its own copy constructor. For example, the vector<T> copy constructor behaves something like the following:

```
template<class T>
vector<T>::vector(const vector<T> & original)
{
    mySize = original.size();           // copy size info.
    tPtr = new T[mySize];               // get a distinct array
    for (int i = 0; i < mySize; i++)    // copy original's array
        tPtr[i] = original[i];          //   into our new one
    ...
}
```

Unlike the default copy constructor, this one will copy the non-pointer data members, allocate a distinct anonymous array for the pointer data member, and then copy the values from the original object's array into this distinct array. The result will be a completely distinct copy:

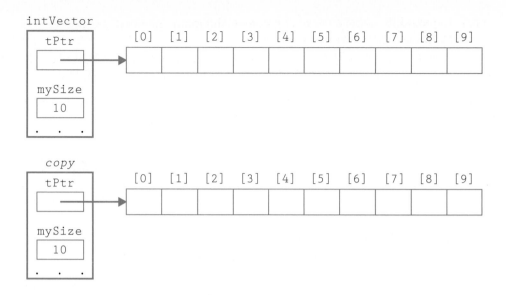

The general form of a copy constructor for an arbitrary class is:

Class Copy Constructor

Form

ClassName(const *ClassName* & *original*)

where:

ClassName is the name of the class containing this function; and *original* is a reference to the object being copied.

Purpose

This function is used by the compiler to construct a copy of the argument corresponding to *original*. The compiler calls this function whenever such a copy is needed, including when:

▸ An object of type *ClassName* is passed as a value parameter

▸ The return value of a function is a value of type *ClassName*

▸ An object of type *ClassName* is initialized when it is declared

▸ The evaluation of an expression produces an intermediate (or temporary) value of type *ClassName*

Note that the parameter of a copy constructor *must* be a reference parameter (and should be a const reference parameter, as well) because if it is defined as a value parameter, then a call to the function will

1. Pass *original* as a value parameter, which means that a copy of *original* must be made

2. To make a copy of *original* as a value parameter, the copy constructor is called again (with *original* as its argument)

3. To pass *original* as a value parameter to that copy constructor, a copy of *original* is needed

4. To make a copy of *original*, the copy constructor is called again (with *original* as its argument)

and so on, resulting in an infinite recursion! Defining *original* as a reference parameter avoids this infinite recursion because the reference (address) of *original* is passed, instead of a copy of *original*.

THE delete OPERATION

When execution of a program begins, the program has available to it a "pool" of unallocated memory locations, called the **free store** or **heap.** The effect of the new operation is to request the operating system to

1. Remove a block of memory from the free store

2. Allocate that block to the executing program

The block can be used by the executing program if it stores the address of that block (the value produced by the new operation) in a pointer variable.

The size of the free store is limited, and each execution of new causes the pool of available memory to shrink. If a call to new requests more memory than is available in the free store, then the operating system is unable to fill the request and new returns the null address 0.

Memory that is no longer needed can be returned to the free store by using the **delete operation.** Just as new is a request by the executing program for memory from the free store, the delete operation is a request to return memory to the free store. Such memory can then be reallocated to the program by a subsequent new operation. The new and delete operations are thus complementary:

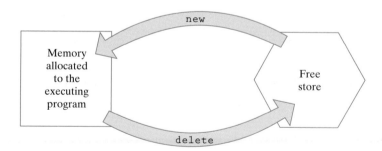

The general form of the delete operation is as follows:

Form
 delete *pointerVariable*
or
 delete [] *arrayPointerVariable*

> **Purpose**
> The first form frees the run-time allocated object whose address is stored in *pointerVariable*. The second form frees the run-time allocated array object whose address is stored in *arrayPointerVariable*.

For example, if `intPtr` has been allocated memory from the free store with

```
int * intPtr = new int;
```

then the statement

```
delete intPtr;
```

will release the memory location pointed to by `intPtr`, making it available for allocation at a later time. Following the operation, the value of `intPtr` will be undefined, and so the result of any attempt to dereference it,

```
*intPtr
```

is unpredictable, possibly producing a run-time error. To avoid such problems, it is considered good programming practice to always set the value of such pointers to the null address,

```
delete intPtr;
intPtr = 0;
```

so that a statement of the form

```
if (intPtr != 0)
    // ... ok - IntPtr can be safely dereferenced
else
    // ... not ok - IntPtr's memory has been deallocated
```

can be used to guard access to the memory pointed to by `intPtr`.

Similarly, if `dPtr` is a pointer to the first element of an array allocated at run time, as in

```
cin >> numValues;

double *dPtr = double[numValues];
```

then that array's memory can be returned to the free store with the statements

```
delete [] dPtr;
dPtr = 0;
```

Memory Leaks. It is important for programs that allocate memory using new to deallocate that memory using delete. To see why, consider the following innocent-looking code:

```
do
{
    int * intPtr = new int[10];
    assert(intPtr != 0);

    // ... use the array via intPtr to solve a problem

    cout << "\Do another (y or n)? ";
    cin >> answer;
}
while (answer != 'n');
```

The first time the loop executes, an array of 10 integers will be allocated:

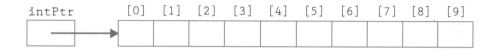

The second time the loop executes, a second array will be allocated and its address stored in intPtr. However, delete was not used to return the first array to the free store, and so it is still allocated to the program:

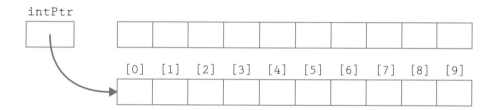

Since intPtr was the only means of accessing the first anonymous array and we overwrote its address in intPtr, that array is now "lost" or "marooned" memory—it can neither be accessed by the program, nor returned to the free store.

The third time the loop executes, a third array is allocated and its address stored in intPtr, marooning the second anonymous array:

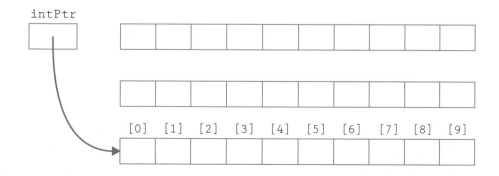

With each repetition of the loop ten more memory locations will be lost. If the loop executes enough times, the assertion (intPtr != 0) will fail and terminate the program. Because such code loses memory over time, this situation is called a **memory leak.**

To avoid memory leaks, the memory to which a pointer points should always be deallocated before the pointer is assigned a new address:

```
do
{
   int * intPtr = new int[10];
   assert(intPtr != 0);

   // ... use the array via intPtr to solve a problem

   delete [] intPtr;

   cout << "\Do another (y or n)? ";
   cin >> answer;
}
while (answer != 'n');
```

This will ensure that the memory pointed to by a pointer is released to the free store and thus avoid a memory leak.

Destructor Functions. We saw earlier that the vector<T> constructor could use new to request an anonymous array at run time. Since the pointer by which this array is accessed is a private data member, how is this anonymous array deallocated? Stated differently, how does vector<T> avoid a memory leak?

In addition to *constructor* functions that are used to define objects of the class, C++ also allows a class to have a special **destructor** function to do any necessary "clean-up" activities at the end of a class object's lifetime. These activities include using delete to release memory allocated at run time. For example, the vector<T> destructor might be written as follows:

```
template<class T>
vector<T>::~vector()
{
   delete [] tPtr;    // deallocate array
   tPtr = 0;          // reset pointer to NULL
   mySize = 0;        // update size
   // ...
}
```

The compiler will automatically insert calls to this destructor at the end of a vector<T> object's lifetime, so that the object can "clean up after itself." This illustrates the primary role of a destructor function, which is to reclaim any storage that was allocated to the object at run time.

The name of a destructor is always the name of the class preceded by the tilde (~) character:

Form

~*ClassName*()

Purpose

The compiler calls this function to destroy objects of type *ClassName* whenever such objects should no longer exist:

- ▶ At the end of the main function for *ClassName* objects that are defined within `main()` as static or global objects
- ▶ At the end of each block in which a non-static *ClassName* object is defined
- ▶ At the end of each function containing a *ClassName* parameter
- ▶ When a *ClassName* object allocated at run time is destroyed using `delete`
- ▶ When an object containing a *ClassName* data member is destroyed
- ▶ When an object whose type is derived from type *ClassName* is destroyed (see section 12.4)
- ▶ When a compiler-generated *ClassName* copy (made by the copy constructor) is no longer needed

Note that like a constructor, a destructor has no return type. However, unlike a constructor, a destructor cannot have parameters, and thus can only have a single definition.

By providing a destructor for any class that uses run-time allocated memory, a class object will automatically release that memory at the end of its lifetime, avoiding a memory leak. This makes class objects self-contained, which is another characteristic of good design.

The Assignment Operator.   In addition to a default copy constructor, the compiler also provides for each class a default definition for the assignment operator (=) that, like the default copy constructor, simply does a byte-by-byte copy of the object being assigned. As with the copy constructor, this works fine unless the class has a pointer data member.

The problem is similar to the copy constructor problem: If v1 and v2 are two vector objects defined by

```
vector<int> v1(10),
            v2;
```

and we subsequently assign v1 to v2,

```
v2 = v1;
```

the default assignment operator will simply copy the data members of v1 into those of v2. This works fine for the mySize data member, but not for the tPtr data member:

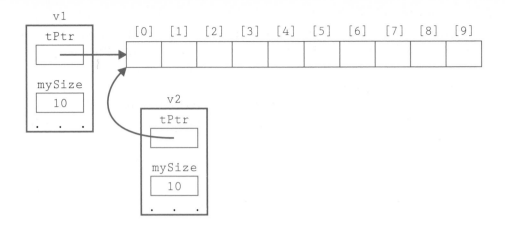

 That is, the default assignment operator does not make a distinct copy of a class object that contains a pointer data member. This means that the class designer must overload the assignment operator, which must be defined as a function member. For example, class `vector<T>` has overloaded the assignment operator to behave something like the following:

```
template<class T>
vector<T> & vector<T>::operator=(const vector<T> & original)
{
   if (mySize != original.size())        // if necessary
   {
      delete [] tPtr;                    //   deallocate old array
      tPtr = new T[original.size()];     //   get a distinct array
   }
   mySize = original.size();             // copy size info.
   for (int i = 0; i < mySize; i++)      // copy original's array
      tPtr[i] = original[i];             //   into our new one
                                         // copy any other data members...
   return *this;                         // return ourself
}
```

The behavior is similar to that of the copy constructor, with two main differences. One difference is that whereas the copy constructor builds a *new* object and thus can simply build the copy, the assignment operator may be applied to an *existing* object. If that object already has a run-time allocated array whose size is different from that of `original`, then that array should be replaced with one whose size is the same as that of `original`. To do this, the old array must be deallocated with `delete`, to avoid a memory leak.

The second difference is that the copy constructor returns no value and thus has no return type, but the assignment operation should return the object on the left-hand side of the assignment to support chained assignments. That is, an assignment like

```
v3 = v2 = v1;
```

must first assign `v1` to `v2`, and then assign `v2` to `v3`. Since such a call will be processed as

```
v3.operator=(v2.operator=(v1));
```

the expression `v2.operator=(v1)` must return `v2`. From an internal perspective, when an object receives the `operator=` message, it must return *itself*. Two different actions must be taken in order for this to occur correctly:

1. As we saw in chapter 10, C++ allows a class object to refer to itself by providing every message sent to the object with the predefined local variable `this`, which is a pointer to the object receiving the message. The statement

    ```
    return *this;
    ```

    dereferences this pointer and returns the object to which the `operator=` message was sent.

2. Normally, a `return` statement in a function,

    ```
    return object;
    ```

    first uses the copy constructor to build a copy of *object*, and then returns this copy. This extra copying can be avoided by *declaring the function's return-type as a reference:*

    ```
    ReturnType  &  FunctionName( Parameters );
    ```

    This tells the compiler to return the actual *object* named by the `return` statement, rather than a copy of it.[7]

Given such a function, the preceding vector assignment

```
v2 = v1;
```

will replace the previous contents of `v2` with a distinct copy of `v1`:

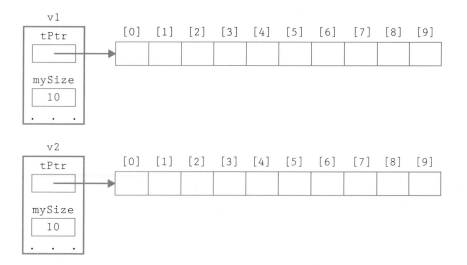

---

[7] It follows that the object being returned cannot be a local variable if the return type of the function is a reference, since its lifetime ends when the function terminates. The reference return type can thus be used to return reference parameters (e.g., see the definitions of `operator<<` and `operator>>` in previous chapters), or the object receiving the message (e.g., `*this`).

The general form of the assignment operation can be described as follows:

Assignment Operation

Form

```
ClassName & ClassName::operator=
                    (const ClassName & original)
{
    // ... make a copy of original


    return *this;
}
```

where:

  ClassName is the name of the class containing this function; and

  original is a reference to the object being copied.

Purpose

For classes that have pointer data members, overload `operator=` to make the object receiving this message a distinct copy of `original`. `operator=` **must** be defined as a function member of the class.

SUMMARY

The following is a general rule of thumb to remember when designing a class:

If a class allocates memory at run time using `new`, then it should provide:

▸ a *copy constructor* that the compiler can use to make distinct copies

▸ an *assignment operator* that a programmer can use to make distinct copies

▸ a *destructor* that releases the run-time allocated memory to the free store

---

Remembering this rule will help you to build classes whose objects are self-contained, that are free of memory leaks, and that behave in the way a user expects.

✔ Quick Quiz 13.2

1. (Run or compile) Memory for a C-style array is allocated at _____ time; memory for a `vector<T>` object is allocated at _____ time.

2. The _____ operation is used to request memory during program execution. If not enough memory is available, it returns the _____; otherwise it returns the _____ of a block of memory. The newly-allocated memory location is a(n) _____ variable.

3. The _____ operation is used to release memory during program execution.

4. The base address of a run-time allocated array is stored in a _____ .

5. Given the declarations

```
int a[] = {44, 22, 66, 11, 77, 33};
int * p = a;
```

what is the value of p[2]?

6. Write a prototype for the copy constructor of a class named C.

7. Write a prototype for the destructor of a class named C.

8. (True or false) The parameter of a copy constructor should always be a value parameter to ensure that a distinct copy is made.

9. (True or false) The assignment operator for a class must be a function member.

10. When the compiler needs to make a copy of a class object, it uses a _____ copy constructor that simply copies the object's members _____ by _____ .

11. When is it essential that a class have its own copy constructor and why?

12. The problem of run-time memory getting marooned is called a _____ .

13. When an object's lifetime is over, the compiler calls the object's _____ .

14. When is it essential that a class have its own destructor and why?

15. When is it essential that a class have its own assignment operator and why?

EXERCISES 13.2

For exercises 1–10, write C++ statements to do what is asked.

1. Declare a char pointer variable named charPtr.

2. Allocate an anonymous char variable, storing its address in charPtr.

3. Input a character value and store it in the anonymous variable of exercise 2.

4. Display the value of the anonymous variable of exercise 2.

5. Convert the case of the value of the anonymous variable of exercise 2 using character-processing functions such as isupper() and tolower() from ctype.

6. Declare a double pointer variable named doublePtr.

7. Allow the user to enter n, the number of values to be processed; then allocate an anonymous array of n double values, storing its address in doublePtr.

8. Fill the anonymous array of exercise 7 with n input values, entered from the keyboard.

9. Compute and display the average of the values in the anonymous array of exercise 7.

10. Deallocate the storage of the anonymous array of exercise 7.

11. Find the base address of the anonymous array allocated in exercise 7 and draw a memory map showing the addresses of its first few elements.

12. Describe the output produced by the following statements:

```
int * foo, * goo;

foo = new int;
*foo = 1;
```

```
cout << (*foo) << endl;
goo = new int;
*goo = 3;
cout << (*foo) << (*goo) << endl;
*foo = *goo + 3;
cout << (*foo) << (*goo) << endl;
foo = goo;
*goo = 5;
cout << (*foo) << (*goo) << endl;
*foo = 7;
cout << (*foo) << (*goo) << endl;
goo = foo;
*foo = 9;
cout << (*foo) << (*goo) << endl;
```

13.3 THE STL `list<T>` CLASS TEMPLATE

In our description of the C++ Standard Template Library in section 9.4, we saw that it provides a variety of other storage containers besides `vector<T>` and that one of these containers is named `list<T>`. Now that we have seen anonymous variables and how C++ pointers provide indirect access to them, we are ready to examine the `list<T>` class template and its implementation.

A LIMITATION OF `vector<T>`

Although `vector<T>`s are easy to use to store sequences of values, they do have limitations. One limitation is that values can be efficiently added to the sequence only at its *back*. If there are empty elements at the end of its run-time allocated array,[8] the `push_back()` function permits values to be appended to the *back* of the sequence, without the existing values having to be copied:

Before			
v.push_back(55)			
88	77	66	
[0]	[1]	[2]	

After			
v.push_back(55)			
88	77	66	55
[0]	[1]	[2]	[3]

Consequently, when a value is appended to a vector using `push_back()`, any values already in the vector will stay in the same positions.

Why is it that `vector<T>` provides no corresponding `push_front()` (or `pop_front()`) functions to manipulate the *front* of the sequence? Because insert-

---

[8] To make sure that this is usually the case, each time `push_back()` is used to append a value to a vector whose run-time allocated array is full, a new array that is twice as large is allocated and the elements of the old array are copied into it. If the vector has no run-time allocated array (i.e., its capacity was zero), then an array whose capacity is one memory page (typically 4K bytes) is allocated.

ing and deleting values at the front of a vector requires extensive copying of values, which takes time. To insert a value at the front, all of the values in the vector must be shifted one position to make room for the new value:

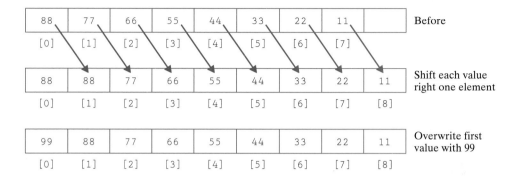

In fact, if a problem requires that values be inserted anywhere except at the back of a sequence, a vector<T> is not the best container for storing that sequence, because of the copying required in shifting values to make room for the new value.

The same problem occurs when any element other than the one at the end of the sequence must be removed. In the vector, all of the elements that follow it must be shifted one position to the left to close the gap. The following diagram illustrates this when the first element is removed:

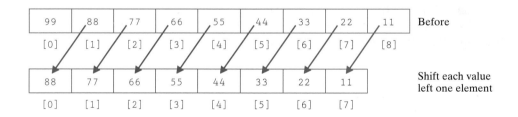

For problems where many such within-the-sequence insertions and deletions are required, STL provides the list<T> container. It allows values to be inserted or removed anywhere in a sequence without any of the copying that plagues vector<T>.

Organization of list<T> Objects. To see how list<T> stores a sequence of values, suppose that aList is defined by

```
list<int> aList;
```

and consider the following sequence of insert operations:

```
aList.push_back(77);
aList.push_back(66);
aList.push_front(88);
```

A simplified picture of the resulting object aList is

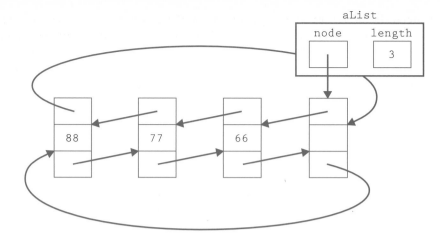

As indicated by the diagram, a sequence of values can be stored within a series of **nodes** linked together by pointers, producing a container called a **linked list.** In addition to space for the data being stored, each node has two pointers, one to the node containing the preceding value and one to the node containing the next value. The STL `list<T>` class template declares the type `list_node` as a protected struct,[9] as follows:

```
template<class T>
class list
{
   // ... previous part of class list ...

 protected:
   struct list_node
   {
      list_node * prev; // address of the node containing
                        //    the previous value
    T data;             // the value being stored in
                        //    this node
      list_node * next; // address of the node containing
                        //    the next value
   };

   // ... remainder of class list ...
};
```

Linked lists that use nodes containing two pointers are called **doubly-linked lists.**

---

[9] A **struct** is exactly the same as a class, except that all of its members are by default public, whereas those of a class are by default private. By declaring a `list_node` as a *struct* within class `list`, the `list` operations can directly access the `list_node` data members. By declaring `list_node` *protected* within class `list`, casual users of class `list` are prevented from accessing it or its data members, while classes derived from `list` are permitted to do so.

Although the designers of STL chose this organization for their list<T> class template, other organizations are possible. One of these is a **singly-linked list,** consisting of a pointer to the first in a sequence of nodes, each containing the value being stored and just one link, a pointer to the next node in the sequence. The final node in the sequence is marked by the null address in its link member:

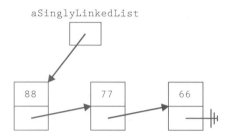

Another arrangment is a **circular linked list,** which is a singly-linked list, but contains a pointer to the last node. In this arrangement, the final node's link consists of a pointer back to the first node, providing easy access to both the last and first values in the sequence:

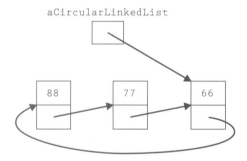

As we shall see next, regardless of its organization, the linked structure of a list allows insertion and deletion operations to be performed that do not require the extensive copying that characterizes its vector<T> counterpart.

SOME list<T> OPERATIONS

In the remainder of this section, we examine a collection of list<T> operations that illustrate the flexibility provided by pointers. A complete table of the list<T> operations is given in appendix D.

The list<T> Default Class Constructor. Perhaps the most basic list<T> operation is the default class constructor. When a programmer writes

```
list<int> aList;
```

the default class constructor builds an empty linked list aList, for which a (simplified) picture is

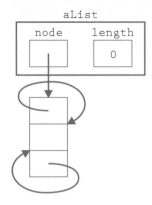

As shown in the diagram, the default class constructor allocates an empty node, called a **head node,** and stores the address of this node in its node data member. In the STL list<T> class template, this head node plays a central role:

- ▶ Its next member always points to the node containing the *first* value in the sequence (or to the head node, if the list is empty);
- ▶ Its prev member always points to the node containing the *last* value in the sequence (or to the head node, if the list is empty); and
- ▶ Its data member is unused.

The main advantages of this organization is that there is always at least one node in the list (i.e., the head node) and every node has a predecessor and a successor. These properties simplify several of the list<T> operations.

The size() and empty() Members. Two of the simplest list<T> operations are size() and empty(). The size() function member is a simple accessor function for the length data member; it returns the number of values currently stored in the list. It might be defined as follows:

```
template<class T>
inline int list<T>::size() const
{
    return length;
}
```

The empty() function member is nearly as simple, returning true if there are no values in the list and false otherwise. Its definition might be

```
template<class T>
inline bool list<T>::empty() const
{
    return length == 0;
}
```

The begin() and end() Iterator Members. As with vector<T>, the list<T> class template provides two functions, begin() and end(), that return iterators to the front and past the end of the list, respectively. In the list<T> class template, these functions are implemented using the pointer data members of the head node. More precisely, the begin() function returns a pointer to the first node, by returning the address stored in the next member of the head node:

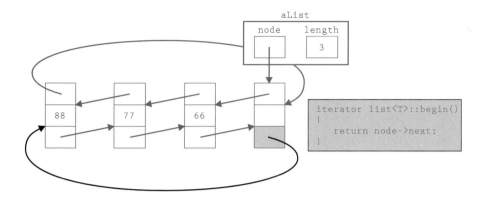

By contrast, the end() function returns a pointer pointing beyond the last node that contains a value by returning the address of the head node:

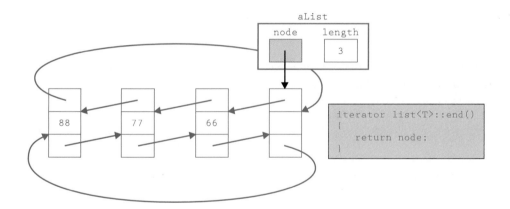

The begin() function thus returns an iterator to the first value in the list, and the end() function returns an iterator that points beyond the final value in the list.

Iterators and Pointers. From our discussion of iterators in preceding chapters and our discussion of pointers in this chapter, it should be evident that an iterator is an *abstraction* of a pointer, hiding some of its details and eliminating some of its hazards.

To illustrate, the list<T> class template declares a list<T>::iterator as an object containing its own list_node pointer named node as a data member. With much of the detail omitted, the class can be thought of as having a structure somewhat like the following:

```
template<class T>
class list
{
  // ... previous list members omitted ...
```

```
public:
  class iterator           // ... some simplification here ...
  {
   protected:
     list_node * node;     // ... and here ...

   // ... other iterator members omitted...
  };

 // ... other list members omitted ...
};
```

The `iterator` class overloads `operator*` so that it returns the value of the data member in the `list_node` pointed to by the iterator's `node` member. Here is a simplified definition:

```
template<class T>
inline T list<T>::iterator::operator*()
{
    return node->data;
}
```

The `iterator` class also overloads `operator++` to "increment" the iterator to the next node in the list:

```
template<class T>
inline iterator list<T>::iterator::operator++()
// prefix version
{
    node = node->next;
    return *this;
}

template<class T>
inline iterator list<T>::iterator::operator++(int i)
// postfix version
{
    iterator tmp = node;
    node = node->next;
    return tmp;
}
```

and overloads `operator--` similarly to "decrement" the iterator to the previous node in the list.

The `front()` and `back()` Members. Like `vector<T>`, `list<T>` provides function members to access the first and last values in the class. These are implemented by dereferencing the iterators returned by the `begin()` and `end()` operations:

```
template<class T>
inline T & list<T>:: front()
{
    return *begin();
}
```

```
template<class T>
inline T & list<T>:: back()
{
    return *(--end());
}
```

Since the list<T>::iterator class overloads operator* to return the data member of the list_node whose address is stored in its node member, an expression like

```
*begin()
```

can be used to access the first value in the sequence, and an expression like

```
*(--end())
```

can be used to access the last value in the sequence. Note that operator* has higher precedence than operator--, so parentheses must be used in this last expression to ensure that the iterator returned by end() is decremented before it is dereferenced.

The insert(), push_front(), and push_back() Members. To add a value to a sequence, the list<T> class template provides several operations, including:

- ▶ *aList*.push_back(*newValue*); which appends *newValue* to *aList*;
- ▶ *aList*.push_front(*newValue*); which prepends *newValue* to *aList*; and
- ▶ *aList*.insert(*anIterator, newValue*); which inserts *newValue* into *aList* ahead of the value pointed to by *anIterator*.

Of these three, insert() is the most general operation—the push_back() and push_front() operations are implemented using insert()—and we will therefore focus our discussion on it.

To illustrate its behavior, suppose that aList is the following list<int>, and position is a list<int>::iterator that has been positioned at the node containing 55 (perhaps by using the STL find() algorithm):

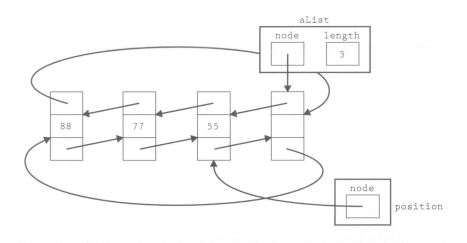

Now suppose that the following statement is executed:

```
aList.insert(position, 66);
```

The `insert()` operation gets a new node,[10] assigns its `data` member the value 66, assigns its `prev` member the address of the node containing 77, and assigns its `next` member the address of the node containing 55:

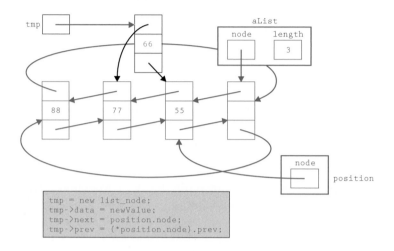

```
tmp = new list_node;
tmp->data = newValue;
tmp->next = position.node;
tmp->prev = (*position.node).prev;
```

The `next` pointer in the node before `position` is then assigned the address of the new node:

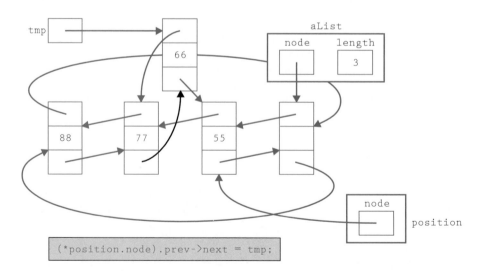

```
(*position.node).prev->next = tmp;
```

---

[10] We show the new node being allocated using `new`; however, the STL list class actually manages its own collection of `list<T>` nodes. Only when this pool of nodes becomes empty does it use `new` to add more nodes to the pool. The `insert()` operation issues a call to `get_node()`, a function that gets the next available node from this pool of nodes, refilling it with more nodes when it is depleted.

Finally, the prev member of the node pointed to by position is updated to point
to the new node, and the length member is incremented:

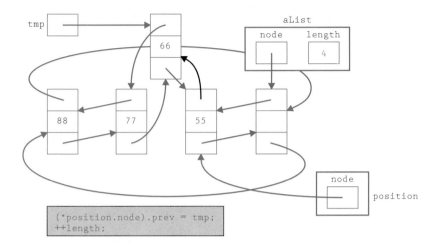

```
(*position.node).prev = tmp;
++length;
```

All we have done is change the values of four pointers, but this has inserted the
value 66 into the sequence between the values 77 and 55. Although the nodes containing the sequence values could be anywhere in memory, we can picture the resulting list as follows:

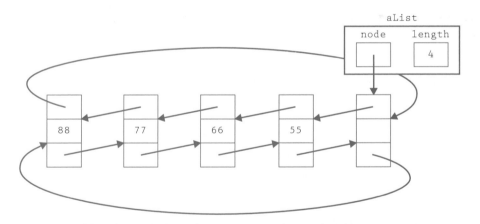

The push_front() and push_back() operations behave in a similar manner. push_front() effectively uses insert() and begin() to insert its value
at the beginning of the sequence,

```
template<class T>
inline void list<T>::push_front()
{
    insert(begin(), newValue);
}
```

while push_back() uses insert() and end() to insert its value at the end of
the sequence:

```
template<class T>
inline void list<T>::push_back()
{
    insert(end(), newValue);
}
```

The pop_back(), pop_front(), erase() and remove() Members. To remove a value in a sequence without any copying, list<T> provides several different operations:

- ▶ aList.pop_back(); removes the last value from aList
- ▶ aList.pop_front(); removes the first value from aList
- ▶ aList.erase(anIterator); removes the value pointed to by
  anIterator from aList
- ▶ aList.remove(aValue); removes all occurrences of aValue from
  aList

The pop_back(), pop_front(), and remove() operations are implemented
using the erase() function, so we will focus on this operation.

To illustrate it, suppose that aList is the list<int> we just examined and
that position is a list<int>::iterator pointing at 66, the value we wish
to erase:

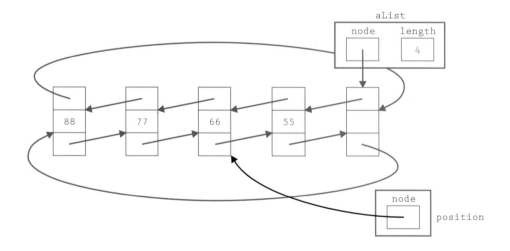

The call

```
aList.erase(position);
```

begins by making the next member of the node containing 77 point to the node
containing 55 and the prev member of the node containing 55 to point to the node
containing 77:

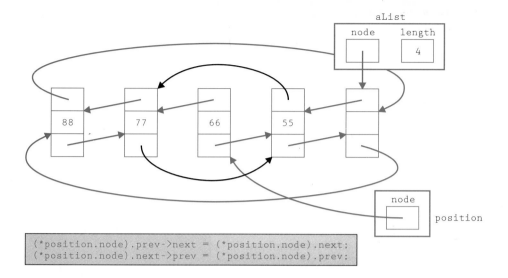

```
(*position.node).prev->next = (*position.node).next;
(*position.node).next->prev = (*position.node).prev;
```

These two statements cut the target node out of the sequence, so that all that remains to do is deallocate that node,[11] and decrement the list's length member:

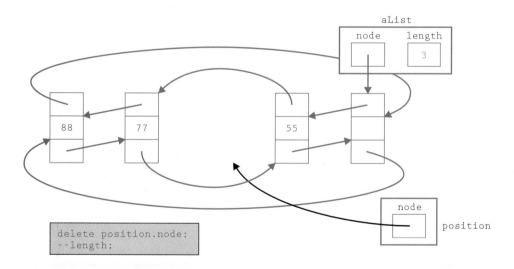

```
delete position.node;
--length;
```

Note that the erase() operation removes the value pointed to by position simply by changing two pointers. No copying of values is required, thanks to the flexibility of the linked nodes.

---

[11] We show the node being deallocated using delete; however erase() actually uses a call to a local function put_node() that stores the node in the list's pool of nodes (see footnote 10). This approach allows a subsequent insert() operation to *recycle* that node, thus avoiding the overhead of deallocating the node now, and reallocating it later. The nodes in the list_node_buffer are deallocated by ~list(), the list destructor.

As described earlier, the `pop_front()` and `pop_back()` operations are implemented using this `erase()` function: `pop_front()` erases the node at position `begin()`, and `pop_back()` erases the node at position `--end()`. The `remove()` operation can be implemented using `erase()` and a simple `while` loop, as follows:

```
template<class T>
void list<T>::remove(const T & value)
{
   iterator first = begin(), // begin at first node
            last = end(),    // stop at head node
            next = first;    // save current node address

   while (first != last)
   {
      ++next;                   // save address of next node
      if (*first == value)      // if value in current node
         erase(first);          //    erase it
      first = next;             // reset first to next node
   }
}
```

These are just a few of the `list<T>` operations. A complete list can be found in appendix D.

EXAMPLE: INTERNET ADDRESSES

The PART OF THE PICTURE that follows this section describes the TCP (Transmission Control Protocol) and IP (Internet Protocol) communication protocols that are used to specify the rules computers use in exchanging messages in networks. TCP/IP addresses are used to uniquely identify computers in the Internet; for example, `titan.ksc.nasa.gov` is the address of a site at the NASA Kennedy Space Center. These addresses are made up of four fields that represent specific parts of the Internet,

host.subdomain.subdomain.rootdomain

which the computer will translate into a unique TCP/IP address. This address is a 32-bit value, but it is usually represented in a dotted-decimal notation by separating the 32 bits into four 8-bit fields, expressing each field as a decimal integer, and separating the fields with a period; for example, `128.159.4.20` is the TCP/IP address for the above site at the NASA Kennedy Space Center.

Problem. A gateway is a device used to interconnect two different computer networks. Suppose that a gateway connects a university to the Internet and that the university's network administrator needs to monitor connections through this gateway. Each time a connection is made (for example, a student using the World Wide Web), the TCP/IP address of the student's computer is stored in a data file. The administrator wants to check periodically who has used the gateway and how many times they have used it.

Solution. The TCP/IP addresses will be read from the file and stored in a linked list of nodes that will store an address and the number of times that address appeared in the data file. As each address is read, we check if it is already in the list. If it is, we increment its count by 1; otherwise, we simply insert it at the end of the list. After all the addresses in the file have been read, the distinct addresses and their counts are displayed.

The program in Figure 13.2 uses this approach to solve the problem. The addresses are stored in a list<TCP_IP_Address> object addressList, where TCP_IP_Address is a small class containing two data members (address and count), input and output function members, and a function member Tally() to increment the count of an address. Also, operator==() is overloaded so that STL's find() algorithm can be used to search the list.

 FIGURE 13.2   INTERNET ADDRESSES.

```
/* internet2.cpp reads TCP/IP addresses from a file and produces a list
 * of distinct addresses and a count of how many times each appeared
 * in the file.  The addresses and counts are stored in a linked list.
 *
 * Input (keyboard): name of file containing addresses
 * Input (file):     addresses
 * Output:           a list of distinct addresses and their counts
 ********************************************************************/

#include <assert.h>                 // assert
#include <string>                   // string
#include <iostream.h>               // cin, cout, >>, <<
#include <fstream.h>                // ifstream, isopen()
#include <list>                     // list<T>
#include <algorithm>                // find

//-------------- Begin class AddressItem --------------------------------
class AddressItem
{
 public:
   void Read(istream & in)
   { in >> address; count = 0; }

   void Print(ostream & out) const
   { out << address << "\t occurs " << count << " times\n"; }

   void Tally()
   { count++; }

   friend bool operator==(const AddressItem & addr1,
                          const AddressItem & addr2);

 private:
   string address;
   int count;
};
```

```cpp
inline bool operator==(const AddressItem & addr1,
                       const AddressItem & addr2);
{ return addr1.address == addr2.address; }

//---------------- End class AddressItem ----------------------------

typedef list<AddressItem> TCP_IP_List;

int main()
{
   string fileName;                    // name of file of TCP/IP addresses
   TCP_IP_List addressList;            // list of addresses

   ifstream inStream;                  // open stream to file of addresses
   cout << "Enter name of file containing TCP/IP addresses: ";
   cin >> fileName;
   inStream.open(fileName.data());
   assert(inStream.is_open());

   AddressItem item;                   // one of the addresses & its count
   for (;;)                            // loop:
   {
      item.Read(inStream);             //    read an address
      if (inStream.eof()) break;       //    if eof, quit

      TCP_IP_List::iterator it =       //    check if item already in list
         find(addressList.begin(), addressList.end(), item);
      if (it != addressList.end())     //    found
         (*it).Tally();                //    increment its count
      else
         addressList.push_back(item);  //    else add it to the list
   }                                   // end loop

   cout << "\nList of addresses:\n\n";    // output the list
   for (TCP_IP_List::iterator it = addressList.begin();
                       it != addressList.end(); it++)
      (*it).Print(cout);
}
```

Listing of `file13-2.dat` used in sample run:

```
128.159.4.20
123.111.222.333
100.1.4.31
34.56.78.90
120.120.120.120
128.159.4.20
123.111.222.333
123.111.222.333
77.66.55.44
100.1.4.31
123.111.222.333
128.159.4.20
```

Sample run:

```
Enter name of file containing TCP/IP addresses: file13-2.dat

List of addresses:

128.159.4.20      occurs 2 times
123.111.222.333   occurs 3 times
100.1.4.31        occurs 1 times
34.56.78.90       occurs 0 times
120.120.120.120   occurs 0 times
77.66.55.44       occurs 0 times
```

✔ Quick Quiz 13.3

1. Why doesn't vector<T> have functions for inserting and removing elements at the front of a vector?
2. In a linked list, values are stored in _____ that are linked together by _____.
3. (True or false) Values can be inserted at the end of a vector<T> more efficiently than at its front.
4. (True or false) Values can be inserted at the end of a list<T> more efficiently than at its front.
5. What advantages do linked lists have over vectors?
6. What advantages do vectors have over linked lists?

EXERCISES 13.3

Exercises 1–7 assume the following declarations (which are used to process singly-linked lists as described in this section),

```
class Node              or equivalently,     struct Node
{                                            {
 public:                                         int data;
   int data;                                      Node * next;
   Node * next;                              };
};
                                             Node * p1, * p2, * p3;
Node * p1, * p2, * p3;
```

and that the following statements have been executed:

```
p1 = new Node;
p2 = new Node;
p3 = new Node;
```

Tell what will be displayed by each of the code segments or explain why an error occurs.

1.
```
p1->data = 123;
p2->data = 456;
p1->next = p2;
p2->next = 0;
cout << p1->data << "   " << p1->next->data << endl;
```

2.
```
p1->data = 12;
p2->data = 34;
p1 = p2;
cout << p1->data << "  " << p2->data << endl;
```

3.
```
p1->data = 12;
p2->data = 34;
*p1 = *p2;
cout << p1->data << "  " << p2->data << endl;
```

4.
```
p1->data = 123;
p2->data = 456;
p1->next = p2;
p2->next = 0;
cout << p2->data << "  " << p2->next->data << endl;
```

5.
```
p1->data = 12;
p2->data = 34;
p3->data = 34;
p1->next = p2;
p2->next = p3;
p3->next = 0;
cout << p1->data << "  " << p1->next->data << endl;
cout << p2->data << "  " << p2->next->data << endl;
cout << p1->next->next->data << endl;
cout << p3->data << endl;
```

6.
```
p1->data = 111;
p2->data = 222;
p1->next = p2;
p2->next = p1;
cout << p1->data << "  " << p2->data << endl;
cout << p1->next->data << endl;
cout << p1->next->next->data << endl;
```

7.
```
p1->data = 12;
p2->data = 34;
p1 = p2;
p2->next = p1;
cout << p1->data << "  " << p2->data << endl;
cout << p1->next->data << "  " << p2->next->data << endl;
```

 Part of the Picture: The TCP/IP Communications Architecture

BY WILLIAM STALLINGS

The key to the success of distributed applications is that all the terminals and computers in the community "speak" the same language. This is the role of the underlying interconnection software. This software must ensure that all the devices transmit messages in such a way that they can be understood by the other computers and terminals in the community. With the introduction of the Systems Network Architecture (SNA) by IBM in the 1970s, this concept became a reality. However, SNA worked only with IBM equipment. Soon other vendors followed with their own proprietary communications architectures to tie together their equipment. Such an approach may be good business for the vendor, but it is bad business for the customer. Happily, that situation has changed radically with the adoption of standards for interconnection software.

TCP/IP ARCHITECTURE AND OPERATION

When communication is desired among computers from different vendors, the software development effort can be a nightmare. Different vendors use different data formats and data exchange protocols. Even within one vendor's product line, different model computers may communicate in unique ways.

As the use of computer communications and computer networking proliferates, a one-at-a-time special-purpose approach to communications software development is too costly to be acceptable. The only alternative is for computer vendors to adopt and implement a common set of conventions. For this to happen, standards are needed.

However, no single standard will suffice. Any distributed application, such as electronic mail or client/server interaction, requires a complex set of communications functions for proper operation. Many of these functions, such as reliability mechanisms, are common across many or even all applications. Thus, the communications task is best viewed as consisting of a modular architecture, in which the various elements of the architecture perform the various required functions. Hence, before one can develop standards, there should be a structure, or *protocol architecture,* that defines the communications tasks.

Two protocol architectures have served as the basis for the development of interoperable communications standards: the TCP/IP protocol suite and the OSI (Open Systems Interconnection) reference model. TCP/IP is the most widely used interoperable architecture, and has won the "protocol wars." Although some useful standards have been developed in the context of OSI, TCP/IP is now the universal interoperable protocol architecture. No product should be considered as part of a business information system that does not support TCP/IP.

TCP/IP LAYERS

The communication task using TCP/IP can be organized into five relatively independent layers: physical, network access, internet, transport, and application.

The **physical layer** covers the physical interface between a data transmission device (e.g., workstation, computer) and a transmission medium or network. This layer is concerned with specifying the characteristics of the transmission medium, the nature of the signals, the data rate, and related matters.

The **network access layer** is concerned with the exchange of data between an end system and the network to which it is attached. The sending computer must provide the network with the address of the destination computer, so that the network may route the data to the appropriate destination. The sending computer may wish to invoke certain services, such as priority, that might be provided by the network. The specific software used at this layer depends on the type of network to be used; different standards have been developed for circuit-switching, packet-switching (e.g., X.25), local area networks (e.g., Ethernet), and others. Thus it makes sense to separate those functions having to do with network access into a separate layer. By doing this, the remainder of the communications software, above the network access layer, need not be concerned about the specifics of the network to be used. The same higher-layer software should function properly regardless of the particular network to which the computer is attached.

The network access layer is concerned with access to and routing data across a network for two end systems attached to the same network. In those cases where two devices are attached to different networks, procedures are needed to allow data to traverse multiple interconnected networks. This is the function of the **internet layer.** The internet protocol (IP) is used at this layer to provide the routing function across multiple networks. This protocol is implemented not only in the end systems but also in routers. A *router* is a processor that connects two networks and whose primary function is to relay data from one network to the other on its route from the source to the destination end system.

Regardless of the nature of the applications that are exchanging data, there is usually a requirement that data be exchanged reliably. That is, we would like to be assured that all of the data arrive at the destination application and that the data arrive in the same order in which they were sent. As we shall see, the mechanisms for providing reliability are essentially independent of the nature of the applications. Thus, it makes sense to collect those mechanisms in a common layer shared by all applications; this is referred to as the **host-to-host layer,** or **transport layer.** The transmission control protocol (TCP) is the most commonly-used protocol to provide this functionality.

Finally, the **application layer** contains the logic needed to support the various user applications. For each different type of application, such as file transfer, a separate module is needed that is peculiar to that application.

OPERATION OF TCP/IP

Figure 13.3 indicates how these protocols are configured for communications. To make clear that the total communications facility may consist of multiple networks, the constituent networks are usually referred to as *subnetworks*. Some sort of network access protocol, such as the Ethernet logic, is used to connect a computer to a subnetwork. This protocol enables the host to send data across the subnetwork to another host or, in the case of a host on another subnetwork, to a router. IP is implemented in all of the end systems and the routers. It acts as a relay to move a block of data from one host, through one or more routers, to another host. TCP is implemented only in the end systems; it keeps track of the blocks of data to assure that all are delivered reliably to the appropriate application.

For successful communication, every entity in the overall system must have a unique address. Actually, two levels of addressing are needed. Each host on a subnetwork must have a unique global internet address; this allows the data to be delivered to the proper host. This address is used by IP for routing and delivery. Each application within a host must have an address that is unique within the host; this allows the host-to-host protocol (TCP) to deliver data to the proper process. These latter addresses are known as ports.

Let us trace a simple operation. Suppose that an application, associated with port 1 at

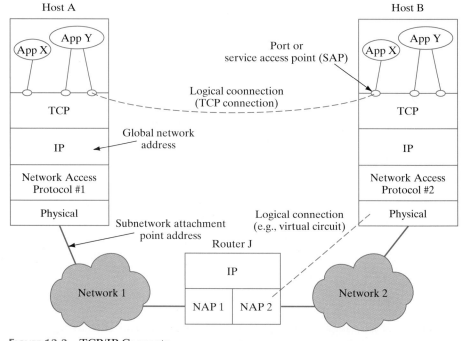

FIGURE 13.3   TCP/IP Concepts

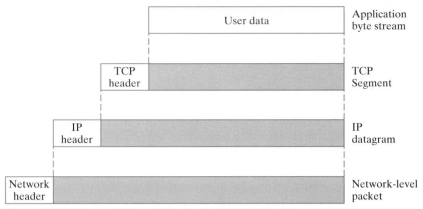

FIGURE 13.4   Protocol Data Units in the TCP/IP Architecture

host *A*, wishes to send a message to another application, associated with port 2 at host *B*. The application at *A* hands the message down to TCP with instructions to send it to host *B*, port 12. TCP hands the message down to IP with instructions to send it to host *B*. Note that IP need not be told the identity of the destination port. All it needs to know is that the data is intended for host *B*. Next, IP hands the message down to the network access layer (e.g., Ethernet logic) with instructions to send it to router *X* (the first hop on the way to *B*).

To control this operation, control information as well as user data must be transmitted, as suggested in Figure 13.4. Let us say that the sending process generates a block of data and passes this to TCP. TCP may break this block into smaller pieces to make it more manageable. To each of these pieces, TCP appends control information known as the TCP header, forming a *TCP segment*. The control information is to be used by the peer TCP protocol entity at host *B*. Examples of fields that are part of this header include:

- ▶ **Destination port:** When the TCP entity at *B* receives the segment, it must know to whom the data are to be delivered.

- ▶ **Sequence number:** TCP numbers the segments that it sends to a particular destination port sequentially, so that if they arrive out of order, the TCP entity at *B* can reorder them.

- ▶ **Checksum:** The sending TCP includes a code that is a function of the contents of the remainder of the segment. The receiving TCP performs the same calculation and compares the result with the incoming code. A discrepancy results if there has been some error in transmission.

Next, TCP hands each segment over to IP, with instructions to transmit it to *B*. These segments must be transmitted across one or more subnetworks and relayed through one or more intermediate routers. This operation, too, requires the use of control information. Thus IP appends a header of control information to each segment to form an *IP datagram*. An example of an item stored in the IP header is the destination host address (in this example, *B*).

Finally, each IP datagram is presented to the network access layer for transmission across the first subnetwork in its journey to the destination. The network access layer appends its own header, creating a packet, or frame. The packet is transmitted across the subnetwork to router J. The packet header contains the information that the subnetwork needs to transfer the data across the subnetwork. Examples of items that may be contained in this header include:

- ▶ **Destination subnetwork address:** The subnetwork must know to which attached device the packet is to be delivered.

▶ **Facilities requests:** The network access protocol might request the use of certain subnetwork facilities, such as priority.

At router J, the packet header is stripped off and the IP header examined. On the basis of the destination address information in the IP header, the IP module in the router directs the datagram out across subnetwork 2 to *B*. To do this, the datagram is again augmented with a network access header.

When the data are received at *B*, the reverse process occurs. At each layer, the corresponding header is removed, and the remainder is passed on to the next higher layer, until the original user data are delivered to the destination application.

A SIMPLE EXAMPLE

Figure 13.5 puts all of these concepts together, showing the interaction between modules to transfer one block of data. For simplicity, the example shows two systems connected to the same network, so that no router is involved. Let us say that the file transfer module in computer X is transferring a file one record at a time to computer Y. At X, each record is handed over to TCP. We can picture this action as being in the form of a command or procedure call. The arguments of this procedure call include the destination computer address, the destination port, and the record. TCP appends the destination port and other control information to the record to create a TCP segment. This is then handed down to IP by another procedure call. In this case, the arguments for the command are the destination computer address and the TCP segment. The resulting IP datagram is handed down to the network access layer, which constructs a network-level packet.

The network accepts the packet from X and delivers it to Y. The network access module

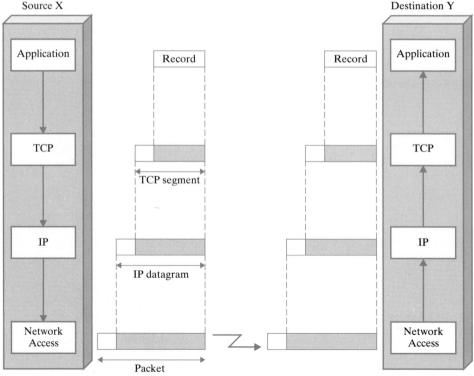

FIGURE 13.5   Operation of TCP/IP

in Y receives the packet, strips off the header, and transfers the enclosed transport PDU to Y's IP module, which strips off the IP header and passes the resulting TCP segment to TCP. TCP examines the segment header and, on the basis of the destination port field in the header, delivers the enclosed record to the appropriate application, in this case the file transfer module in Y.

TCP AND UDP

For most applications running as part of the TCP/IP protocol architecture, the transport layer protocol is TCP. TCP provides a reliable connection for the transfer of data between applications.

Figure 13.6a shows the header format for TCP, which is a minimum of 20 octets, or 160 bits. The Source Port and Destination Port fields identify the applications at the source and destination systems that are using this connection. The Sequence Number, Acknowledgment Number, and Window fields provide flow control and error control. In essence, each segment is sequentially numbered and must be acknowledged by the receiver so that the sender knows that the segment was successfully received. The Windows field is passed from one side to the other to indicate how many data the other side may send before receiving additional permission. Finally, the checksum is a 16-bit frame check sequence used to detect errors in the TCP segment.

In addition to TCP, there is one other transport-level protocol that is in common use as part of the TCP/IP protocol suite: the user datagram protocol (UDP). UDP provides a connectionless service for application-level procedures. UDP does not guarantee delivery, preservation of sequence, or protection against duplication. UDP enables procedures to send messages to other procedures with a minimum of protocol mechanism. Some transaction-oriented applications make use of UDP; one example is SNMP (Simple Network Management Protocol), the standard network management protocol for TCP/IP networks. Because it is connectionless, UDP has very little to do. Essentially, it adds a port addressing capability to IP. This is best seen by examining the UDP header, shown in Figure 13.6b.

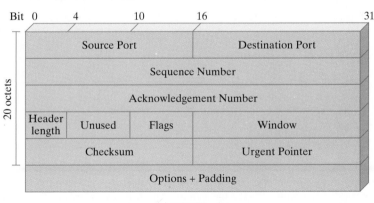

(a) TCP Header

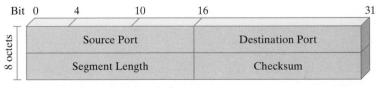

(b) UDP Header

FIGURE 13.6   TCP and UDP Headers

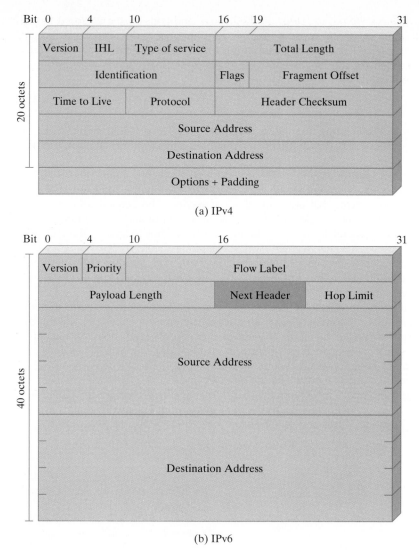

FIGURE 13.7   IP Headers

IP AND IPv6

For decades, the keystone of the TCP/IP protocol architecture has been the Internet Protocol (IP). Figure 13.7a shows the IP header format, which is a minimum of 20 octets, or 160 bits. The header includes 32-bit source and destination addresses. The Header Checksum field is used to detect errors in the header to avoid misdelivery. The Protocol field indicates whether TCP, UDP, or some other higher-layer protocol is using IP. The Flags and Fragment Offset fields are used in the fragmentation and reassembly process.

In 1995, the Internet Engineering Task Force (IETF), which develops protocol standards for the Internet, issued a specification for a next-generation IP, known then as IPng. This specification was turned into a standard in 1996 known as IPv6. IPv6 provides a number of functional enhancements over the existing IP, designed to accommodate the higher speeds of today's networks and the mix of data streams, including graphic and video, that are becoming more prevalent. But the driving force behind the development of the new protocol was the need for more addresses. The current IP uses a 32-bit address to specify a source or destination. With the explosive growth of the Internet and of private networks attached to the Internet, this address length became insufficient to accommodate all of the systems needing addresses. As Figure 13.7b shows, IPv6 includes 128-bit source and destination address fields.

Ultimately, all of the installations using TCP/IP are expected to migrate from the current IP to IPv6, but this process will take many years if not decades.

TCP/IP APPLICATIONS

A number of applications have been standardized to operate on top of TCP. We mention three of the most common here.

The **simple mail transfer protocol (SMTP)** provides a basic electronic mail facility. It provides a mechanism for transferring messages among separate hosts. Features of SMTP include mailing lists, return receipts, and forwarding. The SMTP protocol does not specify the way in which messages are to be created; some local editing or native electronic mail facility is required. Once a message is created, SMTP accepts the message, and makes use of TCP to send it to an SMTP module on another host. The target SMTP module will make use of a local electronic mail package to store the incoming message in a user's mailbox.

The **file transfer protocol (FTP)** is used to send files from one system to another under user command. Both text and binary files are accommodated, and the protocol provides features for controlling user access. When a user wishes to engage in file transfer, FTP sets up a TCP connection to the target system for the exchange of control messages. These allow user ID and password to be transmitted, and allow the user to specify the file and file actions desired. Once a file transfer is approved, a second TCP connection is set up for the data transfer. The file is transferred over the data connection, without the overhead of any headers or control information at the application level. When the transfer is complete, the control connection is used to signal completion and to accept new file transfer commands.

TELNET provides a remote logon capability, which enables a user at a terminal or personal computer to logon to a remote computer and function as if directly connected to that computer. The protocol was designed to work with simple scroll-mode terminals. TELNET is actually implemented in two modules: User TELNET interacts with the terminal I/O module to communicate with a local terminal. It converts the characteristics of real terminals to the network standard and vice versa. Server TELNET interacts with an application, acting as a surrogate terminal handler so that remote terminals appear as local to the application. Terminal traffic between User and Server TELNET is carried on a TCP connection.

TO PROBE FURTHER

The topics in this section are covered in detail in *Data and Computer Communications, Fifth Edition,* by William Stallings (Prentice Hall, 1997). Links to web sites with further information can be found at http://www.shore.net/~ws/DCC5e.

*13.4 POINTERS AND COMMAND-LINE ARGUMENTS

In section 2.1, we saw that every C++ program has a function whose name is `main`. The main function differs from other programmer-defined functions in a number of ways. One of the differences is that arguments are passed to the main function, using an array of pointers. How this is done is the topic of this section.

The main function cannot be called directly. Instead, we can think of it as being *called* when a program is *executed*. In **command-line environments** such as the UNIX operating system, a program is executed by entering its name following the operating system prompt. For example, to invoke the text editor `emacs` on a computer running UNIX , we might enter the command

```
emacs
```

and the program will begin executing. In any command-line environment, entering the name of a C++ program on the command-line can be thought of as issuing a call to the main function of that program.

To edit a C++ source file in the UNIX environment, we can enter a command of the form

```
emacs SourceFileName
```

When invoked in this way, the program (`emacs`) begins execution, searches for the file named *SourceFileName*, and (assuming that it is found) opens it for editing. In this example, the file that we wish to edit (*SourceFileName*) is an example of a **command-line argument.** Just as entering the name of the program (`emacs`) is like calling the main function of a program, entering the name of the program followed by *SourceFileName* is like calling the main function of a program and passing it *SourceFileName* as an argument.

Command-line arguments are used with many of the system commands in command-line environments such as UNIX. For example, the command

```
mkdir projects
```

is used in UNIX to create a new subdirectory named `projects`. Similarly, the command

```
cd projects
```

will change location in the directory structure to the subdirectory `projects`. In each case a program is being executed (one named `mkdir`, and the other named `cd`), and the name `projects` is passed to that program as an argument. In this section we examine the mechanism by which a main function can receive and process command-line arguments. The techniques discussed can be used in any C++ command-line environment.

PARAMETERS OF THE MAIN FUNCTION

The general form of the main function is

```
int main(parameter_list)
{
    statement_list
}
```

In all of our programs up to this point, the *parameter_list* has been empty:

```
int main()
{
    // ... body of the main function ...
}
```

But this need not be the case. A main function can be declared with a parameter list consisting of two predefined parameters:

- argc (the argument count), an integer; and
- argv (the argument vector), an array of pointers to characters.

As a legacy from C, the standard way to declare these parameters in a main function is:[12]

```
int main( int argc, char * argv[] )
{
    // ... body of the main function ...
}
```

When a C++ program with the parameters argc and argv declared in the parameter list of its main function is executed from the command line, two things occur automatically:

1. If n character strings were entered on the command line, then the value of argc is set to n

2. The value of argv[0] is the address of the first character string of the command line.
   The value of argv[1] is the address of the second character string of the command line
   :
   :
   The value of argv[n-1] is the address of the nth character string of the command line.

To illustrate, consider the following simple C++ program:

FIGURE 13.8   INTRODUCING argc AND argv.

```
/* commline8.cpp introduces the predefined parameters argc and argv.
 *
 * Output: The value of argc, followed by each string in argv.
 ****************************************************************/

#include <iostream.h>

int main(int argc, char * argv[])
{
    cout << "\nThere are " << argc
         << " strings on the command line:\n";

    for (int i = 0; i < argc; i++)
        cout << '\t' << "argv[" << i << "] contains: "
             << argv[i] << endl;
}
```

---

[12] C has no classes, and thus has no string class. Instead, C permits character strings to be stored in character arrays (char []), and passed to functions via character pointer (char *) parameters, with the value of a character string literal being the address of its first character. Hence the close relationship between character strings, arrays, and pointers in C.

In this program the parameter list of the main function contains declarations of `argc` and `argv`. If the compiled version of this program is stored in a file named `commline,` then `commline` can be executed by entering the command

    commline

which produces the output:

```
There are 1 strings on the command line:
    argv[0] contains: commline
```

Thus, within `commline,` `argc` has the value 1, and `argv[0]` refers to the character string `commline.` If we execute `commline` by entering the command

    commline Argument

then the output produced will be:

```
There are 2 strings on the command line:
    argv[0] contains: commline
    argv[1] contains: Argument
```

In this execution, we see that `argc` has the value 2, `argv[0]` contains the character string `commline,` and `argv[1]` contains the character string `Argument.` If we execute `commline` by typing

    commline I want an argument

then the output will be:

```
There are 5 strings on the command line:
    argv[0] contains: commline
    argv[1] contains: I
    argv[2] contains: want
    argv[3] contains: an
    argv[4] contains: argument
```

From these examples it should be evident that the values of `argc` and `argv` depend on what the user enters on the command line when invoking the program. If the user enters the name of the program followed by i arguments, then the value of `argc` will be $i + 1$, the number of character strings entered on the command line; `argv[0]` will refer to the name of the program; and `argv[1]` through `argv[i]` will refer to the i arguments that were entered.

EXAMPLE: A SQUARE ROOT CALCULATOR

As a simple illustration of the use of `argv` and `argc,` consider the problem of designing a square root calculator, that allows the user to enter the value(s) to be processed on the command line.

Problem. Construct a program `sroot` that, given a real value, displays the square root of that value; the input value is to be entered on the command line. For example, if the command

    sroot 4

is entered, the value 2 will be displayed; and if

```
sroot 4 9 16 25
```

is entered, the values 2, 3, 4, and 5 will be displayed.

Objects. From the problem description, we can identify the following data objects:

Object	Kind	Type	Name
A sequence of command-line arguments	variable	`char * []`	*argv*
The number of command-line arguments	variable	`int`	*argc*
A particular command-line argument	variable	`double`	*inValue*
The square root of an argument	variable	`double`	—

Since the program must process command-line arguments, it *receives* the arguments through the parameters of the main function (i.e., `argc` and `argv`). We can thus specify the problem as follows:

Receive: One or more command-line arguments.

Precondition: The command-line arguments are positive, numeric values.

Output: The square roots of those values.

On the basis of this specification, we can write the following stub for the program:

```
#include <iostream.h>

int main(int argc, char * argv[])
{
}
```

Operations. In designing the solution, we identify the following operations:

i. Retrieve any command-line arguments

ii. Take the square root of each argument

iii. Output the resulting value(s)

Taking the square root of each argument and outputting the resulting value are straightforward, but retrieving the arguments requires the use of `argc` and `argv`. Consider what the user might enter:

```
sroot        // error–no data to process (argc is 1)
sroot A      // error — non-numeric data (argc is 2, argv[1] is "A")
sroot 9      // one value (argc is 2, argv[1] is "9")
sroot 4 9    // two values (argc is 3, argv[1] is "4", argv[2] is "9")
```

Generalizing, we see that if the user supplies i values to be processed, then `argc` will equal i+1, `argv[1]` will refer to the first value, `argv[2]` will refer to the second value, and so on. We can thus use `argv[i]` to retrieve the ith value, with i varying from 1 through `argc-1`.

However, each `argv[i]` refers to a character string, and we must take the square root of a value of type `double`. This means that the character string stored in `argv[i]` must be converted to the corresponding `double` value. Fortunately,

C++ provides the `strtod()` function in `stdlib` that performs this operation.[13] That function can also be used to make our program more foolproof by checking its return value—`strtod()` returns 0 if it is unable to convert the string to a numeric value, which will be the case if the user supplies a non-numeric value on the command line.

Once we have converted the character string to the corresponding `double` value, all that remains is to find its square root, which is easy, using the `sqrt()` function declared in `math`. We then simply display the value and its square root.

We can thus construct the following algorithm, which checks that at least one command-line argument has been given and if so, uses a loop to process each argument.

Algorithm for `sroot`.

1. If *argc* is less than 2, display an "incorrect usage" error message and quit.
2. For each integer *i* in the range 1 through *argc* − 1:
   a. Get *inValue*, the double equivalent to argument *i*.
   b. If *inValue* > 0
         Display *inValue* and its square root.
      Else
         Display an "invalid data" error message.

Coding. Given this algorithm, we can encode it in C++ as shown in Figure 13.9.

FIGURE 13.9   ENCODING `sroot`.

```
/* sroot9.cpp displays the square roots of a sequence of values,
 *     specified by the user on the command line.
 *
 *    Receive: One or more numeric (double) values
 *    Output:  The square roots of the input values
 ***********************************************************************/

#include <iostream.h>                    // cin, cout, <<, >>
#include <math.h>                        // sqrt()
#include <stdlib.h>                       // strtod()

int main(int argc, char * argv[])
{
   if (argc < 2)
   {
      cout << "\n*** Usage: sroot List-of-Positive-Numbers \n\n";
      return 1;
   }

   double inValue;                        // double equivalent of an argument
```

---

[13] More accurately, the `strtod()` function is a legacy from C, the parent language of C++.

```
   for (int i = 1; i < argc; i++)
   {
      inValue = strtod(argv[i], 0);
      if (inValue > 0)
         cout <<"\n--> The square root of " << inValue
              << " is " << sqrt(inValue) << endl;
      else
         cout << "\n*** " << argv[i] << " is not a valid data item;"
              << "\n*** must be numeric and greater than 0.\n"
              << endl;
   }
}
```

Sample runs:

<u>sroot</u>

*** Usage: sroot List-of-Positive-Numbers

<u>sroot 4</u>

--> The square root of 4 is 2

<u>sroot 4 ABC 7 9</u>

--> The square root of 4 is 2

*** ABC is is not a valid data item;
*** must be numeric and greater than 0.

--> The square root of 7 is 2.64575

--> The square root of 9 is 3

The program in Figure 13.9 is a simple illustration of how `argc` and `argv` can be used, but it barely scratches the surface of the powerful capabilities they provide. We now describe a few of these capabilities.

COMMAND-LINE ARGUMENTS: FILES AND SWITCHES.

The main function parameters `argc` and `argv` allow the programmer to retrieve whatever arguments were entered on the command line, and then use those arguments to determine how the program should behave. For example, suppose that we are working on a UNIX system. To remove a file from the file system, we might enter the command:

`rm` *FileName*

In this usage of the `rm` command, the file to be removed, *FileName*, is the argument to the command. It should be clear that the `rm` command can retrieve the name of this file using `argc` and `argv`.

Another example stems from `emacs`, a popular UNIX text editor. One of its features is that if you are editing a file named *FileName*, it creates a backup file named *FileName~*. Because such files take up disk space, they should be removed periodically. To remove all such files from the current directory, one can use the command

```
rm *~
```

Because UNIX treats the asterisk (*) as a **wild card** that matches any character string, the arguments to the `rm` command become all files of the form *FileName~*. The `rm` command then removes all such files from the file system.

Using wild cards can be risky, because it is easy to remove files inadvertently. To reduce this risk, an alternative form of the `rm` command can be used:

```
rm -i *~
```

Instead of blindly removing all files that end with a tilde (~), the command-line argument `-i` causes the `rm` command to prompt the user for the removal of each file (i.e., to removes files interactively). For example, execution of this command might produce the following queries from the operating system and user replies:

```
delete mystats.cpp~? y
delete change.cpp~? n
delete minimum.cpp~? n
delete minmax.cpp~? y
delete sroot.cpp~? y
```

It should be clear that the `rm` command can use `argc` and `argv` to check for the presence of the `-i` argument and behave interactively if it is present but non-interactively if it is absent.

Command-line arguments like `-i` that alter the behavior of a program are called **switches** and are common in command-line operating systems such as UNIX.

In summary, most command-line arguments fall into one of three categories:

1.   *Values* that the program processes
2.   *Files* that the program reads from or writes to (see chapter 8)
3.   *Switches* that in some way alter the behavior of the program

The main function parameters `argc` and `argv` provide a mechanism whereby a program can retrieve such arguments.

Part of the Picture: Data Structures

In this chapter, we have provided an introduction to pointers and how they can be used to build sophisticated classes like `vector<T>` and `list<T>`. These are two of the many new structures for storing data provided by the Standard Template Library (STL). By permitting data to be efficiently stored and manipulated, these **data structures** can greatly simplify the solutions to many problems.

As we saw, different data structures have different uses. For example, although both `vector<T>` and `list<T>` can be used to store a sequence of values, `vector<T>` should be used if direct access to values in the middle of the sequence is needed—`vector<T>` permits this via the subscript operator, but `list<T>` does not—and `list<T>` should be used if many insertions and deletions must be performed within the sequence and not just at the end. Both `list<T>` and `vector<T>` provide for these operations via `insert()` and `erase()`, but the times required by the `vector<T>` versions of these operations are proportional to the number of values in the list, whereas the times for their `list<T>` counterparts are independent of the number of values in the sequence.

STL provides other containers for data storage, including the **set, multiset, map, multimap, stack, queue,** and **priority queue** containers, most of which are implemented using pointers. Selection of the container most appropriate for a particular problem depends on the kinds of operations needed to solve the problem as well as a thorough understanding of the time efficiency of the operations for a given container. The study of these data structures and their relative efficiencies will be the focus of a planned sequel to this text.

The STL containers can be used to solve so many problems that the beginning (or even intermediate) programmer may be tempted to relegate pointers to the past and avoid developing expertise in their use. It is indeed the case that, thanks to STL, the most commonly used data structures can be used as "off-the-shelf" components, without the work of building them from scratch using pointers. Nevertheless, pointers remain an important tool for the advanced C++ programmer, because the full benefits of inheritance (a simple form of which we saw in chapter 12) can be achieved only when an object is accessed via a pointer or reference. Although the details are beyond the scope of our present discussion, much of **object-oriented design** consists of designing objects that share a common interface and yet behave independently (or **polymorphically,** in object-oriented terminology). In C++, such objects must be allocated at run-time using `new`, and then accessed via a pointer or reference. The sequel to this text will expand our understanding of the STL containers, pointers, and inheritance, and their roles in object-oriented design.

☞ *PROGRAMMING POINTERS*

✍ PROGRAM STYLE AND DESIGN

Pointers permit the implementation of flexible data structures like `vector<T>` and `list<T>` from the Standard Template Library. When using such objects, we must select the data structure that best fits the problem to be solved. More precisely, if one is storing a sequence of values and the problem requires access to arbitrary values within the sequence, then a `vector<T>` is an appropriate container for storing the sequence. However, if one is storing a sequence and the problem requires many insertions and deletions anywhere except at the end of the sequence, then a `list<T>` provides an efficient means of storing and manipulating such a sequence.

The pointers used to implement `list<T>` and `vector<T>` have memory addresses as values. Consequently, the manner in which pointer variables are used is quite different from that in which other kinds of variables are processed, and this can cause special difficulties for both beginning and experienced programmers. Pointers are used to store the addresses of objects whose memory is allocated at run time. Consequently, operations on such objects that:

- ▶ Create the object require that its memory be explicitly allocated using `new`
- ▶ Destroy the object require that its memory be explicitly deallocated using `delete`
- ▶ Modify the size of the object require that its old memory be deallocated and then new memory of the correct size be reallocated.

When designing classes that have pointer data members, *always* define a **copy constructor** (by which the *compiler* can make copies of an object, as needed), the **assignment operator** (by which a *programmer* can make a distinct copy of an object, as needed), and a **destructor** (that the compiler can use to deallocate an object's run-time memory at the end of its lifetime).

⚡ POTENTIAL PROBLEMS

The operations used to process pointers are quite different from those used to process objects whose memory is allocated at compile time. Some of the main features to remember when using pointer variables and run-time allocation in C++ programs are:

1. *Use the* `typedef` *mechanism and descriptive identifiers to declare pointer types.* **This** increases the readability of programs, which reduces the likelihood of errors and makes errors easier to find when they do occur.

2. *Each pointer variable is bound to a fixed type; a pointer is the address of a memory location in which only a value of that type can be stored.* **For example, if** `pPtr` **and** `qPtr` are pointer variables declared by

   ```
   int * pPtr;
   double * qPtr;
   ```

   then `pPtr` is bound to the type `int` and `qPtr` to the type `double`. Memory locations pointed to by `pPtr` can store only integer values, whereas those to which `qPtr` points can store only real values.

3. *Care must be used when operating on pointers because they have memory addresses as values.* **In particular:**

   ▶ *A pointer* `ptr` *can be assigned a value in the following ways:*

`ptr = &obj;`	(where `obj` is an object of the type to which `ptr` points)
`ptr = 0;`	(the null address)
`ptr = anotherPtr;`	(where `anotherPtr` is a pointer bound to the same type as `ptr`)
`ptr = new Type;`	(where `Type` is the type to which `ptr` points)

   ▶ *Arithmetic operations on pointers are restricted.* **For example, pointer values** (memory addresses) cannot be added, subtracted, multiplied, or divided. However, an integer value `i` can be added to or subtracted from the value of a pointer variable, which changes the address in the pointer by `i * sizeof(Type)`, where `Type` is the type to which the pointer is bound.

   ▶ *Relational operators can be used to compare pointers, but the two pointers must be bound to the same type or one or both may be the null address.*

   ▶ *Pointers may be used as parameters, but corresponding parameters and arguments must be bound to the same type.* **A function may also return a pointer as** its return value, but the type to which that pointer is bound must be the same as the type to which the function is declared to point.

4. *Do not confuse memory locations with the contents of memory locations.* **If** `ptr` **is a** pointer, its value is the address of a memory location; `*ptr` refers to the contents of that location. Both `ptr++` and `(*ptr)++` are valid (if `ptr` is bound to a type for which `++` is defined), but the first increments the address in `ptr`, while the second increments the contents of the memory location at that address.

5. *The null address ≠ undefined.* **A pointer becomes defined when it is assigned the ad**dress of a memory location or the null address. Assigning a pointer the null address is analogous to initializing a numeric variable to zero.

6. *If* the value of a pointer `ptr` *is undefined or the null address, then an attempt to dereference* `ptr` *is an error.* **Doing so may produce cryptic run-time error messages.**

7. *When memory is allocated at run time with the* `new` *operation, the value returned by* `new` *should be tested before proceeding, to ensure that the operation was successful.*

The `assert()` mechanism provides a convenient way to do this. For example, if `ptr` is a pointer in which we are storing the address of a newly allocated block of memory,

```
ptr = new SomeType;
```

then the assertion

```
assert(ptr != 0);
```

can be used to verify that the `new` operation returned a valid (non-null) address.

8. *Memory locations that were once associated with a pointer variable and that are no longer needed should be returned to the free store by using the* `delete` *function.* Special care is required so that memory locations are not rendered inaccessible. For example, if `pPtr` and `qPtr` are pointer variables bound to the same type, the assignment statement

```
pPtr = qPtr ;
```

causes `pPtr` to point to the same memory location as that pointed to by `qPtr`. If the program should execute

```
delete qPtr;
```

then the memory previously pointed to by `qPtr` is deallocated, leaving an invalid address in `pPtr`, so that any attempt to dereference `pPtr` (i.e., `*pPtr`) will usually generate a run-time error. This difficulty occurs so frequently, it has a special name—the **dangling pointer problem.**

9. *Never rely upon the default copy constructor or assignment operator for a class containing a pointer data member.* When a class contains a pointer data member, these default operations will not make distinct copies of an object. The **aliasing problem** can result, since changes to a copy of an object can inadvertently change the original object, producing a difficult-to-find logical error.

Programming Problems

SECTIONS 13.1–13.3

1. Design and implement a class `BigInt` whose values are large integers with perhaps hundreds of digits. Overload the addition and subtraction operators. Treat each number as a list, each of whose elements is a block of digits of the number. Then add the integers (lists) element by element, carrying from one element to the next when necessary. Write a two-function `BigInt` calculator program to test your class.

2. Extend class `BigInt` from problem 1 by overloading the multiplication and division operators to multiply and divide two large integers.

3. A limited number of tickets for the Hoops championship basketball game go on sale tomorrow, and ticket orders are to be filled in the order in which they are received. Write a program that a box-office cashier can use to enter the names and addresses of the persons ordering tickets together with the number of tickets requested, and stores this information in a list. The program should then produce a sequence of mailing labels (names, addresses, and number of tickets) for orders that can be filled. Check that no one receives more than four tickets and that multiple requests from the same person are disallowed.

4. A *polynomial of degree n* has the form

$$a_0 + a_1x + a_2x^2 + \cdots + a_nx^n$$

where $a_0, a_1, \ldots, a_n$ are numeric constants called the *coefficients* of the polynomial and $a_n \neq 0$. For example,

$$1 + 3x - 7x^3 + 5x^4$$

is a polynomial of degree 4 with integer coefficients 1, 3, 0, -7, and 5. Design and implement a `Polynomial` class that can represent any such polynomial. Store only the nonzero coefficients and the corresponding exponents in a list. Provide input and output operators, displaying polynomials in the usual mathematical format with x^n written as $x \uparrow n$ or $x \char94 n$. Use your class in a program that reads a polynomial and then reads values for x and evaluates the polynomial for each value.

5. Extend the class `Polynomial` in problem 4 to add two polynomials.

6. Extend the class `Polynomial` in problems 4 and 5 to multiply two polynomials.

7. In an ordered list, all operations that modify the list are designed to ensure that its elements remain in ascending order. Build an `OrderedList` class template derived from class `list<T>` that exhibits this characteristic.

8. Suppose that jobs entering a computer system are assigned a job number and a priority from 0 through 9. The numbers of jobs awaiting execution by the system are kept in a *priority queue*. A job entered into this queue is placed ahead of all jobs of lower priority but after all those of equal or higher priority. Write a program to read one of the letters R (remove), A (add), or L (list). For R, read a job number and remove it from the priority queue; for A, read a job number and priority and then add it to the priority queue in the manner just described; and for L, list all the job numbers in the queue.

9. Write a "quiz-tutor" program, perhaps on a topic from one of the early chapters, or some other topic about which you are knowledgeable. The program should read a question and its answer from a file, display the question, and accept an answer from the user. If the answer is correct, the program should go on to the next question. If it is not correct, store the question in a list. When the file of questions is exhausted, the questions that were missed should be displayed again (in their original order). Keep a count of the correct answers and display the final count. Also, display the correct answer when necessary in the second round of questioning.

10. Write a program to read the records from the file `Student` (see the file descriptions at the end of Chapter 8) and construct five linked lists of records containing a student's name, number, and cumulative GPA, one list for each class. Store these records in a vector of `list<T>`s. After the lists have been constructed, sort each list and then print each of them with appropriate headings. *Note:* If `aList` is a `list<T>` object, then `alist.sort();` will sort `aList` provided `<` is defined for type T objects. In this exercise, you must overload `operator<()` to define what it means for one student record to be less than another.

11. The number of elements in a list may grow so large that finding a value in the list cannot be done efficiently. One way to improve performance is to maintain several smaller linked lists. Write a program to read several lines of uppercase text and to produce a text concordance, which is a list of all distinct words in the text. Store distinct words beginning with A in one linked list, those beginning with B in another, and so on. After all the text lines have been read, sort each list (see problem 10 and then print a list of all these words in alphabetical order.

12. Modify the program of problem 11 so that the concordance also includes the frequency with which each word occurs in the text.

13. In addition to the words in a section of text, a concordance usually stores the numbers of selected pages on which there is a significant use of the word. Modify the

program of problem 11 so that the numbers of all lines in which a word appears are stored along with the word itself. The program should display each word together with its associated line numbers in ascending order.

14. Design and implement a program that acts as a screen-oriented text editor (*Hint:* Assume that the first line of the file to be edited contains the number of lines in the file, and build a class that uses a list of lists to store the file). The editor should display:

> ▶ fifteen to twenty numbered lines at a time,

> ▶ the current cursor position (line and column), and

> ▶ a menu of the commands that allow the user to replace, insert, delete, and find the position of text strings in the file, as well as loading and storing a file.

Optionally, allow the user to enter the name of the file to be edited on the command line.

SECTION 13.4

15. Write a program `binary` so that the command

```
binary DecimalValue
```

will calculate and display the binary representation of `DecimalValue`.

16. The *median* of a list of *n* numbers is a value such that $n/2$ of the values are greater than that value, and $n/2$ of the values are less than that value. The usual procedure to find the median is to sort the list and then pick the middle number as the median if the list has an odd number of elements, or the average of the two middle numbers if the number of elements is even. Write a program to find the median of a list, so that the command

```
median FileName
```

will calculate and display the median of the values in file `FileName`, but the command

```
median
```

will calculate and display the median of a list of numbers entered from the keyboard.

17. Write a program so that the command

```
copy File1 File2
```

will make a copy of `File1` with the name `File2`.

18. Write a program so that the command

```
page File
```

will display the specified file on the screen, one page (23 lines) at a time, waiting between pages until the user presses some key.

ASCII CHARACTER SET

ASCII CODES OF CHARACTERS

Decimal	Octal	Character	Decimal	Octal	Character
0	000	NUL (Null)	29	035	GS (Group separator)
1	001	SOH (Start of heading)	30	036	RS (Record separator)
2	002	STX (Start of text)	31	037	US (Unit separator)
3	003	ETX (End of text)	32	040	SP (Space)
4	004	EOT (End of transmission)	33	041	!
5	005	ENQ (Enquiry)	34	042	"
6	006	ACK (Acknowledge)	35	043	#
7	007	BEL (Ring bell)	36	044	$
8	010	BS (Backspace)	37	045	%
9	011	HT (Horizontal tab)	38	046	&
10	012	LF (Line feed)	39	047	' (Single quote)
11	013	VT (Vertical tab)	40	050	(
12	014	FF (Form feed)	41	051	)
13	015	CR (Carriage return)	42	052	*
14	016	SO (Shift out)	43	053	+
15	017	SI (Shift in)	44	054	, Comma
16	020	DLE (Date link escape)	45	055	– (Hyphen)
17	021	DC1 (Device control 1)	46	056	. (Period)
18	022	DC2 (Device control 2)	47	057	/
19	023	DC3 (Device control 3)	48	060	0
20	024	DC4 (Device control 4)	49	061	1
21	025	NAK (Negative ACK)	50	062	2
22	026	SYN (Synchronous)	51	063	3
23	027	ETB (EOT block)	52	064	4
24	030	CAN (Cancel)	53	065	5
25	031	EM (End of medium)	54	066	6
26	032	SUB (Substitute)	55	067	7
27	033	ESC (Escape)	56	070	8
28	034	FS (File separator)	57	071	9

Decimal	Octal	Character	Decimal	Octal	Character
58	072	:	93	135	]
59	073	;	94	136	^
60	074	<	95	137	_ (Underscore)
61	075	=	96	140	`
62	076	>	97	141	a
63	077	?	98	142	b
64	100	@	99	143	c
65	101	A	100	144	d
66	102	B	101	145	e
67	103	C	102	146	f
68	104	D	103	147	g
69	105	E	104	150	h
70	106	F	105	151	i
71	107	G	106	152	j
72	110	H	107	153	k
73	111	I	108	154	l
74	112	J	109	155	m
75	113	K	110	156	n
76	114	L	111	157	o
77	115	M	112	160	p
78	116	N	113	161	q
79	117	O	114	162	r
80	120	P	115	163	s
81	121	Q	116	164	t
82	122	R	117	165	u
83	123	S	118	166	v
84	124	T	119	167	w
85	125	U	120	170	x
86	126	V	121	171	y
87	127	W	122	172	z
88	130	X	123	173	{
89	131	Y	124	174		
90	132	Z	125	175	}
91	133	[	126	176	~
92	134	\	127	177	DEL

B

C++ KEYWORDS

The following table lists all of the keywords in C++, together with a brief description of the context in which they usually appear.

Keyword	Contextual Description
asm	Used to declare that information is to be passed directly to the assembler
auto	Used to declare objects whose lifetime is the duration of control within their block
bool	Used to declare objects whose values are `true` or `false`
break	Used to terminate processing of a `switch` statement or loop
case	Used in a `switch` statement to specify a match for the statement's expression
catch	Used to specify the actions to be taken when an exception occurs (see `throw`, `try`)
char	Used to declare objects whose values are characters
class	Used to construct new types encapsulating data and operations (default `private`)
const	Used to declare objects whose values should not change during execution
const_cast	Used to add or remove the `const` or `volatile` property of a type
continue	Used in a loop statement to transfer control to the beginning of the loop
default	Used in a `switch` statement to handle expression values not specified using `case`
delete	Used to deallocate memory allocated at run-time, returning it to the free store
do	Used to mark the beginning of a `do-while` statement, providing repetitive control
double	Used to declare objects whose values are (double precision) real numbers
dynamic_cast	Used to cast pointer or reference types in a class hierarchy
else	Used in an `if` statement to mark the section to be executed if the condition is false
enum	Used to declare a type whose values are programmer-specified identifiers
explicit	Used to prevent constructors from being called implicitly for conversion purposes
extern	Used to declare objects whose definitions are external to the local block
false	A `bool` value
float	Used to declare objects whose values are (single precision) real numbers
for	Used to mark the beginning of a `for` statement, providing repetitive control
friend	Used to declare `class` operations that are not member functions
goto	Used to transfer control to a label
if	Used to mark the beginning of an `if` statement, providing selective control

inline	Used to declare a function whose text is to be substituted for its call
int	Used to declare objects whose values are integer numbers
long	Used to declare 32-bit integer, or extended double precision real numbers
mutable	Used to declare class data member as modifiable even in a const object
namespace	Used to a control the scope of global names (to avoid name conflicts)
new	Used to request memory allocation at run-time
operator	Used to overload an operator with a new declaration
private	Used to declare class members that are inaccessible from outside of the class
protected	Used to declare class members that are private, except to derived classes
public	Used to declare class members that can be accessed outside of the class
register	Used to declare objects whose values are to be kept in registers
reinterpret_cast	Used to perform type conversions on unrelated types
return	Used to terminate a function, usually returning the value of some expression
short	Used to declare 16-bit integer numbers
signed	Used to declare an object in which the value's *sign* is stored in the high order bit
sizeof	Used to find the size (in bytes) of an object, or of the representation of a type
static	Used to declare objects whose lifetime is the duration of the program
static_cast	Used to convert one type to another type
struct	Used to construct new types encapsulating data and operations (default public)
switch	Used to mark the beginning of a switch statement, providing selective control
template	Used to declare type-independent classes or functions
this	Used within a class member to unambiguously access other members of the class
throw	Used to generate an exception (see catch, try)
true	A bool value
try	Used to mark the beginning of a block containing exception handlers (see catch)
typedef	Used to declare a name as a synonym for an existing type
typeid	Used to obtain type information during run time
typename	Can be used instead of class in template parameter lists and to identify qualified names as types
union	Used to declare a structure, such that different objects can have different members
unsigned	Used to declare an object in which the high-order bit is used for data (see signed)
using	Used to access members of a namespace
virtual	Used to declare a base-class function, that will be defined by a derived class
void	Used as to indicate the absence of any type
volatile	Used to declare objects whose values may be modified by means undetectable to the compiler (such as shared-memory objects of concurrent processes)
while	Used to mark the beginning of a while statement, as well as the end of a do-while statement, each of which provides repetitive control

C++ Operators

The following table lists all of the operators available in C++, ordered by their precedence levels, from highest to lowest—higher precedence operators are applied before lower precedence operators. Operators in the same horizontal band of the table have equal precedence. The table also gives each operator's associativity—in an expression containing operators of equal precedence, associativity determines which is applied first—whether they can be overloaded, their arity (number of operands), and a brief description.

Operator	Associativity	Overloadable	Arity	Description
`::`	right	no	unary	global scope
`::`	left	no	binary	class scope
`.`	left	no	binary	direct member selection
`->`	left	yes	binary	indirect member selection
`[]`	left	yes	binary	subscript (array index)
`()`	left	yes	n/a	function call
`()`	left	yes	n/a	type construction
`sizeof`	right	n/a	unary	size (in bytes) of an object or type
`++`	right	yes	unary	increment
`--`	right	yes	unary	decrement
`~`	right	yes	unary	bitwise NOT
`!`	right	yes	unary	logical NOT
`+`	right	yes	unary	plus (sign)
`-`	right	yes	unary	minus (sign)
`*`	right	yes	unary	pointer dereferencing
`&`	right	yes	unary	get address of an object
`new`	right	yes	unary	memory allocation
`delete`	right	yes	unary	memory deallocation
`()`	right	yes	binary	type conversion (cast)
`.`	left	no	binary	direct member pointer selection
`->`	left	yes	binary	indirect member pointer selection
`*`	left	yes	binary	multiplication
`/`	left	yes	binary	division
`%`	left	yes	binary	modulus (remainder)
`+`	left	yes	binary	addition
`-`	left	yes	binary	subtraction

Operator	Associativity	Overloadable	Arity	Description
<<	left	yes	binary	bit-shift left
>>	left	yes	binary	bit-shift right
<	left	yes	binary	less-than
<=	left	yes	binary	less-than-or-equal
>	left	yes	binary	greater-than
>=	left	yes	binary	greater-than-or-equal
==	left	yes	binary	equality
!=	left	yes	binary	inequality
&	left	yes	binary	bitwise AND
^	left	yes	binary	bitwise XOR
|	left	yes	binary	bitwise OR
&&	left	yes	binary	logical AND
||	left	yes	binary	logical OR
? :	left	no	ternary	conditional expression
=	right	yes	binary	assignment
+=	right	yes	binary	addition-assignment shortcut
-=	right	yes	binary	subtraction-assignment shortcut
*=	right	yes	binary	multiplication-assignment shortcut
/=	right	yes	binary	division-assignment shortcut
%=	right	yes	binary	modulus-assignment shortcut
&=	right	yes	binary	bitwise-AND-assignment shortcut
|=	right	yes	binary	bitwise-OR-assignment shortcut
^=	right	yes	binary	bitwise-XOR-assignment shortcut
<<=	right	yes	binary	bitshift-left-assignment shortcut
>>=	right	yes	binary	bitshift-right-assignment shortcut
throw	right	yes	unary	throw an exception
,	left	yes	binary	expression separation

D

LIBRARIES AND CLASSES

C LIBRARIES

Many of the C++ libraries were originally C libraries. The following describes some of the most useful items in the more commonly used libraries.

assert.h (OR cassert)

`void assert(bool expr)`	Tests the boolean expression `expr` and if it is true, allows execution to proceed. If it is false, execution is terminated and an error message is displayed.

ctype.h (OR cctype)

`int isalnum(int c)`	Returns true if `c` is a letter or a digit, `false` otherwise
`int isalpha(int c)`	Returns true if `c` is a letter, `false` otherwise
`int iscntrl(int c)`	Returns true if `c` is a control character, `false` otherwise
`int isdigit(int c)`	Returns true if `c` is a decimal digit, `false` otherwise
`int isgraph(int c)`	Returns true if `c` is a printing character except space, `false` otherwise
`int islower(int c)`	Returns true if `c` is lowercase, `false` otherwise
`int isprint(int c)`	Returns true if `c` is a printing character including space, `false` otherwise
`int ispunct(int c)`	Returns true if `c` is a punctuation character (not a space, an alphabetic character, or a digit), `false` otherwise
`int isspace(int c)`	Returns true if `c` is a white space character (space, `'\f'`, `'\n'`, `'\r'`, `'\t'`, or `'\v'`), `false` otherwise
`int isupper(int c)`	Returns true if `c` is uppercase, `false` otherwise
`int isxdigit(int c)`	Returns true if `c` is a hexadecimal digit, `false` otherwise

`int tolower(int c)`	Returns uppercase equivalent of `c` (if `c` is lowercase)
`int toupper(int c)`	Returns the lowercase equivalent of `c` (if `c` is uppercase)

float.h (OR cfloat)

The following constants specify the minimum value in the specified floating-point type.

FLT_MIN ($\leq -1E+37$)	`float`
DBL_MIN ($\leq -1E+37$)	`double`
LDBL_MIN ($\leq -1E+37$)	`long double`

The following constants specify the maximum value in the specified floating-point type.

FLT_MAX ($\geq 1E+37$)	`float`
DBL_MAX ($\geq 1E+37$)	`double`
LDBL_MAX ($\geq 1E+37$)	`long double`

The following constants specify the smallest positive value representable in the specified floating-point type.

FLT_EPSILON ($\leq 1E-37$)	`float`
DBL_EPSILON ($\leq 1E-37$)	`double`
LDBL_EPSILON ($\leq 1E-37$)	`long double`

limits.h (OR climits)

The following constants specify the minimum and maximum values for the specified type.

SCHAR_MIN (≤ -127)	`signed char`
SCHAR_MAX (≥ 127)	`signed char`
UCHAR_MAX (≥ 255)	`unsigned char`
CHAR_MIN (0 or SCHAR_MIN)	`char`
CHAR_MAX (SCHAR_MAX or USHRT_MAX)	`char`
SHRT_MIN (≤ -32767)	`short int`
SHRT_MAX (≥ 32767)	`short int`
USHRT_MAX (≥ 65535)	`unsigned short int`
INT_MIN (≤ -32767)	`int`
INT_MAX (≥ 32767)	`int`
UINT_MAX (≥ 65535)	`unsigned int`
LONG_MIN (≤ -2147483647)	`long int`
LONG_MAX (≥ 2147483647)	`long int`
ULONG_MAX (≥ 4294967295)	`unsigned long int`

math.h (OR cmath)

`double acos(double x)`	Returns the angle in $[0, \pi]$ (in radians) whose cosine is `x`

`double asin(double x)`	Returns the angle in $[-\pi/2, \pi/2]$ (in radians) whose sine is `x`
`double atan(double x)`	Returns the angle in $(-\pi/2, \pi/2)$ (in radians) whose tangent is `x`
`double atan2(double y)`	Returns the angle in $(-\pi, \pi]$ (in radians) whose tangent is `y/x`
`double ceil(double x)`	Returns the least integer $\geq$ `x`
`double cos(double x)`	Returns the cosine of `x` (radians)
`double cosh(double x)`	Returns the hyperbolic cosine of `x`
`double exp(double x)`	Returns e^x
`double fabs(double x)`	Returns the absolute value of x
`double floor(double x)`	Returns the greatest integer $\leq$ `x`
`double fmod(double x, double y)`	Returns the integer remainder of `x / y`
`double frexp(double x, int & ex)`	Returns value `v` in $[\frac{1}{2}, 1]$ and passes back `expo` such that `x` = `v * ` 2^{ex}
`double ldexp(double x, int ex)`	Returns `x * ` 2^{ex}
`double log(double x)`	Returns natural logarithm of `x`
`double log10(double x)`	Returns base-ten logarithm of `x`
`double modf(double x, double & ip)`	Returns fractional part of `x` and passes back `ip` = the integer part of `x`
`double pow(double x, double y)`	Returns `x`^{y}
`double sin(double x)`	Returns the sine of `x` (radians)
`double sinh(double x)`	Returns the hyperbolic sine of `x`
`double sqrt(double x)`	Returns the square root of `x` (provided `x` $\geq$ 0)
`double tan(double x)`	Returns the tangent of `x` (radians)
`double tanh(double x)`	Returns the hyperbolic tangent of `x`

stdlib.h (OR cstdlib)

`int abs(int i)` `long abs(long li)`	`abs(i)` and `labs(li)` return the `int` and `long int` absolute value of `i` and `li`, respectively
`double atof(char s[])` `int atoi(char s[])` `long atol(char s[])`	`atof(s)`, `atoi(s)`, and `atol(s)` return the value obtained by converting the character string `s` to `double`, `int`, and `long int`, respectively
`void exit(int status)`	Terminates program execution and returns control to the operating system; `status` = 0 signals successful termination and any nonzero value signals unsuccessful termination

`int rand()`	Returns a pseudorandom integer in the range 0 to `RAND_MAX`
`RAND_MAX`	An integer constant (≥ 32767) which is the maximum value returned by `rand()`
`void srand(int seed)`	Uses `seed` to initialize the sequence of pseudo-random numbers returned by `rand()`
`int system(char s[])`	Passes the string `s` to the operating system to be executed as a command and returns an implementation-dependent value.

THE `string` CLASS

The `string` class, which was described in Chapter 4, is defined by

```
typedef basic_string<char> string;
```

The unsigned integer type `size_type` is defined in this class as is an integer constant `npos`, which is some integer that is either negative or greater than the number of characters in a string. The following is a list of the major operations defined on a `string` object `s`; `pos`, `pos1`, `pos2`, `n`, `n1`, and `n2` are of type `size_type`; `str`, `str1`, and `str2` are of type `string`; `charArray` is a character array; `ch` and `delim` are of type `char`; `istr` is an `istream`; `ostr` is an `ostream`; `it1` and `it2` are iterators; and `inpIt1` and `inpIt2` are input iterators. All of these operations except `>>`, `<<`, `+`, the relational operators, `getline()`, and the second version of `swap()` are member functions.

Constructors:

`string s;`	This declaration invokes the default constructor to construct `s` as an empty string
`string s(charArray);`	This declaration initializes `s` to contain a copy of `charArray`
`string s(charArray, n);`	This declaration initializes `s` to contain a copy of the first `n` characters in `charArray`
`string s(str);`	This declaration initializes `s` to contain a copy of string `str`
`string s(str, pos, n);`	This declaration initializes `s` to contain a copy of the `n` characters in string `str`, starting at position `pos`; if `n` is too large, characters are copied only to the end of `str`
`string s(n, ch);`	This declaration initializes `s` to contain `n` copies of the character `ch`
`string s(inpIt1, inpIt2)`	This declaration initializes `s` to contain the characters in the range [`inpIt1`, `inpIt2`)
`getline(istr, s, delim)`	Extracts characters from `istr` and stores them in `s` until `s.max_size()` characters have been exracted, the end of file occurs, or `delim` is encountered, in which case `delim` is extracted from `istr` but is not stored in `s`

`getline(istr, s)`	Inputs a string value for s as in the preceding function with `delim = '\n'`
`istr >> s`	Extracts characters from `istr` and stores them in s until `s.max_size()` characters have been extracted, the end of file occurs, or a white-space character is encountered, in which case the white-space character is not removed from `istr`; returns `istr`
`ostr << s`	Inserts characters of s into `ostr`; returns `ostr`
`s = val`	Assigns a copy of `val` to s; `val` may be a string, a character array, or a character
`s += val`	Appends a copy of `val` to s; `val` may be a string, a character array, or a character
`s[pos]`	Returns a reference to the character stored in s at position `pos`, provided `pos < s.length()`
`s + t` `t + s`	Returns the result of concatenating s and t; t may be a string, a character array, or a character.

`s < t,  t < s`
`s <= t,  t <= s`
`s > t,  t > s`
`s >= t,  t >= s`
`s == t,  t == s`
`s != t,  t != s`
	Returns `true` or `false` as determined by the relational operator; t may be a string or a character array

`s.append(str)`	Appends string `str` at the end of s; returns s
`s.append(str, pos, n)`	Appends at the end of s a copy of the n characters in `str`, starting at position `pos`; if n is too large, characters are copied only until the end of `str` is reached; returns s
`s.append(charArray)`	Appends `charArray` at the end of s; returns s
`s.append(charArray, n)`	Appends the first n characters in `charArray` at the end of s; returns s
`s.append(n, ch)`	Appends n copies of `ch` at the end of s; returns s
`s.append(inpIt1, inpIt2)`	Appends copies of the characters in the range `[inpIt1, inpIt2)` to s; returns s
`s.assign(str)`	Assigns a copy of `str` to s; returns s
`s.assign(str, pos, n)`	Assigns to s a copy of the n characters in `str`, starting at position `pos`; if n is too large, characters are copied only until the end of `str` is reached; returns s
`s.assign(charArray)`	Assigns to s a copy of `charArray`; returns s
`s.assign(charArray, n)`	Assigns to s a string consisting of the first n characters in `charArray`; returns s
`s.assign(n, ch)`	Assigns to s a string consisting of n copies of `ch`; returns s

`s.assign(inpIt1, inpIt2)`	Assigns to `s` a string consisting of the characters in the range [`inpIt1, inpIt2`); returns `s`
`s.at(pos)`	Returns `s[pos]`
`s.begin()`	Returns an iterator positioned at the first character in `s`
`s.c_str()`	Returns (the base address of) a `char` array containing the characters stored in `s`, terminated by a null character
`s.capacity()`	Returns the size (of type `size_type`) of the storage allocated in `s`
`s.clear()`	Removes all the characters in `s`; return type is `void`
`s.compare(str)`	Returns a negative value, 0, or a positive value according as `s` is less than, equal to, or greater than `str`
`s.compare(charArray)`	Compares `s` and `charArray` as in the preceding function member
`s.compare(pos, n, str)`	Compares strings `s` and `str` as before, but starts at position `pos` in `s` and compares only the next `n` characters
`s.compare(pos, n, charArray)`	Compares string `s` and `charArray` as in the preceding function member
`s.compare(pos1, n1, str, pos2, n2)`	Compares `s` and `str` as before, but starts at position `pos1` in `s`, position `pos2` in `str`, and compares only the next `n1` characters in `s` and the next `n2` characters in `str`
`s.compare(pos1, n1, charArray, n2)`	Compares strings `s` and `charArray` as before, but using only the first `n2` characters in `charArray`
`s.copy(charArray, pos, n)`	Replaces the string in `s` with `n` characters in `charArray`, starting at position `pos` or at position 0, if `pos` is omitted; if `n` is too large, characters are copied only until the end of `charArray` is reached; returns the number (of type `size_type`) of characters copied
`s.data()`	Returns a `char` array containing the characters stored in `s`, terminated by a null character.
`s.empty()`	Returns `true` if `s` contains no characters, `false` otherwise
`s.end()`	Returns an iterator positioned immediately after the last character in `s`
`s.erase(pos, n)`	Removes `n` characters from `s`, beginning at position `pos` (default value 0); if `n` is too large or is omitted, characters are erased only to the end of `s`; returns `s`

`s.erase(it)`	Removes the character at the position specified by `it`; returns an iterator positioned immediately after the erased character
`s.find(str, pos)`	Returns the first position $\geq$ `pos` such that the next `str.size()` characters of `s` match those in `str`; returns `npos` if there is no such position; 0 is the default value for `pos`
`s.find(ch, pos)`	Searches `s` as in the preceding function member, but for `ch`
`s.find(charArray, pos)`	Searches `s` as in the preceding function member, but for the characters in `charArray`
`s.find(charArray, pos, n)`	Searches `s` as in the preceding function member, but for the first `n` characters in `charArray`; the value `pos` must be given
`s.find_first_not_of(str, pos)`	Returns the first position $\geq$ `pos` of a character in `s` that does not match any of the characters in `str`; returns `npos` if there is no such position; 0 is the default value for `pos`
`s.find_first_not_of(ch, pos)`	Searches `s` as in the preceding function member, but for `ch`
`s.find_first_not_of (charArray, pos)`	Searches `s` as in the preceding function member, but for the characters in `charArray`
`s.find_first_not_of (charArray, pos, n)`	Searches `s` as in the preceding function member, but using the first `n` characters in `charArray`; the value `pos` must be given
`s.find_first_of(str, pos)`	Returns the first position $\geq$ `pos` of a character in `s` that matches any character in `str`; returns `npos` if there is no such position; 0 is the default value for `pos`
`s.find_first_of(ch, pos)`	Searches `s` as in the preceding function member, but for `ch`
`s.find_first_of(charArray, pos)`	Searches `s` as in the preceding function member, but for the characters in `charArray`
`s.find_first_of(charArray, pos, n)`	Searches `s` as in the preceding function member, but using the first `n` characters in `charArray`; the value `pos` must be given
`s.find_last_not_of(str, pos)`	Returns the highest position $\leq$ `pos` of a character in `s` that does not match any character in `str`; returns `npos` if there is no such position; `npos` is the default value for `pos`
`s.find_last_not_of(ch, pos)`	Searches `s` as in the preceding function member, but for `ch`
`s.find_last_not_of (charArray, pos)`	Searches `s` as in the preceding function member, but using the characters in `charArray`

`s.find_last_not_of` `(charArray, pos, n)`	Searches s as in the preceding function member, but using the first n characters in `charArray`; the value `pos` must be given
`s.find_last_of(str, pos)`	Returns the highest position ≤ pos of a character in s that matches any character in `str`; returns `npos` if there is no such position; `npos` is the default value for `pos`
`s.find_last_of(ch, pos)`	Searches s as in the preceding function member, but for `ch`
`s.find_last_of(charArray,` `pos)`	Searches s as in the preceding function member, but using the characters in `charArray`
`s.find_last_of(charArray,` `pos, n)`	Searches s as in the preceding function member, but using the first n characters in `charArray`; the value `pos` must be given
`s.insert(pos, str)`	Inserts a copy of `str` into s at position `pos`; returns s
`s.insert(pos1, str,` `pos2, n)`	Inserts a copy of n characters of `str` starting at position `pos2` into s at position `pos`; if n is too large, characters are copied only until the end of `str` is reached; returns s
`s.insert(pos, charArray, n)`	Inserts a copy of the first n characters of `charArray` into s at position `pos`; inserts all of its characters if n is omitted; returns s
`s.insert(pos, n, ch)`	Inserts n copies of the character `ch` into s at position `pos`; returns s
`s.insert(it, ch)`	Inserts a copy of the character `ch` into s at the position specified by `it` and returns an iterator positioned at this copy
`s.insert(it, n, ch)`	Inserts n copies of the character `ch` into s at the position specified by `it`; return type is `void`
`s.insert(it, inpIt1,` `inpIt2)`	Inserts copies of the characters in the range [`inpIt1, inpIt2`) into s at the position specified by `It`; return type is `void`
`s.length()`	Returns the length (of type `size_type`) of s
`s.max_size()`	Returns the maximum length (of type `size_type`) of s
`s.rbegin()`	Returns a reverse iterator positioned at the last character in s
`s.rend()`	Returns a reverse iterator positioned immediately before the first character in s
`s.replace(pos1, n1, str)`	Replaces the substring of s of length n1 beginning at position `pos1` with `str`; if n1 is too large, all characters to the end of s are replaced; returns s

`s.replace(it1, it2, str)`	Same as the preceding but for the substring of s consisting of the characters in the range [`it1`, `it2`); returns s
`s.replace(pos1, n1,)` `       str, pos2, n2)`	Replaces a substring of s as in the preceding reference but using n2 characters in `str`, beginning at position pos2; if n2 is too large, characters to the end of `str` are used; returns s
`s.replace(pos1, n1,)` `       charArray, n2)`	Replaces a substring of s as before but with the first n2 characters in `charArray`; if n2 is too large, characters to the end of `charArray` are used; if n2 is omitted, all of `charArray` is used; returns s
`s.replace(it1, it2,` `       charArray, n2)`	Same as the preceding but for the substring of s consisting of the characters in the range [`it1`, `it2`); returns s
`s.replace(pos1, n1, n2, ch)`	Replaces a substring of s as before but with n2 copies of `ch`
`s.replace(it1, it2, n2, ch)`	Same as the preceding but for the substring of s consisting of the characters in the range [`it1`, `it2`); returns s
`s.replace(it1, it2,` `       inpIt1, inpIt2)`	Same as the preceding, but replaces with copies of the characters in the range [`inpIt1`, `inpIt2`); returns s
`s.reserve(n)`	Changes the storage allocation for s so that `s.capacity()` $\geq$ n, 0 if n is omitted; return type is `void`
`s.resize(n, ch)`	If n $\leq$ `s.size()`, truncates rightmost characters in s to make it of size n; otherwise, adds copies of character `ch` to end of s to increase its size to n, or adds a default character value (usually a blank) if `ch` is omitted; return type is `void`
`s.rfind(str, pos)`	Returns the highest position $\leq$ pos such that the next `str.size()` characters of s match those in `str`; returns npos if there is no such position; npos is the default value for pos
`s.rfind(ch, pos)`	Searches s as in the preceding function member, but for `ch`
`s.rfind(charArray, pos)`	Searches s as in the preceding function member, but for the characters in `charArray`
`s.rfind(charArray, pos, n)`	Searches s as in the preceding function member, but for the first n characters in `charArray`; the value pos must be given
`s.size()`	Returns the length (of type `size_type`) of s

`s.substr(pos, n)`	Returns a copy of the substring consisting of n characters from s, beginning at position `pos` (default value 0); if n is too large or is omitted, characters are copied only until the end of s is reached
`s.swap(str)`	Swaps the contents of s and `str`; return type is `void`
`swap(str1, str2)`	Swaps the contents of `str1` and `str2`; return type is `void`

THE `list<T>` CLASS TEMPLATE

The `list<T>` class template from the Standard Template Library (STL) was introduced in Chapter 13. The following is a list of the operations defined on `list<T>` objects; n is of type `size_type`; l, l1, and l2 are of type `list<T>`; val, val1, and val2 are of type T; ptr1 and ptr2 are pointers to values of type T; it1 and it2 are iterators; and inpIt1, and inpIt2 are input iterators.

Constructors:

`list<T> l;`	This declaration invokes the default constructor to construct l as an empty list
`list<T> l(n);`	This declaration initializes l to contain n default values of type T
`list<T> l(n, val);`	This declaration initializes l to contain n copies of val
`list<T> l(ptr1, ptr2)`	This declaration initializes s to contain the copies of all the T values in the range [ptr1, ptr2)
`list<T> l(l1);`	This declaration initializes l to contain a copy of l1
`l = l1`	Assigns a copy of l1 to l
`l1 == l2`	Returns `true` if l and l2 contain the same values, and `false` otherwise
`l1 < l2`	Returns `true` if l1 is lexicographically less than l2—l1.size() is less than l2.size() and all the elements of l1 match the first elements of l2; or if val1 and val2 are the first elements of l1 and l2, respectively, that are different, val1 is less than val2—and it returns `false` otherwise
`l.assign(n, val)`	Erases l and then inserts n copies of val (default T value if omitted)
`l.assign(inpIt1, inpIt2)`	Erases l and then inserts copies of the T values in the range [inpIt1, inpIt2)
`l.back()`	Returns a reference to the last element of l
`l.begin()`	Returns an iterator positioned at the first element of l
`l.empty()`	Returns `true` if l contains no elements, `false` otherwise

`l.end()`	Returns an iterator positioned immediately after the last element of `l`
`l.erase(it)`	Removes from `l` the element at the position specifed by `it`; return type is `void`
`l.erase(it1, it2)`	Removes from `l` the elements in the range [`it1, it2`); return type is `void`
`l.front()`	Returns a reference to the first element of `l`
`l.insert(it, val)`	Inserts a copy of `val` (default `T` value if omitted) into `l` at the position specified by `it` and returns an iterator positioned at this copy
`l.insert(it, n, val)`	Inserts `n` copies of `val` into `l` at the position specified by `it`; return type is `void`
`l.insert(it, inpIt1, inpIt2)`	Inserts inserts copies of the `T` values in the range [`inpIt1, inpIt2`) into `l` at the position specified by `it`; return type is `void`
`l.insert(ptr1, ptr2)`	Inserts copies of all the `T` values in the range [`ptr1, ptr2`) at the position specified by `it`; return type is `void`
`l.max_size()`	Returns the maximum number (of type `size_type`) of values that `l` can contain
`l.merge(l1)`	Merges the elements of `l1` into `l` so that the resulting list is sorted; both `l` and `l1` must have been already sorted (using `<`); return type is `void`
`l.push_back(val)`	Adds a copy of `val` at the end of `l`; return type is `void`
`l.push_front(val)`	Adds a copy of `val` at the front of `l`; return type is `void`
`l.pop_back()`	Removes the last element of `l`; return type is `void`
`l.pop_front()`	Removes the first element of `l`; return type is `void`
`l.rbegin()`	Returns a reverse iterator positioned at the last element of `l`
`l.remove(val)`	Removes all occurrences of `val` from `l`, using `==` to compare elements; return type is `void`
`l.rend()`	Returns a reverse iterator positioned immediately before the first element of `l`
`l.resize(n, val)`	Sets the size of `l` to n; if $n > l.size()$, copies of `val` (default `T` value if omitted) are appended to `l`; if $n < l.size()$, the appropriate number of elements is removed from the end of `l`
`l.reverse()`	Reverses the order of the elements of `l`; return type is `void`
`l.size()`	Returns the number (of type `size_type`) of elements `l` contains

`l.sort()`	Sorts the elements of `l` using `<`; return type is `void`
`l.splice(it, ll)`	Removes the elements of `ll` and inserts them into `l` at the position specified by `it`; return type is `void`
`l.splice(it, ll, it1)`	Removes the element of `ll` at the position specified by `it1` and inserts it into `l` at the position specified by `it`; return type is `void`
`l.splice(it, ll, it1, it2)`	Removes the elements of `ll` in the range `[it1, it2)` and inserts them into `l` at the position specified by `it`; return type is `void`
`l.swap(ll)`	Swaps the contents of `l` and `ll`; return type is `void`
`l.unique()`	Replaces all repeating sequences of an element of `l` with a single occurence of that element; return type is `void`

ANSWERS TO QUICK QUIZZES

QUICK QUIZ 1.3

1.	program	**2.**	comment
3.	curly braces, main	**4.**	`return`
5.	Design Coding Testing, execution, and debugging Maintenance	**6.**	State program's behavior Identify the objects Identify the operations Arrange operations in an algorithm
7.	objects	**8.**	operations
9.	variables	**10.**	`cout`, `ostream`
11.	`cin`, `istream`	**12.**	`<<`, `>>`
13.	debugging	**14.**	syntax errors and logic errors

QUICK QUIZ 2.2

1.	integers, integer variations, reals, characters, booleans	**2.**	`short`, `int`, `unsigned`
3.	`float`, `double`, `long double`	**4.**	literal
5.	false	**6.**	true
7.	true	**8.**	single quotes
9.	false	**10.**	true
11.	escape	**12.**	double quotes
13.	`'\n'`	**14.**	not legal—must begin with a letter
15.	legal	**16.**	not legal—identifiers may contain only letters, digits, and underscores
17.	not legal—same reason as 16	**18.**	integer
19.	neither	**20.**	real
21.	real	**22.**	neither
23.	real	**24.**	integer
25.	neither	**26.**	character
27.	cneither	**28.**	string
29.	string	**30.**	character
31.	character	**32.**	character
33.	neither	**34.**	`const int gravity = 32;`

35.	`const double`
	`    EARTH = 1.5E10,`
	`    MARS = 1.2E12;`
		36.	`int distanceTraveled;`

37.	`unsigned idNumber;`
	`float salary;`
	`char employeeCode;`
		38.	`int distanceTraveled = 0;`

39.	`unsigned idNumber = 9999;`
	`float salary = 0;`
	`char employeeCode = ' ';`		

QUICK QUIZ 2.3

1.	0	**2.**	2.6
3.	2	**4.**	5
5.	8	**6.**	3
7.	2	**8.**	36.0
9.	3.0	**10.**	8.0

11.	2.0		**12.**	3.0
13.	11.0		**14.**	1
15.	7.0		**16.**	5.1
17.	8.0		**18.**	10.0
19.	3.0		**20.**	32.0
21.	`10 + 5 * B - 4 * A * C`		**22.**	`sqrt(A + 3 * pow(B, 2))`

QUICK QUIZ 2.4

1. `false, true`

2. `<, >, ==, <=, >=, !=`

3. `!, &&, ||`

4. `false`

5. `true`

6. `false`

7. `false`

8. `true`

9. `true`

10. `true`

11. `true`

12. `true` (for all values of `count`)

13. `true`

14. `x != 0`

15. `-10 < x && x < 10`

16. `(x > 0 && y > 0) ||`
`(x < 0 && y < 0)`
or more simply,
`x * y > 0`

QUICK QUIZ 2.5

1. single quotes

2. `false`

3. `true`

4. `assert`
`('0' <= c && c <= '9');`

5. `assert(isdigit(c));`

6. `assert`
`(c == 'a' || c = 'A' ||`
`c == 'e' || c = 'E' ||`
`c == 'i' || c = 'I' ||`
`c == 'o' || c = 'O' ||`
`c == 'u' || c = 'U');`

QUICK QUIZ 2.6

1. valid

2. not valid—variable must be left of assignment operator

3. valid

4. not valid—variable must be left of assignment operator

5. valid

6. not valid—can't assign a string to an integer variable

7. valid

8. not valid—`'65'` is not a legal character constant

9. valid

10. valid

11. valid

12. valid

13. valid

14. not valid—no assignment operator

15. not valid—`++` can only be used with integer variables

16. `xValue: 3.5`

17. `xValue: 6.1`

18. `jobId: 6`

19. `xValue: 5.0`

20. `jobId: 1`

21. `jobId: 5`
`intFive1: 6`

22. `jobId: 6`
`intFive2: 6`

23. `intEight: 64`

24. `letter: a`

25. `check: true`

26. `distance = rate * time;`

27. `c = sqrt(a*a + b*b);`

28. `++x;`
`x++;`
`x += 1;`
`x = x + 1;`

QUICK QUIZ 2.8

1. streams

2. `true`

3. `cin, istream`

4. `cout, cerr, ostream`

5. `>>`

6. `<<`

7. `cin`

8. `cout`

9. right

10. format manipulators

11. `12323.4568`

12.   ← blank line
`␣␣123124␣␣125127`

13.
```
⎵⎵⎵⎵⎵23.
⎵⎵⎵⎵23.5
⎵⎵⎵23.46
⎵⎵⎵23.46
23.5
```

14.
```
number1:  11
number2:  22
number3:  33
```

15.
```
real1:  1.1
real2:  2.0
real3:  3.3
```

16.
```
number1:  1
Input error:  attempting to read a
period for integer variable
```

17.
```
number1:    1
real1:      .1
number2:    2
real2:      3.3
number3:    4
real3:      5.5
```

QUICK QUIZ 3.2

1. objects received from the calling function
objects returned to the calling function

2. parameters

3. double

4. void

5. no statements

6. argument

7. 6

8. true

9. false

10. `int What(int n);`

11.
```
#include <math.h>
double Func(double x)
{
    return x*x + sqrt(x);
}
```

12.
```
int Average(int num1,
int num2)
{
    return (num1 + num2)
    / 2;
}
```

13.
```
void Display(int num1,
int num2, int num3)
{
    cout << num1
          << "\n\n\n"
          << num2
          << "\n\n\n"
          << num1
          << endl;
}
```

QUICK QUIZ 3.3

1. 6

2. 5

3. 6

4. 10

5. 10

6. 10

7. excellent

8. excellent

9. good

10. fair

11. bad

12.
```
if (number < 0 ||
    number > 100)
    cout <<
    "Out of range\n";
```

13.
```
if (x < 1.5)
    n = 1;
else if (x < 2.5)
    n = 2;
else
    n = 3;
```

QUICK QUIZ 3.4

1.
```
Hello
Hello
Hello
Hello
Hello
```

2. `HelloHelloHello`

3.
```
Hello
Hello
Hello
```

4.
```
1 2
2 3
3 4
4 5
5 6
6 7
```

5.
```
36
25
16
9
4
1
```

6. `Hello`

7. No output produced.

8.
```
1
3
5
7
9
```

9. 25

10. A pretest loop checks the termination condition at the top of the loop; a posttest loop checks it at the bottom.

11. false

12. true

13.
```
1
2
4
8
16
32
64
```

14. **(a)** 0   **(b)** no output produced
```
1
2
3
4
```

15. **(a)** 0   **(b)** 0
```
1
2
3
4
```

QUICK QUIZ 3.6

1. false

2. header (or interface), implementation, and documentation

3. 1. Functions in a library are reusable.
3. They make programs easier to maintain.
5. They support independent coding.
2. They hide implementation details.
4. They provide separate compilation.
6. They simplify testing.

4. header (or interface)

5. implementation

6. header

7. public, private

8. `<lib>`

9. `"lib"`

10. compilation and linking

11. false

12. true

13. Information hiding

QUICK QUIZ 4.2

1. encapsulation

2. data, function

3. overloading

4. dot

5. `month, day, year`

6. `Display()`

7. `birth.Display();`

QUICK QUIZ 4.3

1. Bjarne Stroustrup

2. Jerry Schwarz

3. `istream` and `ostream`

4. stream

5. `istream`

6. `cin`

7. good, bad, and fail

8. `good()`

9. `clear()`

10. `ignore()`

11. true

12. false

13. `ostream`

14. `cout, cerr`

15. `endl, flush`

16. false

17. true

QUICK QUIZ 4.4

1. empty

2. `string label;`

3. `const string`
`    UNITS = "meters";`

4. `"ABC","DEF"`

5. `'e'`

6. 8

7. 0	**8.** false
9. true	**10.** true
11. false	**12.** "seashoreshell"
13. "she"	**14.** 10
15. 27	**16.** 12
17. 29	**18.** 0
19. 35	**20.** "bell"
21. "seal on the shore"	**22.** "She sells the seashore."

QUICK QUIZ 5.4

1. 198	**2.** 198 98 default
3. default	**4.** default
5. -2	**6.** -2 default
7. 123	**8.** 456
9. no output produced	**10.** error—x must be integer (or integer-compatible)

QUICK QUIZ 6.4

1. counting (or counter-controlled) loops, for	**2.** initialization expression, loop condition, step expression, loop body
3. if-break (or if-return)	**4.** pretest
5. posttest	**6.** posttest
7. pretest	**8.** 2*0 = 0 2*1 = 2 2*2 = 4 2*3 = 6 2*4 = 8 2*5 = 10 2*6 = 12 2*7 = 14 2*8 = 16 2*9 = 18
9. 1 3 5 7 9 11	**10.** 11 22 1 33 2 1
11. 000 112 228 18	**12.** 4 5 6
13. 3 2 1 0 -1	**14.** 0 1 1 2 2 5 3 10 4 17
15. ***** 4 12 3 5 2 0 1 -3	

QUICK QUIZ 6.6

1. sentinel, counting, query-controlled	**2.** end-of-data flag, sentinel
3. true	**4.** end-of-file (or eof)
5. eof()	**6.** false
7. false	**8.** query

QUICK QUIZ 7.3

1. value	**2.** value
3. value	**4.** reference

5. ampersand (&)
7. true
9. false
11.
```
void F(const int & x,
       int & y, int & z)
{
   z = y = x * x + 1;
}
```

6. false
8. false
10. false
12. `String = batbatelk`

Quick Quiz 7.4

1. true
3. That it replace each call to this function with the body of the function, with the arguments for that function call substituted for the function's parameters.
5. header (or interface)
7. false

2. `inline`
4.
```
cout << number *
        (number + 1) / 2;
```

6. true

Quick Quiz 7.5

1. scope
3. end of the block
5. a scope error message (perhaps a warning) indicating that i in the last line is not declared
7. name
9. template
11. Generate an instance of `Print()` with type parameter `something` replaced everywhere by `int`.

2. false
4. the body of the function
6. signature

8. signature
10. type

Quick Quiz 7.6

1. recursion
2. 1. An anchor or base case that specifies the function's value for one or more values of the parameter(s).

3. true
5. 0
7. infinite recursion results

2. 2. An inductive or recursive step that defines the function's value for the current values of the parameter(s) in terms of previously defined function and/or parameter values

4. 15
6. 0

Quick Quiz 8.2

1. `istream, cin`
3. `istream`
5. `fstream`
7.
```
ifstream inputStream;
inputStream.open
   ("EmployeeInfo");
```
9.
```
ofstream outputStream;
outputStream.open
   ("EmployeeReport");
```
11.
```
string inFileName,
       outFileName;
cout <<
  "Name of input file? ";
cin >> inFileName;
ifstream inputStream;
inputStream.open
  (inFileName.data());
```
or replace the last two lines with:
```
ifstream inputStream
  (inFileName.data());
```

2. `ostream,  cout` (or `cerr`)
4. `ostream`
6. false
8.
```
ifstream inputStream
   ("EmployeeInfo");
```
10.
```
ofstream outputStream
   ("EmployeeReport");
```

12. false
13. true
14. ```
    assert
      (inputStream.is_open());
    ```
15. ```
    get_line
      (inputStream, str);
    ```
    where str **is of type** string
16. ```
    if (inputStream.eof())
      cout << "End of file\n";
    ```
17. ```
    inputStream.close();
    ```

QUICK QUIZ 8.4

1. false
2. true
3. random
4. ```
   tellg(), seekg()
   ```
5. ```
   inputStream.seekg
     (3, ios::beg);
   ```
6. ```
   inputStream.seekg
     (3, ios::cur);
   ```
7. ```
   inputStream.seekg
     (0, ios::end);
   ```
8. ```
   char ch;
   inputStream.get(ch);
   cout << ch;
   ```
9. ```
   char ch;
   inputStream.peek(ch);      or      inputStream.get(ch);
   cout << ch;                        cout << ch;
                                      inputStream.putback(ch)
   ```
10. formatting manipulators

QUICK QUIZ 9.2

1. false
2. false (not necessarily)
3. true
4. false
5. true
6. false
7. false
8. 5
9. true
10. true
11. true (not necessarily)
12. false
13. true
14. base
15. false
16. true
17. false
18. reference
19. ```
    xValue[0]:  0.0
    xValue[1]:  0.5
    xValue[2]:  1.0
    xValue[3]:  1.5
    xValue[4]:  2.0
    ```
20. ```
    number[0]:  0
    number[1]:  3
    number[2]:  4
    number[3]:  7
    number[4]:  8
    ```
21. ```
    number[0]:  1
    number[1]:  2
    number[2]:  4
    number[3]:  8
    number[4]:  16
    ```
22. ```
    number[0]:  0
    number[1]:  0
    number[2]:  0
    number[3]:  0
    number[4]:  0
    ```

QUICK QUIZ 9.5

1. `int`
2. 0,0
3. 5,5
4. 5,5
5. 10,7
6. 1 1
7. `0 88`
8. true
9. false
10. true
11. `1 1 1 1 1`
12. `0 0 0 0 0 77`
13. 0
14. 88
15. true
16. 0 0, 0, 0, 0, 0, 0.5, 1.0, 1.5, 2.0
17. 1, 1, 1, 1, 1, 0, 3, 4, 7, 8
18. 1, 1, 1, 1, 1, 2, 2, 2, 2
19. 1, 1, 2, 2, 2
20. Alex Stepanov and Meng Lee
21. containers, algorithms, and iterators
22. iterators
23. stack
24. queue

QUICK QUIZ 10.5

1. class, class library
2. operations
3. data
4. false
5. I-can-do-it-myself
6. encapsulation
7. to prevent programs from accessing the data
8. private
9. preprocessor
10. #

11. conditional-compilation
13. false
15. constant, `const`
17. default-value constructors, explicit-value constructors
19. friend

12. function
14. name of the class, scope (`::`)
16. `Student`
18. public

20.
```
class Student
{
  public:
    void Print
      (ostream & out);
    void Read
      (istream & in);
  private:
    int myID;
    string myName;
};
```

QUICK QUIZ 11.2

1. integer
3. true
5. 3
7. 6
9. 8
11. `Nonsense`
13. true
15. true
17.
```
enum WeekDays
  {Sunday = 1, Monday,
   Tuesday, Wednesday,
   Thursday, Friday,
   Saturday};
```

2. false
4. false
6. 3
8. 0
10. 4
12. enumerator
14. false
16. true
18. To store a type declaration and the operations on objects of that type.

QUICK QUIZ 11.3

1. 1. Operations on a C-style enumeration cannot be defined as function members, and so C-style enumerations are not consistent with the I-can-do-it-myself principle
2. true

4. explicit-value

1. 2. Because there is no class invariant, operations on a C-style enumeration cannot assume that valid values will be passed to an enumeration parameter

3. So that other operations that use the class' members can be assured that the invariant holds.

5. `()`, `(int)`

QUICK QUIZ 12.2

1. two-dimensional
3. square
5. 33
7. 33
9. 1, 2, 3, 4
11. 999
13. 1326
15. self-contained

2. three-dimensional
4. 82
6. −1
8. 12
10. 95
12. 29
14. 1326

QUICK QUIZ 12.3

1. true
3. 5, 4
5. 5
7. `qqTab[1].push_back(99.9);`

2. true
4. `qqTab[1][3] = 1.1;`
6. 4
8. `TableRow bottom(4, 0.0);`
   `qqTab.push_back(bottom);`

QUICK QUIZ 12.4

1. $m \times n$ matrix
2. 2, 2
3. $\begin{bmatrix} 5 & -2 \\ 8 & 8 \end{bmatrix}$
4. $\begin{bmatrix} 1 & 2 & 0 \\ -1 & 3 & -3 \\ 10 & 5 & 9 \end{bmatrix}$
5. parent
6. child
7. false
8. member list initialization
9. `this, *this`

QUICK QUIZ 13.1

1. address
2. `&`
3. `*`
4. `*`
5. `->`
6. address
7. `double` value
8. address
9. address
10. `double` value
11. `double` value
12. address
13. null
14. `1.1`
15. `3.3`
16. true
17. true
18. `012a50`

QUICK QUIZ 13.2

1. compile, run
2. `new`, null address, address, anonymous
3. `delete`
4. pointer variable
5. 66
6. `C(C & original);`
7. `~C();`
8. false
9. true
10. default, byte, byte
11. A class should have a copy constructor when the class allocates memory at run-time This is to ensure that a distinct copy of the run-time object is constructed.
12. memory leak
13. destructor
14. A class should have a destructor when the class allocates memory at run-time. This is to ensure that such memory is not marooned.
15. A class should have an assignment operator when the class allocates memory at run-time. This is to en-sure that a distinct copy of the value being assigned is constructed.

QUICK QUIZ 13.3

1. Because inserting and deleting values at the front of a vector is too inefficient because it requires extensive copying of values.
2. nodes, links
3. true
4. false
5. Items can be efficiently inserted or removed at any point in a linked list. Items can be efficiently inserted and removed only at the back of a vector.
6. Each element of a vector is directly accessible. Accessing an element in a linked list requires traversing the list to reach that element.

abs(), 80
Abstraction, 144, 217
Accessibility, identifiers, 412–13
Accessor functions, 605–9
accumulate(), 562
Accumulator (AC), 303
acos(), 80
Ada, 167, 330
Addition operation, 74
Address, 20, 764
Address-of operator, 763–64
Address registers, 301
Aiken, Howard, 6
ALGOL, 9
Algorithm analysis, 373–75
Algorithms, 2, 7, 10–11
  bouncing ball problem, 334
  Color-wavelength program, 652
  depreciation calculation prob-
    lem:
    straight-line depreciation
      algorithm, 367–68
    sum-of-the-years'-digits
      depreciation algorithm, 368
  DigitsIn(), 341
  8–function calculator problem,
    176–77
  Einstein's equation, 53
  Factorial(), 161
  factorial problem, 427–29
  "Farmer in the Dell" problem,
    209–12
  letter grade problem, 287
  for MakeChange(), 400
  mean time to failure problem,
    351
  mileage between cities example,
    697
  Minimum(), 149–50
  modeling temperatures problem,
    589
  one-step integer division prob-
    lem, 386
  patenting, 25
  phone number decoding prob-
    lem, 249
  PrintVerse(), 210
  processing test scores problem,
    569–71
  quality control problem, 521–23
  recursive exponentiation prob-
    lem, 434
  result calculation function,
    178–79
  revenue calculation problem,
    16–17
  road construction problem, 452
  school mascot program, 265–66
  sorting employee information
    problem, 545
  sroot program, 820
  Standard Template Library
    (STL), 559
  Sum(), 322
  temperature conversion prob-
    lem, 275–76
  truck fleet accounting program,
    116
  weather data analysis problem,
    464–65
  year code conversion problem,
    282
Aliases, 770
Aliasing problem, 770, 825
American National Standards In-
  stitute (ANSI), 52, 72–73
Analytical Engine, 5–6, 19
AND gate, 297
Anonymous variables, 776
*ANSI/ISO C++ Standard Draft
  Working Paper*, 52
ANTI virus, 489
Apple II, 7
Apple Macintosh interface, 8
Arbitrary temperature conversions
  program, 276–78
Architecture:
  computer, 2, 300–9
  protocol, 809
  Systems Network Architecture
    (SNA), 808
  TCP/IP communications, 809
  See also Computer architecture
Arguments, 79
  pointers as, 773
Arithmetic-logic unit (ALU), 19, 21
Array of arrays declarations,
  708–11
Array indices, 676–77
Array initialization, 528–29
Arrays:
  array declaration, 526
  array of arrays declarations,
    708–11
  capacity, 525
  character, 529
  C-style, 520, 522, 525–43
    array initialization, 528–29
    arrays as parameters, 532
    character arrays, 529
    non-OOP approach,
      537–40
    object-oriented approach,
      540
    out-of-range errors, 534–36
    predefined array operations,
      536–37
    processing with for loops, 531
    specifying capacity of, 527
    subscript operation, 530–31
    typedef mechanism, 532–33
  elements, 525
  fixed-capacity, 526
  fixed-size, 520
  indices, 676–77
  initialization, 528–29
  jagged, 720
  multidimensional, 695–760
  as parameters, 532
  processing test scores problem,
    567–74
    algorithm, 569–71
    algorithm for PrintResults(),
      570
    algorithm for PromptAnd-
      Read(), 569
    behavior of PrintResults(), 570
    behavior of PromptAnd-
      Read(), 568
    coding/testing PrintResults(),
      570–71
    coding/testing PromptAnd-
      Read(), 569–70
    objects, 567
    objects for PrintResults(), 570
    operations, 568–69
    operations for PrintResults(),
      570
    operations for PromptAnd-
      Read(), 568–69
    problem description of, 567
    program behavior, 567
    program coding, 572–74
  program style and design, 579
  quality control problem,
    520–25
    algorithm, 521–23
    coding, 523–24
    objects, 521
    operations, 521
    problem description, 520–21
    program behavior, 521
    quality control failure
      frequency distribution pro-
      gram, 523–24
  size of, 525
  sorting employee information
    problem, 544–47
    algorithm, 545
    coding, 545–47
    objects, 544
    operations, 544–45
    problem description, 544
    program behavior, 544
    test score processing program,
      572–74
  square, 699–700
  varying-capacity, 526
  vector<T> class template,
    547–67
    array and vector<T> limita-
      tions, 566–67
    class templates, 548–53
    function templates, 547
    Standard Template Library
      (STL), 558–65
    vector<T> operators, 553–58
    vector<T> vs. C-style array,
      565–66
  and vector<T>s, 519–84
  See also C-style arrays; C-style
    multidimensional arrays;
    Multidimensional arrays
ArraySum(), 532–33, 537
*Artificial Intelligence: A Modern
  Approach* (Russell/Norvig), 642
Artificial intelligence (AI), 2,
  636–43
  intelligence, 636–38
  Not-One Game, 638–42
    driver for, 639
    sample output of, 641–42
    turn-taking member function
      for, 640

Artificial intelligence *(cont.)*
    programming techniques, 638
Ascending form, for statement,
    325–26
ASCII character set, 59
asin(), 80
Assembler, 21
Assembly language, 21
assert(), 88–89, 501
Assignment, 92–104
    as an operation, 96
    chaining assignment operators,
        96–97
    increment/decrement operations,
        97–99
    pointer variables, 769–70
    semicolons, 101
    shortcuts, 99–101
Assignment operator, 823
    and delete operation, 787–90
        general form of operation, 790
    and string objects, 235–36
Association for Computing Ma-
    chinery (ACM), 23
Associativity, operators, 76
Asterisk (*), 764
    before name of object in declara-
        tion, 763
    as wild card, 822
atan(), 80
Atanasoff, John, 6
Attribute identification, 591
Augmented matrix, 739
Augusta, Ada, 5–6
Automatic objects, 142
Autosave feature, word proces-
    sors/text editors, 462
Auto VacC (Robosoft), 637
Auxiliary memory, 19

Babbage, Charles, 1, 5–6, 19
back() member, 553, 798–99
Backus, John, 9
bad(), 491
Bad flags, 219
Base address, arrays, 535, 777
Base class, 731
BASIC, 9
begin() iterator member, 796–97,
    804
Behavior identification, 591
Bell Labs, 10
Berry, Clifford, 6
Beta testing, 27
Binary files, 462, 489
Binary half-adder, 297–299
    program, 299
Binary scheme, 20
binary_search(), 563
Bit masks, 654
Bits, 20
Blocks, 153–54
    and body of a function, 154
    wrapping multiple statements
        into single statement with,
        154
Body:
    of functions, 135, 154
    loop, 165
bool, 55
boolalpha manipulator, 226
Boolean expressions, 82–90
    common error in producing,
        271–73
    compound, 84–86
    operator precedence, 86–87
    preconditions/assert(), 88–89
    relational operators, 83–84
    short-circuit evaluation, 87–88
    simple, 83–84
Boolean logic:
    circuit design, 297–99

digital circuits, 297
    and digital design, 296–99
    early work in, 296–97
Booleans, 55, 73
    data representation, 73
Boole, George, 82, 296
Bouncing ball problem, 333–37
    algorithm, 334
    coding, 334–35
    objects, 333–34
    operations, 334
    program behavior, 333
Bound pointers, 765
break statement, 167
Building classes, 585–647
    designing a class, 590–93
        attribute identification, 591
        behavior identification, 591
        external/internal perspectives,
            591
        phases in, 590
        Temperature attributes,
            592–93
        Temperature behavior, 592
    friend functions, 621–26
        use of, 624
    implementing class attributes,
        593–97
        class invariants, 595
        conditional compilation,
            595–97
        encapsulation, 593–94
        implementation decisions,
            593
        information hiding, 594–95
    implementing class operations,
        597–621
        accessor functions, 605–9
        constant function members,
            599–600
        constructor functions, 600–602
        conversion functions, 609–10
        default-value constructor, 600
        explicit-value constructors,
            602–5
        Fahrenheit() function mem-
            ber, 609
        full function names, 598–599
        I/O operators, 615–20
        overloading operators, 610–19
        relational operators, 612–15
        Temperature addition/subtra-
            tion, 610–12
        Temperature explicit-value
            constructor, 603
        Temperature input, 603
        Temperature output, 597–600
    modeling temperatures problem,
        586–90
        algorithm, 589
        coding, 589–90
        extending object-centered de-
            sign, 587–88
        object-centered design,
            588–90
        objects, 588
        operations, 589
        preliminary analysis, 586–87
        problem description, 586
        program behavior, 588
        programming style/design,
            643–44
    retrieving student information
        problem, 626–35
        algorithm, 628–31
        Class Student header file,
            629–31
        Class Student implementation
            file, 631–32
        coding, 633–35
        objects, 627–28
        operations, 628

problem description, 626–27
    program behavior, 627
    See also Classes
Bullet-proof interfaces, 27
Bytes, 20

C++, 4–7, 9–10, 11–14
    assignments as expressions,
        271–73
    character escape sequences,
        59–60
    class types, 650
    coding in, 11–12
    comment, 5
    compiler directives, 5
    double type, 9
    expressions, definition of, 73–74
    function definitions, 134–38
    function prototypes, 138–40
    GNU implementation of, 13
    integer constants, 57
    keywords, 61
    opening documentation, 5
    semicolon in, 101
    string values, 8
    true and false in, 271
    type hierarchy, 690
C++ inheritance mechanism, 10,
    730–32
C, 9–10
Calculating wages program,
    110–11
    revised version, 114
Call-by-reference mechanism, 390,
    393
Calling a function, 134, 140
C with Classes, 10
ceil(), 80
Central processing unit (CPU), 19,
    300
cerr, 468
CERT (Computer Emergency Re-
    sponse Team), 26
Chained function calls, 615
Chain mail, 26
char, 55, 59, 175
Character arrays, 529
Character expressions, 90–91
Characteristic, 71
Character literals, 59
Characters, 55, 58–59, 72–73
charcodes8.cpp, 355–56
CheckValidity(), 249–51
    coding, 250–51
Child class, 731
cin, 9, 468
Circuit design, 297–99
Circular linked list, 795
Class attributes, implementing,
    593–97
    class invariants, 595
    conditional compilation, 595–97
    encapsulation, 593–94
    implementation decisions, 593
    information hiding, 594–95
Class Color declaration, 677–78
Class declaration, 593, 621
Classes, 10, 205–61, 650
    building, *See* Building classes
    class interface, 620–21
    data encapsulation, 213–15
    declaration statement, 593, 621
    "Farmer in the Dell" problem,
        206–12
    function members, 215–16
    istream class, 217–22
        >> operator, 218–19
        clear() member, 220
        ignore() member, 220
        status functions, 219–20
        streams, 218
        white space, 220–22

ostream class, 222–29
   << operator, 223–25
   flushing, 223–24
   flush manipulator, 224
   format control, 225–28
   output manipulator, 224
phone number decoding problem, 247–52
   algorithm, 249
   CheckValidity(), 249–51
   coding/testing, 251–52
   objects, 248
   operations, 248–49
   program behavior, 248
   private portion of, 620
   public portion of, 620
   simulation, 252–57
   string objects, 230–47
      declaring, 231
      input, 232–33
      output, 232
      string operations, 233–47
   structure of, 620
   See also string; Types/expressions
Class interface, 620–21
Class invariants, 595, 666–67
Class objects, pointers to, 768–69
Class operations, implementing,
   597–621
   accessor functions, 605–609
   constant function members,
      599–600
   constructor functions, 600–602
   conversion functions, 609–10
   default-value constructor, 600
   explicit-value constructors,
      602–5
   Fahrenheit() function member,
      609
   full function names, 598–599
   I/O operators, 615–20
   overloading operators, 610–19
   relational operators, 612–15
   Temperature addition/subtra-
      tion, 610–12
   Temperature output, 597–600
Class pointer selector operator
   (->), 768
Class templates, 548
clear(), 356, 491, 496, 500
Clementine (ISL), 637
close(), 470, 484–86
COBOL, 9
CODE 252 virus, 489
Code of ethics, 23
CodeWarrior, 12, 189, 741
Coding stage, software develop-
   ment, 6
Coefficient matrix, 739
Coin dispenser design problem,
   398–405
   data objects, 399
   MakeChange(), 400–402
      algorithm for, 400
      driver program for, 402–3
Color.cpp, 656, 658–61, 663,
   668–69
Color decrement operators, 673–76
Color default value constructor,
   667
Color explicit value constructor,
   667–68
Color.h, 656, 658–63, 667, 670
Color header file, 677–79
Color increment operators, 673–76
Color input (function member),
   669–70
Color input (non-member func-
   tion), 671
Color input operation, 656–59
Color interface file, 662
Color output operation, 659–63

Color relational operators, 671–73
Color successor function, 661
Color-to-int converter, 676–77
Color (type), 651, 657
Color-wavelength program,
   651–52, 668–69
   algorithm, 652
   coding, 652
   object-oriented version, 678
   objects, 651
   operations, 651–52
   program behavior, 651
   See also Computing Color wave-
      length
Columns, 696
Command-line arguments:
   and pointer variables, 815–22
   argc and argv, 817–22
   files and switches, 821–22
   parameters of the main func-
      tion, 816–18
   sroot program, 818–21
   See also sroot program
Command-line environments,
   815–16
Comment, 5
Comparison, pointer variables,
   770–71
Compiler directives, 5
Compilers, 9, 12–13, 21–22
Complex number, 645
Component programming, 577–79
   computer hardware, 578
   computer software, 578–79
Compound boolean expressions, 85
Compound statements, *See* Blocks
Computability Theory, 193–94
Computer architecture, 2, 300–309
   central processing unit (CPU),
      19, 300
   instruction execution, 303
   instruction fetch and execute,
      303–4
   I/O function, 304–5
   I/O module function, 307–8
   I/O modules, 19–20, 300
   I/O organization, 307
   main memory, 300
   memory hierarchy, 305–7
   processor registers, 301–3
   system interconnections, 300
Computer crime, 23–24
Computer graphics, 741–50
   density plots, 745–48
   function graphing, 742–45
   GUI Windows application pro-
      gramming, 748–50
Computer organization, 19–22
   computing systems, 19–20
   memory organization, 20–22
*Computer Organization and Archi-
   tecture: Designing for Performance* (Stallings), 309
Computer science:
   areas of, 2
   definition of, 3–4
Computer viruses, 488–90
Computer vision, 637
Computing:
   and ethics, 23–27
   history of, 4–17
      C++ and OOP, 9–10
      early computing devices, 4–5
      early electronic computers,
         6–7
      mechanical computers, 5–6
      modern computers, 7–8
      stored program, 5
      system software, 8–9
Computing Color wavelength program, 656–63
   algorithm for color input, 658

Color input operation, 656–59
Color output operation, 659–63
input function:
   algorithm, 658
   coding, 658–59
   objects, 657
   operations, 658
   program behavior, 657
Computing Curricula 1991 Report, 4
Computing systems, 19–20
Concatenation, 237–38
Conditional compilation, 595–97
Conditional expressions, 293–95
Condition codes, 302
Conditions, *See* Boolean expressions
Connectionist systems, 638
Constant declaration, 62
Constant function members,
   599–600
Constant objects, 62–64
Constant pointer, 780
Constants, 61, 62–64
const reference parameters, 392–95
Constructor functions, 600–602
Containers, Standard Template Li-
   brary (STL), 558
Control and status registers, 301,
   302–3
Control unit, 19
Conversion functions, 609–10
Copy constructor, 823
   for an arbitrary classs, general
      form of, 782
   default, 780–83
Copyrights, 24–25
cos(), 80
cosh(), 80
count(), 563
Counting approach, input loops,
   358–59
Counting loops/counter-controlled
   loops, 323–24
cout, 5, 8, 9, 468
C standard library, 536
C-style arrays, 520, 522, 525–43
   array initialization, 528–29
   character arrays, 529
   non-OOP approach, 537–40
      array input, 538–39
      array output, 539–40
   object-oriented approach, 540
   out-of-range errors, 534–36
   as parameters, 532
   predefined array operations,
      536–37
   problems with, 537, 540
   processing with for loops, 531
   specifying capacity of, 527
   subscript operation, 530–31
   typedef mechanism, 532–33
C-style enumerations, 653–64
   defining objects, 655
   drawbacks of, 664
   enumeration declarations,
      653–55
   operations, 656–64
      input, 656–49
      output, 659–63
   using, 655–56
C-style multidimensional arrays:
   drawbacks of, 711–12
   higher-dimensional arrays,
      707–10
   three-dimensional arrays:
      declaring, 705–6
      operations on, 706–7
   two-dimensional arrays:
      defining, 699–701
      defining operations, 702–5
      predefined operations, 701–2
Curve fitting, and numerical methods, 447

Dahl, Ole-Johan, 10
Dangling else problem, 270
Dangling pointer problem, 825
Data, 505
Databases, 2, 505
Database systems, 505–10
  relational model, 506–7
  select() function, 507–10
    driver program to test, 508–9
    nested loops for, 509–10
Data buffering, 308
Data and Computer Communications, Fifth Edition (Stallings), 815
Data dictionary, 66
Data encapsulation, 213–15, 593–94
Data members, 593
Data mining, 637
Data registers, 301
Data representation, 69–73
  booleans, 73
  characters/strings, 72–73
  integers, 69–71
  reals, 71–72
Data structures, 2, 822–23
Debugging, 6, 12–13
Declarations, 55–73
  constant objects, 62–64
  functions, *See* Prototypes, functions fundamental types, 55–61
    booleans, 55, 73
    characters, 55, 58–59
    integers, 55, 56–57
    integer variations, 55, 56
    reals, 55, 58–59
    identifiers, 61–62
    variable initialization, 66–67
    variable objects, 64–66
Declaration statement, 62
Declared types, 55
dec manipulator, 226
DEC PDP-11, 9
Decrement operator, 561
Deep Blue, 636–43
Default copy constructor, 780–83
Default-value constructor, 600
delete operation, 783–90
  assignment operator, 787–90
  destructor functions, 786–87
  general form of, 783–84
  memory leaks, 784–86
DeMorgan's Laws, 296–97
densityplot20.cpp, 746–47
Density plots, 745–48
  definition of, 746
  ploting (program), 746–48
Depreciation calculation problem, 366–73
  coding, 368
  Depreciation Functions (program), 369–70
  Methods of Depreciation (program), 370–73
  objects, 367
  operations, 367
  program behavior, 367
  straight-line depreciation algorithm, 367–68
  sum-of-the-years'-digits depreciation algorithm, 368
  testing, 368–70
Dereferencing, 766–67
Dereferencing operator, 561
Derived class, 731
Descending form, for statement, 326–27
Designing a class, 590–93
  attribute identification, 591
  behavior identification, 591
  external/internal perspectives, 591

phases in, 590
Temperature attributes, 592–93
Temperature behavior, 592
Design stage, software development, 6
Destructor, 786–87, 823
  general form of, 787
Detection and recovery programs, for viruses, 488–89
Deterministic processes, 252
dice<4>.cpp, 255–56
Dice-roll simulation, 255–56
Difference Engine, 5
Differential equations, and numerical methods, 447
Digital circuits, 297
Digital design, and boolean logic, 296–299
DigitsIn(), 339–43
  algorithm, 341
  coding, 341
  driver program for, 342
  execution of loop in, table tracing, 342–43
  operations, 340–41
  program behavior, 339
  specification, 339–40
  testing, 342
Direct access, 492
Direct memory access (DMA), 305
Distance learning, 27
Division operation, 74
Documentation file, 184
  building, 186–87
do loop, 339–50
  construction warning, 344–45
  DigitsIn(), 339–43
  loop conditions vs. termination conditions, 344
  posttest loop, 339, 343–44
Dot notation, 598
double, 8, 9, 10, 15, 16, 52–53, 55, 58–59, 131, 175, 463, 567, 568, 570, 651
Doubly-linked lists, 794
Driver program, 138
Dry Bones! problem, 435–39
  drybones11.cpp, 437–39
  song structure, 436–37
Dual-branch form, if statements, 155–56, 268
Dynamic sequences, 567

Early computing devices, 4–5
Early electronic computers, 6–7
EBCDIC (Extended Binary Coded Decimal Interchange Code), 72
Eckert, J. Prespert, 6
8–function calculator problem, 175–82
  algorithm, 176–77
    refinement of, 177
  objects, 175–76
  operations, 176
  program behavior, 175
  program to solve, 180–82
    testing, 182
  result calculation function, 177–79
    algorithm, 178–79
    coding, 179
    objects, 177–78
    operations, 178
    program behavior, 177
Einstein's equation, 52–54
  algorithm, 53
  coding, 53
  energy<1>.cpp, 54
  execution, 53
  objects, 52
  operations, 52–53

program behavior, 52
testing, 53
Electronic Communications Privacy Act (ECPA), 26
emacs text editor, 12, 816, 822
Email, 25
emprecords5.cpp, 545–47
empty(), 235, 796
Empty vector<string>, 548
Encapsulation, 213–15, 593–94
end() iterator member, 796–97, 801, 804
endl manipulator, 226, 503
End-of-data flag, 351
End-of-file (eof), 471
  as sentinel value, 355–56
energy1.cpp, 54
ENIAC, 6–7
Enumerations, 649–93
  Color interface file, 662–63
  Color-wavelength program, 651–52
    algorithm, 652
    coding, 652
    objects, 651
    operations, 651–52
    program behavior, 651
  computing Color wavelength program, 656–63
    algorithm for color input, 658
    Color input operation, 656–59
    Color output operation, 659–63
    function behavior, 657
    input function algorithm, 658
    input function coding, 658–59
    input function objects, 657
    input function operations, 658
  C-style, 653–64
    defining objects, 655
    drawbacks of, 664
    enumeration declarations, 653–55
    operations, 656–64
    using, 655–56
  declaration statement, 654–55
  definition of, 653
  enumeration objects, defining, 655
  geological classification problem, 679–89
    class Rock header file, 681–83
    class Rock implementation file, 687–89
    class RockKind header file, 683–85
    class RockKind implementation file, 685–87
    rock classification program, 680–81
  libraries and types, 662–63
  object-oriented, 664–79
    Color header file, 677–79
    declaring enumeration classes, 664–66
    defining color operations, 666–77
    predecessor functions, 662
    program style and design, 690–91
    successor functions, 661–62
    using, 655–56
    See also C-style enumerations; Object-oriented enumerations
eof(), 470, 478, 481–82, 491
EQP, 637
Equation solving, and numerical methods, 447
erase(), 566, 802–4
Error detection, 308

Error messages, 12
Errors:
    common reference parameter errors, 391–92
    logic, 13
    out-of-range, 534–36
    roundoff, 72
    syntax, 12
Escape sequences, 59–60
Ethics, 23–27
    computer crime, 23–24
    future of, 27
    health concerns and the environment, 24
    information ownership, 24–25
    "netiquette" and hoaxes, 25–26
    privacy, 26
    quality control and risk reduction, 26–27
    security, 23–24
    and society, 23
Executable program, 22
Executing programs, 6, 12–13
exit(), 182–86
Exit condition, 169
exp(), 80
Expert systems, 638
Explicit-value constructors, 602–5
    class object initializaiton, 604–5
Exponent, 71
Exponential notation, 58
Expressions:
    computing with, 130–32
    definition of, 73–74
    temperature-conversion problem, 130–32
Expression statement, 101
External memory, 19
Extraction operator, 219

factorial9.cpp, 162–63
factorial10.cpp, 168–69
Factorial(), 159–63, 182
    algorithm, 161
    coding, 161–62
    objects, 160–61
    operations, 161
    program behavior, 160
    testing, 162–63
Factorial problem, 426–33
    algorithm, 427–29
    coding, 429–33
    objects, 426
    operations, 426–27
Fahrenheit() function member, 609
fail(), 476fn, 491
Fail flags, 219
failuretime10.cpp, 358–59
failuretime<11>.cpp, 360–61
false, 55
"Farmer in the Dell" problem, 206–12
    algorithm, 209–12
    objects, 208
    operations, 208–9
    preliminary analysis, 207–8
    PrintVerse(), 209–12
        algorithm for function, 210
        objects, 209
        operations, 209
        program behavior, 209
    program behavior, 208
Fields, 503, 506
Files, 461–62
    fstream objects, 468–86, 491–504
    program style and design, 511–12
    weather data analysis problem, 462–68
        algorithm, 464–65
        coding, 465–66
        objects, 463

operations, 463
    processing of meteorological data, 462–63
    program behavior, 463
    testing, 467–68
    See also fstream objects
File transfer protocol (FTP), 815
fill(), 563
Fill characters, 227–28, 504
find(), 563, 805
Firewalls, 24
First Course in Database Systems, A (Ullman/Widom), 510
First-generation computers, 7
firstName variable, 5
Fixed-capacity arrays, 526
fixed manipulator, 226
Fixed-point real literal, 58
Fixed-size arrays, 520
Flags, 219, 302
Flame wars, 25
float, 55, 59
Floating-point form, 71
Floating-point notation, 58
Floating-point real literal, 58
floor(), 80
Flow lines, 151
Flushing, 223–24
Flushing an ostream, 223–24
Flush manipulator, 224
flush manipulator, 226, 503
for_each(), 563
Forever loops, 167, 170, 330–32
    returning from, 332–33
    and sentinels, 351–53
for loop, *See* for statement
Format manipulators, 111–14, 225–28
for statement, 163–66, 323–33
    ascending form, 325–26
    construction warning, 329–30
    descending form, 326–27
    forever loops, 330–32
    multiplication table, program for printing, 327–28
    nested loops, 327
    processing arrays with, 531
    returning from, 332–33
Fortran 88, 167, 332
FORTRAN, 9
Fourth-generation computers, 7
Fractional part, 71
Free store, 783
Frequency distribution, 520
friend functions, 621–26
    use of, 624
front() member, 553, 798–799
Front of a stack, 566
fstream objects, 468–86, 491–504
    bad(), 491
    basic operations, 469–85
    clear(), 491, 500
    close(), 484–85
    declaring, 468–69
    eof(), 481–82, 491
    fail(), 491
    fstreams as parameters, 485
    get(), 491
    getline(), 478–81
    good(), 491
    ignore(), 491
    initialization at declaration, 472–73
    input operator, 476–78
    InteractiveOpen() function, 475–76
    is_open(), 474–75
    manipulators:
        requiring arguments, 503–4
        without arguments, 502–3
    open(), 470–72
        general form of, 471

output operator, 483
    peek(), 491, 498–500
    putback(), 491, 500
    seekg(), 491, 492–97
    seekp(), 491, 498
    setstate(), 491, 500–502
    setting stream-status flags (program), 501
    tellg(), 491, 492, 497–498
    tellp(), 491, 492, 498
FTP, 815
Full function names, 598–599
Fully-qualified name, 598–599
Function graphing, 742–45
    plotting a function (program), 743–45
Function members, 215–16, 597
Functions, 129–203, 383–460
    algorithm, 137–38
    argument, 134
    body of, 135, 154
    calling, 134, 140
    coding, 137–38
    and Computability Theory, 193–94
    computing with, 132–48
    defining, 134–38
    design, 136–37, 194–96
        steps in, 135–36
    driver program, 138
    8–function calculator, 175–82
    expressions, computing with, 130–32
    function stub, 136–37
    inline functions, 408–11
        and libraries, 409
        space-time tradeoff, 410
    objects, 136
        local, 140–42
    one-step integer division problem, 384–88
        algorithm, 386
        coding, 386
        objects, 384–86
        operations, 386
        program behavior, 384
        testing, 386
    operations, 137
    overloading, 420–21
    parameters, 134, 136, 388–407
        coin dispenser design problem, 398–405
        name decomposition problem, 395–398
        reference parameters, 389–95
        using, 394–95
        value parameters, 388–89
    program behavior, 136
    prototypes, 138–40, 184
    recursion, 426–46
        Dry Bones! problem, 435–39
        factorial problem, 426–33
        recursive exponentiation problem, 433–35
        Towers of Hanoi problem, 439–42
    return type of, 136
    return value, 134
    specification of, 136–38
    templates, 421–25
        overloading vs., 425
        parameters for types, 422–23
        Swap() template, 423–24
    that return nothing, 142–44
    that use repetition, 159–75
        Factorial(), 159–63
        for statement, 163–66
        processing multiple input values, 166–71
    that use selection, 148–59
        blocks, 153–54
        if statements, 151

Functions *(cont.)*
    Minimum (), 148–51
    nested if statements, 156–57
    selective execution, 151–53
    sequential execution, 151
    styles used to write if state-
      ments, 155–56
    verification/validation, 138
    WindChill(), 140–41
    See also Recursion
Function stub, 136–37
Function templates, 547

Gates, Bill, 1
Gauss, Carl Friedrich, 320, 373
Gaussian elimination, 738
Generalizations, 8
Generic container classes, 548
Generic functions, 547
Geological classification problem,
    679–89
    class Rock header file, 681–83
    class Rock implementation file,
      687–89
    class RockKind header file,
      683–85
    class RockKind implementation
      file, 685–87
    rock classification program,
      680–81
get(), 491
getline(), 466, 470, 478–81, 485–86
good(), 474, 491
Good flags, 219
Graphical user interfaces (GUIs),
    8, 748–50
Graphics libraries, 741
greeting2.cpp, 4
GUI Windows application pro-
    gramming, 748–50

Hackers, 23
Hardware, 7
Hardware independence, 194
Header file, 78–79, 184
    angle brackets in, 79
    building, 184–85
Head node, 796
Heap, 783
heat.cpp, 185
heat.doc, 186
Hertzfeld, Andy, 1
Heuristic search, 638
Hexadecimal integer, 57
hex manipulator, 226
High-level graphics operations, 741
High-level languages, 8
Hollerith, Herman, 6
Hopper, Grace Murray, 6
Host, virus, 488
Hubbard, Elbert, 1
Human-computer communication,
    2
Huxley, Aldous, 1

IBM (International Business Ma-
    chines) Corporation, 6, 9
    first PCs, 8
IBM System/360, 7
I-can-do-it-myself principle, 591
Identifiers, 61–62, 411–13
    accessibility, 412–13
    scope, 412–19
      example, 413–14
      of for-loop control variables,
        416–17
      name conflicts, 417–19
      objects declared outside all
        blocks, 414–16
      signatures, 419
IEEE Floating Point Format, 71
IEEE (Institute of Electrical and
    Electronics Engineers), 23

if-break combination, 167, 331
if-else-if statements, 155–56,
    268–71
if-else statements, 155–56
if statements, 151, 268–74
    dual-branch form, 155–56, 268
    multi-branch form, 155–56,
      268–71
    nested if statements, 156–57, 270
    single-branch form, 155–56, 268
    styles used to write, 155–56
ifstream, 464, 468–86, 491–504,
    521, 544
    See also fstream objects
ignore(), 491
Implementation file, 184
    building, 185–86
Increment operator, 561
Indefinite loops, 167
Independent coding, and libraries,
    192
Indexed objects, 520
Indexed variables, 520
Index (integer), 233, 497
Index register, 301
Indirection, using, 762–63
Indirection operator, 766–67
Infinite loops, and do statement,
    344–45
Information hiding, 191, 594–95
Information ownership, 24–25
information retrieval, 2
Inheritance, 10, 482, 730–32
Inital value, 66–67
Initialization declaration, 67
Inline functions, 408–11
    and libraries, 409
    space-time tradeoff, 410
inline specifier, 408
Input expressions, 104–7
    input (extraction) operator >>,
      105–6
    streams, 104–5
    truck fleet accounting program,
      115–18
Input loops, 350–63
    counting approach, 358–59
    mean time to failure problem,
      350–59
    query approach, 359–63
    sentinel approach, 351–58
Input manipulator, 222
Input/output expressions, 104–14
Input/output modules, 19–20, 300
insert(), 564, 799–802
Instruction register (IR), 302
int, 10, 15, 16, 53, 55, 69–70, 463,
    521, 568, 570, 650
intdivision2.cpp, 387–88
Integer literals, 56–57
Integers, 55, 56–57, 69–71
    data representation, 69–71
Integer variations, 55, 56
Integrated circuits, 7
Integration, and numerical meth-
    ods, 447
Intel Corporation, 7
InteractiveOpen() function,
    475–76, 523
internal manipulator, 226, 503
Internal memory, *See* RAM (ran-
    dom access memory)
Internal perspective, 591
Internet address program, 805–7
Internet Engineering Task Force
    (IETF), 814–15
I/O address register (I/OAR), 300
I/O buffer register (I/OBR), 300
I/O function, 304–5
<iomanip.h>, 111, 142
I/O module function, 307–8
I/O modules, 19–20, 300
I/O organization, 307

ios::app, 472, 485
ios::ate, 472
ios::badbit, 491, 502
ios::beg, 491, 493, 496
ios::binary, 472
ios::cur, 491, 493, 496
ios::end, 491, 493, 496
ios::eofbit, 491, 502
ios::failbit, 491, 502
ios::in, 472
ios::nocreate, 472
ios::noreplace, 472
ios::out, 472
ios::trunc, 472
<iostream.h>, 111, 142
iostream library, 5, 78–79, 501
iota(), 563
isalnum(ch), 499, 499
is_open(), 469, 474–75
isspace(ch), 499
istream, 8, 9, 10, 15, 16, 52–53, 131,
    175, 217–22, 356, 657
    >> operator, 218–19
    clear() member, 220
    ignore() member, 220
    status functions, 219–20
    streams, 218
    white space, 220–22
Iterators, Standard Template Li-
    brary (STL), 558

Jacquard, Joseph Marie, 5, 6
Jagged tables/arrays, 720
Jobs, Steven, 7–8

Kasparov, Garry, 636–43
Keywords, 61
Knowledge representation, 637
Krishnamurti, Jiddu, 1

Language independence, 194
Language processing, 637
Laptop computers, 8
Lee, Meng, 548
Left-associative operators, 76
left manipulator, 226, 503
Leibniz, Gottfried Wilhelm von, 5
Letter grade problem, 286–91
    algorithm, 287
    coding/testing, 289–91
    grade-computation algorithm,
      287–88
    objects, 287
    operations, 287
    program, 289
    program behavior, 286
Lexical analysis, 498
Lexical analyzer, 498
Libraries, 78, 131, 182–93
    constructing, 183–87
    documentation file, 184
      building, 186–87
    header file, 184
      buildiing, 184–85
    and implementation details, 191
    implementation file, 184
      building, 185–86
    incorporating functions and,
      190–94
    and independent coding, 192
    and inline functions, 409
    organizing principle, identifying,
      183
    and program maintenance,
      191–92
    and reusability, 191
    selecting functions to store in,
      183
    and separate compilation, 192
    Standard Template Library
      (STL), 92–96, 548, 550,
      558–65, 578, 714, 823

and testing, 192
translating, 188–90
 compilation, 188
 from command line, 189
 linking, 188
 using project file, 189–90
 using in programs, 187–88
Linear systems, solving, by numerical methods, 447
Linked lists, 794
 circular, 795
 doubly-linked, 794
 singly-linked, 795
Linkers, 22
list<T> class template, 792–815
 begin() and end() iterator members, 796–97
 circular linked list, 795
 default class constructor, 795–96
 doubly-linked lists, 794
 front() and back() members, 798–799
 insert(), push_front(), and push_back() members, 799–802
 Internet addresses problem, 804–7
  program, 805–7
  solution, 804–5
 iterators/pointers, 797–798
 linked list, 794
 list<T> objects, 793–95
 pop_back(), pop_front(), erase(), and remove() members, 802–4
 singly-linked list, 795
 size() and empty() members, 796
 vector<T>, limitation of, 792–95
lists9.cpp, 357–58
Literal, 55
Locality of reference, 306
log(), 80
log10(), 80
Logical operators, 85
Logic error, 13
Logic programming, 638
long, 55
long double, 55
long int, 55, 56
Loops, 163
 body of, 165
 forever, 167, 170, 330–32
 indefinite, 167, 331
 posttest/test-at-the-bottom, 172, 339, 343–44
 pretest/test-at-the-top, 171
lower_bound(), 563

Machine language, 9, 20
Machine learning, 637
Machine translation, 637
Macintosh computers, 9
Main function, 5
main keyword, 5
Main memory, See RAM (random access memory)
Maintenance, programs, 14–15
Maintenance stage, software development, 6
MakeChange(), 400–404
 algorithm for, 400
 driver program for, 402–3
Manipulators, 491
 requiring arguments, 503–4
 without arguments, 502–3
Mantissa, 71
Map, 823
Mark I computer, 6
Massively parallel computers, 8
Mathematica, 742, 745–46
Math library, 78, 80
matmult8.cpp, 728–29

Matrix class:
 building:
  external approach to, 725–26
  internal approach to, 730–38
  using typedef, 726
 constructor, 732–34
 deriving from vector, 730–31
 inheritance, 730–32
 input operation, 736–37
  input operator >> for Matrix, 737
  Matrix Read() operation, 737
 Matrix multiplication, 737
 output operation, 735–36
 Rows() and Columns() operations, 734
  alternative Matrix Print() operation, 735–36
  Matrix Print() operation, 735
matrix.cpp, 727
matrix.h, 726, 730–31
Matrix multiplication, 724–25, 737
 program to demonstrate, 728–30
Mauchly, John, 6
max_element(), 563
Mean time to failure problem, 350–51
 algorithm, 351
 objects, 351
 operations, 351
 program behavior, 350–51
Mechanical computers, 5–6
Mechanization of arithmetic, 4
Megabyte, 20
Member initialization list, 733
Memory:
 hierarchy, 305–7
 knowledge representation, 637
 leaks, 784–86
 organization, 20–22
 unit, 19
Meteo, 637
meteorology1.cpp, 465–66
Michelangelo virus, 488–89
Mileage between cities problem, 696–698
 algorithm, 697
 coding, 697–698
 objects, 697
 operations, 697
 preliminary analysis, 696–97
 problem description, 696
 program behavior, 697
min_element(), 563
Minicomputers, 7
minimum7.cpp, 150–51
Minimum (), 148–51
 algorithm, 149–50
 coding, 150
 objects, 148–49
 operations, 149
 program behavior, 148
 testing, 150–51
Modeling temperatures problem, 586–90
 algorithm, 589
 coding, 589–90
 extending object-centered design, 587–88
 object-centered design, 588–90
 objects, 588
 operations, 589
 preliminary analysis, 586–87
 problem description, 586
 program behavior, 588
Modern computers, 7–8
Modula-2, 9, 167, 330
Modula-3, 167, 330
Modulus operation, 74
money<5>.cpp, 143–44
Multi-branch form, if statements, 155–56, 268–71

Multidimensional arrays, 695–760
 C-style:
  declaring three-dimensional arrays, 705–6
  defining a two-dimensional array, 699–701
  defining two-dimensional array operations, 702–5
  drawbacks of, 711–12
  higher-dimensional arrays, 707–10
  operations on three-dimensional arrays, 706–7
  predefined two-dimensional array operations, 701–2
 mileage between cities problem, 696–698
  algorithm, 697
  coding, 697–698
  objects, 697
  operations, 697
  preliminary analysis, 696–97
  problem description, 696
  program behavior, 697
 multidimensional vector<T> objects, 714–24
 program style/design, 751
 two-dimensional vector<T> functions, defining, 720
 two-dimensional vector<T> input, 722–23
  Table input operation, 722–23
 two-dimensional vector<T> objects, 715–18
  one-step approach, 717
  two-step approach, 715–17
  using typedef for readability, 717–18
 two-dimensional vector<T> operations, 718–20
  push_back() function, 719–20
  size() function, 718
 two-dimensional vector<T> output, 720–21
  Table output operation, 720–21
 vector<T>-based matrix library, 724–50
  Matrix class, 725–26, 730–38
  matrix multiplication, 724–25
  Matrix operations, 726–30
  object-centered design, 738–40
 See also C-style multidimensional arrays
Multimap, 823
Multiplication operation, 74
Multiplication table, program for printing, 327–28
Multiset, 823

Name decomposition problem, 395–398
Name mangling, 548
Natural language understanding, 637
Nested if statements, 156–57, 270
"Netiquette" and hoaxes, 25–26
Neural networks, 638
new operation, 776–83
 allocating arrays with, 777–80
 copy constructor, 780–83
  general form of, 782
 general form of, 776
Newsgroups, 25
next_permutation(), 563
1989 Task Force on the Core of Computer Science, 1
noboolalpha manipulator, 226
Nodes, 794
 head, 796
Normal distributions, 254
noshowbase manipulator, 226

noshowpoint manipulator, 226
noshowpos manipulator, 226
noskipws manipulator, 222, 226, 503
Notebook computers, 8
NOT gate, 297
Not-One Game, 638–42
  driver for, 639
  sample output of, 641–42
  turn-taking member function for, 640
nouppercase manipulator, 226
Noyce, Robert, 7
NPOS, 242–43
Null address, 765
Null pointer value, 765
Numerical computation, 3
Numerical methods, 446–53
  road construction problem, 450–53
    algorithm, 452
    coding/testing, 452
    objects, 451
    operations, 451
    preliminary analysis, 450
    program, 452–53
    program behavior, 450
  trapezoid method of approximating areas, 447–49
  types of problems used in, 447
Numeric expressions, 73–82
  numeric functions, 78–81
  operators, 74–78
Numeric functions, 78–81
  type conversions, 80–81
Nygaard, Kristen, 10

Object autonomy, 591
Object-centered design (OCD):
  definition of, 7
  revenue calculation problem, 15–20
  steps in, 7–15
    algorithm, 7, 10–11
    objects, 7–9
    operations, 7, 9–10
    program behavior, 7–8
  twine problem, 7–15
Object-oriented enumerations, 664–79
  Color header file, 677–79
    class Color declaration, 677–78
  Color input (function member), 669–70
  Color input (non-member function), 671
  declaring enumeration classes, 664–66
    class design, 665
    class implementation, 665–66
  defining color operations, 666–77
    array indices, 676–77
    class invariant, 666–67
    Color I/O, 669–71
    Color wavelength, 668–69
    default-value constructor, 667
    explicit value constructor, 667–68
    increment and decrement operators, 673–76
    relational operators, 671–73
  object-oriented Color-wavelength program, 678
Object-oriented programming (OOP), 9–10
Object program, 9
oct manipulator, 226
ofstream objects, 464–65, 468–86, 544
  See also fstream objects
One-step integer division problem, 384–88

algorithm, 386
coding, 386
objects, 384–86
operations, 386
program behavior, 384
testing, 386
One-trip behavior, 344
On-line chat, 25
Opcode, 20
open(), 469, 470–72, 485
Opening documentation, 5
Open Systems Interconnection (OSI), 809
Operands, 20, 73
Operating systems, 3, 8
Operator associativity, 76
Operator precedence, 75–76
  boolean expressions, 86–87
Operators, 74–78
  operator associativity, 76
  operator precedence, 75–76
  parentheses with, 76–77
  precedence rules, 77
  type conversions, 75
  unary operators, 77
Operator(SYMBOL PYRAMID), 611, 616
Optimization, 442–43
OR gate, 297
OSI (Open Systems Interconnection), 809
ostream, 8, 15, 16, 52–53, 131, 175, 222–29, 468–86
  << operator, 223–25
  flushing, 223–24
  flush manipulator, 224
  format control, 225–28
  output manipulator, 224
Out-of-bounds exception, 239
outofrange.cpp, 534–35
Out-of-range errors, 534–36
Output expressions, 108–10
  calculating wages program, 110–11
    revised version, 114
  output formatting, 111–14
  streams, 104–5
  truck fleet accounting program, 115–18
Output manipulator, 224
Overflow, 70–72
Overloading, 420–21
  templates vs., 425
Overloading operators, 478, 610–19

Parameters, 134, 136, 388–407
  coin dispenser design problem, 398–405
  name decomposition problem, 395–398
  pointers as, 773
  reference parameters, 389–95
    common errors, 391–92
    const reference parameters, 392–95
    exam analogy, 391
    using, 394–95
  value parameters, 388–89
Parent class, 731
Pascal (unit), 9
Pascal, Blaise, 1, 4–5
peek(), 491, 498–500
Perception, 637
Peripheral devices, 19
Phone number decoding problem, 247–52
  algorithm, 249
    refinement of, 249–51
  CheckValidity(), 249–51
  coding, 250–51
  coding/testing, 251–52
  objects, 248

operations, 248–49
program behavior, 248
Pivot element, 740
Pixels, 741
Platform dependence, 356
plotter19.cpp, 743–44
Pointer arithmetic, 771–73
Pointers, See Pointer variables
Pointer variables, 762–75
  as arguments/parameters, 773
  assignment, 769–70
  basic operations, 765–66
  and command-line arguments, 815–22
    argc and argv, 817–22
    files and switches, 821–22
    parameters of the main function, 816–18
    sroot program, 818–21
    See also sroot program
  comparison, 770–71
  declaring/initializing, 763–65
  definition of, 763
  dereferencing, 766–67
  indirection, 766–67
  using, 762–63
  iterator as abstraction of, 797
  pointer arithmetic, 771–73
  pointers to class objects, 768–69
  program style/design, 823
  typedef, using for readability, 765
pop_back() function, 564, 566, 802, 804
pop_front() function, 792, 802, 804
Portable programs, 9
Postcondition, 600–601
Posttest loops, 172, 339, 343–44
pow(), 80
Precedence, operators, 75–76
Precedence rules, 77
Precision, 226
  numbers, 503
Preconditions, 88–89
Predecessor functions, 662
Preprocessor, 595
Preprocessor directives, 595
Pretest loops, 171
Prevention, viruses, 488
prev_permutation(), 563
Primary memory, See RAM (random access memory)
Primitive graphics opertions, 741
PrintAsMoney(), 142–44
PrintVerse(), 209–12
  algorithm for function, 210
  operations, 209
  program behavior, 209
  objects, 209
Priority queue, 823
Privacy, 26
Private portion, classes, 620
Problem solving, through software engineering, 6–7
Processing sequences of values, 520
Processing test scores problem, 567–74
  algorithm, 569, 571
    for PrintResults(), 570
    for PromptAndRead(), 569
  behavior:
    of PrintResults(), 570
    of PromptAndRead(), 568
  coding/testing:
    PrintResults(), 570–71
    PromptAndRead(), 569–70
  objects, 567
    for PrintResults(), 570
  operations, 568–69
    for PrintResults(), 570
    for PromptAndRead(), 568–69
  problem description of, 567
  program behavior, 567

program coding, 572–74
Processing two lists (program), 357–58
Processor registers, 301–3
　control and status registers, 301, 302–3
　user-visible registers, 301–2
Program behavior, 7–8
　bouncing ball problem, 333
　Color-wavelength program, 651
　computing Color wavelength program, 657
　depreciation calculation problem, 367
　DigitsIn(), 339
　8–function calculator problem, 175
　Einstein's equation, 52
　Factorial(), 160
　"Farmer in the Dell" problem, 208
　functions, 136
　letter grade problem, 286
　mean time to failure problem, 350–51
　mileage between cities problem, 697
　Minimum (), 148
　modeling temperatures problem, 588
　one-step integer division problem, 384
　phone number decoding problem, 248
　PrintResults(), 570
　PrintVerse(), 209
　processing test scores problem, 567
　PromptAndRead(), 568
　quality control problem, 521
　result calculation function, 177
　retrieving student information problem, 627
　road construction problem, 450
　school mascot program, 264
　sorting employee information problem, 544
　summation problem, 320
　temperature-conversion problem, 130
　truck fleet accounting program, 115
　weather data analysis problem, 463
Program counter (PC), 302
Programming languages, 3
Programs, 4, 5
　debugging, 6, 12–13
　executing, 6, 12–13
　maintenance, 14–15
　stored, 4, 5
　style/design, 121–25
　testing, 6, 12–14
Program status word (PSW), 302
Promotion, 75
Protocol architecture, 809
Prototypes, functions, 138–40, 184
Pseudocode algorithm, 10–11
Pseudorandom numbers, 253
Public portion, classes, 620
push_back() function, 554, 564, 719–20, 731, 792, 799–802
　and vector<T> class template function members, 566
push_front() function, 792, 799–802
putback(), 491, 500

qualitycontrol1.cpp, 523–24
Quality control, and risk reduction, 26–27
Quality control failure frequency distribution program, 523–24

Quality control problem, 520–25
　algorithm, 521–23
　coding, 523–24
　objects, 521
　operations, 521
　problem description, 520–21
　program behavior, 521
　quality control failure frequency distribution program, 523–24
Query approach:
　input loops, 359–63
　　disadvantage of, 363
Query functions, 362–63
Query language, 506
Queue, 566, 823

rainbow1.cpp, 652
RAM (random access memory), 19, 300
Random access, 492
RandomInt class, 253–54
　construction, 253
　generation, 253–54
Random number generators, 253–54
random_shuffle(), 563
Ranks, 696
Read position symbol, 471
Reals, 55, 58–59, 71–72
　data representation, 71–72
Rear of a stack, 566
Records, 506
Recursion, 426–46
　Dry Bones! problem, 435–39
　　drybones11.cpp, 437–39
　　song structure, 436–37
　factorial problem, 426–33
　　algorithm, 427–29
　　coding, 429–33
　　objects, 426
　　operations, 426–27
　recursive exponentiation problem, 433–35
　　algorithm, 434
　　objects, 433
　　operations, 434
　Towers of Hanoi problem, 439–42
　　driver program, 441–42
　　solving recursively, 441
Recursive exponentiation problem, 433–35
　algorithm, 434
　objects, 433
　operations, 434
Reference parameters, 389–95, 764
　common errors, 391–92
　const reference parameters, 392–95
　exam analogy, 391
Reference return type, 618
Registers, 19
Relational operators, 83–84, 612–15
　and string objects, 236–37
Remainder operation, 74
remove(), 802
Repeated execution, 163–66
Repetition, 319–81
　depreciation calculation problem, 366–73
　　coding, 368
　　depreciation functions program, 369–70
　　methods of depreciation program, 370–73
　　objects, 367
　　operations, 367
　　program behavior, 367
　　straight-line depreciation algorithm, 367–68

sum-of-the-years'-digits depreciation algorithm, 368
　　testing, 368–70
　do loop, 339–50
　　construction warning, 344–45
　　DigitsIn(), 339–43
　　loop conditions vs. termination conditions, 344
　　posttest loop, 339, 343–44
　forever loops, 167, 170, 330–32
　　returning from, 332–33
　　and sentinels, 351–53
　for loop, 163–66, 323–33
　　ascending form, 325–26
　　construction warning, 329–30
　　descending form, 326–27
　　forever loop, 330–32
　　multiplication table printing program, 327–28
　　nested loops, 327
　　returning from, 332–33
　functions that use, 159–75
　　Factorial(), 159–75
　　for statement, 163–66
　　processing multiple input values, 166–71
　input loops, 350–63
　　counting approach, 358–59
　　mean time to failure problem, 350–59
　　query approach, 359–63
　　sentinel approach, 351–58
　loop decisions, 364–66
　Sum():
　　algorithm, 322
　　coding/testing, 322–23
　　driver program for, 323
　　for loop version, 322
　　no-loop version, 374–75
　　objects, 320–21
　　operations, 321–22
　　program behavior, 320
　summation problem, 320–23
　　algorithm, 322
　　objects, 320–21
　　operations, 321–22
　　program behavior, 320
　while loop, 333–39
　　bouncing ball problem, 333–37
　　construction warning, 338–39
　　loop conditions vs. termination conditions, 337–38
　　and sentinels, 353–54
　　See also Bouncing Ball problem
Repetitive stress injuries, 24
replace(), 563
reserve(), 553
Result calculation function, 177–79
　algorithm, 178–79
　coding, 179
　objects, 177–78
　operations, 178
　program behavior, 177
Retrieving student information problem, 626–35
　algorithm, 628–31
　Class Student header file, 629–31
　Class Student implementation file, 631–32
　coding, 633–35
　objects, 627–28
　operations, 628
　problem description, 626–27
　program behavior, 627
Return value, 134
Reusable code, 130
revenue5.cpp, 17
revenue6.cpp, 19

Revenue calculation problem, 15–20
  algorithm, 16–17
  coding in C++, 17
  objects, 15
  operations, 16
  problem description, 15
  program behavior, 15
  program maintenance, 18–19
  testing/execution/debugging, 18
reverse(), 563
right manipulator, 226, 503
Ritchie, Dennis, 9
Road construction problem, 450–53
  algorithm, 452
  coding/testing, 452
  objects, 451
  operations, 451
  preliminary analysis, 450
  program, 452–53
  program behavior, 450
Robotics, 2, 637
Rogue software, 23
Roundoff error, 72
Rows, 696
Run-time allocation, 775–92
  delete operation, 783–90
    assignment operator, 787–90
    destructor functions, 786–87
    general form of, 783–84
    memory leaks, 784–86
  new operation, 776–83
    allocating arrays with, 777–80
    copy constructor, 780–83

SampApp.h, 749
Scalar, 233
Schema, 507
School mascot program, 264–68
  algorithm, 265–66
  coding, 266
  Mascot(), 266
    driver for, 267
  objects, 264–65
  operations, 265
  program behavior, 264
  testing, 267–68
Schwarz, Jerry, 217–19
scientific manipulator, 226
Scientific notation, 58
Scope, 412–19
  example, 413–14
  of for-loop control variables, 416–17
  name conflicts, 417–19
  objects declared outside all blocks, 414–16
  signatures, 419
Scope operator, 561
Search, 638
Secondary memory, 19
Second-generation computers, 7
Security, 23–24
seekg(), 491, 492–97
seekp(), 491, 498
Segment pointer, 301
select() function, 507–10
  driver program to test, 508–9
  nested loops for, 509–10
Selection, 263–317
  conditional expressions, 293–95
  functions that use, 148–59
    blocks, 153–54
    if statements, 151, 268–74
    Minimum (), 148–51
    nested if statements, 156–57
    selective execution, 151–53
    sequential execution, 151
    styles used to write if statements, 155–56
  if statement, 151, 268–74

letter grade problem, 286–91
  algorithm, 287
  coding/testing, 289–91
  grade-computation algorithm, 287–88
  objects, 287
  operations, 287
  program, 289
  program behavior, 286
proper selection statement, choosing, 285–86
school mascot program, 264–68
switch statement, 274–86
  arbitrary temperature conversions program, 276–78
  and break statements, 279
  cases with no action, 284–85
  drop-through behavior, 279–81
  form of, 278–79
  temperature conversion problem, 274–78
  year code conversion problem, 281–83
year code conversion problem, 281–83
  algorithm, 282
  code, 282–83
  driver to test YearName(), 283
  objects, 281
  operations, 282
  testing, 283
Selective execution, 151–53
Self-documenting program, 66
Semicolon, 101
  and do statement, 344–45
Semicolons, 101
Sentinel approach, input loops, 351–58
Sentinel-based input processing, 169
Sentinels, 169
  definition of, 351
  end-of-file (eof) as sentinel value, 355–56
  and forever loops, 351–53
  problem with, 355
  and while loop, 353–54
Separate compilation, and libraries, 192
Sequential access, 492
Sequential execution, 151
Set, 823
setfill() manipulator, 503
setprecision() manipulator, 503, 504
setstate(), 491, 500–502
setw() manipulator, 503, 504
Shareware, 25
short, 55
Short-circuit evaluation, 87–88
Shortcuts, assignment, 99–101
short int, 55, 56
showbase manipulator, 226
showpoint manipulator, 226
showpos manipulator, 226
Signatures, functions, 419
Sign bit, 56
signed char, 55
Significand, 71
Simple boolean expressions, 83–84
Simple mail transfer protocol (SMTP), 815
Simple Network Management Protocol (SNMP), 813
Simulation, 252–57
  dice-roll simulation, 255–56
  normal distributions, 254
  RandomInt class, 253–54
  random number generators, 253–54
sin(), 80
Single-branch form, if statements, 155–56, 268

Singly-linked list, 795
size() function, 554, 718, 796
  and pointer arithmetic, 771–73
sizeof operator, 771
skipws manipulator, 222, 226, 503
Smalltalk-80, 10
SMTP (simple mail transfer protocol), 815
SNA (Systems Network Architecture), 808
SNMP (Simple Network Management Protocol), 813
Social and professional context, 3
Software:
  and component programming, 578–79
  development, 6
  rogue, 23
  system, 8–9
Software engineering, 1–22
Software life cycle, 6
Software maintenance, 14–15
Software methodology and engineering, 3
sort(), 562–63
Sorting employee information problem, 544–47
  algorithm, 545
  coding, 545–47
  objects, 544
  operations, 544–45
  problem description, 544
  program behavior, 544
  test score processing program, 572–74
Source program, 9
Speech recognition, 637
sphere3.cpp, 11
SPIKE, 637
SQL (Structured Query Language), 507
Square arrays, 699–700
sroot program, 818–21
  algorithm, 820
  coding, 820–21
  objects, 819
  operations, 819–20
  problem, 818–19
Stack, 566, 823
Stack pointer, 301
Standard library, 78
Standard Template Library (STL), 548, 550, 578, 714, 823
  algorithms, 562–64
  container class templates, 559–60
  iterators, 560–62
    objects, 561
    operations, 561–62
    vector<T> function members involving, 564–65
  list<T> class template, 792–815
  organization of, 558–59
  vector<T> class template, 558–65
Static objects, 142
Stepanov, Alex, 548
STL, See Standard Template Library (STL)
Stored program, 4, 5
Streams, 104–5
  opening, 468
string, 8, 15, 16, 52–53, 131, 175, 230–47, 463, 521, 544, 567, 568, 650, 657
  and assignment operator, 235–36
  concatenation, 237–38
  empty() operation, 235
  input:
    using >>, 232
    using getline(), 233
  output, 232

string *(cont.)*
  and relational operators, 236–37
  size() operation, 234–35
  string objects, declaring, 231
  subscript operation, 233–34,
    238–45
  substring, 238–45
    insertion, 241–42
    pattern matching, 242–45
    removal, 241
    replacement, 239–41
string library, 5
String literal, 60
string objects, 230–47
  declaring, 231
  input, 232–33
  output, 232
  string operations, 233–47
Strings, 60–61, 72–73
Stroustrup, Bjarne, 10, 218
Struct, 794
Structured Query Language
  (SQL), 507
Subclass, 731
Subprograms, *See* Functions
Subscripted variables, 520
Subscript operations, 701
Subscript operator [], 233–34
Substring, 238–45
  insertion, 241–42
  pattern matching, 242–45
  removal, 241
  replacement, 239–41
Subtraction operation, 74
Successor functions, 661–62
Sum(), 322–23
  algorithm, 322
  coding/testing, 322–23
  driver program for, 323
  no-loop version, 374–75
  objects, 320–21
  operations, 321–22
  program behavior, 320
Superclass, 731
Supercomputers, 8
Swap() template, 423–24
Switches, 822
switch statement, 274–78
  and break statements, 279
  temperature conversion prob-
    lem, 274–78
    algorithm, 275–76
    coding/testing, 276
    objects, 275
    operations, 275
    program behavior, 275
Symantec C++, 12, 189, 741
Symbolic computation, 3
Syntax errors, 12
System interconnections, 300
Systems Network Architecture
  (SNA), 808
System software, 8–9
Systran, 637

table.cpp, 720–21
Tables, 506
tan(), 80
tanh(), 80
TCP/IP communications, 808–15
  applications, 815
  application layer, 810
  architecture/operations, 809
    example of, 812–13
  host (transport) layer, 810
  internet layer, 809
  IP and IPv6, 814–15
  layers, 809–10
  network access layer, 809
  operation of, 810–12
  physical layer, 809
  TCP segment, 811

  and UDP, 813
Telecommuting, 27
tellg(), 491, 492, 497–498
tellp(), 491, 492, 498
TELNET, 815
tempconversion2.cpp, 589–90
temperature<1>.cpp, 132
temperature<2>.cpp, 133
Temperature accessor functions,
  606
Temperature addition/subtraction,
  610–12
Temperature attributes, 592–93
Temperature behavior, 592
Temperature class declaration,
  619–20
Temperature-conversion problem,
  130–32
  algorithm, 131
  coding and testing, 131–32
  objects, 130–31
  operations, 131
  program behavior, 130
  version 2, 133
  version 3, 187
temperature.cpp, 593, 603
temperature.doc, 593
Temperature explicit-value con-
  structor, 603
Temperature input, 603, 607–8
Temperature output, 597–600
Temperature (type), 588
Templates, 421–25
  overloading vs., 425
  parameters for types, 422–23
  Swap() template, 423–24
Temporary, definition of, 780
Tennyson, Alfred, 205
Terabyte, 506
Terminal condition, 169
Termination condition, 331
Test-at-the-bottom loops, 172, 339,
  343–44
Test-at-the-top loops, 171
Test files, 467
Testing programs, 6, 12–14
testscores11.cpp, 572–74
Text editor, 12
Text files, 462, 471
Text-oriented programs, 748
Third-generation computers, 7
Thompson, Ken, 9
Three-dimensional arrays:
  declaring, 705–6
  operations on, 706–7
Tokens, 498
Top of a stack, 566
Towers of Hanoi problem, 439–42
  driver program, 441–42
  solving recursively, 441
Trace table, 163–64
Transistors, 7
Trapezoid method of approximat-
  ing areas, 447–49
Trojan horses, 23
truck<4>.cpp, 116–18
Truck fleet accounting program,
  115–18
  algorithm, 116
  objects, 115
  operations, 115–16
  program behavior, 115
  Trucking Costs program, 116–18
true, 55
Truth tables, 85
Turbo C++, 12, 189–90, 742
  ObjectWindows Library, 748–49
Turing, 167, 330
Turing, Alan, 6
Twine problem, 7–15
Two-dimensional arrays:
  defining, 699–701

operations, defining, 702–5
predefined operations, 701–2
Two-dimensional vector<T>:
  functions, defining, 720
  input, 722–23
  objects, 715–18
    one-step approach, 717
    two-step approach, 715–17
    using typedef for readability,
      717–18
  operations, 718–20
    push_back() function, 719–20
    size() function, 718
  output, 720–21
Two-pass file processing:
  problem, 492–93
  program, 494
Two's complement representation,
  70
Type conversion function member,
  676
Type conversions, 75
typedef:
  building a Matrix class using, 726
  and C-style arrays, 532–33
  and pointer variables, 765
  and two-dimensional vector<T>
    objects, 717–18
Type hierarchy, C++, 690
Type parameter, 547
Types/expressions, 51–127, 650–51
  assignment expressions, 92–104
  boolean expressions, 82–90
  character expressions, 90–91
  declarations, 55–73
  Einstein's equation, 52–54
    algorithm, 53
    coding, 53
    energy<1>.cpp, 54
    execution, 53
    objects, 52
    operations, 52–53
    program behavior, 52
    testing, 53
  input/output expressions, 104–14
  numeric expressions, 73–82
  See also Classes

UDP, 813
Unary operators, 77
Unicode, 72–73
Uniform distribution, 254
unique(), 563
UNIVAC, 6–7
Universal machine, 5
UNIX operating system, 8, 9, 12
unsigned, 55
unsigned char, 55
unsigned int, 56
unsigned long, 56
unsigned short, 56
upper_bound(), 563
uppercase manipulator, 226
User datagram protocol (UDP),
  and TCP, 813
User-visible registers, 301–2
  address registers, 301
  condition codes, 302
  data registers, 301

Vacuum tubes, 7
Value parameters, 388–89
  problem with, 392–93
Variable declaration, 64–65
Variable initialization, 66–67
Variable objects, 64–66
Variables, 8, 61, 64–66
Varying-capacity arrays, 526
v.back(), 550
v.begin(), 564
v.capacity(), 550
vector<double>, 568, 570

vector<string>, 544, 567, 568, 570
vector<T>-based matrix library,
  724–50
  building a Matrix class:
    external approach to, 725–26
    internal approach, 730–38
  matrix multiplication, 724–25
  Matrix operations, 726–30
  object-centered design, 738–40
vector<T> class template, 547–67
  array and vector<T> limitations,
    566–67
  class templates, 548
  function templates, 547
  Standard Template Library
    (STL), 558–65
    algorithms, 562–64
    container class templates,
      559–60
    iterators, 560–62
    organization of, 558–59
  vector<T> objects, defining,
    548–53
  vector<T> operators, 553–58
  vector<T> vs. C-style array,
    565–66
vector<T> definition, 550
vector<T> function members,
  550–53
  constructors, 551
    accessing first and last values,
      553
    appending and removing val-
      ues, 551–53
    checking size and capacity, 551
  involving iterators, 564–65
vector<T> objects:
  defining, 548–53
  preallocating, 548–49
  and initializing, 549–50
vector<T> operators, 553–58
  assignment operator, 556

equality operator, 556–57
less-than operator, 557–58
subscript operator, 554
  when not to use, 554–55
  when to use, 555–56
vector<T>s, 519–84
  capacity of, 566
  C-style arrays vs., 565–66
Vector of unknowns, 739
v.empty(), 550
v.end(), 564
Venn diagrams, 193–94
v.erase(), 564
Very large-scale integrated (VLSI)
  circuits, 7
v.front(), 550
v.insert(), 564
Viruses, 23
  detection/recovery, 488–89
  prevention, 488
  scanning for, 488–90
Virus warnings, as hoaxes, 26
Visual C++, 12, 189, 742
vi text editor, 12
void, 55
von Neumann, John, 6–7
v.pop_back(), 550
v.push_back(), 550
v.rbegin(), 564
v.rend(), 564
v.reserve(), 550
v.size(), 550

wages.cpp, 114
wchar_t, 55
Weather data analysis problem,
  462–68
  algorithm, 464–65
  coding, 465–66
  meteorological data, processing,
    462–63
  objects, 463

operations, 463
program behavior, 463
testing, 467–68
while loop, 333–39
  bouncing ball problem, 333–37
    algorithm, 334
    coding, 334–35
    objects, 333–34
    operations, 334
    program behavior, 333
  construction warning, 338–39
  loop conditions vs. termination
    conditions, 337–38
  and sentinels, 353–54
White space, 61, 107, 477
Wild card, asterisk (*) as, 822
Windows (Microsoft), 8
  applications, and computer
    graphics, 748
Word, number of bits in, 20
Workstations, 8
Worms, 23
Wozniak, Steve, 7–8
Write position symbol, 471

Xlib, 741
Xt, 741
X Window System, 8

Year code conversion problem,
  281–83
  algorithm, 282
  code, 282–83
  driver to test YearName(), 283
  objects, 281
  operations, 282
  testing, 283

Z-1/Z-2/Z-3/Z-4 computers, 6
Zero-trip behavior, 337
Zuse, Konrad, 6, 8

plug into
Prentice Hall PTR Online!

Thank you for purchasing this Prentice Hall PTR book. As a professional, we know that having information about the latest technology at your fingertips is essential. Keep up-to-date about Prentice Hall PTR on the World Wide Web.

Visit the Prentice Hall PTR Web page at
http://www.prenhall.com/divisions/ptr/
and get the latest information about:

- New Books, Software & Features of the Month
- New Book and Series Home Pages
- Stores that Sell Our Books
- Author Events and Trade Shows

join prentice hall ptr's new internet mailing lists!

Each month, subscribers to our mailing lists receive two e-mail messages highlighting recent releases, author events, new content on the Prentice Hall PTR web site, and where to meet us at professional meetings. Join one, a few, *or all* of our mailing lists in targeted subject areas in Computers and Engineering.

Visit the Mailroom at http://www.prenhall.com/mail_lists/
to subscribe to our mailing lists in...

COMPUTER SCIENCE:

Programming and Methodologies
Communications
Operating Systems
Database Technologies

ENGINEERING:

Electrical Engineering
Chemical and Environmental Engineering
Mechanical and Civil Engineering
Industrial Engineering and Quality

get connected with prentice hall ptr online!

CodeWarrior®
Professional Edition

Academic Pricing $119

With our academic pricing, you can get the same tools professional developers use at prices students can afford!

CodeWarrior Professional Edition features our award-winning integrated development environment (IDE) and includes compilers for C, C++, Java and Pascal— so you won't need to buy or learn a second development environment. You also get **Windows-** and **Mac OS-hosted** tools and cross compilers so that you can develop code for both PCs and Macs, irrespective of your host platform. In addition, you get powerful and easy-to-use reference material including **online books, tutorials,** and **megabytes of sample code.**

Get your copy of CodeWarrior today and start programming like a pro!

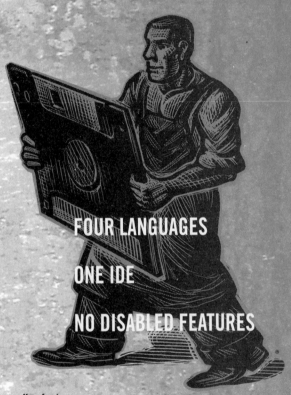

FOUR LANGUAGES

ONE IDE

NO DISABLED FEATURES

Key features:
Microsoft Foundation Classes
Metrowerks PowerPlant
Multiple open projects
Sub-projects
Multiple targets per project
Threaded execution
Integrated error management

Also includes:
Online reference material
Sun Java documentation (API and language specification)
Microsoft IE
Free technical support
One free update
30-day money-back guarantee

metrowerks®

For more information check out our web site www.metrowerks.com

CodeWarrior is available at the bookstore where this book was purchased, or through Metrowerks: 1-800-577-5416 or academia@metrowerks.com